FASHION

Seventh Edition

Mary G. Wolfe

Publisher
The Goodheart-Willcox Company, Inc.
Tinley Park, Illinois
www.g-w.com

Introduction

Fashion brings the exciting world of fashion to life through an in-depth look at how clothing relates to people's lives and how the apparel industries work. It opens your eyes to the many ways that you might be a better consumer and/or employee of fashion-related businesses.

Fashion is full of features to pique your interest. The textbook

➤ discusses couture collections, designer ready-to-wear, private label lines, and computer designing and marketing of fashion goods.

➤ looks at globalization and trends for textile companies, apparel manufacturers, retailers, and consumers, including industry-wide collaboration, multichannel retailing, and cross-channel shopping.

➤ analyzes how Internet technology is changing fashion firms' product development, promotion, and selling through electronics (e-commerce).

➤ analyzes how mobile applications and social media affect consumer comparison shopping and buying practices (m-commerce).

➤ explains how consumers are weighing the dilemma of imports, environmental sustainability, and ethical and social issues about companies when buying their goods.

➤ discusses how to deter, detect, and defend against identity theft.

➤ describes the many career opportunities related to fashion and apparel, including entrepreneurship. Occupations are linked to their relevant Career Cluster fields.

➤ helps you become more fashionable or helpful to others by explaining how to use the elements and principles of design in clothing, telling how to plan the best wardrobe for people's needs, and teaching how to shop and care for clothes.

Fashion is also a great reference guide. Fashion terms are explained, garment styles and parts are illustrated, and popular apparel fabrics are described. The extensive glossary at the end of the text defines other fashion and apparel terms that are used by industry professionals.

This information is presented in an easy-to-understand format. Simple, direct language is supplemented with hundreds of color photographs and illustrations. Each chapter begins with learning objectives and ends with review materials to make your learning more meaningful and enjoyable. The goal of this book is to help you gain knowledge that will be valuable to you whether you become an integral part of the fashion world or a well-informed consumer.

About the Author

Mary Wolfe has worked in all segments of the fashion industry, from textile research to retail sales. She designed for a national sportswear firm before opening her own apparel business. She gained recognition as the personal fashion designer for the wife of a U.S. Vice President. As a consultant to several garment manufacturers, she has assisted with collection designs and pattern specifications.

Mary received the Outstanding Faculty Member Award for her teaching of fashion-related courses at the University of Delaware. She has been a New Jersey Woman of the Year and has been listed in Outstanding Young Women of America and National Dean's List. Mary is also the author of books on fashion merchandising and pattern making. She received her bachelor's degree in Textiles and Clothing from Iowa State University and her Master's of Business Administration degree from West Chester University of Pennsylvania.

WELCOME TO *FASHION*

Welcome to the exciting world of *Fashion* where you will get an in-depth look at how the apparel industries work. Read further to discover key elements that will lead you on the path to career success and become a better consumer.

Chapter Titles introduce the topics covered in each part of your text.

Fashion Terms help you build a fashion vocabulary and appear in blue type in the text where defined. Note the icon that links you to vocabulary activities in the *Companion Website*.

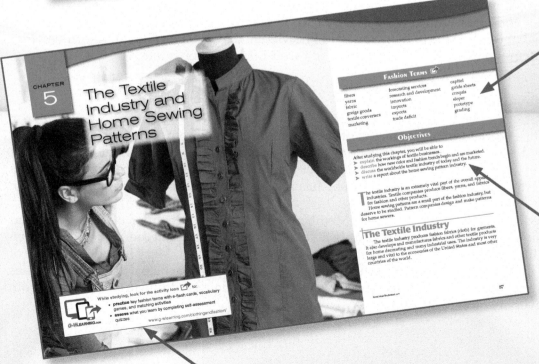

Chapter Objectives provide a framework for concepts and skills you will learn from studying the chapter.

Link to the **Companion Website** activities to reinforce chapter vocabulary and concepts.

CHARTS AND ILLUSTRATIONS

Complex Concepts Presented Simply

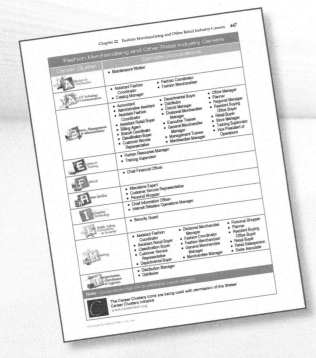

CHAPTER REVIEW AND ASSESS

Enhances and Extends Learning

Chapter 4 Review and Assess

Fashion Recall

Write your answers on a separate sheet of paper.

Short Answer: Write the correct answer to each of the following questions.

1. What three major developments during the Industrial Revolution caused a switch from handmade garments to mass-produced ready-to-wear clothes?
2. What are two common names for the garment industry?
3. Name two trade publications of the apparel industries.
4. Name two trade associations of the apparel industries.
5. The high-fashion garment industry originated with the superior dressmaking industry of what country?
6. How did World War II affect the American design industry?
7. How many major showings of collections do the couture fashion houses present each year?
8. Why was the Chambre Syndicale formed in Paris?
9. Name two designers in the Coty Hall of Fame.
10. Name two reasons for the recent changes in the haute couture industry.
11. A retail shop owned by a couturier that carries accessories designed by the couturier or a member of his or her staff is a _____.
12. In a _____ arrangement, a couturier provides a retailer with a famous name and merchandise in return for a certain amount of money.
13. In a _____ arrangement, a manufacturer pays for the exclusive rights to produce and market goods that bear a designer's name as a stamp of approval.
14. In New York City, the fashion industry centers around _____ Avenue.
15. Which do more retail buyers attend—showings of the couture collections or showings of the prêt collections?

Fashion Vocabulary

16. Read the text passages that contain each of the *Fashion Terms* listed on the chapter opening. Then, write definitions of each term in your own words on a separate sheet of paper. Double-check your definitions by rereading the text and using the text glossary.

Critical Thinking

17. **Compare technologies** Compare the effect the Industrial Revolution had on the apparel industries to what you believe emerging technologies will have on the apparel industries in the future. Write a summary about your comparison to post to the class website for peer and instructor review and discussion.
18. **Assess influence** Assess the influence trade publications and associations have on the fashion industry. What impact do they have on fashion trends? Discuss your assessment in class.
19. **Analyze impact** In the text, the author states that "the single term *couture* has come to mean *top-of-the-line designer fashions*." Analyze the impact of couture fashions in your community. To whom are these fashions marketed? What evidence can you give to support your analysis? Write a short summary or blog post of your analysis.
20. **Evaluate contributions** In your opinion, which fashion designer do you believe has contributed most to the development of fashion? Explain your evaluation in writing.

84

Copyright Goodheart-Willcox Co., Inc.

---

21. **Predict impact** Use online resources to investigate predictions about how technology will impact the development of new fashions 10 years from now. Write a report summarizing your predictions based on your research. Be sure to list the sources of your information.

Core Skills

22. **Reading and speaking** Look for articles and pictures of fashion showings in the United States or abroad in recent newspapers and magazines or on the Internet. Where were the showings held? Which designers were featured? What types of apparel were shown? What distinguishing characteristics and fashion trends were evident? Give an oral, illustrated report of your findings to the class.
23. **Reading and writing** Research website of the Council of Fashion Designers of America (CFDA) to identify the most recent winners of the *CFDA Fashion Awards*. Choose one of the winners to read about. Write a short summary of your findings, including a description of the winning fashions.
24. **Research and speaking** Use online and print resources to learn more about a famous fashion designer of the past. Use school-approved presentation software to prepare an oral report with visual aids on the life, work, and major contributions of the designer. Be sure to credit your photo sources.
25. **Reading and writing** Ask local apparel businesses and libraries that subscribe to trade publications for the apparel industries if you can borrow several publications. Bring copies of as many different publications as possible to class. Notice what kinds of information are presented in each. Compare the content of these publications to the fashion news in

newspapers, consumer magazines, and on websites. Write a brief summary of your comparison.
26. **Technology** Use school-approved video creation software to prepare a digital video presentation about the influence of Hollywood movies on the fashion industry in the United States. Be sure to credit all sources used in your presentation.
27. **CTE career readiness practice** Presume you are an in-store fashion writer for a major department store. Your latest assignment is to write a press release for a *new* brand of designer ready-to-wear that your store will begin to carry for the coming season. Research details about the brand, its target market, and how the brand relates to your customers. Keep a documentation log of all your sources. Then, write the press release about the new brand.

Fashion in Action

28. **Portfolio builder** Create a booklet showing the fashions of at least three current well-known designers. If available, show each designer's unique signature or logo. Add this booklet to your portfolio. As an alternative, create a digital poster showing the fashions and designer logo and save the poster for your digital portfolio.
29. **Design activity** Imagine you are a fashion designer. Describe your design line. To whom would your fashion line appeal? Sketch a sample of a design that might be featured in your collection.

Self-Assessment Quiz ➦

Complete the self-assessment quiz online to help practice and expand your knowledge and skills.

85

Copyright Goodheart-Willcox Co., Inc.

Fashion Recall helps you review important concepts.

Fashion Vocabulary activities help reinforce and assess understanding of chapter vocabulary.

Critical Thinking activities challenge you to use higher-order skills.

Core Skills activities strengthen your reading, writing, research, speaking, listening, and career readiness skills.

Fashion in Action activities provide hands-on practice using your developing *design* skills. *Portfolio* activities guide you in building a portfolio that can help you pursue a career in fashion-related areas.

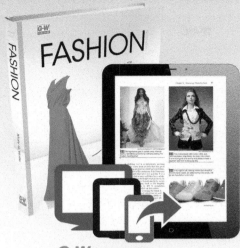

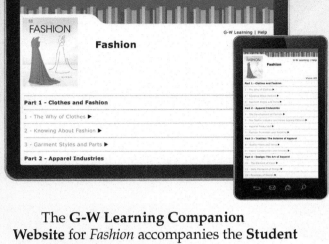

The **G-W Integrated Learning Solution** offers easy-to-use resources for both instructors and students. Both digital and blended (print + digital) teaching and learning content can be accessed through any Internet-enabled device, such as a computer, smartphone, or tablet. From the following options, choose the ones that work best for you and your students.

The **G-W Learning Companion Website** for *Fashion* accompanies the **Student Textbook** and provides content to help students build skills and knowledge, extend textbook content, and reinforce learning. The website complements textbook chapters and is available to students at no charge.

The **Online Learning Suite** for *Fashion* is available as a classroom subscription. It includes the online student text, the companion website content, and the digital workbook.

The **Online Instructor Resources** provide extensive support for instructors. Included in the online resources are Answer Keys, Lesson Plans, ExamView® Assessment Suite, and much more. These resources are available as a subscription and can be accessed at school or at home. They are also available on CDs.

Looking for a **Blended Solution**? G-W offers the Online Learning Suite bundled with the printed textbook in one easy-to-access package for school districts and instructors seeking a combination of print and digital tools. With this option, individual students and instructors have the flexibility of using solely print, solely digital, or a combination of print and digital versions of the *Fashion* educational materials to best meet their particular learning and teaching styles.

Contents in Brief

PART One   Clothes and Fashion

Chapter 1 The Why of Clothes 20
Chapter 2 Knowing About Fashion. 34
Chapter 3 Garment Styles and Parts .50

PART Two   Apparel Industries

Chapter 4 The Development of Fashion 70
Chapter 5 The Textile Industry and Home Sewing Patterns 86
Chapter 6 Apparel Production 102
Chapter 7 Fashion Promotion and Retailing 124

PART Three   Textiles: The *Science* of Apparel

Chapter 8 Textile Fibers and Yarns 144
Chapter 9 Fabric Construction and Finishes 170

PART Four   Design: The *Art* of Apparel

Chapter 10 The Element of Color. 198
Chapter 11 More Elements of Design 216
Chapter 12 Principles of Design 230

PART Five   Consumers of Clothing

Chapter 13 Wardrobe Considerations. 248
Chapter 14 Wardrobe Planning. 260
Chapter 15 Being a Smart Consumer 278
Chapter 16 Making the Right Purchase 298
Chapter 17 Apparel for People with Special Needs 322
Chapter 18 Caring for Clothes. 342

PART Six   Apparel Industry Careers

Chapter 19 A Career for You. 368
Chapter 20 Careers in the Textile Industry 388
Chapter 21 Careers in Apparel Design and Production 408
Chapter 22 Fashion Merchandising and Other Retail Industry Careers . . 428
Chapter 23 Careers in Fashion Promotion 450
Chapter 24 Other Careers and Entrepreneurial Opportunities 466

Contents

PART One — Clothes and Fashion

Chapter 1
The Why of Clothes.........20
Why People Wear Clothes.........22
    Protection....................22
    Adornment....................23
    Identification..................25
    Modesty......................26
    Status 27
Why People Select Certain Clothes...28
    Values and Attitudes............28
    Conformity versus Individuality.....29
    Personality 30

Chapter 2
Knowing About Fashion.....34
Fashion Terms 35
Clothing Construction Terms 38
Clothing Business Terms..........40
    Price Markets.................42
Fashion Cycles 43
    How Cycles Occur 43
    Silhouettes of Fashion Cycles 44
Social and Economic Influences on
    Fashion 45

Chapter 3
Garment Styles and Parts.....50
Basic Dress Styles 51
    Other Dress Styles 52
Neckline Styles.................52
Collar Styles...................53
Sleeve Styles 55
Skirt Styles....................57
Pants Styles...................58
Coat and Jacket Styles 61
Miscellaneous Styles and Parts.....61
Design Options.................64

PART Two — Apparel Industries

Chapter 4
The Development of Fashion.....70
The Scope of the Apparel Industries ..71
    Inside *The Trade* 72
Couture 73
    The Development of High Fashion..73
    The Business of High Fashion.....74
    Fashion Associations and Awards ..76
    Recent Changes for Growth and
        Income......................77
Designer Ready-to-Wear..........79

Chapter 5
The Textile Industry and Home Sewing Patterns 86
The Textile Industry..............87
    Fabric Production and
        Distribution..................88
    The Development of Textile
        Corporations.................89
    Textile Marketing 90
    Fashion Considerations.........90
    Textiles Worldwide 93
    The Future of Textiles 94
Home Sewing Patterns............95
    The Business of Patterns 95
    The Breadth of Pattern
        Companies...................96
    Designing Home Sewing
        Patterns....................97
    Perfecting the Patterns.........97
    Finishing the Patterns..........98
    Innovations for the Future 98

Contents

Chapter 6
Apparel Production 102

The Business of Apparel Production . . 104
   Contracting. 104
Establishing Merchandise Plans. 104
   Calculations and Decisions 105
The Designing Process 106
   Sources of Inspiration 106
   Adapting Designs 107
Preparation for Production. 107
   Making and Using Samples. 108
   Preliminary Production
     Procedures. 108
Factory Production 109
   Cutting. 109
   The Tailor System 110
   The Piecework System 110
   The Latest Production Methods . . 111
   Finishing. 112
Selling the Apparel 112
   Showing the Lines 113
   Promoting the Lines 114
Overseas Manufacturing 115
   Differences in Cost, Fashion, and
     Construction. 115
   Competition of International
     Trade 116
   Using International Trade. 116
   Country of Origin Labeling 117
   No Clear-Cut Answers 117
Ongoing Innovation for Apparel
   Production 118
   Computer Automation. 118
   Reducing Lead and Response
     Times. 119
   Other Industry-Wide Cooperation . . 120
   The Future of the Industry. 120

Chapter 7
Fashion Promotion
and Retailing 124

Promotion. 125
   Advertising 126
   Publicity 126
   Visual Merchandising and Special
     Events 126
   Video and Electronic
     Merchandising 127
How Retail Works. 128
   Retail Terms 128
   Retail Buying 129
   Timing and Pricing for Demand . . . 130
   Private Label Brands. 131
   Retail Business Considerations . . . 132
Types of Apparel Retail Outlets 132
   Department Stores 132
   Branch Stores 133
   Chain Stores. 133
   Discount Stores 134
   Specialty Retailers 135
   Franchises 135
   Mail-Order Houses 136
   TV and Other Retailing 136
Retail Imports 137
Retailers' Future 138

Contents

PART Three — Textile: The *Science* of Apparel

Chapter 8
Textile Fibers and Yarns....144
Natural Fibers....146
Cotton....146
Linen....148
Other Plant Fibers....150
Wool....150
Silk....153
Other Natural Materials for Apparel....156
Manufactured Fibers....157
The Development of Manufactured Fibers....157
Manufactured Fibers Present and Future....158
Categories of Manufactured Fibers..158
Producing Manufactured Fibers...159
Generic Characteristics....160
Using the Characteristics....163
Yarns....164
Yarn Types....166
Combination Yarns and Blends...166
Yarn Textures....167

Chapter 9
Fabric Construction and Finishes....170
Fabric Construction....171
Weaving....172
Knitting....176
Fabrics from Other Construction Methods....179
Fabric Coloring and Printing....181
Bleaching....181
Dyeing....181
Printing....183
Fabric Finishes....185
Mechanical Finishes....186
Chemical Finishes....187
Glossary of Popular Apparel Fabrics....189

PART Four — Design: The *Art* of Apparel

Chapter 10
The Element of Color....198
Color as a Design Element....199
Symbolism of Color....200
Color Terms....201
The Color Wheel....201
Color Schemes....202
Monochromatic Color Scheme....202
Analogous Color Scheme....203
Complementary Color Scheme...203
Split-Complementary Color Scheme....203
Triad Color Scheme....204
Accented Neutral Color Scheme..204
Using Colors in Apparel....204
The Changeability of Colors....205
Creating Illusions with Color....205
Enhancing Personal Coloring....207
Color Tone....207
Find the Best Colors....207
Personal Color Categories....208
Wear the Best Colors....213

Chapter 11
More Elements of Design...216
Shape....217
Using Shape in Clothing....218
The Shape of Fashion....218
Facial Shapes....219
Line....219
Line Types....219
Line Directions....220
Line Applications....222
Creating Illusions with Lines....222
Further Use of Lines in Clothing..223
Texture....224
Using Structural Texture in Clothing....225
Using Added Visual Texture in Clothing....226

Contents

Chapter 12
Principles of Design **230**
  Balance 231
    Types of Balance 232
  Proportion 232
    Proportion in Apparel 233
  Emphasis .234
  Rhythm. 235
  Harmony. .235
  Create the Best Look 236
  The Total Design for Individuals 237
    Tall and Thin. 237
    Tall and Heavy 238
    Short and Thin 239
    Short and Heavy. 239
    Large Upper Body 240
    Thick Middle. 241
    Large Lower Body 241
    General Guidelines 242
    Extra Tips. 243

PART Five — Consumers of Clothing

Chapter 13
Wardrobe Considerations . . .**248**
  Projecting a Positive Image 249
    Clothing as Communication. 250
    Personality 250
    Yin and Yang Traits. 251
    First Impressions. 252
  Appropriate Apparel 253
    Lifestyle .253
    Climate. .254
    Community Standards. 255
  The Benefits of a Well-Planned
    Wardrobe 255
    Project the Best Self-Image 255
    Save Money 256
    Gain Flexibility 256
  Enjoy Apparel Choices 257

Chapter 14
Wardrobe Planning **260**
  Evaluate Current Apparel. 261
  Group Clothes. 263
    Clothing Worn Often. 263
    Clothing Worn Occasionally. 263
    Clothing Needing Repairs or
      Cleaning. 264
    Clothing Not Worn in the
      Past Year 265
  Distinguish Wants from Needs 265
  Choosing Accessories. 266
    Using Accessories to Advantage . .266
    Footwear. 267
    Handbags. 267
    Headwear. 268
    Belts 268
    Scarves .268
    Neckties. 268
    Handkerchiefs 269
    Jewelry. .270
    Eyewear .270
    Gloves 270
    Hosiery .271
  Develop a Total Future Plan. 271
    Basic Garments 271
    Extending a Wardrobe 272
    Write a Plan 273
  Consider Available Resources 273
    Sewing as an Option. 274

Contents

Chapter 15
Being a Smart Consumer...278

Prepare Ahead 280
   Make a List 280
   Gather Information 281
   Evaluate Advertising 282
Where to Shop 282
   Price versus Quality and Service . .282
   Types of Merchandise 283
   Location and Store Hours 283
   Advertising or Loyalty 284
   Cross-Channel Shopping. 284
   Consumer Decisions 285
When to Shop. 285
Shopping Considerations. 286
   Shopping Manners 287
Hangtags, Labels, and Packaging . . .287
   Hangtags 288
   Labels 288
   Packaging 289
Government Legislation 289
   Textile Fiber Products
    Identification Act. 289
   Permanent Care Labeling Rule . . .290
   Wool Products Labeling Act 291
   Fur Products Labeling Act 291
   Flammable Fabrics Act 291
Consumer Rights and
Responsibilities 291
   Right and Responsibility for
    Safety 292
   Right and Responsibility to Be
    Informed. 292
   Right and Responsibility to
    Choose 292
   Right and Responsibility to
    Be Heard 293

Chapter 16
Making the Right Purchase...298

Comparison Shopping. 299
Judging Value and Quality. 300
   General Quality. 301
   Specific Points of Quality 302
Political/Social Viewpoints 304
   The Dilemma of Imports 304
   Environmental Sustainability 305
   Ethics and Social Responsibility. . .306
Evaluate Proper Fit 307
   Determine Size Category 307
   Know and Use Body
    Measurements 307
   Try on Garments. 309
Know Trademarks. 310
   Designer Labels 311
Evaluate Bargains 311
   Shopping at Sales. 311
   Types of Sales 312
   Impulse Buying 313
How to Pay. 314
   Cash Purchases 314
   Layaway Purchases 315
   Credit Purchases 315
   Installment Plans 316
   Electronic Payments 317
   Evaluating the Use of Credit 318
Identity Theft 318

Contents

Chapter 17
Apparel for People with
Special Needs 322
Apparel Needs of Infants. 323
Comfort 324
Practicality 324
Safety 324
The Layette 325
Infant Apparel Sizes 326
Clothing for Young Children. 326
Appropriateness 327
Safety 328
Practicality 328
Growth Features. 328
Children's Self-Esteem 328
Children's Apparel Sizes 329
Sewing Children's Apparel. 330
Clothing for Older Adults. 330
Physical Changes 331
Selecting Apparel for Older
Adults .332
Apparel for People with Disabilities . .332
Specific Garment Features 333
Shape and Fashion. 333
Obtaining Apparel for People
with Disabilities. 334
Maternity Fashions 335
Travel Wardrobes 335
Mix and Match 335
Be Practical 336
Determine Travel Needs 336
Packing Tips. 337
Other Considerations 338

Chapter 18
Caring for Clothes 342
Daily Care of Clothes 343
While Dressing and Undressing. . .343
After Wearing. 344
Until the Next Wearing 345
Weekly Care of Clothes. 345
Home Storage Areas 346
Seasonal Clothing Storage 347
Removing Spots and Stains. 348
Identify the Fiber and the Stain . . .349
Stain Removal Supplies. 349
Stain Removal Methods. 349
Laundering Clothes. 351
Sort Clothes. 352
Choose Correct Products 354
Use Laundry Products Correctly . .356
Use the Right Water
Temperatures 357
Follow the Correct Laundering
Procedures. 357
Hand Washing 358
Drying Clothes 359
Ironing and Pressing 360
Ironing and Pressing Equipment . .360
Ironing Techniques 361
Dry Cleaning. 362

Contents

PART Six — Apparel Industry Careers

Chapter 19
A Career for You 368
Choosing a Career 370
  Find out About Yourself 370
  Research Careers. 371
  Determine Needed Education and
    Training 373
  Consider Earning Levels 374
  Learn About the Employment
    Outlook 375
Landing That Job 375
  Job Hunting 375
  Preparing a Résumé 376
  Creating a Portfolio. 376
  Writing a Cover Message 378
  Filling out a Job Application 378
  The Interview 378
Becoming a Success 381
  Develop Positive Personal Traits . .382
  Other Important Factors 383
Making Job Changes 384

Chapter 20
Careers in the Textile
Industry 388
Textile Research and Development . .390
  Textile Research Scientist 391
  Textile Laboratory Technician 392
Textile Design. 392
  Textile Designer 392
  Textile Colorist 394
  Textile Stylist 394
  Assistant Stylist 395
Textile Production 396
  Textile Converter. 396
  Assistant Converter 397
  Production Supervisor. 397
  Machine Operator. 397
  Quality Control Inspector. 398
  Machine Technician 398
  Plant Engineer 398
  Industrial Engineer 398
Textile Marketing and Sales. 399
  Market Research Analyst 399
  Textile Sales Representative 399
  Sales Trainee 401
  Textile Sales Manager. 401
  Textile Advertising and Promotion
    Specialists 401
Textile Administration 402
  Human Resources Manager 402
  Accounting and Finance
    Employees 402
  Data Processors. 402
  Other Administrative Employees . .403
Textile Careers 404

Contents

**Chapter 21
Careers in Apparel Design
and Production** 408

Apparel Design.................409
  Fashion Designer 410
  Assistant Designer 412
  Sketching Employees 413
  Sample Maker 414
Apparel Manufacturing 414
  Pattern Maker 415
  Pattern Grader 415
  Marker Makers 415
  Spreader 416
  Cutter......................416
  Assorter....................416
  Sewing Machine Operator.......416
  Finisher 417
  Trimmer and Inspector 417
  Alteration Hand 418
  Presser 418
Production Management..........418
  Product Manager 418
  Plant Manager 419
  Production Assistant...........419
  Supervisors 419
  Piece Goods Buyer............419
  Industrial Engineer 420
  Costing Engineer 420
  Quality Control Engineer.......420
  Plant Engineer 420
Sales and Distribution...........420
  Showroom Salesperson 421
  Other Showroom Sales
    Employees 421
  Outside Sales Representative 421
  Sales Manager 422
  Market Research Employees.....423
  Jobs in Distribution............423
Top Management 423
  Division Director 423
Administrative Employees 424
Apparel Design and Production
  Careers 425

**Chapter 22
Fashion Merchandising
and Other Retail Industry
Careers** 428

Retail Job Generalities 430
  Qualifications for Retail Work 431
Merchandise Planning and Buying...431
  Retail Buyer 432
  Assistant Retail Buyer..........434
  Resident Buying Office (RBO)
    Buyer.....................434
  Executive Trainee 435
Direct Selling 436
  Retail Salesperson 436
Other Store Operations..........437
  Training Supervisor 437
  Customer Service Representative..437
  Alterations Expert.............438
  Comparison Shopper 438
  Personal Shopper............438
  Stock Clerk 438
  Head of Stock 439
  Checkout Cashier............440
  Office Support Workers 440
  Maintenance Workers..........440
  Security Guard 441
Retail Management..............441
  Merchandise Manager.........441
  Fashion Coordinator 441
  Assistant Fashion Coordinator....443
  Store or Site Manager..........444
  Other Retail Management.......444
Fashion Merchandising and Other
  Retail Industry Careers 447

Contents

Chapter 23
Careers in Fashion Promotion .450

Fashion Advertising. 452
  Account Executive 452
  Art Director 452
  Graphic Designer 453
  Other Advertising Design
    Employees 454
  Advertising Director 454
Fashion Display. 454
  Display Director 454
  Display Designer. 455
Other Fashion Promotion Careers . . .455
  Fashion Illustrator 455
  Fashion Model 456
  Fashion Photographer. 458
  Fashion Writer 459
  Copywriter 460
  Editor. 460
  Audiovisual Jobs. 461
Fashion Publicity. 461
  Public Relations Specialist. 461
Fashion Promotion Careers. 463

Chapter 24
Other Careers and Entrepreneurial Opportunities 466

Apparel Educators. 467
  Classroom Teacher 468
  Extension Agent. 469
  Adult Education 470
  Consumer Education. 470
The Home Sewing Industry 471
  Commercial Pattern
    Development 471
  Pattern Sales and Promotion. 472
  Fabric Sales 473
  Video Demonstration Work 473
Textile and Clothing Historians 473
Theatrical Costumers 475
Clothing Care 476
  Dry Cleaning and Laundry
    Businesses. 476
  Commercial Laundries 477
  Linen Supply Service 477
Entrepreneurs. 477
  A Home-Based Business 478
  A Retail Store. 479
  A Dressmaking or Tailoring Shop . .480
  An Apparel Production Business . .481
  A Trading Company. 481
  A Mail-Order or Online
    Business 482
  Freelancing and Consulting. 483
Other Careers and Entrepreneurial
  Opportunities 485

Glossary. .488

Index 520

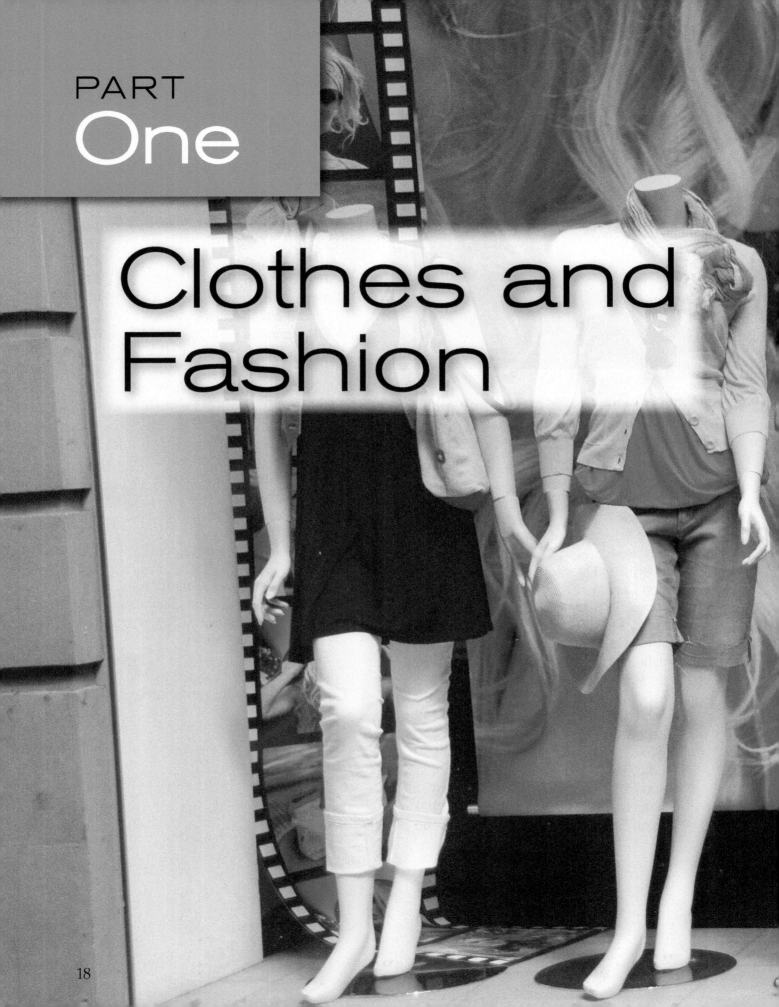

Clothes and Fashion

1   The Why of Clothes

2   Knowing About Fashion

3   Garment Styles and Parts

Gr8/Shutterstock.com

The Why of Clothes

While studying, look for the activity icon to:

- **practice** key fashion terms with e-flash cards, vocabulary games, and matching activities
- **assess** what you learn by completing self-assessment quizzes

G-WLEARNING.com

www.g-wlearning.com/clothingandfashion/

Joel Shawn/Shutterstock.com

Fashion Terms

consumer
cultures
protective clothing
adornment
beauty

identification
dress codes
modesty
status
values

attitudes
conformity
peer pressure
individuality
personality

Objectives

After studying this chapter, you will be able to
➤ explain the various reasons people wear clothes.
➤ analyze how satisfies certain physical, psychological, and social needs.
➤ discuss how values, attitudes, conformity, individuality, and personality affect clothing selections.

Clothing does much more than just cover the body. Your appreciation of clothing will expand as you become more aware of the influences clothing has on you. It can influence you both as a consumer (someone who buys and uses goods and services) and as a future employee of a clothing manufacturing or retailing company.

Throughout history, clothing has had great meaning. It has indicated people's handicraft skills, artistic imagination, and cultural rituals. Cultures are the customs and beliefs of certain groups of people. Clothing also reflects advances in technology.

In ancient times, clothing was made from items found in nature. The first clothes were probably made from animal skins. Today's technology provides many different fibers, fabrics, finishes, and manufacturing processes. Regardless of these advances, however, the reasons to wear clothes are the same as they have been throughout history.

Why People Wear Clothes

People in prehistoric times clothed their bodies over 75,000 years ago. This has been shown by the discoveries of ancient cave drawings, statues, and remains of materials used for making clothing. From the beginning, clothing has served the same basic human needs. Those needs are protection (a physical need), adornment and identification (psychological needs), and modesty and status (social needs).

Protection

Unlike other living creatures, the human body needs protection, or physical safeguards. Clothing can prevent harm caused by the climate and the environment. It supplements the natural body covering like a second skin. Protective clothing gives physical protection to the body. For instance, protection from drowning is provided by life jackets or other flotation clothing. As you will see, some clothing that offers protection is also stylish.

Alexey Losevich/Shutterstock.com

1-1 Water-repellent garments protect people from getting wet when it rains.

Protection from Weather

To preserve good physical health, people use clothing as protection from cold temperatures. It can protect them from sunshine or high winds. It can also protect them from the wetness of rain, as shown in **1-1**. Where people live influences the clothing needed for protection.

Warm sweaters, coats, gloves, and long underwear help bodies retain heat, thus protecting people from frigid weather. Wide-brimmed hats can keep hot sunshine off faces and heads. People wear windbreakers and water-repellent jackets for protection against weather.

Sunglasses and hats are sometimes worn as fashion items as well as for protection. Fur pelts were essential for warmth and protection long ago. Now fur garments might stir controversy as well as provide high fashion and warmth.

Protection from Environmental Dangers

People need physical protection from dirt, insects, and other harmful agents in the environment. Shoes protect feet from soil, hard objects, and hot and cold surfaces. Astronauts must have protective clothing to provide them with the correct atmospheric conditions to keep them alive in outer space. In medical settings, special clothing items, such as sterile gloves, gowns, and face masks, help reduce the transfer of germs and maintain sanitation.

Natives of some geographic regions need protective clothing against insects, worms, and leeches. The swish of a grass skirt is meant to keep insects away. Some people who live in the tropics grease their bodies. Some plaster mud on themselves for physical protection. These body coverings are substitutes for clothing and accomplish similar protective results.

Protection from Occupational Hazards

Some garments protect workers from the specific dangers of their jobs. Unlike turtles that can use their shells for protection, humans must use clothing to guard against bruises, cuts, burns, and other injuries.

As industry and technology have developed, special protective garments have evolved. Hard hats, steel-toed shoes, and safety goggles have been standard equipment at many job sites for years. More recently, special garments to guard against acids, static, lint, fumes, and other potential dangers have been developed. Some specialized clothing can protect against contamination, chemicals, radiation, and fire. These clothes were devised for firefighters, factory workers, miners, and others as in **1-2**.

Athletes often wear protective clothing. The helmets, gloves, and pads pictured in **1-3** provide protection while skateboarding. The special shoes worn by tennis players and basketball players are designed to protect them from slipping. Reflective vests enable workers in roadways to be seen.

Some garments were originally designed for protection while working. Later, they became fashion items. Examples include blue jeans and tall leather boots that were first worn by ranchers and outdoor workers.

Protection from Enemies

Throughout history, clothing has protected people from attackers. Physical protection against human enemies centuries ago was provided by body shields or suits of armor. Current army helmets protect soldiers' heads. Pockets and belts can hold military weapons. Camouflage fabric helps the wearer hide by blending in with the environment.

Tultex Corporation, Swann-Neimann Photography

1-3 Sports and recreational activities can be more fun if the proper physical protection is used to prevent injury.

1-2 Occupational clothing is able to provide protection against possible unsafe conditions of certain jobs.

Diego Cervo/Shutterstock.com

Police officers often wear bulletproof vests, as shown in **1-4**, to protect their bodies from gunfire. Other clothing that protects against enemies may be less obvious. The helmets and pads worn by football players protect against opposing players. The reflective vests and jackets worn by joggers and bikers after dark offer protection from the drivers of motor vehicles.

Some cultures believe items of clothing can give them protection from such enemies as evil spirits, illness, or a bad harvest. Items such as good luck charms and medallions are sometimes used to make people feel luckier, healthier, safer, or braver.

Adornment

Clothing can affect a person's mental attitude or morale in a good way. This is done through adornment or decoration. Adornment provides a psychological feeling of well-being through beauty. It differs between cultures and it changes over time.

Fotokostic/Shutterstock.com

1-4 Police officers can help protect their bodies from gunfire by wearing bulletproof vests under their uniforms.

Beauty is a quality that gives pleasure to the senses. It creates a positive emotional reaction in the viewer. Most psychologists believe beauty is essential to human life. People have a need to make themselves look more attractive. Body adornment enhances self-concept and personality. The winter wear in **1-5** would be just as efficient if it were all black. However, the combination of bright colors adds beauty to it.

1-5 The artistic patterns and colors of these hats, jackets, and scarves make a statement of adornment. They would be just as serviceable in a plain neutral color.

kurhan/Shutterstock.com

Decorative clothing makes people more attractive. People wear clothing that is artistically designed, and combine garments in artistic ways. Then they further adorn themselves with earrings, bracelets, and neck chains. Makeup and nail polish add more decoration. The large sums of money spent each year on jewelry and beauty aids attest to the emphasis people place on personal appearance.

Adornment has been found in various cultures throughout history. Primitive people used colored clay or vegetable dyes to decorate their bodies. Jewelry was carved from animal bones or horns. The body was decorated with what was available.

The decorations people use still depend on their native culture. In some regions, people decorate their bodies with paints and ornaments. Some bodies are intentionally scarred or bound for adornment. People may wear necklaces made of animal teeth, shells, or seeds. Individuals may imitate this type of decoration with tattoos and piercings.

The way one culture views beauty may be very different from how other cultures view it. The desirability of certain decorations is determined by the standards, values, and traditions of each society. For instance, many cultures have popular, but different, hairstyles. Fabrics and garments of different cultures vary in textures, patterns, and colors, as in **1-6**. Often the traditional fabrics a culture uses to create its folk costumes have great importance.

Individuals also have different thoughts about beauty and adornment because of personal experiences. A professional athlete may consider casual attire to be more becoming than formal wear. Someone who enjoys ballet and opera might have dressier adornment preferences.

Ideas also change with time. What is considered beautiful one year may not look attractive at all a few years later.

Clothing worn for adornment gives people a positive way to express themselves. They can express creativity and individuality. Clothing can contribute to increased self-respect, self-acceptance, and self-esteem. When people improve their looks, they attract favorable attention.

Sometimes people adorn themselves in a way that is different from their usual style for change or adventure. This gives relief from

michaeljung/Shutterstock.com

1-6 Traditional apparel used for body adornment in parts of Africa is somewhat different from most American fashions.

© Lilly Pulitzer

1-7 By adorning themselves in ways that are different from their everyday attire, people can receive a psychological lift.

boredom. It adds psychological zest to life. A businessperson who wears dark suits all week might choose a bright outfit for a fun event on the weekend or on vacation, as in **1-7**.

Identification

Identification is the process of establishing or describing who someone is or what someone does. Clothing can identify employees of restaurants, hotels, hospitals, or stores, and people of many other professions.

Group identity is shown when group members dress alike. Clothing can satisfy the psychological need to belong to a group, such as a profession, a social group, an association, or a country of heritage. It indicates the roles people play or their skills. It signals who they are and what they do.

Uniforms are one way of identifying roles, as in **1-8**. Uniforms are outfits or articles of clothing that are alike and specific to everyone in a certain group of people. They act as symbols of group identity. Besides giving a sense of belonging, uniforms can indicate positions of authority and the images companies want to project. People who provide protection to the public, such as police officers, need easily recognized uniforms in order to carry out their duties. Uniforms prove that someone really is a mail carrier, a military officer of a particular rank, a football referee, a flight attendant, or a member of the clergy.

Uniforms can decrease racial, religious, and other perceived barriers. Some schools require students to wear uniforms so individual differences and tensions are minimized. Identifying with that school can then shift students' focus to academics. Uniforms give a unified appearance or public image among those in a particular group.

bikeriderlondon/Shutterstock.com

1-8 These uniforms identify the wearers as cheerleaders for a particular school or team.

The regular clothing of many people can be considered a type of *psychological uniform*, because they tend to dress similarly. Look around at your classmates. Are most of them dressed in the same general kinds of pants or skirts, shirts, sweaters, and shoes? People who are close in age and share similar interests often dress like each other. By doing so, they gain confidence, acceptance, and psychological approval. They feel comfortable and secure. Such rules of dress are not formally written, but understood.

Many adults also dress like their peers. Men in a particular group might all wear dark suits and ties to work. To casual gatherings, they may all wear jeans and sweaters. This conformity, or unofficial uniform, makes them feel secure about being appropriately dressed.

Identification can also be accomplished with emblems, colors, badges, patches, and specific pieces of jewelry. Some students wear their class rings. Members of religious groups might wear stars, crosses, or other religious symbols. This identification gives the wearers a feeling of unity with others in the group. Athletic uniforms, nuns' habits, and nurses' outfits tell the world about those people's special identities. Scottish Highlanders wear particular tartan plaids to show they belong to certain clans.

Ceremonial garments can provide identification. The caps and gowns worn by students indicate they are graduating. A white gown and

veil indicates a woman is a bride, as in **1-9**. Some ceremonies involve the use of elaborate robes, prayer shawls, christening gowns, and other unique garments.

Many businesses and schools have dress codes. Dress codes are written or unwritten rules of what should and should not be worn by a group of people. Although the garments worn are not uniforms, they must fall within a certain range of options. Besides achieving group identity, the clothes help the group members maintain a certain standard of behavior. Sometimes this comes from the symbolic meaning of the clothing. At other times, it is because of how the clothes look or feel. For instance, a business suit helps a person to act in a businesslike manner.

Modesty

Human beings wear clothing to satisfy their social need for modesty. Modesty is the covering of a person's body according to the code of

1-9 A wedding gown clearly identifies the woman wearing it as a bride.

Perry Ellis Formalwear

decency of that person's society. Standards of modesty differ among various cultures and situations, and they change over time.

In many societies, people would be embarrassed to appear without clothes in public. Modesty dictates the proper way to cover the body for social acceptance. Standards of decency are molded by cultures and social systems. Each society has its own accepted standards of modesty.

In the 1800s, it was considered immodest for American women to show their ankles. During the early 1900s, the body was almost completely covered, even for sports. In the 1920s, older people were appalled at the short skirts worn by young women. However, short skirts soon became acceptable. Ladies' swimsuits were once made of thick fabric. They covered most of the body. Now fashionable swimwear exposes more skin. See **1-10**. The standards of society about modesty have changed a great deal.

The situation or event people are attending also influences modesty. Wearing only a swimsuit to school or to an office job would not be appropriate. A man may wear a kilt to play bagpipes at a traditional Scottish gathering. However, wearing a kilt anywhere else might embarrass him. By wearing appropriate or inappropriate clothing, people show their acceptance or rejection of their social environment.

Status

A person's status is his or her position or rank compared with that of others. Good or high status is usually associated with recognition, prestige, and social acceptance. Clothing is sometimes used to gain a higher rank in society, along with achievement and peer approval. Thus, many people are willing to pay more for garments with designer labels or popular logos, as in **1-11**.

Adults may try to achieve a higher status by wearing diamond jewelry or expensive clothing items. Examples might be a cashmere sweater or a beaded gown, as in **1-12**.

Some items have important social meanings and make the people wearing them feel important. The items enable individuals to show others what they have achieved. Service stripes on a military sleeve, merit badges on a Boy Scout's shirt, and a school letter on an athletic jacket all tend to raise the status of the wearer. In ancient times, hunters adorned themselves with the pelts of their prey to impress others with their achievements.

1-11 This man achieves status through both the desirable trade name of the manufacturer and the revered name of the football team.

1-10 Standards of modesty have changed over the years. Today's fashionable swimwear is much skimpier than in past eras.

Joao Virissimo/Shutterstock.com

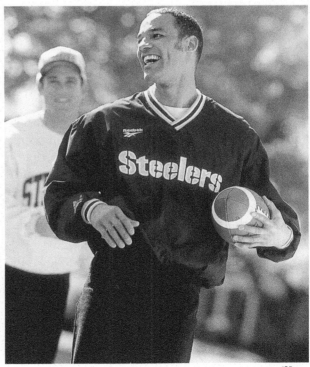

JCPenney

David's Bridal

1-12 A gown with decorative beading, such as this one, gives much more status than a plain long dress made of inexpensive fabric.

Why People Select Certain Clothes

You have just read that people wear clothes to fulfill certain physical, psychological, and social needs. Additional factors that influence people's clothing choices are related to the mental image people have of themselves. Some of the most important factors are people's values and attitudes, their tendencies toward conformity or individuality, and their personalities.

Fashion is a mirror of the times. It reflects the culture at a given time. Historic clothing has revealed many details about the lifestyles of those from various past cultures. Clothes tell others a lot about who people are and how they lived.

If only one current publication could be left from today for people to read in hundreds of years, some experts suggest it should be a fashion magazine. Many believe it would tell more than the volumes written by philosophers, novelists, prophets, and scholars.

Values and Attitudes

Values are the ideals and beliefs important to individuals. They are the underlying motivations for a person's actions. They are the basis of a person's decisions, lifestyle, and personal code of ethics. **Attitudes** are formed from values. They are an individual's feelings about, or reactions to, other people, things, or ideas.

Values and attitudes are learned over a lifetime. They are influenced by cultural customs and traditions. Economic and social conditions of the time also affect them. Values and attitudes can be passed from one generation to another. Family members, friends, and the community are important in forming them.

Some people select comfortable clothing because they value their own comfort, **1-13**. Others always choose bargains because they value economy. Some people value easy care. Others must have the latest fashions in clothes, or expensive items, because they value prestige and want to be noticed. People who are in the businesses of making or selling clothing items try to identify the values and attitudes of their customers. Then they can provide the items that will be preferred, and ultimately bought, by that group of consumers.

What people do with their money shows their personal values. Some like to spend money on many clothes and accessories. Others have few clothes, preferring to spend their money on concerts, movies, ski trips, or other forms of recreation. Still others save their money for a car or other large purchases in the future.

Advertising can influence people's values, attitudes, and purchase decisions. Television commercials try to create a stronger desire for particular products. Fashion ads in newspapers and magazines play to desires for economy, status, easy care, adventure, and comfort. Shopping malls attract many customers who value convenience.

michaeljung/Shutterstock.com

1-13 This young woman has chosen clothing to suit her values and attitudes.

Ken Hurst/Shutterstock.com

1-14 The values and attitudes of this man are determined in part by his age and occupation. An attractive suit is valued as an asset to help his career advance.

Age influences people's clothing selections, too. As people go through life, their values and attitudes change. Students in their middle school years may consider conformity to be important. High school and college students may want to be noticed by other people. They may also have to be budget conscious, but still want to wear the current fashions. Business attire, as shown in **1-14**, might be selected by someone who plans a professional career. Prestige and status may be desired during middle age. Comfort becomes more important as people age.

Conformity versus Individuality

Pressure from other people has a great influence on how people dress. Conformity means obeying, or agreeing with, some given standard or authority. Humans learn early in life what others expect them to wear. Parents, teachers, and other authority figures set some

of the rules of dress. Peer pressure, which is social influence from others in a person's age group, also contributes to conformity. To be accepted by a peer group, people must often conform to group standards of dress and behavior. Those who do not conform risk rejection by the group.

As discussed earlier, conformity can satisfy the needs for identification. By doing this, a safe feeling of belonging is achieved through approval. However, too much conformity can mean a loss of individuality.

Individuality is self-expression. It is the quality that distinguishes one person from another. It is the characteristic of being unique. When people choose styles and colors of clothes that are totally different from those of their friends, they are communicating their individuality. They are satisfying their need for adornment while rejecting peer pressure and conformity. The girl in **1-15** has shown some individuality in her outfit.

Most people balance the influences of conformity and individuality in their clothing. Their clothing choices depend on their moods as well as different settings and situations.

Personality

Personality can be defined as the total unique characteristics that distinguish an individual, especially his or her behavioral and emotional tendencies. A person's basic personality might be happy or sad, shy or outgoing, warm or aloof, kind or mean, relaxed or stiff, or something else. Personalities are influenced by people's in-born characteristics as well as learned by their experiences.

Studies have found that certain ways of dressing give clues about specific personality traits. For instance, tests have shown that people who desire very decorative wearing apparel tend to be very sociable. People who mainly like comfort from their clothes tend to have self-control and confidence. They are often outgoing and secure, as in **1-16**. People who are shown in the personality tests to prefer economy, rather than spending lots of money on their wardrobes, are usually responsible, alert, efficient, and precise.

Summary

People wear clothes today for the same reasons they have worn them throughout history. One reason is for physical protection of the

1-15 Many individuals have fun showing their individuality through the way they put outfits together.

FlashStudio/Shutterstock.com

Monkey Business Images/Shutterstock.com

1-16 These smiles confirm the results of studies concluding that people who choose comfortable clothes tend to be confident and outgoing.

body from weather, environmental dangers, occupational hazards, and enemies. Another reason for wearing clothes is for adornment or decoration that gives a sense of beauty. Clothing is also worn for identification through uniforms, emblems and badges, ceremonial garments, and according to dress codes. Modesty, which follows society's code of decency, is another reason people wear clothes. Finally, clothing is often worn to raise status or to bring a person recognition, prestige, and social acceptance.

People select certain clothes to wear because of their values and attitudes, their tendencies toward conformity or individuality, and their personalities. Values are the basis of people's decisions, lifestyles, and codes of ethics. Attitudes affect people's feelings or reactions to other people, things, or ideas. Conformity and individuality are usually balanced in people's clothing choices. Clothing choices can also give clues about personality traits.

Fashion Recall

Write your answers on a separate sheet of paper.

Matching: Determine the best reason a person would wear each of the items listed below and write the corresponding letter.

1. Designer clothes.
2. Swimsuit.
3. Space suit.
4. Colorful necklace.
5. Hard hat.
6. Uniform.

A. protection
B. adornment
C. identification
D. modesty
E. status

True/False: Write *true* or *false* for each of the following statements.

7. The reasons people wear clothes are different today from those in historic times.
8. Clothes can offer protection from weather, environmental dangers, occupational hazards, and enemies.
9. Folk costumes provide information about how various cultures view beauty and adornment.
10. Uniforms eliminate group identity and take away the feeling of belonging.
11. All societies of the world have the same standards of modesty.
12. Clothing is sometimes used to achieve a higher status.
13. Clothing selection is influenced by people's values and attitudes.
14. Peer pressure encourages individuality.
15. Personality tests have shown that people who wear very decorative clothes tend to be very sociable.

Fashion Vocabulary

16. For each of the *Fashion Terms* at the beginning of the chapter, identify a word or group of words describing a quality of the term—an *attribute*. Pair up with a classmate and discuss your list of attributes. Then, discuss your list of attributes with the whole class to increase understanding.

Critical Thinking

17. **Compare and contrast reasons** Think about the reasons people wear clothes. Categorize the reasons in order of importance to you from most to least important. Compare and contrast your list with the lists of your classmates. How are the lists similar or different? Explain why.

18. **Analyze influences** What part does clothing play in people's lives? Analyze how clothing influences and satisfies certain physical, psychological, and social needs. Discuss your analyses with the class.

19. **Analyze selections** Describe and list factors that affect personal clothing selections. Analyze how your list compares to those of others in the class. Discuss the similarities and differences in factors that impact personal clothing choices.

Core Skills

20. **Speaking and writing** Interview two or more older adults about the clothing they wore when they were your age. Did their clothes reflect traditions of their nationalities? Did they follow different codes of modesty? Did garments provide the physical protection needed for their jobs? What forms of decorative adornment were popular? If possible, ask the interviewees to share photos of the clothing they wore. Write a short, illustrated report about what you learned to share with the class.

21. **Speaking** Take a tour of a museum that features a historic clothing exhibit. Compare clothes worn during that period to clothes worn today. Discuss your

findings in class. As an alternative, take an online, virtual tour of a historic fashion exhibit at a museum and discuss your findings with the class.

22. **Speaking and listening**   As a class, discuss how clothing choices are affected by values, attitudes, desire for conformity or individuality, and personality.

23. **Research and technology**   Locate at least two images online to illustrate protective clothing. Use a school-approved application to create a digital poster of your findings (be sure to credit your images). On your poster, describe the technological advances that have made the clothing possible. Upload your posters to the class website for peer review.

24. **Technology**   Use school-approved infographic software to create an infographic showing the reasons people wear clothes. Be sure to credit any images you use. Print your infographics and ask permission to display them in your school. As an alternative, post your infographics to the class website for peer and instructor review.

25. **CTE career readiness practice**   The ability to read and interpret information is an important workplace skill. Presume you work for a clothing manufacturer who typically manufactures outdoor clothing for all seasons. The company is considering adding a new line of sun-protective clothing to its product line, but wants you to evaluate and interpret some

research on sun-protective fabrics. You will need to locate three reliable sources of the latest information on these fabrics. Read and interpret the information. Then, write a report summarizing your findings.

Fashion in Action

26. **Portfolio builder**   Use presentation software to create a photo essay with written photo descriptions about why people wear clothes. Save your presentation for your print and digital portfolios.

27. **Design activity**   Working in teams, list clothes and accessories that people wear for protection, adornment, identification, modesty, and status.

28. **Design activity**   Find at least two pictures of people wearing uniforms and mount them on paper (or locate the pictures online and create a digital poster). Be sure to credit the source of your pictures. Write your impressions of what each uniform shows or represents to those who see others wearing it. Also explain what *design* aspects of the uniform help the person wearing it.

Self-Assessment Quiz ⤴

Complete the self-assessment quiz online to help practice and expand your knowledge and skills.

Knowing About Fashion

While studying, look for the activity icon to:

- **practice** key fashion terms with e-flash cards, vocabulary games, and matching activities
- **assess** what you learn by completing self-assessment quizzes

www.g-wlearning.com/clothingandfashion/

style	fad	composite garments
fashion	classic	haute couture
apparel	wardrobe	ready-to-wear (RTW)
garment	fit	retailers
silhouette	draped garments	wholesalers
fashion trend	tailored garments	fashion cycle

Objectives

After studying this chapter, you will be able to
➤ **use** correct vocabulary to discuss fashion and clothing.
➤ **identify** and describe the three main methods of clothing construction.
➤ **discuss** the concept of fashion cycles that occur over time.
➤ **analyze** the influence that social and economic factors have on fashions.

Understanding fashion includes knowing many specific clothing terms. Some are already familiar to you. Many may have been written on the labels of clothing you have purchased. Several may have been mentioned by retail store personnel. Some may have described items on retail websites or been used in mail-order catalogs. The subject of fashion cannot be fully understood until these terms become a part of your vocabulary.

Fashion Terms

There are many styles of clothing. A **style** is a particular design, shape, or type of clothing item. The style of a garment is determined by the distinct features that create its overall appearance. Various styles that have been repeated in the history of clothing are recognizable. They have been given names such as A-line skirts, Bermuda shorts, Western shirts, and turtleneck sweaters, such as in **2-1**. Many distinct styles are described in the next chapter of this book.

Yellowj/Shutterstock.com

Pavel L Photo and Video/Shutterstock.com

2-1 Turtleneck sweaters are a particular style with high, knitted collars that fold over onto themselves. The basic turtleneck style is not affected by size, color, or fabric design.

Fashion is the display of the currently popular style of clothing. A fashion is the prevailing type of clothing that is favored by a large segment of the public at any given time. It is the clothing that is most accepted or up-to-date. The styles that are fashionable this year may seem very unfashionable in a few years.

Styles come and go. Fashion is always here in some form. Fashion reflects a continuing process of change in the styles of apparel that are accepted. If people are *stylish*, they are in vogue or are wearing the styles that are currently popular and fashionable.

The term apparel, or wearing apparel, applies to any or all men's, women's, and children's clothing. A garment is any article of apparel, such as a dress, suit, coat, evening gown, or sweater. It is any particular clothing item. *Garment parts* are the sleeves, cuffs, collar, waistband, and other components that make the complete garment.

The silhouette is the shape of a clothing style. It is formed by the width and length of the neckline, sleeves, waistline, and pants or skirt. If you were to squint your eyes and look at a suit, dress, or coat, the outer lines (shape) of the garment would show its silhouette. Look at the straight silhouette in **2-2**.

Silhouettes are always changing in fashion. The general direction that a silhouette takes (becomes wider, narrower, longer, shorter) shows a fashion trend. That is the direction in which fashion is moving. It compares what is in fashion now with fashions of the recent past.

elwynn/Shutterstock.com

2-2 This Chinese *cheongsam* presents a slender, straight silhouette.

High-fashion or *high-style* items are the very latest or newest fashions. They are usually of top quality, with fine workmanship and beautiful fabrics, as in **2-3**. Because of the quality, they are expensive. High-fashion garments sometimes seem extreme and unusual. They originate from name designers in leading fashion cities. They are worn by wealthy or famous people who are fashion pacesetters. Some details of high-fashion garments filter down into generally accepted fashions.

Avant-garde clothes are the most daring and wild designs. They are unconventional and startling. They are too far out to be considered fashions of the times. Most features of these garments disappear completely after a few years. Avant-garde clothes are used to draw attention to the wearer. See **2-4**. They do not appeal to very many people. They are often worn by rock groups on stage. Sometimes teens wear versions of avant-garde clothing and hairstyles. A spiked hairdo with purple and orange streaks is considered avant-garde.

Hong Kong Trade Development Council and Moda Management

2-3 This high-fashion gown is carefully made of fine silk fabrics, real feathers across the top, and hand detailing. The inside is beautifully lined.

Anton Zabielskyi/Shutterstock.com

2-4 This unconventional outfit contains ruffles, lace, extra-long sleeves, large jewelry, and sharp color contrast. It is too avant-garde to be worn by most people. It makes a statement when worn by this young lady.

2-5 A fad might be soft, distinctly colored sport shoes that become popular quickly, are widely worn by many people, and go out of popularity in a short time.

A clothing fad is a temporary, passing fashion. It is a new item or look that has great appeal to many people for a short period of time. It is usually out of the ordinary. A fad becomes popular fast and then dies out quickly. It is a passing fancy that is very well liked for a while. Soon after it reaches its height of popularity, its extreme design causes its popularity to wane. Often it is an accessory, such as the brightly colored shoes shown in **2-5**. It sometimes includes a particular fabric or decoration.

Many teens enjoy wearing the latest fads. Fads provide a feeling of adventure as well as a sense of belonging to the group. Ankle socks with lace ruffles are a fad of the past. Other examples are hot pants and tall, colorful plastic boots. Argyle kneesocks, various types of hats, and patchwork garments are sometimes fad items.

jocic/Shutterstock.com

Fads can be fun as long as they are not too expensive and the money being spent for them is not needed for other, more practical items. If a faddish item is well designed and meets a clothing need, it can become a style or influence fashion. Fashions have more lasting aesthetic value than fads.

A *craze* is like a fad because it is a passing love for a new fashion. However, this has a display of emotion or crowd excitement with it. It is a mania. Sometimes very popular entertainers will start a craze. Advertising on television and in magazines and newspapers can heighten the craze. Stores have a hard time keeping such items in stock because people are so eager to buy them. Advertising on television, the Internet, and in magazines and newspapers can heighten the craze.

A classic item of clothing is one that continues to be popular even though fashions change. It stays in fashion for a long time. Classics were originally fashion items, but their general appeal and simple, stylish lines have kept them popular. They can be worn year after year. Some examples of classic garments are white dress shirts, dark business suits, navy blazers, tuxedos, Chanel suits, shirtwaist dresses, and loafer shoes. Blue jeans are now also a classic. The trench coat shown in **2-6** is a classic garment.

A wardrobe consists of all the apparel a person owns. A wardrobe includes all of the garments and accessories. *Accessories* are the articles added to complete or enhance an outfit. Examples include belts, hats, jewelry, shoes, gloves, and scarves. These are the secondary items added to dress up, or set off, garments. People need accessories in their wardrobes to achieve a total, completed look.

Clothing Construction Terms

The fit of a garment refers to how tight or loose it is on the person who is wearing it. A good fit means the garment is the right size and does not pull tightly or sag loosely when worn. Figure **2-7** shows a well-fitting dress. The design of a garment can, however, give it intentional looseness. Garments can be designed

Robnroll/Shutterstock.com

2-6 Trench coats have remained basically the same in style and use over many decades.

to be loose, semifitted, or fitted (quite tight) to achieve different fashion looks. A *fitted* garment is shaped to follow the lines of the body.

Seams are the lines of stitches that join two garment pieces together. *Darts* are short, tapered, stitched areas that enable the garment to fit the figure. Seams and darts give shape to flat pieces of fabric so they can fit a three-dimensional body.

The *bodice* of a garment is the area above the waist, such as the upper part of a dress or jumpsuit. The bodice is often closely fitted and is distinguished by a seam around the waistline of the garment. Notice the seams, darts, and bodice in **2-8**.

Throughout clothing history, there have been three main methods of making or constructing clothing. They are the draped, tailored, and composite methods. These three basic ways of

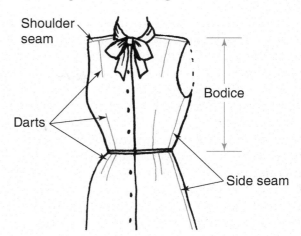

2-8 Seams are located at the shoulders, sides, and other places in garments. Darts stitch fabric together where the garment would be too big if left unstructured.

2-9 This beautiful Indian sari shows that flat fabrics can be draped to create garment designs.

JCPenney

2-7 A well-fitting garment looks good and feels good when worn.

www.exoticindia.com

putting fabric together do not change. Yet the results are styles of clothes that vary from year to year and from culture to culture.

Draped garments are those that are wrapped or hung on the human body. At first, animal skins were thrown over the body. Later, weaving produced pieces of fabric. An uncut square or rectangular piece of woven material was draped either tightly or loosely around the body. The same piece of fabric could be wrapped to achieve different looks or to serve several purposes. For instance, it could be used as a garment, as a bed covering, or for carrying things.

Examples of draped garments are the Roman toga and the Indian sari, as in **2-9**. There are also ponchos and draped skirts and gowns. They have characteristic folds of soft fabric. Draped garments are usually held in place with pins, buttons, toggles, or a sash or belt.

Tailored garments are made by first cutting garment pieces and then sewing them together to fit the shape of the body. The first tailored garments were made when the eyed needle was invented. Seams could then be sewn, such as with thread, to join garment parts together.

Tailoring provided jackets and pants that were warmer than furs thrown loosely over the body. Animal skins were used at first since they do not ravel and are well-suited to this method. Garments were later cut and sewn from fabric. Examples of tailored garments of today include suits, pants, and fitted jackets, as in **2-10**.

Composite garments are made by a combination of the tailored and draped methods. Garment parts are cut and sewn. Some parts may fit close to the body, and some are draped. Folds of fabric often hang loosely from the shoulders, waist, or hips. Examples of composite garments are the Japanese kimono, tunics, bathrobes, caftans, and capes. The evening gown in **2-11** is a composite garment.

2-10 Although wearing ease allows for comfort, this jacket, shirt, and pants are made with shaped garment pieces that have been cut and sewn together.

kostudio/Shutterstock.com

Vogue® Patterns/Bellville Sassoon

2-11 In this composite dress, some garment parts are tailored and others are draped to achieve the overall design and fit.

Clothing Business Terms

Haute couture (pronounced oat koo-tur´) literally means *finest dressmaking* in French. However, it has come to mean the high-fashion industry. It refers to a group of firms or *fashion houses*, each with a designer who creates original, individually designed fashions. Designers of exclusive, high-fashion garments are called *couturiers*.

Haute couture clothes originate in Paris, Milan, New York, or other fashion centers. They are very expensive and are made in limited numbers. They are constructed of luxury fabrics with a great deal of handwork. They have intricate cut and details, and contain the exclusive label of the designer.

Haute couture garments are sometimes *custom-designed* specifically for a particular person. Custom-designed garments have special fit, design, and fabric for the one person who ordered them. *Made-to-order* or *custom-made* garments are not designed for a particular person although they are made for that person. He or she places an order after seeing a sample garment, sketch, or picture.

Copies of some haute couture garments are made in quantity by high-priced manufacturers. They look like the original haute couture garments, but are produced in factories. The quality of construction and fabric may be good, but not as high as a haute couture version. Good copies might sell in better fashion boutiques. Cheap copies sell at bargain shops.

Knockoffs are lower-priced copies of garments. They are produced in great volume with lower-quality materials and construction. Copies and knockoffs are a result of *fashion piracy*. That is the stealing of design ideas without the consent of the originator, such as from Internet coverage of designer showings.

Ready-to-wear (RTW) garments, as in **2-12**, are those that are mass-produced in factories. They are manufactured in quantity according to standard sizes. Thousands of one garment design are made in many sizes. They are available in great numbers on the racks of stores throughout the country and world. They contain the manufacturing company's label rather than the name of the particular designer.

Consumers are the people who buy and use goods and services. Consumers purchase and wear apparel. You, your family, your friends, and all shoppers who buy goods and services are consumers. Consumers are very important in determining what fashions will or will not become popular. Consumers also keep their country's economy strong with their purchases.

2-12 The clothes worn by almost all consumers are ready-to-wear garments offered in quantity on retail racks and shelves.

Mitrofanova/Shutterstock.com

Retailers sell individual items to consumers. They advertise and sell their items directly to the general public. Retail stores include department stores, chain and discount stores, and small shops. Mail-order catalogs, TV shopping channels, and online retailers will all be discussed in Chapter 7.

Wholesalers, on the other hand, sell goods in large lots to retailers. Wholesalers usually distribute their goods from large warehouses. Each item costs less from a wholesaler, but usually dozens of each item must be purchased.

Sometimes retailers sell the extra clothes that were produced by manufacturers but were not ordered for regular selling. These items are called *overruns*. They are in perfect condition but are leftover at the manufacturer at the end of the season, so they are priced lower for consumers.

Stores may also sell irregulars. *Irregulars* have slight imperfections. The irregularities in merchandise are often not noticeable, but the goods must be labeled as such and priced lower than their perfect counterparts. *Seconds* are items that are soiled or have flaws. For instance, they might have missing trim or mended runs and tears. They must also be priced lower than perfect goods.

Promotions to sell particular fashions are done nationally by the manufacturer of the goods, as well as locally by retail stores. The promotional activities are the advertising and merchandising efforts to increase sales.

Price Markets

The apparel industry offers garments at all prices along a sliding scale from high to moderate to low. These are called *price markets*, which are categories into which merchandise is placed according to its retail selling price.

High-priced apparel is sold to the *class market* that is made of the few people who buy high-fashion clothing. These people accept more unusual styles and colors than most consumers. They are willing to spend more money on their wardrobe than most others. They often go to many important social events and like being seen in high-fashion items. The garments are sold only in exclusive salons. Each item has the designer's name on the label.

The high-priced market has only a tiny percentage of the total sales of garments. However, the high-priced designers and their creations receive the most publicity. These designers also tend to be the most creative since they do not have restraints imposed by keeping production costs down. Their designs, and the publicity they receive, keep the general public aware of fashion trends.

The moderately priced market has almost one-third of all clothing sales. These garments are factory-produced in relatively small numbers. They have dependable brand names and are of good fabrics, such as the garments shown in **2-13**. They are sold in small specialty stores or better department stores. Most fashion designers work in this price market. Usually the name of the manufacturing company is on the label instead of the name of the designer. The designer is most often a hired, anonymous talent.

2-13 These moderately priced men's garments of good quality have been produced in relatively small numbers.

In cooperation with Jos. A. Bank

Low-priced apparel is sold to the *mass market*, which is made up of the bulk of people who are average folk. The low-priced market has about two-thirds of all apparel sales. These garments are mass-produced in great volume in common styles and colors. They are sold on racks of discount stores, lower-end department stores, and through inexpensive catalog sales outlets. Not many fashion designers are employed for this market since very little original designing is done. Only the name of the manufacturing company is on the label.

Fashion Cycles

A fashion cycle is the periodic popularity, disappearance, and later reappearance of specific styles or general shapes. It is a rotation of particular styles. The fashion cycle is a regular round of different styles that are fashionable over time and then eventually repeat themselves.

How Cycles Occur

Peoples' desire for new fashions causes garment silhouettes and details to constantly change. Fashions always change with the same series of events: the new style is introduced; it is eventually worn by many people; and finally it is discarded for a newer style. In other words, new fashions eventually peak, become old fashions, and disappear. New fashions are always being created because people want to own the newest and latest items.

In fashion cycles, high fashion is usually introduced by high-priced designers and worn by *fashion leaders* of the time. These are men, women, and trendy young people with enough status and credibility to start new styles. They are not afraid to wear something before everyone else does. Every community has fashion leaders, who are first to accept and wear new styles. They are *trendsetters* who lead by example within their social groups.

In past centuries, the fashion leaders or trendsetters were royalty. They could afford new fashions and discard older styles. Now fashion leaders tend to be public celebrities, such as television and movie stars, rock musicians, sports heroes, and political figures. Some are members of the most prestigious social classes. However, others are members of specific subcultures or simply people who are especially responsive to change.

While fashion leaders are wearing the new styles, other people are watching them. The others are forming opinions about the new fashions and deciding how they would look on them. Their eyes and minds are getting used to the new colors, shapes, and proportions. Soon adaptations of the fashions are worn by people in many social groups. The styles receive greater publicity and promotion. Retail stores carry more of them and prices become more affordable. The fashions become well established, with mass acceptance and popularity among the general public.

Following a fashion's highest level of social acceptance is *social saturation*. This is a period in which the fashion is worn by almost everyone. It is overused. The fashion becomes dull and boring. It is no longer novel or exclusive. It starts to decline in popularity and eventually becomes obsolete.

Meanwhile, a different high-fashion look is emerging. Trendsetting fashion leaders have moved on to new styles being introduced. The attention of consumers turns away from the old styles and focuses on the new. The new style eventually gains popularity with the average person. Consumers acquire, use, and eventually discard clothing items. This process is outlined in **2-14.**

2-14 A fashion item is created and introduced to the public, worn by certain fashion leaders, and spread to masses of consumers, gaining high acceptance. Then it diminishes in popularity and use, ending as an accepted fashion.

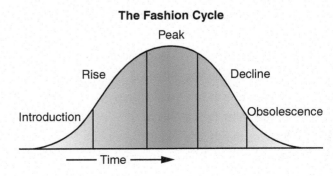

The Fashion Cycle

The life of each fashion look can be quite different. The period might range from several months to several years. The speed with which fashions cycle in and out of style increases with technological innovations. These technologies, including the Internet, increase the speed of communication and the spread of ideas. Other factors can slow down fashion cycles. This includes the aging of the population since older people tend to prefer familiar styles. Clothes from the past look strange today because they are no longer in fashion. However, each style is considered attractive when it is popularly worn as a fashion.

As fashions come and go, they seem to be extreme and daring when first introduced, smart and stylish when they are popular, and dowdy and out-of-date after their peak. Figure **2-15** illustrates the feelings toward styles as they pass into and out of fashion, as developed by fashion historian James Laver. The years listed are approximate.

Silhouettes of Fashion Cycles

This book will not go into depth in describing historic clothing. However, each period has had a characteristic style that set it apart from other times. Some styles became fashionable even though they were uncomfortable or unsafe. For instance, at times women were cinched in so tightly they could hardly breathe. Skirts were sometimes so long and tight that walking was difficult. Fashionable shoes had pinched toes or caused people to trip.

In past centuries, fashion cycles moved slowly. Three specific silhouettes would separately rise, peak, and fall in popularity. This always happened in the same order within about a 100-year span. The three basic silhouettes were bell, back fullness, and tubular. There were variations of dress and coat lengths, positions of the waistline, and styles within each silhouette category. The silhouettes would repeat, but with distinctly new fashion features. The old silhouettes were repeated in new ways. The changes took place gradually. Notice in **2-16** how the same silhouettes cycled in and out of popularity over the years.

The *bell silhouette* dress has a fitted waist and full skirt. It is wide at the bottom. Capes and pants with legs that are wide and full at the bottom are also examples of this silhouette.

2-15 Fashions are disliked before they become popular, then strongly liked when they are at their peak. After their popularity decreases, they are strongly disliked. Eventually old fashions are considered to be charming and gorgeous.

The Swing of Fashion Popularity

10 years before its time — vulgar and indecent

5 years before its time — bold and shameless

1 year before its time — flashy and daring

When it is in fashion — elegant and smart

1 year after its time — tacky and dowdy

5 years after its time — hideous

10 years after its time — outrageous

20 years after its time — funny

50 years after its time — odd

100 years after its time — charming

2-16 The bell, back fullness, and tubular silhouettes used to repeat themselves about every 100 years.

Fashion Cycle Silhouettes

| 1740s | 1780s | 1820s |
| Bell | Back Fullness | Tubular |

| 1850s | 1880s | 1920s |
| Bell | Back Fullness | Tubular |

The *back fullness silhouette* has a skirt that puffs out in back but not in front. For this, there has been draping of fabric at the back hipline or a bustle to give back fullness. Sometimes suit jackets also flare out in back.

The *tubular silhouette* has a slim skirt all around. It sometimes has a high or low waistline. It often hangs from the shoulders to the hem without being belted. It has mostly vertical lines.

Fashion cycles in men's clothing can be seen in the different widths of neckties, lapels, and trouser legs. They fluctuate over time by moving from narrow, to medium, to wide, and then to narrow again. Also, the tops of trousers may have pleats at the waist or be tight from waist to hips. Trouser bottoms sometimes have cuffs and sometimes have no cuffs.

Figure **2-17** summarizes the American fashion trends of the 1900s. Recently, cycles have not been as distinct as in past centuries. The pace of fashion change is tied to the overall pace of the culture. Rapid change takes place now because of new technology in communications, manufacturing, and retailing. Current fashion trends seem to occur in 20- to 30-year cycles, or the span of a generation.

Today most clothes are practical and comfortable. They have freedom of movement and are functional. Fashions seem unpredictable and individualistic. Consumers now think more freely. They buy what they like, what they need, and what they can afford. However, these fashions will also become part of clothing history.

Styles must sell to stay in fashion. Designers try to appeal to the public, so as many clothes as possible will be purchased. Because of varied lifestyles, more clothing styles are popular at a time. Mass production allows a variety of fashion looks to be available to all. Also, worldwide communication, trade, and travel spread fashion ideas quickly. They permit many fashion looks to be popular everywhere. Today, several basic styles may exist at the same time with minor trends of fashion changing quickly.

Social and Economic Influences on Fashion

Fashion has always reflected social and economic conditions, current events, technology, popular entertainment, and people's values and attitudes. The decoration on the clothes of the past related to the general thinking and art forms of the time. In the Victorian period, for instance, small, intricate decoration was

2-17 American fashion trends in the twentieth century were fun and interesting, but silhouettes were not as distinct as in other centuries.

Twentieth Century Fashion Trends

1900s— Edwardian elegance

1910s— Influence of early movie stars

1920s— Carefree, jazzy, "flapper" era

1930s— Clingy, draped, long fashions

1940s— Padded look; World War II influence

1950s— Sloppy; bobby socks and sneakers; poodle skirts

1960s— Pop or mod decade; coordinated costumes; miniskirts; pantsuits for women

1970s— Men's leisure suits; bold neckties; double-knit jackets; pants flared at bottoms

1980s— Preppy look; designer jeans; natural fibers; comfort

1990s— Oversized fit; lack of color—much black; casual office attire

1900s 1920s 1950s 1970s

Karkas/Shutterstock.com

2-18 Today, anyone can wear purple garments; they are not reserved for only the wealthy.

used frequently. In architecture, for example, Victorian homes were decorated with jigsaw cut trim and other ornamentation. In clothing, ribbons, laces, and braids were used.

Historic clothing shows that social and economic factors have always had a great deal of influence on fashion. Long ago, people dressed according to their social class. Members of royalty were the only people who could afford to wear silks, pearls, embroidery, and certain colors. In fact, they were the only ones who were permitted to wear these items. For

example, purple dye was rare and expensive. Thus, it was a status symbol worn only by the wealthy. See **2-18**.

Economic factors still affect fashion. For instance, in an era of hard times, clothing usually gives a serious, conservative image. Fashion trends move slower. In better times, the styles are brighter and more adventurous, since people are more apt to try new, different fashions. Clothing looks perkier and trends move faster during prosperous times.

The *Hemline Index* is a theory that was developed by a research director of a stock brokerage firm. He noticed that when hemlines rose (as in the early 1920s and 1960s), the stock market indexes also went up. When hemlines started to fall (as in the late 1920s and 1950s), the stock market indexes also went down. Hemlines were mixed in the early 2000s. Popular skirt lengths were simultaneously various levels of short and long. This coincided with the volatile stock market that had sharp ups and downs.

Many fashion and stock market experts think the *Hemline Index* is amusing and should be taken lightly. Even so, it reinforces the basic idea that people's moods are reflected in the way they dress. When they are down in the dumps, they tend to lose interest in their appearance. When their spirits are high, they dress in styles that are more fun and provocative. If the standards of dress change quickly, the basic social structure of the society has probably changed.

During wartimes, there is a military influence on apparel. During World War II, the government restricted the amount of fabric to be used for civilian clothing. This was necessary because of the demand for supplies needed for the armed forces. Styles became tight. The widths of hems and seam allowances were skimpy. Men's trousers no longer had cuffs. The country's economic needs made necessary limitations on the fashions of the time.

Summary

To know about fashion, specific fashion terms must be understood. Clothing construction terms refer to how garments fit and are made. Clothing business terms deal with haute couture and ready-to-wear aspects of fashion.

Price markets differ. Price markets of high-priced, moderately-priced, and low-priced apparel have different characteristics.

Fashion cycles occur because of consumers' desire for new garment silhouettes and details. Fashion leaders introduce new looks that are created. The designs gain in popularity to finally achieve very high acceptance for a period of time. Eventually, they lose popularity, diminish in use, and disappear while other fashions are gaining popularity. At some later time, they reappear. Until recently, various silhouettes have recurred in the same order within 100-year spans.

Social and economic influences on fashion are shown historically by people dressing according to their social class. These influences are related to the general thinking and art forms of certain times. Hard times, stock market levels, and wars have influenced society's fashions during various periods.

Chapter 2 Review and Assess

Fashion Recall

Write your answers on a separate sheet of paper.

Matching: Write the letter for the general term that describes each specific term.

1. Stylish.
2. Retail.
3. Classic.
4. Draped.
5. Overruns.
6. Couturier.
7. Seams.
8. Fit.
9. Silhouette.
10. Darts.
11. Avant-garde.
12. Fashion piracy.

   A. fashion term
   B. clothing construction term
   C. clothing business term

Short Answer: Write the correct answer to each of the following questions.

13. What is the difference between a fad and a craze?
14. Describe a fitted garment.
15. Explain the difference between a custom-designed garment and a custom-made garment.
16. What is fashion piracy?
17. What are the three silhouettes that were the basis for fashion cycles in past centuries?

True/False: Write *true* or *false* for each of the following statements.

18. In recent times, fashion cycles have not been as distinct as in past centuries.
19. During a recession, clothes tend to be fun and provocative to try to help people feel better.
20. According to the *Hemline Index*, when hemlines rise, the stock market indexes also go up.

Fashion Vocabulary

21. Working in teams, locate a small image online that visually describes or explains each of the *Fashion Terms* on the chapter opening. To create flash cards, write each term on a note card and paste the image that describes or explains the term on the opposite side of the card. Then, use your cards to review the chapter vocabulary.

Critical Thinking

22. **Assess vocabulary knowledge** Why is it important to know fashion terms and use them correctly? Explain how this knowledge is important, especially to someone working in the fashion field.
23. **Make comparisons** Compare the three main methods of clothing construction. How do these methods influence the style of clothes that are popular today? Write a short summary of your comparison.
24. **Analyze fashion influences** What social and economic factors influenced fashions of the past? What social and economic factors do you believe influence fashions of today?

Core Skills

25. **Speaking** Visit a discount store and an expensive clothing boutique. In an oral report to the class, compare the kinds of clothes promoted in each business. What are the differences between the apparel for the mass market and the class market? What silhouettes and features are most common for each category? Which store sells more fad items? Which sells more classic styles? If possible, show photo examples from the website of each business as you give your report.

26. **History and speaking**   Bring pictures, detailed descriptions, or articles of clothing to class that show a fad of the past. Why do you think the item is no longer in fashion? Show a current fad by clipping fashion ads that picture it. What details about the item indicate it is a fad? Discuss your analysis in class.

27. **Writing**   Write an essay about one or more people whom you consider to be current fashion leaders or trendsetters. Describe the new styles they are wearing. How and where do they display their fashion choices?

28. **Research and speaking**   Search online for technologies that apparel manufacturers are currently using for tracking fashion trends. How do these technologies help manufacturers decide what fashions and how many of them to produce? Discuss your findings with the class.

29. **Math practice**   Use spreadsheet software to analyze the *Hemline Index* theory in relation to stock market indexes. According to your analysis, does the Hemline Index relate to how well the economy is doing? If not, what other factors about fashion influence the stock market? Discuss your findings?

30. **CTE career readiness practice**   Use reliable online or print resources to investigate economic issues surrounding current fashion trends. Read two or more articles and summarize your findings in writing. When evaluating reliability of information, remember the following.

    • *Identify author/writer credibility.* Who is the author or writer (well-known)? Is the author, writer, or publisher known for reliable fact-checking?

    • *Verify details.* Can you verify the facts in the articles for other reliable sources? Is the information current? Is the copyright recent?

    • *Identify bias.* Is the information presented from only one point of view? Is it from a well-known educational institution or other source? Avoid articles that lack objectivity.

Fashion in Action

31. **Portfolio builder**   Create a storyboard showing the basic apparel designs in fashion this year. Collect representative color pictures of items from websites, catalogs, or magazines. Be sure to credit your images. Mount them on heavy paper and label them with the names of the styles. As an alternative, use school-approved software to create a digital storyboard.

32. **Design activity**   Clip or print pictures of draped and tailored garments, two different pictures of each. Roughly sketch a composite design for each of the four pictured garments. For each new design, write a brief paragraph describing the changes you made.

33. **Design activity**   Use your imagination to sketch a possible fad for the future. Share your sketches with the class and describe why you think this a future fad.

Self-Assessment Quiz ↗

Complete the self-assessment quiz online to help practice and expand your knowledge and skills.

Garment Styles and Parts

G-W LEARNING.com

While studying, look for the activity icon to:

- **practice** key fashion terms with e-flash cards, vocabulary games, and matching activities
- **assess** what you learn by completing self-assessment quizzes

www.g-wlearning.com/clothingandfashion/

FASHION TERMS ⤷

asymmetrical	cuff	cardigans
lapel	waistband	pullovers
set-in sleeves	inseam	closures
kimono sleeves	single-breasted	yoke
raglan sleeves	double-breasted	

Objectives

After studying this chapter, you will be able to
- ➤ describe the many styles of dresses.
- ➤ identify neckline and collar styles for men's and women's apparel.
- ➤ describe sleeve, skirt, pants, coat, and jacket styles.
- ➤ discuss how garment parts can be combined in different ways to achieve new and different fashions.

All garments are comprised of a combination of garment parts, such as sleeves and collars. As different garment parts are put together, new designs are created.

As you study this chapter, you will learn to identify basic garment styles and parts. You will develop fashion awareness. You will understand how basic clothing styles are constantly being revived and modified to become current fashions.

Basic Dress Styles

Some basic dress styles are illustrated in **3-1**.

Sheath dresses have no waistline seam. They hang from the shoulders and have inward shaping at the waist.

Shift or *chemise dresses* also have no waistline seam. They are straight and loose fitting with no inward shaping at the waist.

A-line dresses are narrow (fitted) at the shoulders. They have no waistline seam and become wider at the hemline. They are named after the *A* shape of their silhouette.

belkos/Shutterstock.com

| Sheath | Shift | A-line | Tent | Empire | Lowered waistline |

3-1 These dress styles may be made to look different by using various sleeves, collars, fabrics, and trims. However, the basic silhouette of each category remains the same.

Tent dresses are large and billowy. They hang loosely from the shoulders. If sleeveless, they are often worn in hot weather because they do not hug the body.

An *empire* (pronounced om-peer from French fashions) *dress* has a high waistline. Its opposite, the *lowered waistline style dress*, has a long torso. Its seam between the bodice and skirt is down toward the hips.

Other Dress Styles

Other dress styles are formed by using a variety of seams, fullness, or other characteristics. They modify basic dress styles, such as the examples shown in **3-2**.

Princess dresses have seam lines going up and down their entire length. The vertical seaming is from the shoulder or the armhole. Princess seams provide fit as well as fashion. There is no horizontal waistline seam.

Blouson dresses have a blousy fullness above the waist. They are usually belted. They most often have a fitted skirt.

Shirtwaist dresses are like long, semifitted, tailored shirts. They are as long as a regular dress and usually have a belt or sash at the waist.

Coatdresses are heavy dresses that usually close down the front like a coat. However, they are worn as the main garment rather than over another garment.

In an asymmetrical dress (or garment) design, the right side is different from the left side. If divided by a center line, the two halves are not the same. The asymmetrical dress pictured in 3-2 has a typical *surplice closing*, which has a diagonal overlap to one side.

Jumpers and *sundresses* have a brief bodice, often with shoulder straps and a low neckline. They may or may not have a waistline seam, and may be fitted or loose at the waist. A jumper is made of heavier fabric and is worn over a blouse or sweater. A sundress is worn in hot weather alone as a dress.

Neckline Styles

There are many neckline styles. As you read the following descriptions of some of them, look at the drawings in **3-3**.

Décolleté is the French term for a low neckline. It is usually used with bare shoulders, such as in an evening gown or sundress. Sometimes the garment is strapless.

A *jewel* or *round neckline* encircles the base of the neck. It is plain and rounded.

A *boat* or *bateau neckline* goes straight across from shoulder to shoulder. It is high at the front (and usually back) and is wide on the sides.

Princess   Blouson   Shirtwaist   Coatdress   Asymmetrical   Jumper or sundress

3-2 Many dress styles are possible. Each one has a descriptive name.

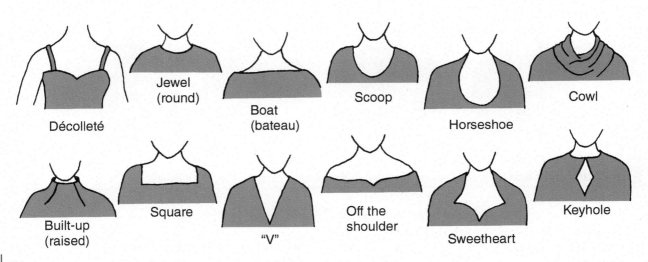

Décolleté   Jewel (round)   Boat (bateau)   Scoop   Horseshoe   Cowl

Built-up (raised)   Square   "V"   Off the shoulder   Sweetheart   Keyhole

3-3 This is only a sampling of the many neckline options that are available for apparel.

A *scoop neckline* is lowered and round. It is usually lower in front than it is in back.

A *horseshoe neckline* is up high at the neck in back but goes down like a *U* in front.

A *cowl neckline* is draped with flowing folds. It gets its name from a medieval monk's hood.

Necklines can be raised, normal, or low. Sometimes they are high in front and low in back. Sometimes they are just the opposite. They can be round, square, V-shaped, or off the shoulder. They can have scalloped edges or special shapes such as the sweetheart or keyhole versions.

Collar Styles

Collars can be designed to have long or short points. Sometimes the corners are rounded. Study the different collars and their names in **3-4**.

Collar styles range from narrow to wide. Some collars lie down flat on the garment, while others stand up around the neck. Most go up somewhat in back, fold over, and then fall back onto themselves and a small amount of the garment. A popular collar for shirts is the *button-down collar* with points that button to the shirt.

3-4 Collars may be wide or narrow. They may lie down on the garment or stand up around the neck.

Collars on garments that fold open at the neckline often have lapels. A *lapel* is a pointed part of the garment below the collar. It turns back at the front neckline. It looks like a continuation of the collar going down from a V-shaped notch along the outer edge. It is shown in 3-4 on a *convertible collar*.

A *stock collar* is an imitation of an ascot. An *ascot* is an accessory added at the neck like a necktie. It is a broad scarf that is looped over itself. A true ascot was originally worn by men and is usually tucked into the front neckline of the shirt.

A *jabot* (pronounced ja-bow) was originally of lace or a ruffle worn on a man's shirt. Now it is worn on the collar front or going down from the neckline of women's garments, as well as on men's tuxedo shirts.

3-5 All sleeve styles are based on these three basic types of sleeves.

Basic Sleeves

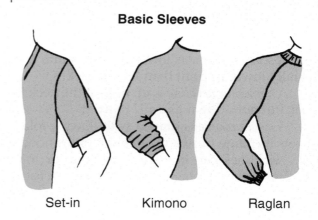

Set-in   Kimono   Raglan

Set-in Sleeve Styles

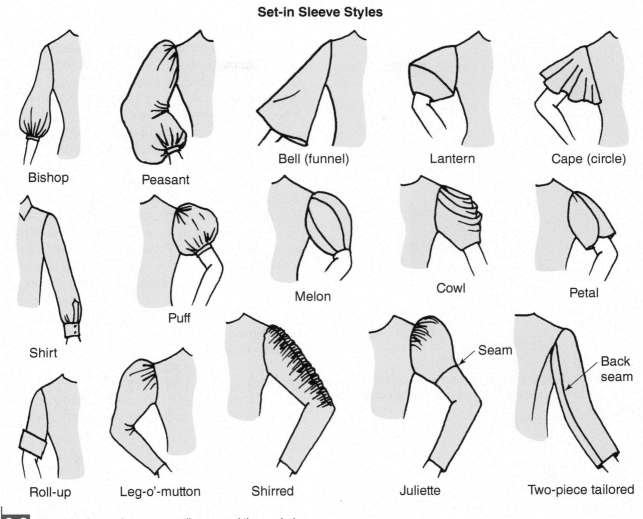

Bishop Peasant Bell (funnel) Lantern Cape (circle)

Shirt Puff Melon Cowl Petal

Roll-up Leg-o'-mutton Shirred Juliette Seam Back seam Two-piece tailored

3-6 All set-in sleeves have a seam line around the armhole.

Sleeve Styles

The three basic types of sleeves are set-in, kimono, and raglan, as shown in **3-5**. Any of these can be short, just above the elbow, three-quarters length (just below the elbow), seven-eighths length, wrist-length, or long (just below the wrist bone).

Set-in sleeves are sleeves that are stitched to the garment around the regular armholes. They offer the best fit for most people. They can be tight (fitted), puffy, long, or short. In all cases, there is a seam in the front and back from the underarm curving up to the shoulder. That seam follows the natural body line that connects the arm to the body. Examples of many set-in sleeves are shown in **3-6**. Take note of the armhole seam joining the sleeve to the garment bodice in each case.

Kimono sleeves, as shown in **3-7**, are continuous extensions out from the armhole areas with no seam lines connecting them to the garment bodice. Kimono sleeves can be long or short and either fitted or loose. Fitted kimono sleeves often have gussets. A *gusset* is a wedge-shaped piece of fabric added to give more ease of movement. Gussets can be used in various places on many garment parts.

If a kimono type of sleeve is designed lower than usual at the underarm, it is called a *dolman sleeve*. *Batwing sleeves* are very low and loose at the underarm with only a gradual curve, if any, between the side waistline and the sleeve bottom. They are almost cape-like.

Stylized kimono sleeves can have many different design lines. In all cases, there is no seam joining the sleeve to the bodice.

Kimono Sleeve Designs

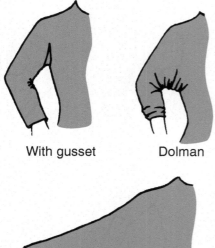

With gusset   Dolman

Batwing

3-7 A tight-fitting kimono sleeve may have a gusset at the underarm. Dolman and batwing styles are kimono sleeve variations.

3-8 A raglan sleeve has a seam line coming up from the underarm in front and back. The seam then turns to form one of a variety of design options.

Raglan Sleeve Design

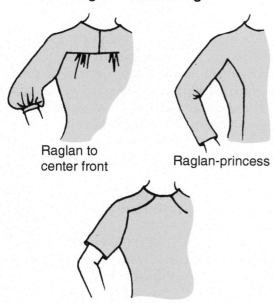

Raglan to
center front   Raglan-princess

Saddle sleeve design

Raglan sleeves have a shaped seam in the garment originating from the underarm. The seam does not continue up to the outer shoulder at the top of the arm. Sometimes it goes directly up to the neckline, as seen in 3-5. Other times it goes across to the center front or jogs down into a bodice princess seam, as in **3-8**.

Raglan sleeves can be any length, just like other sleeve types. The raglan seam line is usually a smoothly curving line. However, it can also be shaped in unusual ways. The *saddle sleeve* design is an example of a specific raglan sleeve. It is also called a *strap-shoulder* or *epaulet sleeve*.

Some garments are designed to be sleeveless, as shown in **3-9**. These are usually for hot weather or for jumpers or vests that are worn over a blouse or shirt. The basic *sleeveless* armhole hits the top of the shoulder where a set-in sleeve would ordinarily join the bodice. Sometimes, for design interest, it is cut in toward the neckline.

Cap or *French sleeves* are very short. They are illustrated in **3-10**. They are like a sleeveless armhole at the underarm and a short kimono sleeve going out from the shoulder. They can

Basic   Cut-in

3-9 Sleeveless garments do not have sleeves. The armhole is sometimes designed with varying shapes.

3-10 Cap sleeves have a small amount of length down from the shoulder and no sleeve at all at the underarm.

Basic cap or   Set-in
French sleeve   cap sleeve

also be an extension of the shoulder dropping down over the upper arm. A very short set-in sleeve is also a cap sleeve.

Dropped shoulder sleeves, as in **3-11**, have a horizontal seam around the upper part of the arm. The lower sleeve can be any length. They can also have any amount of fullness.

A **cuff** is a band at the bottom of the sleeve. A *vent* is an opening that goes from the open end of the cuff up into the sleeve. It enables the cuff to overlap and button. It is often finished with a *placket* that is a decorative strip of fabric over the vent. Often the placket has a point at its upper end. Study these parts in **3-12**.

Skirt Styles

Several skirt styles are illustrated in **3-13**. Become familiar with their shapes and their names.

Straight skirts have no added fullness at the hem. They go down straight from the hipline for a very slim silhouette. They are sometimes called *fitted skirts*.

A-line skirts have extra width at the hem on each side. When viewed from the front or back, the silhouette resembles the letter *A*.

Flared skirts have some fullness at the hem all around. There are soft ripples going upward from the skirt bottom toward the waist.

Circular skirts are very full at the hem. When held out at the sides during wearing, this style of skirt forms a half circle. When opened up and laid flat, it forms a circle.

Full skirts are pleated or gathered. *Pleated skirts* have structured folds of cloth. The pleats

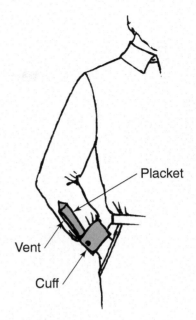

3-12 A long shirt sleeve usually has a cuff, a vent, and a placket.

either hang open from the waist or are stitched down for a snug fit from the waist to the hips. *Gathered skirts* have the fullness of the fabric pulled together at the waist without structured folds.

Slightly gathered skirts that are not very full are called *dirndl skirts*. They are quite straight and often have pockets in the side seams.

Gored skirts have vertical seams all the way from the waistline to the hem. They are similar to the princess seams in a dress. The seam lines cause the skirt to have several panels or gores. The gores are a bit wider at the hem than at the hipline. Skirts can have four, six, or many gores.

Umbrella skirts have many narrow gores. The gores are pressed to have a narrow silhouette, but when the wearer walks or moves, the gores spread open and close like an umbrella.

Wrap skirts wrap around the body and overlap at the side-back or side-front. They are most often fastened with a tie or button. They usually have a straight or slightly flared silhouette.

Some skirts are part of a dress, attached to a bodice with a waistline seam. Other skirts may be held at the top by a **waistband**. A waistband is a band of fabric that goes around the waist and fastens with a button or hook and eye.

All skirt styles also have the option of varying lengths. Notice the names of the most common hem lengths in **3-14**.

3-11 Dropped shoulder designs have a horizontal seam around the upper part of the arm.

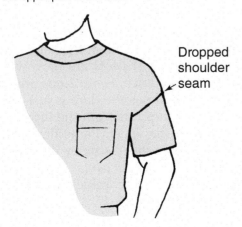

Dropped shoulder seam

Skirt Styles

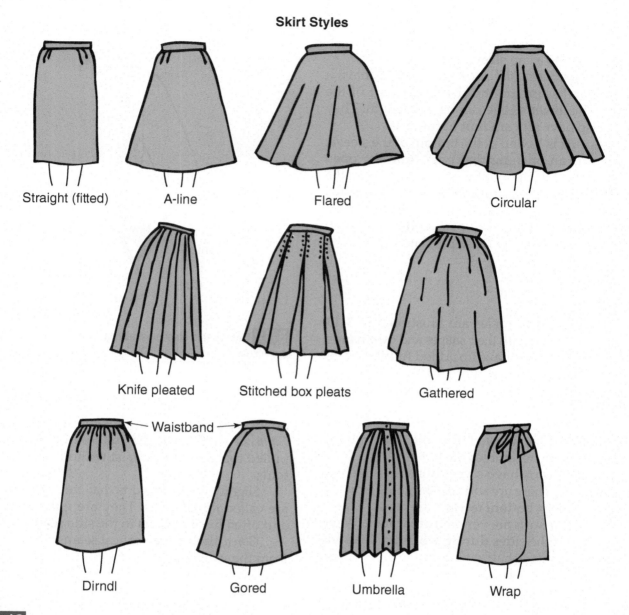

Straight (fitted)   A-line   Flared   Circular

Knife pleated   Stitched box pleats   Gathered

Waistband

Dirndl   Gored   Umbrella   Wrap

3-13 Skirts can be very narrow, extremely full, or shaped in various ways. Fashion interest can be created with gathers, seams, pleats, or an overlap.

Pants Styles

Pants are also called *slacks* or *trousers*. Pants can be many different lengths. Some are short shorts. Others are so long that they drag on the ground. Notice the names of the many lengths indicated in **3-15**. The seam on the inside of the leg (from crotch to pants hem) is called the inseam. The inseam length is an important measurement when buying or hemming pants.

Pants can be many different widths as well as lengths. These are indicated in **3-16**. *Straight pants* are the same width at the hem as they are at the knee. *Tapered pants* are narrower at the hem than at the knee. *Flared pants* are wider at the hem. Sometimes the flare is just below the knee. Other times it is from the hips on down, or even from the waist. Pants flared from the waist are often worn as fancy evening slacks. They are called *palazzo pants*. Flared pants that are gathered in at the ankles are called *harem pants*. Notice these in **3-17**.

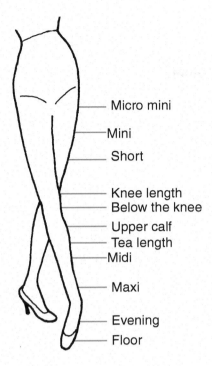

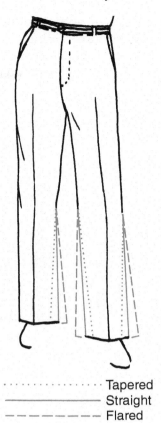

3-14 Skirt designs can be any length that is popular or desired.

.... Tapered
——————— Straight
– – – – – – – – Flared

3-16 The legs of tapered pants get tighter as they go down toward the ankle. Flared pants legs get wider.

3-15 Pants can be almost any length, depending on the dictates of fashion.

3-17 Some pants have special design interest. The ones shown here have excess flare.

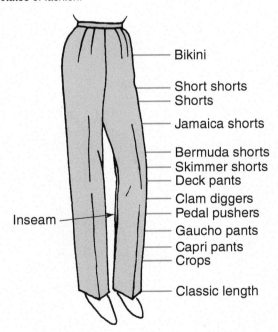

Palazzo pants   Harem pants

Gauchos, knickers, and culottes are shown in **3-18**. They have some fullness and usually end below the knee. The legs of *gaucho pants* are like wide tubes. *Knickers* are gathered to a band or strap below the knee. *Cargo pants* are loose, with pockets on the sides of the legs. *Culottes* are pants that look like a skirt, also called *pantskirts*. *Skorts* combine a skirt with shorts.

One sturdy type of pants is *jeans*, shown in **3-19**. They are comfortable and have become fashionable as everyday wear. They can be casual when worn with a sweatshirt or dressier when worn with a blouse or sport coat. They have heavy double stitching and are usually made of denim. *Cords* are jeans made of corduroy fabric.

The top of *hip-huggers* is lower than the regular waistline. The pants ride on the upper hips. A garment with a bodice, or top, attached to pants is called a *jumpsuit*. Look at these in **3-20**.

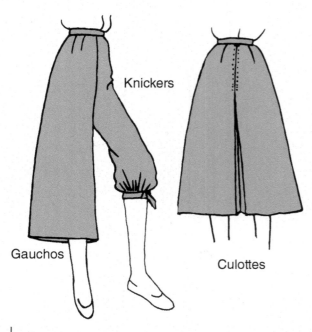

3-18 These pants styles have emerged on the fashion scene at various times through the years.

Knickers

Gauchos

Culottes

3-19 Jeans have become a classic style of pants worn for their sturdiness and versatility.

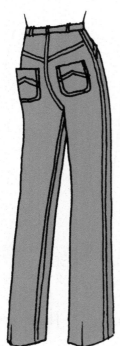

Jeans
(back view)

3-20 Like other garments, pants have a wide variety of design options.

Hip-huggers

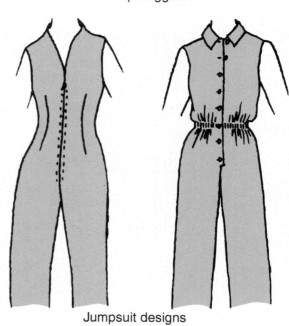

Jumpsuit designs

Coat Styles

Trench   Wrap   Coachman   Polo   Chesterfield

3-21 A coat is needed as an outer garment in cool climates.

Coat and Jacket Styles

Coats are warm or weatherproof garments that are worn over a person's regular clothing. Some popular coat styles are shown in **3-21**.

Capes, as in **3-22**, are coat-like outer garments that hang from the neck and shoulders over the back, front, and arms. They have no sleeves, thus arm movement is restricted. There are usually slits in each front side of capes for the hands to slide through.

3-22 Capes go in and out of fashion. They are usually not worn as an everyday cover-up.

Capes

Jackets are short coats. A few common jacket styles are shown in **3-23**.

Sport coats or *blazers* are classic jackets that are always in fashion. They, along with suit jackets, are either single-breasted or double-breasted. **Single-breasted** garments are held shut with one row of buttons in front. **Double-breasted** garments have a wider overlap and two rows of buttons. An example of each is in **3-24**. European cut blazers and suit jackets are more tightly fitted at the waist than traditional American blazers.

A *poncho* is similar to a blanket with a slit or hole in the middle for the head. It has no sleeves. Sometimes it is made of waterproof cloth and used as a rain jacket. A *parka* is a heavy winter jacket with a hood. It has a warm *lining*. Sometimes the lining is of quilted fabric or real fur. Look at these in **3-25**.

Miscellaneous Styles and Parts

A *hood* is a head covering that is attached at the neckline of a garment. A hood is shown in **3-26** along with garments that are described in the following paragraphs.

Jacket Styles

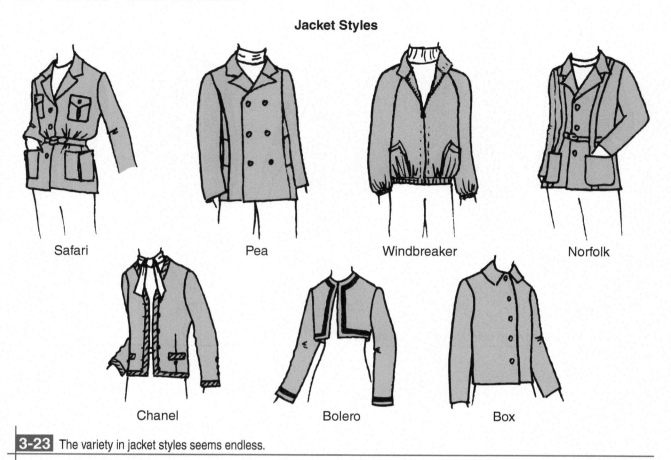

Safari

Pea

Windbreaker

Norfolk

Chanel

Bolero

Box

3-23 The variety in jacket styles seems endless.

3-24 The jacket on the left is single-breasted, with one row of buttons and buttonholes. The coat on the right is double-breasted. It has a wider overlap at center front and two rows of buttons.

Andrey Armyagov/Shutterstock.com

3-25 Ponchos are loose garments that slip over the head. Parkas, on the other hand, can be snug at the waistline and cuffs.

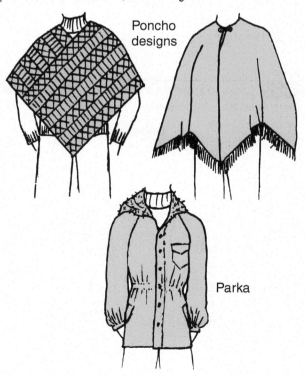

Poncho designs

Parka

3-26 All these apparel items have specific names and characteristics.

Hood

Tunic

Vest

Caftan

Halter

JCPenney

3-27 This robe is a caftan style, which is long and loose-fitting.

A *tunic* is a long blouse or shirt that extends down over pants or a skirt. It is a long upper garment that goes over a lower garment. Tunics are hip-length or longer. Sometimes they are belted.

Caftans are long, flowing, robe-like garments. See **3-27**.

Vests are sleeveless, close-fitting, jacket-like garments. They cover just the chest and back. They do not extend much below the waistline. Some vests are called *weskits*.

Halters are brief garments worn on the upper body, usually in hot weather.

A *sweater* is a knitted (or crocheted) covering for the upper body. It is usually worn for warmth. Sweaters are cardigan, pullovers or partial-closer styles. Cardigans open down the front. Often they button or zip. Pullovers slip over the head when they are put on or taken off, as shown in **3-28**.

The term *lingerie* refers to undergarments, ladies' slips, and feminine nightwear. *Pajamas*, *nightgowns*, and *nightshirts* are forms of nightwear. A *robe* is worn over nightwear when the person is not in bed. It is long and loose. Its name originates from the flowing garments of ancient civilizations.

StockLite/Shutterstock.com

3-28 This pullover sweater, which slips over the head when put on or taken off, has an argyle design on the front.

Closures enable the wearer to get into and out of garments. They include zippers, buttons, snaps, hooks and eyes, Velcro®, or any other fasteners that can open a correctly sized space and close it again. See **3-29**.

A yoke is a band or shaped piece, usually at the shoulders or hips, that gives shape and support to the garment below it.

Pockets are built-in envelopes that hold items. Pockets are usually added onto the outside of garments or are inserted into seams. Pockets sometimes have added tabs or flaps. *Tabs* are decorative fabric pieces that go out from the edge of pockets. *Flaps* are decorative fabric pieces that fall down over the openings of pockets. Illustration **3-30** shows several yokes as well as a pocket, tab, and flap.

Design Options

Fashion designers have almost endless options of garment parts, styles, lengths, and widths to combine in different ways. Thousands—even millions—of new fashions can be created. See **3-31**.

Petinov Sergey Mihilovich/Shutterstock.com

3-29 Zippers, ties, snaps and belt clasps, are fasteners that can open or close garments.

Old styles are continuously put together in new ways. Often, new and exciting names are given to the same old garment styles and parts. This makes them sound like they have never been used before. In these ways, the fascinating world of fashion continues.

Summary

Fashions are formed by how garment parts are designed and combined. Fashion designers have almost endless options of garment parts, styles, lengths, and widths to combine in interesting ways.

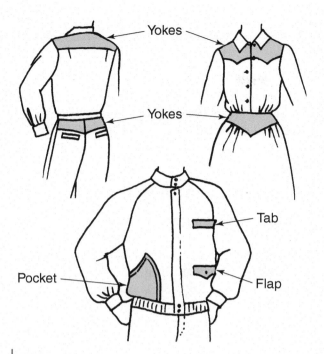

3-30 Yokes, tabs, pockets, and flaps are all features that can be incorporated into apparel designs.

Basic dress styles include the sheath, shift or chemise, A-line, tent, empire, and lowered waistline styles. Other dress styles include princess, blouson, shirtwaist, coatdress, asymmetrical, jumper, and sundress.

Neckline styles include décolleté, jewel or round, boat or bateau, scoop, horseshoe, cowl, and many others. The many different collar styles can have long, short, or rounded points. Collars can be narrow or wide, include lapels, or be a ruffled jabot.

All sleeve designs are based on the set-in, kimono, or raglan types of sleeves. There are also sleeveless designs, cap sleeves, and dropped shoulder designs.

Skirt styles can be straight, A-line, flared, circular, or gored. Fullness can be in pleats or gathers. Some skirts imitate an umbrella or wrap with an overlap.

Pants (slacks or trousers) can also be different widths, such as tapered, straight, and flared. Many lengths offer options for pants styles, such as gauchos, knickers, and culottes. Other pant styles are jeans, hip-huggers, and jumpsuits.

Anita Ford Collection

3-31 This fashion combines a rounded collar, buttons down the center front, princess seam lines, three-quarter length sleeves with bottom ruffles, lowered waistline, gathered skirt, and sash with a bow. It also uses a bright solid color and coordinating plaid in silk fabric. All of these features have been combined with others in different ways to create new fashions for centuries.

Coats, jackets, and capes are worn over other clothing. They can be of many styles and may be single-breasted or double-breasted.

Miscellaneous garment styles include tunics, caftans, vests, halters, lingerie, and nightwear. Additional garment parts include hoods, closures, yokes, pockets, tabs, and flaps.

Fashion Recall

Write your answers on a separate sheet of paper.

Matching: Match the specific terms with one of the four general style categories.

1. Bell.
2. Mandarin.
3. Flared.
4. Leg-o'-mutton.
5. Keyhole.
6. Jewel.
7. Shawl.
8. Horseshoe.
9. A-line.
10. Kimono.
11. Convertible.
12. Dirndl.

A. neckline style
B. collar style
C. sleeve style
D. skirt style

Completion: Write the word or words that correctly complete the sentences.

13. _____ dresses have vertical seam lines going up and down their entire length.
14. The right sides of _____ garments are different from the left sides.
15. A _____ is a pointed part of the garment that turns back at the front neckline below the collar.
16. _____ sleeves are stitched to the garment around the regular armhole.

True/False: Write *true* or *false* for each of the following statements.

17. Raglan sleeves have no seam line connecting the garment bodice to the sleeves.
18. Closures are fasteners that enable the wearer to get into and out of garments.
19. A décolleté neckline is high and usually has a turtleneck collar with it.
20. Gored skirts have vertical seam lines that cause them to have several panels called gores.

Fashion Vocabulary

21. Work with a partner to write the definitions of the *Fashion Terms* at the beginning of the chapter based on your current understanding. Pair up with another pair to discuss your definitions and any discrepancies. After reading the chapter, discuss the definitions with the class and ask your instructor for any necessary corrections or clarification of the definitions.

Critical Thinking

22. **Assess styles**   Describe which basic dress styles seem to be in fashion today. Assess how these styles have been modified to become the current fashions of today.
23. **Analyze clothing**   Analyze the clothing you are wearing. Write a description of the garment styles in your outfit, including neckline, collar, and sleeve styles.
24. **Create fashions**   Imagine you are a fashion designer. Describe to the class how you would combine various garment parts, styles, lengths, and widths to create a fashion.

Core Skills

25. **Research and writing**   Investigate the history of jeans. Write an essay on how they originated, the various groups of people who have worn them at different times, and the types of jeans available today.

26. **Reading and speaking** Choose one of the dress styles discussed in the text and read about the history of the style. For example, you may want to read about the history of the *sheath* dress. Locate image examples online that support your reading and create a digital time line showing how the dress style evolved. Share your digital time lines with the class.

27. **Writing** Mount at least six pictures or drawings of current fashions on pieces of paper. Label the particular garment styles and parts (scoop neckline, raglan sleeve, tapered pants, and so on). Write catalog descriptions for each fashion. As an alternative, use digital images and school-approved software to create a digital poster of current fashion drawings. Label the images and write descriptions for each item as above. Be sure to credit your image sources.

28. **Research and writing** Use the Internet to research the development of various fasteners used on garments. Collect and mount actual samples of the fasteners. Label each and describe where it would be used on garments. As an alternative, collect digital images of the fasteners and use school-approved software to create a digital poster of your findings. Upload your poster to the class website for peer and instructor review.

29. **CTE career readiness practice** Analyzing fashion trends is an important workplace skill for those who work in the fashion industry. Choose one current trend you have observed in garment styles. Analyze the possibility of this trend continuing. Do you think this trend will become a classic design style? What evidence supports your view? Write a short commentary on your analysis and post it to the class website for peer and instructor review.

Fashion in Action

30. **Portfolio builder** Collect photos or sketches of each of the garment styles and parts described in the chapter. Label each one and keep them in a folder to be included in your portfolio.

31. **Design activity** Look up information on different types of pleats. Examples might be knife, inverted, box, accordion, sunburst, kick, and any others you can find. Illustrate and describe each.

32. **Design activity** Choose three different collar and sleeve styles. Combine them into six totally different shirt designs. Use school-approved design software to sketch the designs. Add variety by making the sleeves various lengths and the collar points longer, shorter, pointed, and rounded. Use your creativity. Share your designs with the class.

Self-Assessment Quiz ➦

Complete the self-assessment quiz online to help practice and expand your knowledge and skills.

Two

Apparel Industries

4   The Development of Fashion

5   The Textile Industry and
      Home Sewing Patterns

6   Apparel Production

7   Fashion Promotion and Retailing

The Development of Fashion

rag trade
trade publications
trade associations
collections
fashion piracy

logo
Chambre Syndicale
Coty Awards
designer patterns
house boutiques

franchises
licensing
bridge lines
prêt à porter

Objectives

After studying this chapter, you will be able to
- ➤ discuss the worldwide importance of the apparel industries.
- ➤ list several trade publications and trade associations.
- ➤ describe the development of haute couture.
- ➤ explain how the couture industry is changing.
- ➤ discuss the importance of the designer ready-to-wear industry.

The *apparel industries* center around textiles, garment manufacturing, and retailing. The *textile industry* includes the business firms that produce the fabrics used for apparel and other end uses. The *apparel manufacturing industry* includes the firms that do the designing and factory construction of garments. This wholesale level sells to retail companies. Retailing includes the activities dealing with the direct selling of the items to consumers. Fashion promotion is also an important aspect of the industries. All the business segments concerned with apparel are exciting, yet complicated.

The Scope of the Apparel Industries

The apparel industries have been developing for many centuries. Clothing styles were evident even in ancient Greek and Roman times. However, fashion as it is known today started in Europe during the Renaissance period in the 1500s. Textiles and clothing changed very slowly until about the time of the *Industrial Revolution*, which began in England in the late 1700s and spread to the United States.

In general, the Industrial Revolution caused a switch from handmade garments to mass-produced ready-to-wear clothes. Three major developments contributed to this overall change:

➤ Mechanized textile mills were able to make fabrics of better quality in less time.

➤ The sewing machine was invented, and factory manufacturing of clothing was introduced.

➤ Techniques in mass distribution, advertising, and retail selling were developed and refined.

Today, the apparel industries are one of the top industry types in the world. Textile and apparel production are the largest industries in many nations, especially in developing countries. Retailing is a large industry in all countries, especially in well-developed ones like the U.S.

The influence of apparel businesses goes beyond the design, manufacture, and distribution of textile and clothing items. Many other industries are affected by the fashion field. For instance, advertising firms rely on the apparel industries for a great deal of their work. Publishing companies need fashion news. Also, one part of the apparel industry can greatly affect other sections. Fitted waistline styles increase belt sales. Rising hems boost hosiery sales.

Inside *The Trade*

The *garment industry* is sometimes called the rag trade or the *needle trades*. In the United States, this manufacturing industry started as small tailoring shops in New York City. Immigrants settled there as skilled tailors and assistants before the turn of the twentieth century. The garment industry was located between the textile mills of the North and the cotton fields of the South. Plus, New York was the nation's largest city and the center of fashionable society. Today, New York's fashion industry is centered along *Seventh Avenue*. Other nearby streets and avenues are home to the textile firms, menswear showrooms, fashion accessories companies, and fur district.

Other cities also have their *garment districts*. Apparel businesses provide many jobs in all parts of the United States and the world. In fact, the industry is a leader in hiring and training workers for entry-level positions. The industry also provides a variety of employment opportunities for more advanced positions, which often require a much higher level of education and training.

Many fashion magazines and trade publications are important to the apparel industries. Trade publications are magazines, newspapers, and books that deal specifically with a certain industry or trade. Several trade publications for the apparel industries are shown in **4-1**. Specific trade information is also sent daily via e-mail to individuals in different segments of the industry.

The *Women's Wear Daily* (WWD) newspaper is considered to be the *bible* of the fashion industry. It reports all new apparel trends with photos, fashion illustrations, and stories. It also reports on business and financial news of the apparel industry. Once weekly, the edition features the menswear industry. A few examples of the many other specialized trade publications are *Textile World*, *Apparel Magazine*, *Footwear News (FN)*, *Sportswear International*, *Accessories Magazine*, and *California Apparel News*. Subscribers may also read these publications online. For descriptions of specific trade journals, find their websites by searching each newspaper/magazine title through an Internet search engine.

As in other industries, apparel businesses have trade associations to which workers belong. Trade associations are groups that promote or further the interests of a certain industry or trade. Some examples are the Council of Fashion Designers of America (CFDA), American Apparel

4-1 Trade publications give specific news about particular industries. *Textile World, Apparel, Internet Retailer, Stores, and Retail Information Systems (RIS)* are a few examples of the many trade publications concerned with textiles, apparel manufacturing, and retailing.

and Footwear Association (AAFA), the National Retail Federation (NRF), and the National Textile Association. Such associations try to further the interests of their members. They set standards for their industry and allow constructive communication among their members. They lobby to the government for laws that help their industry and also promote their industry to the public.

Each association has a trade publication that distributes information to its membership. Each also has periodic trade shows. The shows attract thousands of people associated with production of ready-to-wear clothing. Equipment manufacturers, textile firms, and apparel manufacturers participate. They display and give presentations about machines and manufactured goods, in hopes of selling them to others who attend the shows. Meetings and lectures disclose new ideas. With such activities, industry members are kept up-to-date with the latest innovations and products.

Couture

High-fashion couture clothes are very fashionable and expensive. Couture designers and their firms serve the small, but influential, high-priced market.

The Development of High Fashion

The high-fashion garment industry originated with the superior French dressmaking industry. France has led fashions for hundreds of years. Paris has been an international cultural center and is still thought to be the world's fashion center, as shown in **4-2**.

Exquisite *haute couture* (pronounced oat koo-tur′) shops originated in Paris centuries ago. At first, Parisian couturiers dressed dolls in scaled-down versions of their latest creations. They sent them to prospective customers throughout the world. Only when fashion magazines and newspapers began to appear to communicate designs did this practice fade away.

Early American dressmakers went to Paris for their designs, rather than doing original work. They brought back many fine fashions. From

4-2 Many of the best-known haute couture businesses, like Nina Ricci, are in Paris.

those clothes, they learned about French cut and workmanship. They copied and adapted what they needed for their purposes.

Several influential French couturiers of the past are listed in Figure **4-3**. Such designers and their Paris haute couture businesses were located in city houses rather than in commercial buildings. Thus, they became known as *fashion houses*. They had international fashion supremacy until World War II. Then the war cut them off for several years.

As World War II stopped the flow of fashion news and garments from France, the American design industry grew. American fashion ingenuity became recognized in all areas of apparel. Young talents created colorful sportswear. The designers became confident, resourceful, and adventuresome with their creations. Also, Hollywood movies encouraged original designing and became a vehicle to spread fashion ideas throughout the country. Several American high-fashion designers of the past are listed in **4-4**.

When Paris couture houses reopened after the war, they were challenged by fashion designers in the United States, Italy, and England. Today, many cities join Paris as being influential on the apparel scene. In Italy, couture houses are located in Milan, Florence, and Rome. Other important cities are New York, Tokyo, and London. California has centers known for sportswear. Dallas, Chicago, and Montreal are gaining respect for their fashion industries. The Scandinavian countries are known for their native patterned knitwear. Israel has beachwear

French Couturiers of the Past

Louis Vuitton—Luxurious women's and menswear, leather goods, accessories, and shoes; founded upscale luggage company in 1854, family run until 1969; enduring influence due to consistent high quality products and current designs. In 1987, company joined with Moët-Hennessy to become LVMH Group, now a large international retail conglomerate.

Charles Frederick Worth—Of English descent; founder of French couture (1860s).

Madame Paquin—Elegant, tasteful, innovative designs; fur-trimmed suits; fine embroidery; greatest influence 1890s–1920s.

Paul Poiret—Bold colors; looser look; greatest influence 1900s–1920s.

Madelaine Vionnet—Started bias draping; greatest influence 1920s–1930s.

Coco Chanel—Famous for Chanel cardigan-style suit look; mixed fabric patterns and textures; greatest influence 1920s–1971.

Edward Molyneux—Of English descent; classic, elegant Paris design; greatest influence 1919–1950.

Elsa Schiaparelli—Of Italian descent; many types of apparel; creative with prints; greatest influence 1920s–1950s.

Nina Ricci—Important feminine collections from 1932; firm now run by son-in-law.

Cristóbal Balenciaga—Of Spanish descent; outstanding quality of clothing construction; initiated a basic silhouette; greatest influence 1940s–1950s.

Christian Dior—Wide skirts and small waistlines; greatest influence 1940s–1950s. Raf Simons now designs for this label.

Pierre Balmain—Designed elaborate gowns for famous people until his death in 1982; greatest influence 1950s–1960s.

4-3 Haute couture, or the creating and selling of high-fashion designs, started in the 1800s.

American High-Fashion Designers of the Past

Gilbert Adrian—Hollywood costumes from the 1920s; greatest influence 1940s.

Halston—Fashionable hats, then women's wear, airline uniforms, and perfume from 1950s–1980s. First to license his name.

Claire McCardell—Original sportswear; greatest influence late 1930s–1950s.

James Mainbocher—Theater and other clothes; greatest influence 1940s–1960s.

Norman Norell—Won the first Coty Award in 1943; was later the first Hall of Fame winner; fashion influence until the early 1970s.

4-4 American high-fashion designers became recognized in the mid-1900s.

Recently, the term *haute* is used less and the single term *couture* has come to mean *top-of-the-line designer fashions*. Exclusive designers throughout the world now name their highest-priced collections *couture*, even though items are factory produced, but in limited quantities. Upscale retailers have couture departments where they present expensive ready-to-wear suits, dresses, and evening fashions of top design firms.

The Business of High Fashion

Most successful couture designers have had help getting started from wealthy financial backers. Their talents have been recognized, and they have been able to succeed because of the money and promotion of their benefactors. It is also important for designers to have the support of the press and other media that can spread fashion news quickly and make or break a couturier.

French couturiers used to design all their garments specifically for the clients who would wear them. Sometimes a client even contributed creative suggestions. Each fashion had true originality and presented the self-expression of its wearer.

Today fashion designers do collections, which include all of their designs for a specific season. The designs are created for anyone who will buy or order them. The designs are based on the fashion influences that each designer projects as the coming trends.

and leather coats. Hong Kong is high on the list with silks. Dublin features tweed and knit creations. Madrid excels with leather and beading.

Many designers from other cities have branch salons in Paris. Also, most designers of Paris, Milan, and other fashion centers have offices and salons in New York. Most major cities have several talented, exclusive designers.

The couture fashion houses present two major showings of their collections a year. They are the fall-winter showings (held the preceding summer) and the spring-summer showings (held the preceding winter). The showings are held in one common location, often under large tents, with each firm having a specific time slot. This allows buyers and members of the press to attend each one.

The showings are glitzy runway extravaganzas. They are like theater productions that feature high-fashion models parading to music, as in **4-5**. From 50 to 100 outfits might be shown by each designer. The cost of preparing for and producing the showing is exorbitant. The fine fabrics and trimmings, as well as the quality construction of each of the many designs, are expensive. Additionally, there are modeling fees and costs for hair and makeup experts, lighting, and music. The designer makes a traditional walk down the runway at the end of the show.

The exclusive audiences at the collection showings are made up of wealthy private customers, press representatives, and commercial buyers. The commercial buyers represent various retailers, apparel manufacturers, and pattern companies. If a private customer buys a design, it is constructed to that person's measurements. Showings are now sometimes recorded and sent to the couturier's best clients.

Fashion piracy, or the stealing of design ideas, is always a threat to designers. Therefore, clients who are allowed into the showings are carefully screened. Commercial buyers, such as apparel manufacturers and pattern companies, have to pay large cash deposits. If they buy some designs, the deposits are deducted from the purchase prices. However, these companies must pay more for each garment they buy than a private customer pays. This is because they are essentially paying for copying rights as well as the garment. Fewer and fewer commercial buyers attend each year because of the high costs.

Even though no sketching is allowed, the clothes are shown on the Internet and copied in cheaper versions by manufacturers soon after the showings. The couturiers do allow photographs for press releases, which gives them free publicity. The publicity keeps the designers' names famous and their designs in demand.

Couturiers must constantly be original and artistic, **4-6**. They strive to create well-designed fashions of impeccable quality, distinctive styling, and lasting good looks. Most designers want to produce timeless clothing. However, some of their creations selected to be shown by the press have a touch of the outrageous.

To succeed, couturiers should recognize the importance of business decisions, as well as have artistic creativity. The job is strenuous and competitive. Many designers have business partners who watch the finances of the firms so the designers can strictly design. Many fashion houses, especially in Italy, are family-run with the skills passed on from generation to generation.

Top fashion designers have personal trademarks for which they are known. Each designer strives to have his or her signature, initials, logo, or type of garment instantly recognized. A logo is a symbol that represents a person, firm, or

4-5 For collection showings, models wear original fashions that are often unusual and show the flare of the designer.

Gina Smith/Shutterstock.com

Kirill Mikhirev/Shutterstock.com

4-6 Fashion designers often create their own beautiful fabrics, as well as the clothing ideas that are constructed with the highest quality.

organization. In the past, logos and labels were only put on the inside of garments. Now they are often status symbols placed at visible locations on the outside of apparel. Some couturiers even create their own lining or garment fabrics, with their logos or names woven into the designs.

Fashion Associations and Awards

The trade association for top designers of the Paris couture is the Chambre Syndicale (pronounced shom'br sin-dee-kall'). It was formed to determine qualifications for couture houses and to deal with their common problems and interests. A couturier must be recognized as talented and successful to become a member. He or she must agree to abide by rules that include a code against copying. The rules also govern minimum numbers of staff models and production workers, dates of showings, and shipping dates.

The Chambre Syndicale coordinates the dates of the showings and issues admission cards to press people for the openings. It sponsors a school for the education of apprentices for the

couture industry. It also represents its members in relations with the French government, arbitrates disputes, and regulates working hours and uniform wage arrangements.

Most cities or countries that are international fashion centers have similar organizations. For instance, *Fashion Week Tokyo* introduces Japanese designers to buyers, the public, and the press. It operates through a central information office. It gives the designers a structure in which they can compete with each other, such as through scheduled collection showings. Through such organizations, designers can join together to help make their city or country a leader in the fashion world. Besides Paris, Milan, and New York City, organized fashion weeks are held in Sydney (Australia), Mumbai (India), Moscow (Russia), Dubai (United Arab Emirates), and many other international cities.

Many fashion professionals belong to *The Fashion Group International, Inc.* It was organized in 1930 by women who were influential in American women's fashions. They were designers, magazine editors, retail executives, and other professionals. They were committed to promoting American fashions. The Fashion Group International, Inc. helped build the entire American fashion industry to the place of prominence it has today.

The prestigious *American Fashion Critics' Awards*, referred to as the Coty Awards, were presented each year from 1943 to 1978, and then became the *Cutty Sark Awards* through 1988. Such awards were given to the fashion designers recognized as the most creative and outstanding. Awards were given for excellence in women's wear, accessories, and menswear. Voting was done by a national jury of fashion editors of newspapers and magazines. Being named to the *Coty Hall of Fame* was the highest fashion honor in the United States. A designer could achieve that honor only by winning a Coty Award three different years.

Recently, major U.S. fashion awards have been presented by the Council of Fashion Designers of America (CFDA), such as for designers of the year in several categories as well as special awards for other fashion achievements. More than 450 designers are members of the CFDA. See **4-7**. Various awards are also given by well-known retail stores, businesses, and other professional groups.

Council of Fashion Designers of America/© Corina Lecca, photographer

4-7 Ralph Lauren and Michael Kors are prominent, successful fashion designers who are members of the Council of Fashion Designers of America.

sergios/Shutterstock.com

4-8 With such a huge selection of quality apparel of all fashion levels and prices available to consumers these days, there is small demand for couture fashions.

Most countries have their own ways of recognizing talent in fashion design with awards presentations. Examples are the Dutch Fashion Awards, Taiwan Fashion Awards, and British Fashion Awards.

Recent Changes for Growth and Income

Today, consumers have an abundance of mass-produced fashions of excellent quality available to them at many different price points. Thus, the expensive couture industry has only a small number of rich and famous customers. People's lifestyles and attitudes toward clothes have changed. Most people want more clothes and don't feel the need to buy exclusive items. See **4-8**.

Besides the financial crunch of decreasing sales, haute couture houses have had increasing problems in hiring skilled tailors needed to make the clothes. The older tailors are retiring,

and young people are not choosing to go into this field. To survive, many top fashion designers are diversifying. They create ready-to-wear collections and fashion accessories for the moderately priced market.

Several couturiers add to their incomes by selling the patterns of some of their creations to commercial pattern companies. Illustrations of designer patterns can be seen in pattern catalogs at fabric stores where the patterns are sold. Skilled home sewers can use the patterns to make their own designer clothes.

Couturiers also supplement their businesses with boutiques and franchises in cities around the world. Many of them also have licensing agreements with manufacturers of other types of products, such as perfumes and home linens.

House boutiques are small retail shops that are branch stores owned by the couturier, as in **4-9**. They are usually in or near the haute couture premises, but may also be located in fashionable areas of other cities. They feature

4-9 This house boutique in Paris sells shoes that are designed by the staff of Christian Dior.

high-priced, high-quality accessories, such as handbags, shoes, and scarves. The merchandise is usually manufactured for the house by outside producers, but it is designed by the couturier or a member of the staff. It bears the designer's label. The couture house pays the rent and hires the salespeople.

Franchises are arrangements in which a firm, such as a couturier, provides retailers with a famous name and merchandise. In return, the firm (or couturier) receives a certain amount of money. The retail franchise owners do not work for the designer directly. However, they have been granted the right to use the designer's name and trademark to market goods. The designer does not help run the franchises, but the use of his or her exclusive name helps the businesses prosper. Franchises of designer fashions are often located in exclusive shopping areas of major cities. Sometimes they exist as boutique areas within large department stores.

Licensing is an arrangement whereby manufacturers are given exclusive rights to produce and market goods that bear a famous name as a stamp of approval. In return, the person or firm whose name is used receives a

percentage of wholesale sales. These are *royalty fees*. The royalties received by couturiers in licensing agreements are very lucrative. Major couture houses license their names to different manufacturers on a large variety of products. The merchandise includes eyeglasses, home linens, perfume, cosmetics, luggage, candy, shoes, china, and automobile interiors. Tommy Hilfiger, shown in **4-10**, is a highly successful apparel designer who licenses his name for many types of products.

Licensing arrangements began to multiply in America in the 1970s, though they were common in Europe much earlier. This has been called the *name game*. Some designers find it hard to keep tabs on the design or quality of all the products bearing their names. Some have established design studios. Employees of the studios arrange the licensing deals and check to be sure that the products are worthy of their labels. Inferior products would lower the value of designers' names.

The primary purpose of today's couture operations is to maintain the prestige of the designers. The houses must be successful with their couture creations to stay in demand for licensing. Only a slim profit, if any, is made on the couture clothes. The extravagant collection showings often lose money. However, the publicity from the showings keeps the designers' names in the fashion spotlight, so other big business ventures can be pursued.

4-10 Tommy Hilfiger is a successful fashion designer who has licensing agreements for other types of products. He is seen here with a fashion student on a study trip to New York City.

Figures **4-11** through **4-14** list many recently popular American and foreign fashion designers. Become familiar with the names of the designers and their apparel specialties. In some cases, the well-known name of a designer is maintained for the fashion house after that person has died. A new designer is hired to continue the tradition of high fashion with new creations. This is true for the houses of Chanel, Dior, Nina Ricci, Anne Klein, and Perry Ellis.

Designer Ready-to-Wear

The designer ready-to-wear (RTW) industry has become more important than couture. Showings of these bridge lines (designer ready-to-wear apparel priced between better and couture categories) are held as giant trade exhibitions. Showings take place in New York City, Paris, and other cities. In New York City, designer fashion week shows are held twice a year in Manhattan. The event is called *7th On Sixth*. The fall/winter collections are presented in early spring, and the spring lines are shown in the fall. For each fashion season, over 50 shows are staged in six days. Each show is 20–25 minutes long. Retail buyers, celebrities, and press attend. Other RTW lines are presented in corporate showrooms on or near Seventh Avenue. A lower-key trend is to have a breakfast or brunch showing with models walking around the tables wearing collection designs.

Fashion (market) week activities are glamorous, exciting, and exhausting for everyone involved. A great deal of publicity is generated by the designer RTW showings, and new fashion ideas are noted. Depending on orders from retailers, only about half of the designs will be put into production.

There are many RTW designers listed in Figures 4-11 through 4-14. These include familiar names such as Coty Hall of Fame members Donna Karan, Calvin Klein, and Ralph Lauren.

In Paris, the designer RTW industry is called prêt à porter (pronounced pret ah por-tay'). Prêt à porter means *ready-to-wear* in French. (The literal translation is *ready to carry*.) Prêt à porter collections are mass-produced designer fashions. They are often merely called the *prêt collections* (to differentiate them from the couture collections).

The women's wear prêt showings are held twice a year in Paris. The showings are always exciting and busy. They last for a week to 10 days. Over 100,000 fashion professionals come to these

---

4-11   France is still considered to have a great deal of design talent for high-fashion apparel.

Some Top French Fashion Houses

Chloé—Youthful, edgy women's fashions.

Louis Féraud—Excels in colorful, artistic, luxurious women's attire; died in 1999.

Jean-Paul Gaultier—Designs for the young market and does single-sex dressing that both men and women can wear.

Givenchy—Especially big in the 1950s; glamorous evening wear, ladies' suits, and dresses; perfection of cut and lasting quality.

Kenzo—Of Japanese descent; colorful, casual, multilayer silhouettes.

Karl Lagerfeld—Of German descent; he has created many inventive, wearable designs in France, Italy, and the United States for his own collection, and other famous labels.

Guy Laroche—Understated, quality fashions for mature, elegant women; also menswear, accessories, and perfumes; died in 1989.

Claude Montana—Strong on silhouette, color, and texture.

Hanae Mori—Of Japanese descent; fashions with poetic colors and patterns; also accessories; formed a foundation specifically to assist new talent in the fashion industry.

Thierry Mugler—Often creates sexy, clingy dresses.

Sonia Rykiel—The red-haired queen of knits and sweater dressing.

Yves Saint Laurent—Known for stylish, elegant, trendsetting designs; has been called the *king of fashion*; died in 2008.

Emanuel Ungaro—Known for sensuously draped dresses; feminine prints and textures.

Valentino—Italian who moved business from Rome to Paris; ladylike, sophisticated fashions for famous clientele.

Some Top American Fashion Designers and Firms

Adolfo—Cuban born; started with dramatic hats; now tasteful, classic, feminine dresses and suits; some licensing and RTW.

Geoffrey Beene—Sophisticated elegance with unusual details since the 1940s; a Coty Award winner; died in 2004.

Dana Buchman—Beautiful women's fashions for busy lifestyles.

Liz Claiborne—Firm continues with many brands (Dana Buchman, Kate Spade, DKNY, Kensie, etc.) and outlet stores; died in 2007.

Oscar de la Renta—Dominican of Spanish descent; creates romantic, colorful, glamorous fashions with ruffles and flourishes for own label and others; Coty Hall of Fame.

Louis Dell'Olio—Designs several lines with different labels; does furs, shoes, suits, and sportswear.

Carolina Herrera—Elegant women's creations.

Tommy Hilfiger—Classic American styles and jeans updated with unique twists.

Betsey Johnson—Originally based on dance costumes, now in many stores worldwide with fresh, unique designs.

Norma Kamali—Designs avant-garde fashions with unusual materials and ease of movement.

Donna Karan—Designs simple, sensual women's clothes that stretch and move well; also DKNY label at a lower price point; Coty Hall of Fame.

Calvin Klein—All-American sportswear designs with sophisticated simplicity; status jeans; has many famous clients; Coty Hall of Fame.

Michael Kors—Provocative, comfortable women's clothes.

Ralph Lauren—Uses blazers with looks from prairie rugged to English gentry to romantic; home fashions; retail stores; Polo logo; Coty Hall of Fame.

Michael Leva—Young designer known for easy experimental classics.

Bob Mackie—Designs for Hollywood stars; lots of beaded work.

Mary McFadden—Unusual, artistic, eccentric designs in decorative fabrics; luxurious evening clothes; Coty Hall of Fame.

Nicole Miller—Beautifully cut, contemporary, whimsical clothes; generous charitable giving.

Josie Natori—Lingerie and accessories with fine detailing.

Tom & Linda Platt—Irreverent fabric and color combinations; elegant but uncomplicated garments.

Arnold Scaasi—Glamorous gowns; Coty Award winner.

Adrienne Vittadini—Patterned knits; several lines; licenses; boutiques.

Vera Wang—Elegant, sexy wedding gowns and other fine apparel.

4-12 Many American designers have built their design businesses into large, successful firms. Most companies continue after the original designer's death.

4-13 Italy has become well-known for fashion, including leather products, knitwear, and garments with international flair.

Some Italian Fashion Names

Giorgio Armani—Milan; did menswear first, creates masculine, unstructured, layered designs for women; witty; relaxed refinement.

Benetton—Knitwear; many worldwide outlets; corporate advocacy advertising.

Nino Cerruti—RTW knitwear.

Dolce & Gabbana—Design team with sometimes outrageous women's wear and menswear, often in knits.

Fendi—Rome; sisters started with leather accessories; now also furs and RTW.

Salvatore Ferragamo—Florence; a family leather business started with shoes; died in 1960, firm now run by son James.

Gianfranco Ferre—Known for elegant, romantic, chic designs; once designed for House of Dior; died in 2007.

Gucci—Founded in Florence in 1921 by Guccio Gucci (he created the *GG* logo), who died in 1953; family-run until 1987. Now a corporate fashion conglomerate, Gucci Group.

Andre Laug—Rome; very original, wearable women's ensembles still being created; died in 1984.

Mariuccia Mandelli—Milan; designed the Krizia Collection; started hot pants in the 1960s, then created dresses, suits, animal knits, and other sweater dressing. Sold firm and retired in 2014.

Emilio Pucci—Simple structural garment shapes for women; strong artistic prints and signed fabrics; died 1992.

Gianni Versace—Milan; known for slinky, chain mail evening dress; also very original daytime outfits; since his death in 1997, designing has been done by his sister, Donatella.

Other Fashion Names Around the World

Hugo Boss—Of German descent; developed distinctive menswear lines; died in 1948.

Ika Butoni—Hong Kong; decoratively sequined and other artistic dresses.

Robert Burton—Creative Australian designer, mainly 1980s–1990s.

Scott Crolla—British; uses upholstery fabrics and tapestries in apparel.

Victor Edelstein—British; a favorite of the late Princess Diana.

David Emanuel—Feminine British fashions and gowns; designed Princess Diana's famous wedding dress.

Katia Filippova—Moscow; designer of avant-garde, eclectic combinations of colors, textures, and shapes.

Diane Freis—American-born designer in Hong Kong; romantic, feminine dresses with frills, feathers, beads, and tassels; also one-size shirred waistband creations.

Rei Kawakubo—Japanese; unconventional, somber designs in neutrals or earth tones; firm is Comme Des Garçons.

Jurgen Lehl—German who designs a full line in Japan.

Pat McDonagh—Canadian fashion designer; died in 2014.

Antonio Miro—Designs men's and women's lines in Spain.

Mitsuhiro Matsuda—Japanese; mixed many colors and layers of apparel; died 2008.

Issey Miyake—Combines classic Japanese design with unusual knits, draped skirts, and eccentric sculptural layering; uses fabrics with interesting textures.

Pitoy Moreno—Philippines; creates conservative, elegant gowns.

Jean Muir—British; best known for ladylike, jersey knit dresses and eccentric classics; died in 1995.

Bruce Oldfield—Original British designs for women.

Zandra Rhodes—British; trendy, off-beat women's clothes; innovative surface decorations; unusual hemlines.

Jil Sander—German; produces and shows designs in Italy.

Sybilla—New York City-born designer who lives and works in Madrid, Spain.

Alfred Sung—Leading couturier in Canada.

Tamotsu—Japanese; soft, curvaceous designs reveal the body shape.

Zang Toi—Malaysian-born designer creatively uses bright color combinations.

Roberto Verinno—Spanish; simple, elegant, professional women's clothes.

Yohji Yamamoto—Japanese; colorful, avant-garde, jovial creations.

4-14 Original and innovative design talent exists throughout the world. Fashion is truly international big business.

shows. Orders are placed by retail buyers. The buyers and media reporters also assess new directions that the influential French fashions are taking. Menswear, children's wear, and knitwear showings are at other separate times.

The Italians promote their fashions often, with different specialties at different times. In Milan, designers show their lines at prestigious fashion fairs just prior to the Paris prêt showings. See **4-15**. The exhibits are sponsored by two large industrial groups. One group is for ready-to-wear, and the other is for knitwear. There are also individual fabric fairs for silk, wool, leather, and home furnishing fabrics. In Florence, there are major exhibitions for children's wear and menswear. Italy even has fashion fairs devoted to uniforms and work clothes. Other countries do some of this, but to a lesser degree.

Carnaby Street in London has boutiques where colorful, uninhibited fashions for young men were first launched. However, England's ready-to-wear strength today lies in their high

4-15 Italian designer, Gianni Versace, started in Milan. Since his death, his sister, Donatella, has run the international firm.

quality men's tailored apparel, fine rainwear, and fashion-forward women's clothes. British designers show their lines at London Fashion Week.

Other countries are eager to export their fashions, too. Most countries have their own semiannual trade fairs and exhibits. See **4-16**. They also have showings and promotional trade offices in cities in the United States and around the world.

Unknown designers are hired to work on the ready-to-wear lines under the big name designers in the fashion houses. See **4-17**. Eventually, some of the best ones branch off into businesses of their own. Some designers specialize in jewelry, handbags, belts, or shoes. The designer labels in ready-to-wear clothes and accessories indicate to consumers that the items should be of fine quality and in good taste. The showroom in **4-18** contains the ready-to-wear collection of Norma Kamali for retail buyers to see.

Summary

The apparel industries of textiles, garment manufacturing, and retailing developed slowly throughout the world until the Industrial Revolution. Then there was a switch from hand-made garments to mass-produced ready-to-wear clothes. In the U.S., the rag trade started in the garment districts of New York City and other cities. There are many fashion magazines, trade publications, and trade associations tied to the segments of the apparel industries.

Expensive, high-fashion clothes originated in Paris haute couture houses. American dressmakers copied French designs until World War II. Then designers in all major cities of the world became known independently for various types of fashions.

4-16 Some fashion designers and manufacturers participate in trade shows to show their latest designs to potential clients.

Stefano Tinti/Shutterstock.com

4-17 After studying in an apparel design program, many graduates start as assistant designers in industry fashion firms.

Iowa State University/AESHM Department

4-18 Many fashion designers, including Norma Kamali, design ready-to-wear collections.

Most designers have wealthy financial backers or business partners. They present glitzy showings of their collections and promote their exclusive logos. The designers belong to fashion associations. Excellence is rewarded with prestigious awards. Recent changes for design firms to achieve more growth and income include designers' sewing patterns, house boutiques, franchise agreements, and licensing arrangements. Fashion piracy is common.

The showings of designer ready-to-wear (RTW) lines are now more important than couture. Collections of these mass-produced designer fashions are presented on runways and in showrooms in various fashion cities during market weeks. Designer labels in RTW clothes and accessories indicate to consumers that the items should be of fine quality and in good taste.

Chapter 4 Review and Assess

Fashion Recall

Write your answers on a separate sheet of paper.

Short Answer: Write the correct answer to each of the following questions.

1. What three major developments during the Industrial Revolution caused a switch from handmade garments to mass-produced ready-to-wear clothes?
2. What are two common names for the garment industry?
3. Name two trade publications of the apparel industries.
4. Name two trade associations of the apparel industries.
5. The high-fashion garment industry originated with the superior dressmaking industry of what country?
6. How did World War II affect the American design industry?
7. How many major showings of collections do the couture fashion houses present each year?
8. Why was the Chambre Syndicale formed in Paris?
9. Name two designers in the Coty Hall of Fame.
10. Name two reasons for the recent changes in the haute couture industry.
11. A retail shop owned by a couturier that carries accessories designed by the couturier or a member of his or her staff is a _____.
12. In a _____ arrangement, a couturier provides a retailer with a famous name and merchandise in return for a certain amount of money.
13. In a _____ arrangement, a manufacturer pays for the exclusive rights to produce and market goods that bear a designer's name as a stamp of approval.
14. In New York City, the fashion industry centers around _____ Avenue.
15. Which do more retail buyers attend—showings of the couture collections or showings of the prêt collections?

Fashion Vocabulary

16. Read the text passages that contain each of the *Fashion Terms* listed on the chapter opening. Then, write definitions of each term in your own words on a separate sheet of paper. Double-check your definitions by rereading the text and using the text glossary.

Critical Thinking

17. **Compare technologies**   Compare the effect the Industrial Revolution had on the apparel industries to what you believe emerging technologies will have on the apparel industries in the future. Write a summary about your comparison to post to the class website for peer and instructor review and discussion.

18. **Assess influence**   Assess the influence trade publications and associations have on the fashion industry. What impact do they have on fashion trends? Discuss your assessment in class.

19. **Analyze impact**   In the text, the author states that "the single term *couture* has come to mean *top-of-the-line designer fashions.*" Analyze the impact of couture fashions in your community. To whom are these fashions marketed? What evidence can you give to support your analysis? Write a short summary or blog post of your analysis.

20. **Evaluate contributions**   In your opinion, which fashion designer do you believe has contributed most to the development of fashion? Explain your evaluation in writing.

21. **Predict impact** Use online resources to investigate predictions about how technology will impact the development of new fashions 10 years from now. Write a report summarizing your predictions based on your research. Be sure to list the sources of your information.

Core Skills

22. **Reading and speaking** Look for articles and pictures of fashion showings in the United States or abroad in recent newspapers and magazines or on the Internet. Where were the showings held? Which designers were featured? What types of apparel were shown? What distinguishing characteristics and fashion trends were evident? Give an oral, illustrated report of your findings to the class.

23. **Reading and writing** Research website of the Council of Fashion Designers of America (CFDA) to identify the most recent winners of the *CFDA Fashion Awards*. Choose one of the winners to read about. Write a short summary of your findings, including a description of the winning fashions.

24. **Research and speaking** Use online and print resources to learn more about a famous fashion designer of the past. Use school-approved presentation software to prepare an oral report with visual aids on the life, work, and major contributions of the designer. Be sure to credit your photo sources.

25. **Reading and writing** Ask local apparel businesses and libraries that subscribe to trade publications for the apparel industries if you can borrow several publications. Bring copies of as many different publications as possible to class. Notice what kinds of information are presented in each. Compare the content of these publications to the fashion news in newspapers, consumer magazines, and on websites. Write a brief summary of your comparison.

26. **Technology** Use school-approved video creation software to prepare a digital video presentation about the influence of Hollywood movies on the fashion industry in the United States. Be sure to credit all sources used in your presentation.

27. **CTE career readiness practice** Presume you are an in-store fashion writer for a major department store. Your latest assignment is to write a press release for a *new* brand of designer ready-to-wear that your store will begin to carry for the coming season. Research details about the brand, its target market, and how the brand relates to your customers. Keep a documentation log of all your sources. Then, write the press release about the new brand.

Fashion in Action

28. **Portfolio builder** Create a booklet showing the fashions of at least three current well-known designers. If available, show each designer's unique signature or logo. Add this booklet to your portfolio. As an alternative, create a digital poster showing the fashions and designer logo and save the poster for your digital portfolio.

29. **Design activity** Imagine you are a fashion designer. Describe your design line. To whom would your fashion line appeal? Sketch a sample of a design that might be featured in your collection.

Self-Assessment Quiz ➦

Complete the self-assessment quiz online to help practice and expand your knowledge and skills.

The Textile Industry and Home Sewing Patterns

G-WLEARNING.com

While studying, look for the activity icon to:

- **practice** key fashion terms with e-flash cards, vocabulary games, and matching activities
- **assess** what you learn by completing self-assessment quizzes

www.g-wlearning.com/clothingandfashion/

Objectives

After studying this chapter, you will be able to
- ➤ **explain** the workings of textile businesses.
- ➤ **describe** how new color and fashion trends begin and are marketed.
- ➤ **discuss** the worldwide textile industry of today and the future.
- ➤ **write** a report about the home sewing pattern industry.

The textile industry is an extremely vital part of the overall apparel industries. Textile companies produce fibers, yarns, and fabrics for fashion and other products.

Home sewing patterns are a small part of the fashion industry, but deserve to be studied. Pattern companies design and make patterns for home sewers.

The Textile Industry

The textile industry produces fashion fabrics (cloth) for garments. It also develops and manufactures fabrics and other textile products for home decorating and many industrial uses. The industry is very large and vital to the economies of the United States and most other countries of the world.

Fabric Production and Distribution

There are four main steps in the production of finished fabrics. They are

1. *fiber production* from natural or synthetic materials
2. *yarn production* at spinning mills
3. *fabric (cloth) manufacturing* by weaving, knitting, or other methods
4. *fabric finishing* to satisfy the look, feel, and performance demands of the market

These processes involve highly specialized machinery and great skill. All firms strive for peak production and maximum quality at the lowest cost. They are also concerned about not damaging the environment. After production, the finished fabrics must be sold and distributed.

Fiber Production

Fibers are thin, hair-like strands that are the basic units in textiles. Different raw materials are processed into various fibers.

Agricultural industries supply natural fibers such as cotton, wool, flax, and silk. They are made from plant or animal sources.

Chemical companies produce manufactured fibers such as rayon, nylon, spandex, acetate, and polyester. Most are liquid chemical mixtures that form into thin threads as they solidify, as in **5-1**. They are made to have characteristics that suit their end uses. For example, nylon is strong, resilient, and nonabsorbent. It is used to make a wide variety of items from hosiery to carpeting.

Manufactured fibers were first invented in the early 1900s and have grown in popularity and use. Millions of pounds of fibers are sent to mills by fiber producers each year.

Yarn Production

Yarns are continuous strands, usually of multiple fibers, ready for knitting, weaving, or other processing into cloth. Mills spin fibers into yarns, as shown in **5-2**. Several fibers are twisted together to form the long strands of yarns used to make fabrics. Most U.S. textile mills are in the Southeast, especially North Carolina, South Carolina, and Georgia. A great deal of yarn production for U.S. consumption is done in other countries.

5-2 Spinning mills have many rows of specialized machines that twist fibers into yarns quickly and precisely.

International Linen Promotion Commission

5-1 Manufactured fibers are made with special equipment under controlled conditions by many chemical companies.

Trevira Polyester-Hoechst Fibers Industries

Fabric Manufacturing

Fabric is cloth made from textile fibers and yarns. This is done by textile manufacturing plants (also called *mills*) that weave, knit, or produce fabric by other methods. Huge mechanized looms, as shown in **5-3**, and knitting machines produce great amounts of yard goods very fast. However, the cloth is still unfinished. The unfinished fabrics are called greige goods (pronounced *gray goods*).

Fabric Finishing

Finishing is done by bleaching, dyeing, printing, or applying special coatings to the greige goods. Finishing imparts color, texture, pattern, ease of care, and other characteristics to the fabrics. The fabric finish in **5-4** gives denim a worn look.

Textile converters are firms, or individual merchants, who buy or handle greige goods for finishing. They keep close tabs on fashion trends to anticipate demand. They contract with others to dye, print, and finish the goods to their specifications. Then textile converters sell the finished products to apparel manufacturers. A small amount goes to fabric retailers for home sewing. Usually, converters do not own fabric plants or finishing facilities. Instead, they serve as middle agents between these stages and the final-use markets.

Rehan Qureshi/Shutterstock.com

5-4 Modern finishing equipment can create denim surfaces that appear faded and worn.

Distribution

Finally, sales offices are necessary to market the finished fabrics. They sell the fabrics to apparel and accessory producers, fabric retailers, and specialists for home and industrial uses. Many textile firms have showrooms in New York City near the garment district.

The Development of Textile Corporations

Historically, each textile company specialized in a single stage of production. Spinning mills, weaving mills, knitting mills, finishing plants, and selling agents all worked independently. However, after World War II, problems of scarcity and price made this fragmented operation outdated. The industry began to integrate itself. Textile firms started to do several, or all, processes, including direct selling. In some cases, selling agents bought manufacturing and finishing plants. Mergers and acquisitions created large textile corporations.

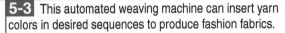

5-3 This automated weaving machine can insert yarn colors in desired sequences to produce fashion fabrics.

sspopov/Shutterstock.com

Today, some companies specialize in one phase of textile production, such as producing manufactured fibers. Other companies specialize in one type of fabric, such as brocades or knits. However, the textile industry is dominated by corporations that handle all processes of production and distribution. Steps from fiber production to sales are done in different plants and locations belonging to, or as divisions of, one corporation. This enables a firm to control its goods through as many processes as are potentially profitable. Also, the many products of a firm are distributed by its different, specialized marketing divisions.

Besides textiles used for apparel, other markets exist for home furnishings and industrial products. Home furnishings textiles include upholstery, carpets, curtains, and drapes, as in **5-5**. There are also tablecloths and napkins, sheets, towels, blankets and bedspreads, lampshades, and other fabric products. These goods are expected to last longer than apparel items. Thus, performance characteristics, such as stain resistance, colorfastness, and durability are important. Home furnishings textiles are slower to change their fashionable colors and patterns than apparel fabrics.

Sales of industrial textiles are based on performance specifications rather than fashion. They vary as to their detailed uses and lifetime expectations. A few examples of industrial textiles include filters, hoses, building insulation, soil erosion barriers, conveyor belts, and safety nets. There are also fiber optics, inflatable buildings, and space suits, as in **5-6**. In the transportation industry, there are seat covers, seat belts, air bags, brake linings, and tire cords. For medical

5-6 Advances in technology have led to new textile products for end uses varying from apparel to space-age electronics.

uses, different textiles are needed for bandages and other wound dressings, surgical gowns and masks, disposable sheets, artificial hearts and arteries, etc. Many other specialized industrial textiles exist, with demand growing each year.

Textile Marketing

Marketing is the process of finding or creating a profitable market for specific goods or services. It identifies customers, determines those customers' wants and needs, and provides satisfying products at acceptable prices to those customers. The prices must also give a profit to the company. Marketing incorporates market research, product design, manufacturing, promotion, sales, and distribution activities.

Marketing is done by fiber and fabric manufacturers, apparel designers and producers, and retailers. However, the textile industry is the first step, so the market must be analyzed. To create and sell fabrics successfully, the marketing strategies of textile firms must ensure that the right fabrics are available at the right time and at the right price.

Fashion Considerations

Before the textile companies can begin to develop their fiber characteristics or fashion fabrics, they must come up with some early projections of colors, weights, textures, and surface designs. Their textiles must meet public fashion acceptance at the time they reach the market. Textile designers make these decisions

5-5 Besides apparel fabrics, textiles are specially produced and readily available for home furnishing uses.

Oleg Doroshin/Shutterstock.com

about a year and a half before the public sees the fabrics. For instance, during the fall of one year, textile designers are designing their fabric lines for apparel that will sell to consumers the spring after next.

Color must be decided first, as in **5-7**. In the final garment, color will be the most important factor in drawing the consumer to the item. A *color line* is determined by logic, research, and gut feeling. The best and worst color sellers of the last season are reviewed with apparel manufacturers and retailers. Colors often change by evolution rather than by sharp changes. The good ones might be kept and altered to go through several seasons. Burgundy may become purple, then magenta, then pink. Colors that have not been used for quite awhile may be brought back if they now seem new.

The fabric designer of a textile firm must be aware of upcoming fashion trends. The weight and construction of fabrics must complement the styles of future garments that will be produced. Companies use market research to discover and analyze, formally (through statistics) and informally, what the future will bring. Companies also use skilled information consultants. **Forecasting services** look forward approximately two years ahead to predict coming trends. They foresee the colors, textures, silhouettes, and accessories of the future.

Forecasting services sell their information to companies that subscribe to their publications and services. As in **5-8**, they present their ideas

The Doneger Group

5-8 Forecasting services offer expert advice about future color trends, fabric textures and patterns, and apparel shapes and designs.

5-7 The colors for textile products are planned well ahead of when the fabrics will be made into apparel and sold to consumers through retail stores.

BASF Corporation, Fibers Division

with trend books, color cards, fabric swatches, videos, slides, and sketches. They also post information on websites that their customers can access with passwords. Forecasting services are invaluable to textile firms, apparel manufacturers, and retailers. Fashion companies sometimes subscribe to more than one service. Through these services, all segments of the industry get the same information, to use in their own ways.

Textile firms design collections of distinctly different groupings of fabrics. The fabrics are created by using different weaves, textures, colors, and surface designs. The finished fabrics must have the right combinations of colors, patterns, and fabric weights for changing fashion trends.

Ideas for prints and textures also come from sources other than forecasting services. They may be inspired by nature, the art and entertainment worlds, or historical research.

Historically, textile designers would prepare technical drawings by hand on graph paper. Now almost all designers create their textile designs by using computers with special software programs. These programs allow designers to draw freehand shapes and lines. They can easily modify their designs by changing colors or motifs, increasing or decreasing brightness, reducing or enlarging various design features, or combining motifs. With a descriptive name, designs are saved for later use. A special camera can be used to photograph designs for permanent viewing. As new trends in fashion emerge, designers can update their computerized designs and give related manufacturing specifications quickly, as in **5-9**.

Fashion Fabric Sales

Fabric collections are created for certain end uses, such as children's wear, men's sport shirts, or bedsheets. The collections are given distinctive names. This enables a strong marketing message to be conveyed to potential clients.

5-9 Trained textile stylists use computer-aided design (CAD) programs to create new patterns and give related manufacturing specifications quickly.

Fashion Institute of Technology

Some textiles are developed exclusively for a fashion designer's apparel or household linens through licensing agreements.

Most textile producers maintain fabric libraries in their showrooms for use by the companies that buy their textiles. They display small amounts of their fabrics to promote and sell them. Fashion boards with sketches and fabric samples are set up as selling aids. Sample garments are sometimes made that feature the company's fibers, yarns, or fabrics. Customers (apparel manufacturers and retailers) and fashion reporters view and discuss the new fabrics with the textile producers. The textile companies hope their products will be selected for apparel manufacturing and publicity.

Fiber and fabric producers assist apparel manufacturers and retailers in every way they can to create final products that please consumers. They help manufacturers with needed market information and other planning data, as shown in **5-10**. Textile producers assist the manufacturers in selling their new apparel lines to retailers. They help retailers sell to consumers with publicity and advertising about their fibers and fabrics. They help train sales associates. They provide consumer education programs and educational materials. They also provide textile trademark tags and labels to be attached to the apparel.

Technology

Technology is important to satisfy the markets for apparel, home furnishings, and industrial

5-10 By using technology and discussing fashion business data, textile producers help their customers (apparel manufacturers and retailers) with marketing ideas.

Pressmaster/Shutterstock.com

textiles. Technology is the creation, modification, or application of products, methods, and systems, usually advanced through research and development. Research and development (R and D) departments provide new knowledge, develop new products, and improve old products. R and D is a vital part of the textile industry. Some R and D activities include the invention of new manufacturing machinery and procedures. Other R and D activities include the development of new manufactured fibers, chemical finishes, and other textile improvements. See **5-11**.

Sometimes the apparel industry requests the production of fabrics with certain characteristics to satisfy market demand. At other times, developments in the textile industry inspire new apparel designs. For instance, water-repellent fabrics enable raincoats to be styled for all-purpose wear. Extra-fine fibers and stretch fabrics allow for the designs of new types of garments. Textiles for activewear can make it easier for people to adjust more quickly to cooler and warmer temperatures. Some textiles also have antibacterial and odor control properties, sun protection, or insect repellency.

Home decorating fabrics are stronger and more resistant to fading and abrasion. Specific characteristics are available for industrial and medical uses of textiles. *Quality standards* rate textiles according to levels of defects. *Performance standards* rate the suitability of textiles for specific uses.

Innovations of computerized machines make textile manufacturing faster and better. Innovation is the creative, forward-thinking introduction of new ideas. Innovation has resulted in electronic spinning, knitting, weaving, dyeing,

and finishing machines. Waste is reduced, since only the needed amounts of materials are used. Sometimes completely new applications for textiles are discovered.

At manufacturing technology centers, industry workers learn skills on the latest equipment. Some textile science colleges research new textile technology. Professors and graduate students work in the fields of

> *nanotechnology*—altering materials atom by atom, such as at the molecular level of chemicals

> *microelectronics*—miniature electronic components, which can result in smaller, faster, cheaper computerized devices

> *robotics*—mechanical equipment that automates tasks, thereby removing heavy lifting and difficult and repetitive tasks from human workers

Textile companies and researchers subscribe to such magazines as the *Textile Research Journal* and *Textile World*. Most belong to the American Fiber Manufacturers Association, Inc. (AFMA). Through these channels, they learn about the latest textile developments and communicate them to others.

Textiles Worldwide

The textile industry is worldwide in scope. The United States manufactures some textiles, but increasingly brings in (imports) greater amounts of textile fibers, yarns, and fabrics from other countries. Imports are goods that come into the country from foreign sources. Some of the imports are superior fibers and fabrics from countries known for their high-quality production. Most other textiles are imported simply because the prices are low. Some textiles come from countries with low labor and factory operation costs. Textiles from those countries can then be sold for lower prices, even after shipping costs and tariffs (taxes on imports) are added.

Manufactured fibers and knitted goods come into the United States from Japan. Wool fibers and fabrics come from the United Kingdom and Belgium. Cotton fibers are imported from Egypt, and flax from Ireland. Silk fabrics come from China and Italy. Laces come from France.

5-11 When textile researchers arrange polymers into different molecular structures, new fibers can be manufactured.

yurok/Shutterstock.com

Countries promote their textile industries to encourage trade. International fabric fairs and trade shows are held in many countries. They promote textile machinery as well as fibers, fabrics, and apparel. Trade journals are distributed throughout the world. See **5-12**.

Firms in the United States also export some textile goods to other countries. Exports are commercial products sent out of a country to other countries. However, the U.S. imports far more than it exports. This creates a trade deficit—a negative economic condition because the amount of imports is greater than the amount of exports.

Growing competitive pressures, largely from lower-priced imports, have severely cut into the textile industry of the United States. Large amounts of profits and many jobs have been lost. Textile firms have been forced to make drastic changes. Plants have been closed. Low-profit and diminishing product lines have been discontinued. Improvements in technology and production efficiencies have been implemented. Textile firms are striving to create goods that will please consumers, sell well, and make money.

The Future of Textiles

Due to increasing marketing skills and global competition, the U.S. textile industry has become more innovative and progressive. This competitive spirit is helping the industry adapt to rapid changes, resulting in a higher degree of computer technology, **5-13**. Textile firms are closing outdated plants, automating newer ones completely, and establishing American-owned plants in other countries.

In the future, small, weak firms will fail or be purchased by larger companies. Such acquisitions and mergers are already creating fewer, stronger companies. Those with top-quality products and customer service will flourish.

Demand for textiles will continually increase as worldwide standards of living rise. Experts predict polyester to be the predominant fiber. Cotton will remain popular. Environmentally friendly textile processing will increase. Modifications to existing fibers and newer mixtures of fibers are more likely to emerge than totally new fibers. Nonwovens and disposable textiles will become more common, especially in medical and food service uses. Also, textile imports will continue to increase as more production is done in lower-wage countries.

Textile World magazines/www.textileworld.com

5-12 Some trade journals are published in several languages that concentrate on specific parts of the world. *Textile World* magazine publishes *Textiles Panamericanos* for Latin America and *Textile World Asia* for the Far East.

5-13 Computerized automation simulates and oversees color accuracy, technical design, and all production machinery operations.

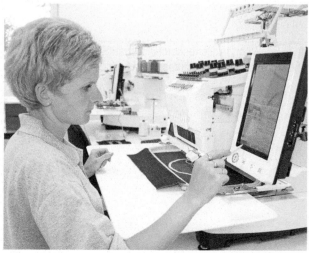

branislavpudar/Shutterstock.com

Predictions imply that the production of knits will grow, with fewer woven materials produced. Yarn production will create greater popularity of novelty yarns. Manufacturers use knitting machines, which use less energy than weaving looms. Also, knitting mills have lower capital requirements than weaving mills. (Capital is the financial worth, or accumulated investment cash, needed to start, expand, or run a business.)

Successful textile firms in the future will use industry changes to their advantage. They will learn to work with imports and compete better. More sophisticated global marketing techniques will give more attention to pleasing retailers and consumers with the right products.

Flexibility and versatility for shorter production runs of different fabrics will be needed to quickly satisfy changing market needs. New computerized methods will enable fast manufacturing changes to provide smaller, more customized orders of unique products. These orders will be filled quicker and more accurately, with direct computer communications between textile firms, apparel manufacturers, and retailers. Production will go up while waste decreases and more environmentally friendly processes are used.

Restructured firms will have fewer levels of workers and management. Automated equipment will require continued retraining of employees. Ambitious young workers can become leaders.

Home Sewing Patterns

Pattern making companies design and make patterns for the home sewing market in the United States and around the world. Every year, new styles appear in the major pattern catalogs. Thousands of fashion and crafts patterns are available to sewing enthusiasts. See **5-14.**

The Business of Patterns

Many people have sewing skills. Few have pattern making skills. Therefore, most people buy patterns to use as guides for their sewing projects.

Pattern making companies offer a large choice of designs for home sewing consumers.

wavebreakmedia/Shutterstock.com

5-14 Different pattern brands are offered to home sewers. They can be found in catalogs at fabric stores and on pattern companies' websites.

The thick catalogs at fabric stores clearly show all pattern designs and their variations. Photos and drawings also show possible combinations with other garments and examples of appropriate fabrics and accessories. The catalogs have sections by category of figure and garment types. Examples are children's patterns, formal wear, misses' dresses, and menswear.

Pattern catalogs arrive in fabric stores many weeks ahead of the wearing season for the garments, allowing time to sew them. Patterns that are popular sellers stay in the catalogs for many seasons. Unpopular patterns are dropped from future catalogs. Some free sewing patterns are available online. Consumers can search for free sewing patterns, and then download and print the ones they like.

To help home sewers, patterns have printed guide sheets, with illustrated directions for all cutting and sewing steps. Fabric layouts are shown. Needed *notions*, such as zippers, trimmings, and buttons, are listed on the envelope for each design. Appropriate fabrics are suggested, too.

Pattern companies continually tabulate sales of patterns to see how well each is selling. This tracking system tells them which designs are in demand and in what sizes. Pattern preferences generally follow the trends of ready-to-wear (RTW) fashions. Most patterns stay in the catalogs for a year or two. Those patterns that continue to sell well are kept in the catalogs longer. Those that do not sell are dropped to make room for new patterns.

The Breadth of Pattern Companies

Designer patterns are available to give home sewers access to some couture designs, as shown in **5-15**. Sophisticated designer lines are replicas of actual couturier fashions. They are bought from designers through licensing agreements.

Signature lines have the endorsement of celebrities. Usually the celebrity is an actor or model. The styles in such lines are typical of what that person likes and wears. The celebrity helps develop the line through a licensing agreement. The celebrity is shown wearing the fashions in photographs in counter catalogs and promotional materials.

Easy-to-sew patterns are of designs that are simple to cut and make. They are developed for beginning or busy sewers. They are also specially marked, as shown in **5-16**.

The major pattern companies offer helpful sewing information to their customers. They research fashion trends and spread fashion news to the fabric retailers that sell their patterns. Their education departments produce articles and tutorial videos on sewing techniques, resolving common issues, and other types of advice for customers to view online. Customer service departments respond to electronic inquiries as well as phone calls, while also promoting their company's patterns.

5-16 Easy-to-sew patterns from different companies have various names, such as *Easy McCall's*, *Jiffy* by Simplicity, and *Very Easy Vogue®*.

5-15 As shown on the envelope of this Vogue® Pattern for home sewers, the dress is by fashion designer Oscar de la Renta.

Designing Home Sewing Patterns

Home sewing patterns are designed in much the same way as ready-to-wear fashions. The staff designers are inspired by American and foreign fashions. They follow the advice of trade publications and fashion magazines, and they use information gathered at fabric fairs. They consider requests from home sewers and imitate the latest in ready-to-wear. They also evaluate what has or has not sold well in previous lines.

Both easy-to-sew and challenging designs are created. The company also tries to come up with the right mix of dressy, casual, athletic, and specialized patterns. Design ideas are coordinated with marketing plans to create something for almost everyone.

The rough first sketch, or croquis (pronounced crow-key), of each design shows both front and back views. It also shows any special details the designer wants included in the pattern. It is presented to management and pattern makers in a construction meeting. Details about fullness and length of garment parts, structural needs (linings, interlinings, etc.), and sewing methods for the design are discussed. Then notes are written on the croquis about when the design will appear in the counter catalog. The figure-type category and special construction techniques are also noted.

Suitable fabric samples are chosen for each design from the pattern company's fabric library. The library has swatches of fabrics that are available to home sewers. Then the design is put into a final artist's sketch showing it in a fashionable fabric.

Perfecting the Patterns

Making patterns requires a combination of design talent and technical expertise. A member of the pattern making staff makes the first pattern, usually with a computer program. To keep sizing consistent, the work is done from a basic pattern, called a *sloper*. The sloper is in the company's basic size, programmed into the software, from which all designs in a category start. For complicated or fluid designs, the first pattern may be made by draping muslin onto a body form of the basic size, rather than from the flat pattern sloper.

Next, a partial muslin proof of the pattern is sewn and fitted on a body form. Only one side of the design is made, as in **5-17**. Then the designer is asked to check the work. The original sketch has been transformed into three-dimensional form. Fit and design corrections are made as needed.

A full muslin prototype is then sewn together. A prototype is the first full-scale trial garment of a new design. The prototype is worn by a model with the same proportions as the pattern company's standard client. The model walks, bends, and sits in the garment to test its wearing comfort. The designer makes final fit, drape, and design changes at that time.

The next step is to gain the approval of a committee of company management. Then all planned views (showing, for example, sleeve and collar variations) are penciled onto the muslin sample. Notches and other construction markings are noted, as well as recommended notions and fabrics.

The muslin pattern pieces are used to make a hard paper master pattern for the design. The pattern pieces are marked with notches and construction symbols. A descriptive name is put on each piece, such as pants front, back pocket, or waistband.

The garment is then cut and constructed in fashion fabrics for photographs and fashion shows. If the design is planned for striped or plaid fabric, it is made with that type of fabric.

5-17 The muslin proof of each pattern is checked to be sure it accurately represents the designer's ideas.

The McCall Pattern Company

If it is designed *for stretchable knits only*, a sample is made in a stretchable knit. Every effort is made to show consumers how to achieve good results when they use the pattern.

Finishing the Patterns

Next, the pattern is graded. Grading is the making of each pattern piece in all the sizes that will be sold. It is a scientific process that is now done by computer. Every pattern piece is printed in each size or several sizes, with different lines showing the outline for each size.

Fabric layout charts are made using outline drawings of the individual pattern pieces. They show how the pieces should be placed on fabric for cutting. Various layout charts are devised for different standard widths of fabric. Also, yardage needs are recorded for each garment option and fabric width.

A guide sheet is prepared with sewing instructions and drawings. Pattern procedure instructions about how to construct different kinds of garments and details are stored on computer systems. They are constantly updated. The appropriate codes are entered into the computer, and generic sketches with how-to instructions appear on the guide sheet.

The pattern envelope must be developed, too. The design is drawn in watercolor to look like it was made in a specific fashion fabric. The artist's painting, or a fashion photograph, is used on the envelope front, as in 5-15 and 5-16, and in the catalog. The back of the envelope tells the amount of fabric, in each standard fabric width, needed to make the garments. It also gives the amounts of lining, interfacing, buttons, and other supplies needed.

The tissue pattern pieces, guide sheets, and envelopes are printed on printing presses. Machines fold the patterns and guide sheets and insert them into the envelopes. The final product pieces are shown in **5-18**.

5-18 Each final sewing pattern has an envelope (upper left), guide sheet (lower left), and tissue paper pattern pieces (upper right).

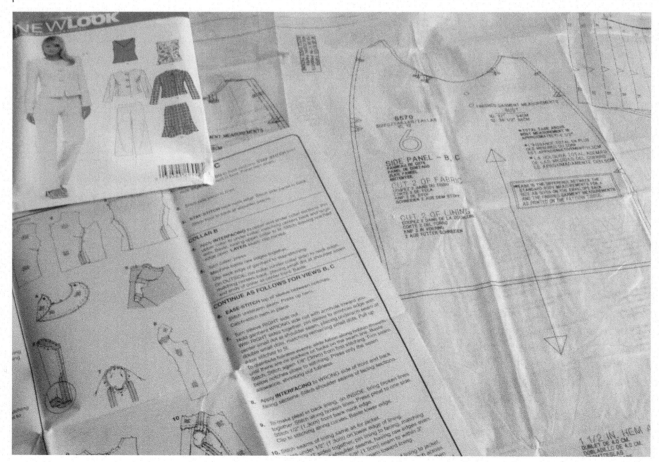

Innovations for the Future

The patterns of the major companies will probably become more generalized in the future. Pattern markings and instructions will be bilingual. This feature eliminates the printing costs of separate sets of pattern pieces and guide sheets in different languages for international use. European patterns will be readily available in the United States. There will also be more *multisize patterns*. These are patterns with several sizes printed together on the same pieces.

More patterns in the future will probably be for use with knits, since textile companies will be producing more knit fabrics. Also, guide sheet directions may be written for *serger* (or overlock) sewing machines. These sewing machines duplicate ready-to-wear manufacturing techniques. See **5-19.** They are very effective in sewing knits and newer types of fabrics.

Companies that make *custom patterns* already exist. They make patterns to fit individual measurements. Some are basic patterns for use as slopers that fit an individual's measurements.

5-19 A serger, as shown below, allows home sewers to produce a factory-like finish on various types of fabrics and products.

Dmitry Kalinovsky/Shutterstock.com

The customer fills out information in a measuring kit from the company. From that, electronic patterns are made for basic pants, skirt, and bodice versions. Specialized apparel patterns are also available, such as for ballet or ice skating costumes.

Software to make basic and design patterns is currently available for personal computers. Home sewers can use this type of software to see how all angles of a garment will look. They can also make changes and print the pattern with their proper measurements. Technological advances will continue to provide the home sewer with more pattern-making resources than ever before.

Summary

The textile industry produces fibers, spins yarns, manufactures fabrics, finishes fabrics, and distributes the finished fabrics. Some textile corporations do only one of those steps, while others handle all processes of production and distribution. To succeed with textile lines, companies emphasize marketing skills with fashion, sales, and technology considerations.

Today, the textile industry is worldwide. The U.S. imports great amounts of textiles, creating a trade deficit. In the future, the textile industry will be more innovative and flexible to meet increasing demands and changing market needs.

Companies that make home sewing patterns are an important segment of the home sewing industry. Pattern companies sell designer patterns, signature lines, and easy-to-sew patterns. The patterns are designed by sketching ideas and calculating construction details. After samples of the designs are sewn and approved, the patterns are graded into sizes and printed, along with guide sheets and envelopes.

In the future, there will be more multisize patterns and duplication of RTW manufacturing techniques.

Fashion Recall

Write your answers on a separate sheet of paper.

Short Answer: Write the correct answer to each of the following questions.

1. List and briefly explain the four main steps in the production of finished fabrics.
2. Give three examples of how new manufactured fibers and chemical finishes have revolutionized the textile and garment industries.
3. When textile companies develop their lines, what factor do they decide first? Why?
4. List three sources of ideas for prints and textures in textile designs.
5. Explain how textile patterns can be designed on a computer.
6. Explain the difference between quality standards and performance standards as they relate to textiles.
7. Usually, are more textile products exported to other countries or imported into the United States?
8. In the future, which is likely to grow more: the production of knits or the production of wovens?
9. Explain how the major pattern companies act as information centers.
10. What does a croquis show?
11. True or false. The grading area of a pattern company sews prototypes.
12. In the future, are the patterns of the major companies likely to become more generalized or more specific?

Fashion Vocabulary

13. Individually or with a partner, create a T-chart on a sheet of paper. List each of the *Fashion Terms* from the chapter opening in the left column. In the right column, write the definition of each term in your own words after reading the chapter.

Critical Thinking

14. **Assess skills**   Assess how marketing, fashion, and technology skills are interrelated in the textile industry. Share your assessment through class discussion.
15. **Critique trends**   Critique the current color and fashion trends. Use online or print resources to document these color trends. How do these trends influence the textile industry? Write a short summary of your findings.
16. **Analyze evidence**   Use online or print resources to analyze evidence about home sewing patterns. Do you believe the use of home sewing patterns is rising in popularity or declining? Give evidence to support your answer.

Core Skills

17. **Writing**   Tour a local fabric store. Take notes on what types of fabrics are available. What colors, textures, and fabric weights are most common? Study the pattern catalogs. Which pattern companies are represented? Note the categories of patterns available. Are designer, signature, and easy-to-sew patterns offered? Which categories of patterns interest you the most? Are magazines and pamphlets from pattern companies available? Write a report on your findings.
18. **Research and speaking**   Use online or print resources to research the history of sewing patterns. Use school-approved presentation software to prepare an illustrated oral report on the influential people and important developments in

the industry. Include details and pictorial examples about the first patterns. Be sure to credit the sources of all images. Explain when patterns started to be used by the general public. Give your presentation to the class.

19. **Research and writing** Use online and print resources to research sizing methods for home sewing patterns and ready-to-wear fashions. Compare the standardized size measurements of the pattern industry with ready-to-wear sizing. What are the similarities and differences? Is a size 10 in ready-to-wear fashions the same as a size 10 in pattern? What issues surround sizing methods? Write an essay detailing your findings.

20. **Writing** Suppose you are a textile chemist who works for a major textile manufacturer. You have been assigned to scientifically develop a new textile fiber for a fashion, home decorating, or industrial end use to meet a specific market need. In writing, describe the textile fiber's technological specifics (such as aspects about dyeing or finishing) in a short report. Identify some possible marketing information describing how this textile fiber might be promoted to consumers.

21. **Math practice** Go to the website of a pattern company and select a sewing pattern for an outfit you like. What type of fabric is recommended for the garment? Using your size, read the fabric-requirements chart to determine how much fabric you would need for each standard width.

22. **CTE career readiness practice** Suppose you are a fashion journalist who works in the educational division of a major pattern company. Your current assignment is to write a full-page public service announcement (PSA) that captures consumers' attention regarding the company's new, celebrity signature line of patterns. Research the fashion details about this signature line, details about the celebrity and why he or she likes and wears this style, and locate illustrations of the designs that are sure to be a hit for the upcoming fashion season. Then, write the copy for the public service announcement.

Fashion in Action

23. **Portfolio builder** Select one aspect of the worldwide trade of textile products (low cost fabrics or garments from developing nations, a textile specialty from a specific country, impacts of having a trade deficit, etc.). Do further research and present your findings in a report to be filed in your portfolio.

24. **Design activity** Imagine you are a textile designer. Create color drawings or paintings on paper showing a collection of at least five different textile designs. (As an alternative, use your school-approved drawing software to create your color drawings.) Make sure the motifs are clear and easy to reproduce. Describe the texture and fabric weight of each. Give the collection a distinctive or catchy name. Write a paragraph describing the intended end uses of the fabrics.

Self-Assessment Quiz ➦

Complete the self-assessment quiz online to help practice and expand your knowledge and skills.

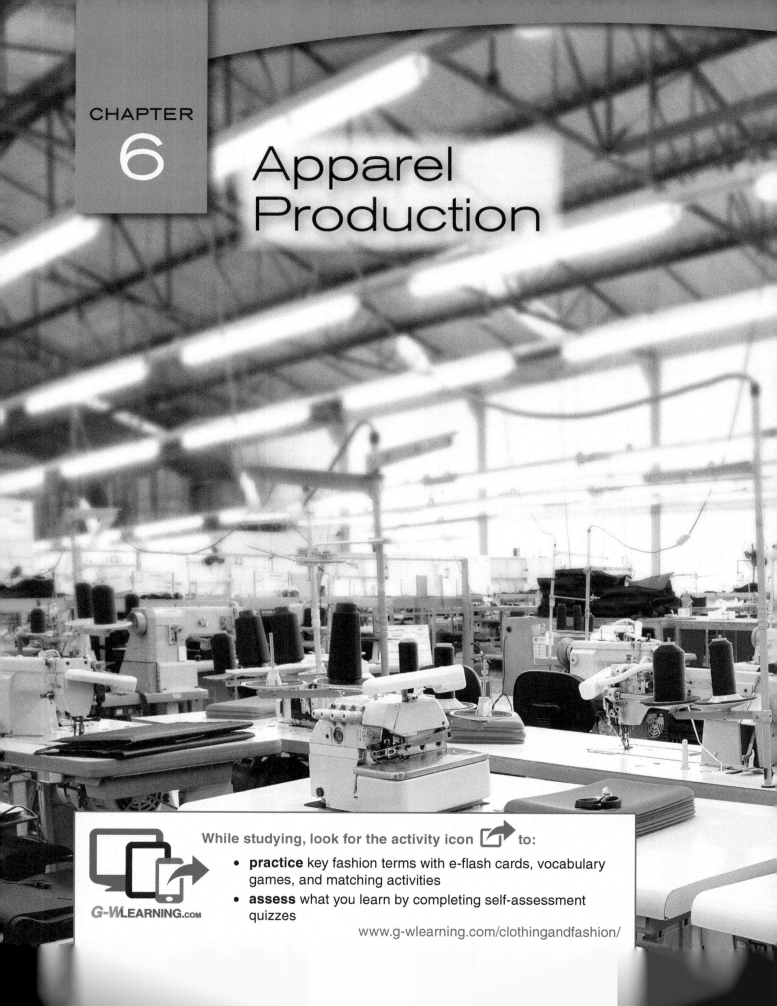

CHAPTER
6

Apparel Production

While studying, look for the activity icon to:

- **practice** key fashion terms with e-flash cards, vocabulary games, and matching activities
- **assess** what you learn by completing self-assessment quizzes

G-W**LEARNING**.com

www.g-wlearning.com/clothingandfashion/

Fashion Terms

profit
contractors
merchandise plan
line
samples
stylists
costing
computer-aided
  design (CAD)
marker
mass production
piecework system

unit production
  system (UPS)
computer-aided
  manufacturing
  (CAM)
modular
  manufacturing
productivity
ergonomics
benchmarking
apparel marts
quotas

offshore production
domestic production
joint venture
computer imaging
computer-integrated
  manufacturing
  (CIM)
collaboration
business-to-business
  (B2B) e-commerce
agile manufacturing

Objectives

After studying this chapter, you will be able to
➤ discuss the business aspects of apparel production.
➤ distinguish between the production processes of ready-to-wear
  clothing.
➤ describe selling methods used by apparel manufacturers.
➤ compare various viewpoints about overseas manufacturing.
➤ discuss possible future directions of apparel production.

After doing marketing analyses, the factory production of garments includes all the steps needed to turn fabrics into finished wearing apparel. These steps are the buying of fabric and the designing, pattern making, cutting, sewing, assembling, and distribution of garments. Ready-to-wear garment manufacturers produce apparel in large quantities according to projected amounts of consumer demand within given price ranges. Consumer whims present high risks. Most companies have some very good years and also some lean years.

103

The Business of Apparel Production

Apparel manufacturers must struggle to keep their costs low, quality high, and selling prices competitive. Manufacturers must buy fabrics and pay their employees' wages. They must buy new equipment and pay for the upkeep of old equipment. They have overhead expenses, such as gas and electricity, for their factories and offices. They must pay rent or a mortgage, as well as taxes.

Manufacturers try to sell products at or lower than their competitors' prices, while maintaining their standards of quality and design. However, the companies must be able to make a profit to stay in business. Profit is the incoming money that is left over after all the outgoing costs have been deducted. Firms use their profits for expansion and improvements. The money is used to buy new equipment, hire more people, conduct research, and pay dividends if the firms have stockholders.

Apparel producers vary widely as to size, variety of products, and type of business operation. The largest firms are publicly owned by stockholders. They produce many lines under different labels. Smaller garment manufacturing companies are often privately owned. They usually specialize in one or two apparel categories in a particular size range. They also stay within a certain price level.

Over the years, apparel manufacturing firms have expanded and diversified by adding or acquiring subsidiary divisions. Some small manufacturers were bought to become divisions of large conglomerates, or parent firms. Many firms are global companies with production plants located in low-wage countries around the world and sales offices in major cities. However, there are still many prosperous small businesses run by enterprising, creative individuals.

Contracting

Some firms do all stages of production, from fabric purchasing to the distribution of finished garments. Other firms handle designing, pattern making, and fabric selection, but not the cutting and sewing. They contract those parts of production to other, independently owned sewing factories called contractors. Contractors produce the garments according to the manufacturing firm's designs and specifications.

The contracting process has been done since people were hired to do sewing in their homes over a century ago. Today, many firms hire contract factories during the height of their production season. This enables the apparel firm to produce a variety of products. Companies can meet changing consumer demands without making large financial investments in new equipment. See 6-1. Also, newcomers to the apparel industry who have design ideas can go into production quickly without much capital. The contractors must deal with labor, equipment, and maintenance costs. Contractors may choose to work with more than one company. Almost all apparel firms contract out some of their sewing for extra capacity during busy times.

Establishing Merchandise Plans

A merchandise plan is each season's plan for a manufacturer's line of designs. It is a business plan for how many apparel or accessory groups and items are needed to satisfy both the demands of retailers and consumers, and the financial goals of the producer. As part of marketing, it involves varying degrees of planning, buying, manufacturing, and selling.

6-1 Monogramming apparel is a specialized job done by trained operators who use machines made specifically for the task.

Alen Thien/Shutterstock.com

Merchandise plans are aimed at demands of the final consumers of the goods, even though many steps move apparel from concept to retailers. Consumer needs and demands must be determined in order to provide retailers with the right goods. The proper amounts of supplies must be acquired to do the manufacturing. Production must be planned, so the finished garments can be delivered at the right price and at the proper time.

Clothing producers develop merchandise plans to help them estimate and meet these needs. In small companies, this is done by the president or the designer, or both. In large firms, a merchandise planning staff carries out these duties.

First, companies look at their primary consumer markets to see what kinds of clothes their clients prefer. They study past sales. They analyze the winners and losers of previous seasons. This has become easier with the use of technology. Sales by style number, color, fabric, size, and so on can be calculated quickly and accurately. Sudden or gradual changes in customer preferences can be noted. Sometimes changes show in one part of the country and not in other parts. Design and production are planned accordingly.

The merchandise staffs of manufacturing firms also do research to decide what directions fashions will take. To do this, they note the trends of couture fashions. They study the current arts, including movies, television, and museum showings. They subscribe to fashion forecasting services. They even buy popular items from retail stores—to copy.

Successful clothing manufacturers seem to have a sixth sense for judging fashion trends. Although the element of gut feel is unscientific, it is very important in fashion. Occupational guessing is a game that puts millions of dollars at stake.

Calculations and Decisions

Merchandise planners for apparel firms must also figure out manufacturing details, as in **6-2**. They must decide when and where to order fabrics, and at what prices. Production capabilities are calculated for the company or contract factories. Some of the work might be done in Kentucky, Alabama, Hong Kong, Korea, South and Central America, or other places.

Kzenon/Shutterstock.com

6-2 Each detail on a garment requires a sewing procedure that costs money to perform. Methods of construction must be calculated for each style to be produced.

With this information and the ideas from the firm's designers, the preliminary lines are developed. A line is a collection of styles and designs that will be produced and sold as the firm's selections for a given season. Each line contains a group of garments that are somewhat similar. The garments in a line are usually all for the same time of day or type of occasion. Sometimes they are color coordinated. Large manufacturers might have several related lines. For instance, they might produce ski, tennis, sweat suit, and swimwear lines.

After the lines are established, samples are made of the chosen designs. Samples are trial garments, or *prototypes*, made exactly as they are intended to look when sold.

The next step in apparel company merchandise planning is communicating with the firm's key retail accounts. All samples are shown. The retail buyers respond with specific remarks about strong and weak points in the line. After these meetings, designs may be altered and manufacturing details may be changed. The amounts of each style to be manufactured are decided. Some items may be dropped from the line and never produced.

Finally, merchandise planners must decide when, where, and how to show and sell the lines. Should they be shown in several cities? Should the showings be big, splashy events, or quiet and small? How many trade showings should there be? Should road salespeople take the lines around to show retail buyers at stores? What advertising should be done?

Merchandise planners keep tabs on garment acceptance all the way to the final consumers who buy from retail stores. They try to reduce risks with market surveys, computer analysis, and samplings. *Samplings* (not sample garments) are small quantities of garments that are made and placed in retail stores. At the first indication of consumer reaction, acceptable styles are reordered by the stores and produced in large quantities by the manufacturer. Unpopular styles are discontinued. Consumer reaction is the most important input.

The Designing Process

One or many apparel designers may work for a garment manufacturing firm, depending on its size. They work months or a year ahead of when the apparel will be bought by consumers. The design and production time is becoming shorter with faster technology. Design team members coordinate their ideas with the merchandise plans of the company. They use design software to experiment with design ideas. They can print their designs as color sketches. Expensive dress designs might be draped over a mannequin (dressmaker's form).

When one line is ready for production, designing plans are started for the next season. The styles that are selling well in one season are modified and repeated for the next season. Sometimes the same design is done in cotton with short sleeves for summer and in a wool blend with long sleeves or layered for winter. Some new garment designs are added to each new line.

Sources of Inspiration

Even though ready-to-wear designers borrow ideas from others, the upscale lines also include new ideas of their own to move fashion forward. Designers use many different sources for inspiration. Forecasting services are very influential. They even offer private design work and consultations, for a fee, to manufacturing firms. Historic revivals and art movements influence fashion designs. Nature contributes to some

designs. A popular movie or television series can cause great consumer demand for certain fashions. The design of the jacket in **6-3** is based on military wear from the past.

News events can also create interest in clothing. For example, when Alaska and Hawaii became states in the mid 1900s, Eskimo jackets and muumuus became fashion trends. When the United States resumed relations with China, mandarin collars became popular. Wars can create a military influence in fashions. New lifestyle patterns also influence fashion. For instance, the fitness craze has brought about the popularity of exercise attire.

Royalty and prestigious people sometimes set fashion trends. A rock group might wear something that starts a design trend. *Fashion-forward* young people on the streets sometimes invent their own extreme looks that designers notice. Designers are keen observers of people and the way they put outfits together.

6-3 Bomber jackets of the First World War and Second World War have inspired the many leather jackets that have been popular fashions.

Early Spring/Shutterstock.com

Designers also get inspiration from national and international fashion magazines and fashion shows. Fabrics from textile firms have a large influence. Trade shows enable designers to show their lines and to see the lines of other manufacturers. The designers also talk to store owners and buyers about what kinds of garments their retail customers would like.

Designers must have a feel for changing economic, social, and political conditions which affect fashion. Today's fashion designs must be functional. For sports, they must allow freedom of movement. A garment designed for jogging on the road at night must reflect light for safety. A jacket designed for sailing must repel water. These garments must also have a pleasing look for social acceptance. The fabric, design, and construction must all be in harmony.

Adapting Designs

The ready-to-wear garment design industry includes much adaption of higher-priced fashions. Specific designs are simplified for less expensive production, or toned down so they will have widespread appeal. Clothing that reflects the latest trends is manufactured in all the price points and size ranges to suit the current consumer market.

Manufacturers of low-priced garments employ fashion stylists instead of designers. The stylists redesign existing garments into knockoffs, rather than create new designs. They adapt current fashions to meet the mass production abilities and price ranges of their companies. This reduces the risk of producing unsuccessful designs, and it saves time and money.

Fashion piracy is considered common to ready-to-wear designers. Copying dominates the industry. In the United States, there is no legal copyright protection against it. Apparel designs are not registered with the government.

There are practical reasons why copying has become prevalent. Producers must get fast-selling lines out immediately, or the time span of popularity will be lost. Another reason is that firms are highly specialized in terms of apparel type, size, and price range. This means many different firms must produce versions of a design for that design concept to reach all potential customers.

To finalize a design, a stylist may make several different sketches of a garment until it looks just right and is suitable for production. The sketch is then shown to managers who suggest changes or approve it. They consider if it will sell in their market(s). They also do preliminary costing to figure the expenses of producing the design. They tabulate the price per yard of fabric and how much yardage will be needed. They figure labor costs and production capabilities of the firm.

Contractors' costs are calculated for apparel companies. If there will be foreign production, shipping costs must be included. Design and management personnel consider the costs of trimmings, such as embroidery and buttons. They calculate production costs for design details, such as sewing pleats, tucks, yokes, pockets, and topstitching. Sometimes design details must be eliminated. Inexpensive copies of higher-priced garments often have simplified style lines, fewer seams, no linings, and cheaper fabrics and trimmings.

Preparation for Production

The fashion designer or a pattern maker makes the first pattern, as in 6-4. Most companies use computer-aided design (CAD) software to

6-4 Pattern making takes precision and concentration to get each part perfect for the garment design and size, and to fit with other pattern pieces.

Iowa State University/AESHM Department

create new designs for textiles, apparel, or other products. Hundreds of options are available using this technology. When these options are combined just right, the program produces the pattern. See **6-5**. The use of CAD significantly reduces the time and number of people needed to make a pattern and prepare it for cutting.

CAD software also saves designers' time when revising patterns. For example, designers trained to use CAD can move darts or include gathers, pleats, or flares. Designers can also make design changes, add seam allowances, and print the final pattern pieces. Many previously time-consuming hand manipulations are done quickly and accurately with CAD software.

CAD use is best for designing sportswear and children's clothes with flat patterns. It is also helpful for designing knitwear, such as sweaters. The designer uses CAD to design the knitwear and then, in a matter of hours, the system programs the knitting machines to produce them. The programming previously took weeks. CAD is not as useful for designing garments that are draped, such as evening gowns made of soft, flowing fabrics.

There is a growing demand for designers with CAD training. Universities and trade schools have CAD instruction in their apparel curriculums. Companies realize it is a must if they are to stay competitive.

6-5 With CAD technology, specifications can be entered into the software to generate patterns. Changes can be made quickly and as often as necessary. Work is stored in the system and can be sent electronically to other locations.

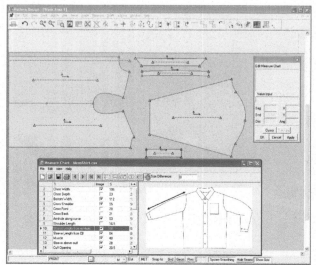

Gerber Technology

Making and Using Samples

Sample garments are made by sample makers, or *sample hands*. These people are skilled in all sewing techniques. They make all design samples (prototypes) in their firm's one standard size. The sample garments are made in fashion fabrics. The sample hands work closely with the designer to make any needed revisions.

Styling and fit are checked by putting the samples on a mannequin or a live model. Samples are revised until they are just right. Specifications are finalized, and tricky construction details are made clear. Management must approve the new styles. They recheck the costs, availability of materials, and profit potential. The approved samples are later used as examples for production and for sales promotion.

Apparel firms have four main production seasons. They are usually called *Spring*, *Summer*, *Fall I*, and *Fall II (Winter)*. The *Winter* line is often directed toward the holiday season, including Christmas, Hanukkah, and New Year's celebrations. Sometimes a beach or resort wear line is considered to be a fifth production season.

Only a fraction of the designs first intended for a line are actually produced. Some are eliminated because the merchandise plan indicates they will not sell well. Other designs cost too much to produce in relation to the retail price range of the company's market.

The final garment selections are given style numbers. A master production pattern is made for each design in the firm's standard size, usually by computer. Final production details are arranged.

Preliminary Production Procedures

The master pattern in the firm's standard size is *graded* into smaller and larger sizes. Most grading is done by computer. Computer grading is especially good for producers who use similar styles over and over again. The computer can then be programmed to grade that type of garment expertly. Grading that used to take three days by hand can be done in an hour or less with technology.

Final fabric selections are ordered from textile firms whose quality can be trusted and whose prices are reasonable. The fabric suppliers must be able to deliver the goods on time and supply more fabric if production is increased.

Fasteners, thread, and trims are ordered in volume for the chosen designs. Special sewing machine attachments are sometimes ordered or made for new design processes.

The layout of pattern pieces is drawn to become a marker. A marker is a long piece of paper that lays out all the various pieces and sizes of the pattern for cutting. It is the plan of how every pattern piece will economically fit onto the fabric. It is used as a guide for the cutter. It has to be planned for the most efficient cutting of garment parts. No fabric should be wasted.

Manufacturing firms use technology to determine the best layout. Miniature pattern pieces and their layout arrangement are displayed on a computer screen. The layout is calculated for the fabric width. The program can determine where the end of one bolt and the beginning of the next falls. It can match plaids and stripes, and can avoid flaws (fabric defects). It minimizes waste.

When the best layout is established, the computer can print the full-size marker. However, most production cutting is now done simply by having the marker in the electronic system. Systems have a special telecommunication feature. This feature allows a company to do the grading and marking at its main location and instantaneously send markers to a manufacturing operation elsewhere. There are also computer pattern firms that can be hired to make the patterns and the markers for a manufacturer's designs.

Factory Production

Apparel manufacturing is done throughout the United States and around the world. The cutting and sewing of the chosen designs have traditionally started about six months before the clothes are in retail stores. However, production time is shorter now, getting apparel to retailers and consumers faster. Usually large numbers of orders are taken by the apparel firm before production of a garment begins. This assures that a market exists for what is made.

The garments are mass-produced. The manufacturing of large numbers of the same items at the same time is called mass production. Garments are manufactured and sold by dozens. They go step-by-step through the assembly line. Production costs are high. Every unnecessary procedure is eliminated in an effort to keep production costs down.

Apparel production labor costs are based on companies' wholesale prices. Companies that produce cheaper, lower-quality garments pay lower wages and require less skill than upscale garment manufacturers. Although most apparel manufacturers run good operations, there is an ongoing campaign against sweatshops in the U.S. and abroad. *Sweatshops* are manufacturing plants that pay less than the required minimum wage, use child labor, do not recognize overtime worked, have unclean conditions, or violate workers' rights in other ways. It is believed that solving this problem requires cooperation and coordination throughout the fashion industry. Government crackdowns as well as consumer awareness and response are also needed.

The U.S. government raised the conditions of manufacturing workers many decades ago by setting labor standards. Unions have won higher pay and better workers' rights. The public must also understand that these improvements create higher apparel manufacturing expenses that have, in turn, increased consumer prices.

Cutting

To begin production, cutters unroll layers of flat fabric into high stacks. They control large machines, called *spreaders*, to move bolts of yard goods back and forth on very long tables. The stacks are quite high. They might have 100 layers of fabric. A long paper marker might be placed across the top, but now computerized cutting is usually done directly from the marker in the CAD system. Garment parts in all sizes, programmed into the computer, are cut perfectly.

Electric straight-knife cutting machines, like large power saws, are manipulated by hand or computer along the outlines of the pattern pieces of the marker. The number of garments cut at one time varies, depending on the thickness of the fabric, the equipment used, the price of the garments, and the number of orders. The entire thickness of the stack is cut at once. This results in fabric stacks of garment parts.

With technology, computerized knife cutters, like manual cutters, cut multiple layers of fabric. Some even sharpen themselves automatically. Water-jet cutters cut smaller stacks of fabric layers.

A *laser cutter* is a device that generates an intense, powerful beam of light. It vaporizes the fabric almost instantaneously. Laser cutting is done on a single layer of fabric and cuts one garment a piece at a time. Laser cutters are economical because they are very fast and accurate. They can cut as many garments per unit of time as a human operator using a manually controlled multiple-layer cutter. They are precise at cutting intricate shapes. They offer great style flexibility since they can cut 100 or more different styles in one hour.

The Tailor System

The *tailor system* is a manufacturing system in which all sewing tasks for a garment are done by one person. Today it is only used for custom sewing jobs, such as expensive gowns, tailored suits, and coats. It is slow and expensive. The person sewing the garment must be skilled in all sewing and tailoring tasks, as in **6-6**. Much handwork and extensive pressing are done.

Faster methods that involve less handwork have been developed for suits. They include more built-in shaping from the pattern, rather than from hand sewing or steam pressing. Also, some garment parts are fused together. Unstructured styles are offered in sizes such as small, medium, and large, which are less precise than regular sizing. *Section construction* is sometimes used by manufacturers, in which sections of a garment are made by operators rather than one operator sewing an entire garment.

The Piecework System

The piecework system is a manufacturing procedure in which each specific task is done by a different person along an assembly line. This divides the total manufacturing process into small, individualized jobs. Every sewing machine operator does only one job on a specialized machine, as shown in **6-7**. This procedure attempts to make production time per item as short as possible while the work moves along.

Piecework has been done by the *progressive bundle system* since mass production began in

Levent Konuk/Shutterstock.com

6-6 The tailor system, in which a person with expert sewing skills makes the entire garment, is sometimes used for expensive suits and coats.

the industry. Cut garment parts are packaged into bundles of dozens to go through the sewing operations. Work tickets are put on the bundles. The bundles are put into canvas bins with wheels called *handling trucks*.

The handling trucks are rolled to the different production stations in the factory. Bundles of collars are delivered to one station, sleeves to another, with fronts and backs delivered to other stations. The bundles are moved through the assembly line. Pockets are put on by one person; buttonholes are made by another worker, all with special machines or attachments for those jobs. Further down the line, the parts come together and are joined by other workers.

The most efficient use of time and people on the assembly line is figured out ahead of time by engineers. Workers are paid at a set rate per task, determined by the difficulty and time required to do their specific sewing tasks. This piecework rate is multiplied by how many times they accomplish the task, such as how many collars or sleeve cuffs they assemble.

Lucian Coman/Shutterstock.com

6-7 Machine operators use specialized sewing machines to do specific tasks along an assembly line.

Kzenon/Shutterstock.com

6-8 Unit production is a computerized system that carries unconnected garment parts to the proper sewing machine operators until each garment is completed.

The goods are inspected periodically during the production process. Almost no hand finishing jobs are done. Hems and fasteners are put in by machine during assembly. Any hand sewing that is required falls under the heading of trimming. It is done at the end by workers who specialize in such tasks.

The **unit production system (UPS)** is a computerized piecework arrangement, used now by many apparel manufacturers. See **6-8**. The cut pieces of each garment are hung (loaded) together onto an overhead product carrier, which is moved through the manufacturing steps by a conveyor system. Time is saved since bundles do not need to be untied, retied, ticketed, or manually moved along as work is done. Also, operators can better see how the garments look overall.

The unit production system is a method of **computer-aided manufacturing (CAM)**, which utilizes electronics for the production of apparel. Each workstation has a computer terminal. When a task has been completed, the operator presses the *send* button on the workstation terminal or scans a bar code on the garment holder. This directs the carrier to automatically take the items to the next station.

With CAM, work is routed in such a way that the sewing line is continuously and automatically balanced. Garment parts are fed to the workstations with full consideration of the skill and speed of each operator. Each terminal feeds information into the main system. The computer tracks all inventory and piece rate data for better production planning. Supervisors can

continually monitor the production line with a central computer. They can make changes when needed. They can also check on operator efficiency, payroll information, operating costs, inventory control, and style data.

The Latest Production Methods

Modular manufacturing is the latest method being used in apparel production. This method is mostly used by large manufacturers who can afford to implement it and train employees to use it. The modular system divides the production employees into independent teams, or module work groups. The module members choose a leader and hold weekly meetings (usually one hour long) on company time to sort out problems and agree on their own work assignments and schedules.

Modular manufacturing has improved the flexibility and productivity of apparel manufacturing. **Productivity** is a measure of how efficiently or effectively resources, such as labor supply, machines, and materials, are used. Improved productivity results in higher amounts of output in relation to the amounts of input.

Modular manufacturing also improves product quality and employee morale, while reducing employee grievances and *production throughput time*. This is the time required to turn raw materials into a completed product. Peer pressure reduces absenteeism and encourages nonperformers to leave on their own. Companies share the resulting profits with the operators through higher pay. Individual piece rate pay is replaced with pay based on total module production.

The modular manufacturing system *empowers* the workers. In other words, it gives them the authority and autonomy to make the decisions needed to ensure the highest group productivity. For this to be successful, top managers and production supervisors must be willing to trust their employees to meet the manufacturing challenges.

Emphasis is also now being placed on ergonomics and benchmarking. Ergonomics matches human performance to specific tasks being done, workplace equipment used, and the environment for efficiency and safety. It is also called *human engineering*. To prevent repetitive motion injuries, occupational health problems, and worker fatigue, equipment is designed and arranged for the most effective and safest interaction with those who use it. For instance, the height of sewing machine stands is adjustable, worktables can tilt, and footrests have been added.

Benchmarking is the continuous process of measuring a company's products, services, and practices against other companies' extremely good products, services, and practices. The best ideas of the apparel industry and related industries are identified and improved upon. For example, one company might have an innovative method for attaching sleeves. Other companies notice that benchmark and adopt it. Each company strives to do the best job in each operation, so the total manufacturing process is as efficient as possible. Also, industry training opportunities are available to workers who want to learn the latest techniques, as in **6-9**.

Finishing

After manufacturing, finished garments are inspected inside and out. If flaws or mistakes are found, and if they can be fixed, the garment is returned to the operator responsible. In some cases, the inspector may decide it would take too much time or effort to fix the problem. Then the garment is sold cheaply as a second.

To finish production, pressers give a complete final steam pressing to the garments. Labels or hangtags listing fiber content and care instructions are attached to all garments. If a large order is being made for a particular store,

Kzenon/Shutterstock.com

6-9 Training in the latest apparel manufacturing techniques is offered at universities and industry technology centers.

the factory may attach the store's price tags. The garments are finally ready for distribution to the stores that ordered them.

To ship garments to other cities and states, folded garments are packed flat in corrugated containers. Hanging garments are hung on bars in stand-up boxes. Some items have special packaging, as in **6-10**. Then the cartons of garments or accessories are sealed and addressed to distribution centers or retail stores for shipping.

For apparel manufactured in the New York City garment district, rolling hang-up racks, as in **6-11**, are used to move the clothes. The racks are rolled along the streets from factories to shipping rooms. Sometimes the racks go directly to nearby department stores that are desperate to receive their orders.

Selling the Apparel

Sales promotion by apparel producers is far ahead of the wearing season. Apparel companies present their new lines to retail store buyers by showing them sample garments about six months before the merchandise will be bought by consumers.

Because of the speed needed to get fashions into the stores, most apparel goes right from producer to retailer. The wholesale jobbers of past eras, who distributed manufacturer's goods to retailers, have almost disappeared. Modern transportation systems move merchandise to stores in fast and dependable ways. This direct-shipment system also helps to keep prices as low as possible since no middle people have to be paid.

© iStock.com / 36clicks

6-10 Packaging and shipping is an important aspect at the end of apparel production.

6-11 In the garment district of New York City, racks of garments are rolled from place to place.

Showing the Lines

During the period known to the trade as *market weeks*, retail store buyers from all over the country go to fashion market centers. They look at the new collections in the manufacturers' showrooms. Some manufacturers show their collections accessorized and professionally modeled in elaborate fashion shows. Others simply hang their garments on racks in their showrooms and show them to individual retail buyers, as in **6-12**. Some firms hold press previews for fashion reporters and editors in hopes of getting publicity. Some produce videos of their lines.

All companies hope that buyers will place orders for their retail stores before they leave the showrooms. As orders are taken, production is scheduled. Many manufacturers start producing some of the goods before the openings. They rely on their merchandising projections to estimate initial market demand.

New York City is the largest U.S. fashion market center. Los Angeles, Chicago, and Dallas are also very important, as are Atlanta, Seattle, and Miami. Various cities are known for certain types of merchandise. Market weeks are held on different dates in different cities, so manufacturers can show their lines to retail store buyers in many regional locations.

6-12 Retail buyers visit apparel manufacturers' showrooms to look at lines from which they might place orders.

Seattle International Trade Center

Apparel marts are buildings or complexes that house permanent showrooms and sales offices. They offer apparel manufacturers the opportunity to all be in one convenient location, so buyers can see and buy the lines at any time. Marts are usually departmentalized to concentrate the same type of merchandise, such as children's wear, in a particular area. Apparel marts are located in several cities. Company showrooms are often positioned like stores in a mall, as in **6-13**.

In addition to their periodic new lines, firms also introduce new styles as a season progresses. Highly accepted styles may be made in a wider assortment of fabrics or colors than originally shown. New fads may come into demand and be produced. Unpopular styles are dropped from the line completely.

Besides having sales staff in their showrooms, some firms have sales representatives (reps) showing and selling their lines around the country. See **6-14**. The manufacturers show the new styles to their sales representatives at fashion shows and sales meetings. The reps then travel within their assigned territories with sample lines to show to retailers. Sometimes a certain label of goods from a manufacturer is *confined*. That means it is sold to only one retailer in a certain trading area on an exclusive basis.

For small manufacturers without their own sales reps, there are independent sales reps who

Adriano Castelli / Shutterstock.com

6-14 An apparel manufacturer's sales representatives display their company's new lines at trade shows to generate interest and take orders.

maintain permanent showrooms or travel in different parts of the country. They sell collections of several different manufacturers' lines that are not in competition with one another.

Promoting the Lines

Manufacturers advertise in trade publications to bring their names and products to the attention of retailers. These ads are less expensive than ads in consumer publications. Some apparel producers do *cooperative advertising* with retail stores. They might advertise their merchandise in national fashion magazines along with a list of the regional stores that carry their lines. Other times, retailers advertise in local newspapers and promote a particular manufacturer's products. Either way, the businesses share the advertising expenses and both benefit.

Manufacturers sometimes provide retailers with selling aids. Examples are large photographs for store displays, newspaper advertising mats, and customer mailing pieces. Manufacturers also have in-store programs for the retailers who sell their lines. They provide training talks to salespeople, personal appearances by the firm's designer, fashion shows, and trunk shows, as in **6-15**. During a *trunk show*, a complete collection of samples is brought into a store for a limited amount of time. There is heavy local advertising. Orders are taken directly from customers by a key company salesperson.

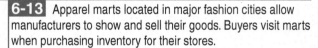

6-13 Apparel marts located in major fashion cities allow manufacturers to show and sell their goods. Buyers visit marts when purchasing inventory for their stores.

California Market Center

Manufacturers' promotions in stores provide consumer feedback. It is important for companies to listen and respond to constructive criticism. If orders are not coming in as well as expected, or fall off, there must be a cutback in production. Manufacturing has to be stopped as early as possible to keep costs down. On the other hand, production must be increased for popular items. Reorders provide the best chances for making big profits since all the designing and preliminary details have already been done.

Overseas Manufacturing

Much manufacturing competition is coming from outside the United States. Taiwan, Hong Kong, and South Korea have been major apparel

6-15 Apparel lines are sometimes presented to customers of retail shops through special trunk shows. Often the designer is at the location of the trunk show to talk with shoppers.

Anita Ford Collection

producing locations for several decades. Mainland China is now the largest producer. Caribbean and Latin American countries are gaining in production, as shown in **6-16**. Also, developing countries in the Middle East, Africa, and other parts of Asia have increased apparel manufacturing.

Imports of goods that come into the country from foreign sources have risen because of the intense competition in the apparel industry. Imports often fill certain voids in the U.S. domestic industry for unusual or low-priced items.

Differences in Cost, Fashion, and Construction

In general, American-made apparel has high costs of production compared to many other countries. Manufacturers worldwide compete for price advantages. Low-wage countries can mass-produce garments at a low cost. This allows them to sell their garments at lower prices than comparable items produced in the U.S. Thus, they have a market in the U.S.

The lower labor rates overseas usually include no overtime pay or *fringe benefits*, such as vacation time or health insurance. Overseas government *export incentives*, to encourage sending products out of the country, also reduce companies' production costs in those countries. Examples of export incentives are tax exemptions, rebates, and preferential financing

6-16 These marketing materials are promoting the apparel manufacturing facilities and expertise of a Latin American country to fashion companies in other parts of the world.

plans offered by governments to producers who export goods. Conversely, U.S. manufacturers must comply with government regulations regarding such matters as safety and benefits for workers.

The savings from overseas production more than compensates for the shipping costs of bringing the goods to the United States. The savings are great even after *tariffs*, or government *import taxes (duties)*, are paid when the merchandise enters the U.S. to be sold. Most goods travel across the oceans via container shipping freighters.

The second void filled by some overseas apparel producers is fashion innovation. Firms in the United States tend to mass-produce *safe* styles that are sure to sell. Overseas sources, on the other hand, often produce small amounts of more adventurous garments. Producers worldwide compete for new and different fashions. European fashions, for instance, are often innovative and of fine quality. They have appeal just because of their European origin. The name of the designer or firm on such imported apparel is a drawing card for American demand, even though the price may be higher.

The third reason to import apparel is related to handwork. Hand embroidery, beading, and knitting are examples. The highly paid U.S. labor force cannot spend time on such tasks. U.S. industry is most profitable with large scale, fast, machine production.

Competition of International Trade

Clothing imports and exports have become major economic issues in international trade. In the United States, imports have been steadily and rapidly increasing for many years.

Apparel production is a *labor-intensive* industry. In other words, a big portion of the total costs of finished products is due to large amounts of human effort compared with other expenses. Since many people are needed, wage rates make a big difference in production costs. There is little difference in the amount of time it takes to make apparel in the U.S. or abroad. It takes about the same number of minutes to make a shirt in Tennessee as it does in Haiti.

Apparel manufacturers in the United States are at a disadvantage when competing for international trade against low-wage countries. Textile and apparel industries are among the first to be set up in developing countries. Garment production requires what they have: cheap labor and low capital expenses. Clothing factories can be started in places where technology and money are limited.

In recent years, the importance of the apparel industry, in relation to overall manufacturing in the United States, has declined. Its share of the nation's total industrial activity has fallen. The number of people working in the industry has been reduced. Experts cite imports as the major cause for these economic facts.

The textile and apparel industries have fought for varying degrees of government protection to control the level of imports. The United States has some agreements with countries to limit imports by a quota system. Quotas are limitations set by the government on certain goods that can enter the country during a particular time span. They have been established on categories of products, such as specific fibers or types of finished garments.

The government, however, has to be careful about restricting trade. Curbing imports of fashion merchandise may bring retaliation with other countries refusing to accept goods the U.S. wants to export to them. The government must look at the total picture of trade. International diplomacy, which involves the balancing of political and economic issues, is important in trade negotiations. Borders of most countries are becoming more open, encouraging trade.

Using International Trade

The apparel industry in the United States sometimes uses cheap foreign labor instead of competing against it. Some American firms now have their own production facilities in developing countries. However, most firms contract with companies owned in those countries to manufacture their garments. Large firms may have an American supervisor stationed in a foreign country. This person keeps tabs on all of the contract production in that country or in that particular area of the world. The production for an American apparel firm may be spread among several different countries. All garments cannot be produced in the same country because of production capabilities and U.S. import quotas or other regulations.

Sometimes garments that are cut in America are shipped overseas for sewing and finishing. Then they are shipped back. In this procedure, only a minimum duty is paid on the value that has been added while the merchandise was out of the United States.

Manufacturers who have their goods produced overseas (called offshore production) are constantly looking for countries with lower wage rates, better innovations, and unrestricted quotas. Today, the fact that a garment has the name of an American designer or firm is no assurance that the item is American made (called domestic production).

American apparel producers export some goods. However, they have not been able to match their exports to the rising tide of imports. Thus, the deficit in the balance of trade has continued to grow.

Instead of exporting goods from the United States, some major apparel producers have set up licensing agreements with foreign producers. Apparel is produced overseas with an American firm's label and specifications. It is sold overseas without coming to the United States. In return, the firm receives a percentage of sales.

Another method is with a joint venture arrangement. That is when two firms form a partnership for combined advantages. For international trade, an American firm and a foreign producer enter into a partnership for production and sales overseas. The American company provides the designs, patterns, technical expertise, and use of its brand name. The foreign producer employs the labor to produce and market the goods in that country.

Major American apparel producers have licensing agreements or joint ventures in many countries. Their goods are made and sold worldwide. Some even have wholly owned manufacturing plants in foreign countries.

Country of Origin Labeling

Legislation in the mid-1980s required textile and apparel products to have labels indicating where they were made. *Made in the USA* labels are placed in domestically produced apparel.

At the same time, the textile and apparel industries unified themselves by forming the *Crafted with Pride in U.S.A. Council, Inc.* They

conducted nationwide efforts to bring the industries' message to the American people. The council, made up of every segment of the textile and apparel industries, sponsored public awareness campaigns. It spread the *Buy American* message through television and other media. It also encouraged the use of hangtags and labels such as those in **6-17**. American clothing manufacturers are listed online.

No Clear-Cut Answers

There are no clear-cut or easy answers in dealing with apparel imports. *Economic* views differ. Some people feel there should be stronger government controls to try to help the U.S. apparel industries. Others feel that the industries must make themselves competitive in world markets or else dissolve. They say it is a fact that developing countries can produce textiles and apparel more cheaply than the United States. They also say that many of the developing countries critically need apparel industries for their livelihoods. Therefore, they believe that the United States should be moving into industries where it would not compete with developing countries. The U.S. could be more competitive in world markets, they predict, if focused on industries that require more capital and technology.

Political views question whether import protection of the apparel segment would alienate other countries that trade with the U.S. Textile and apparel manufacturing companies and unions have campaigned against imports to save their jobs. They want government help.

Humanistic viewpoints compare the jobs of apparel workers in the U.S. with those in developing countries. Without apparel jobs,

6-17 American textile and apparel industries hope that labels such as this one will encourage consumers to notice the country of origin and buy domestically produced apparel.

many people in developing countries would have no way of obtaining the basic necessities of life. Unemployment in the U.S. apparel industry has sad consequences as well. Hard times spread to nearby stores and businesses and whole communities. Government expenses increase for the relief and welfare of many people. Also, the pride and self-respect of the unemployed workers are lowered.

Ongoing Innovation for Apparel Production

In the future, the trend of apparel imports is expected to continue, but the pace of increase should slow down. To compete, American production facilities will become even more automated. They will use more computerized pattern designing, laser-beam cutting, sonic (fused) joining, and robotic sewing.

High-tech equipment and the competition of imports will reduce the number of workers in the industry. However, the economic hardships of the resulting unemployment should eventually subside. Some present workers will retire, and others will be retrained to operate computerized equipment. Fewer new workers will seek jobs in apparel production.

Firms from other countries, such as Japan, may set up apparel production operations in the United States. Likewise, American firms will also continue to invest in overseas production facilities. The apparel industry's scope is becoming totally global (worldwide).

Computer Automation

High-tech computer automation is revolutionizing the entire apparel production industry. Computer-aided design enables computer imaging to be done on a screen in three dimensions. The graphics allow the sketch to turn to any angle so all sides of the fashion design can be seen. Fabric draping grids, as in **6-18**, help with *fluid* designing. Then the computer automatically converts the three-dimensional work into a two-dimensional flat pattern.

Unlike machines that must be retooled to change, computer-controlled automation is flexible. The programming is changed on software rather than altering the machinery. This reduces setup costs and time. It allows smaller quantities of apparel to be produced economically. Forecasting mistakes can be fixed faster. Fewer risks are taken. Automated sewing, which can rapidly produce small quantities of garments in various styles, also allows for more innovative designing.

Robotic machines are being developed to do whole piecework operations with little or no human intervention. Computerized workstation machines first pick up a garment part. They align it, sew it, trim it, and take it to the next station. One specialized machine might place a pocket onto a garment, stitch around it, and pass it to the next machine.

The best present applications for robotics are in repetitive sewing procedures. A pillowcase can be totally made and packaged by a machine. A cowboy boot machine just has to be loaded with leather. Finished, decoratively stitched boots, as in **6-19**, are unloaded.

Computer-integrated manufacturing (CIM) is revolutionizing the industry. It combines CAD, CAM, robotics, and company information systems. It is being called *hands-off production*, since the entire production process is controlled by computer. For the future, planners foresee bolts of fabric entering one end of a robot assembly line and emerging at the other end of the line as finished garments. Fashion designers would create their designs on computers, and the machines would do the rest.

6-18　Fabric draping can be shown on photos that are scanned into the computer, using a flexible three-dimensional grid.

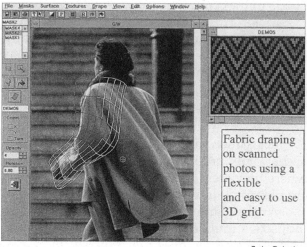

Fabric draping on scanned photos using a flexible and easy to use 3D grid.

Gerber Technology

6-19 After looking at these boots, imagine all the specific procedures done robotically from the beginning to the end of manufacturing.

Reducing Lead and Response Times

Industry-wide cooperation has reduced *lead times* (for customers ordering ahead) and *response times* (for manufacturers' production and delivery). All segments of the apparel industries have joined forces to make the whole supply chain work better. The program involves collaboration with all companies sharing information and working together. It ties together all parts of the textile, apparel, and retail industries into one unified industry rather than as individual segments.

With collaboration, *electronic data interchange (EDI)* linkages are set up via the Internet. Standardized software programs have been developed so companies' computers can communicate with each other. Secure websites connect partnered textile, apparel, and retail companies with business linkages, as shown in **6-20**. Textile mills set up a computer system that measures, color codes, and inspects fabric as it comes off the loom. The information is transmitted to computers at the apparel factories before the bolts of cloth arrive. Thus, the sewing factory does not need to inspect, color code, or measure the fabric. The fabric moves directly from the delivery truck to the cutting

room for swift processing without any repetition of tasks. The sewing plant then uses computers to inform retail stores about production and delivery of their orders. *Invoicing*, or billing for the materials sent, is also done automatically by computer.

Information also flows backward through the chain. As selling data are recorded through check-out technology at retail locations, they trigger manufacturers to produce more of the items that are selling. This also prompts textile firms to automatically send more of the required fabric to the apparel manufacturers. Because products are automatically made to replenish those that have been sold, inventory levels can be lower, meaning smaller amounts of items are kept on hand.

As a result of collaboration, communications are improved and processing costs are reduced. There is less duplication of functions, which means a faster response to market trends than before. Therefore, the right merchandise is available for demand, and costs are lower. Retailers have fewer missed sales and markdowns because of extra unwanted merchandise. Also, with long-term partnerships, suppliers maintain

6-20 This simplified illustration shows that with collaboration, linkages can be established with businesses from each segment into chains of suppliers and buyers.

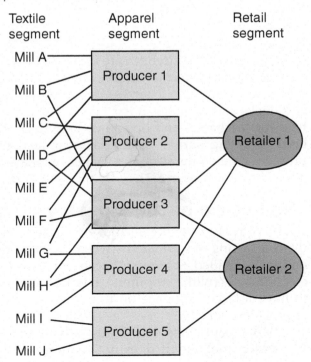

the promised quality and expected on-time delivery. The fear of sharing information electronically with other companies is diminishing. This makes domestically produced apparel more competitive against imports. The domestic apparel manufacturing process that has normally taken one year (longer for offshore production) is now much shorter, as well as more accurate.

Global supply chain collaboration is also being used for *fast fashion*. This is when small lots of new designs are brought to market quickly, with a 10-week or less turnaround from design to retail selling. With automatic information-transfer, collaborating partners do fast production in close proximity to the market. Thus, shipping costs are lower. Consumers are eager to get the latest fashions and are willing to pay full price for these limited-edition fashions that are only available for a short time.

Other Industry-Wide Cooperation

The *Textile/Clothing Technology Corporation*, called *(TC)²*, researches high-tech innovations in apparel production processes and helps the industry implement them. This results in better quality, service, and cost from American apparel sources than from their overseas competitors. By pooling industry resources, financial responsibility and leadership are shared. Research and development duplication is eliminated, since member companies are not working independently from one another. Industry unity and strength are improved.

(TC)² has a tech center in Cary, North Carolina that offers education courses, demonstrations, and books and manuals. It has interactive video help for mechanics and operators. Its *Size USA* body scanning survey of the U.S. population provides data on the sizes and shapes of today's adult consumers, as in **6-21**.

The Future of the Industry

Business-to-business (B2B) e-commerce is the transacting of business between companies online. It is called *e-commerce* because it is done electronically (with computers). It will continue to have a large influence on the future of the apparel industry.

B2B e-commerce has many advantages. It operates globally. It does not require setup

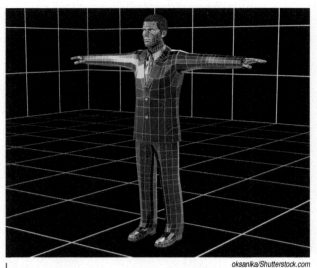

oksanika/Shutterstock.com

6-21 The body scanning of 11,000 individuals across the U.S. provided statistically accurate shape and sizing data for manufacturers, brands, and retailers to improve fit.

time because the Internet is already in use and available. Direct communications can be easily established between collaborating companies by using passwords on secure websites. Also, time zone differences are insignificant since people can receive and send messages at their own convenience. Language differences are less of a barrier, since nations are teaching and using more English, which has become the universally accepted language of the Internet. Cultural differences are being minimized. Additionally, news or updates can be sent as they occur so there is no lost time in business dealings. However, some security of information privacy may be compromised.

In the future, apparel industry innovation will use *virtual product development (VPD)*, the practice of developing products in a fully digital environment. Collaborative digital environments will bring together designers, customer firms, and consumers. This will enable faster design, less risk of product failure, and decreased development costs.

Apparel production will become a marketing as well as a manufacturing industry. The focus will be on pleasing customers. Company-owned facilities will be cost effective and use the latest technology. CAD work will interface with sourcing and quality specifiers that are online worldwide. Textile providers, product developers, manufacturing sites, and retailers will be networked. Unified tracking systems will tell at what stage and where products are at all times.

United States manufacturers will move into agile manufacturing, a seamless data capture system of information, production, and delivery. The system will combine collaboration partnership alliances, EDI e-commerce linkages, and wireless (radio frequency) transmission of consumer purchase data and trends. It will provide custom garments for individuals with design features selected by the consumer and to fit each consumer's body.

Agile manufacturing will use precise three-dimensional body scanning and interactive design stations. Customized production will remove forecasting risks while meeting specific needs of individual consumers. Virtual or live fit sessions will take place via computers. A garment will be cut and produced exactly for each person's dimensions.

Production of the custom garments will use single-ply laser cutting as well as textile printing onto the garment parts. More seams will be fused together rather than sewn. This will be done by *sonic* (radio-wave, supersonic sound) *joining*. Another method, electronic injection sewing, is done with liquid chemical thread that solidifies. Also, technology may fabricate apparel automatically in the form of seamless garments. These garments might be knitted, formed, or molded, rather than sewn.

Another possibility for the future is apparel that might contain heat-sensitive body coils to heat or cool the wearer. This is already available for the military. Climate-controlled suits can be powered by solar cells.

Summary

Clothing manufacturers try to keep their costs low, quality high, and selling prices competitive to make a profit. Companies may do all stages of production themselves or hire contractors to do some or all production processes.

Merchandise plans try to satisfy consumer needs and demands so retailers have the right goods at the right price at the right time. Manufacturing details and production capabilities are calculated to develop the apparel lines.

Merchandise planners keep tabs on consumer acceptance of each garment.

Garment designers do digital sketches or drape ideas onto mannequins. Their ideas are from forecasting services, history, art, nature, popular entertainment, news events, and other influences. Much adapting of higher priced fashions is done, simplifying designs for lower production costs.

Garment patterns are made on CAD equipment. Samples are sewn to check styling and fit. Production procedures, such as grading and marker-making, are done for the final garment selections.

Factory production in world locations depends on costs and quality. Cutting garment parts might be with hand saws or by computer-driven cutters. The piecework system is preferred by most manufacturers rather than the tailor system of manufacturing. Bundles of dozens of garment parts move among operators of specialized sewing machines. CAM systems are being used, and modular manufacturing incorporates ergonomics and benchmarking. Finally, finished garments are inspected and pressed.

To sell the apparel, manufacturers show their lines to retail store buyers during market weeks. This is done in company showrooms or apparel marts, or by sales representatives. Manufacturers promote their lines to retailers in trade publications, and may offer benefits of cooperative advertising, selling aids, and trunk shows.

Much labor-intensive apparel manufacturing is done overseas, where labor costs and fringe benefits are lower. There may be better fashion innovation overseas, since the U.S. mass-produces safe styles. Many American apparel producers are now using offshore production through licensing agreements and joint ventures. There are no clear answers about apparel imports because of varying economic, political, and humanistic viewpoints. Country of origin labeling is required on apparel.

In the future, apparel production will be even more global. High-tech computer automation will utilize robotics and CIM. Lead and response times will be reduced as all parts of the industry cooperate through B2B e-commerce, virtual product development, and agile manufacturing.

Fashion Recall

Write your answers on a separate sheet of paper.

Matching: Match the following aspects of apparel production with the appropriate terms.

1. Piecework system.
2. Stylists.
3. Trunk shows.
4. Costing.
5. Grading.
6. Offshore production.
7. Market weeks.
8. Marker.
9. Low labor rates.
10. Tailor system.

A. designing
B. preparation for production
C. factory production
D. selling and promoting
E. overseas manufacturing

Short Answer: Write the correct answer to each of the following questions.

11. Name three reasons why a manufacturer might choose to use contractors for production processes.
12. What are samplings (not samples), and what is their function?
13. Name five factors that are considered during the costing process.
14. *True* or *false*. CAD is especially useful for designing evening gowns and other garments of soft, flowing fabrics.
15. *True* or *false*. CAM is being used in more and more tailor system sewing shops.
16. *True* or *false*. Apparel marts are huge factories for apparel production.
17. Which provide better chances for making big profits, first-time orders or reorders? Why?
18. Imports of apparel fill voids in U.S. markets because of differences in _____, _____, and _____.
19. Why are textile and apparel industries among the first to be set up in developing countries?
20. What is the goal of (TC)^2?

Fashion Vocabulary

21. With a partner, use the Internet to locate photos or graphics that depict each of the *Fashion Terms* listed on the chapter opening. Print the graphics or use presentation software to show your graphics to the class, describing how they depict the meaning of the terms.

Critical Thinking

22. **Make predictions** Why is planning crucial to apparel production? Predict what would happen if decisions were not based on well-developed plans. Share your predictions with the class.
23. **Formulate ideas** Imagine you are a fashion designer. From where would you draw your inspiration for ideas? What people, places, or environments do you find most inspiring? Explain your response in class.
24. **Analyze considerations** What are the pros and cons of overseas manufacturing? What factors did you consider in your analysis when forming your opinions? Write a blog post of your analysis to upload to the class website for peer and instructor review.

Core Skills

25. **Research and writing**   Collect *three* pictures of current garment designs that you think were influenced by particular people or events. For each, write a description about what you think the influence was and how the garment displays this influence. In addition, write a paragraph about some current events that could influence upcoming apparel designs.

26. **Reading and writing**   Write a report on the production of a pair of jeans. List all the different steps you think took place to produce the jeans. What different skill levels were needed for the different jobs?

27. **Speaking and listening**   Team up with other students to hold a class debate about apparel imports. Decide who will be pro-American and who will be pro-imports. Debate the economic, political, humanistic, and other areas of concern about the subject. Ask the class to vote on whether they favor more or fewer government regulations on trade.

28. **Technology demo**   Locate an online video that demonstrates a *computer-aided design* program used in the fashion industry. Present an oral report to the class in which you replay the demo and describe the features of the design program.

29. **Research and speaking**   Do further research related to recent technological advances that are affecting apparel production. If possible, interview people who work in the industry. Present an oral report of your findings to the class.

30. **CTE career readiness practice**   Imagine it is five years in the future and you are starting your first full-time job. Your new employer is a major apparel manufacturer, and you know the work is fast-paced and demanding. You have watched some family members and friends suffer the effects of workplace stress on their health and wellness over the years. Your goal is to maintain health and wellness by developing a plan for handling workplace stress. Investigate and evaluate the resources on the *National Institute for Occupational Safety and Health* link on the Centers for Disease Control website. Then, write your plan for preventing job stress.

Fashion in Action

31. **Portfolio builder**   After researching apparel production, prepare a flowchart that diagrams apparel production from fabric to garment. Keep this diagram in your print or digital portfolio to demonstrate your understanding of the apparel production process.

32. **Design activity**   Target a group of customers and develop an imaginary line of men's or women's sportswear. Trace fashion illustrations from newspaper ads or pattern catalogs to show your line of garments. Gather color and fabric swatches for your line. Mount them to make an attractive display. Give a marketing pitch to the class, describing why you think the styles, fabrics, and colors are good for your line.

Self-Assessment Quiz ↗

Complete the self-assessment quiz online to help practice and expand your knowledge and skills.

Fashion Promotion and Retailing

While studying, look for the activity icon **to:**

- **practice** key fashion terms with e-flash cards, vocabulary games, and matching activities
- **assess** what you learn by completing self-assessment quizzes

G-WLEARNING.com

www.g-wlearning.com/clothingandfashion/

FASHION TERMS

indirect selling
direct selling
promotion
advertising
publicity
visual merchandising
video merchandising
electronic
  merchandising

channel of
  distribution
fashion
  merchandising
markup
markdowns
open-to-buy
resident buying
  offices (RBOs)

private label
anchor stores
electronic retailing
offshore sourcing
omni-channel
  retailing
niche retailing

Objectives

After studying this chapter, you will be able to
➤ describe fashion promotion in terms of advertising, publicity, visual merchandising, and video merchandising.
➤ define many retail terms.
➤ distinguish between different types of apparel outlets.
➤ discuss the pros and cons of retail imports.
➤ describe possibilities for the future in retail sales of apparel.

Once textile and clothing items are designed and produced, they must be sold. This is done with a combination of indirect and direct selling. Indirect selling is promotion to the general public. Direct selling is the exchange of merchandise to individual consumers in return for money or credit.

Promotion

Promotion is indirect, or nonpersonal, selling aimed at a large general audience. It tries to catch the public's eye by appealing to the needs and wants of consumers. Promotion includes all efforts to inform people about new and desirable products.

125

The purpose of fashion promotion is to make people interested in particular apparel products, so they will want to buy them. Promoters want people to feel as if they have to have the latest items. Fashion promotion includes advertising, publicity, visual merchandising, special events, video merchandising, and electronic merchandising.

Advertising

Advertising is a paid promotional message by an identified sponsor. Advertisements appear in media such as websites, applications (apps), newspapers, magazines, television, and radio. Local and regional retail stores use mostly local newspaper, online, and radio ads. The ads are usually prepared by each store's advertising department. Nationwide retailers and textile and apparel manufacturers often use television and national magazine ads, which are more expensive than local newspaper and radio ads. The TV and magazine ads are generally prepared by advertising agencies. Companies may also use apps and online advertising, such as banner ads or search engine advertising, as a way to attract customers.

Sometimes textile and apparel manufacturers share the costs of *cooperative advertising* with retailers. The retailer benefits by paying only part of the advertising costs. The manufacturer shares the costs and benefits by having its name or product linked with a known and respected retailer.

Publicity

Publicity is free promotion. It includes nonpaid messages to the public about a company's merchandise, activities, or services. An example might be a newspaper story about a store or its branches. Another example might be a fashion magazine's layout of photographs taken at a manufacturer's collection showing, such as in **7-1**.

Public relations departments of businesses try to get publicity through various media sources. Sometimes individuals promote their firms during speeches to live audiences. Sometimes they hold press conferences to promote their products or services.

Press kits are distributed by some manufacturers. The kits include photos and written copy about the companies' lines in the hope of

FashionStock.com/Shutterstock.com

7-1 Including this photograph as part of a fashion story in a magazine would give the manufacturer publicity, or free promotion.

being included in fashion news articles. A press kit is shown in **7-2**.

Visual Merchandising and Special Events

Visual merchandising is presenting goods in an attractive and understandable manner. The way goods are placed on view can be a key to achieving high sales. Displays and exhibits are ways that clothing items are visually promoted. *Mannequins* are commonly used in both window

7-2 Press kits include pictures and words that can easily be placed into newspapers or magazines, sent out to try to obtain publicity for the company.

displays and interior displays, as in **7-3**. Some displays have special effects such as moving parts, lights, or mirrors. Fashion shows, contests, and other special events add visual excitement. Malls often have special displays, entertainment, or fun activities, such as in **7-4**.

Some department stores and upscale retailers have special promotional activities. Colored spotlights accent displays. Celebrity appearances are scheduled. Purchases are placed in high-profile shopping bags. Departments have catchy names. Floors are arranged as arcades or streets of shops. Some stores hold art shows. Stores want to be regarded as exciting or entertaining places to be. Then there is a better chance that consumers will want to come and the retailers will sell more goods.

Retailers are becoming more talented and aggressive with visual merchandising activities and special events. They sometimes have their own special events departments. Retailers are becoming entertainment, service, and news-making businesses. They are developing images for their companies. Having an image helps a retailer attract customers. Since many stores may carry the same merchandise, the presentation of the goods is often what makes the difference.

7-4 Amusement rides, movie theaters, and other entertaining activities are part of the Mall of America.

Video and Electronic Merchandising

Video merchandising uses videos in retail stores to show new fashion trends, promote merchandise, and build customer traffic. Videos are sometimes set up in retail store departments near the merchandise they are showing. They attract the attention of passing customers with sound and movement. Videotaped fashion shows and interviews with designers encourage shoppers to stay in the department or store. However, they have not had a strong sales effect.

Some fashion tapes are educational to train salespeople. They describe the philosophy, facilities, and lines of manufacturers. Other videos are educational for consumer information. They may explain how to select jewelry or how to build wardrobes that will help them look successful. Videos may play silently, or have spoken words or music. Short videos hold customers' attention best.

Fashion rock videos tell a story while presenting promotional information. They are very creative and usually only three to five minutes long. Instead of presenting a sales pitch, they have lots of action and music with bright, fun clothing. The clothes might have a subtle outside logo or label. A manufacturer's name might be flashed casually in the background. This is called *soft sell*.

7-3 This window display uses oval frames in three different sizes as props to create interest for accessories next to the dressed mannequins.

Electronic merchandising is promotion via electronic devices, such as computers and mobile technology. Retailers alert their customers about special sales or new merchandise through e-mails, social media messages, or other applications (apps). In these ways, businesses try to have personal conversations with their customers. Often the retailer provides a linked website address, so the consumer can click to see the goods being promoted. Items with the chosen styles, colors, and sizes can be selected for purchase and check-out. Retailers can evaluate the success of each promotion by analyzing how many people clicked through from the e-mail to the retail website. They can even trace who those people are.

How Retail Works

Retailing is direct selling. It is the exchange of merchandise in return for money or credit. *Retailers* sell goods directly to the final consumers who will use them. This is done through stores, mail-order catalogs, websites, or other methods. It completes the channel of distribution.

A channel of distribution is the route that goods and services take from the original source, through all the middle people, to the ultimate user. A standard channel of distribution, or *supply chain*, is shown in **7-5**. The more specific apparel channel of distribution, or *textile/apparel pipeline*, starts with textile producers and ends with retailers selling to consumers who wear the clothes. See **7-6**.

7-5 The channel of distribution takes basic materials through all steps of production and handling to the ultimate users of the final products.

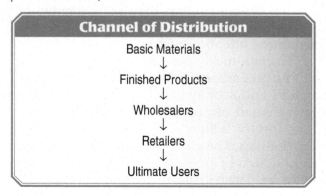

Channel of Distribution

Basic Materials
↓
Finished Products
↓
Wholesalers
↓
Retailers
↓
Ultimate Users

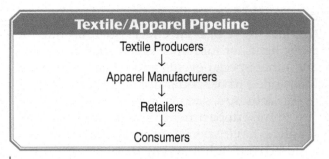

Textile/Apparel Pipeline

Textile Producers
↓
Apparel Manufacturers
↓
Retailers
↓
Consumers

7-6 The textile/apparel pipeline is the channel of distribution for fashion items. After being made, garments usually go from manufacturers to retailers, without a separate wholesaler.

Retailers buy large amounts of apparel and other goods, usually directly from manufacturers. They, in turn, sell small quantities of the goods, or individual apparel items, to many different consumers.

Retail Terms

Fashion merchandising is also called *apparel retailing*. It involves the planning, buying, promoting, and selling of apparel and other fashion merchandise to consumers who will wear the goods. It tries to satisfy customer demand as to price, quantity, quality, style, and timing.

The difference between the retail company's cost of goods bought (purchase price) and the retail price of goods sold is called the markup. Some of that money is profit. Most of the markup, however, must be used toward operating expenses and overhead costs. It must also cover losses from damaged goods, unsold merchandise, and shoplifting. Shortages from customer and employee theft can be shockingly high.

Markdowns are price reductions made in the hope of selling certain goods. Markdowns are most often made at the end of a season. They enable stores to move otherwise unsalable, excess merchandise. They are necessary, but they cause retailers to lose a great deal of potential revenue. Sometimes retailers receive *markdown money* from manufacturers to compensate for losses when the selling prices of the goods must be reduced.

Odd-figure pricing is the pricing of retail merchandise a few cents lower than the next higher dollar. Examples are $2.99 and $19.98. The purpose is to make the merchandise seem less expensive in shoppers' minds.

Many retailers offer *loss leaders*. These are low-priced articles on which retailers make little to no profit. They are popular items to attract shoppers to retail sites. Retailers hope that shoppers will also buy other goods at their regular prices to increase profits.

Stock control or *inventory control* is the receiving, storing, and distributing of merchandise. Large retailers have computerized conveyors to move the received merchandise into the proper sections of warehouses or storage areas. Inventory is marked with *bar codes* of dark bars and white spaces, so each piece can be recorded electronically. The goods are prepared for the selling floor and taken to the proper areas when requested. As merchandise sells, electronic check-out scanners automatically record inventory changes in the system.

Other than fashion lines, *basic stock* is merchandise that is constantly in demand. It includes mostly staples, such as underwear or men's business shirts. It has a predictable and constant customer demand.

Retailers place *purchase orders* with manufacturers. These are written documents authorizing manufacturers to deliver certain goods at specific prices. Each purchase order has a unique number for identification. When a manufacturer finishes producing the items specified for a purchase order, the goods are shipped to the retailer.

Retailers can also buy *odd lots* (or *job lots*). These are incomplete assortments of goods, that might be discontinued or overrun items a manufacturer has left at the end of a season. Not all sizes or styles are available. They are bought for reduced prices to clear out the manufacturer's inventory. Retailers use these goods as sale items.

The *completion date* is a date designated on a purchase order by a retailer. Any merchandise that has not left the manufacturer by the completion date is subject to cancellation. If the completion date cannot be met, the retailer could grant the manufacturer an extension.

As ready is an expression used by manufacturers regarding the estimated delivery time of merchandise ordered by retailers. This is a promise to fill (ship) orders when they are completed. It takes the place of the commitment for an exact shipping date. Decisions about how firm or open the agreement should be depend a great deal on the past relationship between the product manufacturer and retailer.

Retail Buying

Thousands of buyers go to New York City or other regional apparel marts to place orders for their retail companies. Marts have permanent manufacturers' showrooms, as shown in **7-7**. They may also rent additional space to manufacturers for use during *market weeks*. Fashion shows and special displays, as in **7-8**, feature manufacturers' lines during market weeks.

Regional marts save retailers the time and expense of going to New York City for buying trips. This matters especially to small, independent retailers that may be located far from New York. In addition, manufacturers' salespeople periodically call on retail buyers at their stores.

Retail companies limit their buyers to a specific open-to-buy. Open-to-buy is the amount of merchandise (in dollars or units) that buyers are permitted to order for their store, department, or apparel category. The open-to-buy is for a specified time period, such as for fall or spring goods.

Retailers order apparel about six months ahead of the wearing season. With computerization and collaboration, the lead and response times are becoming shorter. The merchandise is promoted to consumers about three months ahead. Buyers specialize in certain types of merchandise with a targeted customer audience in mind.

7-7 Each showroom in a regional mart contains the line of a specific apparel manufacturer.

California Mart: In-Wear/Matinique, Inc.

A.Krotov/Shutterstock.com

7-8 During market weeks, manufacturer's showrooms display all merchandise as nicely as possible to entice retail buyers to order goods for their stores, catalogs, and websites.

Resident buying offices (RBOs) are service businesses located in major market centers where there are many sources of goods, such as New York City, Los Angeles, Hong Kong, etc. *Independent* resident buying offices are hired by noncompeting member retailers from many parts of the country that sell similar goods. Another type, *retailer-owned* resident buying offices, is operated by large retail companies only for their stores or sites. Most of the merchandise purchased for all of the company's branches is done centrally at these buying offices.

Resident buying offices provide their member retailers with trend forecasting and global supply information. They send news bulletins electronically about new items, best sellers, price changes, supply conditions, and other developments. They sometimes set up market appointments with certain apparel firms for visiting buyers. They may recommend suppliers and accompany buyers on calls.

If requested, resident buying offices will do the actual buying for retailers. They will follow up on shipments of orders, place reorders, and fill in orders for fast delivery. They will also prepare sample advertising, direct mailing pieces, and promotional ideas for their member stores.

Fees charged by resident buying offices vary in relation to the types and amounts of services provided. Group buying is most important to small merchants. The clout of all the retailers together as a larger group can result in lower prices (through quantity discounts) and more reliable deliveries.

Timing and Pricing for Demand

Merchandise is offered by retailers well ahead of the wearing season. Thus, consumers are urged to buy their summer garments in the spring. Retailers try to sell all of their shorts, swimsuits, and other summer attire by July 4th. Fall clothes are made available in midsummer. Retailers like to be sold out of their seasonal merchandise early, as insurance against consumers changing their minds when the season arrives. However, consumers are now objecting to this type of timing. They prefer items to be available during the season of wear rather than only before the season.

Retailers must constantly be aware of consumer desires. They must notice changes in consumer lifestyle patterns and tastes. Consumers make the final decisions about what will or will not sell. If the public is not ready for certain styles, they will not move. To encourage sales, the presentation of items by retailers must educate consumers about how to wear or combine articles of clothing. Retailers must show how to put together and accessorize outfits. In this way, they can create consumer demand through understanding.

Retail buyers must try to order the correct number of *stock keeping units (SKUs)*. SKU numbers give the style, color, size, vendor, and other chosen information for each item. See **7-9**. The items that sell quickly may not be available for reorder because manufacturers may already be working on the next season's line. That causes the retailer to lose the opportunity of additional sales dollars. Buyers must also try not to order more than consumers will purchase. Goods left over will be sold at reduced prices. This causes

7-9 Each different item in the inventory of this store, such as red-and-white shirts, green jerseys, and yellow pullovers, has a different SKU number.

by the same factory. Sometimes retailers purchase a manufacturer's line and put on their own private label. Some retail companies even have their own manufacturing plants.

Through private labels, retailers are entering the apparel production business. *Product development directors* are assisted by buyers in establishing the basic items and fashion copies to be made for their companies, as in **7-10**. Product developers need a thorough knowledge of fabrics and manufacturing methods.

There are various *advantages* to private label programs for retailers.

➤ Retailers have exclusive design control. They can specify the quality, fit, price, and packaging of their items.
➤ Retailers pay less than the regular prices for the goods. Expenses for the merchandising, designing, and selling functions of a manufacturing firm have been eliminated. The retail company can then have higher markups and better profits.

financial losses. Good buyers seem to have instincts about what and how much their stores will need. Also, sales data from check-out systems tell them which items are increasing or decreasing in popularity.

Some markdowns are planned for sales promotions, hoping to attract more shoppers. However, some retailers have been criticized for overdoing price promotions. In the effort to provide marked down merchandise to please consumers, retailers sometimes first mark up the goods to higher-than-normal prices. This means the *sale* price is really the retailers' regular price. This practice allows their *margin* (money made or *profit*) to be acceptable financially. In the long run, if such promotions run constantly, retail companies lose their credibility with customers. The pricing policies and ethics of the retailers are questioned.

Private Label Brands

Private label merchandise is produced specifically by or for a retailer. The trademark or brand name on the label is owned by the retail company that sells the goods, rather than by the manufacturer. The merchandise is produced exclusively in the colors, patterns, styles, and fabrics the retailer specifies.

Retailers provide specifications (specs) and usually samples of the designs they want produced by the contracted sewing shop. Sometimes they supply the fabrics. Often the goods are very similar to national brands and made

7-10 Retail product developers plan private label merchandise and arrange for production of the items.

- Many lower-priced knockoffs are made by copying fast-selling, higher-priced styles. Slight changes can be made to update them for each future season, if they stay popular.
- Retailers have an opportunity to build an image for themselves through distinct private label goods.

There are also several *disadvantages*.

- Private label manufacturing requires large financial investments. It ties up money in production that could be used to buy goods from other manufacturers.
- A great deal of private label manufacturing is done overseas. Thus, there may be a long time from making design and production arrangements until the goods actually arrive at the stores. This can cause problems with fashion timing, as well as price changes, if money exchange rates fluctuate.
- There may be slow customer acceptance of products until the labels are recognized.
- No markdown money is available from manufacturers. The retailers must absorb the losses if there are quality, fit, or other problems.

Retail Business Considerations

Location is an important aspect for retail businesses. The most successful stores are conveniently located for their customers. Mail-order companies send catalogs to their *target market—* consumers who are most likely to buy their goods. Online retailers are convenient for their customers through technology. Exposure to the best potential customers results in the highest volume of sales. With a continuous fast stream of sales, a retailer can afford to use smaller markups and offer lower prices, while still making good profits.

Mass retailing has encouraged customers to shop without help from salespeople. Most retailers no longer wait on clients one at a time. Instead, vast amounts of merchandise are put on racks and shelves, in catalogs, or are available on websites. Customers are free to view and evaluate merchandise. Clothes are *package priced.* That means that each garment, or package of items, has an individual price marked on it. Customers can do their shopping without asking for help. This impersonal selling is used by

retailers to save money, since fewer salaries need to be paid. The savings are passed on to customers in the form of lower prices.

In most retail companies, technology records the goods purchased as inventory and then sold to customers. Cash registers are computerized, allowing sales trends to be detected hourly and daily. Central computers gather the sales information immediately from all chain or branch stores in the system. Weekly, monthly, and yearly sales reports are also calculated and analyzed.

Retailers measure an individual store's business in different ways by using these facts and figures on purchased inventory and goods sold. They can easily calculate the productivity of each square foot of selling space. All retailers analyze stock turnover, financial assets, promotional efforts, and salespeople's activities. They also try to determine merchandising success in terms of correct predictions on goods ordered, pricing, and timing for their customers.

Besides attending trade shows and subscribing to trade publications and resident buying services, retailers belong to other organizations. Examples of these are the *National Retail Federation (NRF)*, local Chambers of Commerce, and shopping mall merchant groups. *STORES Magazine* is the trade publication of the NRF. *Internet Retailer* and *Direct Marketing (DM) News* join other trade journals in offering print or digital editions. Daily and weekly news also comes to subscribers via e-mail.

Types of Apparel Retail Outlets

There are many sizes and types of apparel retailers. Through them, goods are sold to consumers. Specific retailers may fall under more than one of the following categories.

Department Stores

Department stores offer large varieties of many types of merchandise placed in appropriate departments. Almost all clothing and household items are sold in a wide range of colors, sizes, and styles. The goods are categorized into areas such as menswear, juniors, infants, jewelry, and shoes. The departments may also define various price ranges. For instance, there may be a *ladies' better dresses* department and a *budget sportswear* area. Designer labels and well-known manufacturer brands are usually offered in addition to private label lines. Each department has salespeople and a place to pay for the goods being purchased. Each department is a separate profit center for record-keeping purposes.

Department stores may offer credit and return or exchange privileges. Other conveniences may include liberal payment plans, gift wrapping, pleasant restrooms, and customer service desks. They may even have bridal registries and personal shopping assistants.

Department stores stress customer satisfaction. They try to maintain a reputation for quality and integrity. They want customers to regard them as dependable. Often they serve as anchor stores in shopping malls, as in 7-11. Anchor stores are large, well-known retailers that provide the attraction needed to draw customers to malls.

Department stores appeal to various income levels due to their wide range of products and pricing. However, most department stores target the majority of their merchandise to people in the middle to upper-middle income brackets.

Department stores have somewhat higher operating expenses than most other stores. That is because they have more personnel, bookkeeping, and extra services. They advertise and have promotional activities. Their prices must cover the costs of the extra services and promotions they offer. However, they also have large buying and sales volumes that help to keep their prices low. Many small- and medium-size department store chains of the past have been purchased by larger firms and merged into their businesses.

Branch Stores

When a well-established department store opens a store in another location, the new one is called a *branch*. Branches receive merchandise and operations direction from the original *flagship store*. See 7-12. The buying, advertising, and control of the branches can be done centrally to lower operating expenses. If an item is not available at a branch store, it may be obtained on short notice from the flagship store or another branch.

Retailers first established suburban branches in widening circles around a main downtown store. Now branches can be located a great distance from the home base. Many large stores have expanded nationally.

Chain Stores

A *chain* is a group of stores owned, managed, and controlled by a central office. All the stores in the chain handle the same goods at similar prices. All of a company's chain stores look very much alike. No store is considered to be the main store.

7-11 Bloomingdale's, Macy's, Nordstrom, Dillard's, and other department stores serve as anchor stores in many malls. They are often at the corners or ends of large malls, with many small shops on aisle walkways between them.

7-12 Saks & Company has its flagship store on Fifth Avenue in New York City. Many Saks Fifth Avenue branch stores are located around the country.

Some chains are centered in various regions of the country. Others are nationwide. Merchandising and operating decisions are made in the central office. Some chains are big enough to have regional offices overseeing certain stores, as well as the central office to which all regions report.

Prices in chain stores are often lower than those in upscale department stores. Since large chains have enormous buying power, manufacturers can afford to produce merchandise to the chain's specifications. Thus, private label merchandise may be styled and made exclusively for them at lower prices.

Chains include retailers that are in other categories. Examples of general merchandise chain stores are Walmart, Sears, Target, and JCPenney. Examples of specialized apparel chains are The Gap, The Limited, T.J. Maxx, Ross Stores, and Talbots.

Discount Stores

Discount stores, as in **7-13**, sell clothing and other merchandise in large, simple buildings with low overhead. Large amounts of garments are crowded onto racks and shelves. Some items are well-known brands, and some are lesser known or the discount chain's private label brands. The merchandise is sold at low prices.

Manufacturers give discount stores special pricing for buying in large quantities. They sell huge amounts of lower-priced apparel and accessories to customers with modest clothing budgets. Discount stores earn profits from small markups because they sell large quantities of merchandise and have lower operating expenses. They use mass retailing methods. They expect customers to shop without assistance. Merchandise from all departments is paid for at

checkout areas just inside the store exits. No extra customer services, such as telephone orders or gift wrapping, are offered.

In the past few years, discount store companies have grown rapidly. Most are chains. They are open in the evenings, on Sundays, and most holidays. They underprice other kinds of stores, thus creating stiff competition.

Dollar stores have also grown in popularity in the past several years. Shoppers find a variety of items and more convenience. Dollar stores generally offer a smaller retail venue, more locations closer to home, close-in parking, and smaller discount layouts. Bargain prices with a treasure trove atmosphere contribute to the growing success of these chain stores.

Off-price discounters sell moderate- to higher-priced brand name apparel at lower-than-normal prices. They carry quality goods, often with the labels cut out to protect the manufacturers' regular goods sold elsewhere.

Off-price discounters do not place advance orders with manufacturers for specific merchandise to be produced. They buy whatever is available, such as overruns, odd lots, irregulars, and end-of-season goods. They pay cash for the inventory rather than asking for credit. They buy this season's extra items when most other stores are thinking about the next season. Goods are put out in the stores to be sold and worn immediately.

Factory outlets are discount retail stores owned by manufacturers. Each store sells only the manufacturer's merchandise. This eliminates the middleman and the related expenses.

A factory outlet was originally a single, small store near a factory. The store sold the manufacturer's surplus production or seconds. Recently, many new factory outlet malls have opened that offer manufacturers' lines nationally. They are usually located in outlying areas and must be careful not to compete against the full-price retailers to whom they sell their lines. Thus, many manufacturers now produce some lower-price lines only for their factory *outlet stores*.

Other types of discount stores are wholesale warehouse clubs and hypermarkets. *Warehouse clubs* specialize in bulk sales of nationally branded merchandise. *Hypermarkets* are large stores that sell almost every type of merchandise, including apparel and groceries.

7-13 Discount stores sell large volumes of items at low prices in simple buildings.

Specialty Retailers

Specialty retailers handle a specific kind of merchandise or one category of goods. They might carry only golf equipment or women's apparel, or they might specialize even further into a specific type of apparel. Examples are maternity catalog companies, bridal boutiques, children's apparel websites, and shoe stores, as in **7-14**.

Some small specialty stores have lower volumes of sales and need to charge higher prices than larger stores to make a profit. Small quantities of goods are stocked. The employees must perform all of the stock control, promotion, and direct selling functions that big stores split among their specialized personnel.

Upscale specialty stores provide many personal services that appeal to some shoppers. They stress customer service and personal contact. They give advice about the selection of goods within their specialties. The personal preferences of regular clients are known. Returns are usually accepted, but customers may be given credit toward other purchases rather than cash.

Boutiques are a type of specialty store. They are small shops that sell few-of-a-kind apparel and accessories. Their merchandise is often fashion-forward, pricey, and presented in a creative way. They have a distinct image and give individualized attention to their clients.

Many specialty shops are located in malls and shopping centers. Some are chains and some are independently (privately) owned. Sometimes they are quite small, with only one or a few employees.

7-14 This specialty store concentrates on selling all kinds of shoes.

Small specialty stores that are not well established sometimes go out of business. Others are starting all the time. Successful specialty stores become loyal customers of particular manufacturers. The buyer for the store is the same year after year, quite different from large firms in which employee turnover is common.

Franchises

Franchise stores are individually-owned businesses that use the name and merchandise of an established firm. The *franchisor* (brand parent company) provides a *franchisee* (retail owner-operator) with exclusive use of the name and goods in a specified city or area. Sometimes the parent company offers assistance in organizing, training, and management. After meeting the financial obligations to the parent firm, the franchisee keeps the remaining profits.

The franchisee can expect quick acceptance because of the well-known name attached to the merchandise. The brand parent company, on the other hand, can spread the locations of its goods without large capital expenditures. Designers and manufacturers have franchise shops all over the world, owned and run by independent business people in each location.

Mail-Order Houses

Mail-order houses sell to consumers through catalogs. Mail-order customers select merchandise by looking at catalog pictures and reading the descriptions. Orders are placed by mail, telephone, or online. Catalog firms usually have toll-free numbers and extended order-taking hours. Most accept credit card payment over the phone and have websites so customers can order online or use mobile technology for convenience.

In many mail-order distribution centers, technology systems track inventory and control warehousing. Careful packaging techniques are used to distribute the merchandise. Sometimes gift wrapping is offered, as in **7-15**.

Mail-order houses may sell goods at lower prices, but sometimes charge high shipping and handling fees. They purchase goods in large quantities, have low overhead, and sell to a mass market. They have a large volume of business and offer few services. They usually offer money-back guarantees to ensure customers are satisfied.

Lands' End Direct Merchants

7-15 Apparel items must be carefully packaged to prevent wrinkling, and are sometimes gift wrapped, before being sent to the recipients.

Mail-order retailing (also known as *direct-mail marketing*) includes every type of merchandise—from practical, low-budget items to unique, luxurious ones. The trend in mail-order is toward specialty catalogs aimed at narrow segments of the consumer market. Computerized mailing lists provide companies with names of people in particular market niches, such as various income levels or hobby interests. Catalogs are prepared with target audiences in mind.

Mail-order retailing especially suits busy people with little time or desire to go out to shop. These people can study the catalogs during their spare moments. Mail-order customers can call a toll-free number or order through the mail-order company's website.

TV and Other Retailing

Television retailing combines entertainment and sales. It shows and describes merchandise on certain home shopping television channels. Viewers order by telephone or online, pay by credit card or other means, and have the merchandise delivered to them.

Some less common types of retailing are thrift shops, variety/dollar stores, personal selling, and leased departments.

Thrift shops (sometimes called *resale shops*) sell items that have been owned and used by others. They may be run by nonprofit organizations. Merchandise is usually donated by members of the community. Volunteers sometimes staff the shops. Some of the goods have old styling or look used. Other times, beautiful almost-new suits and gowns are donated and sold. This win-win situation allows shoppers to get some great items at very low prices, while the proceeds go to charity. Some resale shops sell apparel on consignment, so the previous owner receives some money. In all cases, recycling saves resources.

Variety stores started as five-and-ten-cent stores, selling goods at discounted prices. They have now evolved into very popular *dollar stores*. They sell wide ranges of inexpensive home goods, personal goods, apparel, garden tools, seasonal decorations, toys, stationery and office supplies, food and beverages, pet supplies, and other merchandise for one dollar or just a few dollars. Checkout counters are near the exits. Dollar stores previously appealed to low- and fixed-income consumers. However, high-income shoppers now frequent the stores for fill-in purchases or occasional specific purchases.

Personal selling is done without a store. It moves cosmetics, jewelry, clothing lines, and other merchandise directly to customers through parties or showings in homes. Orders are taken and the items are delivered to the customer later. The merchandise is usually of high quality, but may also be quite highly priced.

A *leased department* is a department within a store operated by an outside firm. Usually the store supplies the space and essential services in return for a fee or percentage of the sales. Name-brand designers sometimes lease a department within a retail store. Shoes, fine jewelry, and restaurants are other examples of leased departments.

Electronic Retailing

Electronic retailing (*e-tailing*) offers online shopping via computer and mobile devices, such as tablets and smartphones. Online retailing allows consumers to view merchandise on their personal screens. Consumers can do research, comparing features and prices of specific items. They can view three-dimensional digitized images of apparel and other items, with detailed written descriptions. This type of shopping is steadily increasing. Busy consumers can shop any time, day or night.

Retail websites offer a *shopping cart* into which consumers electronically place their selected items. To make the final purchase, after reviewing the selections in the shopping cart, a checkout system requires input of credit card information or another payment method. An electronic verification is immediately given for the order, and also to the customer's e-mail address. The merchandise is delivered according to provided instructions.

Customer service can be a problem for online e-tailers. Consumers cannot go to an actual salesperson to ask questions about the merchandise or to clarify buying procedures. To combat this, companies hire customer service representatives to answer consumer questions via "live chat" online or by phone.

E-tailing is challenging traditional store retailing. Department stores and malls have experienced a decrease in foot traffic. The profitability of physical retail space has gone down because of new technologies being favored by consumers. From a business viewpoint, e-tailing provides retail companies with an overview of what consumers are researching. As sales occur, there is also instant electronic tracking—in units and dollars—of style, size, and color preferences of the market.

Rafael Ramirez Lee/Shutterstock.com

7-16 Container ships loaded with internationally-made apparel and other goods arrive in U.S. ports daily. Imports make up a large percentage of retail inventories.

Retail Imports

Offshore sourcing is the term used when goods are bought from overseas producers. Most large retailers do some direct importing from abroad. Some retailers produce their own private label goods in overseas contract factories.

There has been a fast rate of growth in apparel imports. A larger percentage of offshore sourcing is done each year. See **7-16**.

Many retailers are in favor of imports. As mentioned previously, imports are cheaper for retailers to buy, and they can be sold to consumers at about the same prices as domestic goods. Thus, imports allow retailers to have higher markups and bigger profits.

There are other reasons why many retailers like imports. Sometimes a retailer can import new and different merchandise that no one else has. Also, garments that require much handwork may not be available from domestic sources. If retailers want these garments, they may have to be imported.

There are risks for companies doing offshore sourcing. Long lead times require early buying decisions, since orders are placed much farther ahead of when they will be received and sold. Retailers are forced to order next year's seasonal merchandise before they know what is selling well this year. It is hard to order the right merchandise or the right quantities. With early ordering, imported goods must be financed with loans for a longer time than domestic orders. This leaves less money available for retailers to buy other goods to sell in their stores.

Imports limit retailers' abilities to respond quickly to market developments. Often stores cannot reorder. There are shipping delays, magnified by customs inspections, which can result in late merchandise arrivals. There are quota uncertainties. Often surprises occur in the quality of delivered goods. Communications are difficult between the retailer and offshore producers. Staff travel costs are high.

Commissionaires are hired around the world by retailers. They are usually native to the countries in which they reside. They know the customs, laws, and production capabilities of their countries. They also know the tariff quotas of the United States. They function like an overseas buying office, often working for many firms.

As discussed in Chapter 6, retailers have been encouraged by U.S. apparel industries to seek domestic sourcing. Manufacturers are striving for more efficient production to give fast response and delivery times. For retailers, that would mean lower inventory costs and more accuracy in buying the items that will sell in the correct quantities. Also, reorders can be placed more easily.

Everything/Shutterstock.com

7-17 With omni-channel retailing, companies can serve their customers seamlessly, offering the same goods and process through all venues of their company.

Retailers' Future

In the future, retailers will reposition themselves by recognizing market and technology changes. Retailers will probably attract shoppers in the following three main ways:

➤ provide products and services seamlessly through all types of selling venues, so consumers can buy goods any way that is convenient for them at any time

➤ use technology and efficiency to satisfy busy consumers' shopping tasks faster, easier, cheaper, and more enjoyably

➤ offer unique products to satisfy out-of-the-ordinary tastes of specific consumers

➤ Retailers will get better at omni-channel retailing, which is selling goods seamlessly across all channels. Identical products and services are offered through stores, catalogs, mobile apps, TV, and websites of the retail company. Consumers can view the same merchandise at the same prices via all venues. A combination might be used, such as seeing an item in a catalog, buying it online as in **7-17**, and picking it up at a store. With omni-channel retailing, company data incorporates all marketing, sales, inventory, shipping, servicing, and other information. Plus, the information is available to every employee at any time and place through technology.

Technology will greatly enhance retail efficiency. Shoppers will scan items themselves in retail stores, either to purchase them or to record them for gift-giving to friends and relatives. Online shopping will promote and sell more products via electronic means. Shopping will be easier for consumers to do from home or wherever they are. Technology will reduce long checkout lines and facilitate payment processing. "One-stop retailers" will offer goods that are instantly available and organized in the store to find quickly.

Consumers become bored with stores that look alike and sell similar merchandise. They tend to make more purchases if they are in a good mood. Shoppers want socialization, recreation, and an enjoyable escape while they shop. This *shoppertainment* draws people for the entertainment value, such as with high-tech interactive computer simulations, convenient movie theaters and restaurants, and other amusements.

Retailers will offer more unique products of higher quality. They will market to tiny *niches*, identified by specific customers' credit card purchases and other database information. Niche retailing is dividing the total consumer market into narrow target markets with specific tastes or lifestyles. There is less competition in niche markets, but also fewer customers. By clearly understanding and focusing on their target customers, niche retailers can operate with less stock, make more sales, and gain higher profits. In this way, small retailers will complement mass merchandisers rather than compete against them. They will have to stay flexible and creative to fill observed gaps with innovative merchandising methods.

The concentration of large retailers will continue, with buyouts of smaller retail chains resulting in fewer, but larger retail corporations. Large retailers will have more efficient central buying and distribution procedures. More private label brands will be carried. Merchandise and shipping containers will all be marked with *Universal Product Code (UPC)* bars to be scanned for instant computerized inventory and sales tracking.

Nonstore formats, such as computer and mobile commerce, direct (mail-order) marketing, and TV retailing will take market share from traditional single-channel stores. Selling will be done directly to consumers globally. However, with these consumer-direct formats, consumers will lose the experience of actually seeing, touching, and trying on merchandise. Although these experiences will be computer simulated, customers may still return large amounts of merchandise.

In the future, more consumers will have and use more mobile apps and evolving new technology, which will also become more user-friendly. Online security systems and encrypted payment methods will continue to provide more confidentiality and security for shoppers. More screen-based catalogs and online shopping will continue to evolve.

Eventually, televisions and computers will combine into one piece of electronic retailing equipment. This equipment can be used for body scanning, which will collect individual sizing information electronically. The information will be stored on smart cards that can be updated as often as needed and inserted like credit cards to be read.

Consumers will be able to electronically redesign garments. Lengths, colors, and patterns will be changed until the perfect fashion selection is created. When garments are just right, shoppers will see how they look in them with virtual reality images of themselves on the screen wearing the creations. When approved, a radio-frequency transmission of data will begin the fast computer manufacturing process. The finished items will be shipped directly to the consumers who ordered them.

Summary

Fashion promotion, or indirect selling, is done through advertising, publicity, visual merchandising, and video merchandising. Advertising is done locally, nationally, or cooperatively. Public relations departments seek publicity by distributing press kits. Visual merchandising presents goods with displays, exhibits, and special events. Videos and electronic merchandising attract and educate shoppers, train salespeople, and try to sell merchandise.

Retailing, or direct selling, completes the apparel channel of distribution to consumers. Retail vocabulary includes pricing, stock, and purchasing terms. Retail buying is done in New York City or regional apparel marts, often assisted by resident buying offices. The merchandise must be timed and priced for demand. Product developers plan private label goods and arrange for production of the items. Many business details must be considered for retail success.

There are many types of apparel retail outlets. Chain stores or branches of department stores often serve as anchor stores in malls. Discount stores sell large quantities of goods at low prices. Specialty retailers cater to specific markets. Franchise stores have well-known names and merchandise. Mail-order houses, TV retailing, and electronic retailing enable consumers to shop from home or elsewhere. They are increasing in popularity. Other types of retail outlets include thrift shops, variety/dollar stores, personal selling, and leased departments.

Retail merchandise will continue to be sourced offshore. In the future, retailers will provide products and services seamlessly through all the venues of their companies. There will be more technology and efficiency to help busy shoppers, as well as unique products for specific consumer tastes. Both apparel manufacturers and retailers will increase selling worldwide through the Internet. Eventually, consumers will redesign garments electronically for themselves.

Fashion Recall

Write your answers on a separate sheet of paper.

Matching: Match the following terms with their definitions.

1. Low-priced articles on which stores make little to no profit; used to attract shoppers into stores.
2. Store merchandise that is constantly in demand.
3. The retail pricing of merchandise a few cents less than a dollar denomination.
4. Incomplete assortments of goods that retailers buy from manufacturers.
5. The difference between the store's cost of goods bought and the retail price of goods sold.
6. A written document authorizing manufacturers to deliver certain goods at specific prices.

A. odd-figure pricing
B. markup
C. odd lots
D. basic stock
E. purchase order
F. loss leaders

Short Answer: Write the correct answer to each of the following questions.

7. What is the purpose of fashion promotion?
8. Describe two ways an apparel firm might get publicity.
9. How does developing an image with visual merchandising help stores attract customers?
10. Name three reasons why retailers use video merchandising.
11. List the four steps in the textile/apparel pipeline.
12. What is the difference between independent resident buying offices and retailer-owned RBOs?
13. Name two advantages and two disadvantages of private label programs for retailers.
14. Name and describe five types of apparel retailers.
15. What do commissionaires do?
16. In the future, in what three ways will retailers probably attract shoppers?

Fashion Vocabulary

17. In teams, play *picture charades* to identify each of the *Fashion Terms* on the chapter opening. Write the terms on separate slips of paper and put the slips into a basket. Choose a team member to be the *sketcher*. The sketcher pulls a term from the basket and creates quick drawings or graphics to represent the term until the team guesses the term. Rotate turns as sketcher until the team identifies all the terms.

Critical Thinking

18. **Compare and contrast** Compare and contrast the forms of fashion promotion. Which form of fashion promotion do you think is most effective? What evidence from the text and other sources can you give to support your view?
19. **Analyze pros and cons** Based on the chapter content, analyze the pros and cons of retail imports. How do retail imports impact the economy? As a consumer, which do you prefer—imported or domestic goods? Why? Write a summary citing text and reliable online resources to support your response.
20. **Make predictions** Predict the future of retailing. Write a description of retailing 10 years from now. What factors are likely to prompt changes in the industry?

Core Skills

21. **Speech**   Find examples of apparel promotion by walking through stores, examining websites, and looking through newspapers, magazines, and fashion publications. In an oral report, describe examples of advertising, publicity, visual merchandising, and video merchandising.

22. **Math practice**   Compare the apparel price ranges and labels in various retail outlets. Do you see markdowns, imports, and private label merchandise? What goods are package priced? Prepare a cost comparison chart and share your findings in class.

23. **Writing**   Visit a shopping center or mall. What types of stores are included? What other attractions are offered? Prepare a written report about your findings to post to the class website for peer and instructor review and comments.

24. **Research and speaking**   After obtaining permission from store management, use a digital camera to photograph a variety of apparel displays in several retail stores. Choose photos of the five best displays and explain why they work together. Use presentation software, or a school-approved web application, to combine your photos and explanation to share with the class.

25. **Technology**   Find a website that creates a virtual model of yourself from information you provide. Select fashions and "try them on" your model. Compare this way of shopping for clothing with shopping for apparel at a local retail establishment. Write an illustrated report summarizing your conclusions.

26. **CTE career readiness practice**   Presume you work for a major fashion retailer that is considering the development of a *private label* line of women's and men's fashions. As a marketing researcher, your employer has asked you to investigate the private labels of at least three other fashion retailers. What private labels appear to be the strongest in the fashion industry? What issues do other retailers have with their private labels? Do the labels draw a strong customer base to the store? Do the private labels make a significant contribution to the retailers' profit margins? Why or why not? Write a summary of your findings to submit to your employer.

Fashion in Action

27. **Portfolio builder**   Interview two or more local store managers. Ask them if their stores belong to chains or parent retail companies. How is their buying done? Do they work with resident buying offices? Do they go to New York City often, or do they work mostly with regional marts? How are the stock control functions done? Prepare a written report of your findings and add this information to your portfolio.

28. **Design activity**   Collect five mail-order catalogs that offer apparel. Describe the size, type of paper, presentation of merchandise, and price range of each catalog. How does a person place orders and make payments? How are goods delivered? What are the added shipping costs and return policies? Based on this information, describe how you would design an apparel mail-order catalog. Present your ideas to the class.

Self-Assessment Quiz

Complete the self-assessment quiz online to help practice and expand your knowledge and skills.

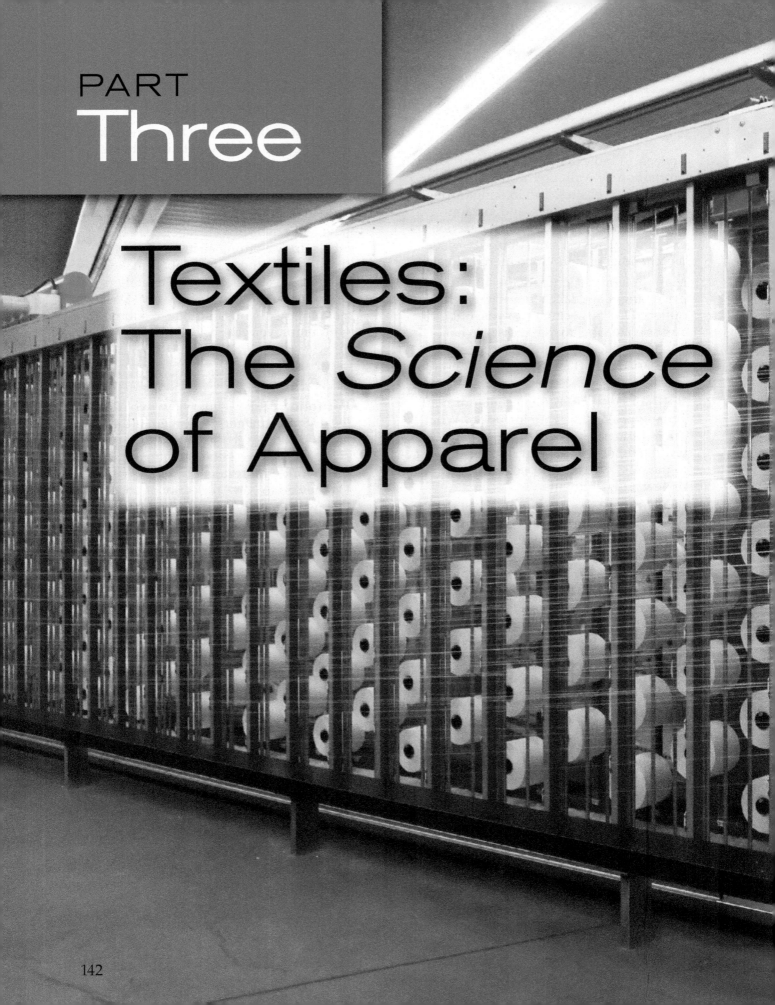

PART
Three

Textiles: The *Science* of Apparel

8 Textile Fibers and Yarns

9 Fabric Construction and Finishes

Textile Fibers and Yarns

While studying, look for the activity icon **to:**

- **practice** key fashion terms with e-flash cards, vocabulary games, and matching activities
- **assess** what you learn by completing self-assessment quizzes

www.g-wlearning.com/clothingandfashion/

cotton
pill
linen
wool
woolen yarn
worsted yarns
silk

filament
sericulture
polymers
generic name
denier
spinneret

staple fibers
wicking
ply yarns
combination yarns
blend
texturing

Objectives

After studying this chapter, you will be able to
➤ **describe** the sources and processing of natural fibers.
➤ **explain** how manufactured fibers are made.
➤ **identify** the characteristics and uses of individual fibers.
➤ **discuss** how different types of yarns are made.

As stated in Chapter 5, *fibers* are long, thin, and hairlike. They are very small in diameter. They are the basic units in making textile products.

Fibers are spun into continuous strands called *yarns*. Yarns vary in size. Some are coarse and fluffy, while others are finer than sewing thread. Yarns are woven, knitted, or pressed into fabrics. Then fabrics are finished with dyes, prints, and coatings before being made into apparel or other items.

Some fibers are obtained from natural sources. They are called *natural fibers*. Others are made in factories from chemical and other sources. They are called *manufactured fibers*.

Each fiber has specific properties. No fiber is perfect. Each has some good, fair, and poor characteristics that make it suitable or unsuitable for certain uses. The basic properties of a fiber can be slightly altered but never totally changed. Fiber properties determine the appearance, performance, and comfort of fabrics. They include absorbency, shrinkage, warmth, strength, wrinkle resistance, and other characteristics. These also influence the appearance, performance, and comfort of finished garments. Thus, an understanding of fibers, yarns, and fabrics is basic to the study of apparel.

Vedran Vidovic/Shutterstock.com

Natural Fibers

Natural fibers are made from natural sources, mainly plants and animals. Natural fibers are listed in **8-1**.

Cellulosic natural fibers, such as cotton and linen (flax), are from plants. Less common cellulosic natural fibers are jute, kapok, sisal, straw, hemp, and ramie.

Protein natural fibers, such as wool, are from animals. Specialty hair fibers, such as mohair, vicuña, alpaca, cashmere, camel's hair, horsehair, and angora are protein fibers. Silk is also a natural protein fiber.

All cellulosic and protein natural fibers are *absorbent*, or able to take up moisture. This provides wearing comfort, since perspiration is absorbed, and body heat is controlled. Absorbency also provides good dyeability.

Natural fibers vary in quality due to weather conditions, soil fertility, and animal disease. Also, their quality depends on their varieties or breeds.

Cotton

Cotton is a natural fiber obtained from mature seed pods of the cotton plant. It is the most widely used natural fiber. China leads the world in cotton production, with the United States being second. This crop is important to the nation's economy. It is grown in the South, sometimes called the *cotton belt*. Some cotton is exported from the United States to other countries. Cotton is also grown in India, Brazil, Greece, Pakistan, Turkey, and many other countries.

Eco-friendly *organic cotton* is grown with no chemical fertilizers or pesticides and is from plants which are not genetically modified. However, end products from organic cotton are more expensive for consumers because of necessary crop rotation and the use of beneficial insects, compost, and other natural farming methods.

Cotton Production and Processing

Cotton fibers come from the seed pods of the plant as it ripens. First, flower blossoms ripen, wither, and fall off. Then they leave green seed pods, called cotton *bolls*. Inside the bolls, moist fibers grow and push out from newly formed seeds. Either chemicals or natural frost causes the leaves to fall off the plant. Once exposed to more sunlight and air, the fibers continue to expand until they split the boll apart, as in **8-2**. The cotton boll is then plucked off the plant, usually by a mechanical stripper or picker. See **8-3**.

After harvesting, the cotton bolls go to the gin where the fibers are separated from the seeds. Cleaning machines remove burrs, dirt, and leaf trash. The ginned fiber is called *lint*. It is pressed together and made into large *bales*. Before going to a spinning mill, samples are taken from each bale to determine the cotton's value, as shown in **8-4**. Each bale is classed according to length and fineness of fibers, as well as strength, color, luster, and cleanness.

8-1 The most popular natural fibers are cotton, linen, wool, and silk.

Natural Fibers	
Cellulosic (from plants)	
Cotton—most common	
Linen (flax)—quite common	
Others:	
Hemp	Ramie
Jute	Sisal
Kapok	Straw
Protein (from animals)	
Wool—most common	
Silk—quite common	
Specialty hair fibers:	
Alpaca	Horsehair
Angora	Llama
Cashmere	Mohair
Camel's hair	Vicuña

8-2 The cotton boll bursts open to expose fluffy cotton when it is ready for harvest.

National Cotton Council of America

National Cotton Council of America

8-3 When cotton bolls are ready to be picked, they can be mechanically harvested.

National Cotton Council of America

8-5 At the textile mill, cotton bales are opened after being shipped from cotton merchants.

At the mill, cotton is processed by a continuous, automated system. Cotton from several bales is blended together. See **8-5**. This provides uniformity and maintains constant yarn quality. Also, any fiber lumps are reduced.

The loosened fibers then receive more cleaning and fluffing. The cotton is formed into a continuous wide sheet called a *lap*. The lap is rolled around and around a cylinder. From there, it is fed into the *carding* machine where it receives final cleaning and is separated into individual fibers. It is eventually drawn through a funnel-shaped device that molds the fibers into a sliver. A *sliver* is a round, rope-like strand of fibers about the diameter of a person's finger.

8-4 The USDA uses high-volume instrumentation to class cotton at its location in Bartlett, Tennessee.

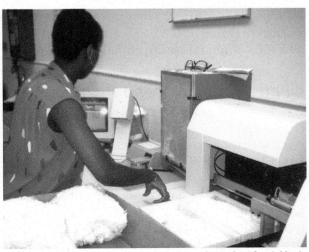

National Cotton Council of America

Combing is done for high-quality fibers of exceptional smoothness, fineness, and strength. This combs out short fibers. Long fibers remain. This high-quality fiber is again formed into a sliver.

After carding, and possibly combing, cotton goes through *drawing*. Several slivers are combined into a strand that is drawn out, without twisting, and reduced to about the same diameter as the original sliver. This further blends the fibers, arranges them in parallel order, and increases uniformity.

Slivers are then fed into the *roving* frame where the cotton is twisted slightly and drawn into a smaller strand. The roving, or twisted sliver, is fed to the *spinning* frame where it is drawn out to its final size and twisted into yarn. The twist holds the fibers together and gives strength to the yarn that is then wound onto bobbins. Refer to **8-6** to review the steps of cotton processing.

Pima cotton fibers are of very high quality with naturally long fibers. Cotton fibers termed *Egyptian* (originally grown in Egypt) have a smooth, silk-like texture.

Cotton Incorporated is the marketing and research organization for cotton growers. It acts as a product development and promotional center for cotton producers to improve the demand for and profitability of cotton. It prepares and distributes fashion forecast information to designers, manufacturers, the fashion press, and retailers. It advertises cotton products in consumer and trade media. It also encourages manufacturers and retailers of cotton products to use the Seal of Cotton, shown in **8-7**, on their identification and promotional materials.

Cotton Processing

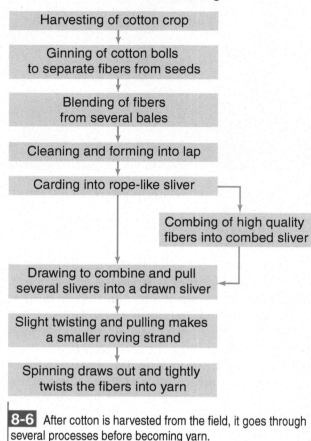

Harvesting of cotton crop

↓

Ginning of cotton bolls
to separate fibers from seeds

↓

Blending of fibers
from several bales

↓

Cleaning and forming into lap

↓

Carding into rope-like sliver

→

Combing of high quality
fibers into combed sliver

↓

Drawing to combine and pull
several slivers into a drawn sliver

↓

Slight twisting and pulling makes
a smaller roving strand

↓

Spinning draws out and tightly
twists the fibers into yarn

8-6 After cotton is harvested from the field, it goes through several processes before becoming yarn.

National Cotton Council of America

8-7 The Seal of Cotton is the registered trademark/service mark of Cotton Incorporated for products made of 100 percent cotton.

A different organization, the National Cotton Council, distributes educational materials and lobbies for advantageous trade legislation on behalf of the cotton industry.

Cotton Characteristics and Uses

Cotton has many good characteristics. It is relatively inexpensive. It is soft and absorbent. Cotton is comfortable to wear in hot weather. It takes dyes and prints very well. It does not cling. Cotton launders well and is strong even when wet.

Cotton can be treated to become fire resistant, mildew resistant, and water repellent. It is strong and durable to wear for a long time. It does not pill, or form an accumulation of little balls, on the surface from rubbing or wearing. It also blends well with other fibers.

Cotton also has disadvantages. One disadvantage of cotton is that it wrinkles easily. To counteract this, it is often treated or blended with manufactured fibers to reduce its wrinkling characteristics. Another disadvantage is that cotton shrinks. Because of its absorbency, it tends to pick up spots and stains. It is not elastic (stretchable) or resilient (able to spring back to its original condition).

Cotton is very versatile. In other words, it can be used in many different ways. It is used for clothes ranging from baby diapers to high-fashion garments to heavy denim. Household uses range from towels to upholstery to awnings. Apparel and household items have the largest uses for cotton, but thousands of bales are also used by industry.

Linen

Linen is a natural fiber obtained from fibrous materials of the stalk of the *flax* plant. It is the oldest known fiber. Flax is grown in cooler regions of the world, with the western hemisphere only growing it for linseed oil, not fiber. Major flax growing countries are Russia, Ukraine, Argentina, France, and other parts of northern Europe. Belgium and Ireland make beautiful linen fabrics from flax.

Linen Production and Processing

Flax is a grass that looks like tall, slender reeds. The linen fibers are taken from the long, wiry stem. Long ago, the stem was beaten by hand to produce the fiber that could be spun into yarns.

Harvesting of flax plants takes place three to four months after planting. When the plants are mature, they are pulled out of the ground by machine, as shown in **8-8**, rather than being cut.

8-8 At harvest time, machines pull the flax plants from the ground, remove seeds and leaves, and lay them flat to dry.

International Linen Promotion Commission

8-10 In flax spinning, the fibers are drawn out and then tightly twisted into yarns.

Threshing machines remove the seeds and leaves. The flax stalks are allowed to dry in the sun. Then they are tied into bundles and soaked in *retting* tanks. This lasts for one or two days. Bacterial action loosens the outside flax fibers from the rotting woody center stem. Then the flax is untied and dried again in the fields.

Later, the flax is *scutched*, as in **8-9**. In this step, rollers crush the stalks to complete the separation of the soft flax fibers from the harsh, woody parts. Then they are *hackled* or combed, to straighten and clean the fibers. A drawing machine then combines the fibers into a continuous wide ribbon. The drawing process is repeated until all the fibers are parallel in small, rope-like slivers ready for spinning. Figure **8-10** shows flax spinning.

Linen fibers are drawn and twisted together in a way similar to cotton. Finally, a continuous, strong, uniform, and workable strand of yarn wound on bobbins results. Refer to **8-11** to review the steps of linen processing.

8-11 The fibrous materials from the stalk of the flax plant are processed into linen yarns.

Linen Processing

Pulling of flax plants from the ground
↓
Threshing removes seeds and leaves
↓
Drying of stalks in the sun
↓
Soaking of stalks in retting tanks
↓
Second drying done in fields
↓
Scutching crushes stalks to separate fibers from unwanted parts
↓
Hackling combs fibers to straighten and clean them
↓
Drawing combines fibers into continuous slivers
↓
Spinning draws out and tightly twists the fibers into yarn

8-9 This man is working at a scutching machine, which crushes stalks to separate the fibers from the unwanted parts.

International Linen Promotion Commission

Linen Characteristics and Uses

Linen fibers look like bamboo sticks when magnified. They have a variety of thicknesses. Fiber bundles tend to cling together, giving linen its characteristic thick-and-thin appearance.

Compared to cotton, linen is expensive. Its higher price is due to limited production and the hand labor still involved in its processing. Also, it is imported from higher-wage countries, which adds to the final price.

The quality of linen is determined by the length and fineness of the fibers. The finer and longer fibers (from the taller plants) are used in better-quality linen fabrics. They are thinner, smoother fabrics. Also, the degree of bleach, if white, or the fastness of the dyes, if colored, affect the quality. The colors of pure linen are neutral.

Linen has many advantages, including its strength. Linen is very strong. It is also known for its durability and luster. Linen wears evenly; it is more likely to become thin, rather than to develop holes. The luster of linen often increases with continued use. It gets softer the more it is washed and worn. It is also cool and absorbent.

Linen also has disadvantages. Linen wrinkles and creases more easily than cotton. Thus, it is popular for apparel designed to have a crushed look. Since flax fibers are longer than cotton ones, there are fewer fiber ends in a yarn. Thus, less lint, or fuzz, from fiber ends is at the fabric surface. Therefore, linen does not attract or hold soil the way cotton does. It sheds stains and dirt easily.

Fabrics made of linen usually *ravel* (come unwoven at the edges) easily, since linen yarns are coarse and must be woven loosely. Seam allowance edges in garments should be finished, so no raw edges are exposed. Linen garments should be dry-cleaned, or washed if they have been preshrunk. For a smooth surface, they should be pressed while damp with a hot iron under a pressing cloth.

Linen fibers are made in lightweight to heavyweight fabrics. Some are thin and airy; others are crisp and smooth. Still others are heavier or thick and rustic. There are sheer linens, linen suit fabrics, as in **8-12**, and heavy linen canvas. In addition to clothing, linen is used for handkerchiefs, tablecloths, kitchen towels, upholstery, and draperies.

Linen is often blended with other fibers, especially cotton, polyester, rayon, and silk.

Talbots

8-12 Linen suiting fabric has the right weight to be made into jackets and pants.

These combinations can give better resistance to wrinkles and softer, richer textures. Using certain finishes on linen can also improve its wrinkle resistance.

Other Plant Fibers

Other plant fibers are related to flax. Most are *bast fibers* that lie in bundles just under the bark in the stems of various plants. They are strong, woody fibers. Many are used for twine, rope, braided rugs, and burlap. In apparel, they are used for hats, bags, belts, and shoes.

Ramie is a fiber that is sometimes used as a linen or cotton substitute. It adds strength when combined with other fibers. Since it is from Asia, it has been nicknamed *China grass*. Examples of other bast fibers are *hemp*, *bamboo*, and *jute*, which are inexpensive and weaken with age. Jute is in burlap fabric. Fibers from leaves or seed pods are *sisal* and *kapok*.

Wool

Wool is obtained from the fleece of sheep or lambs. It is the most commonly used animal fiber. Merino sheep are said to produce the finest wool fibers. Sheep are raised for wool throughout the world. The leading producers are China, India, and Australia. The United States ranks first in the consumption (use) of wool. The U.S. raises sheep in every state, but the industry is concentrated in the West.

For *organic wool*, chemical pesticides may not be used on the sheep. Genetic engineering of animals is prohibited. Farms can only graze a certain number of sheep on various amounts of land. Also, no chemical processes are used from farm production to finished garments.

Wool Production and Processing

To be processed, first the fleece is *sheared* off the sheep by experts, who use large power clippers. It is removed close to the skin and in one piece, as in **8-13**. The *fleece* is usually one year of wool growth for the sheep. Most shearing is done during the spring months, just before warm weather arrives and after the fleece is thick from a cold winter. Sheep are put back out to pasture unharmed, to grow another coat of wool.

Wool pools are organized throughout the country as collection points for fleece from many producers. The fleece is sorted, packaged, tied, and stored in sacks. Then it is sent to a wool mill for processing. At the mill, the fibers are graded and sorted. A trained worker separates the different grades depending on length, strength, color, amount of curl, and feel of the fibers. The fibers vary in length from one-half inch to over one foot. Quality is a result of the health of the sheep, the climate, and the fiber's location on the sheep. The highest quality is from the shoulders and sides of the sheep. The poorest is from the lower legs.

The wool is *scoured* (washed), as in **8-14**, to remove sand, dirt, and natural oil. The removed oil is lanolin, which is used in cosmetics, shampoos, and ointments. The fibers are put through squeeze rollers and dried. Then several lots of wool are blended mechanically to attain uniformity. The wool may be dyed at this point or later during processing.

Carding further removes impurities while straightening the fibers. The carding machine has a series of various-sized rollers with fine wire teeth revolving at different speeds in opposite directions. The fibers are straightened and interlaced. See **8-15**. They then leave the machine in the form of a thin, wide, continuous web.

American Sheep Industry Association

8-14 After wool is graded and sorted at the mill, it is scoured to remove impurities and capture its oil for other uses.

8-13 Shearing, to remove the wool fleece from sheep, is done very fast by experts who are trained and experienced at doing the job. The sheep are not hurt when getting this haircut.

8-15 The process of carding wool further purifies and straightens the fibers to form a continuous, wide web.

Gail Johnson/Shutterstock.com

American Sheep Industry Association

The short fibers (less than two inches) are put aside for less expensive woolen yarn. The long staple fibers will become higher-priced worsted yarns.

For woolens, the web is divided into narrow strips that form roving for spinning. The yarns contain short and long fibers that lie in random directions. They have a twisted, loose effect. Fabrics from these yarns are relatively dense and have soft, fuzzy surfaces.

For worsteds, combing straightens the long fibers and places them parallel to each other. The resulting sliver is drawn through a series of machines, gradually reducing it to a thin, slightly twisted roving. It is placed on large spools, ready for spinning. Fabrics from worsted wool are smooth and compact.

Yarns for both woolens and worsteds go through spinning processes. In each case, the roving is pulled (drawn) and twisted into the final yarn. The finished yarn is wound onto revolving bobbins or spools after twisting. Refer to **8-16** to review the steps of woolen and worsted processing.

Wool Characteristics and Uses

The wool fiber is durable and versatile. It is made into featherweight fabrics, bulky tweeds, and plush carpets. Wool fabrics have endless varieties of weights, textures, finishes, and colorations.

Wool fibers have natural *crimp*, or curl that looks like wavy lines or coil springs under a microscope. Better quality wool fibers have more crimp per inch. It gives the fiber *elasticity* to stretch, compress, and recover to its original shape without damage. This resiliency enables wool garments to return to their original size and shape after a rest. Crimp is what causes wool to be wrinkle resistant.

Wool is a warm fiber. It has good insulating qualities since it traps air among the fibers. This inhibits the rapid transfer of temperature. It is lightweight, too. Wool garments have always been popular for military use because of their light weight and warmth.

Wool is somewhat water resistant, as well as absorbent. Wool fibers have a thin film over scale-like cells that overlap like roof shingles. This covering helps to shed water, as well as spots and stains. However, with prolonged exposure to wetness, wool is absorbent. Wool fabric can

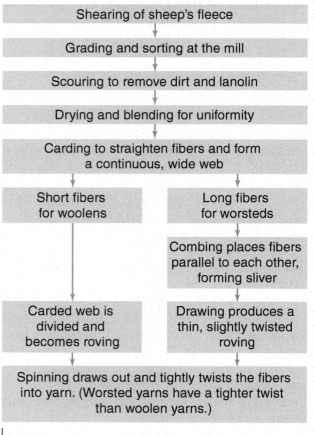

Wool Processing

Shearing of sheep's fleece

↓

Grading and sorting at the mill

↓

Scouring to remove dirt and lanolin

↓

Drying and blending for uniformity

↓

Carding to straighten fibers and form a continuous, wide web

↓

Short fibers for woolens	Long fibers for worsteds
	Combing places fibers parallel to each other, forming sliver
Carded web is divided and becomes roving	Drawing produces a thin, slightly twisted roving

Spinning draws out and tightly twists the fibers into yarn. (Worsted yarns have a tighter twist than woolen yarns.)

8-16 Wool processing turns the sheared fleece of sheep into either woolen yarns or worsted yarns.

absorb moisture, or perspiration, to quite a degree without making the wearer feel wet. Like all natural fibers, wool fibers allow the fabric to breathe. This makes wool comfortable to wear. Wool takes readily to dyes. It can be dyed in a wide range of colors and intensities. Wool also resists fading. Wool is long wearing because it is strong. However, when soaked in water, wool fibers weaken.

Wool is static resistant because of its moisture content. It does not spark or cling from static electricity. Wool also has flame-retardant characteristics. It will extinguish itself if it is not kept in direct contact with a flame. Dense weaves are especially flame retardant, since they have less air in them.

Wool is easy to tailor. During garment construction, it eases, stretches, and shapes well. With steam, creases can be removed and reset. Worsted fabrics hold their shape and a sharp crease much better than woolens do. See **8-17**.

8-17 Top brand suits and sportcoats, such as these, and other high-quality wool garments are made of 100 percent worsted wool.

There are some disadvantages to wool. It is harmed by bleach, sunlight, and dry heat. It absorbs odors. Wool fabric will shrink with the hot water and agitation of conventional washing. The scales of the fibers compress, interlock, and stay that way. Wool should be dry-cleaned or hand washed in cold water. Today some wool is processed to be shrink-resistant and machine washable to some degree.

Some people find wool garments to be scratchy if placed next to the skin. Some wool garments, especially those made of worsted fabrics, may become shiny with wear. Another disadvantage of wool is that it can be destroyed by moths and beetles. Now, however, wool can be chemically treated so moths and other insects shun it. Also, wool can be reused rather than discarded.

Categories of Wool

There are different categories of wool. Also, wool is often blended with less expensive fibers. To inform and protect consumers, the Wool Products Labeling Act requires the label on wool products to give the percent of fiber content and also to give the source. The Act does not say anything about quality. It is enforced by the Federal Trade Commission (FTC).

The terms *virgin wool*, *pure wool*, and *100% wool* are used interchangeably. They indicate fabrics that are made from all-wool fibers or yarns that have never before been used. These wools are softer, stronger, and more resilient than recycled wool.

Recycled wool refers to wool fibers from previously-made wool fabrics. They might be from cutting scraps, mill ends, or garments. These are shredded back into fibers. They are not as soft, strong, or resilient as those from new wool. They are used mostly in thick, stiff utility fabrics. They often go into winter gloves, interlinings for coats, and picnic blankets. Wool products must be labeled *recycled* when not made of virgin wool.

The International Wool Textile Organization (IWTO) is a global association representing the interests of the world's wool textile industry. Members include wool growers, traders, primary processors, spinners, weavers, garment makers, and retailers of wool products. It offers a network for business contacts in the sectors of wool apparel, technical textiles, and interior decorating textiles. The American Sheep Industry (ASI) is the national organization representing the interests of tens of thousands of sheep producers throughout the United States.

Specialty wools are from such animals as goats, camels, and llamas. Their limited supplies are imported from rural regions of several countries. Specialty wools are more expensive than sheep's wool and used less. Some specialty wools are from coarse, long, outer animal hairs. They are used in interlinings, rough coatings, and upholstery fabrics. Others are fine, soft, undercoat hairs. They are used in luxury coatings, sweaters, shawls, suits, and dresses.

Some examples of specialty wools are luxurious cashmere from the cashmere goat and camel's hair from the two-humped Bactrian camel. Silky *mohair* is from the Angora goat. *Angora* (from the Angora rabbit), *vicuña*, and *alpaca* are other specialty wools.

Silk

Silk is a luxurious natural fiber obtained by unwinding the cocoons of silkworms. The silk fiber is the only natural filament fiber. A filament is a very long, fine, continuous thread, rather than many threads of short lengths. Silk filaments may be a thousand yards or more in length.

Silk Production and Processing

Silk originated in China. Its revered silkworm cocoon and method of production were kept a secret for over 2,000 years. Eventually, silkworm eggs and mulberry seeds were smuggled to other countries. China is currently the leading producer of silk fiber. Japan and Eastern Europe are also major suppliers. The United States consumes more silk than any other country of the world. Many fine silk products are made in the United States from the imported fibers.

The raising, or cultivation, of silkworms is the science of sericulture. It carefully controls the cycle from moth to silk fiber.

A silk moth lays several hundred eggs that eventually hatch. The resulting tiny worms feed on the leaves of mulberry trees, as in **8-18**, until they are fat and about two inches long. Then they stop eating and spin a protective cocoon around themselves, shown in the upper part of **8-19**. A silk filament is released from each silkworm to spin the cocoon. The filament hardens in the air. A gum, called *sericin*, is released at the same time and holds the cocoon together.

In silk processing, the worm inside the cocoon is intentionally killed by heat before it turns into a moth and forces its way out of the cocoon. The resulting hole would ruin the continuous silk filament. The cocoon is soaked in hot water to allow for the *reeling* process, as in **8-20**. During this process, the cocoon becomes

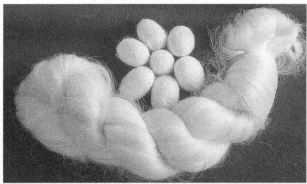

China External Trade Development Council, Taiwan

8-19 A mature silkworm takes about three days to spin a cocoon around itself, held together with sericin. Silk fibers for apparel are obtained from this cocoon.

soft and easy to unwind. The unbroken silk threads are unwound from cocoons and put onto large reels.

The sericin that originally bound the fiber to the cocoon is boiled off either before or after weaving. Silk does not need to be spun into a yarn like cotton or wool because it is already a continuous filament. However, most silk, except coarse sizes, must have many filaments tightly twisted together for a heavier weight before it is woven into fabric. This process is called *throwing*. It is solely to provide the weaver with a yarn of large enough width and proper weight for the particular fabric being made. Refer to **8-21** to review the processing of silk.

Used alone, the term *silk* refers to the cultivated silk from carefully tended silkworms. *Wild silk* fibers come from uncultivated silkworms. The wild silkworms eat the leaves of trees other

8-18 Cultivated silkworms eat 150 to 200 pounds of mulberry leaves during the 40 days until they mature.

China External Trade Development Council, Taiwan

8-20 Hot water is used to loosen the silk filaments, so they can be unwound by automatic reeling machines.

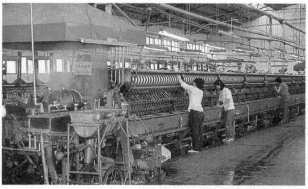

China External Trade Development Council, Taiwan

Silk Processing

Silkworm spins cocoon around itself

↓

Cocoon is soaked in hot water; silkworm dies; silk filament loosens

↓

Reeling of several filaments off cocoons while slightly twisting them together onto reels

↓

Sericin is boiled off now or after weaving

↓

Throwing tightly twists more filaments together into yarn

8-21 Silk, known for its luxurious beauty, is the only natural fiber in filament form.

Anita Ford Collection

8-22 Silk has a natural luster that gives a beautiful sheen to garments made from the fiber.

than mulberry. They spin cocoons under natural conditions. The fiber is strong with a distinctive rugged appearance when woven. It is uneven in texture and is somewhat stiff and coarse. It is usually used in its natural tan color. It is difficult to bleach or dye. *Tussah* fabric is woven from wild silk fibers.

Doupion silk comes from two silkworms that have spun their cocoon together. It has irregular, thick-thin filaments producing a slubbed effect. It is used in making *shantung* fabric.

Spun silk is made from pierced cocoons (cut filaments) or waste silk. The tangled fibers on the outer layers of leftover cocoons, along with imperfect ones, are used to make spun silk. The fibers are several inches long. They are cleaned, combed, and spun into yarn the same as cotton and wool. Spun silk is not as strong or lustrous as reeled silk.

Silk Characteristics and Uses

Silk has always been a status symbol. In past eras, it was known as the *cloth of kings*. Elegant, expensive silk fabrics are synonymous with luxury.

Silk is made into fabrics of various degrees of crispness and softness, thickness or transparency. It has a natural shine or luster, as shown in **8-22**. Silk fabrics drape nicely. They are absorbent and can resist permanent wrinkles. Silk fibers are strong and will last a long time.

Silk is a *natural insulator*. It is warm in the winter and cool in the summer. It is light and comfortable. Also, silk takes dyes very well, since it is highly absorbent.

Silk requires some special care. Silk garments should be dry-cleaned unless the care label says they can be hand washed. Silks can shrink and some dyes that are used may bleed during laundering. Sunlight and alkaline soaps can damage silk. High iron temperatures weaken silk and cause the color to fade or to yellow. Also, silk has a tendency to water-spot. Perspiration harms silk, and deodorants may cause it to deteriorate.

When the sericin is washed out, some silk becomes very thin and lightweight. Salts from tin, lead, or iron can be added to make the resulting fabrics heavier. These *weighted silks* often rustle when shaken. Labels must indicate the percentage of weighting. Weighted silk is usually cheaper, weaker, and less serviceable. These days silk is most often blended with other fibers for weight or performance improvements rather than being weighted with metal salts.

Pure silk must contain no metallic weightings. It can have no more than 10 percent by weight of dyes or finishing materials. However, black silk may have 15 percent.

The four most popular natural fibers are shown in **8-23**. The characteristics of each fiber can be reviewed and compared to the others.

Other Natural Materials for Apparel

Horsehair is being used in fashion textiles to give strength without weight. Hair from the mane of horses is softer and shorter than tail hair, which is longer and thicker. The hard-wearing fabric made from horsehair may also be called *haircloth*. Some expensive designer handbags are made of lightweight horsehair from Mongolian ponies.

Miscellaneous materials such as fur and leather are from the hides of animals. They are not fibers; however, they are used for apparel.

8-23 All natural fibers have characteristics that make them suitable for various types of apparel.

Popular Natural Fibers			
Fiber Name and Source	**Fiber Advantages**	**Fiber Disadvantages**	**Typical Apparel Uses**

Cotton
 	
Boll of cotton plant
	strong, durable
	absorbent, cool
	quite inexpensive
	versatile uses
	soft, comfortable
	no static buildup
	stands high temperatures
	dyes and prints well
		affected by mildew
		wrinkles unless treated or
		   blended
		shrinks in hot water
		weakened by finishes,
		   perspiration, sun
		burns readily
		no elasticity
			underwear
			socks
			shirts
			jeans
			sportswear
			dresses
			blouses
			outerwear

Linen
 	
Stem of flax plant
	very strong
	resists dirt, stains
	absorbent, cool
	comfortable
	durable over time
	stands high temperatures
	smooth, lustrous
	lint-free: for dish towels and
	   medical cloths
		affected by mildew,
		   perspiration
		wrinkles easily
		hard to remove creases
		expensive if good
		shines if ironed on
		   right side
		burns readily
		ravels, shrinks
			handkerchiefs
			suits
			dresses
			skirts
			shirts

Wool
 	
Fleece of sheep
	very warm
	lightweight
	durable
	very absorbent
	comfortable
	resilient
	resists wrinkles
	creases well
	dyes well
	resists static
	easy to tailor
	can be reused
		weakened when wet
		affected by moths
		shrinks and mats with heat,
		   moisture, and
		   agitation
		needs special care, dry
		   cleaning
		absorbs odors
		harmed by bleach,
		   perspiration
		scratchy on skin
		pills
			sweaters
			suits
			coats
			skirts
			socks
			slacks
			outerwear

Silk
 	
Cocoon of silkworm
	lustrous
	smooth, luxurious
	very strong
	absorbent
	lightweight
	resists wrinkles, soil, mildew,
	   and moths
	comfortable
	dyes well
	drapes well
		expensive
		needs special care, dry
		   cleaning
		water spots
		yellows with age
		weakens with perspiration,
		   sun, soaps
		attacked by insects,
		   silverfish
			evening gowns
			wedding gowns
			lingerie
			blouses
			scarves
			dresses
			neckties
			suits

These materials are quite expensive since their supply is limited. They have been used since before recorded history. They are durable and weatherproof. Today they are fashionable, but controversial since animals must be killed to obtain the hides. Artificial substitutes have been developed to copy their looks.

Down is a light, fluffy feather undercoating that protects geese and ducks from extremely cold temperatures. The best quality is on the breast and underbody of large birds during the winter months. It is lightweight and extremely effective as an insulator. Down's microscopically thin fibers have millions of tiny insulating air pockets in each ounce. Down-filled comforters, sleeping bags, ski jackets, winter coats, and other products offer maximum warmth. The down is placed between the outer fabric and the lining of these items.

Manufactured Fibers

Manufactured fibers are made by industrial processes from substances such as wood cellulose (the fibrous substance in plants), oil products (petroleum), and chemicals. They try to duplicate and improve on the characteristics of natural fibers. Manufactured fibers are often cheaper, stronger, and more durable than the natural products they replace. They are more uniform in size and quality than natural fibers, since their processing is controlled. Manufactured fibers can be carefully engineered and modified to have characteristics that fit specific end-use needs. As with all fibers, each manufactured fiber has both advantages and disadvantages.

In general, manufactured fibers tend to offer easy-care *resilience*, retaining their shape or bouncing back when crushed. They are wrinkle-resistant and often require no ironing. In fact, high temperatures will soften those that are heat sensitive. Fabrics of heat-sensitive fibers have a low melting point and can be heat-treated to set pleats, mold shape, or emboss fabric designs.

Most manufactured fibers are versatile, nonallergenic, strong, and resistant to *abrasion* (surface wear and rubbing). Most do not absorb moisture or breathe for wearing comfort. Thus, sometimes they feel clammy when worn, especially in hot, humid weather. However, this same characteristic enables them to dry quickly.

Manufactured fibers that are nonabsorbent build up static electricity that causes them to spark and to cling to the wearer. They can be surface cleaned with a damp sponge since their smooth, nonporous surfaces do not allow dirt and grime to become imbedded. However, oil and ground-in stains are hard to remove. Moths and mildew do not usually affect these fibers.

The trade organization for producers of manufactured fibers is the American Fiber Manufacturer's Association, Inc. (AFMA).

The Development of Manufactured Fibers

After thousands of years with only natural fibers, experimental production of manufactured fibers started in Europe around 1850. By copying nature, scientists first changed natural fiber materials into liquids. Then they copied the silkworm by forcing the liquid out through tiny holes. Cellulosic material was taken from plants and formed into fibers.

The first commercial manufactured fiber was produced in the United States in 1910. This fiber was sold as artificial silk for several years. It was given the name *rayon* in 1924. That same year, commercial production of an *acetate* fiber was started.

Later, textile chemists made their own fiber-like materials by duplicating the molecules of plant and animal fibers. In 1939, *nylon* was introduced as the first noncellulose, test-tube fiber. It was made totally from chemicals. Women's hosiery was one of the first products made with nylon. It was used for military purposes during World War II because of its strength.

In the 1940s, '50s, and '60s, more manufactured fibers were developed. Fiber blending became widespread, bringing together the best properties of two or more fibers into fabrics that offered easy care. Also, sophistication of manufactured fibers took place for specific end-use products. The fibers were modified to give greater comfort, more flame resistance, better soil release, easier dyeability, and so on. Qualities were built into fibers to satisfy consumer textile needs.

As time passed, there were also more production facilities for manufactured fibers. By the start of the 1970s, fibers produced at chemical plants accounted for well over half of America's textile usage.

Manufactured Fibers Present and Future

Today, manufactured fibers account for the majority of all fibers used in fabrics. Most of the fibers are produced in Asia. They are made into a wide range of textile products. They are used in medicine, transportation, space travel, environmental control, and many other industries.

Fiber innovations and new fabrics are being developed by technology to fill apparel needs. For instance, swimsuit fabrics now resist fading from sunlight, saltwater, and swimming pool chlorine. They are fast drying and resistant to mildew, mold, and silverfish.

Other fabrics, used in exercise and active outdoor wear, do not absorb moisture. Instead, they pull it away from the skin to the surface of the fabric where it can bead up and evaporate. See 8-24. The wearer stays fairly dry.

Gore-Tex® membrane is a fluorocarbon material. It contains billions of tiny pores per square inch as a result of stretching it as thin as possible during production. The membrane is too thin to be used alone, so it is *laminated* (joined with an adhesive) to a sturdy outer fabric. Garments made from Gore-Tex® laminate are waterproof, yet breathable. This means they block wind and rain, but perspiration can pass through the garment, keeping the wearer dry and comfortable.

The future of textile technology may be even more amazing. Apparel may be made with materials that can automatically adjust to different environmental conditions, such as heat, cold, or rain. The possibilities are endless.

Categories of Manufactured Fibers

There are two basic types of manufactured fibers: cellulosic and synthetic (noncellulosic).

Cellulosic fibers are produced from cellulose, the fibrous substances found in plants such as softwood trees and bamboo. These sources have the advantage of being *renewable*, or able to regrow fairly fast. After harvesting, they are processed with chemicals. Manufactured cellulosic fibers are rayon, acetate, lyocell, and triacetate.

Synthetic (noncellulosic) fibers are made from molecules containing various combinations of carbon, hydrogen, nitrogen, and oxygen. These are obtained from petroleum, natural gas, air, and water. Textile chemists link these molecules into chemical compounds called polymers.

Manufactured fibers have been grouped for identification. A generic name is given to a group of fibers of similar chemical composition. Manufactured fibers are classified into generic groups by the Federal Trade Commission. A new generic name is established only when a fiber is developed that is different in chemical composition from other fibers. The present generic categories are listed in 8-25. Some are more familiar than others. Also, not all of these are commonly used in apparel. Some are used mainly for home furnishings, industrial, or medical products.

Within each generic group, there can be many individual fibers developed by fiber manufacturers. They are modified versions of the generic composition and are called *variants*. Each is slightly different from the others. They are engineered to have specific properties for certain purposes. They may offer greater comfort, flame resistance, soil release, or blending

Syda Productions/Shutterstock.com

8-24 Certain fibers used in exercise apparel are resistant to perspiration and odors, and remain breathable for the wearer.

8-25 Manufactured fibers can be grouped as cellulosic or synthetic (noncellulosic), depending on their composition.

Manufactured Fibers		
Cellulosic	**Noncellulosic**	
acetate	acrylic	olefin
lyocell	aramid	polyester
rayon	melamine	rubber
triacetate*	modacrylic*	spandex
	nylon	

* Not currently produced in the U.S.

qualities. Each brings specific desirable qualities to a finished product.

When a fiber producer develops a new variant, it is given its own identifying brand name, or *trademark*. Such names are always capitalized. The trademark, and the process for making the particular fiber, are registered with the U.S. Patent Office. New trademarks appear as modified manufactured fibers are developed. Old ones are discontinued and replaced.

The individual fiber producers own, advertise, and should stand behind their trademarked fibers. Sometimes fiber producers have several trademarks within a generic category because they have several fibers with slight differences. No other producers can make that exact variant unless they are licensed to do so by the company holding the patent. Some generic fiber categories, such as nylon and polyester, have many different manufacturers and trademarks.

Producing Manufactured Fibers

All manufactured fibers are made by forcing a syrupy substance through tiny holes. Solid fiber-forming substances (the raw materials) must first be converted into a liquid state. To do this, they are dissolved in a chemical solvent or melted with heat.

Extruding

The syrupy liquid is *extruded*, or forced out, in the desired thickness. The term used to describe fiber thickness or diameter is denier. The smaller the denier of the fiber, the softer and more pliable it is. An 840-denier is used in truck tires, while a 15-denier filament is used in sheer panty hose.

Fine, *microdenier fibers* that are half the denier of silk are now being produced. They are soft, luxurious, and drapable. Fabrics made from them are wrinkle-resistant and water-repellent, yet breathable.

A device called a spinneret is used to extrude the liquid. It is similar in principle to a bathroom showerhead. It has from one to hundreds of tiny holes. A spinneret is usually made from corrosion-resistant metals. Each tiny hole forms one fiber.

Manufactured fibers can be extruded from the spinnerets in shapes such as round, octagonal, trilobal (three-sided), and so on. The holes in the spinneret are shaped the way the fiber will be formed for varied end uses. The shape of a fiber can make it more or less lustrous, or to help it hide dirt. (Variations of shape are not possible for natural fibers.)

Certain additives put into the extruding solution can give the finished fiber such characteristics as resistance to static or flame-retardancy. *Solution dyeing* is the process of adding color to the solution before it is extruded. This gives a high degree of colorfastness, since the pigment is an integral part of the fiber.

Chemical Spinning

Chemical spinning causes the extruded solutions to become fibers. The filaments of continuous strands coming from the spinneret are hardened or solidified. There are three methods of spinning manufactured fibers—wet, dry, and melt spinning. Some fibers may be produced by more than one method.

Wet spinning hardens the filaments in a chemical bath. As the filaments emerge from the spinneret, they pass directly into the bath where they are solidified or regenerated. Acrylic and rayon fibers are produced by this method, shown in **8-26**.

Dry spinning solidifies the extruded filaments by drying them in warm air. The chemical that was used to change it to a liquid is evaporated away. This process, shown in **8-27**, is used for acetate, acrylic, modacrylic, spandex, and triacetate.

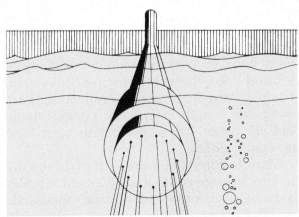

American Fiber Manufacturers Association, Inc.

8-26 In wet spinning, the filaments emerge from the spinneret directly into a chemical bath for solidification.

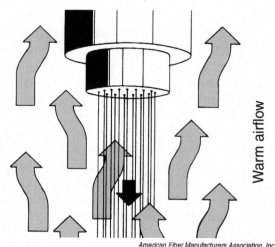

American Fiber Manufacturers Association, Inc.

8-27 In dry spinning, the filaments coming from the spinneret solidify by drying in warm air. The original liquefying chemical evaporates.

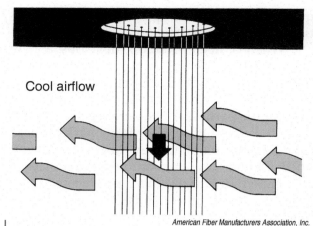

American Fiber Manufacturers Association, Inc.

8-28 Melt spinning solidifies the melted, extruded filaments by cooling them.

Melt spinning extrudes melted substances. They are hardened by cooling, as indicated in **8-28**. Nylon, olefin, polyester, aramid, polylactide, and glass fibers are produced by melt spinning.

Stretching

During or after hardening, manufactured fibers are stretched. This makes the denier smaller. It also causes the fiber molecules to become arranged, or *oriented*, into a more orderly pattern. This gives added strength. Fibers can be stretched to a consistent diameter. They can also be made thick and thin by varying the stretching pressure during spinning.

Cutting

Sometimes, manufactured fiber filaments are cut into staple. **Staple fibers** are short pieces, usually between one and four inches. Cotton, wool, and linen fibers occur naturally as staple. All staple fibers (natural or manufactured) are classed into length categories. Longer staple fibers are better for weaving into yarn than short staple lengths.

Manufactured fibers are extruded from the spinneret in large continuous filament bundles called *tow*. Filament tow may contain thousands of parallel filaments in rope form, as shown in **8-29**. The tow is usually mechanically *crimped* (curled or waved) and cut into the desired staple

Trevira Polyester Hoechst Fibers Industries

8-29 Each of the lines going into these barrels contains many continuous filaments of a manufactured fiber.

lengths. Some crimped staple is used as filling without being made into yarns. It is called *fiberfill*. Study **8-30** to review the steps in manufactured fiber processing.

Generic Characteristics

Each generic classification of manufactured fiber has its own chemical composition and set of characteristics. The most widely used manufactured fibers in apparel are polyester, nylon, rayon, and acrylic.

Manufactured Fiber Processing

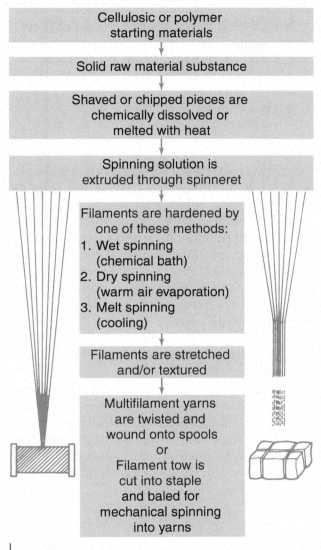

Cellulosic or polymer starting materials

↓

Solid raw material substance

↓

Shaved or chipped pieces are chemically dissolved or melted with heat

↓

Spinning solution is extruded through spinneret

↓

Filaments are hardened by one of these methods:
1. Wet spinning (chemical bath)
2. Dry spinning (warm air evaporation)
3. Melt spinning (cooling)

↓

Filaments are stretched and/or textured

↓

Multifilament yarns are twisted and wound onto spools
or
Filament tow is cut into staple and baled for mechanical spinning into yarns

8-30 Manufactured fiber processing uses specific raw materials that are melted or dissolved into a liquid. The liquid is extruded through a spinneret, solidified, stretched, and twisted or cut.

Polyester

Polyester has become the most widely used of all manufactured textile fibers. It has outstanding wrinkle-resistance and easy-care qualities. Polyester does not shrink or stretch. It is strong and quick-drying. Heat-set pleats and creases stand up extremely well under everyday wear. Also, water-based stains are easy to remove from fabrics made of polyester fibers. Polyester gives these properties to permanent press blends, especially when combined with cotton, rayon, or wool.

Polyester is extremely versatile. It can be made to have the look and feel of any natural fiber while adding easy care, durability, and low price. Polyester is used in woven, knitted, and nonwoven fabrics. It is also used for all kinds of apparel, home furnishings, and industrial products. Polyester insulating fiberfill fibers have hollow cores that act as tiny air-trapping shafts. They are soft and compressible like down, but they remain fluffy when wet. Some fiber companies produce many different variations of polyester.

Polylactic (PLA) is a polyester fiber developed in the early 2000s. Lactic acid is its polymer material, which is derived from fermenting sources of natural sugars, such as corn or sugar beets. These crops are annually renewable. PLA is very lightweight and provides excellent color characteristics. It has low flammability, low moisture absorption, and high wicking ability. It is also highly resistant to ultraviolet light. It is especially good for sports and performance apparel.

Nylon

Nylon is a very strong synthetic fiber that is made from petroleum chemicals (petrochemicals). It has great versatility. Nylon gives strength and abrasion resistance to many blends. It washes easily, dries quickly, needs little pressing, and holds its shape well since it does not shrink or stretch. Monofilament nylon is knitted into hosiery. See **8-31**. Multifilament nylon is used as yarn for apparel. Spun staple nylon yarns add strength to blends with other fibers.

8-31 Nylon is often used for hosiery. Because dyes can be added to the solution before being extruded, nylon is available in a variety of colors.

© iStock/zimindmitry

Rayon

Rayon is composed of regenerated cellulose, mainly from wood pulp. Bamboo has also become a quickly renewable resource for rayon because it grows so fast. Rayon dyes very well due to its high absorbency. The fibers are soft and comfortable. They are versatile, creating fabrics with different looks, weights, and performance. They can have beautiful luster. When given a high twist, they are used in crepe fabrics. Rayon fibers also blend well with almost all other fibers.

Acrylic

Acrylic has wool-like qualities as well as easy care. These fibers are not scratchy and do not shrink or mat. However, they do build up static electricity and pill. They are most commonly used to make soft, high-bulk, textured yarns. Such yarns are used in sweaters and fur-like fabrics. They are warm and lightweight. Acrylic fibers have resistance to common chemical solvents, bleaches, and weathering. They are used alone or in blends, and from fine fabrics to heavy work clothing.

Modacrylic

Modacrylic is a modified acrylic fiber. Its heat sensitivity permits it to be manipulated for different results. It can be stretched, embossed, and molded into special shapes. Modacrylic is often made into dense, high pile, fur-like fabrics. It also resists flames and most chemicals. Modacrylic is often blended with other fibers to reduce their degree of flammability. It is used extensively for flame-retardant sleepwear.

Acetate and Triacetate

Acetate and *triacetate* are made from cellulose acetate, a derivative of cellulose. Fabrics from these fibers drape beautifully, and look and feel luxurious. They often have crisp body. Their natural luster can be adjusted from dull to bright for a wide variety of rich textures. They take special dyes well and are colorfast. Also, they blend well with other fibers.

Acetate and triacetate have low wet strength and low resistance to abrasion. They must be dry-cleaned or carefully hand washed. They may be heat treated to help them resist wrinkles and maintain their stability. In fact, triacetate has resistance to damage or glazing by heat, thus it may be safely ironed at higher temperatures. Heat-setting treatments can give triacetate pleat retention by permanently changing the crystalline structure of the fiber. Triacetate is stronger than acetate and more shrink resistant.

Olefin

Olefin is very nonabsorbent. Thus, it is shrink-resistant and difficult to dye. It is available only in limited colors and resists fading. Its great advantage is its wicking power. In other words, it can pull moisture away from the body to the surface of a fabric where it can evaporate quickly. Because of this, it is used next to the skin for exercise and outdoor wear, ski underwear, and knitted sportswear. It is also very effective in disposable diapers.

Olefin is very lightweight, yet bulky enough to trap air for insulating purposes. It is less expensive than other manufactured fibers. It does not deteriorate from chemicals, mildew, perspiration, rot, or weather. Consequently, it is used to make protective clothing for many industries. One disadvantage is that it is sensitive to light and to heat, which causes it to melt. However, modifications to the olefin fiber have improved these characteristics.

Spandex

Spandex has great elasticity. It is strong and lightweight. Garments containing spandex retain their holding power through constant stretching and recovery. Spandex was first used in swimsuits and foundation garments since it provides softness and comfortable fit with freedom of movement. However, now it is popular in all types of apparel, from casual jeans to high-fashion designs. Spandex fibers are always used with other fibers since only a small amount is needed to give the desired holding power and recovery characteristics. See **8-32**.

Lyocell

Lyocell is a cellulosic manufactured fiber. It is biodegradable and heralded as being environmentally friendly. It is made from wood

8-32 With only a small amount of spandex, this pants fabric has good stretch and recovery, providing comfortable fit and freedom of movement.

pulp from trees grown in managed, constantly replanted forests. The chemical agents used to manufacture it are recycled. Lyocell fibers are strong, highly absorbent, and blend well with other fibers. They are used in many types of fashion fabrics.

Aramid

Aramid fibers are lightweight, tough, and resistant to flames and chemicals. They can stop bullets. These fibers are used in protective clothing for firefighters, police officers, military personnel, and others in hazardous occupations.

PBI

PBI (Polybenzimidazole) does not burn, melt, or drip. It provides garment comfort, since it retains high amounts of moisture. PBI has excellent resistance to chemicals, solvents, fuels, and steam. It resists oils and stains and has good insulating properties. PBI is used for firefighters' protective apparel and industrial work clothing. Flight suits and racecar driver uniforms are its other uses.

Melamine

Melamine is flame resistant, has low thermal conductivity, and is stable at high heat. It is white and dyeable. It is processed on standard textile equipment for use in protective clothing such as firefighters' wear, for aircraft seating, and for other high-risk fabric needs.

Rubber

Rubber fibers are made from the sap (latex) of certain plants. They are usually used as a core around which other fibers are wrapped to protect the rubber from abrasion. Rubber fibers have good elasticity to stretch and recover. They have low resistance to bleach, heat, and sunlight. Rubber fibers are used in such items as rubber boots, raincoats, and elastic.

Using the Characteristics

Different fibers are sometimes combined in the manufacturing process to take advantage of the good characteristics from each fiber. For instance, *bicomponent fibers* result from extruding two polymers in filaments through a spinneret. Both polymers are within the same filament. Extruded bicomponent filaments may have the two fibers lying side by side or one fiber may be placed as a core inside the other fiber. Almost any cross-sectional shape or geometry can be done for various elasticity or appearance. Sometimes bicomponent fibers are called *conjugate fibers*, especially in Asia where most bicomponent fibers have been produced so far. Fiber producers predict significant growth of this process in the future.

A close relative to bicomponent fibers is *co-spun fibers*. In this case, different polymers are extruded through different holes in the same spinneret. Each filament contains one solid type of fiber, with all fibers being spun at the same time from the spinneret.

Figure **8-33** shows the more popular manufactured fibers used in apparel. Use it to review and compare the characteristics of the different fibers. Basic knowledge of these fibers is important for smart clothing decisions. In addition to the trademarks shown, generic (unbranded) fibers are often used in less expensive apparel. They are usually imported from lower-wage countries, where they are mass produced in huge amounts.

Yarns

Natural and manufactured fibers are made into *yarns*. These continuous strands of textile fibers are in a form suitable for processing into yard goods. Raw fibers are converted into several different types of yarns. The yarns, in turn, are made into fabrics by weaving, knitting, or other methods.

8-33 The many manufactured fibers available today allow great variety in the production of apparel and other items.

Popular Manufactured Fibers*			
Generic Name: Some Trademarks	**Fiber Advantages**	**Fiber Disadvantages**	**Typical Apparel Uses**

polyester
 	
Coolmax
Dacron
Diolen
Fillwell
Fortrel
Loftguard
Microlux
Microtherm
Serelle
Tairilin
	resilient
	colorfast
	strong, durable
	easy care
	resists wrinkles, abrasion,
	    bleach, perspiration,
	    mildew, moths
	can be heat-set
	easy to dye
	does not stretch or shrink
	very versatile
		low absorbency
		spun yarns pill
		takes oily stains
		static buildup
			permanent press fabrics
			fiberfill insulation
			shirts
			blouses
			dresses
			slacks
			suits
			underwear
			sportswear
			children's wear

nylon Anso Antron Cordura Micro Supplex Silky Touch Stainmaster Supplex TACTEL Ultron Wear-Dated	very strong lightweight dries quickly durable resilient resists mildew, moths, chemicals, wrinkles lustrous colorfast elastic	low absorbency surface pills damaged by sun picks up oils and dyes in wash static buildup heat sensitive	sweaters hosiery lingerie skiwear slacks windbreakers dresses raincoats swimwear blouses sportswear
acrylic Acrilan BioFresh Creslan Duraspun Evolutia MicroSupreme Pil-Trol Wear-Dated WeatherBloc	resembles wool lightweight soft, fluffy warm, bulky resilient resists weather, moths, chemicals, mildew, wrinkles shape retention easy care colorfast	low absorbency static buildup surface pills heat sensitive	sportswear sweaters infant wear socks knitted garments pile fabrics jackets skirts slacks bathrobes

(continued)

8-33 *(continued)*

Generic Name: Some Trademarks	Fiber Advantages	Fiber Disadvantages	Typical Apparel Uses
rayon Bemberg Modal Zantrel	very absorbent dyes/prints well soft, pliable, drapable comfortable/versatile inexpensive colorfast no static or pilling	wrinkles/shrinks unless treated low resiliency heat sensitive will mildew stretches weak when wet	blouses dresses sport shirts lingerie sportswear neckties jackets
acetate Celanese Celstar Chromspun Estron MicroSafe	silk-like look/feel drapes well does not shrink resists moths, mildew, pilling inexpensive easy to dye versatile	poor abrasion resistance weak heat sensitive needs special cleaning care dissolved by nail polish remover	dresses blouses linings lingerie shirts scarves neckties
olefin Angel Hair Crowelon Duron Herculon Impressa Marquesa Lana Nouvelle Trace	resists abrasion, chemicals, stains, mildew, pilling, wrinkles, static not affected by aging, weather, perspiration excellent wicking thermal warmth strong, durable very lightweight	heat sensitive poor dyeability nonabsorbent	knitted sweaters, socks, sportswear nonwoven fabrics for industrial apparel filler in quilted goods disposable diapers
spandex Dorlastan Glospan Lycra	very elastic resistant to lotions, oils, perspiration, sun, flexing lightweight strong, durable soft, smooth	yellows with age heat sensitive harmed by chlorine bleach nonabsorbent	swimwear/skiwear foundation garments support hose slacks exercise and dance wear fashion apparel
lyocell Tencel	biodegradable absorbent strong resists sunlight, aging, abrasion	attacked by mildew	soft denims shirts reusable nonwovens many fashion fabrics
aramid Kevlar Nomex	strong no melting point resists abrasion, most chemicals resilient, supple flame-resistant	no stretch nonabsorbent	protective clothing
PBI	flame-resistant comfortable chemically stable		firefighters' coats astronauts' space suits

* Information from the American Fiber Manufacturer's Assoication, Inc. (AFMA)

Yarn Types

Monofilament yarns are simply single filaments, usually of a high denier. One example of monofilaments is the single strand yarns in women's hosiery. Another is the clear, plastic-like sewing thread used to hem some ready-to-wear garments.

Most often, filaments are combined and used as *multifilament yarns* in apparel. The yarns are formed by twisting the many continuous strands of fiber being extruded through the spinneret at the same time. As the degree of twist is increased in any yarn, the yarn becomes harder, more compact, and less lustrous. A low twist is used for most multifilament yarns, so they are soft and lustrous.

Spun yarns are made with staple fibers. The fibers are usually bound together by *mechanical spinning*. This process pulls (draws) and twists the fibers together to obtain a continuous length sufficient for weaving or knitting. Generally, for spun yarns, a tighter twist produces a stronger yarn. However, too tight a twist can weaken the final yarn.

Yarns spun from staple fibers are more irregular than filament yarns. The short ends of the fibers produce a fuzzy effect on the yarn surface. Spun yarns are more bulky than filament yarns of the same weight. They are also more porous and warmer. The resulting fabrics often have a more natural feeling and snag less than fabrics made from filament yarns. However, spun yarns have a tendency to pill after some wear. Look at **8-34** to see a monofilament yarn, a multifilament yarn, and a spun yarn.

Ply yarns are formed by twisting together two or more single yarns. Each yarn strand is called a *ply*, as in three-ply yarn. Ply refers to the number of yarns twisted together. This is usually done when extra strength, added bulk, or unusual effects are desired. When a number of ply yarns are twisted together, they form a *cord*, as seen in **8-35**.

Combination Yarns and Blends

Combination yarns are ply yarns composed of two or more different yarns. They can be formed by putting spun staple and filament yarns together in different ways. This gives softness from the spun staple and added strength from the filament fibers.

Another form of combination yarn is made with two or more yarns that vary in fiber composition, content, or twist level. They are put side by side to twist into a yarn.

A *blend*, on the other hand, is made when two or more fibers (usually in staple form) are put together before they are spun into yarns. This uniformly mixes fibers with different physical characteristics. The best performance feature of each fiber is sought. When blended properly, the positive qualities of one fiber can decrease the negative properties of another fiber. The resulting fabrics have better performance, nicer appearance, or lower prices.

8-35 When single yarns are twisted together, a ply yarn is made. If two or more ply yarns are twisted together, a cord yarn is produced.

Two-ply   Cord yarn
yarn

8-34 Yarns may be monofilament, multifilament, or spun.

Monofilament   Multifilament   Spun
yarn   yarn   yarn

Most natural and manufactured fibers blend well. This can increase strength and durability, prevent shrinkage, or provide other advantages. The most desired performance characteristics sought in apparel fabrics are wrinkle resistance, shrinkage control, and colorfastness. The cost of the fabric is less when natural fibers are blended with less expensive manufactured fibers.

By knowing the advantages and disadvantages of individual fibers, the performance of fabrics containing them can be judged. For instance, when blended, nylon adds strength and stability to fabric. Rayon and cotton provide absorbency and comfort. Acrylics improve softness and warmth without adding weight. Spandex gives elasticity. Silk gives beautiful luster. Acetate adds drapability and texture. Polyester contributes easy care, permanent-press qualities, as well as abrasion resistance. Polyester/cotton blends are popular for easy-care, comfortable apparel.

Yarn Textures

Textured yarns are illustrated in **8-36**. Texturing of manufactured filaments is done by processing with chemicals, heat, or special machinery. Texturing turns the straight, rod-like filaments into crimped, coiled, or looped forms. It creates a different surface texture, since the filaments no longer lie parallel to each other in the yarn. It is a permanent treatment that gives the yarns bulk, softness, stretch, and wrinkle resistance. When made into fabrics, textured filament yarns have more resemblance to spun yarns but give better durability.

8-36 Textured yarns have more bulk, stretchability, and wrinkle resistance than yarns of straight filaments.

Crimped   Coiled   Looped

Summary

Cotton and linen/bast fibers are cellulosic natural fibers from plants. Cotton is harvested from seed pods (bolls), cleaned, and drawn into strands for spinning. It is quite inexpensive, soft, absorbent, and versatile, but also wrinkles. Linen is from the stalk of flax plants. It is more expensive than cotton, and is strong, durable, and lustrous. Linen wrinkles and ravels.

Wool and silk are protein natural fibers from animals. Wool is from the fleece of sheep, which is sheared and scoured before being made into woolen or worsted yarn. Wool is versatile, warm, easy to tailor, and has resiliency from its crimp, but shrinks and can be scratchy. Wool can be used, pure, blended, or recycled. Specialty wools from other animals are also available. Silk is a cultivated filament fiber unwound from silkworm cocoons. Other silks are wild, doupion, and spun silks. Silk is luxurious and strong, but requires some special care.

Other natural materials are fur, leather, and down. They are not fibers, but have specific uses in apparel. Artificial substitutes have been developed to copy them.

Manufactured fibers are engineered for improved characteristics. Textile chemists developed them by duplicating the molecules of plant and animal fibers. Today, innovative manufactured fibers have many apparel, medical, and industrial uses.

The two basic manufactured fiber types are cellulosic, from plant substances, and noncellulosic, from chemical polymers. Most generic groups contain many trademarks. Generic groups include polyester, nylon, acrylic, modacrylic, rayon, acetate, olefin, spandex, lyocell, and others. All manufactured fibers are made by extruding liquid materials through a spinneret. The material is then dried by chemical spinning (wet, dry, or melt spinning), stretched, and cut if staple is desired.

Yarns are continuous strands of fibers suitable for making fabrics. They might be monofilament, multifilament, spun, or ply yarns. Combination yarns and blends can change performance characteristics. Textured yarns have added bulk, softness, stretch, and wrinkle resistance to resemble spun yarns.

Fashion Recall

Write your answers on a separate sheet of paper.

True/False: Write *true* or *false* for each of the following statements.

1. Cotton, linen, jute, and ramie are protein natural fibers.
2. Combing is an extra processing step done for high-quality cotton fibers.
3. The United States leads the world in the production of linen.
4. Linen is known for its durability and luster.
5. Short wool fibers of less than two inches are used to make worsted yarns.
6. The terms virgin wool, pure wool, and 100% wool can be used interchangeably.
7. Silk is the only natural filament fiber.
8. Highly absorbent manufactured fibers tend to build up static electricity.
9. Denier is the term used to describe fiber length.
10. A blend is made when two or more fibers are put together before they are spun into yarns.

Short Answer: Write the correct answer to each of the following.

11. Name two advantages, two disadvantages, and two end uses of cotton.
12. Name two advantages, two disadvantages, and two end uses of linen.
13. Name two advantages, two disadvantages, and two end uses of wool.
14. Name two advantages, two disadvantages, and two end uses of silk.
15. Name a manufactured fiber. Then name two advantages, two disadvantages, and two end uses of that fiber.

Fashion Vocabulary

16. Work in teams, to locate a small image online that visually describes or explains each of the *Fashion Terms* on the chapter opening. To create flash cards, write each term on a note card and paste the image that describes or explains the term on the opposite side of the card.

Critical Thinking

17. **Evaluate fibers**   Name a natural fiber and a manufactured fiber that would be good choices for sportswear. Explain why these would be good choices during class discussion.

18. **Compare fibers**   Suppose you are shopping for a shirt or blouse. Would you want the garment to be made of natural or manufactured fibers or a blend of these? Which fibers do you prefer? Write a summary explaining your choices.

19. **Identify characteristics**   If you were a textile engineer developing a new textile fiber for outerwear for mountain climbing, what characteristics would you want in that fiber?

20. **Analyze environmental responsibility**   Some fiber manufacturers are trying to use sustainable processes that help to save the environment. Should world governments and consumers encourage fiber manufacturers to use sustainable practices? Why or Why not? How might consumers identify whether fiber manufacturers demonstrate environmental responsibility? What actions might consumers take to support sustainability practices among fiber manufacturers?

Core Skills

21. **Research and speaking**   Research the source of a specialty wool fiber. In an oral report, describe the animals that produce the fiber. Tell where the animals are raised. Try to find out how many animals are needed to give enough fibers for one sweater or one coat. Explain why you think these fibers are fashionably desirable and why they are so expensive.

22. **Research and writing**   Research the history of a manufactured fiber. Write a report on its development and its past and current uses.

23. **Reading and writing**   Read the fiber content labels of five different garments. This information may be found in mail-order catalogs or listed on websites. In a written report, explain how the fibers used affect the appearance, performance, and comfort of each garment.

24. **Research and writing**   Visit the website of the American Fiber Manufacturers Association, Inc. (AFMA). One of its valuable features is a list of news releases and articles about important innovations and current events. Read one release or article and write a summary to post to the class website for peer and instructor review.

25. **Technology**   Go to the website of a textile museum, such as The Textile Museum in Washington D.C., or a university textile department. Browse an online gallery or exhibition. Choose three textile items of interest to you. Investigate details about the textile items, including their history, how they were made, and how they were possibly used. Use a school-approved web application to create a digital poster about your findings to upload to the class website for peer review.

26. **CTE career readiness practice**   Use online or print resources, or the help of a chemistry teacher, to learn about the chemical composition of a manufactured fiber such as polyester and the process for making the fiber. Prepare a storyboard showing how the fiber is manufactured from raw materials to finished yarn, including its performance qualities. Share your storyboard with the class.

Fashion in Action

27. **Portfolio builder**   Obtain as many fabric samples as possible. Note the appearance and feel of each. Then unravel the yarns to find textured filaments, staple fibers, or other discoveries. Analyze the twist and fiber lengths of each type of yarn. Mount the fabric pieces, yarns, and fibers on note cards along with your written descriptions of them. Keep these in your portfolio for future reference.

28. **Design activity**   Using various fabric scraps and yarns, create a collage. Write a brief description of the various types of fibers and yarns used to create the collage. Display the collage in the classroom.

Self-Assessment Quiz ↗

Complete the self-assessment quiz online to help practice and expand your knowledge and skills.

Fabric Construction and Finishes

While studying, look for the activity icon to:

- **practice** key fashion terms with e-flash cards, vocabulary games, and matching activities
- **assess** what you learn by completing self-assessment quizzes

www.g-wlearning.com/clothingandfashion/

weaving

loom

warp yarns

shuttle

filling yarns

selvage

plain weave

twill weave

satin weave

nap

knitting

gauge

weft knits

warp knits

nonwoven fabrics

dyeing

roller printing

screen printing

finishes

hand

Objectives

After studying this chapter, you will be able to
➤ describe how fabrics are made from fibers and yarns.
➤ identify what fabric characteristics result from the different types of fabric construction.
➤ explain how fabrics are given color and surface designs.
➤ discuss fabric finishes, how they are applied, and the effects they give.

The appearance and performance of textiles depend on their fiber content, type of yarn, fabric construction, and added color and finishes. These factors can be varied to make millions of individual fabrics with different characteristics.

Fabric Construction

Fibers and yarns can be held together in various ways to make *fabric*. The two most common methods of making fabric are weaving and knitting. Other methods, such as felting, bonding, braiding, netting, and lace making, are used less often. Most apparel is made of either woven or knitted fabrics. Many modern textile mills start with raw fibers at one end and go through all processes that result in finished *yard goods* at the other end.

Weaving

Weaving is a procedure of interlacing two sets of yarns placed at right angles to each other. The yarns are sometimes also called *threads*. The machine for weaving is called a loom. A basic hand loom is shown in **9-1**.

Two sets of yarns are used for weaving. The lengthwise yarns are threaded onto the loom side by side and pulled tight. These are called warp yarns. They must be strong and durable to withstand the strain of the weaving process.

The crosswise yarns weave back and forth from edge to edge with a shuttle that pulls the threads through the warp yarns. This forms the fabric. Crosswise yarns are called the filling yarns (or *weft* or *woof yarns*). They pass over and under the warp yarns. Where they turn at the fabric's edge to go back the other direction is called the selvage, as shown in **9-2**. The selvage runs along both edges of the fabric. It is strong and will not ravel.

Automatic looms, as shown in **9-3**, have power shuttles that move at tremendous speeds. When the appropriate warp yarns are raised, the filling yarn shoots from one side to the other. Different warp yarns are then raised by the loom, and the shuttle propels the filling yarn back to the original side. This continues as the fabric is woven. It all happens so quickly that it appears to be a smooth, continuous operation.

Other types of looms include shuttleless looms and dart looms. A *shuttleless loom* carries the filling yarns by steel bands attached to wheels on each side of the loom. A *dart loom* has many darts that shoot across at the right time with individual lengths of yarn from a package

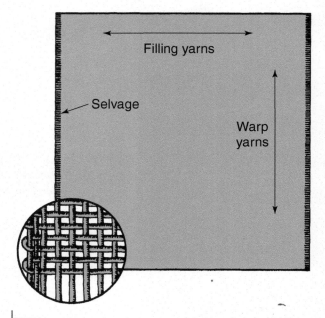

9-2 Filling yarns pass over and under warp yarns to weave fabrics. They turn and go back the other way at the selvage.

beside the loom. In still other looms, the filling yarn is carried very fast by a tiny jet of water or air.

Weaving plants have rows of machines (looms) producing fabrics at high speeds, shown in **9-4**. Sophisticated, computerized weaving techniques are becoming more widely used.

Fabric Grain

The direction that yarns run in a fabric is called the *grain*. Warp yarns form the *lengthwise grain*. They run parallel to the selvages. Filling

9-1 This person is weaving fabric using a simple loom. Huge, mechanized looms work on the same principle—weaving a set of yarns over and under a perpendicular set of yarns.

Mikhail Olykainen/Shutterstock.com

9-3 Automatic looms are guided by computers to produce plain or fancy woven fabrics. Half the warp yarns have been lifted for the shuttle to take a filling yarn to the other side.

Pendleton Woolen Mills

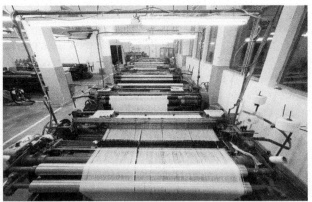

9-4 Large looms produce woven fabrics quickly and efficiently for use in garments and other finished textile products.

yarns run along the *crosswise grain*. In woven fabrics, the *filling* (crosswise grain) stretches more than the *warp* (lengthwise grain). The grain is important in apparel, since garments need to stretch more around the body than up and down. Warp yarns should go up and down in garments for strength and stability.

Bias grain goes diagonally across the fabric. *True bias* runs at a 45 degree angle, or halfway between the lengthwise and crosswise grains. The greatest amount of stretch in a woven fabric is along the true bias. Note the grain lines indicated in **9-5**.

9-5 Various grains can be determined by the direction of the yarns in woven fabrics.

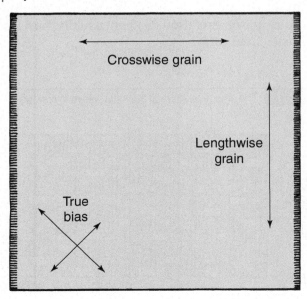

The result of weaving the yarns closely together is a strong, dense fabric. When the yarns are woven loosely, the fabric is lighter and more porous. If the fabric has low-twist or *special effect* yarns, these run in the filling direction. A textured effect is achieved by weaving some low-twist and some high-twist yarns together. *Stretch* woven fabrics are woven of stretchable yarns.

Types of Weaves

There are three basic weaves for making fabric—plain, twill, and satin weaves. These are all made by passing the filling yarns over and under the warp yarns. However, the number of warp yarns is different in each weave. Weaves also differ in appearance and durability. Every other weave is a variation of one or more of the three basic weaves.

The simplest and most common weave is the plain weave. It is shown in **9-6**. In most cases, the lengthwise and crosswise threads are the same denier. The filling yarns pass alternately over and under the warp yarns as in a tennis racquet, only much closer together. This creates a fabric that is strong, reversible, and durable. Examples of plain-weave fabrics include muslin, percale, gingham, chiffon, poplin, and broadcloth.

The appearance of a plain weave can be changed by using large yarns with small yarns, using textured yarns, or applying a special finish. The *rib weave*, shown in **9-7**, uses coarser yarns along with regular ones. The result is a corded effect. The *basket weave* is a common variation of the plain weave. It is formed by using two or more yarns as one. Illustration **9-8** shows a common 2 x 2 basket weave. Two filling

9-6 The plain weave is the simplest weave. Each filling yarn passes alternately over and under each warp yarn at right angles to it.

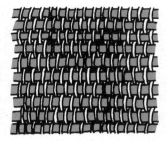

9-7 The rib weave uses filling yarns that are quite different in size from the warp yarns. Thus, a ribbed look results.

9-8 The basket weave is a plain weave with multiple yarns.

yarns pass over and under two warp yarns. Hopsacking, monk's cloth, and oxford cloth are examples of basket-weave fabrics.

In the twill weave, a yarn in one direction *floats* (passes) over two or more yarns in the other direction at regular intervals. Each float begins one yarn over from the last one. A dominant yarn can be seen on the surface of the cloth. It creates a diagonal rib or cord pattern, called a *wale*, as shown in **9-9**.

Twill-weave fabrics are usually very firm and tightly woven. The weave is often used to produce strong, durable fabrics. Twill-weave fabrics resist wrinkles and hide soil. Examples

of twill-weave fabrics are denim, gabardine, and surah.

There are many ways to vary twill weaves. The floats can be long or short. The angle of a wale may vary from a reclining slope to a very steep slope. Large, high-twist or textured yarns also create different looks.

A common variation of the twill weave is the *herringbone* pattern. In this weave, the wale changes direction at regular intervals to produce a zigzag effect.

The satin weave, as shown in **9-10**, has long yarn floats on the surface. They go over four or more opposite yarns and under one. Each float begins two yarns over from where the last float began. The face of a satin-weave fabric is composed almost entirely of yarns running in only one direction. This creates a surface that reflects light and has a lustrous sheen.

The satin weave is smooth, slippery, and drapable. It is good for linings and formal wear. If the yarns are woven together closely, the fabric is stiffer and stronger. If they are woven more loosely, the fabric resists wrinkles and is more pliable. However, this type of weave is generally the least durable of the three weaves. When worn, the floating threads are likely to catch other surfaces, which may cause snagging, pulling, and friction. Friction causes the fabric to pill and dulls the sheen.

The satin weave is used to make both satin and sateen fabrics. In *satin*, the floats run in the warp direction. For the highest luster, the long floats are made of filament fibers with low twist. In *sateen*, the floats run in the filling direction. Spun yarns are used. Sateen usually has less luster than satin.

9-10 The smooth surface of the satin weave is created by floating yarns.

9-9 A twill weave causes the fabric surface to have a diagonal wale.

Wale

Variations

There are many variations of the basic weaves. *Pile* fabrics have loops or yarn ends projecting from the surface. An example of a fabric with loops is terry cloth. Some fabrics with clipped yarn ends are corduroy, velvet, and fake furs. Notice the difference between the looped pile illustrated in **9-11** and the cut pile in **9-12**.

Woven-pile fabrics are made by varying either a plain weave or a twill weave. Extra filling yarns are woven into the basic weave. In some cases, such as for velvet, fabrics are woven double, face-to-face. They are then cut apart between the layers to make two separate pieces of pile fabric.

Pile and brushed-surface fabrics have nap. Nap is a layer of fiber ends raised from a fabric surface. Nap appears differently when viewed from different directions. This is because fiber ends lying at various angles reflect varying amounts of light. In apparel, the nap must run the same direction throughout an entire garment. If one garment part is cut from fabric with nap going the opposite direction, a difference in color, shading, or pattern will result.

Other variations of the three basic weaves create patterns in woven fabrics. Stripes, checks, and plaids, as in **9-13**, are the oldest woven patterns. They are made on a *box loom*. Shuttles carrying different colors of yarn are housed in boxes at the sides of the loom. Specific shuttles are used at certain times to produce the desired pattern in the fabric. Other symmetrical or geometric patterns can also be produced in this way.

Large and intricate designs are woven on a *Jacquard loom*. The fabric pattern is programmed on a computer that controls when each individual warp yarn is raised for every passage of the shuttle. Although this process provides the flexibility to make a desired pattern, it is more expensive and slower due to the more complicated loom procedure. Damask, tapestry, and brocade fabrics are woven in this way. See **9-14**. Fabrics with a woven pattern that contain a name or logo are also done on a Jacquard loom.

Smaller designs, such as geometric forms in a sequence, can be woven into a fabric with a *dobby attachment*. This is an electronic attachment for a regular loom. It is faster and less expensive than Jacquard weaving for simple, small, geometric designs. An example of a dobby weave pattern is illustrated in **9-15**.

9-11 A looped-pile fabric, such as terry cloth, has loops of yarn extending out from the fabric surface.

9-12 Cut-pile fabrics, such as corduroy or velvet, have yarn ends projecting from the fabric surface. To achieve this, extra yarns are woven into the fabric and then cut.

9-13 A plaid pattern can be woven into fabrics by inserting yarns of different colors where the lines are wanted.

9-14 Large, intricate fabric patterns, such as brocades, are woven on Jacquard looms.

In the *leno weave*, the warp yarns do not lie parallel to each other. Instead, they are used in pairs, and one crosses over the other before the filling yarn is inserted. The leno weave is illustrated in **9-16**.

A special loom attachment is needed to produce leno-weave fabrics. The fabrics have an open effect. The crossing of the warp yarns adds strength and prevents slippage of the yarns. Leno-weave fabrics are used to make shirts, curtains, thermal blankets, mosquito netting, and bags for laundry, fruits, and vegetables.

9-15 This weave is one of several patterns produced on an industrial dobby weaving loom.

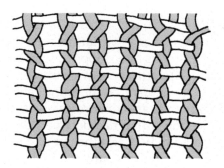

9-16 Because leno-weave fabrics have open spaces, they may look fragile. However, the crossings of the warp yarns give them strength and stability.

Knitting

Knitting is a fabric construction method of looping yarns together. In knitting, one yarn can form the entire fabric. A series of loops in the same, continuous yarn are interlocked. This can be done a row at a time or in a continuous circular pattern. Loops of yarn are pulled through other loops of yarn. The knitted fabric or garment grows longer as rows of loops are interlocked into the previous loops. The loops, or stitches, can be varied to create numerous patterns and textures.

Lines of loops that run the length of knitted fabrics are called *wales*. Lines of loops that run crosswise are called *courses*. Both are illustrated in **9-17**. **Gauge** is the number of stitches, or loops, per inch in a knitted fabric. A higher gauge number indicates a closer and finer knit.

Knit fabrics are popular for apparel, **9-18**. They tend to move with and fit the body shape comfortably. They are versatile and wrinkle resistant, so they are good choices for travel clothes. Most natural and manufactured fibers are suited to knitting.

Knits do not ravel the way woven fabrics do. However, they can get lengthwise runs from broken threads, as seen in nylon stockings. They can also snag or come unknitted if the yarn is pulled. They are usually flexible and stretchy. Their stretch is built in by the knitting process. (This differs from stretch wovens that are made with elastic fibers or yarns.)

Almost all knitting for garments sold in retail stores is done on knitting machines in commercial knitting mills. Circular knitting machines make knitted fabrics in tube forms. Flat knitting machines make flat, knitted fabrics.

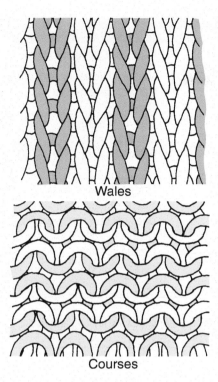

9-17 In knits, wales run in the lengthwise direction and courses run across the fabric.

kurhan/Shutterstock.com

9-18 Knitwear can be casual or high fashion. It is popular because of its comfort, versatility, and ease of care.

Commercial knitting is faster than weaving on looms. In fact, it happens faster than the eye can follow. Technicians develop knit patterns on computers. The computers control the knitting machines. The result might be knit yard goods, or finished socks, sweaters, and other knitted garments.

Types of Knits

The two methods of knitting fabrics are weft knitting and warp knitting. The difference is in the way the loops are formed. Their structures and characteristics are described in **9-19**.

Weft knits (or *filling knits*) have one strand of yarn that runs across, forming a horizontal row of interlocked loops. The commercial process is essentially mechanized hand knitting.

Weft knits can be made either on a circular machine or on a flat machine. Specially designed circular knitting machines are used to make the right-sized tubes for such items as hosiery, underwear, and T-shirts. Large widths of circular knits are cut open and used as flat fabric.

With flat machines, the number of stitches can be automatically increased or decreased

to shape the finished fabric. Shaping during the knitting operation reduces garment seam construction and is considered to make a finer garment. The resulting shaped product is described as being *full-fashioned*. Where stitches have been dropped or added is slightly noticeable, as shown in **9-20**. Sweaters and dresses are often full-fashioned and may have separate shaped collars, cuffs, and trim pieces.

Single-knit fabrics, such as jersey, are usually made with cotton, rayon, nylon, or blends. They are made on single-needle, weft knitting machines. They stretch in both directions and may tend to stretch out of shape. They have lengthwise wales on the right side and crosswise courses on the wrong side.

To determine whether a fabric is single knit, pull it crosswise. If the fabric rolls toward the right side, it is a single knit. This type of knit is lightweight, soft, and drapable. Its cut edges may curl or roll, and it will often run if snagged. It is most often found in formal wear, lingerie, and T-shirts.

Basic Knits and Their Characteristics

Type of Knit	Structural Drawing	Fabric Names	General Characteristics
Weft Yarns run across		Single knit Jersey Purl knit Ribbed knit Double knit Interlock knit Sweater knit	Made on circular or flat machine Can be full-fashioned Stretchy May run if snagged Cut edges may curl Great versatility
Warp Yarns run lengthwise		Tricot Raschel knit	Made only on flat knitting machine Stable and durable Does not ravel; has selvage edges Quite run-proof Limited stretch Versatile

9-19 In weft knitting, the yarn forms interlocking loops in horizontal rows across the fabric. In warp knitting, interlocking stitches carry the yarn lengthwise in a zigzag pattern.

9-20 Full-fashion marks occur where shaping is done through the knitting process rather than by the stitching of seams.

Double-knit fabrics are made on a weft machine with two needles and two yarns. Loops are drawn through from both directions to knit two fabrics as one. Plain double knits look the same on both sides, with rows of fine wales. The crosswise direction stretches more than the lengthwise one. They are firmer and more stable than single knits. They have give, but they will not sag or stretch out of shape. Double knits are usually made from polyester, triacetate, or wool. They are used for garments such as suits, coats, slacks, and dresses.

To identify a double knit, look at the edge and pull it crosswise. It will not roll, and you will see two separate layers of loops. However, it cannot be separated into two individual layers.

There are many varieties of double knits, including *interlock knits*. Interlock knits are lightweight and stretchy. They have a smooth surface on both sides and a very fine lengthwise rib. Most will run along an unfinished edge. They are used to make underwear, T-shirts, golf shirts, and dresses.

Purl knits have pronounced horizontal (crosswise) ridges. They have superior stretch and recovery in both directions. Also, they are usually reversible since the back is identical to the face of the knit.

Rib knits have pronounced vertical (lengthwise) ridges. They have great crosswise stretch. They are usually used for waistbands, neckbands, and cuffs rather than for whole garments.

Sweater knits are very stretchy and are usually loosely knitted. They have large denier yarns to resemble hand knitting. Textured knits are made from filament yarns that have been permanently crimped, coiled, curled, or looped.

Other patterns are created by changing the placement of smooth and bumpy stitches. Sometimes stitches are dropped, added, alternated, or crossed. A Jacquard knitting machine makes complex designs and textures. Tremendous pattern variety can be achieved with combinations of these stitches.

Warp knits are made only on flat knitting machines. Many yarns and needles are used to produce them. Interlocking loops are formed in the lengthwise direction, a whole row at a time. Each yarn is controlled by its own needle and follows a zigzag course.

Warp knits are stable, durable, and relatively run-proof. They can be produced fast, inexpensively, and in great quantity. Most warp knits are lightweight and tightly knit. They stretch only in the crosswise direction. In yard goods form, warp knits can be recognized by their straight selvage edges.

Tricot is the most familiar warp knit. It is used for drapable or clingy dresses, shirts, and lingerie. It does not run or ravel, but raw, cut edges have a tendency to curl.

Raschel knits are made on the raschel knitting machine. This machine makes all kinds of fabrics from heavy, crochet-like knits to sheer net or lace effects. It knits stripes, checks, and diagonal patterns. Raschel knits can be made of every possible fiber, and they usually have a lot of texture. They often have limited stretch.

Fabrics from Other Construction Methods

Although weaving and knitting are the most popular ways of constructing fabrics, yard goods can also be produced by several other methods.

Nonwovens

Nonwoven fabrics are made directly from fibers rather than from yarns. The fabrics are made from a compact web of parallel, cross-laid, or randomly dispersed fibers. The fibers are held together in a web (or sheet) through a combination of moisture, heat, chemicals, rubbing, needle punching, and/or pressure. Sometimes a chemical binder is added as a glue-like substance. Manufactured fibers can be melted together. Also, a few nonwoven fabrics are produced by machines that mechanically tangle the fibers into a mat. They are used for padding and as *batting* in quilting.

Nonwovens have no grain line and limited stretch. Their edges do not ravel. They are relatively inexpensive. Many are used for industrial and medical purposes. They are often disposable. Others are used in garment *interfacings*. Interfacings are placed inside certain parts of garments, such as collars and cuffs, to give strength and support.

Felt is a type of nonwoven fabric. Wool fibers are used to make some felt fabrics. Wool is the only fiber that *felts* naturally. When a combination of heat, moisture, chemicals, and pressure are applied, the scales of the wool fibers interlock and mat together. Cotton, rayon, and other fibers are also used in felts.

Felt fabrics are thick and somewhat stiff. They are not as strong as woven or knitted fabrics, but they can be molded into shapes. They are often used for hats and craft projects.

Vinyl and urethane *films* are thin, nonwoven sheets that are not made from fibers. However, they can be finished to look like leather or woven fabrics. Often films are used as coatings on other fabrics. The coated fabrics are used for raincoats, umbrellas, purses, shoes, and household textiles, such as tablecloths.

Artificial suedes, such as Ultrasuede® and Facile®, are nonwoven fabrics composed of polyurethane with fine fibers of polyester. When they are made into garments, raw-cut edges can be left exposed like real suede or leather, since they do not ravel or fray. Also, they can be stamped, embossed, painted, or perforated for unique textures.

Some nonwovens are *needle punched* to hold their fibers tangled together. Needle punching creates a mechanical interlocking of fibers with a needle loom, as shown in **9-21**. Small holes, regularly placed, are evident in the fabric.

Bonded Fabrics

Bonding is a method of permanently fastening (laminating) together two layers of fabric in some way. A chemical adhesive may be used, or the layers may be fused with a web of fibers that melts when heat is applied. Bonding provides stability, strength, body, or opacity. One layer of fabric may serve as a lining to eliminate the need for a separate lining in the garment.

The layers of bonded fabrics may be similar or different. For instance, two knitted fabrics or two woven ones may be fastened together, or a knitted fabric may be bonded to a woven or lace fabric. Sometimes a layer of foam is attached to a layer of fabric to add warmth. Other times, a stable fabric is bonded to a knit to limit stretch.

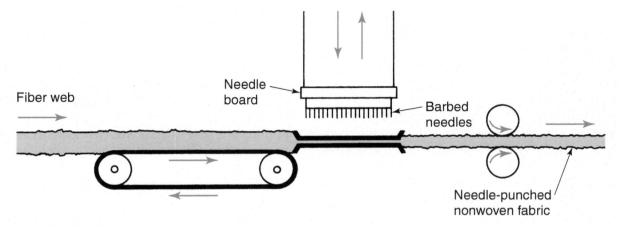

Fiber web

Needle board

Barbed needles

Needle-punched nonwoven fabric

9-21 A needle-punching loom punches needles into the fiber web and then withdraws, leaving the fibers entangled as a nonwoven fabric.

Tricot knit is often used as a backing fabric. It is inexpensive and allows some stretch. A bonded fabric is shown in **9-22**.

Bonded fabrics wrinkle less and have more body than single fabrics. They do not fray or ravel. They are easy to sew and do not need to be lined. They are warm without being heavy. They are often used for skiwear and winter coats.

9-22 This bonded fabric, made for skiwear, is warm, stretchable, and colorfast. The different outer and inner layers of the fabric can be seen in the upper-right corner.

BASF Corporation, Fibers Division

Fusible web, another type of bonded fabric, is sold in fabric stores for home use. It is a sheet of binder fibers that can act as an adhesive because its softening point is relatively low. It can fuse two layers of fabric together when it is placed between them and pressed with a heated iron. It is sometimes used for hemming or other garment construction processes. Iron-on patches and interfacings have a fusing substance only on the wrong side. This enables them to stick to other fabrics when applied with a hot iron.

Quilted Fabrics

The construction of *quilted fabrics* consists of a layer of padding (or batting) sandwiched between two layers of yard goods. The three layers are usually held in place by machine stitching around decorative areas or shaped spaces. See **9-23**. Sometimes fabrics are quilted by *pinsonic thermal joining.* This is done by a machine that uses ultrasonic energy to join layers of thermoplastic materials. (*Ultrasonic energy* is sound energy that is higher in frequency than can be heard by the human ear. *Thermoplastic materials* are materials that soften when heated and harden again when cooled.) The ultrasonic vibrations generate localized heat by causing one piece of material to vibrate against the other at an extremely high speed. This results in a series of welds that fuse the materials together in a chosen quilted design.

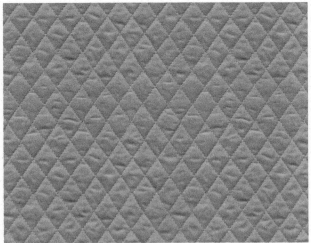

Donna Wells/Shutterstock.com

9-23 Quilted fabrics are usually assembled with two layers of plain-weave fabric—one on the top and the other on the bottom—and a layer of batting between them. A design is made with stitches. Puffy areas show between the stitched lines.

Braided Fabrics

Braided fabrics are made by *braiding*, also called *plaiting*. This is the process of interlacing three or more yarns to form a regular diagonal pattern down the length of the resulting cord. Braided fabrics are usually narrow. They are used for decorative trims and shoelaces. Braids are often joined together to make rugs.

Laces and Nets

Laces and nets are openwork fabrics made by knotting, twisting, or looping yarns. Knots may hold threads together when they cross each other. In other cases, continuous coils of thread loop through each other to form a mesh. Laces and nets can be constructed by hand or machine. They can be fine or coarse.

Fabric Coloring and Printing

Coloring and printing processes for fabrics include bleaching, dyeing, and printing. Sometimes fibers or yarns are dyed before being made into fabrics. However, the largest volumes of fabrics, especially wovens, are bleached and/or dyed after the fabric is produced.

Bleaching

Bleaching is a chemical process that removes any natural color from fibers or fabrics. This is done when pure white yard goods are wanted. Fabrics may be bleached before being dyed or printed to make sure the applied colors are true. This procedure, or a boiling rinse, is needed for some cottons and linens to remove impurities. Such impurities may include sizings, oils, and waxes that may have accumulated during the manufacturing process.

Dyeing

Dyeing is a method of giving color to a fiber, yarn, fabric, or garment. See **9-24**. It is done with coloring agents called *dyes*. Some dyes are from natural sources, such as bark, roots, leaves, flowers, insects, and animals. Others are produced chemically. No one dye is best for every textile fiber. Some dyes that color one type of fiber are useless on others. Dyes are applied according to the type of fiber used and the desired result.

Dyes can create millions of different colors. Computers are programmed to mix specific colors. This technology enables uniformity and saves time.

The term *colorfast* implies that the color in a fabric will not fade or change. Conditions that test colorfastness include laundering, dry cleaning, sunlight, perspiration, and rubbing.

9-24 These nylon yarns were dyed in bright, clear colors while they were in fiber form.

BASF Corporation, Fibers Division

The care label on a garment should state if the product is not colorfast under certain conditions. Colorfastness depends on the chemical makeup of the dye, the fiber content of the textile product, and the method of dyeing. Textiles can be dyed at the fiber, yarn, yard goods (piece), or garment stages.

Fiber Dyeing

Fiber dyeing imparts color to fibers before they are spun into yarns. This allows the mixing of colored yarns for almost unlimited fabric patterns and effects. Natural fibers are said to be *stock dyed*. This means color is added to the loose fibers before spinning. It penetrates the fibers to produce uniform color and provide colorfastness. Manufactured fibers are *solution dyed*, as in **9-25**. Dye is added to the syrupy fiber solution before it is extruded through the spinneret. This results in clear, rich colors with excellent colorfastness, since the dye becomes a structural part of the fibers.

9-25 These freshly extruded acrylic fibers have been solution dyed. The pink dye was part of the solution that came through the spinneret when the fibers were made.

BASF Corporation, Fibers Division

Yarn Dyeing

Yarn dyeing is done by placing spools of yarns into a dye bath, as shown in **9-26**. Yarn dyeing gives good color absorption and an opportunity for fabric designing. The threads of woven stripes, checks, plaids, and Jacquard patterns are yarn dyed before the fabric is made.

Piece Dyeing

Piece dyeing is the most common and least expensive method of coloring textiles. Greige goods are placed in a dye bath before being cut and made into garments. Piece dyeing is a very fast process. The fabric travels at a high speed through the steps of dyeing, setting, rinsing, and drying. Piece dyeing achieves less complete dye penetration than fiber or yarn dyeing does. However, it does allow fabric manufacturers to respond quickly to fashion trends. Large volumes of fabric can be stored undyed. Then, just before the fabric is cut into garment pieces, it can be dyed in the latest fashion colors. Most piece-dyed fabrics result in solid colors.

Cross dyeing is a form of piece dyeing. Two or more fibers with different dyeing properties are combined in a fabric. The dye bath may contain one dye that each fiber takes in a different way or a separate dye for each fiber. Fibers react to the dyes in different ways to create different looks. A single-dyeing operation can dye the background of a woven or knitted fabric one color and the pattern a different color. Simple plaids and checks or two-tone, heathery looks can be produced from cross dyeing.

9-26 Large amounts of yarn are dyed together in baths containing the desired color, which is usually mixed by computer.

Burlington Industries, Inc.

Vat dyeing is used mainly with cellulosic fibers. It is done by the piece-dyeing method. The term *vat* refers to the dyes that are used. The color develops (oxidizes) after the vat dyes are inside (or have combined) with the fiber. Vat-dyed fabrics are very colorfast.

Garment Dyeing

Garment dyeing is becoming more common, enabling garment producers to make fast deliveries of orders to retailers. It can also assure that the colors of separate tops and bottoms match. In garment dyeing, apparel is manufactured in various styles, but with undyed yarns. Garments manufactured as *P.F.D. (prepared for dye)* are preshrunk, or made larger to allow for shrinkage. They are made with fabric, thread, and trimmings that will have identical appearance from dyes to be used. When specific orders are received, the garments are dyed in the requested colors, labeled, and shipped.

Garments can be dyed at home with powdered or liquid dyes that are sold in stores. This can be tricky and may or may not produce the desired results.

Dyeing to Create Designs

Resist dyeing is done to create fabric designs on a very small scale. In this procedure, areas to be colored are left exposed to the dye. Areas that are not to be colored are shielded from the dye. They might be shielded by applying wax, paste, or chemical agents, or by stitching, clamping, or tying in knots. The most common types of resist dyeing are batik and tie dyeing. *Batik* is a form of resist dyeing in which wax is used to cover the area where dye is not wanted. *Tie dyeing* is also resist dyeing. Garments to be dyed are twisted, tied, or knotted, so the tight folds of the fabric form barriers to the dye. This creates patterns on the fabric.

Printing

Printing is a process for adding color, pattern, or design to the surface of fabrics, as shown in **9-27**. This is different from woven or knitted designs that are part of the fabric structure. On printed fabrics, the design can be seen distinctly only on the right side. The wrong side is much lighter. If printed poorly, the design may not be even with the grain of the fabric.

Amnarj Tanongrattana/Shutterstock.com

9-27 This electronically controlled printing bed has been programmed by a computer to do its work.

Printing is most successful on fabrics made of absorbent fibers. The dyes in the print can penetrate deeply into the fibers of the fabric, as for the shirt in **9-28**. If special colors or designs are requested by an apparel manufacturer, huge yardages must be ordered to make production runs profitable for fabric producers. Smaller orders are filled by offshore companies.

Overall prints are the same across all of the fabric. *Border prints*, as in **9-29**, have a design that forms a distinct border, usually along one or both sides of the fabric. *Directional prints* have an up-and-down direction to them. They must be used going the proper direction. *Even*, or

9-28 This rayon camp shirt takes print dyes very well because the fiber is absorbent.

JCPenney

China External Trade Development Council

9-29 Border prints show a definite edge to all four sides of most silk neck scarves. In yard goods, the border might be along selvage edges and across the fabric at intervals.

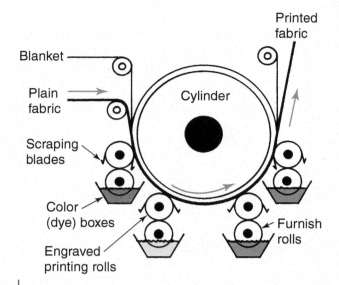

9-30 In roller printing, the fabric moves around a large cylinder. Carefully calculated, small printing rolls put dye onto the fabric in the right amounts and at the right places.

balanced plaids are the same in both the lengthwise and crosswise directions. The design will match if a corner is folded back across the center of any repeat. *Uneven plaids* are different in one or both directions. For instance, they may be different to the right and up than they are to the left and down.

Roller printing and screen printing are the two basic methods of printing. Screen printing is considered to give better quality designs than roller printing.

Roller Printing

Roller printing is sometimes called *direct*, *calender*, or *cylinder printing*. When roller printing is done, color for the design is applied directly to the fabric as it passes between a series of metal rollers. The design to be printed is engraved onto the rollers. A different roller is used for each color. The engraved roller part is full of wet dye paste and transfers the color directly on the fabric. A sharp blade scrapes the paste from the unengraved portion. Machine settings are critical to ensure exact matching in multicolor patterns. A diagram in **9-30** shows how roller printing is done.

Roller printing is a simple, high-speed printing method. It is used to produce large quantities of designs inexpensively. The majority of printed fabrics currently on the market are roller printed. The quality of roller printing depends on the skill of the engraver who etches the design on the roller or designs on a computer. It also depends on the care taken in feeding the fabric through the rollers. Some

roller-printed fabrics are made with more than a dozen separate rollers and colors. When the design is printed off-grain, or the color looks blurred, the print is "out of register".

A variation of roller printing is *discharge printing* (sometimes called *extract printing*). First the fabric is piece dyed a solid color. Then a bleaching paste is applied to the rollers. It removes dye from certain areas, usually resulting in a white design on a colored background, as in **9-31**.

9-31 This fabric was first piece dyed to a blue color. Later, a discharge printing process formed the design by bleaching the dye away from the motif areas.

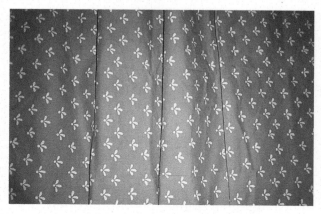

Screen Printing

For many years, screen printing has been an art done by hand on flat screening frames. It is similar to stenciling. Each color requires a separate stretched screen made of a sheer fabric. The background of the screen is painted with a paste or insoluble film to resist the dye. The untreated area of the screen allows the dye to pass through onto the fabric when a squeegee is moved back and forth. Today the screening process is used for printing logos and symbols onto garments. It is also used for very large designs and high-quality apparel prints. It is versatile, but expensive.

Rotary Screen Printing

Rotary screen printing is a mechanized combination of roller and screen printing. It is a fast, modern printing method. The dye is transferred to the fabric through porous, cylinder-shaped, nylon screens. A separate screen is still needed for each color of the design. Each screen has some design areas open and others closed, and screens roll over the fabric separately. Dye is worked through the open sections, printing the design.

Heat Transfer Printing

The *heat transfer printing* method is not used a great deal. In this process, the desired colors and patterns are placed in special ink on special paper. The paper is placed on the fabric and, through the use of heat and pressure, the colors and patterns are transferred from the paper to the fabric. Complicated designs with a good deal of depth and color can be produced. T-shirts are often printed with heat-transfer designs.

Flocking

Flocking prints a glue substance onto the fabric in a pattern. Then small pieces of fluffy material are sprinkled over the fabric. They stick to the glue in the desired pattern to produce designs with texture. Glitter can also be set into the flocking for a sparkle effect.

Block Printing

You may have done *block printing* with cutout blocks in art class. It is mostly used as a hand-craft type of fabric printing. The carved design on the block is inked and then placed onto the fabric.

Ink-Jet Printing

Ink-jet printing is the newest method for printing small lots of fabric more cheaply, with finer detail, and in a wide range of colors. It is similar to ink-jet printing onto paper. Huge, computer-driven, ink-jet textile printers have thousands of micronozzles that spit droplets of the basic colors onto fabrics moving through them. This digital printing from a CAD file eliminates the preparation of printing plates, gives flexibility for short runs, and greatly reduces response time to fashion trends. A customer can design an individual pattern on a computer and transmit the design electronically. The fabric, of chosen fiber content, is then printed in exactly the amount needed. Prints can be designed for the shape of specific garment pieces. Flat, finished garments can even be printed this way. Experimentation is also being done with photocopying machine technology.

Fabric Finishes

Finishes improve the appearance, feel, and/or performance of textiles. In general, finishing refers to any of the processes through which fibers, yarns, and fabrics are passed in preparation for their end uses. Finishes have a great influence on how the final textile products, or garments, will perform.

Finishes are applied mechanically or chemically to textiles to make them more acceptable. Less desirable characteristics of fibers can often be controlled by special finishes. However, finishes cannot improve the basic quality of fabrics. That depends on the quality of the fibers, yarns, and method of construction.

Unfinished cloth may be finished at the mill. It may also be sent to different types of finishing plants to undergo a variety of finishing processes. These processes impart texture, ease of care, and other characteristics. Only after finishing is the fabric ready for sale to apparel manufacturers, fabric retailers, or other end-use producers.

Most textile finishes are *permanent*. They last the life of the garment. Some are *durable*. They last through several launderings or dry cleanings, but they lose their effectiveness over a period of time. A *temporary* finish lasts until the fabric is washed or dry-cleaned. Starch is usually temporary. A *renewable* finish is temporary but can be replaced or reapplied. Some stain- or water-resistant finishes, often sprayed on such items as trench coats and upholstery fabrics, are renewable.

A term that ends in *proof*, such as *waterproof*, means complete protection. A term with *resistant* or *repellent*, such as *water-repellent*, means that the finish provides partial protection.

A combination of fabric construction and finishing creates the hand of a fabric. Hand is the way fabric feels to the touch. Characteristics such as drapability, thickness, softness, firmness, crispness, elasticity, and resiliency can be judged by feeling a fabric carefully. The hand of a fabric can determine how appropriate it is for a certain type of garment or end use.

Nanotechnology has become important in the development of fiber properties and fabric finishes. *Nanotechnology* is the altering of materials atom by atom, such as at the tiny molecular level of chemicals. Nanotechnology is used in the development of new materials and the addition of new properties to already existing ones. New physical, chemical, and biological properties can emerge in materials at the nanoscale. This enables the development of textiles with stain- and germ-fighting properties. Using nanotechnology, scientists have developed fabrics that repel insects without pesticides, absorb and neutralize harmful airborne chemicals, hold color without the use of dyes, and store energy.

The great many finishes used on fabrics today fall into two main categories: mechanical finishes and chemical finishes. Fabrics can receive finishes from one or both categories, in addition to being colored and printed.

Mechanical Finishes

Mechanical finishes affect the size and appearance of fabrics. They alter such factors as the amount of surface fiber and fabric thickness. They can give the fabric surface a smooth and flat look, or a napped or flocked texture. They are done by mechanical, rather than chemical, methods.

Drying and Stretching

After being made, cloth is usually given its correct width and length by drying and stretching, as in **9-32**. This is called *heat setting* when applied to manufactured fibers, *crabbing* when applied to wools, and *tentering* for other fabrics. Drying and stretching gives the fabric its final shape by passing it through heat and sometimes moisture while it is in a stretched condition.

Compressive Shrinking

Trademarked as *Sanforized®*, *compressive shrinking* is a process of permanent shrinkage control for fabrics made of cellulosic fibers. This assures consumers that the product will shrink less than 1 percent in final use. The fabric is compressed lengthwise and crosswise while it is in a damp and softened state.

Preshrinking is done with heat and moisture. Garments labeled preshrunk will not shrink more than 3 percent in either direction.

Fulling shrinks some wool fabrics lengthwise and widthwise under carefully controlled conditions. It makes the fabrics stronger and gives them body by tightening the weave. *Sponging* of wool fabrics also shrinks them, so they will not get smaller with dry cleaning. The fabric is dampened to allow the fibers to relax. The fabric is then dried. These procedures add to the price of quality woolens and worsteds.

Calendering

Calendering presses the surface of fabrics flat with heat and pressure. The fabric is passed

9-32 Large, fabric-drying equipment is used to straighten fabrics after they have been produced.

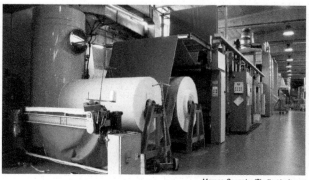

between heated cylinders or rollers. This gives the fabric a lustrous, smooth, polished surface.

Calendering can also *emboss* the fabric, which gives a permanent raised and indented design. For embossing, the heated rollers have engraved sections that form the design. Calendering can also produce a watermark, or *moiré*, pattern on fabrics.

Rubbing is a friction caused by passing fabric between calender rolls that are revolving at different speeds. The side of the fabric against the faster roll results in a soft surface, such as in polished cottons.

Singeing

Singeing is passing the cloth over a series of gas jets, a flame, or heated copper plates to singe off any protruding fibers. This gives a smooth, uniform surface. When done to worsted fabrics, it gives them their characteristic hard finish.

Cutting

Cutting is done for some napped fabrics, such as corduroy, to create a cut pile. The ribs of floating filling yarns are cut down the center with razor-sharp cutting discs. This cutting exposes the yarn ends and makes them stand up.

Brushing

The *brushing* process, sometimes called *napping*, raises the fabric surface by pulling up fiber ends. It tends to hide the weave. The fabric is swept mechanically with stiff, metal-bristled brushes. This removes loose fibers, threads, and lint from the surface of the fabric. More importantly, it pulls up low-twist, spun yarn fibers from the fabric surface. This produces a soft, fuzzy, napped finish. Flannel fabrics have brushed finishes.

Shearing

Shearing, as shown in **9-33**, trims any fiber or yarn ends that are sticking out from the fabric. If done close to the fabric surface, it causes the weave to become more distinct. If done after the surface nap has been raised on a cloth, it gives the pile a uniform length much like mowing a lawn.

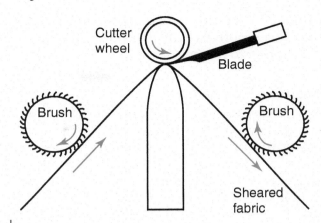

9-33 For shearing, revolving brushes raise fiber or yarn ends, so the sharp blade can trim the surface for the desired appearance.

Pressing

The *pressing* procedure places the fabric between heavy, electrically heated plates or cylinders. The hot plates press the cloth, with steam if necessary.

Beetling

In *beetling*, linen or cotton fabric is pounded to give a flat effect. It gives a harder surface with increased sheen.

Chemical Finishes

Chemical finishes generally affect fabric performance. They enable fabrics to better serve their intended purposes. The finishing agents become part of the fabrics through chemical reactions with the fibers. Some finishes for manufactured fibers are designed to lessen their plastic feeling by making them more absorbent and softer to the touch. Some fabrics are now manufactured dual-sided. They are absorbent on the inside, but repel soil and stains on the outside.

Antistatic

An *antistatic* finish prevents the buildup of static electricity, so garments will not cling to the body of the wearer.

Crease Resistance

With *crease resistance*, some fabrics, especially cottons, rayons, and linens, are baked with a resin that helps them resist and recover from wrinkles. However, the fabrics become weaker and less absorbent with the finish. Stains are also harder to remove.

Flame Resistance

A *flame-resistant* finish prevents fabric from supporting or spreading a flame. The fabric is self-extinguishing when removed from the source of the flame, but it is not fireproof. As the fabric burns, the finish cuts off the oxygen supply or changes the chemical makeup of the fibers. The Flammable Fabrics Act sets standards for the flammability of household items and clothing, especially for children's sleepwear. See **9-34**. The finish must withstand laundering. Flame-retardant fibers, such as wool, aramid, modacrylic, and polybenzimidazole fibers, do not need this finish.

Mercerization

Mercerization is a caustic soda treatment used on cellulosic textiles, such as cotton, linen, and rayon. It is also used on cotton thread. It increases the luster, strength, absorbency, and dyeability of the fibers.

Micro-Encapsulation

The *micro-encapsulation* process, used to develop performance textiles, can modify fibers as well as apply a finish. It can surround tiny (core) fibers with a uniform coating, resulting in useful properties. Micro-encapsulation finishes on textiles are used to impart desirable properties that may be difficult to apply using other finishing methods. Examples are moisturizing products for the skin, mosquito repellent, and aromatherapy. These finishes often last for several washes before the coating is gone from the core. A glossary of many popular apparent fabrics is provided to aid you in your study of textiles.

Mildew Resistance

For *mildew resistance*, a metallic chemical is applied to fabrics to prevent mildew from forming.

Moth Resistance

A *moth-resistant* finish discourages moths and carpet beetles from attacking wool fibers. The moth-resistant chemicals can be added to the dye bath.

Permanent Press

Permanent press is sometimes called *durable press*. A *resin* is applied to polyester/cellulosic blends and other fabrics. It is heat-set onto the fabric. This finish helps the fabric retain its original shape and resist wrinkling. It also retains creases or pleats that have been heat-set in manufacturing. Ironing should not be necessary if care instructions are strictly followed, such as removing the garment from the dryer when still tumbling, and hanging it on a hanger. Sometimes stains are difficult to remove from fabrics with this finish. Some wrinkle-free fabrics are made of yarns that wrap cotton fibers around a polyester core rather than using a baked-on resin.

Shrinkage Control

Dimensional stability, comparable to that obtained by compressive shrinkage, can be gained through the use of special *shrinkage control* chemical finishes.

Sizing

Sizing is a solution of starch or resin used to fill up spaces between yarns. It is applied to fabrics to increase weight, body, and luster. It is sometimes added to cheaper fabrics to improve their appearance. This is becoming less popular. It is usually not a permanent finish.

9-34 Children's sleeping garments, such as those shown in this picture, are required by law to have flame-resistant finishes.

iofoto/Shutterstock.com

Glossary of Popular Apparel Fabrics

A

argyle (*arg-ile*). Fabric of diamond design with contrasting, diagonal overstripes. Originally knitted, now also woven or printed.

B

barathea. Fine cloth, originally of silk or wool, with a broken-rib pattern.

barre (*bah-ray*). Knit or woven fabric with crosswise stripes of texture or color.

batiste (*bah-teest*). Sheer, lightweight fabric that has high texture, softness, and fine, plain-weave construction.

Bedford cord. Strong, woven fabric with lengthwise ribs.

Benares (*beh-narh-eez*). Lightweight fabric from India, usually woven with metallic threads.

bengaline (*beng-uh-leen*). Strong fabric with defined, crosswise ribs.

bird's-eye. Has a diamond-shaped weave with a center dot that resembles a bird's eye.

bouclé (*boo-klay*). Fairly thick fabric, woven or knitted, with a rough-looped or nubby surface, usually with a spongy effect.

broadcloth. Closely woven fabric with fine, imbedded ribs. It is made in many weights, fibers, and blends.

brocade. Heavy, luxurious, Jacquard-weave fabric that has an elaborate, raised design, usually of contrasting colored threads.

brocatelle (*bro-kuh-tel*). Brocade-type fabric with blistered or puffed appearance.

buckram. Coarse, stiff, open-weave fabric used for stiffening.

burlap. A coarse, plain-weave fabric made from jute.

butcher linen. Coarse, homespun linen or an imitation made with manufactured fibers.

C

calico. Smooth, plain, closely woven, lightweight, cotton cloth with small-print design.

cambric (*kaym-brik*). Plain-weave fabric with slightly glossy surface.

canvas. Strong, heavyweight, hard-wearing, plain-weave fabric.

cavalry twill. Strong, twilled fabric for uniforms and riding breeches.

hallis (*shal-ee*). Soft, lightweight, plain-weave fabric, often printed with delicate floral, Persian, or necktie effects on a dark background.

chambray (*sham-bray*). Plain-weave, cotton fabric combining colored warp and white filling yarns, usually creating a pastel color.

charmeuse (*shar-moose*). Soft and lightweight silk, cotton, or synthetic satin-weave dress fabric that drapes well.

cheviot (*shev-ee-ut*). Rough-surfaced coating fabric, usually with heavy nap.

chiffon. Dressy, plain-weave fabric that is very light, transparent, and drapable.

China silk. Lightweight silk or manufactured-fiber lining fabric.

chino (*chee-no*). Twilled, cotton fabric made of combed, two-ply yarn, with slight sheen; used for uniforms, sportswear, and hobby clothing.

chintz. Glazed, closely woven, plain-weave, cotton fabric often printed with birds or florals.

ciré (*seer-ay*). Fabric with a smooth, flat, glossy, and slippery surface produced by heat calendering or a wax process.

cloque (*kloh-kay*). Fabric with a raised design.

cord. A strong fabric of heavy wool or cotton-warp yarns and lengthwise ribs, often woven in stripes.

corduroy. Durable, cut-pile fabric with wide or narrow wales formed with extra filling threads that are cut and napped.

covert cloth. Durable, medium-weight fabric of tightly twisted, two-ply yarns; in a twill weave with a finely flecked look.

crash. Coarse fabric with a rough, irregular surface made from thick, uneven yarns.

crepe (*krape*). Fabric with a dull, crinkled surface obtained by chemical treatment, tightly twisted yarns, or novelty weaves.

crepe de chine (*krape duh sheen*). Fine, lustrous, lightweight fabric of silk or manufactured fibers that is made like crepe.

crinoline (*krin-uh-lin*). Stiff, open fabric with heavy sizing applied.

D

damask (*dam-usk*). Firm, heavy, reversible fabric woven in Jacquard designs.

denim. Strong, washable, cotton or blend, jeans fabric in twill weave. The warp yarns are colored, and the filling yarns are white.

dimity (*dim-uh-tee*). Quite sheer, lightweight, cotton fabric with fine, woven stripes, checks, or designs.

dobby (*dah-bee*). Fabric with small figures, such as dots or geometric designs, in the weave. Made on a dobby loom.

doeskin. Fabric of wool or manufactured fibers with a soft, often napped, finish. Also, soft leather from an animal skin.

Donegal (*dohn-eh-gahl*). Woolen, homespun tweed with colorful, woven slubs from uneven yarns.

dotted swiss. Fine, sheer fabric with small dots applied by weaving, flocking, or using a clipped spot loom.

double knit. Weft-knit fabric of double construction.

drill. Firm, sturdy, durable, tightly woven, cotton fabric; used for work clothes, pockets, and khaki or olive drab uniforms.

duck. Heavy, plain-weave fabric that is very durable.

duffel cloth. Thick, heavy, napped coating fabric, usually tan or green.

E

eyelet. Fabric embroidered with openwork patterns.

F

faille (*file*). Dressy fabric of silk or manufactured fibers with flat, crosswise ribs.

fake fur. Slang term for pile fabrics that imitate animal fur.

felt. Compact sheet of matted fibers that are interlocked by a combination of chemicals, heat, moisture, and pressure.

flannel. Soft, plain- or twill-weave cloth with a brushed surface made in many fibers and weights.

fleece. A bulky, knitted or woven fabric used for sweat suits and other soft, warm apparel.

foulard (*fool-ard*). Soft, lightweight, silky, necktie or scarf fabric of plain or twill weave, printed with a small, all-over pattern.

G

gabardine (*gab-ur-deen*). Hard-and-smooth- or soft-and-dull-surfaced, twill-weave fabric of medium to heavy weight.

gauze (*gawz*). Thin, sheer, open-weave fabric.

georgette. Sheer, creped, dressy fabric with good stiffness and body for its weight.

gingham (*ging-um*). Cotton or blended fabric, usually with woven, check design, but sometimes with woven, stripe or plaid.

glen plaid. Squares of small, woven checks alternating with larger checks to simulate a plaid in one or two muted colors and white. Sometimes called a glen check.

granite cloth. Fabric that has pebbled effects like the grainy surface of unpolished granite.

H

Harris Tweed. Soft, flexible, all-wool tweeds handwoven on islands off the coast of Scotland. They are expensive and of high quality.

herringbone (*hair-ing bone*). Fabric with broken, twill weave giving a zigzag effect.

homespun. Heavy, nubby, plain-weave fabric from uneven yarns.

Honan (*hoh-nan*). Silk or manufactured-fiber pongee, with occasional thick-thin effect.

hopsacking. Rough, open fabric with ply-yarn basket weave.

houndstooth. Fabric with medium-sized, broken check that resembles a four-pointed star.

I

illusion. Very fine mesh of silk or nylon used in bridal veils.

insertion. Narrow fabric, often lace, finished on both edges to use as a decorative strip.

intarsia (*inn-tar-see-uh*). Reversible, flat knit with a geometrical, colored design.

interlock. Closely knit, smooth, stretchy, fluid, double-knit fabric; identical on both sides.

J

jersey. Knitted fabric with smooth, dull finish, that is elastic and drapable.

K

kersey (*kur-zee*). Woven fabric with a fine nap, used for overcoats and uniforms.

khaki (*ka-kee*). Fabric of various fibers usually in an earthy tan.

L

lace. Decorated, openwork fabric, often of floral design.

lamé (*lah-may*). Dressy fabric, woven or knitted, with metallic threads.

lawn. Fine, sheer, crisp-finish fabric in a plain weave.

leno (*leen-oh*). Open, lacy, woven fabric with a mesh effect.

loden cloth. Heavy, napped, coating fabric woven from rough, oily wool with natural water repellency and a dull green color.

M

mackinaw. Thick, coarse fabric with some natural water repellency, usually plaid or checked, used for hunting jackets.

madras. Plain-weave, cotton fabric in colored plaids, stripes, or checks, with dyes that run together during washing.

Marseilles (*mahr-say*). Firmly woven, reversible, cotton or blend fabric with raised, geometric designs.

matelassé (*mat-la-say*). Fabric with raised patterns that look quilted or puffed.

matte jersey (*mat jur-zee*). Dull tricot made of fine, crepe yarns.

melton. Thick, heavy, nonlustrous, coating fabric with a nap that is raised straight and then sheared.

mesh. Open fabrics of various construction and fibers.

middy twill. Sturdy, often navy-blue, cotton, twill-weave fabric.

moiré (*mwa-ray*). Fabric, usually taffeta, produced by engraved rollers with a wavy, rippling, watermarked appearance.

momie cloth. Fabric with a crepey, pebbled effect from the weave.

monk's cloth. Heavy, coarse, loosely woven, basket-weave fabric.

moss crepe. Crepe with a moss-like surface.

mousseline (*moo-seh-leen*). Sheer, crisp, evening-wear fabric of different fibers.

muslin (*muhz-lin*). Inexpensive, durable, plain-weave, cotton-type fabric.

N

nacré velvet (*na-kray vel-vit*). Velvet with back of one color and pile of another, giving a changeable appearance.

nainsook (*nayn-sook*). Soft, lightweight, plain-weave, cotton fabric.

net. Open, knotted, sometimes stiff, fabric of various weights.

ninon (*neen-ohn*). Sheer, open-mesh, plain-weave fabric.

O

organdy. Sheer, lightweight, stiff, plain-weave cotton.

organza. Sheer, crisp organdy in silk or manufactured fibers.

ottoman. Fabric of various fibers with wide, horizontal ribs.

outing flannel. Soft, lightweight, cotton fabric; napped on both sides.

oxford cloth. Smooth, shirting fabric of basket weave, often with colored warp and white filling threads.

P

paisley (*payz-lee*). Any fabric with a multicolored cone or scroll-like design.

panne (*pan-ay*). Very lustrous velvet with pile pressed flat in one direction.

paper fabric. Slang for nonwoven fabrics, often disposable.

patchwork. Fabric resulting from joining small, geometric pieces of other fabrics together, or printed to look that way.

peau de soie (*po deh swah*). Soft, closely woven, silk-like fabric with dull sheen; usually used in fancy gowns.

percale (*per-kayl*). Tight, plain-weave, smooth, cotton fabric; finer than muslin.

piqué (*pic-kay*). Medium-weight fabric with raised, lengthwise, woven cords or patterns.

plissé (*plih-say*). Thin, cotton fabric with puckered stripes or pattern in an overall blister effect caused by selective shrinkage.

polished cotton. Cotton fabrics with a shiny surface, from a slight sheen to a high glaze.

pongee (*pon-jee*). Fairly lightweight, plain-weave fabric made from irregular yarns; originally handwoven of silk.

poodle cloth. Loopy or bumpy, knotted-yarn fabric.

poplin. Medium to heavy fabric with a fine, crosswise rib.

power net. Elastic, net fabric that stretches in one or both directions; used mainly for support undergarments.

R

raschel knit (*ra-shel nit*). A type of coarse or open knit; often lace or net.

rep. Woven, slippery fabric with crosswise design or stripe; usually used for neckties.

S

sailcloth. Strong, durable, cotton fabric.

sateen. A satin-weave fabric of cotton with a high-luster finish.

satin. Slippery, lustrous fabric of silk or manufactured fibers with floating surface yarns. The wrong side is dull.

seersucker. Medium-weight, cotton fabric with woven, puckered stripes formed by tight and loose warp yarns.

serge (*surj*). Smooth, twill-weave fabric with a diagonal on both sides.

shantung. Plain-weave fabric of silk or manufactured fibers with a rough, nubbed surface.

sharkskin. Medium- to heavy-weight fabric with a textured, lustrous surface.

suede cloth. Woven or knitted fabric with napped surface that looks like suede leather.

surah (*soir-ah*). Soft, lustrous, silky fabric of fine, twill weave.

T

taffeta. Crisp, smooth, plain-weave fabric used for evening wear and linings. It rustles and has a slight, crosswise rib.

tapestry. Ornamental fabric with slight, looped piles and a pictorial design.

tartan. Cloth, often wool, woven in distinctive, colored plaids of Scottish Highland clans.

tattersall. Checked fabric with two sets of dark lines on a light background.

terry cloth. Absorbent fabric with raised, uncut loops on one or both sides.

Thai silk. Fairly heavy, slubbed, brightly colored, silk fabric made in Thailand.

ticking. Strong fabrics, usually having narrow, woven stripes.

toile (*twahl*). Fabric printed with one-color, fine-line, pictorial designs.

tricot (*tree-koh*). Drapable, warp-knit fabric with fine, vertical wales on the front and crosswise ribs on the back.

tropical suiting. Crisp, lightweight, suiting fabric, often of linen.

tulle (*tool*). A sheer, fine, net fabric.

tussah (*tuss-ah*). Tan fabric woven from silk of wild, uncultivated silkworms.

tweed. Rough-surfaced fabric, often wool, with mixed-color slubs of yarn forming a speckled effect on a somewhat hairy surface.

U

uncut velvet. Velvet with pile left in looped form.

V

velour (*vel-ouhr*). Thick-bodied, close-napped fabric with a velvety look.

velvet. Rich, soft fabric of silk or manufactured fibers, with short, thick pile. Usually woven double, face-to-face, and cut apart on the loom.

velveteen. Fabric with dull, velvety pile, woven singly with full, close-cut, filling yarns; of cotton or manufactured fibers.

voile (*voyl*). Lightweight, sheer, crisp, woven fabric of high-twist yarn.

whipcord. Strong, often twill-weave fabric of various fibers used for uniforms, riding clothes, and hard-working apparel.

woolen. Fabric made of wool fibers, usually somewhat fuzzy, such as wool, flannel, fleece, melton, serge, or tweed.

worsted. Smooth, closely constructed fabric of firm, strong, combed, long-staple, wool yarns. Examples include gabardine, challis, crepe, serge, and sharkskin.

Z

zibeline (*zib-eh-leen*). Heavy, coating fabric with nap pressed in one direction.

Soil Release

A *soil release* finish makes it possible to remove stains. It is often used on polyester or permanent-press fabrics. It helps water-resistant fibers be more absorbent, so detergents can release soil and oily stains from them during laundering.

Stain Resistance

Stain resistance makes fibers less absorbent, so it is easier to lift off or sponge away spills of food, water, and other substances. Protection is given against water-based and oily stains. Some stain-fighting solutions are applied at the nanotechnology (molecular) level, protecting each fiber rather than coating the fabric. This type of finish will not interfere with other fabric features, such as nap or wrinkle-resistance.

Waterproof

Waterproof finishes fill the pores of a fabric, so water cannot pass through it. A rubber or plastic coating is usually used. Waterproofed fabrics are often uncomfortable to wear since air cannot pass through the fabric for circulation or the evaporation of body moisture.

Water-Repellent

A *water-repellent* finish coats fabrics with wax, metals, or resins. It causes fabrics to shed water in normal wear, but it does not make them completely waterproof. It repels water-based stains while remaining porous. It may have to be renewed after laundering.

Summary

There are various methods of making fabric. Weaving interlaces warp and filling yarns at right angles to each other on a loom. Diagonally between the lengthwise and crosswise grains is the bias grain. The plain, twill, and satin weave types have variations for different surface appearances. Variations also include pile fabrics with nap, Jacquard and dobby designs, and leno weaves.

Knitting loops yarns together as wales or courses. Weft knits can be made on circular or flat machines and as single or double knits. Warp knits, made only on flat knitting machines, might be tricot, raschel, or other knits.

Other fabric construction methods include nonwovens, bonded, quilted, and braided fabrics, as well as laces and nets.

Bleaching removes color or impurities from fabrics. Dyeing gives color at the fiber, yarn, piece (yard goods), or garment stages. Printing adds color, pattern, or design to the surface of fabrics by roller printing, screen printing, rotary screen printing, heat transfer printing, flocking, block printing, or ink-jet printing.

Finally, finishes are applied to fabrics. Mechanical finishes affect the size and appearance of fabrics. Chemical finishes affect fabric performance.

Fashion Recall

Write your answers on a separate sheet of paper.

Short Answer: Write the correct answer to each of the following questions.

1. What are the two most common methods of making fabrics?
2. What is the grain of a fabric?
3. Name the three basic weaves.
4. Large and intricate brocade designs are woven on a _____ loom.
5. Name the two methods of knitting fabrics.
6. What procedure permanently fastens together two layers of fabric with an adhesive or with heat?
7. What does the term *colorfast* mean? What conditions test colorfastness?

True/False: Write *true* or *false* for each of the following statements.

8. Weaving yarns closely together results in a strong, dense fabric.
9. Denim is a plain weave fabric.
10. Satin usually has more luster than sateen.
11. Knit fabrics are usually stretchy, flexible, and wrinkle-resistant.
12. Warp knits are made on circular knitting machines.
13. Stock dyeing and solution dyeing are forms of fiber dyeing.
14. Finishes improve the appearance, feel, and/or performance of textiles.
15. Finishes improve the basic quality of fibers, yarns, and fabrics.
16. Brushing is a finishing process that creates nap by pulling up fiber ends on the fabric surface.
17. Mercerization is a finish that increases the luster, strength, absorbency, and dyeability of cellulosic fibers.

Fashion Vocabulary

18. Work with a partner to write the definitions of the *Fashion Terms* on the chapter opening based on your current understanding before reading the chapter. Then, pair up with another pair to discuss your definitions and any discrepancies. Finally, discuss the definitions with the class and ask your instructor for any necessary correction or clarification.

Critical Thinking

19. **Analyze fabric construction** Analyze the various types of fabric construction and determine which would be best for children's playwear. Explain why this type of construction would be best, citing the text and other reliable resources as evidence to support your choice.
20. **Assess colorfastness** What factors could affect the colorfastness of a dye? Explain why knowing this information is important for those who work in the fashion industry and for consumers.
21. **Draw conclusions** Use online resources to research the significance of the Flammable Fabrics Act. What conclusions can you draw about how this act influences the ways in which fabrics are produced? Discuss your conclusions in class.

Core Skills

22. **Writing** Obtain a piece of woven fabric. Label the lengthwise, crosswise, and bias grains. If it has a selvage, compare that to an edge that ravels. Identify the type of weave. Then find a piece of knitted fabric. Identify the wales and courses. Determine the gauge. Identify the kind of knit. Mount the fabrics on paper and write descriptions about them.

23. **Online textile showroom**   Examine the fabrics offered by an online fabric shop or fashion textile showroom. What are the name, address, and website of the business? What types of fabrics does it sell? Who are its customers?

24. **Speaking**   Research one of the finishes described in this chapter. How and where was it invented? On what kinds of textile products is it used? What characteristics does it give to textile products? How is it applied? How durable is it? Give a comprehensive, illustrated oral report to the class.

25. **Fabric presentation**   Choose three of the fabrics listed at the end of the chapter. Visit stores to find clothing made using the fabrics. With permission of store management, photograph five garments for each fabric listed. Using presentation software, give a presentation using the photos and explain why the particular fabric is suitable for each garment.

26. **CTE career readiness practice**   Imagine you work for an employer who manufactures a major line of outdoor sportswear. Suppose your supervisor presents you and your team the following dilemma: locate a woven fabric that is waterproof, lightweight, porous, and durable. Your team assignment is to develop a creative and innovative plan for solving this problem. Use the following process to produce your plan:
    A. Analyze the problem.
    B. Apply past learning and brainstorm possible options.
    C. Gather new information to solve the problem.
    D. Organize data and compare all options.
    E. Choose an option for solving the problem.
    F. Summarize the actions necessary to solve the problem.

Fashion in Action

27. **Portfolio builder**   Collect samples of as many of the fabrics listed in this chapter's glossary as possible. They might be from fabric stores, unsewn textiles at home, or old garments. Mount them along with descriptions of their fabric constructions, color applications, and finishes. Add this to your portfolio for future reference.

28. **Design activity**   To strengthen your understanding about types of woven and knitted fabrics, complete the following activities.
    A. *Weaving samples.* Use thin strips of paper in two different colors to make examples of the plain weave, twill weave, and satin weave. First lay down the warp yarns in one color. Then weave in the filling yarns of the other color. Glue your examples to paper. Label each weave and list fabrics made with it. Try to create interesting combinations of weave designs.
    B. *Knitting samples.* Use a square hand-knitting loom and yarn to create two knitted sample squares—one *purl knit* (crosswise ridges) and one *rib knit* (lengthwise ridges). Follow the guidelines for the loom to create your samples.

Self-Assessment Quiz ↗

Complete the self-assessment quiz online to help practice and expand your knowledge and skills.

Design:
The *Art*
of Apparel

10   The Element of Color

11   More Elements of Design

12   Principles of Design

197

CHAPTER

10

The Element of Color

While studying, look for the activity icon to:

- **practice** key fashion terms with e-flash cards, vocabulary games, and matching activities
- **assess** what you learn by completing self-assessment quizzes

www.g-wlearning.com/clothingandfashion/

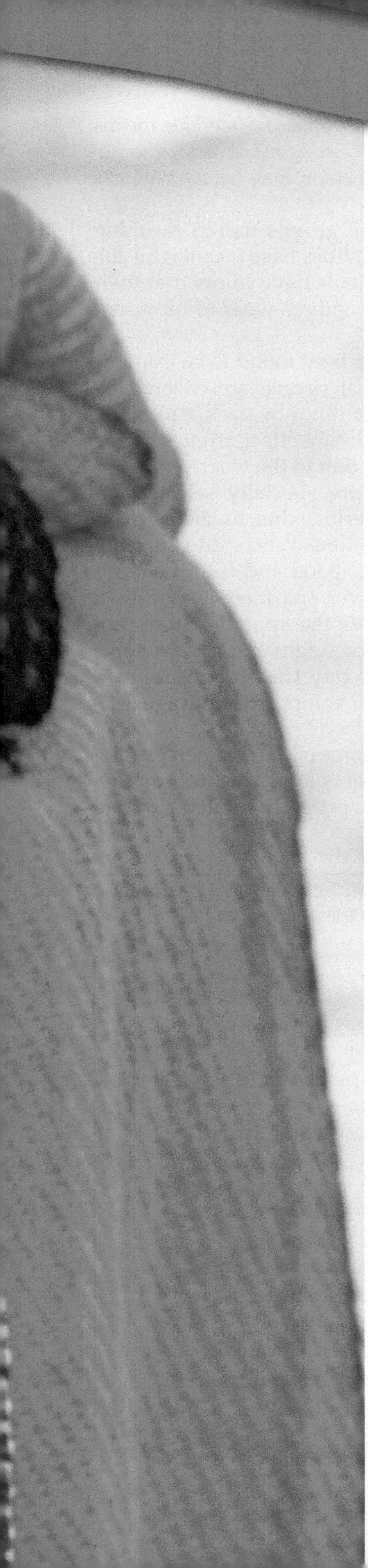

hue
value
tint
shade
intensity
neutrals
color wheel
primary hues
secondary hues

intermediate hues
warm colors
cool colors
color schemes
monochromatic
  color scheme
analogous color
  scheme

complementary color
  scheme
split-complementary
  color scheme
triad color scheme
accented neutral
  color scheme
undertone

Objectives

After studying this chapter, you will be able to
- ➤ identify color as a design element.
- ➤ explain the symbolism and terms related to color.
- ➤ describe how the color wheel can be used to show relationships among colors.
- ➤ discuss how to use color schemes and illusions effectively in apparel.
- ➤ choose clothes in colors that flatter a person's hair, eyes, and skin tone.

The elements of design are color, shape, line, and texture. They are the building blocks of design. They are put together in different ways to form the design of a building, a car, a painting, or a pair of shoes. You can use the elements of design to achieve the best look.

Color as a Design Element

Color is the most exciting design element. It is used and noticed everywhere. Just think how drab the world would be without it.

Color enables people to express themselves. It affects how people feel. It can make clothes seem warm or cool, perky or drab. It can create illusions by making a person look taller or shorter, larger or smaller. It can emphasize or play down personal features. The

elina/Shutterstock.com

best colors for people are the ones that make the most of people's natural looks.

Knowing how to use color is important in achieving a well-dressed appearance. Color is probably the most personal and important aspect of fashion. It is what first catches the eye. It sets the stage. Clothing is usually selected because of its color.

The apparel industries like to stress new colors and color combinations each season, as shown in **10-1**. When colors become popular, designers and promoters give them fashionable names. Examples include royal blue, salmon pink, sunburst yellow, ruby red, lime green, lilac, peach, coral, and rose. The colors, however, are not new. Their new names are used to grab attention and convince people that they *need* to wear these colors to be in fashion. This is a play on emotions. Having a few items in the new, fashionable colors might lift someone's spirits. However, having a whole new wardrobe in the latest fashionable colors is unnecessary.

Symbolism of Color

Some say the colors people wear reveal their personalities. This is true in many cases.

Colors do have definite symbolism. This gives them communication value. Certain colors have come to mean certain things. *Feeling blue* means feeling sad or gloomy. *Seeing red* describes someone who is angry. A person may be described as *green with envy*.

Certain religious groups assign meaning to various colors. Countries have meaningful colors in their flags. Schools have colors that their athletes and band members wear to represent them.

Some colors have been found to be calming. Some stimulate. Most people are cheered by bright, clear colors, but not by dark, dull ones. Colors can have a calming effect, trigger happy feelings, or call attention to the wearer.

Various colors are specially selected for certain building interiors due to their effects on feelings and emotions. When red is used, it can make people feel good and full of energy. Red can indicate power, spark emotion, attract attention, and activate the appetite. Store promotion areas might be bright and cause people to be cheerful and to buy. Classrooms are usually in soft or neutral colors to encourage serious study.

Figure **10-2** lists some of the common psychological associations of colors. This information can help you pick the properly colored clothing

10-2 Studies have shown that humans tend to associate certain traits and emotions with specific colors.

Common Psychological Associations of Colors
Red—Hot, dangerous, angry, passionate, sentimental, exciting, vibrant, aggressive
Orange—Lively, cheerful, joyous, warm, energetic, hopeful, hospitable
Yellow—Bright, sunny, cheerful, warm, prosperous, cowardly, deceitful
Green—Calm, cool, fresh, friendly, pleasant, balanced, restful, lucky, envious, immature
Blue—Peaceful, calm, restful, highly esteemed, serene, tranquil, truthful, cool, formal, spacious, sad, depressed
Violet—Royal, dignified, powerful, rich, dominating, dramatic, mysterious, wise, passionate
White—Innocent, youthful, faithful, pure, peaceful
Black—Mysterious, tragic, serious, sad, gloomy, dignified, silent, old, sophisticated, strong, wise, evil
Gray—modest, sad, old

10-1 New, fashionable colors and color combinations appear in apparel each season.

crystalfoto/Shutterstock.com

to suit the occasion for which it is being worn. In some cultures, people wear black for funerals and white for weddings, baptisms, and confirmations. They might wear orange to a party and blue to visit a friend in the hospital. Color has a great deal of influence in people's lives and in their clothes.

Color Terms

Color has three dimensions or qualities. They are hue, value, and intensity.

Hue is the name given to a color, such as red, yellow, green, or violet. It distinguishes one color from another.

Value is the lightness or darkness of a color. The values of colors range on a gradation scale from almost white to almost black. A tint is made when white is added to the color so it is lighter than the pure hue. Pink is a tint of red. A shade is made when black is added to make a hue darker. Burgundy is a shade of red. Value is summarized in **10-3**. You can often see the value of a color better if you squint your eyes to look at it.

Intensity is the brightness or dullness of a color. Very strong, bright colors are said to have high intensity. Dull, faded, or dusty colors are low in intensity. Intensity can be lowered by mixing a hue with its complement on the color wheel.

Black and white are neutrals. They are really not colors. White reflects all light and thus has

no color. It is the absence of color. Black, on the other hand, absorbs all light and all colors. When white and black paints or dyes are mixed, they become the neutral gray. Beige is also usually considered to be a neutral in apparel since it can be used with almost all colors.

White and black, which are used alone, are also used to lighten or darken colors. Since white reflects light, it feels cooler in hot climates. In summer, most clothing is white or lightly colored, showing that people want to stay cool. Black brings warmth to the wearer. In winter, people tend to wear dark colors that help them feel warm.

The Color Wheel

A color wheel, shown in **10-4**, is a circle that is segmented to show hues and how they can be mixed or used with each other. Use the wheel as a guide to study how to choose and combine colors.

There are three pure, or basic, hues. These primary hues—red, yellow, and blue—cannot be made from any other colors. They need their own pigments, or coloring matter. All other colors can be made by mixing them. The three primary hues are placed equal distances from each other on the color wheel.

The three secondary hues are orange, green, and violet (purple). They are made by mixing equal amounts of two primary hues together. They are found halfway between the primary hues on the color wheel. Orange is made by mixing red and yellow. Green is made from equal amounts of blue and yellow. Violet is a combination of red and blue.

Intermediate hues (sometimes called *tertiary hues*) result when equal amounts of adjoining primary and secondary colors are combined. When naming these hues, it is customary to state the name of the primary hue first. Intermediate colors are blue-violet, blue-green, yellow-green, yellow-orange, red-orange, and red-violet.

The color wheel can be divided into warm and cool sides. Warm colors are red, orange, and yellow. They appear to be hot like the sun, or like fire. Cool colors are green, blue, and violet. They remind us of water or the sky. Orange is the warmest color. Blue is the coolest color.

10-3 The value of a color or hue is changed by adding either white to make a tint or black to make a shade.

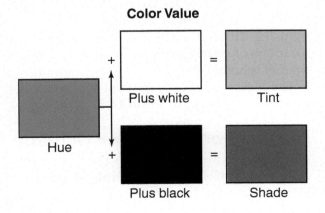

Color Value

Hue + Plus white = Tint

Hue + Plus black = Shade

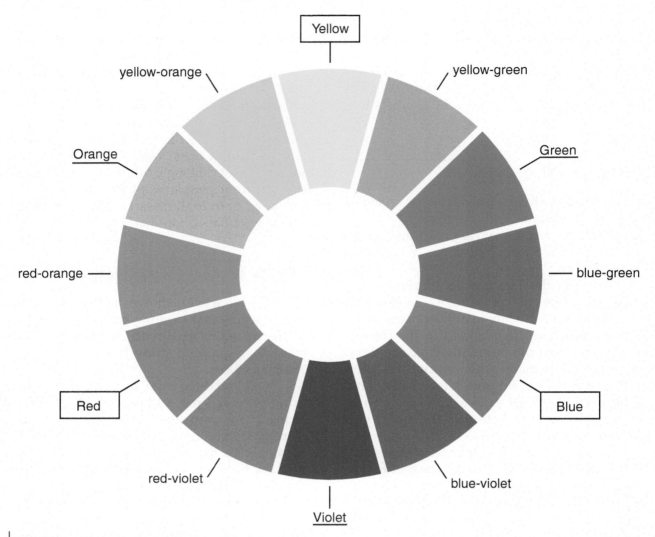

10-4 The color wheel shows how hues are related. The names of the primary hues have boxes around them. The names of the secondary hues are underlined. Intermediate hues have their names written in lowercase (small) letters.

Warm colors convey activity and cheerfulness. They can create an outgoing, lively mood. However, if overdone, they can be too stimulating.

Warm colors appear to advance, or to come toward the observer. They make the body look larger. White and light colors also make objects look larger.

Cool colors give a feeling of quietness and restfulness. They suggest a subdued mood. If overdone, they can be depressing.

Cool colors appear to recede, or to back away, from the observer. They make the body look smaller. Designers often use cool colors for garments in large sizes so the people wearing them look smaller.

Color Schemes

Color schemes are the ways that colors are used together. Different results are achieved by using different combinations of colors. The locations of colors on the color wheel can help predict whether the colors will be harmonious when combined. The following six basic color schemes are diagrammed in **10-5**.

Monochromatic Color Scheme

A monochromatic color scheme is a one-color plan that uses different tints, shades, and intensities of the same hue. It is usually restful to the eyes because of the unity that results from using just one color. A pair of navy slacks with a

Color Schemes

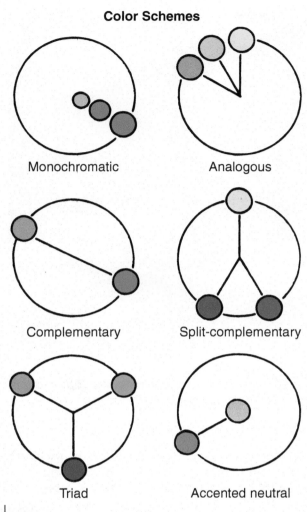

Monochromatic   Analogous

Complementary   Split-complementary

Triad   Accented neutral

10-5 Different hues may be used in these six color schemes, but the relative positions of the hues on the wheel do not change.

Nejron Photo/Shutterstock.com

10-6 This monochromatic outfit not only has different shades of the same violet hue, but also uses different textures to accentuate the color scheme.

pale blue shirt is an example of a monochromatic color scheme. Brown slacks with a beige shirt is also monochromatic. See **10-6**. Neutrals are sometimes added to a monochromatic scheme for contrast and interest.

Analogous Color Scheme

An analogous color scheme uses neighboring, or adjacent, colors on the wheel. It is sometimes called a *related color scheme* since two or three related colors are used. To avoid monotony in clothing, different values and intensities might be used for some contrast. This plan is used when blue and green are put together, or orange and yellow, or pink and violet. The combination of yellow, yellow-green, and green is an analogous scheme with three hues. In

nature, the yellow, orange, and red of autumn is an analogous color scheme. Also, the blue, aqua, and green of sky, water, and grass is analogous.

Complementary Color Scheme

A complementary color scheme uses opposite hues on the color wheel. Complementary colors are across from each other on the wheel. They have great contrast. In fact, the colors look even brighter when they are used side by side. Examples of complementary color combinations are red and green, violet and yellow, and orange and blue, as in **10-7**.

School colors are often of complementary schemes, so uniforms and banners look vivid and exciting. Be careful when considering this plan for daytime clothing. Worn together in full strength, these colors can be jolting. However, when used in tints and shades, they can be sophisticated and pleasing. A soft tint of one is usually attractive with a deep shade of the other. Also, intensities can be dulled, or a large area of one hue and a small amount of the other can be used.

Split-Complementary Color Scheme

A split-complementary color scheme uses three colors. It combines one color with the two colors on the sides of its complement. For

10-7 This complementary color scheme combines orange with blue. These hues are opposite each other on the color wheel.

10-8 These dresses have an accented neutral color scheme. They use hot pink for the accent with black and white.

instance, blue might be used with yellow-orange and red-orange. This is also a bright color scheme, so it should be used with care in apparel.

Triad Color Scheme

A triad color scheme combines three colors equidistant on the wheel. Examples are red, yellow, and blue or violet, green, and orange. This color scheme provides a great deal of contrast. To soften the contrast, pleasing values and intensities might be combined. A large area of one of the colors in a tint or shade might be worn with small amounts of the other two for accents.

Accented Neutral Color Scheme

An accented neutral color scheme combines white, black, gray, or sometimes beige with a bright color accent. An example would be a gray and black striped suit and white shirt with a red necktie or scarf, or the dresses shown in **10-8**.

The accented neutral color plan is pleasing to the eye and very versatile in clothing. The color that looks best on a person can be used for the accent. Depending on the type of outfit, the accent can be placed at the most attractive location, such as near the face, at the shoulders, or around the waist.

Using Colors in Apparel

All colors are beautiful, depending on personal taste. However, if not used wisely or combined well, color can cause apparel to look gaudy or very drab. Harmony results when hues, values, and intensities are combined in a pleasing way. Otherwise a clash might occur, which causes discord.

Opinions about color combinations that are considered harmonious change as fashion changes. It is best for each person to strive for a fashionable image with harmony and variety in the color schemes that are well suited to him or her.

Although fashion often bends the rules, colors in clothing are usually best used according to the following guidelines.

➤ Black is good for formal wear. It suggests sophistication.

➤ Brown is casual, natural, and informal.

➤ Navy looks good on almost everyone. It is good for sportswear or classic styles.

➤ Beige and gray give a professional or tailored image. Both of these neutrals are quiet and unassuming, and they can be accessorized well.

➤ White looks good with all colors. Off-white is better for most people than pure white.

➤ Red, green, and blue have many tints, shades, and intensities that make these hues suitable for almost all occasions.

➤ Yellow is good for casual, fun clothes, but it is not pleasing with every skin tone.

➤ Bright colors are fun for active sportswear or as accents with neutrals.

The Changeability of Colors

Colors appear to change when viewed under different lighting. Additional light makes colors look brighter. Fluorescent and incandescent lights give different effects from those of natural light. Fluorescent light makes colors look bluer. Incandescent light can give a yellow cast and tends to soften or fade some colors. People should try to choose colors that look good on them in the environments where they are worn.

Colors of contrasting value are often exciting when used together. A combination of black and white gives the strongest contrast. Black and yellow is a very distinct, dramatic color combination. Extreme contrast makes colors look brighter.

Using a color with a neutral makes the color appear brighter. Also, white and gray look brighter when placed beside black.

Colors with medium or dark values look even darker when used next to a light area. Light colors appear even lighter next to a dark area, as shown in **10-9**.

Texture, or the roughness or shininess of a material, affects color. The appearance of a hue in a corduroy fabric is different from that of the same hue in satin.

From a distance, the colors in narrow stripes and small plaids will appear blended. Small red and white stripes may look pink from across

Ekaterina Rainbow/Shutterstock.com

10-9 When a plaid skirt is worn with a white top, the contrast is emphasized. The skirt looks even darker, and the top looks whiter and brighter.

the room. This may or may not be favorable. It depends on the desired effect and the colors of the accessories being worn.

Clothing outfits are generally more attractive if they do not have equal areas of light and dark. They might be mostly dark with an accent of light, or the other way around. In most cases, colors in clothes seem better balanced if light ones are used above dark ones.

Creating Illusions with Color

Colors can set a mood of liveliness or quietness. They can create feelings, brighten eyes, or highlight the hair or complexion. The effects they give depend on how light, dark, or strong the colors are. The effects also depend on how the colors are combined with other colors in a total outfit. Think about these factors when choosing the colors for clothing.

Colors can appear to change the size and shape of the person wearing them. To use color to advantage, there are many pointers to be followed. These *color tricks* were used by artists for centuries and apply equally well when choosing clothing colors.

Dark, cool, and dull colors make a form seem smaller. Physical attributes can be diminished by using cool colors, dark shades, and dull intensities. These colors appear to recede and seem to decrease the size of the area where they are used. Slimming colors are black, navy blue, dark blue-violet, charcoal gray, chocolate brown, burgundy, and dull dark green.

Light, warm, and bright colors make a form seem larger. These colors advance and seem to increase the size of the wearer. Such colors are white, yellow, orange, and red.

Certain colors trick the eye into either minimizing or enlarging areas of the body, depending on where they are placed. For example, when a light- or bright-colored shirt is combined with dark, dull pants, the upper part of the body will look larger and the bottom part will look smaller.

Bright colors draw attention. Some people look great in them, but it is usually best to use them in small areas. Since bright colors are eye-catching, they are best used to draw attention to certain areas. For instance, people will notice the face more when there is a brightly colored scarf, tie, or collar positioned near it. See **10-10**.

Bright colors are also more easily remembered. Bright articles of clothing should not be worn as often as more subdued outfits. Less intense colors are easier to combine in outfits and can be worn more often because they are more subtle.

Wearing a one-color outfit lengthens and thins a form. By wearing all close values, the *eye of the beholder* follows an unbroken line. A business suit of all one color is more slenderizing than slacks and a sport coat of different hues or values. See **10-11**.

When combining two colors in an outfit, special care should be taken. Sharply contrasting colors appear to shorten the body by breaking it up into separate parts. This is because the color-contrast line stops the eye from moving along the figure in a vertical direction. Strong contrasts call attention to where the form has been broken. A wide belt or waistband of a sharply contrasting color also has this effect. To shorten a form, an outfit can be broken up with different colors on the top and bottom, or a brightly colored belt can be worn.

To emphasize certain physical features, a small amount of a light or bright color can be used in an advantageous location on an otherwise subdued outfit. White collars are often put at the neckline of dark dresses to draw attention to the face. A light or bright stripe is often put on men's sport shirts to emphasize the chest. The attention is then automatically pulled away from other areas.

In most cases, no more than three major colors should be used in one outfit. It is best to use one color for a large area and another color, or two, for smaller areas. The split-complementary and triad color schemes, described earlier in this chapter, are both three-color schemes.

When choosing colors for clothing, the wearer's personality should be considered. A quiet and shy person may be more comfortable wearing *quiet* hues, such as pale, cool, and neutral colors. Bright colors would overpower a subdued personality. On the other hand, dramatic and vivacious people might enjoy wearing *bolder* colors. Outgoing people tend to wear warm, bright hues, often with striking contrasts.

10-10 A brightly colored neck scarf and jewelry draw attention up to the face.

Dragon Images/Shutterstock.com

Copyright Lilly Pulitzer

10-11 An outfit of all the same color makes the wearer look taller and thinner than an outfit that divides the body with different colors on the top and bottom.

Enhancing Personal Coloring

The proper use of color in a person's clothing will enhance his or her natural personal coloring. People can wear almost any color and look okay. However, they can look *super* in the best colors. When wearing the right colors, people appear brighter and more alert. Skin imperfections are reduced so less makeup is needed, and the skin, eyes, and hair have a healthier glow. With the wrong colors, people look drained and tired. Physical irregularities and skin imperfections are more apparent.

Sometimes the influences of peer pressure and fashion advertising cause people to pick the wrong colors. However, with awareness, the most flattering hues, values, and intensities for apparel can be chosen.

Color Tone

Personal coloring includes the natural color of a person's hair, skin, and eyes. The combination of these features results in a total color tone.

Clothing colors should be chosen to make a person's color tone look as pleasing as possible.

The colors in the skin are most important, because they cover the largest area. They are coordinated by nature with a person's eyes and hair. They always harmonize well together. Changing hair color with dyes or eye color with colored contact lenses can be tricky. A poorly chosen color may look unnatural. It could take away some of a person's inherent good looks.

There are many variations in people's skin tones, but they are basically in one color family–orange. Skin tones may be given different labels, such as *black*, *red brown*, *yellow brown*, *yellow*, *olive*, or *white*. Other labels are *fair*, *medium*, or *dark*. The most important consideration in choosing colors to wear is the warm or cool undertones of the skin.

An **undertone** is a subdued trace of a color seen through another color or modifying the other color. Everyone's skin color has an undertone of either blue or yellow. The easiest way to test for the undertone is to cut out a two-inch circle from a white sheet of paper. When that is placed over the skin of the inner lower arm, the undertone of blue or yellow should show. Compare the test picture arm with others to see the big difference between the cool and warm skin undertones. Warm undertones in the skin have a more yellow cast. Cool undertones are present if the skin looks a bit bluish.

Find the Best Colors

There are books and color consulting services that analyze skin tones. They advise people about what colors are the most flattering for them to wear. This is called *color analysis*. When finished, each individual is given 30 or more color swatches, in fabric or on printed cards. The swatches, or color cards, can be used as guides when shopping for clothes or cosmetics. See **10-12**.

If a professional color analyst is not used, this same method can be done free online. This might seem hard to do objectively but can be worth the effort. To start, type "seasonal color analysis" into a search engine and peruse the choices. Of the many sources available, click on the best website for you. Additionally, if you have lots of pieces of colored fabric, drape them around your neck and shoulders to see which ones look best. Stand in front of a mirror to

10-12 Fabric swatches can be used to show which colors look best. This can help in choosing the most flattering fashions.

analyze the effect of this important experiment. Try to use daylight instead of artificial lighting, if possible.

When draping the fabric, try hues in different values and intensities to find the right ones. Notice the effect of each on your skin tone, hair, and eyes. Have helpers to give you their truthful opinions. Which colors make your hair and eyes look bright and lively? Does your complexion look more yellow or brown or red with some colors? The right colors for you will bring out your best natural coloring. They will hide any drab, sallow tones. Also, you can now help others to find their best colors.

Personal Color Categories

For easy reference, personal coloring types have been put into four main categories with the names of the seasons: winter, spring, summer, and autumn. See these color categories beginning on the next page. These have nothing to do with a person's birth date. They are just helpful titles. The system was developed in the 1930s and '40s and has grown in acceptance ever since. Two seasons have cool (blue) undertones and two have warm (yellow) undertones. There are varied shades of skin, eyes, and hair within each season.

More information and help is now available to help people of various ethnicities, such as Latinos, Asians, Africans, and those from Mediterranean areas, make color choices. For many ethnicities, subcategories of the main color palettes have been developed based on the intensity and degree of tan, olive, or dark skin color. These palettes range from light to dark within each seasonal category.

The largest number of people in the world are of the *winter season* type. Their ancestry is Asian, Indian, Polynesian, South American, African, or Southern European. Their hair is usually dark and may turn gray prematurely. Most have brown eyes. A few have hazel, gray, dark blue, or green eyes. Their skin has a blue (cool) undertone.

Winter people can wear true black or white in their clothing. Clear, true, vivid colors from light to dark make them look good. Any colors with blue undertones are recommended. Dull or dusty colors should be avoided. Silver jewelry looks best.

People in the *spring season* type have heritage from Scandinavia, Britain, and Northern Europe. Their hair is flaxen or strawberry blond to medium or reddish-brown. Most have blue eyes. A few have aqua, golden brown, or green eyes. Their skin has a yellow (warm) undertone. They should wear hues with yellow undertones. Medium to light colors are better than dark shades. Gold jewelry looks best.

People in the *summer season* type also have backgrounds from Scandinavia and Northern Europe. They have rosy, delicate coloring with a blue undertone. They may blush and sunburn easily. Their hair is ash blond, which often darkens with age. Blue eyes are the most common. A few have green, grayish, hazel, or brown eyes. Their skin has cool coloring. They should wear dusty, muted shades with blue or rose undertones. Cool, soft colors are the best. Silver jewelry is most flattering.

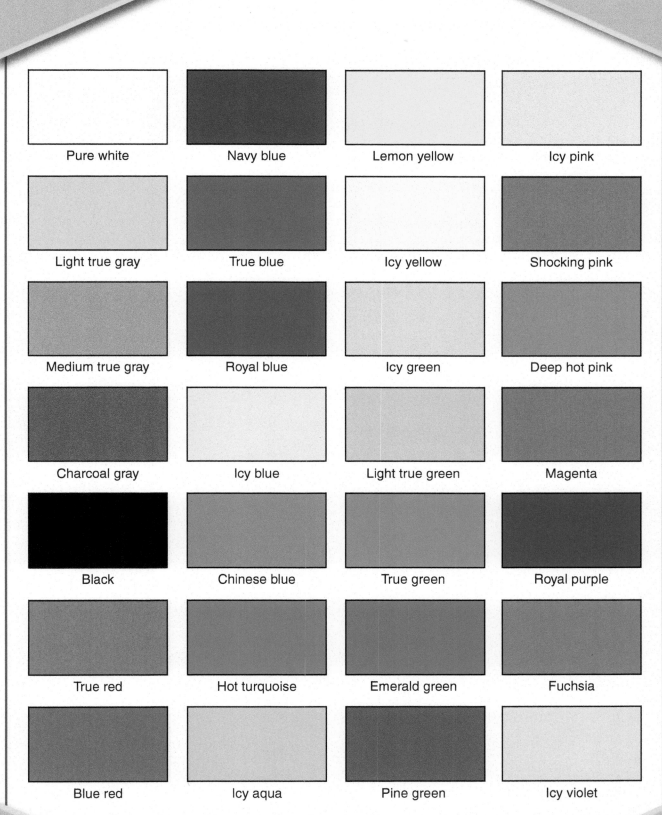

Pure white	Navy blue	Lemon yellow	Icy pink
Light true gray	True blue	Icy yellow	Shocking pink
Medium true gray	Royal blue	Icy green	Deep hot pink
Charcoal gray	Icy blue	Light true green	Magenta
Black	Chinese blue	True green	Royal purple
True red	Hot turquoise	Emerald green	Fuchsia
Blue red	Icy aqua	Pine green	Icy violet

SPRING

Light warm gray	Apricot	Light orange	Medium violet
Ivory	Clear salmon	Light clear gold	Light periwinkle blue
Buff	Bright coral	Bright golden yellow	Dark periwinkle blue
Light warm beige	Warm pastel pink	Pastel yellow-green	Light true blue
Camel	Coral pink	Bright yellow-green	Light clear navy
Golden tan (honey)	Clear bright red	Medium yellow-green	Clear bright aqua
Medium golden brown	Orange-red	Warm turquoise	Light warm aqua

SUMMER

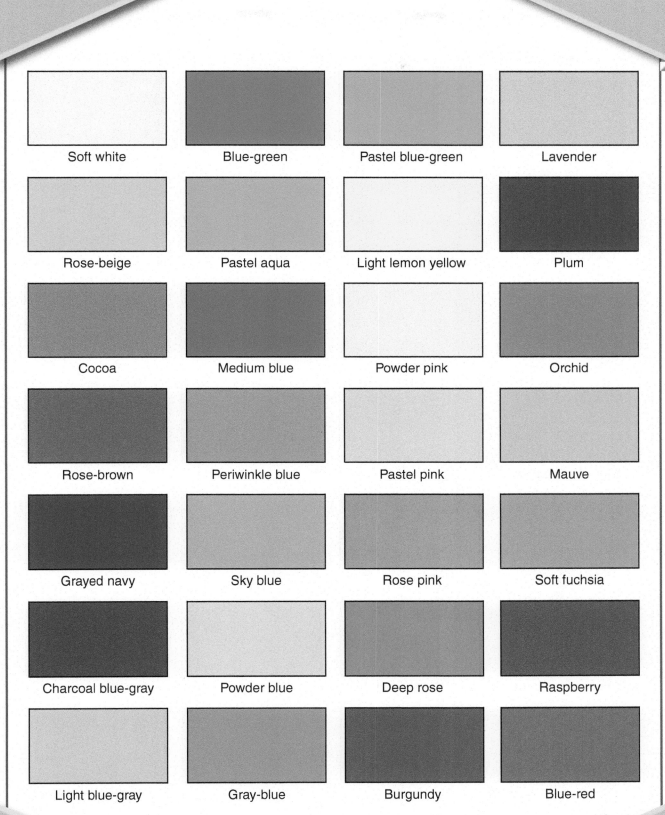

Soft white	Blue-green	Pastel blue-green	Lavender
Rose-beige	Pastel aqua	Light lemon yellow	Plum
Cocoa	Medium blue	Powder pink	Orchid
Rose-brown	Periwinkle blue	Pastel pink	Mauve
Grayed navy	Sky blue	Rose pink	Soft fuchsia
Charcoal blue-gray	Powder blue	Deep rose	Raspberry
Light blue-gray	Gray-blue	Burgundy	Blue-red

AUTUMN

Oyster white	Apricot	Salmon	Deep periwinkle blue
Warm beige	Rust	Orange	Teal blue
Coffee brown	Terra cotta	Orange-red	Turquoise
Dark chocolate brown	Mustard	Dark tomato red	Forest green
Mahogany	Pumpkin	Bright yellow-green	Jade green
Medium warm bronze	Yellow-gold	Lime green	Olive green
Camel	Gold	Moss green	Grayed yellow-green

People in the *autumn season* type are from many diverse backgrounds. Redheaded Irish are typical of this category. People with dark skin tones are autumns if they have a truly golden undertone. Autumns have reddish highlights in hair ranging from blond to dark chestnut brown. Their eyes are usually brown, but some are green, hazel, or blue-green. Their skin may have freckles and yellow undertones. These people should wear strong, but dusty, colors with orange and yellow undertones. Earthy, muted shades such as the colors of wood and metal are good. Yellows, oranges, and browns are accented nicely with gold jewelry.

In summary, the personal coloring categories with blue undertones are winter and summer. These people should wear clothes in cool colors. The categories with yellow undertones are spring and autumn. These people look best in warm colors. Those who wear clear colors the best are winter and spring. Those who look good in dusty, muted colors are summer and autumn.

Wear the Best Colors

A desirable hue in personal coloring may be emphasized by contrasting personal coloring with its complement. This is why many people look so nice wearing blue; it brings out the orange (blue's complement) or brownness in their skin. To intensify a faint pink tinge in the cheeks, use a shade of green in clothing. But don't use green or murky shades if the cheeks are flushed or sallow.

If a person is fond of a color that does not flatter his or her coloring, use it with a becoming hue. Put the flattering color near the face to show off the skin, hair, and eyes. Use the less attractive color in slacks, skirt, or accessories.

For most people, wearing a light color next to the face gives more color to the skin. White and light tints reflect light and make the face appear to have more color.

Dark colors absorb light and tend to drain the skin of color. If a dark value, such as black, is placed directly next to a pale skin, it will drain color away to make the skin look even lighter. That is why light-colored collars are often used on dark shirts or dresses.

It is wise to avoid highly intense colors near the face, except for a small amount. A subdued blue shirt will make blue eyes sparkle, but a bright blue shirt may detract from eye color. Brown eyes are not influenced by color as much as other eye colors.

Sometimes a somber or business occasion calls for a neutral, even if a person prefers to wear a certain color. In this case, look for the favorite color tone in combination with a neutral. If he or she likes blue, try blue-gray. A necktie or pocket handkerchief containing orange will make the gray look even bluer. This is because a color brings out its complement, even in a neutral.

Has this information shown you that the ways color is used in a wardrobe affect a person's appearance? The right combination of colors creates a great look. Keep these pointers in mind. Do not merely reach for the latest fashionable colors. Use this year's colors to maximum advantage, and if any of them do not seem right, reject them. Use only the good ones; next year will bring some more.

Summary

Color is the most exciting design element, especially for fashion. Color has a great deal of symbolism, and it affects feelings and emotions.

Color has hue, value of tints and shades, and intensity. Black, white, gray, and sometimes beige are neutrals. The color wheel shows primary, secondary, and intermediate hue relationships. It has warm and cool sides.

How colors are used together includes monochromatic, analogous, complementary, split-complementary, triad, and accented neutral color schemes. Colors are usually used in apparel according to accepted guidelines. Colors can appear altered under different lighting and in different combinations and textures. Use color to create desired illusions of size, feelings, or attention.

To flatter personal coloring, know if a person's skin undertone is blue or yellow. Find that person's best colors through color analysis. All people can be placed within a winter, spring, summer, or autumn season type that offers attractive apparel color options. Wearing the best colors creates an attractive appearance.

Fashion Recall

Write your answers on a separate sheet of paper.

Short Answer: Write the correct answer to each of the following questions.

1. What are the three dimensions, or qualities, of color?
2. Name the three primary hues.
3. Name the three secondary hues and explain how they are made.
4. Name the six intermediate hues and explain how they are made.
5. Which colors appear to advance, warm colors or cool colors?
6. Everyone's skin color has an undertone of either _____ or _____.
7. The largest number of people in the world are of which personal color season type?

True/False: Write *true* or *false* for each of the following statements.

8. Colors appear to change when viewed under different lights.
9. In outfits with contrasting color values, the light garment will look even lighter, and the dark garment will look even darker.
10. Texture has no effect on color.
11. Clothing outfits are generally more attractive if they have equal areas of light and dark.
12. Dark, cool, and dull colors make a form seem smaller.
13. Wearing light or bright colored pants will make large hips look smaller.
14. A single color for an entire outfit makes a person look thinner and taller.
15. A wide belt or waistband of a sharply contrasting color makes a person look taller.
16. A small amount of a light or bright color can be used to draw attention to a person's best physical features.
17. In most cases, no more than one major color should be used in an outfit.

Fashion Vocabulary

18. For each of the *Fashion Terms* at the beginning of the chapter, identify a word or group of words describing a quality of the term—an *attribute*. Pair up with a classmate and discuss your list of attributes. Then, discuss your list of attributes with the whole class to increase understanding.

Critical Thinking

19. **Infer assumptions** What is the significance of color in design? What assumptions can you infer about how color trends affect fashion? Discuss your assumptions in class.
20. **Analyze symbolism** Choose three colors and describe what they symbolize to you. Then, use the text and online resources to investigate and analyze the symbolism of these colors to people in other cultures. What are the similarities and differences?
21. **Draw conclusions** Based on your hair, eyes, and skin tone, which colors are flattering to you? Use the text and other reliable resources to cite evidence for your conclusions.
22. **Analyze color schemes** Use current online or print fashion magazines to analyze color schemes used in the fashions. Which color schemes appear to be most popular in this season's fashions? Which hues are used in these schemes? Use a school-approved digital poster application to create a digital poster highlighting your findings. Upload your poster to the class website for peer review.

Core Skills

23. **Writing**   Make a list of several fashionable names for the 12 hues of the color wheel. Use names that would impact people's emotions and make them feel good about wearing clothes of those colors. Locate pictures of clothing online that illustrate your descriptive names for colors. Then, use a school-approved web application to create a digital poster illustrating your descriptions and upload your poster to the class website for peer and instructor review.

24. **Research and writing**   Conduct research about one of the main subjects of this chapter as it relates to fashion. Write an essay about that aspect of the element of color. Cite evidence to support your statements. Create a bibliography of your information sources and include it in your report.

25. **Writing**   Determine the personal color season for someone you know (perhaps yourself). Write a description of the hues, values, and intensities that are the best choices for this person's clothing. Describe how these colors can best be used for this person. Put together a guide for this person's use in future dressing and shopping.

26. **Research and writing**   Locate and view video of a recent fashion show. Fashion magazines often post these videos on their websites, or they can be downloaded as podcasts. Imagine you are a fashion reporter covering the event. Write a short news story about the use of color in clothing on the runway that could be used in a podcast.

27. **Research and speaking**   Color, or visible light, is part of something scientists call the *electromagnetic spectrum*. Investigate more about the spectrum and visible light by visiting the website of the National Aeronautics and Space Administration (NASA). Create an illustrated report based on your findings to present to the class.

28. **CTE career readiness practice**   Presume you write a fashion column for a regional online newspaper. For your latest assignment and based on reader requests, your managing editor wants to write an article about ways to use color illusion when choosing clothing to enhance a person's best features. Research illusions with color and write your column in about 500 words.

Fashion in Action

29. **Portfolio builder**   Illustrate each of the six different color schemes for clothing described in this chapter. From magazines, catalogs, or websites, cut out or print a picture to show each. Mount the pictures in a booklet with a color scheme title for each. Add the booklet to your portfolio. As an alternative, use a school-approved application to create a digital poster illustrating the six color schemes and save the poster in your digital portfolio.

30. **Design activity**   Using white poster board and tempera or watercolor paint, make a color wheel of 12 hues using only the primary hues of *blue*, *red*, and *yellow*. Make a value scale of tints to shades for one of the hues. Show a gradual dulling of the intensity of a different hue by adding varying amounts of its complementary color. Label your work.

Self-Assessment Quiz ↗

Complete the self-assessment quiz online to help practice and expand your knowledge and skills.

More Elements
of Design

While studying, look for the activity icon to:

- **practice** key fashion terms with e-flash cards, vocabulary games, and matching activities
- **assess** what you learn by completing self-assessment quizzes

G-WLEARNING.com

www.g-wlearning.com/clothingandfashion/

shape	diagonal lines	texture
line	structural lines	structural texture
vertical lines	decorative lines	added visual texture
horizontal lines	optical illusion	motif

Objectives

After studying this chapter, you will be able to
- ➤ describe the effect that clothing shape has on appearance.
- ➤ list line types, directions, and applications.
- ➤ explain how to use lines to the best advantage in garments to enhance the appearance of body shapes.
- ➤ discuss texture and how to use it effectively to improve appearance through clothing.

All four *elements of design*—color, shape, line, and texture—contribute to the overall design of a garment. A garment of good design is pleasing to the eye. It makes the wearer look his or her best. It has a good combination of design elements.

Fashion designers combine the elements of design in different ways to produce various garment styles. Architects, painters, landscapers, and others use the same design elements in their artistic endeavors.

By observing and experimenting with design, people can develop skills and good taste. Once people know how to use the elements of design effectively, they can dress themselves and others to look their best.

Shape

The shape of a garment is its form or silhouette. It is the overall outline. It is created by the cut and construction of the garment. The shape of an outfit is the outline when seen from a distance or in a shadow.

Since shape can be seen at a distance, it is noticed early. Thus, it is a major factor in a viewer's first impression of a person. This is why it is important that clothes have a becoming shape. The cut of a jacket, the fit of a shirt, or the fullness of slacks should flatter the figure or physique of the wearer.

Clothes can reveal or disguise the natural body contour. The outer shape of a garment can enhance or hide much of the figure underneath. Some silhouettes draw attention to specific parts of the body. Clothing shapes that are most flattering to a person emphasize his or her good features and hide others, if desired.

Using Shape in Clothing

Full, wide clothing shapes make people look larger. They look best on narrower figures, as in **11-1**. Conversely, trim, compact clothing silhouettes make people appear smaller.

Straight, tubular shapes seem to lengthen a form, as in **11-2**. Tubular shapes add to the appearance of height, while bell or back fullness silhouettes would serve to emphasize width. A straight silhouette also gives the impression of slimness and draws attention away from waistlines. Tubular dresses usually fall straight from shoulder to hem.

Form-fitting clothing reveals all body contours. If clothes are too tight, they can make people look as if they have outgrown their clothes. When choosing clothes, people should decide which silhouettes accentuate features they would like noticed. They might also try to minimize attention to some other areas.

The Shape of Fashion

Shape also reveals whether or not apparel is in fashion at any given time. As discussed in Chapter 2, the three basic silhouettes of clothes throughout history have been tubular, bell, and back fullness. However, many variations of shapes are possible within these main categories.

The shapes of fashion are more prominent in high-style designs than in those for the mass market. Depending on the era, sometimes the fashionable silhouette had big, wide (padded) shoulders and a narrower look at the hips. At other times, the "in" look accentuated height with tall, stand-up collars and longer hem lengths. At

Rasstock/Shutterstock.com

11-1 A full silhouette is best for a slim person who can look good with apparent added width.

other times, the silhouette seemed to be cut by a jacket length below the hips, above the waist, or somewhere in between. The longest lasting fashions have shown the natural contour of the figure to some degree.

Review some of the shapes of previous and present fashions. Decide which ones flatter or disguise various parts of the human body. Then decide which silhouettes you might prefer.

11-2 Straight, slim clothing silhouettes make people look taller and narrower than wide silhouettes.

Facial Shapes

The shape of the face should also be considered to achieve the best look. To determine your facial shape, hold your hair back. Close one eye and trace the reflection of your face in a mirror with the edge of a piece of soap.

The neckline of apparel frames the face. Necklines should complement and flatter facial shapes. Strive for necklines that balance the face's structure. For example, someone with a longer face looks best wearing wide, horizontal neckline designs. Pointed chins appear more pronounced with V-necklines. On the other hand, someone with a rounder face would look attractive wearing a V-neckline. In summary, if someone wants to reinforce or strengthen a facial shape, the neckline should repeat that shape. If a different appearance is desired, the opposite shape should be worn.

Line

Line is a distinct, elongated mark as if drawn by a pencil or pen. Lines have direction, width, and length. The element of line can shorten or lengthen form just like color and shape can.

Eyes follow lines. Lines suggest movement or rhythm when they lead the eyes. Lines lead the eyes up and down, side to side, or around.

Lines both outline form and create outer and inner spaces of garments. They break larger areas into smaller ones and connect parts. Lines can emphasize or create height and de-emphasize or focus attention on certain areas. Use lines to fashion advantage in apparel.

Garment lines can be categorized in three ways: by type, by direction, and by application. All garments contain a combination of lines from each of these categories.

Line Types

The three types of lines are straight, curved, and jagged. These line types are shown in **11-3**.

Straight lines are bold and severe. They suggest dignity, power, and formality. They give steadiness or stability. If over used, they can give a stiff look.

All clothes have some straight lines in them. Pants have straight lines in the seams going down the legs. The bottom of a hemmed skirt forms a straight line.

Curved lines can be rounded and circular, or somewhat flattened out. Circles and curves give a soft appearance, but make spaces look larger than they really are. They increase the size and shape of the figure. Circles are closed lines, so they stop the eye entirely. Somewhat flattened curves are the most flattering to the human shape.

11-3 The three main types of lines are straight, curved, and jagged.

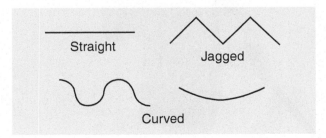

Curved lines are less conservative, formal, and powerful than straight ones. They add interest and smoothness. They give a soft, gentle, youthful, charming, graceful, and flowing feeling. They accent the natural curves of the body.

Curved lines are found in round scoop necklines and along scalloped edges. Fabric prints sometimes contain them. The stronger or more abrupt a curve, the more powerful and moving the feeling it creates. Long, sweeping curves seem smooth and pleasant. Notice the curved lines in **11-4**.

Use curved lines sparingly in apparel. Too many of them used at once can become confusing.

Jagged lines change direction abruptly and with sharp points like zigzags. They are designed into clothing with rickrack, fabric prints, or intentional seaming. A V-neckline and the outer notch of suit collar lapels are mild forms of jagged lines. See **11-5**.

Overused jagged lines can create a jumpy, confused feeling. Use them sparingly, since they are very noticeable. Those who wear clothing with dominantly jagged lines often possess lots of self-confidence. Jagged-line designs are appropriate for fun-loving people to wear at events that do not call for a serious image.

11-4 Curved lines are in the neckline of this dress, as well as the print of the fabric.

StockLite/Shutterstock.com

McCall Pattern Company, Vogue® American Designer/Tracy Reese New York

11-5 This fashionable dress has a zigzag print in the fabric, a V-neckline, and jagged edges on the shoulder ruffles. It creates a dramatic, self-confident look.

Line Directions

Line direction may be vertical, horizontal, or diagonal. Line directions are shown in **11-6**.

Vertical lines are those that go up and down. In clothes, vertical lines lead the eye up and down. They give the impression of added height and slimness. In other words, they can make the body appear taller and thinner. They also give a feeling of dignity, strength, poise, and sophistication.

11-6 Lines can go many different directions in apparel.

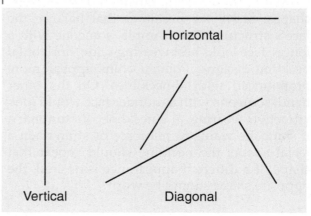

Vertical lines are found along the front line of a shirt, a center back seam, and in princess seam lines. Notice the vertical lines in the shirt pictured in **11-7**. To appear taller and slimmer in an area of the body, use vertical lines there.

Horizontal lines go from side to side like the horizon. In clothes, they move the eye from side to side. They give the impression of less height and more width. In other words, they make the body appear shorter and wider. Also, horizontal lines tend to give a relaxed and calm feeling. They suggest rest and gentleness.

Put horizontal lines across parts of the body where the appearance of width is desired. People who are tall and thin may like clothing with horizontal lines to balance a longer form. When used across the upper body, as in **11-8**, the chest will look wider or bigger. Horizontal lines are found where a belt goes around the waistline and at the bottom edge of a jacket or skirt.

Diagonal lines are slanted. The degree of slant determines their visual effect in clothing. If clothes contain lines with a more vertical slant, they are narrowing. If they have a more horizontal slant, they have a widening effect.

11-7 Strong vertical lines are present in this fabric design, as well as along the sleeve edges and at the shirt center front.

Pressmaster/Shutterstock.com

Alexander Image/Shutterstock.com

11-8 One or more horizontal stripes going across the chest and arms give the illusion of more width in the upper body.

Diagonal lines are versatile and interesting. They are strong and draw attention to the areas where they are used. Diagonals convey action and strength and can make the wearer seem dramatic and/or eccentric.

Diagonal lines are found in V-necklines, along collar lapels, and down the edges of surplice closings. They are seen along the outer edges of flared skirts and trousers that are wide toward the bottom. Stripes on a fabric that is cut on diagonal grain (bias) can be matched at seam lines. This creates angles known as *chevrons*.

Line Applications

Lines are incorporated into clothing in two basic ways. There are structural lines and decorative lines.

Structural lines are formed when parts of the garment are constructed. They are the seams, darts, pleats, tucks, and edges of the garment that were created when it was made. They are the assembly details that also create visual interest. They can look very decorative but are structural, since they are a necessary part of the garment's construction. Structural lines are most noticeable if the fabric of the garment is plain. Also, more of them can be used with a plain fabric.

Decorative lines, or *applied lines*, are created by adding details to the surface of the clothing. They are added simply to decorate the outfit and make it more interesting. They add style and personality.

Decorative lines can be formed with ruffles, braid, fringe, edgings, top-stitching, lace, tabs, flaps, appliqués, or buttons. Decorative lines can also be created with accessories, such as scarves and necklaces.

The decorative lines of an outfit should be in harmony with its structural lines. Decorative lines often accentuate structural lines through repetition or contrast, as in **11-9**. They may accent cuffs, necklines, seams, hemlines, or openings. For instance, a row of top-stitching down the front of a shirtwaist dress emphasizes the long straight structural edge of the dress, adding to the narrowing effect.

Too much detail causes competition between the lines and is confusing. It is not pleasing. The more elaborate the structural and decorative lines are, the more attention is drawn to the body.

Creating Illusions with Lines

As mentioned earlier, garments contain many different lines. The ways lines are combined produce various, predictable effects. They lead the eyes in certain directions. The dominant line catches the gaze first. Skillfully used lines can create various optical illusions. An optical illusion is a visual impression or perceived image that is misleading.

Figure **11-10** shows how lines can play tricks with the eyes. In *A*, the straight lines are the same length. However, the one on the left

11-9 The applied ruffled edge on this dress forms decorative lines that accentuate the structural lines at the seams of the different-colored fabrics.

looks shorter because the diagonal lines added to each end bring the eye back toward the center. The line on the right looks longer because the diagonal lines on each end keep the eye moving.

In *B*, both rectangular boxes are the same size. However, the box on the left looks taller and narrower than the one on the right. The vertical stripe in the left box gives it height and cuts width by making the eye move up and down through its center. The line in the box on the right moves the eye across the horizontal width of the box, which gives the illusion of more width and less height.

In clothing, lines are often combined in designs that appear to form an arrow, or the letters *T*, *I*, or *Y*. These configurations cause certain optical illusions. Look at the examples of corresponding clothing designs in **11-11**. The garments in these examples have only simple drawn lines. However, most real garments have many lines. With study, you will learn to pick out the most important lines in garments and to consider the effects created by those lines.

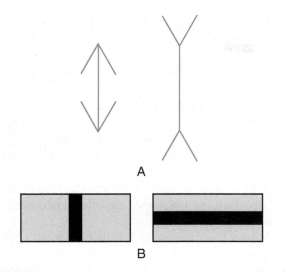

A

B

11-10 These are standard examples of how lines can play tricks, or create illusions, when used in certain ways.

Lines that form an arrow tend to deflect the gaze downward. They appear to reduce the height of a person. Lines that form a *T* also stop the upward movement of the eye. The height is again cut, but more width appears at the top, giving the illusion of broader shoulders. Attention is drawn to the shoulder area, which helps create the illusion of smaller hips.

Lines that form an *I* tend to elongate height between a contained top and bottom. They carry the gaze upward and make the body look somewhat taller and thinner. Lines that form a *Y* keep the gaze moving upward even further. The appearance of more height is given to the body with a raised collar or a V-neckline.

In summary, for a taller, narrower look, select lines that keep the eye moving up the figure without interruption. For a shorter, wider look, choose clothing with horizontal lines, especially where width is desired.

Further Use of Lines in Clothing

Apparent size is affected by how the garment lines divide the figure. To create the illusion of increased height and slimness, choose a narrow overall shape with vertical lines. This can be achieved with a narrow center panel or button placket, vertical trimming, neck-to-hem closing, or princess seam lines. An accented line down the center front, plus vertical princess seam lines, divide the body lengthwise and give a strong vertical feeling.

Lines spaced far apart make the figure look larger. A wide panel, even though it runs vertically in the garment, can make the body appear wider. This is because the viewer's eye hops back and forth across the panel, as in **11-12**.

11-11 The ways lines are used in apparel can create optical illusions.

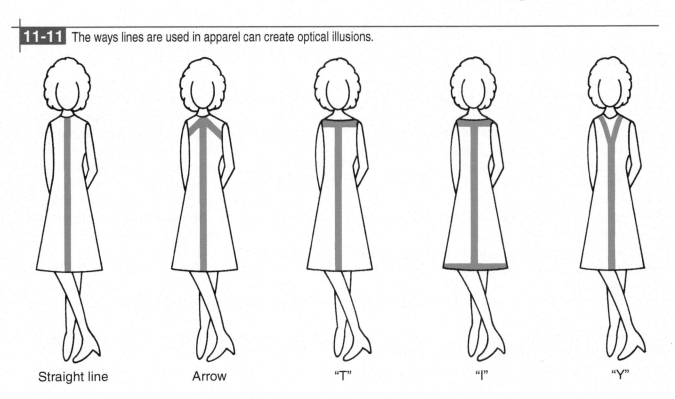

Straight line   Arrow   "T"   "I"   "Y"

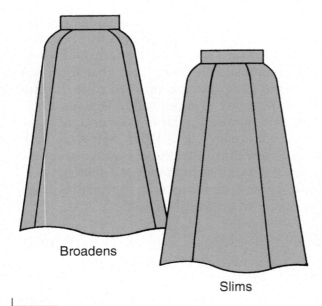

Broadens

Slims

11-12 The skirt shown here with a narrow center panel is more slimming than the one with a wide panel.

When lines are used in a series, the space between them determines what illusion is created. Widely spaced vertical lines create the illusion of width, while narrowly spaced lines produce a narrowing effect. The spaces play tricks by the way the area is divided by the lines. For instance, the wider center front space on a double-breasted jacket is less slimming than just one row of buttons in the center.

The more elaborate or bold the lines of a garment are, the more attention will be drawn to the wearer. Large, bold lines make a person appear larger than he or she actually is. Wide lines are more noticeable and have more widening effect than narrow ones. Large stripes emphasize the area where they are used. They make an individual look bigger, even if they are running up and down the garment.

If lines are all the same width, and evenly spaced, the eye will move the opposite way. The equal lines and spaces cause the eye to move easily from one line to another without stopping. For example, when looking at all equally spaced horizontal lines, the eye will move vertically.

Long, unbroken lines give the feeling of continuity. Broken lines give a spotty effect compared with continuous lines.

V-shaped lines are slenderizing if they are long and narrow. If V-lines are horizontally

flat, they give a widening image. For instance, a wide V-neckline would make the shoulders look broader.

If you want to create the illusion of more body width and less height, use a wide overall shape with horizontal effects added. This can be done with a full garment and uneven horizontal stripes, full or short contrasting sleeves, or pockets or flaps on both sides of the garment. A wide contrasting belt would also give width by forming a line that cuts the body horizontally. Square necklines or wide collars add width, as do yokes.

When lines cross each other, such as at the waistline, hip, or hemline, attention is drawn to that area. A contrast of line direction at the hem of a skirt (possibly created with trim) directs attention to the legs. A mismatched plaid at a seam attracts attention and will make that area look larger. If apparel contains very plain lines, the lines will not be as noticeable, and the attention will go to the face.

Two-piece outfits add width by cutting the body with a horizontal line. The horizontal line gives the greatest shortening and widening effect if it is placed low in the outfit, because the eye is drawn downward. Horizontal lines high on the figure, such as a shoulder yoke or an empire waistline, produce less shortening of the image. For fun, analyze the shirt in **11-13**.

Texture

Texture is the surface quality of goods. Fabric texture is how the fabric's surface feels and looks. It is the quality of roughness or smoothness, dullness or glossiness, or stiffness or softness. Texture is determined by a fabric's fibers, yarns, and method of construction, such as weaving or knitting. Fabric texture is also affected by mechanical and chemical finishes, including any applied designs that are added. Thus, texture may be described as the *character* of the fabric, as in **11-14**.

Some words to describe the texture of fabrics are: rough, smooth, dull, shiny, firm, crisp, fuzzy, bulky, nubby, soft, shaggy, flat, harsh, sheer, loopy, furry, scratchy, pebbly, delicate, sparkling, and fine. Textures can also be described as lightweight, medium-weight, or heavyweight. You can probably think of a few more descriptive

11-13 Discuss the effects of the lines in this shirt, which include a strong vertical center front, a "Y" at the front neckline, a strong horizontal line between the black and white of the fabric, stripes in the fabric, accentuated diagonal collar edges, and decorative tabs.

11-14 Notice the textures of the shiny jacket, fringed bodice, plain woven skirt, and dull hose.

11-15 Notice the smoothness of this jacket, the soft-looking texture of the jeans, and the shininess of the sandals. These are all structural textures.

terms for fabric textures. Tweed is usually rough; silk is most often smooth and glossy.

Structural texture is created when fabrics or garments are manufactured, as shown in **11-15**. Added visual texture is printed onto the surface of fabrics or garments, as shown in **11-16**.

Using Structural Texture in Clothing

Garments made of bulky fabrics that are heavy, fuzzy, or shaggy add visual size when worn. They make a person's shape look bigger and can overpower a small person. However, bulky garments can be used to disguise aspects of the wearer's shape. The main advantage of bulky fabrics is the warmth they provide.

Smooth, flat textures make forms appear smaller. They are suitable for almost all figures and physiques. They can usually de-emphasize some body contours because they hold their own shape. Fabrics such as percale, wool crepe, and soft linen have this texture.

The McCall Pattern Company, McCall's

11-16 The black flowered print on this white dress fabric is an example of added visual texture.

Shiny textures make the body look larger because they reflect light. Shiny textures emphasize body contours. They make fabric colors seem lighter and brighter.

Rough textures have the opposite effect. They tend to subdue the colors of fabrics. This is caused by light hitting their uneven surfaces at different angles.

Sheer fabric also subdues colors because the skin of the wearer is seen through the fabric. Sheer fabric reveals the true body shape. It softens the figure when used over a soft lining.

Dull textures make a person look smaller because they absorb light. They do not have highlights, so heavier body areas look thinner. Dull-textured fabrics in medium weights are almost always flattering.

Clinging, soft textures reveal the body's silhouette and call attention to all contours. They are good for draped designs for people who choose revealing fashion shapes.

Stiff, crisp textures make the total shape look bigger. Since they stand away from the body, contours are de-emphasized. They should not be used in draped styles. Stiff textures require seams and other shape controllers to give form to garments and are good for bell silhouettes.

Textures chosen for various outfits must be suited to the occasions for which they will be worn. They should be appropriate for the garment and for the wearer. Rich and luxurious velvets and brocades are dressy, formal, and dignified. Glossy satin and fine silk are usually for fancy clothes. Heavyweight fabrics are for hard work or for warmth.

Strive for interesting combinations of textures in apparel. Often just one main texture is used, with an accessory providing an accent texture. For instance, a rough tweed coat might have a smooth leather belt. Try not to combine too many textures in one outfit to avoid creating a confusing appeerence.

Harmony is achieved when related textures are used together. Variety and added interest are provided with a combination of unlike textures as long as they do not look too busy together. Medium textures can be easily combined in clothes with heavyweight or lightweight fabrics.

Use texture to advantage. Use a bulky sweater to make small shoulders look bigger. Smooth-textured slacks tend to de-emphasize hips. Combine the knowledge of texture with the best use of color, shape, and line to achieve the optimum look.

Using Added Visual Texture in Clothing

Added visual texture is design that is printed onto the textile surface. The print is the overall pattern created by design motifs. A *motif* is one unit of a design that is usually repeated. Patterned prints applied to the fabric add textural interest. In fact, the applied design is often more noticeable than the structural texture of the fabric.

Added visual texture can affect the apparent size of the wearer just as structural texture does. Added prints can give an overall vertical, horizontal, diagonal, curved, or jagged feeling. If most lines of the added design move in a vertical direction, the body wearing it will look taller. Dominant horizontal lines will shorten the apparent body height. Stand away from the fabric and study the direction its design seems to take.

Added prints can be small, medium, or large. They can be quiet and subtle, or loud and bold. If added designs are large and bold, the structural texture will be secondary.

An added print will diminish the effect of structural and decorative garment design lines. A busy print would diminish the appearance of these lines a great deal. A plain, subdued texture will emphasize apparel design features. The more interesting the texture, the simpler the garment lines should be.

Large, bold patterns emphasize the area where they are used. They increase the apparent size of the wearer. This is compounded if the print has bright colors or sharp color contrasts. Small, subdued, overall prints tend to make a person look smaller, especially if they are in closely related colors.

What is fashionable is always changing. Good structural and added visual textures must be planned and organized in interesting ways, as in **11-17**.

crystalfoto/Shutterstock.com

11-17 Analyze the interesting textures that are combined in this high-fashion outfit.

Line directions can be vertical, horizontal, or diagonal. Line applications are structural and decorative, and these lines should coordinate with each other in garments. The ways lines are combined in outfits can produce predictable effects with optical illusions. The apparent size of the wearer is affected by how apparel lines divide the figure.

Texture, or the surface quality of goods, can be structural or added. Bulky, shiny, and stiff structural textures make people appear larger, while smooth, dull surfaces achieve the opposite effect. Printed motifs or added visual texture can also affect the apparent size of the wearer.

Summary

Besides color, other elements of design are shape, line, and texture. The shape, or silhouette, of a garment can form an outline to enhance or hide body contours. Shape also reveals whether or not apparel is in fashion at any given time. Facial shape should be considered when deciding on necklines and collars.

Lines have direction, width, and length. Line types are straight, curved, and jagged.

Fashion Recall

Write your responses on a separate sheet of paper.

True/False: Write *true* or *false* for each of the following statements.

1. Full, wide clothing shapes make people look slimmer.
2. A tubular shape makes a person look taller.
3. Clothes that are too tight can make people appear to have outgrown their clothing.
4. Someone with a pointed chin would look most attractive wearing a garment with a V-neckline.
5. Straight lines provide a feeling of steadiness or stability.
6. Jagged lines provide a gentle, youthful, and graceful feeling.
7. Vertical lines give a feeling of dignity, strength, poise, and sophistication.
8. Horizontal lines make a person look taller and thinner.
9. Diagonal lines give a feeling of action and strength and can seem dramatic.
10. Structural lines can be formed with ruffles, edgings, top-stitching, lace, tabs, flaps, appliqués, or buttons.
11. Decorative lines are formed by seams, darts, pleats, and tucks.
12. To create the illusion of more height and slimness, choose a narrow overall shape with vertical lines added.
13. Lines spaced far apart make the figure look larger.
14. Two-piece outfits add height by cutting the body with a horizontal line.

Short Answer: Write the correct answer to each of the following questions.

15. Name the four elements of design.

16. Texture is determined by a fabric's _____.
    A. fibers and yarns
    B. method of construction
    C. mechanical and chemical finishes
    D. All of the above.
17. Explain the difference between structural texture and added visual texture.
18. How do bulky fabrics affect the wearer's appearance?
19. How do shiny textures affect the wearer's appearance?
20. How do large, bold patterns affect the wearer's appearance?

Fashion Vocabulary

21. With a partner, create a T-chart. Write each of the *Fashion Terms* from the chapter opening page in the left column. In the right column, write a *synonym* (a word that has the same or similar meaning) for each term. Discuss your synonyms in class.

Critical Thinking

22. **Analyze shape** Analyze the design element *shape* in current fashions. Then, describe the role of shape in the design of today's fashions during class discussion.
23. **Create illusions** When shopping for clothes for yourself, what types of illusions do you like to create with the design element *line* in the garments you select? Write a brief summary describing the design illusions you prefer.
24. **Create harmony** Give an example of how you could use the design element of *texture* to create harmony in an outfit. Use online or print resources to locate an outfit image to support your example.

Core Skills

25. **Speaking** Prepare a speech about which shapes, lines, and textures would be most flattering over the various parts of an imaginary person's body. Describe the person in terms of height and body shape. Include drawings or pictures of at least six garments that would have the best elements of design to enhance this person's features.

26. **Research and writing** Use online or print resources to locate at least five pictures of clothing that show straight, curved, jagged, vertical, horizontal, and diagonal lines. Mount the pictures on paper and write descriptions of the effect of the lines. (As an alternative, use a school-approved web application to create a digital poster of the same.) Identify the lines as structural or decorative.

27. **Technology** Locate websites that show pictures of optical illusions. Use online tools or your school-approved drawing software to create an optical illusion of your own based on the online examples and information in the text. Share your illusion drawing with the class.

28. **Research and speaking** Locate five fabric swatches that exemplify different structural and visual textures. Using a digital camera and presentation software, illustrate and explain each fabric's textural features and how texture would affect the garments made with it.

29. **CTE career readiness practice** Presume you are a fashion consultant for a well-known department store. Your interpersonal skills—your ability to listen, speak, and empathize—are great assets in working with your clients. Your latest client, Elena, is starting a new job and needs help selecting a few key wardrobe pieces for her new job with a design firm. Elena would like her new clothing items to make her look a little taller with more emphasis on her face. As you listen to Elena, some ideas come to mind for her new wardrobe. Describe to Elena what you are thinking in regard to how line, shape, and texture can be used in her new garments to meet her wardrobe goals. Locate images of several mix-and-match items your store offers to give Elena a visual idea of what you are thinking. Then, put together a presentation folder with the images and descriptions for Elena to review before making a final purchasing decision.

Fashion in Action

30. **Portfolio builder** Mount four pictures of garments on paper. Below each picture, analyze the elements of design in the garments. Compare the relationship between outer shape and inner structural and decorative lines. Describe the structural and added visual texture as well as the illusions created by each garment's color, shape, line, and texture. Add this project to your portfolio to demonstrate your understanding of the elements of design. As an alternative, locate digital images of garments and use presentation software to complete this activity as described and save this project in your digital portfolio.

31. **Design activity** Cut out the shape of a garment from the inside of a large piece of cardboard. You will then have cardboard edging around the open silhouette of a shirt, dress, jacket, skirt, or pair of slacks. In front of the class, place it over pieces of fabric with various lines and textures. Include printed motifs. Discuss the effects of the different pieces of fabric on the apparent shape of the garment.

Self-Assessment Quiz ↗

Complete the self-assessment quiz online to help practice and expand your knowledge and skills.

Principles of Design

While studying, look for the activity icon  **to:**

- **practice** key fashion terms with e-flash cards, vocabulary games, and matching activities
- **assess** what you learn by completing self-assessment quizzes

www.g-wlearning.com/clothingandfashion/

G-WLEARNING.com

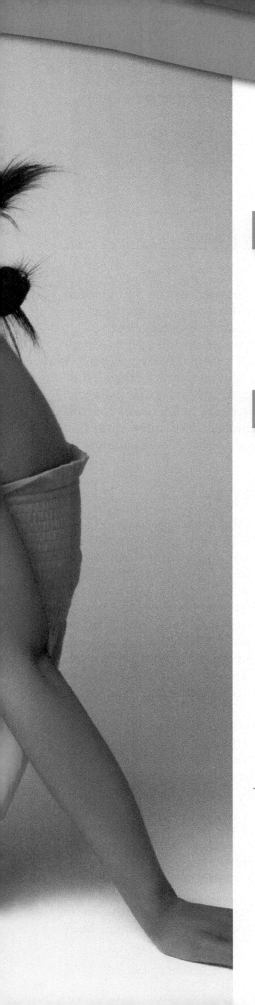

FASHION TERMS ☞

principles of design	proportion	transition
design	emphasis	opposition
balance	rhythm	radial arrangement
formal balance	repetition	harmony
informal balance	gradation	body build

Objectives

After studying this chapter, you will be able to
➤ **name** the four principles of design.
➤ **give** examples of the use of each principle of design.
➤ **explain** how the principles of design can be used to produce harmony in clothing.
➤ **describe** apparel outfits that have the best design for various body shapes.

The **principles of design** are balance, proportion, emphasis, and rhythm. They are guidelines for the use of the elements of design: color, shape, line, and texture. When the elements of design are used effectively, according to the principles of design, the goal of harmony is created. This is true for buildings, paintings, landscapes, interiors, and sculpture, as well as apparel.

Design is the plan, or artistic arrangement, used to put an idea together. The process of designing includes selecting and combining the design elements according to the principles of design in order to achieve harmony. The design process is illustrated in **12-1**.

Balance

Balance, an important principle of design, implies an equilibrium or steadiness among the parts of a design. It involves the distribution of visual weight and is achieved by the way details are grouped. Balance brings overall stability to a design. It produces a feeling of rest or lack of movement.

To achieve proper balance, a garment should have an equal amount of visual weight on each side. The parts, or spaces, of a garment

231

Design

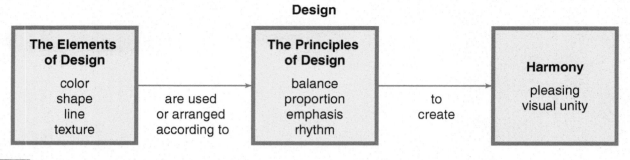

The Elements of Design		The Principles of Design		Harmony
color shape line texture	are used or arranged according to	balance proportion emphasis rhythm	to create	pleasing visual unity

12-1 When the elements of design are used according to the principles of design, harmony is created.

should relate well to each other. If the visual weight of one side is heavier than that of the other, the garment or outfit is out of balance.

A garment's structure, as well as added decoration, creates balance. Balance should also be present in fabric design.

Color plays an important part in achieving balance. Warm and dark colors appear heavier than cool and light colors. A small amount of a bright color balances a large amount of a dull color. A small area of a warm color balances a larger amount of a cool color. Large amounts of tints or neutrals balance smaller areas of shades or bright colors.

Line and texture are also important to achieve harmonious balance. For instance, one long line balances two short ones. One wide stripe balances two thin ones. A larger area of fine or soft texture balances a smaller area of heavy or coarse texture.

Types of Balance

There are two main types of design balance. They are formal and informal balance.

Formal balance is *symmetrical*; both sides are the same to create a centered balance, as in **12-2**. Identical details are arranged the same distance from the center on both the right and left sides. One example would be having the same number of tucks or pleats on each side of a pair of trousers. Another would be similar pockets on both sides of a dress.

Formal balance is the most common type of balance in clothes. It is the simplest and least expensive to produce.

Informal balance is *asymmetrical*; both sides are not the same. The design details are divided unequally from the center. An arrangement of colors, shapes, lines, and textures on one side balances a different arrangement on the other side, as in **12-3**. Informal balance is often achieved with diagonal lines and off-center closings.

The distribution of visual weight should appear balanced in informal balance. One side should not appear heavier than the other. If done properly, the design appears to be balanced, even though the two sides are different. Informal balance is more unusual and interesting than formal balance, and can be quite dramatic.

Proportion

Proportion is the spatial, or size, relationship of all the parts in a design to each other as well as to the whole. Proportion is sometimes called *scale*. The sizes of all the parts of an outfit should be related.

Proportion is determined by the way in which total space is divided and by how the inner lines are arranged. One part of an outfit should not be out of scale with the others. When all the parts work well together, the garment is well proportioned rather than out of proportion.

Proportion is not as pleasing when all areas are exactly equal in size. Unequal parts are more interesting. Also, an odd number of parts is more interesting than an even number. For example, three parts are more interesting than two or four.

Styles that complement the body's natural proportions are pleasing and remain in style longer. Those that make the body appear distorted, or out of proportion, are sometimes popular as fleeting fads.

Garment designs should be relative to the structure and proportion of the human body.

The McCall Pattern Company, Vogue® Patterns, Adri

12-2 This outfit has formal, or symmetrical, balance. If it were folded in half lengthwise, the right side would be the same as the left side.

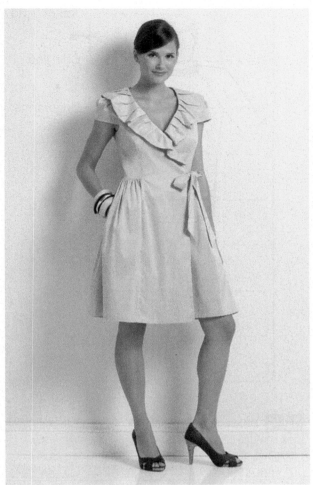

McCall Pattern Company, Butterick Pattern / Suzi CHIN maggy boutique

12-3 This dress has informal balance, with its right and left sides different from each other. The bow on one side balances the larger fabric area on the other side. ✦

Throughout art history, the human body has been drawn as eight heads tall, with ⅜ of that height from the waist to the top of the head and ⅝ from the waist to the soles of the feet, as shown in **12-4**. To coordinate with the actual proportion of the human form, most fashion outfits are divided unequally. For instance, a dress usually has a bodice area smaller than its skirt area.

Proportion in Apparel

When combining garments and accessories in an outfit, the proportion of each variable should be weighed. For instance, consider the length of a jacket in relation to the length of the pants, the length of the whole outfit, and the height of the wearer.

Garment parts, such as yokes, collars, and pockets, must be in proportion to the total design and the wearer. A tiny pocket would look out of proportion on a large, heavy overcoat. The size of details, such as buttons and trimmings, should also be related to the overall size of a garment.

Accessories should be in proportion to the garment and body build of the wearer, too. A large belt would look fine on a tall person, but would be out of proportion on a person with a small frame. Likewise, a tiny purse would look fine if carried by a petite woman, but would look out of proportion if carried by a woman with a large frame.

It is important that the design of the fabric be in proportion to the garment and the wearer. Prints and other textures must be scaled to their

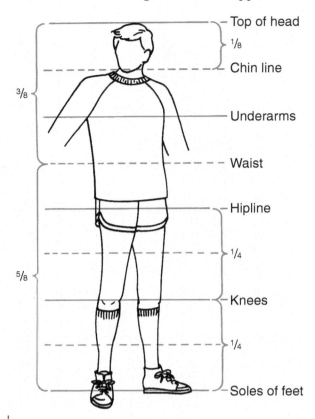

12-4 Historically, the proportions of the human body have been divided into eight sections. Fashions are generally designed, or outfits put together, with a smaller area above the waist and a larger area below the waist.

use. Large prints, plaids, or checks would overpower a small person. On the other hand, a tiny print would become lost on a larger person. The print would be so out of proportion that it would make the wearer appear even larger.

When considering the proportions of an outfit, always use the person's body that is being clothed as your guide. It is most pleasing to divide a garment or outfit at a natural body division such as the chest, waist, or hips.

Emphasis

Emphasis is a concentration of interest in a particular part or area of a design. One part becomes more important or noticeable than all the others, as in **12-5**. The emphasis is the center of attention of an outfit. It is the focal point that first attracts the eye. All other parts of the design are subordinate to the area of emphasis.

Without any center of interest, an outfit looks unplanned and monotonous. It is best to have one main area of emphasis. A secondary emphasis may be included, if carefully chosen. However, too many focal points create a cluttered, confusing design. It is best, for instance, to leave the cuffs, hemline, and other areas of a dress fairly plain if the neckline is being emphasized.

Emphasis can be used in apparel to draw attention to a favorite personal feature. It can also draw the eye away from a feature. Emphasis is most commonly used to call attention to the face. However, it may spotlight the waist, chest, arms, one shoulder, or another area.

Emphasis can be created with contrasts of colors or textures. Light, bright colors and shiny textures attract attention. Structural lines and decorative trimmings, such as an area of tucks, gathers, ruffles, or buttons can provide emphasis. The unusual shape of an area or a contrasting design outline will also attract attention.

12-5 The black bow on this white dress is a point of emphasis and is more noticeable that other parts of the garment.

A center of interest can be achieved with one large item or with a group of small ones. A bow, an appliqué, or a monogram on a contrasting background can create emphasis. Accessories, such as belts, scarves, neckties, or jewelry, can add emphasis to otherwise plain outfits.

Rhythm

The elements of design should be arranged to produce a feeling of continuity or easy movement. That is called rhythm. Rhythm is the pleasing arrangement of the design elements so the eye moves easily over the apparel. Rhythm directs the flow of the eye movement steadily and smoothly through the lines and spaces of the design. The gaze unconsciously moves from one part to another. Rhythm can be created with repetition, gradation, transition, opposition, or radial arrangement.

Repetition repeats lines, shapes, colors, or textures in a garment. This can be done by using the same shaped edges on all parts. These edges might be squared, rounded, or scalloped. Repetition of colors can create good rhythm, especially if the colors are distributed in an interesting way. Rhythm in an outfit can also be achieved by repeating buttons, tucks, pleats, or trim.

Gradation, sometimes called progression, implies a gradual increase or decrease of similar design elements. Colors can go from light to dark, or textures from fine to coarse. Lines may range from thin to thick, and shapes may range from small to large, as in **12-6**. The gradual changes provide continuity while giving a feeling of movement.

Transition is a fluid rhythm created when a curved line leads the eye over an angle. The curved lines of transition cause the eye to change direction gradually rather than abruptly. Transition is found in puff sleeves, cap sleeves, and dropped shoulder designs. Transition can also be achieved by using scarves, shawls, ascots, jabots, ruffles, and gathers.

Opposition is the rhythm created when lines meet to form right angles. Opposition may be found in fabric designs such as checks and plaids. See **12-7**. It is also found in square necklines, square pockets, waistbands, yokes, collars, and cuffs.

Karlova Irina/Shutterstock.com

12-6 The garment's fabric areas start small at the top and become larger at the bottom, producing rhythm through gradation.

Radial arrangement, in which lines emerge from a central point like rays, also produces rhythm. It is created when gathers, tucks, seams, darts, flowing lines, or colors fan out from a central area, as in **12-8**.

Rhythm is broken when lines, trimmings, or fabric designs are not matched at the seams or at other construction points. For instance, it is upsetting to the eye when the lines of plaids, checks, or stripes are broken. If patterns cannot be matched at all seam lines, they should at least be matched at center front and center back.

Harmony

Harmony is pleasing visual unity. It is the tasteful relationship among all parts within a whole. It is created when the elements of design are used effectively according to the design principles.

Iakov Filimonov/Shutterstock.com

12-7 The rhythm of opposition occurs here in the lines of the fabric plaids as well as the horizontal seam across the back at right angles to the vertical lines of the sides of the dress.

Harmony gives the feeling that all the parts of an outfit belong together and suit the wearer and the occasion. The garments and the accessories work together to help the wearer look his or her best. A value judgment, or subjective evaluation, tells people if harmony has been achieved. The person doing the evaluating can be the wearer or someone silently looking at the wearer. Sometimes the assessment about harmony reveals more about the values of the person making the assessment than about the garment or outfit. People generally try to look their best and achieve harmony in their apparel.

The creative use of clothing and accessories is both an art and a science. Through observation and experience, you can learn to use the design elements according to the design principles to achieve harmony in apparel. An outfit is harmonious when it is complementary to the person wearing it.

Create the Best Look

People come in a variety of sizes, shapes, and proportions. Body size is usually measured at the chest, waist, and hips. However, the proportion of the body gives a better indication of shape. This relationship among the different areas of the total human form is called body build. The body build of a female is referred to as her *figure*. The body build of a male is called his *physique*. There is no perfect body shape.

A well-designed garment enhances the attributes of the wearer's body build. By using the elements and principles of design effectively in a wardrobe, anyone's appearance can be enhanced. The rest of this chapter will describe how to attractively dress each particular body build. This information is used by fashion consultants, wardrobe coordinators, and personal shoppers to help clients look their best.

The latest fashions may flatter some people but not everyone. *Personal style* is achieved when design is used to the best advantage. Figures **12-9** and **12-10** summarize ways to utilize design in apparel.

12-8 Rhythm flows through this design in radial arrangement, or from the center outward.

hifashion/Shutterstock.com

Avoiding and Attracting Attention

To Avoid Attention to Areas	To Attract Attention to Areas
Dark, dull colors	Light, bright colors
Cool hues	Warm hues
Minimal structural garment design	Structural accents there
No applied decoration there	Applied decoration there
Flat, dull fabrics	Shiny or textured fabrics
Soft fabrics	Clingy fabrics
Plain, unpatterned fabrics	Large, busy prints

12-9   Use design in clothes to highlight some physical attributes and camouflage others.

12-10   To create body shape illusions with apparel design, follow these suggestions.

Creating Height and Width Illusions

To Look Taller and Thinner	To Look Shorter and Wider
Wear straight silhouettes	Wear wide silhouettes
Use vertical lines	Use horizontal lines
Shape with seams or darts	Shape with gathers or pleats
Use smooth, flat textures	Use bulky, heavy textures
Wear one-color outfits	Contrast colors (top/bottom)
Wear a small, matching belt	Wear wide, contrasting belts
Have fit that skims the body easily	Have tightly fitting clothes
Use dark, dull, cool colors	Use light, bright, warm colors
Wear subtle prints, plaids, etc.	Wear bold prints, plaids, etc.
Create a simple, uncluttered look	Wear full sleeves, wide pants
Use emphasis to lead the eye upward	Use emphasis to lead the eye downward

The Total Design for Individuals

The body has height, width, and depth (thickness). Actual measurements are not as important as total appearance. Clothes can help or hurt that appearance.

In design, the shoulders should be balanced with the chest and hips. Decide what type of a look—taller, shorter, broader, or narrower—is desired for various areas. Decide where and how to use color, shape, line, and texture to create the desired illusions. Use garment designs and fabrics to play up the best features.

Current fashions always include enough variations to give a choice of many looks and designs. People have the opportunity to choose what is most flattering. Everyone can look his or her best by wearing the right clothes.

The seven most common body-build types are discussed in the following sections. Specific apparel recommendations are made for each. Suggestions for what should be avoided are also given.

Tall and Thin

People with a tall-and-thin body build can wear gathered or pleated full skirts, flared or wide-legged pants, and horizontal stripes and seams. Multicolored outfits with large patterns and prints are also good.

Garments for this body build can have shaping with tucks, pleats, gathers, or shirring. Double-breasted jackets and coats can be worn well. Blouson, A-line, and bell silhouettes give width. Long, full sleeves can hide thin arms. Belted tunics, overblouses, and wrist-length or waist-length jackets cut the height. This is especially true if the top and bottom are of contrasting colors, as shown in **12-11**.

HighKey/Shutterstock.com

12-11 The contrasting colors and values cut height where they meet and are attractive on this woman who is tall and thin.

Almost all fabrics can be worn well by people with this build, including heavier fabrics, and those with large weaves and nubby, napped, and pile surfaces. High-fashion garments and fabrics, bold accessories, and some exaggerated details can be tried. Wide belts and horizontal stripes help to minimize height, if desired. Light or brightly colored slacks with a plaid or tweed jacket would be attractive.

People who are tall and thin may want to avoid wearing tight, straight dresses, skirts, or pants. Severely tailored lines, tiny fabric patterns, frilly fashions, and bold verticals should be avoided. Tight, high turtlenecks and clingy jerseys are not good. Slacks that are not long enough are poor choices. Sleeveless styles and small accessories should be avoided.

Tall and Heavy

This statuesque frame can look stunning, but can also be overpowering. People with this body build tend to look their best in garments with simple lines and little decoration. This is often called *understated design*. Subtle and muted prints, stripes, and patterns in scale with the body should be used. Easy fitting, A-line skirts

that are smooth at the hips should end below the knee. Pants should have straight or only slightly flared legs.

The shaping of garments for this body type should be done with seams or darts. Vertical or diagonal lines should be used. Asymmetrical closings look great, as in **12-12**. Flat, firm fabrics are best in grayed or dulled shades. A simple, smooth-fitting tunic or uncluttered suit can be worn. Details at the neck can be used to draw attention to the face.

Loud prints, checks, plaids, and stripes should be avoided by people with tall or heavy body types. Tight clothes, fussy details, ruffles, and delicate accessories can look out of proportion. Clingy, bulky, or heavy fabrics can be unflattering. Boxy overblouses, untucked shirts, and tent dresses should not be worn. Gathers or excess fullness add visual size and should be avoided.

12-12 The easy fitting, asymmetrical, and vertical lines of this dark, one-piece dress are perfect for someone with a tall, heavy figure.

Draper's & Damon's

Short and Thin

A person with a short-and-thin build tends to look best in soft, fluid, lightweight fabrics. Small-scale prints, subtle patterns, and smooth textures are flattering, as are unbroken vertical or diagonal lines. Bell, blouson, and flared silhouettes are good if they are not too wide.

Shirtwaist dresses and business suits look nice on people with short, thin body builds. Pants should have straight or only slightly flared legs. Shape can be given with tucks, shirring, or gathers. Light or bright, one-color outfits are attractive. Clothing should be simple and uncluttered with limited and small-scale construction details—collars, lapels, pockets, and so forth. Hip-length jackets, and moderate-length tunics and vests can be worn well, as in **12-13**. Small, neat accessories are desired.

12-13 A person who is short and thin looks great in outfits with subtle patterns and limited construction details. The appearance of more height is also added here with cropped pants and a stand-up collar.

Draper's & Damon's

People with body builds that are short and thin should avoid bulky textures, large prints and plaids, and large pockets, collars, and cuffs. Heavy looking accessories are overpowering. Wide, contrasting, horizontal bands or belts are not good because they reduce height. Layering clothing items can produce an awkward bulkiness. Skirts should not be too long.

Short and Heavy

A person with a short-and-heavy build looks best in garments providing the illusion of height. Lots of vertical lines give height as well as narrowness. Empire, A-line, or narrow-and-straight silhouettes are good. Long, asymmetric closings are attractive. A sheath dress with long, straight sleeves and no belt creates the illusion of height. If a belt is needed, a thin one of a matching color will not detract from the long, vertical image. Pants should be narrow- or straight-legged. Construction shaping lines and darts should be vertical. High heels can add height. However, extremely high heels can look out of proportion with the body.

Fabric patterns should be subtle with vertical designs for this body build. Otherwise, fabrics should be plain and not stiff. Smooth, flat fabrics should be of dark or dull colors without any sharp contrasts. Stockings and shoes look best when they are colored in relation to the outfit.

Clothes for people with short, heavy body builds should fit well, but not be too tight. Dark gray suits and straight-cut dresses are good choices. One-color suits with matching vests are also good. Perk up one-color outfits with scarves, pins, neckties, or other accessories. Trim near the face brings the eye of the beholder up. Open or collarless V- or U-necklines are also good.

People with this body build should avoid two-piece or two-colored garments that cut them in half visually. Cuffed pants, turtlenecks, double-breasted jackets, and horizontally striped shirts are not recommended. Clunky shoes or boots, and wide, stiff belts should be avoided. Clingy styles, tight clothing, cluttered looks, and shiny fabric finishes are not flattering. Large prints, horizontal lines, extra fullness, and bulky fabrics should not be worn since they give the appearance of added width.

Large Upper Body

A person with this body build has an upper body that is large in proportion to the lower body. Fashion magazines, mail-order catalogs, and sewing patterns sometimes refer to this as the *inverted triangle* figure or physique. Simple, slim, tailored shirts or long cardigan jackets are becoming. They create a vertical line over the top of the body. V-necklines are flattering, as are open collars with lapels. Slim sleeves are good.

Dark, dull, plain fabrics that are smooth or soft are best used on top. See **12-14**. Light, bright, or patterned fabrics are best for the bottom, as in **12-15**. Also, napped and bulky textures can be used on the bottom.

Low waistlines, hipline interest, A-line silhouettes, and full or flaring skirts are good for this body build. Pants should have slightly

StudioOneNine/Shutterstock.com

12-15 This outfit decreases the size of the upper body by using a darker color there. Width is given to the lower body with lighter pants, which are also pleated for fullness.

12-14 A large upper body can be disguised with dark, plain colors over the top and light-colored fullness and interest on the bottom.

Chirtsova Natalia/Shutterstock.com

flared legs. Hip-length tunics or vests are good. A belt or band of contrasting color at the hips is very effective, especially if the hips are small.

Horizontal lines at the chest level, low yokes, or smocking at the bustline should be avoided. Shaping above the waist is best done with vertical seams or darts. Garments that are tapered gently under the chest can be tried. Gathers, pleats, or shirring can be used below the waist.

A person with a larger upper body should avoid wearing clingy or shiny fabrics, large prints, and bright colors above the waist. High or fussy necklines, large collars, and ruffles, bows, or trimmings on the upper garment should also be avoided. Short, full sleeves, breast pockets, and tightly fitted or short tops are not recommended since they give the illusion of width across the chest and upper arms. A dark-colored top and light-colored bottom is becoming. Tight skirts or pants emphasize the large upper body.

Thick Middle

People with this body build do not have well-defined, or indented, waistlines. The waist measurement is similar to measurements of the chest and hips. These people tend to look their best in unfitted but not full garments, such as overblouses, empire lines, tunics, and long sweaters. Tubular silhouettes are attractive. Garments, such as jackets that hang slightly loose from the shoulders, are good.

Vertical lines that move the eye up toward the face can be flattering for people with this build. Fashion details should be kept above the waist, including attractive neckline interest. Skirts can flare a bit at the hemline, and pants can be slightly flared. Shaping should be done with darts or seams. A vest or sweater that is somewhat loose, as in **12-16**, can camouflage bulges.

Smooth, lightweight fabrics in solids or subtle prints are best. Other textures may be used if they give a streamlined effect. Colors should be of medium shades that flatter the face and hair.

A person with an undefined waistline should not wear clingy styles and clothes with fitted waists or tight belts. A baggy or bulky fit around the middle can contribute even more thickness to the midsection. Styles with trim or contrasting buttons at the center front, as well as clothes with bold prints or obvious horizontals, are not recommended.

Large Lower Body

People with this body build have broader hips in proportion to their upper bodies. The fashion industry sometimes refers to this as a *triangular* figure or physique. Thin arms or narrow shoulders can contribute to this appearance. Flattering looks for them include garments with vertical lines pointing up toward neckline interest. Attractive collars, wide shoulder lines, and yokes can be used. Gathered-sleeve tops that become narrow toward the wrist are also good.

Flashon Studio/Shutterstock.com

12-16 A thick middle can be hidden with a dark garment that has no defined waistline and an open jacket that forms a vertical area leading up to added interest near the face.

Skirts and pants should not have excessive fullness at the hips. Pants should not taper at the bottom. See **12-17**. Skirts should have a bit of flare at the hem, such as the A-line styles. Skirts and pants should be shaped with darts and seams. Necklines and tops can have gathering and other fullness.

People who have this body type should wear light, bright, or printed tops with dark, dull-colored skirts or pants. Belts, if used, should match the bottom garments. Smooth and firm fabrics in solids or subtle prints are best.

People who have large hips should avoid tight-fitting pants or skirts as well as over-blouses or shirts that end at the hips. Wide belts and horizontal bands at the hipline, and long, full sleeves with big cuffs are unflattering. They should also avoid wearing the following below the waist: shiny or clingy fabrics, large prints or plaids, and details such as patch pockets. Tight, skimpy tops make the hips appear larger.

The McCall Pattern Company, Vogue® Patterns, Adri

12-17 This outfit camouflages large hips with top interest; fluid, vertical draping; and straight pant legs.

General Guidelines

With this knowledge, you should be able to create the illusions you desire in apparel. In addition, consider the following guidelines.

Pockets in the shape of vertical or slanted slits are slimming. Patch pockets add width. A yoke across the bodice front appears to broaden the shoulders. Wide cuffs at the wrist make arms look shorter.

A person with broad shoulders looks taller because his or her width appears high on the body. A person with broader hips looks shorter. The closer the width is to the ground, the shorter a person appears. Also, hips usually look wider in pants than in a skirt.

Use V lines at the top of a vertical line to give sloping shoulders an upward lift. Use the downward slant of raglan sleeve seam lines to soften or modify square shoulders. A raglan line should not be worn by someone with sloping or narrow shoulders because it accentuates these features. For narrow shoulders, wear tops with extended or padded shoulders. For rounded shoulders, wear set-in sleeves.

If a person has a curved figure with chest and hips that are balanced, tucked-in shirts, belted garments, or a sheath dress that is fitted from bust to hips can accent the proportion. A person who is short waisted can use beltless styles combined with lengthening tricks on the top. For example, choose a cardigan, dropped-waistline style, or tunic, as in **12-18**. If legs seem too long for the rest of a body, use shortening tricks there with color, shape, line, and texture.

If someone is long waisted and has short legs, the natural waistline can be disguised and the lower body elongated. Chemise silhouettes, empire-style dresses, or soft skirts and pants are good choices. Use stockings and shoes in colors that match the skirt or pants.

Textured hose, or pants of bright and heavy fabrics, help to round out legs that are thin. Corduroy or tweed fabrics are good choices. On the other hand, pants in medium or dark tones and longer skirts can disguise legs that are heavy. Keep fashion interest above the waist, and wear simple shoes with enough bulk to balance heavier legs.

12-18 This fluid dress hides the location of the true waist. It gives the illusion of a longer upper body to someone who is short waisted.

NDT/Shutterstock.com

De-emphasize heavier thighs and a larger seat with easy fitting (but not full) pants or with bias-cut or A-line skirts. Put fashion interest near the face.

To lengthen and slim the appearance of a short, thick neck, V-necklines are good, as shown in **12-19**. Avoid turtlenecks, high collars, scarves, or ascots at the neckline.

Extra Tips

Make sure the design of the fabric is related to the structural design of each garment. Straight lines in the fabric design are best when used with a garment having straight structural lines. Medium and large prints should be used in garments with large, unbroken areas and a minimum of construction details. That is because seams, darts, and pleats break up the design motifs. Tiny prints, such as small polka dots, can be used in garments with more structural details. Circular prints give an illusion of roundness, which is good for thin bodies.

To reinforce the design concepts you have learned in this chapter, go shopping for clothes. (Leave your money or credit cards at home.) Try

12-19 This V-neckline dress elongates the neck. Its straight silhouette, front vertical pleating, and one-color fabric make the wearer appear taller and more slender.

McCall Pattern Company, Vogue® American Designer / Anne Klein New York

on garments that have various colors, shapes, lines, and textures. Try many different styles, shapes, lengths, and fabrics. Take note of the garments that are most flattering for your particular body build. Look for balance, proportion, emphasis, and rhythm in the garment designs, too. Some outfits are more harmonious than others.

Don't forget to consider the visual effects of shoes. Wide feet look best in simple, one-color shoe styles. A buckle or other decoration on a shoe may make the foot look shorter or wider. Ankle straps cut the illusion of body height and call attention to heavy ankles.

In general, clothing should not overpower the wearer. For most people, extreme fashions are hard to wear. They distract from body shape and personality. People should wear what is best for them rather than just what is fashionably new.

Summary

The principles of design are guidelines for the use of the elements of design. They are used to put ideas together for every design. Harmony, or pleasing visual unity, is created when the elements of design are used effectively according to the principles of design.

To create balance in a garment, details are grouped in a way that visually distributes weight. Formal balance is symmetrical while informal balance is asymmetrical. The proportion or scale of clothing should be related to the structure and proportion of the human body. Proportion should relate all parts of a garment and accessories to each other and to the whole. Emphasis concentrates interest in a particular area of a design with a center of interest. Rhythm arranges the design elements for pleasing eye movement over the apparel through repetition, gradation, transition, opposition, or radial arrangement.

To create the best look for a woman's figure or a man's physique, apparel designs should emphasize the best features. Different designs are best for various individual body builds.

General guidelines can be followed to create the desired illusions in apparel. Fabric design should be relative to the structural design of each garment. Try on and analyze outfits to reinforce the design concepts for your particular body shape.

Fashion Recall

Write your responses on a separate sheet of paper.

Matching: Match the terms listed below.

1. Gradation.
2. Formal.
3. Repetition.
4. Asymmetrical.
5. Scale.
6. Transition.
7. Focal point.

   A. balance
   B. proportion
   C. emphasis
   D. rhythm

True/False: Write *true* or *false* for each of the following statements.

8. The principles of design are guidelines for the use of the elements of design.
9. Proportion is a visual distribution of weight in the way details are grouped.
10. A large area of a bright color balances a small area of a dull color.
11. Formal balance is the most common type of balance in clothes.
12. Throughout history, the human body has been drawn with ⅜ of it from the waist to the top of the head and ⅝ of it from the waist to the soles of the feet.
13. Yokes, collars, pockets, and other apparel parts must be the right size for the total design and for the wearer.
14. Opposition is a concentration of interest in a particular part of clothing outfits.
15. Emphasis can be created with contrasts of textures or colors.
16. Radial arrangement is one way to achieve rhythm in an outfit.
17. Harmony gives the feeling that all parts of an outfit belong together and suit the wearer and the occasion.
18. People who are tall and thin should wear bold verticals.
19. People who are short and heavy look best in two-piece or two-colored garments that cut them in half visually.
20. The closer a person's width is to the ground, the shorter a person will look.

Fashion Vocabulary

21. Read the text passages that contain each of the *Fashion Terms* from the chapter opening. Then, write the definitions of each term in your own words. Double-check your definitions by rereading the text and using the text glossary.

Critical Thinking

22. **Critique design** Critique garment examples that illustrate the roles *balance, proportion, emphasis,* and *rhythm* play in clothing design. Use online or print fashion resources to locate two garment examples, and print or clip the images. Write a summary of your critique of these garments.

23. **Analyze design** Choose one of the body types discussed in the chapter. Analyze how you can use design elements and principles to enhance the personal attributes of this specific body type. Write a summary of your analysis to share with the class.

24. **Contrast designs** Collect pictures of good and poor examples of the use of the design elements and principles. Contrast the use of the design elements and principles among the images. Write a brief explanation for each picture summarizing the good or poor use of the design elements and principles.

Core Skills

25. **Speaking**   Collect fabric swatches of different colors, textures, and designs. Examples might include velvet, satin, tweed, linen, corduroy, and various printed fabrics. In an oral presentation, explain how each could be used to advantage in apparel for the various body builds discussed in this chapter.

26. **Math practice**   Using one inch for the height of a head, sketch a human body with the proportions that have been used by artists throughout history. Then, using thin or transparent paper, draw at least two fashion sketches using that basic body as a guide.

27. **Research and writing**   Find and mount pictures of garments that would improve the appearance of any five of the seven most common body types. Provide a written explanation of why each garment design would be good for a particular body type.

28. **Technology**   Find a school-approved website that creates a virtual model from information entered by a user. Create models for the seven common body types described in the text. "Dress" each virtual model in clothing appropriate for his or her figure or physique. Print out your dressed models or incorporate the images into presentation software. Give an oral report explaining your clothing choices for each figure or physique type.

29. **Speaking, listening, and writing**   Ask five adults that you know who always look well dressed to comment on their biggest clothes-buying mistakes for their body types. What did they learn from past experiences? Record their responses on a recording device, with their permission, and turn in a transcription of the interviews.

30. **CTE career readiness practice**   Suppose you work in product development for a local fashion design firm. Your employer has assigned you and your design team the task of designing a line of clothing that is flattering to a range of body types or physiques. The clothing designs, for both women and men, must use a range of fabrics, textures, and design elements. You and your team decide to interview your customers (your classmates) to determine their needs for beauty, movement, and wearability in fashion to begin your design process. After your interviews, write a summary of your customer responses and create an illustrated proposal of garment designs that flatter a range of body types.

Fashion in Action

31. **Portfolio builder**   Obtain four pictures of complete outfits from catalogs, magazines, or websites. Mount the pictures and describe the elements and principles of design used in each. Judge the designs as having good, medium, or poor harmony and cite reasons and text evidence that support your opinions. Add this to your portfolio to illustrate your design opinions.

32. **Design activity**   Write a report that includes a brief analysis of a hypothetical body build. Explain what design features would be best for that person's apparel. Sketch three outfits that would work well for that person.

Self-Assessment Quiz ➦

Complete the self-assessment quiz online to help practice and expand your knowledge and skills.

PART
Five

Consumers
of Clothing

13 Wardrobe Considerations

14 Wardrobe Planning

15 Being a Smart Consumer

16 Making the Right Purchase

17 Apparel for People with Special Needs

18 Caring for Clothes

247

CHAPTER 13

Wardrobe Considerations

While studying, look for the activity icon 📲 to:

- **practice** key fashion terms with e-flash cards, vocabulary games, and matching activities
- **assess** what you learn by completing self-assessment quizzes

G-WLEARNING.com

www.g-wlearning.com/clothingandfashion/

image	self-concept	first impression
grooming	yin	lifestyle
communication	yang	mix-and-match items

Objectives

After studying this chapter, you will be able to
- **give** examples of how people use clothes to project images and communicate messages.
- **explain** the importance of dressing appropriately for a person's lifestyle, climate, and community standards.
- **describe** the benefits of a well-planned wardrobe.
- **discuss** the enjoyment that can be gained from choosing the right apparel.

The best clothing choices are those that help a person project a positive image, express personality, and make good first impressions. Wardrobe considerations should be appropriate for a person's lifestyle and for the climate in which he or she lives. Discovering which clothes are most suitable can make it easier to organize a well-planned wardrobe and be a smart consumer. It is important to know how to make wise purchases and care for clothes properly. Additionally, you will be able to guide others to dress in the best ways.

Projecting a Positive Image

The image a person projects is what others see when they look at the person and remember them later. It is the mental picture people form of an individual. To project a positive image, it is important to develop good personal grooming skills and select clothes that fit and flatter.

Good grooming includes having clean nails, hair, teeth, and a clean body. Try to maintain a healthful lifestyle and a body weight. Eat a balanced diet, get plenty of physical activity, and get enough rest and sleep. Sit, stand, and walk with straight posture. Keep hair styled in a way that complements the face and the shape of the head. Try to develop a personality that is cheerful and alert. Remember that pleasant facial expressions and gestures can also help project a positive image. See **13-1**.

For the best image, select clothes that fit properly, without being too tight or too loose. Clothes should be the right length and should flatter a person's physical assets. They should be neat, clean, and in good repair.

To project the best possible image, combine good grooming and clothing sense. Without proper grooming and posture, clothes will not appear as flattering. Developing good grooming skills and making wise clothing selections can help a person feel good—physically and mentally.

Clothing as Communication

Communication is the giving and receiving of messages. Not all messages are spoken or written. *Nonverbal communication* is expressed through facial expressions, hand gestures, body movements, and clothes. How much do clothes say about someone? A person can speak with a powerful voice through clothing selections.

13-1 Individuals look and feel good if they are groomed well and present themselves in a cheerful way. This projects each person's best possible image.

OLJ Studio/Shutterstock.com

You may have heard the saying "You are what you wear." The clothes people choose and the ways they wear them express visual messages that tell others about themselves. Just as a traffic light sends a message without speaking, a person's appearance communicates in a nonverbal way. People often draw conclusions about others based on appearance. Apparel speaks a silent, but clear, language. The best clothing choices are those that convey positive messages.

The colors of the clothes a person wears at particular times can help to express certain moods. On happy occasions, the wearer might choose bright, cheerful, colored clothing. If a person is sad or feels down, dark, dull-colored clothing might be worn.

Clothing can convey different messages about the wearer at different times. If a person is wearing dirty and ripped clothing, what message is the wearer sending to others? The message could be one of low self-image. On the other hand, what message is a person sending to others when wearing clean, well-maintained clothes? Dressing like peers communicates that a person is part of that group. Choosing to dress very differently from others expresses individuality. Conformity to the group and individuality expressed by dressing differently pull in different directions. Most people communicate varying amounts of each.

Sometimes communication with apparel is not successful. If a 50-year-old tried to dress like a teen, the message might be misinterpreted. The 50-year-old might be trying to say "See how young I am!" However, the message received by others could be "See how foolish that person looks!" The same thing might happen if someone were to imitate the clothing style of a popular actor or celebrity. Just because a clothing style looks good on the celebrity does not mean it will look good on everyone. It is important to keep communication in mind when selecting and wearing clothing.

Clothing is an important language, or code, that often projects the wearer's talents and goals. Apparel can imply that a person can be reliable. When considering wardrobe choices, keep these messages in mind so your clothes will speak for the real you.

Personality

An individual's *personality* is made up of personal thoughts, feelings, and actions. It is the total of the unique characteristics that distinguish an individual, especially behavioral and emotional tendencies. Everyone's personality is unique. One way a person can express personality is through clothing choices.

A person's self-concept (the mental image people have of themselves) can also affect clothing choices. Clothes are an outward expression of how individuals feel about the world around them, as well as how they feel about themselves. The way people dress is a projection of how they see themselves and how they want to be viewed by others.

Personality and appearance are what sell an individual to others. Judgments about personality are often based on clothing choices. People who have a negative self-concept often do not take pride in themselves. They may convey this message to others through their clothing choices and appearance. People who have a positive self-concept often take pride in their clothing and appearance. They care about the image they are presenting to others. Having a positive self-concept can help people succeed in other areas, too. It can help a person be elected to a student government office, get a special date, or land a good job. Careful consideration of clothing choices can boost self-confidence and send a positive message to others.

Yin and Yang Traits

Yin and yang traits combine personality and physical characteristics. For centuries, these traits have dealt with the order of the universe. Chinese philosophers used yin and yang to describe the opposite, but equally important, forces existing in the world. Yin and yang represent opposite complementary qualities. They represent the balance between the contrasts found in the universe and relate to personality, body builds, and clothing choices. They are pictured by the ancient symbol shown in **13-2**.

Yin represents the passive, timid, sensitive, and delicate elements of personality. Yin physical traits are pictured as being feminine and relating to shorter stature. Traits may include a small bone structure, graceful features, delicate coloring, and soft, gentle speech.

Yang represents the active, rugged, extroverted elements of personality. Yang physical traits are pictured as being masculine and of large

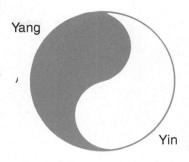

Yang

Yin

13-2 The yin/yang circle illustrates the balance of opposite forces in the universe.

stature with strong, prominent features. Traits may include pronounced coloring; a low, firm voice; and a tall, angular frame.

No one is completely yin *or* yang. Every person has a complex blend of personality traits. Usually, either yin or yang is dominant with some characteristics of the other. People tend to fluctuate in their amounts of yin and yang characteristics as their daily roles and activities change. As a person matures, there must be a balance of yin and yang in the personality. For example, a person may be assertive in business and sports (showing yang characteristics), but gentle and caring in a personal relationship (showing yin traits).

Yin forces are represented by clothing with graceful, flowing lines. Intricate details and curves are used, as well as soft, sheer textures. Fabrics often have small, delicate designs and are in light colors, as in **13-3**. Jewelry is often delicate. Examples of yin forces in nature are the weeping willow tree, the trailing vine, and the tiny hummingbird.

Yang forces are represented by apparel with bold designs. There is a minimum of detail. Straight lines are used. Fabrics have forceful design motifs and are in strong or neutral colors, as in **13-4**. They have heavy, rough textures. Jewelry is often bold and bulky. Examples of yang forces in nature are the sturdy oak tree, the rugged mountains, and the fierce eagle.

In apparel, yin and yang qualities are evident in fabrics, garments, accessories, colors, shapes, lines, and textures. Some people may choose to balance the yin and yang in their clothing with the yin and yang in their personalities and body structures. They feel more comfortable this way and can project a truer image of themselves.

HUANG Zheng/Shutterstock.com

13-3 A dominantly yin person would prefer this outfit with a pastel floral print, puff sleeves, slim matching belt, and tiny purse.

JCPenney

13-4 This outfit shows yang influences with its dark colors, straight lines, and bold details. A dominantly yang person would prefer to wear it.

First Impressions

A **first impression** is what people think of others when they first see or meet them. An *impression* is a feeling or a reaction. The human mind receives and acts on signals very quickly. These signals or impressions work both ways. When people meet, they form first impressions of one another based on their immediate feelings or reactions. At first glance, some people may appear to be handsome, friendly, intelligent, sad, sloppy, or shy. Most people agree that it is what is inside a person that matters most. Whether fair or unfair, first impressions are usually made on the basis of appearance.

First impressions are determined to a great extent by what people wear. That is because the first view of someone consists of about 90 percent clothing. Clothing covers the largest area and is easily noticed. What people wear is the first statement they communicate about themselves. Clothes are often an outward expression of an individual's inner identity.

A favorable first impression leads to good feelings. People want to get to know one another better. A poor first impression has the opposite effect. If the first impression is negative, then people may not want to meet again. They may never get a second chance to prove their worth, especially if meeting for only a short time. For instance, you may have an interview with a prospective employer, and you may have excellent qualifications for the job. If your appearance does not make a good first impression, however, you could lose out to someone who makes a better impression.

First impressions are very important, especially in new social groups, in new schools, and in business. Therefore, it is important to pay attention to the messages clothes send to others. Try to make a good first impression, then reinforce it with words and actions.

Appropriate Apparel

To be appropriate, clothes should be comfortable, clean, and stylish. However, they do not necessarily have to be in the very latest styles. How appropriate they are depends on several factors. Clothes should suit a person's lifestyle. They should meet the needs of the seasons of the regional climate. They should also correspond with community standards of dress.

Lifestyle

Lifestyle is made up of all the activities a person does and the places he or she goes. It is influenced by a person's job, sports, travel, friends, income, and attitudes. It includes school, work, social, and leisure activities. Taking up a new sport, starting a new job, or assuming a new social responsibility alters a person's lifestyle. Apparel may have to change accordingly. New clothing requirements may have to be followed to dress appropriately.

You should be aware of your activities so apparel is geared to your lifestyle. To evaluate your lifestyle, write your usual routine over a normal two-week period. Include a job, evening events, hobbies, sports, and other occasions you attend. What are your specific activities? How many are casual, and how many are dressy? Do you swim, bowl, play tennis, read, watch movies, or go on picnics? Try to make a complete list of your activities.

Next, analyze how you should dress for your activities. Try to develop your sense of what to wear when. Notice how others dress for certain occasions. Which kinds of clothes are needed for what you do? Do you have suitable attire for the special events you attend? Do you have clothes that can double for school wear as well as for movies, shopping, or hobbies? Fortunately, many garments are suitable for more than one type of activity.

Many sports require special ways of dressing. Sports clothes must be ready for action. Special garments provide protection and safety, as well as comfort and freedom of movement, **13-5**. Footwear that provides support, comfort, and durability might be necessary.

Clothing choices are very important in the working world. Dressing appropriately for a job means wearing the right type of clothes for the work to be done. This might mean sturdy and practical garments for hard physical labor. Conservative apparel might be best for a law office, while a uniform is required for some types of official duties or at schools, as in **13-6**. Trendy outfits may be best for working in a fashion boutique. Clothing should conform to the generally accepted standards of the workplace.

In a job, people will take you as seriously as you present yourself. The power of positive dressing causes people to treat you with respect. This, in turn, raises your status and encourages your success. Dress for the kind of job you seek. Fair or not, job advancement often depends on a well-groomed appearance. If your image is sloppy, people may assume that your work and attitude will be that way, too.

13-5 This type of apparel may be needed in the wardrobe of people who have an active lifestyle that includes exercising.

Blend Images/Shutterstock.com

13-6 Many schools require uniforms, partly so students feel serious about concentrating on their studies.

Climate

Different climates create different clothing needs. Garments in summer and winter wardrobes vary in terms of texture, weight, and color. Clothes need to feel cool in the hot weather of summer or in southern states. They must provide warmth when cold temperatures hit in winter, especially in northern areas. Energy conservation has caused houses and offices to be cooler in winter and warmer in summer. This has changed people's wardrobes.

To keep warm when the weather is cold, cover the torso with several clothing layers. The layered look is perfect for adjusting clothing to meet body needs. Each layer traps a pocket of air. This keeps body heat in and lets moisture out. However, do not use so many layers that movements are restricted. Also, the outer layer must be big enough to go over the rest.

The fabrics of garments should be chosen according to the climate. To gain warmth, plan to have fuzzy, bulky, wool-like garments in a wardrobe. Double knits, quilted fabrics, and laminated fabrics provide extra warmth. Down or fiberfill are used in garments to give warmth, too. Garments that fit snugly at the neck, wrists, and ankles keep out drafts of cold air. Avoid clothing that is extremely loose or extremely tight.

For hot weather, garments of cotton or linen are good choices. The outfit in **13-7** is appropriate for warm weather conditions.

When outdoors, people sometimes need protection against wind and rain. Apparel must keep the head, hands, and feet warm and dry. In cold weather, long underwear worn under clothes can provide a surprising amount of warmth.

Northern, colder climates demand higher spending costs for clothing. Items are needed to protect against the cold, such as coats, boots, hats, scarves, gloves, and sweaters, as in **13-8**. People need more variety in their wardrobes

13-7 A sleeveless, collarless dress of a light color, with a loose skirt and cotton fabric, is perfect for hot weather. A hat to block the sun is a great addition.

Dudarev Mikhail/Shutterstock.com

13-8 Colder climates require added costs for heavy outerwear, such as jackets, hats, and scarves.

when they live in geographic regions with distinctly different seasons. A mild climate, where temperature variations are less severe, means fewer clothing needs and is easier on the budget.

Community Standards

Community standards influence the appropriateness of certain clothing. There are different standards of dress in different parts of the country and the world. The tempo of life in a community near a resort area is different from that of one near a major business or financial center. Tastes can be more conservative in smaller towns and rural areas than they are in big cities. Appropriate dress for one activity might differ from place to place.

Particular rules of dress are followed in communities. When worn in the wrong situations, clothes can cause disfavor. For instance, at a rock concert, jeans are probably preferred.

However, at a symphony performance, jeans would show disrespect in most cities. What is considered to be acceptable dress by your friends, school, or employer? Clothes should conform to the times and to social groups, as well as to one's originality or creativity.

The Benefits of a Well-Planned Wardrobe

As discussed in earlier chapters, a wardrobe includes all the clothes and accessories a person owns. With a well-planned wardrobe, people have enough of the right clothes for their lifestyle, climate, and community standards.

You may have a lot of clothes. Are they in style? Do they fit you? Do they need repair? Do you often say, "I don't have a thing to wear," even though your closet and dresser drawers are full? You and others can unclutter and use planning to gain control and create an enduring wardrobe with thrifty, mix-and-match apparel.

Project the Best Self-Image

With a well-planned wardrobe, people can look and feel their best. They have apparel that suits their body shape and coloring, by using the elements and principles of design to advantage. Clothing also suits personality and lifestyle. A well-planned wardrobe reduces frustrations about clothing. People have the clothes they need; clothes fit well and are stylish.

A well-planned wardrobe helps people feel comfortable and confident. The ideal wardrobe plan lets them dress to forget their clothing. They can then pay attention to more important matters. When people know they look good, they feel attractive, secure, and self-confident. They are sure the first impressions they make are always the best ones. They are then able to concentrate on the activity or job at hand. Thoughts and attention can be turned toward others.

When planning your wardrobe, try to establish the right blend of conformity to peer group pressure and individuality. Individualize your clothes enough to express your own personality. Use your clothes to tell others who you are and how you feel in a positive way. Identify yourself through your clothes. Let your clothes conform to current fashion and meet your needs to belong. However, clothes should also be different enough to express your true self.

Dressing should be fun and creative. Clothes should be able to give people a lift and change a mood. This is good for an individual's psychological well-being. People should enjoy wearing the clothes in their wardrobe. They must feel comfortable about their clothes and in them. Aim for an appearance that expresses personality and makes the most of it. Personal satisfaction is gained with a well-planned wardrobe.

Save Money

The least expensive way to dress is to avoid making wardrobe mistakes. Careful planning and wise purchases allow consumers to do this. It is best to plan for a smaller, but well-chosen wardrobe. Having too many clothes is confusing. A closet should contain a well-coordinated, well-edited, complete wardrobe that works, yet is economical.

Looking great does not necessarily mean spending too much money. A well-chosen wardrobe provides a collection of flattering garments and accessories, to keep a person suitably dressed for all activities, at a reasonable cost. The goal should be to have a nice appearance with a minimum expenditure of time and money. It is unnecessary to buy a whole new wardrobe for a new look each season.

A well-planned wardrobe also provides a solid basis for continuous changes or updates. A wardrobe should be in a slow state of change. Keep working on it, replacing a few items at a time. With good planning, needs and expenditures are known ahead of time. It is possible to keep a wardrobe up-to-date without sudden costs.

Gain Flexibility

Planning and having mix-and-match items gives flexibility and extends a wardrobe. These are garments and accessories that can be combined in different ways with several other wardrobe items. For instance, if garments and accessories are based on a particular color scheme, they can be mixed and matched to create many different outfits, as shown in **13-9**. All parts of the wardrobe become harmonious.

13-9 Discuss how many different outfits can be assembled from these pieces (there is an unseen white shirt under the green jacket).

Decide on one or more color schemes that look good with your coloring. Plan the wardrobe around those colors. Examples might be khaki and navy; gray and burgundy; or red, white, and black. Through planning, garments can be put to better use. The color schemes become the foundation for the whole wardrobe. Apparel items coordinate automatically as they are mixed and matched for increased wardrobe flexibility. Bring in brighter or different colors with accessories. Use prints, plaids, or patterned fabrics containing colors of the solid garments with which they are worn.

Reassemble and wear the same clothing items for different occasions and to fit different lifestyle needs. A well-planned wardrobe is easy to coordinate and accessorize for many different looks.

Fewer clothes are necessary when each garment is useful to the maximum extent. For instance, a navy blazer could go with many different sweaters, shirts, and slacks (or blouses and skirts) for more versatility. A pair of blue jeans with a good cut and proper fit can be worn with many different shirts and sweaters. A basic dress can be worn to school, religious events, and an important dinner by changing what is worn with it. For school, a cardigan sweater could be worn over a dress. For religious events, a jacket might be added. For an evening out, one might wear a pretty silk scarf at the neck or fancy jewelry.

Enjoy Apparel Choices

Never stop experimenting with clothes. Fashion is always offering something new. Many people choose to wear styles they like even if they are not the newest fashions. There are many different fashion statements from which to choose. There is no one look or silhouette being dictated for a wardrobe. With all the options, the final decision is a personal one based on individual tastes and needs. Besides, people should not wear items that are supposed to be *in*, if the style does not suit them.

Fashion tastes change as people mature. As people get older, they may become more individual in wardrobe selections. They will probably develop a personal style that says who they are through their appearance. People should always be able to look and feel their best, as in **13-10**. A wardrobe plan allows personal style to evolve, by using different strengths as people's situations change.

Besides expressing themselves to others, people's wardrobes influence the way they feel about themselves. Feeling suitably and attractively dressed gives people confidence about their worth and ability. Then they can devote time and efforts to other people or to important activities.

Being well-groomed and properly dressed is not an absolute guarantee of instant success in every situation. However, it will definitely help boost your self-confidence so that your chances of success are greatly improved. Self-assurance comes by knowing you always put your best foot forward. When you look good, you also tend to feel good. When your wardrobe includes styles that play up your best features and express your personality, your clothes seem to say, "There is an awesome, confident person!"

Lands' End Direct Merchants

13-10 As people mature, they develop their own personal styles that help them look and feel their best.

Summary

To project a positive image to others, it is important to combine good grooming and clothing sense. Clothing communicates messages to others. A person's personality is expressed through clothing choices. Yin and yang traits combine personality and physical characteristics. They describe delicate versus rugged images and relate to people's clothing choices.

First impressions are often determined by what a person is wearing. The right apparel should be comfortable, clean, and stylish, but does not need to be of the latest fashion. Apparel should be geared to lifestyle activities. Different climates create different needs for garments and fabrics. Community standards also influence the appropriateness of certain clothing.

There are many benefits to a well-planned wardrobe. Project the best self-image with clothes that fit nicely and are stylish. Save money by avoiding wardrobe mistakes. Gain flexibility by having mix-and-match garments based on sensible color schemes. People enjoy apparel choices if they wear the styles they like and that are best for them.

Fashion Recall

Write your answers on a separate sheet of paper.

True/False: Write *true* or *false* for each of the following questions.

1. To look good, a person needs good personal grooming plus clothes that fit and flatter.

2. Clothes help people express visual messages that tell others about themselves.

3. One way people express their personalities is through the way they dress.

4. The way people dress is a projection of how they see themselves (their self-concept) and how they want to be viewed by others.

5. Yin and yang represent opposite complementary qualities that balance each other.

6. Yin forces are represented in clothing with bold designs, straight lines, and rough textures.

7. Yang physical traits include a small bone structure, graceful features, delicate coloring, and soft, gentle speech.

8. A first impression is what people think of others when they first see or meet them.

9. A person's lifestyle influences the types of clothes he or she needs.

10. Tight-fitting garments of cotton are good choices for cold, winter weather.

Short Answer: Write the correct response to each of the following items.

11. Why is it important to make a good first impression?

12. Why is proper apparel so important in the working world?

13. How can a well-planned wardrobe save money?

Fashion Vocabulary

14. Create a T-chart on a separate sheet of paper. Write each of the *Fashion Terms* from the chapter opening in the left column. For each term, quickly write a word you think relates to the term in the right column. In small groups, exchange papers. Have each person in the group explain a term on the list. Take turns until all terms have been explained.

Critical Thinking

15. **Analyze roles** Analyze the role that clothes play in the image people project. In what ways can people project a positive image through the clothes they wear? Is it possible to dress in a way that projects no image? Explain your answer during class discussion.

16. **Contrast standards** Contrast the ways in which lifestyle, climate, and community standards persuade people to dress differently in different regions of the country. In writing, cite the text and other reliable resources as examples to support your responses.

17. **Evaluate benefits** Evaluate how having a well-planned wardrobe can positively impact a person's appearance, time, and budget. Through class discussion, describe other benefits of having a well-planned wardrobe.

Core Skills

18. **Reading and speaking** Read an article or book on career dressing for achieving success. Take notes on the key points presented in the article or book. Then, present an oral report about your findings to the class.

19. **Research and writing** Locate at least five magazine or Internet photos of people who are sending out messages by the way

they are dressed. Mount them and explain what messages you are receiving in each case. Describe the social implications of the way people dress. As an alternative, use a school-approved digital infographic application to create a poster with your digital images and descriptions. Upload your poster to the class website for peer and instructor review.

20. **Writing** Write an essay describing experiences you have witnessed concerning first impressions and appearance. Have you seen people treated badly because of their appearance? What kinds of reactions have you seen to well-dressed people who made good first impressions? Have you witnessed occasions when first impressions turned out to be inaccurate?

21. **Writing** Using a school-approved social media site, contact someone your age living in another part of the country or the world. Ask him or her to describe clothing styles that are popular in his or her location. Write a report comparing and contrasting those styles with the popular styles in your area. Explain the differences, if any.

22. **Listening and speaking** Interview a parent, guardian, or older relative about his or her fashion choices over the years. Ask to see photos. How does clothing reflect the historical periods in which the photos were taken? Does clothing in the photos reflect something about climate, lifestyles, community standards, personality, and self-image? Use presentation software and digital photos to share a photo essay reflecting the results of your interview with the class.

23. **CTE career readiness practice** Suppose you are a volunteer for your local affiliate of *Dress for Success*®—a global nonprofit organization that "…empowers women to achieve economic independence by providing a network of support,

professional attire, and the development tools to help women thrive in work and in life." Your new client is Leila, a single mom with two young children. Leila, a recent community college graduate, has an upcoming interview at a fashion design firm and needs a suit for the interview. Along with providing encouragement, you will assist Leila with selecting and fitting a suit appropriate for this professional work environment. What questions might you ask Leila regarding her taste in clothing and the impression she would like to make? Consider Leila's needs and preferences by selecting two suit options (photos) for her interview.

Fashion in Action

24. **Portfolio builder** Prepare a comprehensive lifestyle chart. Determine the time you spend in a week on each of your activities. List the days of the week and activity categories. Record the amount of time spent on each activity in fractions or decimals. Then, write a separate description of the apparel needed for your wardrobe. Add these documents to your portfolio.

25. **Design activity** Obtain five pictures from magazines, catalogs, or websites of clothes that show *yin* design styling and five that show *yang* design styling. Mount the pictures and write descriptions of their yin and yang characteristics. As an alternative, use a school-approved application to create a digital poster with your images and descriptions to share with the class.

Self-Assessment Quiz ➔

Complete the self-assessment quiz online to help practice and expand your knowledge and skills.

G-WLEARNING.com

While studying, look for the activity icon to:

- **practice** key fashion terms with e-flash cards, vocabulary games, and matching activities
- **assess** what you learn by completing self-assessment quizzes

www.g-wlearning.com/clothingandfashion/

Developing a well-planned wardrobe takes careful thought as well as knowledge and skill. To plan a wardrobe, it helps to have knowledge of fashion, fabrics, and clothing construction. Smart consumers think carefully about what apparel items they already have and what they want to add. You need the skills to shop wisely and to select items that will enhance your appearance. Wardrobe planning takes time and effort, but the results are worthwhile.

Evaluate Current Apparel

To develop a well-planned wardrobe, evaluate current apparel by taking a wardrobe inventory. An inventory is an itemized list of current possessions. When completing a wardrobe inventory, you will be able to decide what clothing items to keep, what to eliminate, and what to add for the best possible wardrobe.

Make a wardrobe inventory like the one in **14-1**. List all garments and accessories from closets and drawers by category. Do not forget the garments in the dirty-clothes hamper or at the cleaners. Add other categories to the wardrobe inventory if needed. Write all pertinent remarks in the spaces.

AVAVA/Shutterstock.com

14-1 Filling out a wardrobe inventory like this one is the first step in successful wardrobe planning.

Wardrobe Inventory			Date	
Current Apparel	**Description**	**Condition**	**Like/Dislike**	**Action to Take**
Dresses (girls/women)				
Skirts (girls/women)				
Suits	———			Buy a gray suit?
Blazers/Jackets	1 Navy 1 Gray	Good Too small	OK Don't like	Save for brother.
Dress shirts/Blouses	2 Striped 1 Blue 1 White	Good (1 missing button) Like new Frayed collar	Like striped ones best	Sew on missing button. Buy new white shirt.
Pants	2 Pr. Cords 3 Pr. Jeans	New 2 Wearing out	Good Favorites	Buy 1 pr. dress slacks and 1 pr. jeans.
Shorts	1 Pr. Cargo	Old	Comfortable	
Casual shirts	3 T-shirts 1 Turtleneck 2 Polo shirts	OK Good 1 New	Good OK Fit my needs	
Sweaters	1 V-neck 2 Crew-neck	Old, but OK Good	Don't like Good	Trade/give away?
Coats	1 Tan trench coat 1 Down ski coat	Old Good	Don't like Wear the most	Keep for emergencies.
Shoes/Boots	1 Pr. sneakers 1 Pr. cowboy boots	Poor Good	Really like Really like	Replace sneakers. Buy dress shoes for suit?
Athletic attire	1 Pr. shorts 1 Sweat suit 2 Swimming suits	Good Good 1 with ripped seam	Like OK Like	Fix ripped seam.
Underwear	9 briefs	3 Getting old	Fine	Buy a pkg. of 3.
Socks	6 Pr. white 2 Pr. dress	3 Pr. getting old	Fine Fine	Buy 3 pr. soon.
Sleepwear	2 PJ pants	Old	Comfortable	
Hats/Gloves	Knit hat Leather gloves	Good Good	OK Good	
Neckwear	Navy print tie Gray/red tie	Good Good	OK OK	
Belts	1 Brown leather	Good	OK	Buy one black dress belt?
Jewelry	ID bracelet Cuff links	Broken clasp Like new	Like Never wear	Fix clasp. Give to Dad?
Other (purses, formal wear, work clothes)	1 Sweatshirt	Really old and faded	Super	

As you complete the wardrobe inventory, try to visualize separates being put together as outfits. Keep in mind which clothes can be worn for various activities. Some items might be mixed and matched in new ways. It may even be possible to rediscover some lost or forgotten items.

You may want to analyze a wardrobe just once or twice a year, such as before the beginning of a season. Keep a wardrobe inventory posted inside the closet door. Then it will be easier to develop a well-planned wardrobe.

Group Clothes

Once you have made a list of everything in the wardrobe, consider which items are most suitable and usable. To do this, sort apparel into four groups:

➤ Clothing worn often.
➤ Clothing worn occasionally.
➤ Clothing needing repairs or cleaning.
➤ Clothing not worn in the past year.

Clothing Worn Often

Look at the apparel placed in the first group. These are often favorite clothing items. They are usually well suited to personality, lifestyle, and geographic location needs. They are probably the most flattering to your body type and coloring.

Note the styles, textures, and colors of wardrobe favorites. What makes them pleasing, practical, and appropriate? This information will help you make wise purchases in the future. Look for similar designs when buying new apparel items. Double-check the condition of favorite clothes for signs of wear. Then return these items to their places after cleaning closets and drawers.

Clothing Worn Occasionally

Now look at the clothing in the second group. Try on the garments and carefully check style and fit in a mirror. Are the clothing items flattering, or is there something not quite right about the colors, textures, lines, or fit of the clothes? Do some items seem fine, but not match anything else in the wardrobe? Do some look out-of-date?

Try to create new outfits by combining separates in this group with some favorite items in the first group. Mix and match jackets, shirts, and sweaters with different pants or skirts, as in **14-2**. Try to identify the reasons why some clothes are just okay rather than great. Once again, this will help you be a wise consumer in the future.

Determine if there are some creative ways to perk up the clothes in the second group. Would adding new accessories make these clothes more appealing? Are new tops or a new belt needed to wear with slacks or skirts?

Recycle Garments

To recycle means to use again, often in a new and different way or after reprocessing. Figure out if some items that are worn only occasionally need to be altered or restyled. Should the width or length of pants legs be changed? Should a wide necktie be made narrow? Would new buttons perk up a drab blazer?

14-2 Combine separates worn occasionally with favorite items to create wonderful new combinations.

J. Jill

Should extra fullness of a skirt be removed to make it straighter so it will be more fashionable and worn more often? Should shoulder pads be added to, or eliminated from, a garment? Could some trim add interest as shown in **14-3**?

Most outdated garments can be modified to reflect current trends. Even with minimal sewing skills, repairs, alterations, or updates can enhance existing apparel. Remember that it is almost always easier to take in or shorten a garment than to let it out or lengthen it. If the previous crease line is obvious after lengthening a garment, consider applying braid or another decorative trim over it. Also, the simpler a garment design is, the easier it is to change.

You may decide to dye some washable apparel. Changing colors can be fun and coordinate with a wardrobe in new ways. Liquid or powdered dyes are sold at stores that sell fabrics and crafts. Dye items in hot water. Then rinse

and dry items according to package directions. Tie-dyeing can also achieve special effects.

Some clothes can be recycled by being changed into different types of garments or by being worn in different ways. Pants that have worn-out knees can be made into shorts. Old shirts can be dyed to freshen their colors or to add decorative touches. Long sleeves can be changed to short sleeves. A comfortable summer skirt that is too short may be shortened even more and worn as a tennis skirt. A jumper that is too short can be restyled as a tunic. Jeans that are too small can be made into a tote bag. Be creative!

Clothing Needing Repairs or Cleaning

Now look at the clothes in the third group. These items need repairs or cleaning. They are probably worth saving, but need attention before they can be worn. Fixing them will give you more clothes for less money. A little time and effort can work miracles to help the garments look new again.

Clothing should be repaired as soon as a problem becomes apparent. A small rip will become a big rip if worn over and over. Laundering a garment before it is repaired may cause further damage. Thus, delaying a repair job only makes the job harder, or impossible, to do.

Resew loose buttons before they fall off. Otherwise, buttons might be lost, and it could be very difficult to find identical ones as replacements. Also, reattach loose hooks and eyes before they no longer fasten. Use tape and safety pins to hold clothing together temporarily and/or in emergencies.

Figure out how to make each article of clothing wearable. Then be sure to take the time to work on the garments. Fix that hem. Resew and reinforce ripped seams. Attach all missing buttons.

Holes may be patched with matching pieces of fabric. Apply iron-on patches to the inside of the garment, over a rip or hole, or appliqués to the outside. Appliqués are cutout decorations. They are often shapes of contrasting fabric in various designs. They are applied by stitching or fusing with an iron. New garments sometimes have them. For repair purposes, appliqués and iron-on patches can be bought at notions counters of fabric or craft stores. To express creativity, design and create appliqués with fabric scraps.

14-3 The addition of appliqués and lace to otherwise plain shorts is a fun way to make a different fashion statement.

Shabby Datwin/Shutterstock.com

Keep all necessary supplies in a sewing box or repair box. This box should include thread in several colors, needles, a thimble, buttons, snaps, hooks and eyes, scissors, and iron-on patches. Tears in expensive clothing should be rewoven by specialists. This may be costly, but repairs will be almost invisible.

Remove spots and stains immediately so they do not become permanent. Then launder dirty items or take them to a dry cleaner. Always keep clothes repaired, clean, and pressed. Then they are ready to be worn whenever they are needed.

Clothing Not Worn in the Past Year

The apparel in this group is usually not right. Maybe the garments are not comfortable. Maybe they do not match lifestyle needs. Maybe they do not fit or are outdated.

If there are some specialty items in this group that are well liked, but have not yet been worn, such as ski pants or an evening gown, put those back in the closet. Dispose of the rest of the apparel items in this group, unless it is possible to think of three good reasons to keep any of them.

Clothes that are not worn are not worth the space they take in closets or drawers. They can be better used by someone else. Maybe some items can be traded with a friend for other apparel. Some can be donated to charitable organizations that will give them to people in need. It may even be possible to receive a tax deduction for such donations. Some clothes may be sold at a yard sale or by consignment through a resale shop. See **14-4**. When items are sold on consignment, you are paid a percentage of the retail selling price. As another option, some garments can be saved and handed down to a younger relative.

Items that no one would want to wear may be used for rags after the buttons and zippers have been removed from them. If the fabric is good, other items can be made from it, such as children's clothes, cloth purses or tote bags, makeup pouches, or stuffed animals. Use your imagination. Any jewelry of good quality that is out of style may be stored in a plastic bag. It might return to fashion.

After grouping clothes and making them all as usable as possible, you may have to revise the wardrobe inventory. Do your best to keep the wardrobe inventory up-to-date.

14-4 When you sell items through a consignment shop, you get money from the sale. The shop takes a percentage of the selling price. In this way, good items can also continue to be used by others.

Distinguish Wants from Needs

A want is a desire for something that gives personal satisfaction. The item would be wonderful to have, but an individual can get along without it.

A need is something that is required for a person's continued existence or survival. It is necessary for basic protection, modesty, comfort, or livelihood. For instance, a person who lives in a cold climate needs a heavy coat to stay warm in winter weather. If the person already owns a suitable coat that is a bit out of style, purchasing a new one is not a need. It is a want, because the old coat can provide the needed warmth.

Sometimes it is hard to distinguish between wants and needs. When something is craved, obtaining that item seems to be a need in that person's mind, rather than a want. Also, there are varying degrees of need. The most basic needs provide protection from the environment. Other needs are determined by a person's values, culture, lifestyle, resources, peer group, and standard of living. A college graduate who is beginning a new career may need a business suit for the job, even though he or she could live without it. A teen may need a certain uniform in order to participate in a sport.

People usually have many more wants than needs. Wants are endless. People often want certain clothes or items similar to those of others, even though they don't really need them. To persuade consumers to want certain items, advertisements heighten the appeal of products and encourage people to discard the old for the new. Store displays try to convince consumers they should have particular garments in the latest colors. The clothes worn by celebrities often create desires for certain apparel, too.

Wants are also influenced by personal philosophy. People who are practical may want their apparel to be comfortable and durable. Others may want expensive clothes that will give them high status. Some people like the attention received with many clothes of the latest fads. Evaluate your philosophy. If it does not result in smart wardrobe planning, consider changing it.

Organize wardrobe planning so it can be carried out in order of need. When planning, think about needs first. They have top priority. In other words, they are most important and should be considered first. After that, wardrobe additions should be made according to the degree of want. One garment may even fill both a need and a want. For instance, an all-weather coat with a zip-in lining can meet the need for a winter coat. It can also satisfy the want for an extra spring and fall coat. A new pair of jeans might be the pair of pants needed for a part-time job. They can also double as those wanted extra school pants.

Choosing Accessories

Accessories, as in 14-5, are the items worn with garments to create complete outfits. When choosing accessories, try to achieve a coordinated, yet interesting, look. Show your personality or mood. Add an individual touch with accessories to keep outfits from being plain and uninteresting.

Accessories can work fashion magic. Some are bright; some are subdued. They help to put the finishing touch on an outfit for a fashionable look. Accessories can make the difference between a mediocre wardrobe and a marvelous one.

The right accessories can turn an old outfit into a new, up-to-date one. Accessories can extend a mix-and-match wardrobe. They offer

MaraZe/Shutterstock.com

14-5 Hats, shoes, and other decorative accessories can be coordinated with garments for different fashion looks.

an easy, and often inexpensive, way to pull different garments together. Accessories can also add variety to a wardrobe. They can make the same outfit look either dressy or casual. They make it seem as if a person owns more clothes than he or she really does.

Using Accessories to Advantage

Some accessories are functional as well as decorative. Examples of these are watches and handbags. Other accessories, such as bracelets and neckties, are purely decorative. Evaluate the types and colors of accessories that would be useful before shopping.

To choose and use accessories with flair, make sure they are appropriate for the outfit and occasion. The entire ensemble or outfit might be tailored, sporty, or dressy. Any outfit can be accessorized. When *big* looks are fashionable, accessories generally become bolder and larger in scale. Light, slender fashion silhouettes call for smaller-scale accessories. Sometimes people accessorize in creative ways for a fun event.

When thinking about the size and style of accessories, also consider body build. A person's accessories should be in proportion to his or her body. A person with a small body build should wear smaller accessories, since large items would overpower him or her. Likewise, a person with a large body build looks best with larger accessories.

Accessories can create optical illusions to improve a person's appearance just like garment designs can. Draw attention to one area of the body and away from another by wearing bright, shiny jewelry. Add height with a long necklace or tie. Decrease height with a wide, contrasting belt.

Experiment with accessories by using them in new ways. A pin might be used on a fabric purse. Try accessories with different outfits and in new combinations. Express your individuality. This is one way to make a statement about yourself.

Accessories should never detract from clothing or from a person's overall appearance. They should not draw too much attention. All parts of the design are necessary to balance the whole. Accessorizing is an elaboration on the art of dressing.

Keep accessories simple; do not overdo. If you are not sure an accessory looks right, leave it off. Using too many accessories can make an outfit appear cluttered. A lot of small accents may make an outfit look too spotty or confusing. For example, an outfit accessorized with gold earrings, several gold necklaces, a gold belt, a gold bag, and gold shoes would probably look overdone. It also may not be appropriate for the occasion.

Plan accessories just as carefully as you plan the rest of a wardrobe. Note how accessories are used in fashion magazines, advertisements, and store displays. It takes time and practice to learn to accessorize well. If a garment is intended to be the center of interest, play down the accessories. If a garment is plain, add flair with accessories.

Since accessories usually do not cost as much as clothing items, you can buy them more often to be fashionable. There are endless choices of accessories. When selecting them, consider how often and with which garments you will be able to use each one.

Footwear

A footwear wardrobe might include dress shoes, casual shoes, boots, flip-flops, slippers, and athletic shoes. Shoes are important accessories. Many are quite expensive, so choose them with care. Try to buy shoes that provide support as well as comfort and durability.

Plan footwear selections in neutral or basic colors first. Shoes should blend with, not dominate, outfits. Depending on what is fashionable, shoes should probably be the same color or value as, or darker than, pants or skirts. If shoes are lighter, attention will be drawn to the feet. Bulky footwear makes feet look bigger. Men's shoes should usually coordinate with the color of their belts.

Handbags

Handbags should coordinate with footwear, as in **14-6**, although they do not need to match. If not the same color as the shoes, then the bag should be lighter. Plan to have a handbag in a neutral or basic wardrobe color. Its size should be scaled to body size.

A *shoulder bag* has a long enough strap to go over a person's shoulder. A *hipster* is a small bag on a long strap that can go diagonally across the body from the opposite shoulder. A *fanny pack*, usually for casual or athletic use, is worn around the waist with a buckle strap. A *belt pack*, often for a camera or other small device, has loops to attach to a belt.

14-6 Accessories look good together when they are coordinated in terms of color, scale, and style.

Buturlimov Paul/Shutterstock.com

Purses, billfolds, and briefcases should have simple designs. They are often made of leather, with fabric interior compartments. See **14-7**. Straw bags are usually just for warm weather. Canvas bags are sporty. Smaller purses and clutch bags are used with dressy attire.

Headwear

A hat can complete an outfit in a special, chic way. It can also keep the head warm in winter or offer protection from the sun in summer. A hat should fit the shape and size of the head. A headwear wardrobe might include baseball caps, knit ski caps, sports visors, and straw hats for summer.

Belts

Belts, to go around the waist, are available in various widths, colors, and materials, as in **14-8**. They may be made of metal, leather, fabric, macramé cord, or other materials. They can be wide, skinny, stretchy, plain, or very decorative. They correspond with the waist measurement. *Buckles* to fasten the belt ends, may also be plain or elaborate. They may give a Western flair or an Egyptian touch. They may even display trademarks or designers' logos.

MARGRIT HIRSCH/Shutterstock.com

14-8 Belts can be interesting accessories, especially if they have unusual colors or patterns, or are worn in a creative manner.

Some buckles are detachable, so different strips of belting can be inserted into them for great versatility. Some belts are reversible with combinations such as a black side and a brown side. Remember that color contrast at the waist will draw attention there. People with thicker middles look best when their belts match the color of their outfits. Wide belts look best on people who are tall.

Scarves

Scarves are versatile accessories. They come in all sizes of squares, triangles, and long rectangles. They are available in many assortments of colors, designs, and fabrics, such as heavy wool, medium-weight blends, or thin silks. Scarves can be used to give warmth or protect the inner collar of a jacket or coat, or they can be worn strictly for decoration. Scarves can be worn around the neck, on the head, or in other ways as shown in **14-9**. Fashion changes the sizes of scarves and how they are worn. Scarves can add color near the face. Multicolored scarves can tie together all the parts of an outfit.

Neckties

Neckties are strictly decorative and can express the personality of the wearer with conservative or bold patterns, textures, and colors. The width of neckties swings from narrow to wide and back to narrow as fashion changes. Sometimes bow ties are in style.

14-7 Purses come in many materials, sizes, colors, and price ranges. When buying a purse, coordinate it with a wardrobe.

Neckties come in many fabrics and surface designs. Most have to be dry cleaned rather than laundered. They can be complemented with a tie tack or clasp when those items are fashionable.

Handkerchiefs

Handkerchiefs, meant for blowing the nose, can also be fashionable. A handkerchief peeking from the pocket of a suit can perk up a person's appearance. Some handkerchiefs are made of linen and are monogrammed. Others are made of silk or have border designs.

14-9 These are only a few of the ways that scarves can be tied and used.

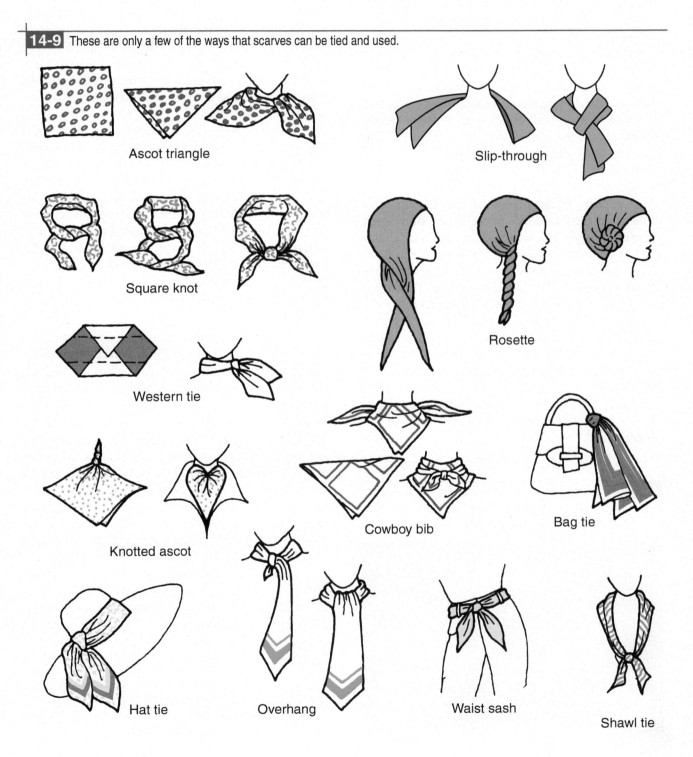

Ascot triangle

Slip-through

Square knot

Rosette

Western tie

Knotted ascot

Cowboy bib

Bag tie

Hat tie

Overhang

Waist sash

Shawl tie

Jewelry

Pieces of *jewelry* are decorative accessories for personal adornment. Examples are necklaces, rings, pins, bracelets, and earrings.

Fine jewelry is expensive. It is usually made of gold, silver, or platinum. It may contain precious stones, such as diamonds, emeralds, rubies, or sapphires. Fine jewelry should be bought from a reputable jeweler and be of a simple style that will not become dated.

Bridge jewelry is made to look like fine jewelry, but it is less expensive. It is made of good metals and may have semiprecious gems, such as opal, jade, garnet, or amethyst. See **14-10**.

Costume jewelry is less expensive. Sometimes it is plated with gold or silver. Sometimes it is made of plastic, shells, wood, or unusual materials. It can be fun, showy, inexpensive, trendy, and obviously fake.

Certain classic pieces of jewelry are wise choices for most people's budgets and don't seem to go out of style. These include simple neck chains, button or loop earrings, ID bracelets, medium-width rings, pearl necklaces, and circle bracelets. Watches come in many styles and price ranges.

Choose jewelry that is suitable to the wearer's personality and age. Some jewelry is dignified; some is striking or bold; some is youthful and fun. Like other accessories, scale jewelry to body size. Earrings should be scaled to the size of the face. Rings should be in scale with the hand. A person who is tall can wear longer necklaces. Heavy bracelets look better on a person with a larger build.

Optical illusions can be created with jewelry. To make a slender neck look wider, wear a necklace of round beads around the throat. To slenderize a thicker neck, choose a chain or necklace of medium length, so there is space between the chin and the jewelry. To widen a longer, thin face, wear round earrings.

To be tasteful, the use of jewelry should not be overdone. Jewelry should be appropriate for the occasion(s). Brushed metal is dressy, especially when used with sparkling stones or pearls. Shiny metal is better for sport or casual wear. Also, the texture and weight of the jewelry should complement the texture and weight of a garment and its fabric.

Other jewelry accessories that come into fashion periodically, or for specific occasions, are lapel pins and cuff links. A *lapel pin* is worn in the buttonhole on the lapel of a suit. It often signifies patriotism, membership in an organization, or an award that has been received. *Cuff links* are worn in place of shirt buttons at the wrist. However, the shirt must have special (French) cuffs with buttonholes through which the cuff links can be inserted.

Eyewear

Eyeglasses should harmonize with a person's eyes, hair, and skin tone. Pick a shape that complements facial contour and features and that suits personality and lifestyle. Glasses should not be overly decorative. Eyeglass frames should not be wider than the widest part of the face. Choose a high, slender, or rounded bridge for a small nose. For a long nose, a low, thick, or straight bridge is best. For glasses that seem to disappear on the face, opt for frameless lenses with no-glare glass and wire temples without designer logos. Some people have more than one pair of glasses for insurance against breakage or loss, as well as for fashion interest.

Sunglasses are not just helpful for glare reduction. They are also fashion items, as shown in **14-11**. They can be more extreme, large, and fun than regular eyeglasses.

Gloves

Gloves are sometimes a high-fashion item. For practical purposes, they are needed for warmth in cold climates. Well-fitting basic gloves made from cloth or leather (with little or no trim)

14-10 If the stones in these jewelry pieces are diamonds, it is expensive fine jewelry. If the jewels are rhinestones, the necklace and bracelet are bridge jewelry.

Syda Productions/Shutterstock.com

14-11 Sunglasses are fun accessories that allow people to make fashion statements.

can be worn with almost anything. Extra gloves can be fancy or bright. Gloves with leather or vinyl palms are best for driving a vehicle.

Hosiery

Hosiery, also called *legwear*, includes panty hose, tights, anklets, knee-highs, leg warmers, and all other stockings or socks. Stockings of various styles, fibers, and colors are available at different qualities and prices. Most are stretchy for good fit.

The texture and color of a woman's hosiery should be related to her shoes and natural skin color. Darker shades make legs look slimmer. Lighter shades and bright colors add size to the legs. Thicker stockings go with low-heeled, sporty shoes. Sheer hose should be worn with dress shoes. Sheer, sandalfoot hose (with no visible reinforcements at the toes or heels) should be worn with shoes that have open toes or heels.

Socks for men should always be of a dark color for dress. For sports, they are usually white. Argyle, striped, and decorated socks gain fashion popularity periodically.

Most hosiery is stretchy. Panty hose are usually made of nylon and are sized by combinations of height and weight. A chart is usually on the hosiery package, so consumers can choose properly. Sport socks are made in natural and manufactured fibers. Their size ranges are based on the distance from heel to toe. Tights usually contain spandex fibers for stretch.

Develop a Total Future Plan

Once you have analyzed a wardrobe, you should know what types of clothes can enhance a person's appearance. You should be aware of personal needs and wants. You should also have some ideas about how to accessorize apparel. The next step is to develop a future wardrobe plan.

Check with the right-hand column (*Action to Take*) of the wardrobe inventory. You will want to build up weak areas of the wardrobe. Make sure to consider any future changes likely to affect lifestyle, such as going to college or beginning a new job. Start planning for new wardrobe needs. As you develop a wardrobe plan, consider the following points.

Basic Garments

Basic apparel provides the core of a wardrobe. These garments are the ones worn most often. They should be classic garments of top quality without faddish details or extreme silhouettes. Well-tailored, traditional styling is best for versatility and long-lasting fashion life. They should be stylish items that have general appeal. Their look can be dressed up or down with a variety of different accessories and by combining them with other garments. The jacket in **14-12** is a basic garment.

When developing a wardrobe plan, first decide which items are basic apparel. A good wardrobe revolves around these few essential garments. They should be of the highest quality that is affordable. They should be of good fabric. These garments should have simple structural lines without many frills or much applied trim. The simpler the design of a basic garment, the more versatile it is.

Having several basic, quality garments, such as jackets, slacks, or dresses that will last a long time without going out of style, is called investment dressing. Basic, quality garments are good investments. They can be worn for many years in various outfits and with different accessories. Investment dressing is especially smart in the business world where fashion changes are slower and more subtle.

conrado/Shutterstock.com

14-12 This jacket is a basic garment that can be coordinated with many different shirts, sweaters, slacks, and jeans to create different fashion looks. It should remain stylish for a long time.

The traditional, classic styles of basic apparel will stay fashionable for many seasons. They can be worn for many years and to many different occasions. You only have to adjust the hem and change the accessories over the years. An inexpensive garment of poor quality would lose its shape after several wearings. It would soon look cheap and would have to be replaced. It would cost more money in the long run to keep replacing those items. Skimping on the basic apparel items is a poor clothing investment. Spend more clothing dollars for styles that will last.

Basic, more expensive apparel items should be in neutral hues or low values of colors. Bright colors would probably be too noticeable, the owner may tire of them, and the garments might lose their fashion interest. With a planned color scheme, only a few accessories and pairs of shoes are needed, since they will go with many outfits.

Extending a Wardrobe

Once you have decided on the basic apparel, consider the less expensive garments and accessories that can expand the wardrobe. These are the extenders or *multipliers*. Plan for versatile pieces that can mix and match with current apparel to make more outfit combinations. An example is pictured in **14-13**.

Extenders add individuality and flair to a wardrobe. If extenders are coordinated, they can be combined in many fashionable ways.

Extenders might include slacks of an unusual texture, a shirt with interesting trim, a patterned or quilted vest, or a brightly colored turtleneck. They can make an outfit look Western, preppy, athletic, or whatever is in style at the moment. If each one can be coordinated with several items in a wardrobe, the number of total outfit combinations multiplies.

14-13 These items—tunic dress, cami top, and double strand of beads—can be mixed and matched with these basic black slacks and jacket or with many other items for numerous different outfits.

Margo Harrison/Shutterstock.com

You will be able to combine more wardrobe items if many of the extenders are solid-colored garments rather than stripes, plaids, or figured designs. A minimum number of shirts, sweaters, pants, skirts, and vests in coordinated colors can be mixed into many outfits.

If budget permits, you can perk up a wardrobe with the latest accessory or fad. Such accents make the wardrobe interesting and even exciting. By adapting new trends to the wardrobe, an up-to-date and individual style of dressing can be achieved.

Plan for *seasonless clothes* whenever possible. They can be lightweight woolens, knits, or good quality corduroys. They can be worn during most of the year: fall, winter, and spring.

Write a Plan

Now you can write a wardrobe plan for the coming seasons and years. This is a blueprint of actions to update or complete the wardrobe in the best way. It might change as you consider the resources available to achieve it, but it will serve as a guide when making purchases. Don't plan garment additions one at a time, even if buying them that way. Plan for several garments that can mix and match to pull together the existing wardrobe. Identify gaps in the inventory. Then include only clothes and accessories that will fill those gaps. Remember, a few carefully chosen additions can make a big change by creating many new outfits.

Make a wardrobe plan like the one shown in **14-14**. It has been partially filled in for use as an example. To complete a wardrobe plan, first list specific activities. Then for each of the activities, select wardrobe inventory items that can be worn and combined with others. Write present apparel (from the wardrobe inventory) under the proper categories.

In the *Needs and Priorities* column of the wardrobe plan, write major future expenditures. (See items shown in red in 14-14.) These are such items as shoes, coats, suits, and other basic apparel that should be of good quality and might be expensive. These purchases can be spread over a period of time. Then, in the same column, list the chosen extenders. (See items shown in blue in 14-14.) They should coordinate with the basics to complete outfits for activities. List occasionally used items only if they are very important. *Needs*

should also include replacement of favorite items that are worn out.

In the wardrobe plan, put a number next to each *need* to show its priority. As you set priorities, decide which additions are the most important. Then you know which items to buy first.

A wardrobe plan is like a blueprint used to build a house. It is rewarding to follow the plan and reach a goal. If you plan well, new purchases will enhance current apparel. It may take several seasons to finally achieve a well-coordinated, compact wardrobe. The result will be well worth the effort.

Consider Available Resources

Available resources, or the money, time, and skills a person has to make wardrobe improvements, should be evaluated. Combine a wardrobe plan with a sound money-management plan to know what is affordable.

If a person doesn't have his or her own source of income, the needs of other family members must be considered. Take into account the family's size, income, other expenses, and attitudes about clothing. Clothing is only one of many needs and wants. Housing, food, medical care, transportation, and recreational activities cost money, too. An unexpected emergency or new responsibilities can limit the amount of money and time available to acquire clothes.

Most people cannot afford to have all the clothes they want. You will want to save toward planned purchases according to the priorities noted in the wardrobe plan.

Small clothing expenses are continuous. They are for clothing upkeep, such as dry cleaning, and for purchases of low-cost extenders and accessories. Large clothing expenses occur only periodically. They are for higher-cost, basic apparel items. Try to plan available resources accordingly. You may want to write a spending plan in order to stay on track to reach goals.

The total amount available to spend on wardrobe items will probably affect the quality of the garments, rather than the styles. Also, your budget and where you shop will determine when additions are made to the wardrobe.

The philosophy about quantity versus quality of clothes is a personal judgment. Young people tend to favor quantity because they like to have a variety of the latest fashions. This may be a good strategy for quickly growing teens. However, as people get older and stop growing, they seem to enjoy having fewer clothes, but of better quality. Buying decisions will depend on a person's situation, guided by a wardrobe plan.

Sewing as an Option

Sewing is one of the best and most economical ways to build a wardrobe. Using sewing skills

14-14 A wardrobe plan should include the basic apparel, extenders, and accessories already owned as well as items needed to fill in any gaps.

Wardrobe Plan				
Season and year: _____		**Basic color schemes:** _____		
Activities	**Basic Apparel**	**Extenders**	**Accessories**	**Needs & Priorities**
School	2 Pr. cords 1 Pr. nice jeans 2 Crew-neck sweaters	2 Striped shirts 2 Polo shirts	Sneakers Cowboy boots	1 Pr. jeans ③ 1 Casual shirt ⑧
Job: Part-time clothing store salesperson	Same 2 cords Same 2 Crew-neck sweaters	Turtleneck Same 2 striped shirts Blue shirt	Brown leather belt Wallet	Loafers ② Dress slacks ⑤ 2 Pr. dark socks ⑦
Religious and special events	Navy blazer Same 2 Pr. cords	Same turtleneck Same blue shirt 2 neckties		White shirt ⑨ Gray suit ⑩
Social activities: Movies	Same 2 Pr. cords	Same 2 Polo shirts Same 2 Striped shirts	Cowboy boots ID bracelet	Same as for school and job.
Sports activities: Swimming	2 Swimming suits 1 Sweat suit	3 T-shirts		

Leisure:
  Bike riding
  shooting baskets
	2 Pr. old jeans
	1 Pr. cargo shorts
		Same 3 T-shirts
		Old sweatshirt
			Sneakers	Sneakers ①
				3 Pr. white socks ④

Lounging and sleeping	2 PJ pants	Old athletic shorts		
Outer clothing	Tan trench coat Down ski jacket		Knit hat Leather gloves	
Other: Prom				Rent formal wear when needed. Could use new underwear. ⑥

Djem/Shutterstock.com

14-15 Sewing skills are valuable resources that can help people build and maintain their wardrobes.

Iakov Filimonov/Shutterstock.com

14-16 Fabrics of many different styles and colors are available in craft stores and on the Internet.

as a resource is a great way to stretch a fashion budget, as in **14-15**. Sewing allows people to get more clothes for their money.

The new sewing machines have a variety of useful features. Patterns and fabrics are available in stores in most communities and on the Internet. See **14-16**. Sewing lessons can be taken. If you develop and use sewing skills, you can make clothes for less than half the cost of buying them ready-made. You can select the colors and styles that achieve a good fit and enhance a person's appearance. You will also be able to express yourself creatively with the apparel you make. You might even appear on a fashion design TV show!

Summary

Developing a well-planned wardrobe takes time, effort, knowledge, and skill. Start by taking a wardrobe inventory to evaluate current apparel. Group clothing, especially noting the features that are most appealing in clothing that is worn often. Analyze the clothing worn occasionally as to what modifications or combinations are needed to wear them more. Take action to do clothing repairs or cleaning. Properly dispose of clothing not worn in the past year. Also, distinguish wants from needs to be able to prioritize wardrobe additions.

Choose accessories that are appropriate for outfits and for the occasions to which they are worn. Consider proper footwear, hosiery, handbags, belts, headwear, and gloves. People can express themselves through scarves, neckties, and decorative handkerchiefs. Evaluate needs for fine, bridge, and costume jewelry. Also, consider harmonious eyewear.

The next step is to develop a future wardrobe plan. The basic apparel for the core of a wardrobe should be top-quality, classic garments. Investment dressing and seasonless clothes are often wise choices. Use less-expensive garments and accessories to extend a wardrobe with many combinations. Write the wardrobe plan as a blueprint to build the best wardrobe over time.

Finally, evaluate available resources to know the money, time, and skills needed to make wardrobe improvements. Think about quality versus quantity, and consider sewing some clothes for yourself or others.

Fashion Recall

Write your answers on a separate sheet of paper.

Short Answer: Write the correct response to each of the following items.

1. It is a good idea to analyze a wardrobe by completing a wardrobe inventory _____.
   A. at least twice each season
   B. every three to five years
   C. once or twice a year
   D. None of the above.

2. Describe two courses of action to take concerning the clothes in a wardrobe that are worn only occasionally.

3. Name three useful ways of disposing of clothes that are never worn.

4. Give two examples of choosing accessories that are in proportion to a person's body.

5. Name two ways people can use accessories to create optical illusions to improve their appearance.

6. Distinguish between fine jewelry and costume jewelry.

7. Describe the kinds of garments that people should choose as their basic apparel, or as the core of their wardrobes.

8. Why is investment dressing especially smart in the business world?

9. Give three examples of wardrobe extenders.

10. List three advantages of having sewing skills.

11. A wardrobe should _____.
    A. be as large as a person can afford
    B. be in a continuous slow state of change
    C. include lots of shoes, since footwear is important
    D. be just like a close friend's wardrobe

12. Clothing expenses _____.
    A. are continuous for upkeep and for low-cost extenders and accessories
    B. are only periodic for expensive basic items
    C. should be part of a sound money-management plan
    D. All of the above.

Fashion Vocabulary

13. Read the text passages that contain each of the *Fashion Terms* on the chapter opening. Then, draw a cartoon bubble to express the meaning of each term as it relates to the chapter.

Critical Thinking

14. **Plan accessories** Give examples of accessories that you could use to extend your wardrobe today and in the future. Also give examples of fad accessories to avoid.

15. **Analyze advantages** For the person who wears a uniform to school or work daily, what do you believe are the advantages of developing a wardrobe plan?

16. **Create a budget** Create an imaginary clothing allowance to be used across a year's time. Use retail websites and clothing catalogs to develop a wardrobe plan based on that amount of money. Write a summary explaining why some months will have larger expenditures than others.

Core Skills

17. **Speaking, listening, and writing** Conduct a phone interview with a wardrobe consultant about the topic of wardrobe planning. (*Note:* Some major department stores employ wardrobe

consultants.) Prepare a list of interview questions in advance of the interview. Share your findings with the class in an oral report.

18. **Technology**   Create a list of community organizations that accept donations of used, but wearable, clothing. Note the address, telephone number, and website for each. Indicate which of them are donation drop-off locations or thrift shops (usually for charity), and which are consignment resale shops. Use a school-approved application to create a flyer for the school newsletter to share with the community.

19. **Math practice**   Describe the latest fad items for teens by completing the following:
    - What is the approximate cost of each item?
    - How long do you think these fads will stay popular?
    - Calculate the approximate cost-per-wearing of the items using this formula: (purchase price + upkeep costs) ÷ number of times worn = cost-per-wearing
    - Do you think these items are wise wardrobe investments? Do you think any will become lasting fashions? Explain your views.

20. **Writing**   Use a spreadsheet program to create a wardrobe planning chart, as shown in 14-14. Fill in the online charts with information about your wardrobe and print it. Then prioritize the items listed under *Needs* and *Priorities*.

21. **Math practice**   Locate price estimates for the items listed in the wardrobe plan chart you created. Report the source of each estimate. Use an online calculator to total the list. Then reduce the total cost by 10 percent by finding appealing substitutes for the items you listed.

22. **CTE career readiness practice**   Most employers value employees that can set and achieve reasonable, attainable goals. Here are a few things you need to remember about goals. Goals should
    - be specific and positive
    - be measurable
    - have a target deadline (either short-term—several months, or long-term—several years)

    Think about your wardrobe goals and financial well-being as related to you as an employee of a fashion retailer. In writing, set a wardrobe goal and way to finance your wardrobe. Determine how you will measure achievement of this goal, and identify a deadline for meeting it.

Fashion in Action

23. **Portfolio builder**   Plan two wardrobes with basic items, extenders, and accessories. Plan one for a high school or college student, and plan another for a young business person. Include your wardrobe plans in your portfolio.

24. **Design activity**   Bring some scarves and neckties to class. Use online resources to investigate various methods for tying and wearing these items. Then, demonstrate the various ways of tying and wearing these items.

Self-Assessment Quiz ↱

Complete the self-assessment quiz online to help practice and expand your knowledge and skills.

While studying, look for the activity icon  **to:**

- **practice** key fashion terms with e-flash cards, vocabulary games, and matching activities
- **assess** what you learn by completing self-assessment quizzes

www.g-wlearning.com/clothingandfashion/

G-WLEARNING.com

Fashion Terms

cross-channel
  shopping
fashion conscious
money conscious
impulse buying

sales resistance
policies
shoplifting
hangtags
labels

packaging
rights
responsibilities
standards
quality control

Objectives

After studying this chapter, you will be able to
- ➤ **plan** ahead as a well-informed consumer.
- ➤ **decide** where and when to shop.
- ➤ **evaluate** the information on hangtags, labels, and packaging.
- ➤ **name** and describe five laws related to apparel.
- ➤ **identify** the rights and responsibilities of consumers.

I t is worth your while to become a competent and well-informed consumer. Making smart clothing buys is a skill that any consumer can learn. By developing good shopping habits, people can dress better for less money. Intelligent buying decisions are made, and a clothing budget is spent more carefully. Smart consumers go past the stage of the beginner who picks apparel on the basis of *I like it; I'll buy it*. Even an attractive item of clothing is worthless if it does not fit the person's body shape, coloring, lifestyle, and wardrobe. Shopping mistakes will dwindle in number as knowledge and experience are acquired.

To improve your shopping techniques, learn how to plan for purchases and shop wisely. Informed people shop with a purpose. They think about their needs in advance and evaluate what is available. After they buy, greater satisfaction is achieved from their purchases.

Clothing purchases consume a sizable portion of a consumer's total budget. Because clothing is necessary, why not make the best choices with available funds? Skilled shoppers can buy much more merchandise than unskilled buyers with the same amount of money. Wise consumers use their resources to the best advantage. They make the decision to buy when they find the best item for the best price.

Prepare Ahead

Apparel is purchased not only as a necessity, but also as a popular form of luxury. To enjoy the luxury of a super wardrobe, learn the techniques to build it intelligently. That starts with good planning before shopping. By selecting and buying apparel wisely, consumers are more likely to be happy with their purchases.

If you have prepared a wardrobe plan, as described in the previous chapter, you are aware of the apparel items needed. Plan to buy only those items in the right colors, textures, and styles. Then you can be confident that purchases will fit into a wardrobe and will be put to good use.

Planning what to buy ahead of time is just as important as the actual purchasing. Shopping is a decision-making process. Make a list and follow it. Gather information and use it. With practice, shopping becomes easier and more enjoyable. A little time spent planning for a shopping trip saves a lot of time and mistakes later.

Make a List

Gain this experience by practicing on yourself. On a piece of paper, list the clothing items and accessories that are your priority needs. Be specific about the color and style of each item. This will become your shopping list after it has been reviewed further.

Estimate the cost of each item on your list of apparel needs. Study catalogs and read advertisements to get an idea of the costs. Write the approximate purchase price next to each item. Will there be extra costs for alterations, unusual upkeep, or credit? If an item needs to be dry-cleaned, how much will that cost over the time you expect to wear the garment? The cost of transportation and parking to buy the apparel might also have to be considered. A sample list is shown in **15-1** to help you get started.

Decide how much money you have to spend on your clothing needs. Then try to spend your money wisely and tastefully. Plan ahead, so expensive items do not have to be purchased all at once. You may discover that to attain your goals, you have to delay some purchases. It might be worthwhile to make some of the items. However, even if you don't sew well, it is still important to know how to buy fabrics and ready-to-wear items intelligently.

You may have to assign different priorities to some clothing needs if your budget can't handle certain costs. Which garments are needed right away? Determine the purchases that could be delayed. Are there some that can be omitted? Purchasing fewer unimportant items leaves more resources for important planned ones or for future purchases.

Learn to put sufficient money into clothes and accessories that wear well and can be worn for several seasons. Consider how many times you will wear each item. Think before you spend a lot on a party outfit that you will wear only once or twice. Such a purchase may force you to skimp on an outfit for school or work that you would wear often. Also, estimate how long the style of each garment will last. Does it have built-in *fashion obsolescence* or fad qualities that will soon date it? Try to recognize the fashions most likely to remain in style for several more seasons.

Plan to invest in *seasonless clothes* whenever possible. For instance, an all-weather coat with a zip-out lining is versatile. A lightweight wool suit or blazer can be worn during most seasons. Items like these extend a wardrobe and help to maximize your budget. Do your plans include basic styles that you can wear to many places?

15-1 Your shopping list should include enough information to allow you to plan your expenditures carefully.

Sample Shopping List			
Needs	**Specifics**	**Estimated Costs**	**Where Available**
Athletic shoes	Light-colored, all-purpose	$50	Mall
Loafers	Brown leather, good quality	$58 + credit costs	Bud's Shoes, Main Street
Blue jeans	Tapered legs	$30	Mall
Dress slacks	Classic lines, gray	$36 + future dry cleaning	Put off until next month?

Do the items mix and match well with what you already have? Buying clothes that will not be worn is a waste of money.

When planning future purchases, wise consumers evaluate past purchases in terms of price, amount of care required, and wearability. They consider pros and cons of brands previously bought. They also consider how pleased they have been with various stores patronized in the past.

Gather Information

In order to plan ahead, become a well-informed consumer. Information inspires confidence and reduces shopping errors. Doing preliminary *armchair shopping* homework saves time and travel costs later. The more knowledge gained before a shopping trip, the better the purchasing decisions will be.

To gather information, read fashion magazines or websites, newspapers, and mail-order catalogs. Also learn about new silhouettes, colors, and fabrics from TV or the Internet. Fashion photographs show how garments and accessories are combined into outfits. Feature articles often give pointers on clothing selection in relation to the use and care of particular apparel items. Fashion writers inform consumers about upcoming fashion trends months before the clothes appear in stores. Learning about new trends helps people adapt a current wardrobe more effectively and plan for future additions.

Browse the various departments of favorite stores. Study their windows, interior displays, and mannequins, as in **15-2**. See how new outfits are assembled. Notice the creative use of accessories. Evaluate the new looks and decide if they suit your personality, body type, and lifestyle. Try to distinguish classic, lasting fashions from passing fads. Although *window shopping* is sometimes a leisure pastime, try not to be tempted into unplanned buying. Leave your cash, credit or debit cards, and checkbook at home when on a tight budget.

Study catalogs, advertisements, and websites to find out the cost of items and where they are available. Get ideas of styles as well as prices. Written descriptions and illustrations show the features of garments and accessories. They also have information about sizes, fabrics, and care of garments.

15-2 Store displays can give you interesting ideas about how items will look when worn.

Take advantage of consumer information resources. Note what well-dressed people are wearing on television and in your community. Friends or relatives, who have had good or bad experiences with clothing purchases, can also offer helpful advice. Also, another great source of information is using the Internet to search a fashion item plus the word *review*. This often provides a wealth of useful information.

Your school or town library should have books and magazines to help plan shopping trips. Consumer reports are available on a wide range of consumer goods, including some types of clothing. The telephone book can help locate certain items, but it does not evaluate the retail stores or merchandise quality. A large ad in the Yellow Pages only indicates that a business has paid the fee for that amount of space in the phone book. Its products or prices are not necessarily better than stores with tiny listings.

Consumer aids also provide information. They are educational pamphlets, booklets, and fact sheets that describe the properties of textile products and give directions for their use and care. This information comes from fiber producers, pattern companies, fabric stores, and trade group associations. Videos and CDs are also available to schools and groups. Most consumer aids are free.

Some help with clothing can be obtained from community classes and workshops. More help can be received by calling the county or state Cooperative Extension Service. As well as providing personal assistance on specific problems, extension agents might have useful printed information.

Evaluate Advertising

A good source of up-to-date shopping information is found in advertisements. Advertising has two purposes. The primary purpose is *to sell*. The secondary purpose is *to inform*. Advertising can be valuable to consumers when viewed this way.

Retailers and manufacturers spend millions of dollars each year to persuade people to buy their products. These businesses use print media, radio, television, websites, apps, displays, demonstrations, fashion shows, and billboards. Advertising catches people's attention with clever slogans, songs, and phrases. Merchandise is described in glowing, sometimes overstated, terms. Advertisers can play on the emotions of consumers. They imply that you will look like the model if you wear what he or she is wearing. Advertisements are meant to entice consumers into buying by creating a desire for the items shown and described.

Advertisements can mislead consumers who have poor planning and shopping habits. Clever ads can even cause some shoppers to buy items they do not need. However, advertising can also provide a great deal of useful information.

Learn to recognize the helpful information in advertisements. Read between the lines and notice the small print. Find ads that present complete views and descriptions of garments, rather than just exciting and glamorous ones. Pay attention to information about fibers, fabrics, and garment care.

Advertisements allow comparisons of similar merchandise from different manufacturers or retail stores, including special sales. They present needed information about new fashions and where they are available.

Reputable media companies will not accept advertisements they know are false. However, any information may be inflated. Learn to judge the content of advertisements carefully and use what is needed for purchasing.

Where to Shop

Decide which stores, shopping centers, or malls to visit before leaving home. Find the most efficient route(s) to prevent wasted travel time and backtracking. Catalog and online purchases are also big time-savers.

Plan to make large, basic purchases first, as in **15-3**, while still fresh and alert. After that, shop for smaller items, if time and budget allow.

Sometimes it is better to shop at different sources for different items. There are pros and cons to shopping at each type of apparel outlet. Refer to Chapter 7 and review the different types of retail stores and their features.

Price versus Quality and Service

Small shops and boutiques provide personal attention and strive for a pleasant atmosphere. Some people are willing to pay more at stores known for their quality merchandise and service. Some stores will even gift wrap. Consumers like the privilege of getting their money back for returned items, instead of store credit. These factors are worth the higher prices to them.

On the other hand, the lower prices of discount stores and manufacturers' outlets are also attractive to many consumers. Stores that order goods in volume offer good buys on basic

15-3 Purchases of major items, such as sport coats and slacks, should be made before smaller items, such as neckties, are bought.

necessities, even on well-known brand names. However, such stores often have crowds of people, long checkout lines, and sparse interiors. Many stores will now "price-match" if the shopper can show that another retailer offers the same item at a lower price.

In general, the stores that offer the least amount of personal service have the lowest prices. However, the quality of the apparel may be low, too. Learn to rely on your own consumer knowledge and awareness to find the right merchandise to fill needs. Determine your expectations of service and quality in relation to what you are willing to pay. Gently used clothing may be available at low prices at clothing exchanges, consignment shops, fairs, yard or garage sales, and thrift shops, as in **15-4**. These sources are sometimes good for seldom-worn party clothes and children's apparel. Interesting finds can create fashionable outfits for bargain prices.

Types of Merchandise

Shopping for specific items can also influence the choice of retailers. For unique merchandise, try a boutique. Items in a certain category may be stocked only at a specialty shop. When shopping for several types of apparel at one time, a big department store can be a good choice. Sometimes items can only be found at several different stores. A large selection of styles can be found online.

Location and Store Hours

Sometimes the locations of stores affect consumers' store choices. It may not pay to travel a long distance just to save a little money on a few low-priced items. However, if buying several expensive items, it may be worthwhile to travel to specific stores for better selections and prices.

Shopping malls and department stores are great options, because they often provide one-stop shopping with wider selections. See **15-5**. Also, public transportation or free parking may be available.

If shopping time is limited, the stores' hours are important. Those who work afternoons and evenings may favor a store that opens at 9:30 a.m. rather than at 11:00 a.m. to shop during time off from work.

It is not convenient for some people to go out to shop at all. They may not have the time, might dislike crowds, or may want to shop without salespeople. The best option is then mail-order or online shopping from home. The conveniences of these options are many. Purchases can be made 24 hours a day, and without the hassle of dressing up to leave home in all kinds of weather. Plus, transportation costs, fighting traffic, and finding a parking space are avoided completely.

Catalogs, TV shows, and retail websites show and describe items in detail. Ordering is done by phone or digital device. The merchandise is

15-4 Thrift shops usually benefit good causes. People donate goods to thrift shops, and other people can buy the goods inexpensively. Good clothing can be purchased at very low prices.

15-5 If your shopping list contains many different items, a large mall, such as this one, might be the best place to find all of them.

delivered to the consumer's address by mail or other parcel delivery services. On the downside, when shopping from home, merchandise cannot be seen, felt, or tried on for size. If the item is wrong or does not fit, arrangements must be made for return delivery. Also, sometimes online retailers sell their customers' information to third parties for their marketing and advertising purposes.

Advertising or Loyalty

Eye-catching advertising can draw people to certain stores. The store may feature the exact item a consumer happens to need, or its advertised prices are lower.

Some people prefer to always patronize the same store because of personal loyalty. A store may be close to home or owned by an acquaintance. It may have the reputation of providing fair policies, truthful advertising, and extra services. This is very important to some people. The store employees may get to know their loyal customers and cater to their needs and tastes.

Cross-Channel Shopping

Cross-channel shopping is now very popular. This means shopping for items across more than one retail channel—combining stores, mail-order catalogs, TV shopping channels, and/or websites. For instance, a consumer might look for sweaters at retail stores and catalogs, yet buy from a website. Conversely, a consumer might search for sweaters (including colors and prices) on several different retail websites. Often mobile apps and social media are used for comparison shopping, peer feedback, product information, and obtaining money-saving coupons. See **15-6**. After doing *e-research*, the shopper might go to the preferred retail store to buy the chosen sweater.

Mail-order and electronic shopping can be done at the best times for each consumer. It is easiest for people who trust the online retailer to provide accurate fabric and color information, know the merchandise, and are easy to fit. When ordered, unlike store purchases, the merchandise may take several days or weeks to arrive. There are usually added shipping charges involved, and someone may have to sign for the items when they arrive. The items

michaeljung/Shutterstock.com

15-6 Retailers are making shopping easier for consumers who want to compare items and buy via mobile apps on smartphones.

can almost always be returned, but some effort and costs are involved in repacking and sending them back. Sometimes the retailer will pay the costs of returning goods. If a store location of that retailer is nearby, goods can be returned there.

Merchandise in catalogs or on websites may not be available in that same retailer's stores. Items can, however, be ordered and sent to the store for pickup by the consumer. This often eliminates shipping charges. Items usually stocked by a store, but sold out, can be ordered at the check-out register and sent to the customer's address. Technologies are always improving, and consumers are becoming more proficient with cross-channel shopping. See **15-7**.

Body scanning is an exciting virtual fit technology that is being perfected. With this technology, correct fit is easier to accomplish remotely, or even in stores, via computer. The consumer's body is scanned with 3-D modeling software to extract the exact measurements and create his/her virtual form. Consumers can then try on various garments using personal virtual forms that look just like them. As a result, changing rooms may become a thing of the past. Custom-made clothing may even become more affordable with this technology. Also, items appearing on TV shows or in commercials in the future might be bought with an electronic click or tap of a finger.

Daniel Korzeniewski/Shutterstock.com

15-7 It is common to see desired merchandise at a store or in a catalog, and then order it on the retailer's website, paying by credit card or electronic payment.

Consumer Decisions

Reports from retailers indicate that most customers are fashion conscious. They are aware of, and want, what is new and fashionable. They usually look in many stores and are loyal to their own tastes, rather than to any one retailer. They want to express themselves and gain approval from peers. When they find what they want, price may not be the deciding factor.

The wisest consumers are not only fashion conscious, but also money conscious. They stay aware of how much each item costs and of their monetary resources. They shop where they can get the best buys and service for their money. They find the retailers that specialize in the kinds of merchandise they need. They know where the buyers' tastes are the same as theirs, so the merchandise will be to their liking.

Consumers, as a group, have *voting power* with their money and purchase choices. Consumer acceptance or rejection of fashion innovations influences the cost, quality, and availability of those specific goods. The consumers' patronage of certain stores gives a vote of confidence to the way those retailers run their businesses. The profits of manufacturers and retailers dwindle when consumers do not purchase their items.

When to Shop

Shopping at different times of the season, called *fashion timing*, can be used in practical ways, as in **15-8**.

For a wide choice of styles, colors, and sizes, shop early in the season. The new fashions will have just come into the stores. There will be a large selection of new clothes, which is especially helpful for people who may be harder to fit. Buying early also allows the longest wearing time while garments are in style. However, clothes are usually most expensive early in the season.

For lower prices, shop late in the season. There will be a smaller selection, but the items may be on sale to clear the stores for next season's new merchandise.

15-8 Shopping early in the season assured this man of a large selection of the latest fashions in outerwear, to be worn throughout the fall and winter.

Tereshchenko Dmitry/Shutterstock.com

If possible, shop ahead of when an item is needed. This allows more time to watch for sales and make intelligent purchases. Try not to buy emotionally or under pressure. Shopping at the last minute tends to invite hurried purchases. If something is needed for that evening, the wrong colors or styles may be a consumer's only choice.

Shop well in advance of holidays to get the best service and selection. Try to avoid shopping just before a store's closing time. Consumers are less likely to make smart shopping decisions when tired or rushed.

Stores are least crowded during bad weather. Consumers who do not mind going out into the elements will find it a good time to browse merchandise and get help from salespeople. Other good times are during the morning hours and the evening around dinner time. In late morning, the clerks have put out the new merchandise. They have marked sale items, and the lunch crowd is not out yet. Also, many stores are almost empty from 6:00 p.m. to 7:00 p.m. They are busiest on weekends and near holidays. Lunchtime and just after office hours are busy times in business areas.

The best time to shop for shoes is after walking a while or in the afternoon. This allows for a good fit over normal foot expansion. Most people's feet are a little bigger later in the day, especially in the summer. However, at the very end of a summer day, or after a great deal of walking, they might be abnormally swollen.

Shopping Considerations

Serious shopping is generally more efficient when done alone, especially when the purchases are planned. However, if an objective, critical opinion is necessary, bring a knowledgeable relative or close friend whose advice you respect. Salespeople may not be reliable or frank with their help. They often give poor advice, since their job is merely to sell merchandise. Some may earn commissions on their sales, so they urge customers to make more purchases. See **15-9**.

Stick to flattering styles, which vary by body build. Consider whether the lines and colors of

15-9 Do not buy an item just because a salesperson tells you to.

garments are becoming and go with an existing wardrobe. Do not guess when matching colors. Carry fabric and color swatches when shopping. Snip small fabric pieces from the seams or hems of garments at home. Attach the swatches to safety pins or glue them on cards. Swatches will help to coordinate any new purchases. If possible, do not carry the actual garments while shopping. They are bulky and might get soiled or lost.

At the store, try to match colors under natural light at a window or doorway, if possible. Store lighting can make colors look different than they look in natural light.

While shopping, be well-groomed and nicely dressed in clothes that are simple to put on and take off. This allows garments to be easily tried on for proper fit at the store. Wear or take along suitable underclothes, accessories, and shoes that complement the planned purchases. They should be the right type and color, if possible. For instance, take or wear brown dress slacks if they will go with a shirt or sweater you intend to buy. This will help you better judge how a purchase will really look.

Stay within your list of preplanned priority shopping needs. Control impulse buying or sudden and not carefully considered purchasing. Rethink buying fads or sale items, if they are not needed. Do not be tempted or talked into making unplanned purchases or ones you may regret later. In other words, develop sales resistance, which is shopping self-control. Consumers have the right to browse and try on garments. They are entitled to shop without being pressured to buy. Salespeople should be providing help as part of their jobs. They are not owed a purchase. Develop the confidence to make the right decisions. Remember, *if in doubt, don't buy*.

Shopping Manners

Use good shopping manners. Shopping will be more fun, and the store personnel more helpful. Always be courteous and polite to salespeople and other shoppers. Wait your turn. State your needs clearly to salespeople for better service and attention. If you do not need help, say, "I'm just looking, thank you."

Responsible consumers handle merchandise carefully. Do not mistreat or damage items. Refold items after looking at them. Pick up merchandise that has fallen. When trying on clothes, make sure they do not get stained from makeup or dirty from shoes. Be careful not to tear openings or break fasteners. After garments are tried on, put them back on their original hangers. See **15-10**.

Cooperate with store policies, which are action plans that guide decisions and outcomes. Policies and rules are often for the consumers' safety and protection. Notice signs that are posted and abide by them. Some garments, such as swimsuits and intimate apparel, have public health requirements.

15-10 Always return the clothes you try on the way you found them on display.

pjcross/Shutterstock.com

Some stores do not allow merchandise to be returned for money back. Sometimes store credit toward the purchase of other items in the store is the only return option. Understand a store's return policies before purchasing goods.

The lack of consideration of some shoppers raises prices for everyone. If an item has been torn, soiled, or returned to the store after being worn, it is damaged merchandise. It cannot be sold at full price. In fact, the store may not be able to sell it at all. Any loss in the retail sales price of goods means an increase in operating expenses for the store. Prices must be raised to make up for those losses.

The practice of shoplifting, or stealing merchandise from a store, adds to the price of goods for everyone else. When items for sale in a store are stolen, the cost of those lost goods must be recovered by the business. Plus, inventory data becomes incorrect and the store's security measures must be increased. Some stores hire security guards, and some buy special detection equipment and tags. All of these provisions create extra costs for the retailers and therefore cause higher consumer prices to cover those costs. Report any shoplifting, if observed directly. It is a serious crime punishable by fine or a prison sentence. Also, anyone with a record of shoplifting will have trouble finding employment with retailers and other companies.

Hangtags, Labels, and Packaging

In shopping venues, hangtags and labels are attached to clothing items. They give information about products, including the size, price, special features, brand name, fiber content, finishes, manufacturer, and care instructions. Hangtags and labels exist to identify products, to help sell them, to help consumers make decisions about them, and to explain proper care.

Hangtags, labels, and packaging information give consumers important facts. This comes from joint efforts of the federal government, fiber producers, fabric and garment manufacturers, the clothing care industry, and consumer groups. As a consumer, read hand-tags and labels carefully when making decisions about buying apparel.

Hangtags

Hangtags are detachable signs, as shown in **15-11**. They are usually affixed to the outside of garments with strings, plastic bands, pins, staples, or adhesives. They are made of heavy paper or cardboard. They are often hung from buttons, buttonholes, zippers, belt loops, or underarm seams. Hangtags are removed before garments are worn.

In general, hangtags tell consumers what manufacturers want to say about their products. Much of that information is voluntary (not required by law). Hangtags are a form of promotion to help sell products. Information about performance features, such as special finishes, reinforced pockets, adjustable button cuffs, etc. is usually on hangtags. Symbols and logos are often displayed to identify the designers, manufacturers, or sellers. Sometimes a seal of approval certifies good test results from a lab. Guarantees may assure replacement or money refunded if items do not perform as expected.

Labels

Labels, as in **15-12**, are permanently attached to garments on the inside, where they do not

STILLFX/Shutterstock.com

15-12 Labels are permanently attached to garments and provide specific types of information.

show during wear. Usually made of ribbon or cloth, they are attached at the back neckline, waistline, side seam, or on a facing. They may be any color or style as long as they do not ravel. A label names the fiber content of a garment and its country of origin. It describes the care required to maintain the longest wear and best appearance of the garment. It also identifies the manufacturer or distributor.

15-11 Manufacturers use hangtags to give promotional information about their products to consumers. Hangtags are removed before garments are worn.

Goodheart-Willcox Publisher

This information may be written on both sides of an attached label, so it can be turned over. Sometimes tagless labels are stamped onto shirttails or inside necklines with indelible ink, or fused onto fabrics. Most of the information on labels is required by law, as explained later in this chapter.

Packaging

Packaging is the covering, wrapper, or container in which some merchandise is placed. Usually, much of the information that is on a garment's inside label is repeated on the outside of the package. The sleeve length, waist, and hip measurements, or chest size may also be printed on the bag, box, or wrapper. There is usually other promotional information printed on the package, too. Sometimes there is additional printed material loose inside the package.

Government Legislation

Laws require that all textile products sold in the United States carry labels showing fiber content and the country of manufacture. Labels must also include the identifying number of the producer, and general care instructions. See **15-13**. The generic names of fibers must be given, since so many trade names now exist. Laws require manufacturers and retailers to attach permanent care and performance labels to almost all textile products. Mail-order catalog descriptions must also state this information.

Several specific laws have been passed and amended over many years to regulate the truthful labeling of clothing, other textile products, and furs. These laws encourage ethical practices to protect consumers against deceptive labeling and advertising. Most are enforced by the *Federal Trade Commission (FTC)*. The FTC can file complaints against violators of these trade practice rules. It works closely with people in the textile industry, retail stores, apparel care businesses, and consumer groups. These individuals and groups help the FTC develop the rules and regulations to interpret the laws and how to apply them.

The laws relating to textiles and apparel give advantages to consumers. They encourage better quality, product safety, reliable service, and truth in advertising. They have added slightly to the cost of clothing production, but the benefits are worthwhile. Permanent labeling is a part of garment manufacturing because business, government, and consumers demanded it.

Textile Fiber Products Identification Act

The *Textile Fiber Products Identification Act* (which also specifies generic names for fibers) requires all fibers to appear on textile product labels. Fibers must be listed in order of content by weight. Both natural and manufactured fibers are listed by their generic group names. Trade names may also be listed, if manufacturers choose to do so.

The percentage of each fiber must be given. If a fiber makes up less than five percent of the total fiber weight, it can be listed as *other fiber or fibers,*

15-13 Government laws specify the information to be included on apparel labels for the protection and benefit of consumers.

Information Required on Sewn-In Labels	
Fiber content by percentage	The generic names of fibers that compose five percent or more of the item must be listed in order of predominance by weight. A fiber under five percent of the total weight must be listed if it affects the fabric characteristics.
Country of origin	The country where the item was assembled, including the United States, must be named. If the materials were imported, but the garment was assembled in the United States, this must be stated on the label.
Identity of producer	The registered number (RN) of the manufacturing plant must be given.
Permanent care requirements	Clear and complete instructions and warnings about care and maintenance of the item must be given.

unless it affects the fabric characteristics. If it does affect the characteristics, then it must be listed by name and its contribution explained. A good example is *4% spandex for elasticity*. Listing the composition of the fabric helps consumers know how the fabric will behave in use and care.

The name or registered number of the manufacturer or persons marketing or handling the product must be given. *Registered numbers* are on file with the FTC and usually appear as *RN* on labels. They are used to identify the responsible parties.

If an item is imported, the country where it was assembled must be listed. This is required for apparel, accessories, and textile products used in the home, such as draperies, upholstery fabrics, and linens. When not imported, garment labels sometimes say *MADE IN THE USA*, as in **15-14**.

15-14 The country of origin must appear on the labels of textile products. American-made items might have MADE IN THE USA labels.

Burlington Industries, Inc.

Permanent Care Labeling Rule

The *Permanent Care Labeling Rule* requires manufacturers to attach clear and complete permanent care labels to domestic and imported apparel. They must give clear and complete instructions for care and maintenance of the items. Care labels must be durable to remain readable in garments. They must withstand wear and cleaning for the normal life of garments.

Care labels specify how to dry-clean, launder, dry, and iron apparel items. They give instructions regarding the use of soap, detergent, and bleach. They recommend the water temperature (hot, warm, or cold). They must be specific about hand or machine washing and the method of drying (tumble dry, drip dry, line dry, lay flat to dry, and so on).

Care labels also give specific warnings, such as avoiding bleaching, ironing, wringing, or twisting, when the appearance or performance of the item would be hurt. If the label does not contain a specific warning, assume it is safe when following normal practice. *Dry-clean only* means the item should not be washed, even by hand. However, washable items can almost always be dry-cleaned.

If an item is packaged when sold, its care label must be positioned for easy reading through the package. If that is not possible, the same instructions must be easy to read on the package itself.

Yard goods for home sewers are also required to have care labels. The information, or a care instruction code from 1 to 9, should be on the end of each fabric bolt. Sometimes the fiber content is printed on the selvage. When fabric is purchased, the salesclerk can provide a free care label for each piece of cloth purchased. These care labels can be sewn into the garments made from those fabrics. See **15-15** to view the labels that are available with fabric purchases.

A few apparel items are not covered by the Permanent Care Labeling Rule. These include some hosiery, headwear, gloves, and footwear, as well as fur goods. Items that are disposable, or that need no maintenance are also exempt from the labels. Other exemptions are for purely decorative items and for remnants (mill ends) cut and shipped by manufacturers. The FTC may exempt (by petition) completely washable

Method Code	Wording
⚠1	Machine wash, warm
⚠2	Machine wash, warm; line dry
⚠3	Machine wash, warm; tumble dry; remove promptly
⚠4	Machine wash, warm; delicate cycle; tumble dry, low; use cool iron
⚠5	Machine wash, warm; do not dry-clean
⚠6	Hand wash separately; use cool iron
⚠7	Dry-clean only
⚠8	Dry-clean; pile fabric method only
⚠9	Wipe with damp cloth only
Note: ⚠3	This applies to most wash-and-wear or permanent-press fabrics. To minimize ironing, remove from dryer immediately after it stops. If touch-up ironing is required, use cool iron.
⚠4 & ⚠6	Certain synthetic fabrics, although rugged, should not be pressed with a hot iron as they may fuse.
⚠5	Dyes used on certain prints, although ordinarily colorfast when washed, do not perform well when dry-cleaned.
⚠7 & ⚠8	Professional dry cleaning is always safest.

Developed by the National Retail Federation

15-15 Each piece of sewing fabric that is purchased should include the correct care label.

garments intended to retail for three dollars or less. They may also exempt apparel that would be impaired by care labels, such as sheer or see-through items.

Wool Products Labeling Act

The *Wool Products Labeling Act* defines the terms *wool*, *virgin wool*, and *recycled wool* as described in Chapter 8. It also defines *lamb's wool* as wool from a lamb up to seven months old. The law protects producers and consumers from misbranding and false advertising.

The law also requires labels to specify the percentage of each type of wool in the fabric.

If fibers other than wool constitute 5 percent or more of the product, they must be named and listed by percentage. Imported wool must be labeled as such and include the country of origin. There is no provision in the law, however, requiring disclosure of the quality of the fibers.

Fabrics cannot be given trade names to imply they are made up of hair from a certain animal unless they really are. For instance, a trade name like *Lambsoft* implies that the yarns in a garment contain lamb's wool. The yarns may be soft, but if they do not contain lamb's wool, that would give a false impression and would be illegal.

Fur Products Labeling Act

The *Fur Products Labeling Act* protects consumers against deceptive information on labels and in ads for fur products. Fur is animal skin with hair, fleece, or fur fibers attached. The label must list the name(s) of the animal(s) and if the fur was bleached, dyed, or otherwise artificially colored. Scrap pieces and *waste fur*, such as from the ears, throats, paws, tails, or bellies of animals, must be disclosed. Labels and ads must also list the country of origin of imported furs. This information is required, even if a garment merely has some fur trim.

Flammable Fabrics Act

The *Flammable Fabrics Act* has flammability, or burning, standards for fabrics and clothing, especially children's sleepwear. It also covers many household textile products, such as rugs, mattresses, and upholstery fabrics. This act has prompted manufacturers to develop new fibers, blends, and finishes to make more flame-resistant fabrics. It helps to ensure safe products for consumers.

Consumer Rights and Responsibilities

Consumers have certain rights, which are legal or moral privileges. These rights include certain expectations from goods and services purchased. Consumers also have responsibilities. These are personal duties for proper courses of action. These rights and responsibilities go hand-in-hand. Consumers must make the effort to carry out their responsibilities, such as using products as directed by the labels.

There has been strong interest in consumer protection during the past several decades. The rights of consumers were defined by the federal government in the 1960s. They were described as the right to safety, the right to be informed, the right to choose, and the right to be heard.

Standards also exist in many categories. Standards are criteria set by authorities, such as those at testing labs or government agencies, who rate products. The standards verify certain levels of quality.

Right and Responsibility for Safety

The consumer's right to safety means that textile products will perform in a safe way under normal use. The Flammable Fabrics Act is one law that provides for safety by denying the sale of highly flammable fabrics and apparel. The government works with public and private agencies to conduct research into the flammability of fabrics and textile products.

Most fabrics are somewhat flammable. A flammability standard is the measure of flame resistance. Higher standards apply to infants' and children's sleepwear in sizes larger than nine months. These garments must be either snug-fitting or flame resistant. If a label says *flame resistant*, it means the garment will not continue to burn once it is removed from the source of the fire.

Other aspects of safety include not having small buttons or decor on children's wear that could cause choking. High lead levels in fasteners and trim and chemicals in some fibers and finishes might be harmful to the skin or eyes. Some added chemicals and finishes might give off unpleasant odors or activate allergies. Health irritants must be controlled under the consumer's right to safety.

The consumer's responsibility is to use products safely. Learn about product safety issues. Guard against personal carelessness with fire and other hazards. Be cautious with matches and around ranges, fireplaces, and candles. Keep clothing, such as loose sleeves, and household textiles away from flame sources. Supervise children when they are near fire-producing products.

Right and Responsibility to Be Informed

The consumer's right to be informed includes the access to true facts needed to make the best purchasing choices. Hangtags and labels give specific information about products being considered for purchase. Advertisements and other sources also provide useful information.

It is the consumer's responsibility to seek and understand product information. Understand the claims made about performance and wear. Use that data wisely to make good buying decisions. Research products online. Find out about the fibers, fabrics, finishes, and features of each garment, as well as the care required. It is good to know where the product was made and by whom. Well-informed consumers make better choices.

Right and Responsibility to Choose

The consumer's right to choose ensures a broad range of merchandise styles, qualities, and prices. Advanced technology has created new standards of performance for textile products suitable for a wide variety of tastes and budgets. Consumers have the right to shop for products and services without being pressured into buying.

Along with the right to choose, it is a consumer's responsibility to select carefully and wisely, as in **15-16**. Keep desired performance

15-16 Consumers have the right to choose from a wide range of products and the responsibility to select thoughtfully.

levels in mind when shopping. Read hangtags, labels, and packaging to find out about special features. Consider how practical the garment is before buying it. Save garments' labels and hangtags to know about any special directions for care. This also helps to remember brand names for future purchases. Saved sales slips provide proof of purchase for the return or exchange of items, if needed.

Right and Responsibility to Be Heard

Finally, consumers have the right to be heard about matters that concern them. Quality and certain standards of performance are consumers' rights. Manufacturers make promises about their products on hangtags, on labels, and in advertisements. If the products do not live up to those promises, consumers have the right to complain without penalty.

Most manufacturers test samples of their products in specially equipped quality control labs before putting them on the market. Quality control strives to reach high standards of product design and manufacturing through product analysis and problem solving. Companies want satisfied consumers and repeat purchases, which depend on the successful performance of the products. Merchandise is rated according to standards set from other products of the same type. Garments are judged according to their features and quality of construction.

Besides manufacturers, many large department stores and mail-order businesses have quality control labs with trained technicians. There are also independent, commercial labs conducting tests of various products. Stores usually order merchandise that meet basic requirements.

Nonprofit consumer testing groups publish test results about many different products. They are supported by memberships and the sale of publications that give the results of their tests. Some testing is also done by service industry groups, such as the International Fabricare Institute. Government *consumer protection agencies* include the National Bureau of Standards and the American Society for Testing and Materials. These agencies work to improve merchandise standards and create new and better products. They run quality and durability tests on fabrics, and they determine the wearability of garments.

Manufacturers' products should live up to the stated or implied promises of their trademarks. Action can be taken when a textile product fails to live up to its claims or consumers' reasonable expectations. However, if the consumer has acted improperly in either the use or care of the item, the return may be denied. Consumers have the responsibility to be fair and honest when complaining about or returning items.

If merchandise must be returned, do it as soon as feasible. Return clothes clean and unworn, if possible, and in their original packaging. Saved sales slips are proof of the date of purchase and price paid. Return garments to the salesclerk, department head, customer service desk, or store manager. Explain why the merchandise is defective or of poor quality. Be pleasant and businesslike. Describe the problem in a specific and factual way. Have hangtags or printed matter with you that support your claim. Manufacturers, retailers, and cleaners are usually reasonable about such claims. Consumers should expect *redress*. This is correction of, or a remedy for, wrongdoing. Redress is usually a refund, a charge credit, or an exchange for another item.

It is the consumer's responsibility to voice reasonable problems. If a product does not live up to its claims or your expectations, a formal complaint may prevent the same problem in the future. The store will inform the manufacturer if the item is faulty in construction. When buyers and sellers work together, products can be improved. By being aware of a product's shortcomings, corrections can be made in the merchandise to please consumers in the future. The complaints and suggestions of responsible consumers can improve textile and clothing products' performance.

Sometimes a store will ignore a consumer's reasonable complaint. In that case, send a letter to the retail store's president or person responsible for consumer complaints, or to the manufacturer of the item. Write your letter carefully, stating exactly what is wrong. Be businesslike and pleasantly firm, as in **15-17**. The letter should be neat and legible. Keep a copy of the letter. Such a letter may not get to the executive to whom it is addressed, but chances are good that the complaint will get attention. If no response is received, write another letter in a month.

15-17 A letter similar to this one should bring fair results when making a reasonable consumer complaint.

Susan A. Smith
902 Loden Grove Road
West Haven, CA 90169

213-555-2498

 June 4, 20xx

Mr. John Doe, President
Smedley Group Retailers Ⓒ
3100 Washington Avenue
Los Angeles, CA 90075

Dear Mr. Doe:

On May 1, 20xx I purchased a cotton sweater from your branch store
in the West Haven Mall. The sweater is white with a red checkerboard
design. The label states that it is part of the *Doberman Collection* by Parker
Fashions. Photocopies of my sales slip and the care label are enclosed. Ⓓ

After wearing the sweater for a short time, I washed it by hand in cold
water according to the directions on the care label. After rolling it in a
towel, I laid it flat to dry as stated. However, when it dried, color from Ⓔ
the red areas had run into the white areas. I can no longer wear the
sweater because it looks so awful.

When I tried to return the sweater to the store, the manager (David Jones)
said he could not take it back because it had been worn. He also implied Ⓕ
that I had ruined it by washing it improperly.

As you can imagine, I am very upset and would like a refund of the
purchase price. Please act on this complaint as soon as possible. Thank Ⓖ
you for your help, and I await your reply.

Sincerely,

Susan A. Smith Ⓗ
Susan A. Smith

Ⓐ Your information (name, address, phone)

Ⓑ Current date

Ⓒ To whom the letter is written (name, title,
company, address)

Ⓓ Purchase and item information

Ⓔ Description of problem

Ⓕ Action already taken

Ⓖ Request for satisfaction

Ⓗ Your signature

For serious consumer grievances, seek guidance from the local Better Business Bureau. Consumers may also contact a local Chamber of Commerce, the state attorney general's office, or a state agency dealing with consumer affairs. Another option is the Bureau of Consumer Protection, which is one of the branches of the Federal Trade Commission.

Responsible consumers should also report false or misleading advertising. Patronize trustworthy businesses and avoid the dishonest ones. Good manufacturers and retailers want satisfied customers. See **15-18**. They deserve repeat business. Through continued purchases, refusals to purchase, or supportable complaints, consumers can apply pressure on retailers. See **15-19**. They, in turn, influence the textile and apparel manufacturing segments of the industry.

Summary

Smart consumers are better dressed for less money. Preparing ahead to buy only needed items in the right colors, textures, and styles is just as important as the actual purchasing. Make a specific list of your priority needs, including cost estimates. Gather fashion information from magazines, newspapers, catalogs, stores, and websites. Try to understand advertisements without being misled about merchandise or prices.

Decide where to shop before leaving home. Plan to make large, basic purchases first. Evaluate low-priced stores versus the quality and services of higher-priced retailers. Also, specific items may influence where to shop. Know the locations and store hours of the various retailers. Consumers may choose to be loyal to trusted retailers. The choice of retailers allows consumers to be both fashion conscious and money conscious.

Shop early in the season for a wide choice of merchandise and maximum wearing time, or late in the season for lower prices. When shopping, use sales resistance. Stick to the planned purchases and be well groomed. Use good shopping manners and cooperate with store policies.

Hangtags, labels, and outside packaging identify and give information about products. Hangtags tell consumers what manufacturers want to say about their products. Labels give information required by law. Packaging might repeat information from the inside, such as size.

U.S. government laws require textile product labels to contain certain information. The Textile Fiber Products Identification Act, the Permanent Care Labeling Rule, the Wool Products Labeling Act, and the Fur Products Labeling Act are examples of these laws.

Consumers should also be aware of their rights and responsibilities.

15-18 Shopping experiences are better when consumers visit honest, quality retailers.
Blend Images/Shutterstock.com

15-19 Whether they know it or not, consumers shape the products and services available at manufacturers and retail stores.
mimagephotography/Shutterstock.com

Fashion Recall

Write your answers on a separate sheet of paper.

Short Answer: Write the correct response to each of the following items.

1. Why is it smart to invest in clothes that are wearable in all seasons?

2. Name three advantages of planning and gathering information before shopping.

3. Describe how reading fashion magazines, fashion sections of newspapers, mail-order catalogs, and viewing TV and Internet sites can help you prepare to shop.

4. What are the two purposes of advertising?

5. Advertisements are good sources of up-to-date shopping information because they _____.

   A. have clever songs and slogans
   B. play on the emotions of consumers
   C. show and describe new apparel items
   D. can entice you into buying

6. Name two times of the day when stores are not likely to be crowded.

7. Distinguish between hangtags and labels.

8. What four kinds of information must appear on the labels of all textile products sold in the United States?

9. Most laws that protect consumers against deceptive labeling and advertising are enforced by which government agency?

10. Which law specifies generic names for fibers and requires labels to list the fibers that are in textile products in order of content by weight?

11. Which law requires domestic and imported apparel to have labels that give instructions for care and maintenance?

12. Which law protects consumers against deceptive information on labels and in advertisements of fur products?

13. Describe the consumer's right and responsibility for safety.

14. Describe the consumer's right and responsibility to choose.

15. List five people or agencies consumers can contact for help with their complaints.

Fashion Vocabulary

16. On a separate sheet of paper, list words that relate to each of the *Fashion Terms* on the chapter opening. Then, work with a partner to explain how these words are related.

Critical Thinking

17. **Analyze factors**   What factors do you analyze and consider before shopping for apparel? List the top 10 factors and rank them from 1 (most important) to 10 (least important) to reflect your priorities. Then, write a summary of your analysis, citing the text as evidence to support your considerations.

18. **Assess options**   Imagine that you are visiting a major U.S. city for the first time. How do you assess where to shop for apparel? In class discussion, describe the factors you assess when making shopping decisions.

19. **Analyze evidence**   Who is responsible for making sure that a child's clothing is safe to wear under normal use? Cite the text and reliable online sources to provide reasons for your choice(s).

Core Skills

20. **Speaking, listening, and writing**   Interview a store manager, security guard, or loss-prevention officer about shoplifting. What is the store's

es...
Ho...
co...
ab...

21. **Re...**
ga...
sto...
sh...
to...
qu...
ser...
atr...
we...

22. **Speaking** Interview a store manager about the behavior of shoppers. Ask him or her about merchandise damaged in the store by shoppers trying the items on and about damage to returned items. Give an oral report to the class about your findings.

23. **Technology** How does online advertising differ from advertising in print, radio, and TV? Look at the sites of online apparel retailers and others. Use a school-approved infographic application to create a digital poster about methods that are unique to online advertising, and showing and describing examples you find. Upload your poster to the class website for peer and instructor review.

24. **Reading and writing** Consumers can post their product reviews online. Find two websites that post customer feedback and read the reviews. Identify the sites and write a summary of the types of comments you find. Anonymously post your own feedback about a recent apparel purchase on an appropriate website. Print a copy of your post to include with your written summary.

25. **CTE career readiness practice** Presume you work for a clothing manufacturer who typically includes only required information on hangtags and labels.

The company wants to include some additional information on hangtags and labels to better inform its customers. You are to research and compare hangtags and labels from three to four competing manufacturers. Read and interpret the hangtag and label information. Then, write a report of your findings. What additional information could you give your employer to help provide a competitive advantage?

Fashion in Action

26. **Portfolio builder** Obtain at least five clothing ads from magazines, newspapers, mail-order catalogs, or websites that give written information and illustrations. Mount these on paper and distinguish between the useful information and the sales pitches. Describe any ads or statements that may be misleading or inflated. Keep this in your portfolio to demonstrate your understanding of clothing ads.

27. **Design activity** Design a display of consumer information sources. Include articles and ads from newspapers, fashion magazines, mail-order catalogs, and the Internet. Sketch store window displays and in-store displays. Include catalogs and library resources. Obtain consumer aids from sources such as fiber producers, fabric stores, and your local extension agent.

Self-Assessment Quiz ➔

Complete the self-assessment quiz online to help practice and expand your knowledge and skills.

CHAPTER 16

Making the Right Purchase

While studying, look for the activity icon 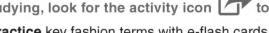 to:

- **practice** key fashion terms with e-flash cards, vocabulary games, and matching activities
- **assess** what you learn by completing self-assessment quizzes

www.g-wlearning.com/clothingandfashion/

comparison shopping
virtual reality
value
quality
cost-per-wearing
environmental
   sustainability

ethics
social responsibility
double ticketing
wearing ease
alterations
trademark
bargain

overdrawn
debit card
layaway purchase
credit rating
finance charge
installment plans
identity theft

Objectives

After studying this chapter, you will be able to
- ➤ **comparison shop** to make the best purchases.
- ➤ **judge** the value and quality of garments.
- ➤ **weigh** political and social viewpoints when buying.
- ➤ **analyze** size and fit considerations.
- ➤ **evaluate** the benefits of trademarks, bargains, and sales.
- ➤ **choose** the best method of payments for purchases.
- ➤ **discuss** how to deter, detect, and defend against identity theft.

The previous chapters of this book discuss how consumers can prepare themselves to shop wisely. Making the right choices in the marketplace, however, also requires level-headed judgments at the time of purchase. Products and prices should be compared and evaluated. Once a decision is made and an item is selected for purchase, consumers must choose among various payment methods.

Comparison Shopping

Comparison shopping involves comparing the qualities and prices of the same or similar items from different retailers before buying. This means looking before buying. Check the fabric and construction of garments. Compare similar garments at different stores and departments, mail-order catalogs, plus retail websites. Read labels and hangtags. By evaluating these details and others, consumers can identify the worth of items and the best purchase prices.

Blend Images/Shutterstock.com

Valuable information to compare merchandise can also be found in mail-order catalogs, newspaper advertisements, and online. Comfort, appearance, durability, and care of garments are important considerations. Wise consumers weigh the pros and cons of alternate choices. Then they choose the retailer and the item that gives them the greatest satisfaction and suits their needs.

Some people study the features of high-quality clothing by browsing in designer departments or expensive stores. They check the construction details, fabrics, colors, and fit. Then they search out similar items in less expensive stores or on websites. In this way, they learn what characteristics are desirable before they buy.

Technology makes comparison shopping easier in many ways. Using the Internet, people can shop from the comfort of their homes or wherever they are at any time of the day or night. Websites often display product reviews and consumer satisfaction ratings of products or businesses. The ratings, which are often based on a 5-star scale, may include written remarks. Product information and images are also available through *social media*, or online tools that allow people to communicate and share information. Many retail sites offer a live-chat option that enables consumers to communicate with service representatives by phone or typed messages. Consumers can get immediate answers to their questions. Product feedback is also available through social media.

Using mobile devices and retail apps, consumers can comparison shop while they are out. Besides checking information on websites, comments from relatives and friends can be evaluated. Prices, store locations, and inventory can be checked and discounts sometimes found.

The growing use of virtual reality allows consumers to interact with computer-simulated objects and environments. Virtual reality is technology that allows users to create and access virtual or artificial worlds, which range from realistic to fantastic. Through technology users can interact with environmental elements in real time. For example, a person can input his or her measurements, hair color, and other information into a computer program. A figure that looks like the consumer appears on the screen. Garments can then be *tried on* the figure

to see how they look. Garments can be mixed and matched into outfits, plus accessories can be added to the simulation.

Although technology has made shopping easier, comparison shopping takes some time. However, consumers who shop this way are usually happier with their purchases. They rarely need to return items. They are more likely than other shoppers to find what they need and want for the best available prices. They save money and get more satisfaction from their purchases.

Judging Value and Quality

Value is the degree to which something is worthwhile or beneficial. When judging the value of clothing, the best value is an item that contains the highest quality of materials, construction, and fashion at the lowest price. Quality is the degree to which a product meets desired standards of excellence and performance.

Apparel purchases are evaluated using many factors. These include design, construction, lasting fashion appeal, fabric durability, ease of care, and suitability for the wearer and his or her lifestyle. See **16-1**. Both the insides and outsides of garments show signs of quality. To get the most for their money, consumers need to become familiar with the marks of quality merchandise. They should not settle for items that are not right.

16-1 High quality, personal suitability, and good price are factors that increase the value of an apparel item.

General Quality

The overall quality of a garment can be described as poor, good, better, or best. Sometimes quality is described as low, medium, or high. A high-quality garment should perform better than one of low quality. Quality has a lot to do with a garment's performance, or its long-term appearance, fit, and wear.

High-quality garments have the best construction, materials, and design. Cut, line, and fabric are emphasized. Since attention is given to construction details, these garments often have extra built-in features and a degree of luxury. See **16-2**.

In high-quality garments, plaids and stripes are matched at the seams. Hems and linings are generous. The linings and buttons are color coordinated with the garments. Seams are straight, with even and secure stitches. Fasteners are secure and located so no gapping or pulling occurs. In knits, many areas have full-fashioned shaping.

Medium-quality garments have reliably good construction, materials, and design. They are usually quite durable. They generally cost less than high-quality apparel, but more than low-quality clothing.

Low-quality garments have only fair standards of construction, materials, and design. They may be priced low, but quickly become worn and unattractive. However, sometimes spending more money for better quality is not necessary. Low-quality garments may be fine if they are fad items that will be outdated soon or items that will be worn only a few times.

Quality is often, but not always, related to price. A low price does not always indicate low quality. Sometimes better-quality merchandise

---

16-2   This hangtag from a high-quality man's dress shirt points out the quality features the manufacturer wants consumers to notice.

CHECK OUT OUR QUALITY FEATURES

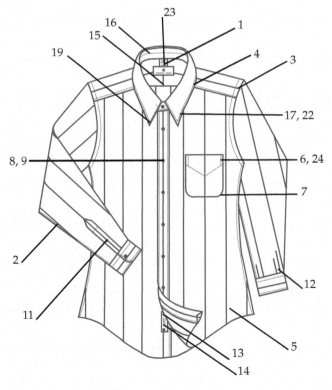

25 QUALITY POINTS TO COMPARE

1. Tailored in America—quality and pride.
2. Long-stitch seams—much stronger than chain stitch and will last longer.
3. Single-needle shoulder, sleeve, and side seams—each seam is sewn twice.
4. 21 topstitches per inch—count them.
5. Extra long shirttails—stay tucked in.
6. Pocket corners are double stitched—very strong.
7. Round corner pockets—looks great.
8. Cross-stitch buttons—very strong.
9. Lock-stitch buttonholes—very strong.
10. Two-ply mercerized cotton thread—very strong.
11. Sleeve placket buttons—neat appearance.
12. Three sleeve pleats—adds comfort.
13. Extra buttons sewn on shirttail—convenience.
14. 800 # for extra button—good service.
15. Split mitered yoke—very comfortable.
16. Broadway-stitched collar band—comfort.
17. Removable collar stays—launders better.
18. Seven-button front—adds comfort.
19. Flat, smooth collar points—looks great and launders better.
20. Die-cut interlining, collar points, neck band and cuffs—consistent fit.
21. Oversized patterns allow for true fit after repeated laundering.
22. Extra collar stays included with each shirt—very convenient.
23. Size label stitched down—no scratching.
24. Extra matching on collar, pocket, and top center patterns—looks great.
25. 100% cotton—best for comfort and wear.

Ferrell Reed

goes on sale or is offered for a reduced price in a store with low overhead costs. An alert shopper can often find good quality products at low prices.

Likewise, not all high-priced garments are of the best quality. Some merchandise prices are raised to help pay for extra store services or high advertising costs. A special feature of a garment, such as fur trim, an unusual braid, or a famous designer's name or logo, can raise its price. Consumers should decide if such details are important and worth the extra money.

People get a good value when they pay only for the quality they want and need. Different garments can require different levels of quality. For specific apparel items, consumers need to decide what quality is important to them. They need to consider the intended use of each garment and the purpose in buying it.

When shopping for basic garments, buying the best quality that is affordable usually results in a good investment. The cost-per-wearing should be considered rather than the actual purchase price. Cost-per-wearing is the purchase price, plus upkeep, divided by the number of times an item is worn. For instance, suppose there are two shirts. A quality, washable, cotton-blend shirt costs $45 and is worn 90 times. It costs 50 cents per wearing. A brightly patterned silk shirt that needs dry cleaning is bought on sale for $30 and worn 15 times. The silk shirt costs $2 or more per wearing. This is four times as much as the other shirt that initially cost $15 more. Likewise, paying a higher price for a good-quality coat or jacket that is worn a great deal for several seasons is usually more economical.

For extenders, occasional wear garments, and accessories, items of lower quality with lower prices may be appropriate. This same thinking applies to fad items. If a fad item is inexpensive, the wearer will not mind discarding it when it is out of fashion. A high-quality, fad item might last longer than the fad itself.

Consumers should develop quality awareness. Well-made, good-looking clothes can be found at many price levels. Smart consumers decide what quality suits their needs. They shop for fashion at prices they can afford. They consider a good buy to be something that meets a need at a price they want to pay.

Specific Points of Quality

When judging the quality of garments, the following specific points should be checked.

The *fabric* should be of an even weave or knit with an even color or pattern. It should be free from spots, streaks, snags, flaws, or irregularities. Its weight and flexibility should suit the garment type and style. The fabric design should be interesting, flattering for the wearer's coloring, and in proportion with his or her size. The fabric care requirements should suit the wearer's lifestyle and budget.

The cut of the garment should use ample fabric so it does not look skimpy. It should be cut *on-grain*. This means that the center line of the garment parts is parallel with the lengthwise or crosswise threads of the fabric. The fabric threads at the garment's front, back, and outer sleeves should run straight up and down. The threads across the chest and hips should run parallel with the floor. If the garment is cut on *true bias*, the fabric threads should be exactly diagonal. Proper grain enables the garment to hang well without twisting.

Garments should also be cut so plaids, stripes, and other fabric patterns are on-grain and matched at the most obvious seams and edges, as in **16-3**. Matching should be done at closures, seams, pockets, sleeves, and collars. However, patterns cannot be matched everywhere. Matching is most important where it is most noticeable.

The *seams* of a garment should be smooth, without ripples or puckers. Seam allowances should be of even widths. They should be generous enough to hold firmly if there is strain on the garment. Reinforcing or double stitching may be needed at areas of strain, such as the underarms or crotch. Extra width is required if alterations will be needed. Raw edges should be finished, for instance with overcasting, so the fabric will not ravel. Seam edges and corners should lay flat. In knit garments, seams should have as much stretch as the fabric.

Stitching should be straight and neat with short and even stitches. They should be sturdy with no broken stitches. The thread should match the fabric color and weight. Thread ends should be securely fastened. Topstitching should be smooth and straight.

16-3 The nicely matched, horizontal lines of this plaid go across the sleeves and bodice front, continuing across the front closure. The subtle, vertical lines are centered.

The *hem* should be of an even width that is proper for the garment style. It should be deep enough to let down if needed. The hem should lie flat and have a finish that is suitable to the fabric. It should not ravel or fray. It should be securely stitched so it is nearly invisible when viewed from the right side.

Reinforcements should be included at points of strain. These include the top corners of patch pockets, the ends of bound pockets, and the sides of shirttails. Reinforcing might be done with extra stitching, bar tacks, or metal rivets (as on the blue jeans in **16-4**). Shoulder seams of knit shirts are often sewn with ribbon or binding reinforcement to prevent stretching. Knees of children's play clothes should also be reinforced.

A *zipper* should be long enough and strong enough for the garment and located for easy use. It should be of a suitable weight and matching color for the garment. A zipper should open and close easily without catching fabric in its teeth or coils. The top should have a locking tab that stays closed when stress is applied. A zipper

should lie smooth and flat, and be free from puckers. Stitching should be secure, even, and inconspicuous in thread that matches the fabric color.

Fasteners such as buttons, snaps, hooks and eyes, and hook and loop tape (such as Velcro®) should be of a suitable size, color, and type for the garment. They should require the same care as the garment. They should be appropriately placed, evenly spaced, and firmly attached. There should be enough fasteners to keep the garment closed without gaps or pulling. Fasteners should open and close easily. Also, they should lie flat and look neat.

Quality garments have an extra button of each size used sewn inconspicuously inside the garment. These may be used to replace lost or damaged buttons.

Buttonholes should look neat. They should be evenly and properly spaced to exactly match the placement of buttons. They should be cut with the grain of the fabric unless they are strictly decorative. The size and type of buttonholes should be suitable for the buttons and for the type of garment. Buttonholes should be firmly stitched with reinforced ends. They should lie smooth and flat on the garment. They should not have loose threads or frayed edges. Bound buttonholes (with fabric pieces forming the slit) and hand-sewn buttonholes in tailored garments are signs of high quality.

Collars should be cut on-grain and centered on the design of the fabric. Backs of collars should fit smoothly close to the neck. The outer

16-4 Some blue jeans that are manufactured for hard wear are reinforced with metal rivets at both ends of the pockets.

part of the collar should turn over far enough to cover the neckline seam at the back. Also, the underside of the collar should not show along the outer edge of the collar. Collar points should be neatly finished and should not curl under or up.

Lapels should lie flat and be stiff enough to hold their shape. They should have a graceful roll and a clean-cut edge, as in **16-5**. They should end at the top button of the garment.

Waistbands should be constructed to prevent stretching and rolling. Belt loops should be well placed and sewn securely.

Pockets should be flat, smooth, and well matched. Corners should be reinforced. Pocket linings should be firmly woven.

A garment's *lining* is an inner layer of fabric sewn into the garment. Lining gives a garment body, helps to retain the shape of the garment, and adds to wearing comfort. Apparel items can be completely or partially lined. A lining should have the same care requirements as the outer fabric. It should fit smoothly into the garment. It should be of the appropriate color, weight, and texture to enhance the garment.

It should never droop or shrink. It should be securely attached, but not so tight that it will rip or come loose if the wearer reaches or stretches. In a jacket, the lining should be attached along the neckline, at the tops of the armholes, along the front facings, and at the hems of the sleeves and jacket bottom.

Interfacings and *paddings* are extra layers inside garments. They support certain parts of garments, such as collars and cuffs, and hold the style lines of the design. They provide extra strength, body, and a smooth finish. Higher-quality garments use more of them. Interfacing and paddings should be properly placed, hidden, and securely attached. They should have the same care requirements and be of a similar color as the garment.

Trimmings and *decorations* are various types of ornamentation added to garments. They should be able to withstand the same care as the garment. Otherwise, they must be easily removable. They should be suitable for the garment, well placed, and neatly and firmly attached. Topstitching should be even and attractive.

Political/Social Viewpoints

Consumers may consider various issues to be important when they make purchases. To support U.S. workers and companies, some consumers try to avoid buying imported goods. Others are not concerned about where goods are made. If they like an item, want it, and can afford it, they will buy it. Some shoppers support manufacturers and retailers that are environmentally or ethically responsible. You may want to weigh these issues when making purchases.

The Dilemma of Imports

Many garments are imported, such as the one shown in **16-6**. Imports have increased sharply over the last several decades. They now account for over 90 percent of the merchandise available to, and bought by, U.S. consumers. People have different views about whether or not clothing should be imported.

As discussed earlier in this text, labor costs are lower in less-developed countries.

16-5 Classic lapels, such as those on suit jackets, should lie flat. They should also hold their shape and have a precise, smooth edge.

Hong Kong Trade Development Council / Virginia Lau, Designer

16-6 High-fashion garments such as this one, as well as inexpensive apparel items, are imported into the U.S. from foreign countries.

Many garments made in these countries can be offered at lower prices in the U.S., even after the addition of shipping costs and duties (tariffs). These products are, therefore, economically attractive to consumers. Some people say that low-cost imports enable retailers to mark up (and make bigger profits on) apparel made overseas. Retailers may sell identical or equivalent products at similar prices, even though the imported ones cost them less to acquire.

Some people think the U.S. federal government should pass stronger laws to limit clothing imports. They cite the fact that the United States has a large *trade deficit* on apparel and other goods. That means more clothing is imported, or brought into the country to sell, than is exported, or shipped out to other countries.

Other citizens want the widest possible choice of goods, which includes imports. Some argue that international trade, including the trade in apparel, fosters goodwill. They say it improves diplomatic relations between the U.S. and its trading partners. Some people believe that jobs in the apparel industry are essential to the survival of workers in many developing nations. Other people believe these jobs pay the workers too little and that many overseas employers take advantage of these workers with poor working conditions and child labor practices.

In some respects, consumers have benefited from the lower prices of imports. Not only do the imported items cost less, but they drive down the prices of similar American-produced apparel. To compete with the lower-priced foreign-made goods, American companies lower their prices. The competition has also caused manufacturers to operate more efficiently, develop new technology, and improve their management.

Some consumers choose to buy items made in the United States whenever possible. By doing so, they hope to support the jobs of domestic workers and help maintain a strong industrial base in the U.S. The consequences of unemployment are severe for individuals, families, and communities. These consequences include poverty and homelessness. Those who become unemployed may have to accept public assistance. That costs everyone money through taxes.

As you can see, there are different sides in the debates about imports. There are no easy, clear-cut answers. Also, today most apparel manufacturing is global. Different production processes are done in various parts of the world. With instant communications and efficient modes of transportation, goods move from country to country for design, materials, and assembly. Finally, they reach their market to consumers.

When you are shopping, read labels to find the countries of origin of the items that interest you. Evaluate the quality, the price, and your own personal viewpoint about where the merchandise was made.

Environmental Sustainability

More consumers are buying goods and services from *green* companies—businesses that are sensitive to environmental issues. Environmental sustainability means preserving the well-being of the planet through responsible processes and uses of resources. Many apparel manufacturers and retailers have *green committees* to evaluate procedures in their operations and educate coworkers about better ways to do things. For example, in many workplaces, employees are urged to communicate electronically, rather than use paper. *Green facilities*, or buildings that use a minimum of energy, water, and chemicals, are built. Some businesses grow plants on their roofs that filter air, absorb storm water, modify interior temperatures, and provide bird habitats. See **16-7**. Transportation emissions are minimized with full trucks and economical routes. Solar power and recycling of disposables are maximized.

To promote environmental sustainability, farmers and ranchers are raising organic cotton and wool. Solvents used in production processes are being recycled as much as possible. Often, substitute solutions are being used in place of toxic chemicals to reduce pollutants. Also, old textile products are reused in mops, home insulation, and other products to keep them out of landfills. Old plastic bottles are being melted and made into polyester fibers that can be continually recycled. Biodegradable fibers are manufactured from wood pulp from trees grown in constantly replanted forests. Some mail-order retailers plant trees to replenish those used to produce their catalogs. Packaging materials are being minimized.

To support environmental sustainability, consumers are encouraged to limit their total consumption of goods. This prevents natural resources from being used up. Also, retailers ask shoppers to provide reusable cloth shopping bags to minimize the use of disposable plastic bags. All of these efforts spread a good message to customers. Consumers think highly of green companies and want to buy their goods. However, many consumers are not willing to pay more for sustainable products. Companies are developing technology to help them maintain green practices and hold prices steady. Some sustainability procedures already save on costs.

Ethics and Social Responsibility

Some consumers prefer to patronize companies that have honest business practices and show social responsibility in the community. Ethics are moral principles, or rules of conduct, that distinguish right from wrong. They include fairness, honesty, trustworthiness, and treating others with respect. Ethical companies advertise truthfully. Their pricing is fair. Their products are safe and labeled properly. They do not sell items produced by factories that use child labor or substandard working conditions.

Social responsibility is the idea that individuals and businesses should contribute to the welfare of the larger society. An individual or a company displays social responsibility by doing what helps society, even if it involves going beyond legal requirements. Socially responsible companies have a corporate culture of caring. They undertake projects or offer services that benefit the community. They encourage employees to do volunteer work and become community leaders. Some sponsor charitable benefits, support cancer research, help build houses for the poor, and give money to good causes in the local community or world. Some companies establish their own charitable foundations.

Socially responsible companies are concerned with the education, family care, health issues, and safety of their employees. Some companies provide high school equivalency programs, continuing education courses, and college tuition assistance for their workers. Some have on-site child care centers and tutors for their employees' children. Other businesses offer their staff free counseling services and

16-7 Green roofs like this one are also called *eco-roofs*.

substance abuse rehabilitation programs. Many offer flexible work hours to help employees juggle work with the demands of family life.

Studies show that a majority of consumers believe corporate social responsibility is important. They prefer to patronize socially responsible firms. Also, people are proud to work for these companies and to promote their merchandise and services.

Evaluate Proper Fit

Clothes do not look their best if they do not fit well. Clothes should not be too tight, too loose, too long, or too short. A good fit has a look of natural ease. If garments fit well, they feel comfortable, look good, and wear well. Improper fit detracts from a garment's attractiveness. Clothes that do not fit well or feel comfortable often stay in closets unworn. They are a waste of money. A well-fitting garment often lasts longer and requires less care than one with poor fit. See **16-8**.

Determine Size Category

Consumers should know what size garments they wear. To determine their size, they must first be aware of their body structure. A person's body structure depends on his or her stage of physical development. It is the relationship of someone's height to his or her weight and bone structure. It also is keyed to the relationship among the chest, waist, and hip measurements.

Sizes are in categories by figure types. Study the size categories described in **16-9** and find the one that best suits you.

Know and Use Body Measurements

After identifying a general size category or figure type, body measurements are needed to determine an exact size. To take their body measurements, people often need help from someone else. A tape measure should be pulled close around the body, but not tight. When having their measurements taken, people should wear the undergarments they wear under their nice clothes. The measurements should be recorded.

To measure his or her *height*, a person should stand without wearing shoes. The measurement

Martin Allinger/Shutterstock.com

16-8 The classic suit worn by this young man will last well into his working career.

is taken from the floor to a ruler placed horizontally across the top of the head.

To take a *chest* or *bust* measurement, the tape measure should be wrapped around the largest part in front of the body and straight across the back. The arms should hang down at the sides.

For female figures, the *waist* measurement is taken at the narrowest or smallest part of the waistline area. That is the natural waistline. For male physiques, the waist may be measured at the position where pants are usually worn. Sometimes that is below the natural waistline.

To obtain the *hip* measurement, the tape should go around the fullest part of the hips.

A shirt with a comfortable collar can be used to find the wearer's *neck* measurement. The collar and band are laid flat on a table. A measurement is taken from the middle of the front button to the far end of the buttonhole at the other front edge. The actual circumference of the neck can also be measured. Sizes are in half-inch increments.

A *shirt-sleeve measurement* is from the back center base of the neck, across the shoulder, and down the arm around the bent elbow to the wrist bone. This is shown in **16-10**.

The *inseam* of pants can be measured from some well-fitting slacks of the right length. The measurement is taken along the inside leg seam, from the crotch to the hem.

16-9 Specific apparel sizes are listed within the various figure types. Figure types and sizes vary according to the manufacturer.

Size Range Categories

(Sizes for infants, toddlers, and young children are listed in Chapter 17.)

Figure Types	Sizes	Proportions
Female Size Categories		
Girls'	7 – 16	For girls whose figures are average; undeveloped in bust and hips. Height approximately 4'2" to 5'2"
(Sometimes Girls' sizes are: Small, size 7; Medium, sizes 8–10; Large, sizes 12–14; X Large, size 16.)		
Girls' Plus	8½ – 16½ 7+ – 16+	For girls whose figures are heavier; undeveloped in bust and hips. Height approximately 4'2" to 5'3"
Girls' Slim	7S – 16S	For slender girls; undeveloped in bust and hips. Height approximately 4' to 5'2"
Juniors'	½ – 13¾14	For girls and women who are short-waisted, have fully developed bust and hips, and small waist. Height approximately 5'3½" to 5'5½"
(Sometimes Juniors' sizes are: X Small, size 1–2; Small, sizes 3–4–5–6; Medium, sizes 7–8–9–10; Large, sizes 11–12–13–14.)		
Misses'	2 – 24	For girls and women, fully developed, with average figures and proportions. Height approximately 5'4½" to 5'7"
Misses' Talls	2 – 24	For tall girls and women. Height from 5'8" to 5'11"
Misses' Petites	2 – 24	For short girls and women. Height from 5' to 5'4"
(Sometimes Misses' sizes are: X Small, sizes 2–4; Small, sizes 6–8; Medium, sizes 10–12; Large, sizes 14–16; X Large, sizes 18–20; XX Large, sizes 22–24.)		
Women's	14W – 32W	Large proportions or a mature figure. Height 5'4" to 5'61/"
Women's Petite	14W – 32W	Large proportions or a mature figure. Height 5' to 5'3½"
Women's Tall	14W – 32W	For tall women with mature figures. height 5'7" to 6'
(Sometimes Women's sizes are: X Small, size 14W; Small, sizes 16W–18W; Medium, sizes 20W–22W; Large, sizes 24W–26W; X Large, sizes 28W–30W; XX Large, size 32W.)		
Male Size Categories		
Boys'	7 – 20	For growing boys of average build. Height approximately 4'2½" to 5'8"
Boys' Slim	7S – 20S	For growing boys of slender build. Height approximately 4'3" to 5'10"
Boys' Husky	7H – 20H	For growing boys of heavier build. Height approximately 4'2" to 5'9"
(Sometimes Boys' sizes are Small, sizes 7–8; Medium, sizes 10–12; Large sizes 14–16; X Large, sizes 18–20.)		
Men's (related to chest measurement)	30 – 52	For boys and men who are fully developed. Height approximately 5'8" to 6'
Men's Tall	30–52	For boys and men who are tall and fully developed. Height approximately 6'1" to 6'3"
Men's Short	30–52	For boys and men who are short and fully developed. Height approximately 5'3" to 5'7"
(Sometimes Men's sizes are: X Small, sizes 30–32; Small, sizes 34–36; Medium, sizes 38–40; Large, sizes 42–44; X Large, sizes 46–48; XX Large, sizes 50–52.)		

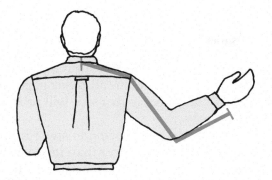

16-10 When measuring for a shirt-sleeve size, start at the center back of the neck (not at the top of the sleeve) and measure to the wrist bone as shown.

Size charts can be found in mail-order catalogs, pattern catalogs, or on websites. People should look for their measurements within a size-range category. If their measurements are not an exact size, they should choose the size that is the closest match.

If a person's top and bottom are different sizes, it is probably best to wear separates most of the time. A top and bottom can be bought in different sizes. For one-piece outfits, clothes that fit the larger part can be chosen, and the other part can be taken in. It is easier to make garments smaller than to make them bigger.

Generally, chest measurements determine the size for suits, tops, and dresses. Waist and hip measurements are used for skirts and women's pants. Men's pants sizes list the waist measurement followed by the inseam length, as in 34–33. Some are sized by the waist measurement in short, medium, or long lengths, such as 36L. Men's shirts are listed by a neck measurement followed by sleeve length, as in 15½–34.

Double ticketing combines two or more specific sizes into more general categories, such as small, medium, and large. This is fine for sweaters or other loosely fitting styles, but is usually unsatisfactory for fitted garments. Consumers should check labels and packages for body measurements and the corresponding size categories. It is also a good idea to try on such garments before buying them.

Try on Garments

Although most people continue to wear a certain size, individual garments vary. Sizes are only a guide to how clothes fit. The only way to know whether or not a garment is right is to try it on. When trying on garments, wear underclothes and shoes that will be worn with the garments. All views in a full-length mirror should be checked, as in **16-11**. A person should move around in a garment the way he or she would if wearing it in the future. This may include walking, bending, sitting, and moving the arms to ensure ample room for movement. Reaching and stretching should be possible without straining the fabric and seams. The garment should fit smoothly without wrinkling or binding anywhere.

The shoulder length should be comfortable and the neckline fit smoothly. When the neckline is buttoned, there should be space for an index finger to slide easily between the collar and the neck. There should be enough ease across the chest and back to prevent pulling or stretching.

Depending on the fashion, the armholes might follow the natural armline. The sleeves should be a good length and wide enough not to bind. Sleeves of blazers and suit coats should end ½ inch above the lower edge of the shirt cuff. There should be proper ease through the hips and seat. Lower garments should hang straight from the waist to the hem. Outer garments should be large enough to go over apparel worn underneath.

16-11 Sizes on apparel in retail stores are indications of which clothes might fit. However, to judge actual fit, it is always wise to try clothes on.

Darts, if present, should go to the proper areas of fitting (shoulder blade, chest or bust, hips, elbows). The center-front and center-back seams of garments should be the correct length. The waistline should be at the right spot. The crotch length of pants should be comfortable when sitting or bending, but not so long that it sags when standing. The length of the garment should be attractive for the wearer's height and for current fashion. The hem should be even.

The fit of garments depends on the fabric. Some fabrics are stiff, some are fluid, and some have a great deal of stretch. Fit also changes with different styles because different designs have varying amounts of built-in ease, as in **16-12**. Wearing ease is the room a person needs to move comfortably in a garment. It is added to garments beyond the actual body measurements. Size and fit also vary among different manufacturers.

All American apparel companies use similar measurements for their sizes, even if their goods are produced offshore. However, they interpret the sizes differently. They use different body proportions and amounts of ease. Each apparel manufacturer cuts its garments for its *target customer*. If a certain size from a particular manufacturer fits a person, all other garments from that manufacturer, in that size, will probably fit the same way.

Often manufacturers of expensive clothing cut their clothing to be bigger than inexpensive clothing. They hope their customers will be pleased when they can fit into garments labeled with smaller sizes than they usually wear.

Inexpensive garments are often skimpier than more expensive ones; less fabric is used. Also, inexpensive fabric may sag or bag when worn. However, consumers should be able to judge the fit of garments regardless of the sizes listed on them. Clothing should be selected according to how it looks and feels on the person wearing it.

Consumers should try to find ready-made clothes that fit. If alterations are necessary, they may cause problems. Alterations are sewing modifications to change the fit of garments. A simple alteration, such as a length change, is usually not a problem. However, extensive or poorly done alterations can change the lines of a garment. They are also an added cost. Consumers should be skeptical of high-pressure salespeople who say tricky alterations can be accomplished easily. They may only be trying to make the sale. Once alterations are completed, the garment cannot be returned.

When trying on shoes, a consumer should check that the shoe is long enough. His or her toes should not touch the ends. A width should be chosen that does not pinch. It is a good idea to walk around in the shoes for several minutes to check their comfort on different surfaces. There should be adequate padding in the heels and soles, and the bottoms should not be too slippery. To avoid foot and posture problems, people should not skimp on shoes they will wear often and for many years.

16-12 Wearing ease allows a person to move comfortably in a garment. Additional fullness may be included as part of the garment's design.

hifashion/Shutterstock.com

Know Trademarks

A trademark is a distinctive symbol or name that identifies the goods of a particular seller or manufacturer. See **16-13**. Trademarks offer information about merchandise quality.

16-13 Manufacturers promote their trademarks so they become instantly recognized by consumers.

The quality of various brands may be high, low, or in the middle. However, within the same brand, quality will almost always be uniform from one article to the next. Trademarks often have performance guarantees. Consumers often choose or reject various brands based on their reputations.

People should note which manufacturers make apparel that best fits their body shape, taste, and quality standards. They can search for the same brands in the future. The merchandise will probably be of the same quality and fit again. In this way, people are assured of getting the type of clothes they want. By making repeat purchases, consumers show loyalty to brands that suit their standards of style and performance.

Every now and then, companies change their production specifications. Sometimes companies are bought by other manufacturers. The quality of their apparel may then change, becoming either of lower quality than before or new and improved. In these cases, comparison shopping can help consumers reevaluate to get the best products and prices.

The quality of big national brands should be compared with lesser-known brands. Sometimes store brands (private labels) are offered at lower prices than national brands. This is because merchandise is often made by large manufacturers. It sells for less because stores buy it in quantity and it is not advertised nationally. Many of these items are quality products and good buys. On the other hand, some may be inferior. If the quality is equal between the national and store brands, the store brand is usually a better buy because it is often priced lower. However, a well-known brand name is usually assurance of good quality.

Designer Labels

Designer labels are trademarks that usually give status to those who wear them. A designer's logo is often placed on the outside of a garment for all to see when the garment is worn. Status symbols are important to some consumers and motivate them to buy such products. However, consumers usually pay more for these items than they would for comparable ones without designer labels and logos.

Evaluate Bargains

A bargain is a favorable purchase. Getting a bargain means getting high-value merchandise for a relatively small amount of money. Sometimes a low price is the sign of a real bargain. On the other hand, a low price can be a sign of poor quality and an item that is not a bargain.

Bargains help people save money and can bring them great satisfaction. Although consumers should look for bargains, they should buy carefully. They should not forget their original shopping plan, priorities, and quality comparisons. Part of the decision-making process in shopping is evaluating whether or not an item is a bargain.

Shopping at Sales

Consumers should not buy something just because it is on sale, **16-14**. A sale item is a bargain only if it is needed. Buying something just because it is on sale is a waste of money if it does not fit into the buyer's wardrobe and is never worn. A garment should be purchased

kurhan/Shutterstock.com

16-14 Some consumers buy merchandise just because it is on sale. These items are not bargains unless they are truly needed and will be used.

because it is right for the consumer and his or her wardrobe plan, not because the price is low.

Before buying sale merchandise, consumers should ask themselves whether or not a purchase fills a genuine need. They should consider whether it has the quality and fit they desire. If an item is damaged, consumers should assess whether or not it can be easily repaired. A sale item should be judged the same way a regularly priced item is judged. It is a bargain if it is of better quality for the same amount of money charged for a regularly priced item. It is a bargain if the consumer gets what he or she wants for less money. Sale items that cannot be used are not bargains at any price. If clothing does not fit, is not needed, and cannot be returned, it does not matter how cheap it is.

Buying at sales has its drawbacks. These can include little personalized service and disorganization. Shoppers may have to dig through piles of merchandise to find the items they want. Crowds and confusion during many sales events can make it hard for consumers to think clearly and make wise decisions. People often get caught up in a frenzy and buy too many items.

Since some sale items cannot be returned, consumers should ask about the return policy before buying. They should also check sale garments carefully for flaws before purchasing. They should look for quality fabrics and construction details. If possible, it pays to shop early before the more popular items are gone. Shopping at sales may take more time, but it is often financially worthwhile.

Types of Sales

Retailers have overused the term *sale*. Consumers should be able to distinguish between sales of quality apparel and promotional sales of cheap garments designed to attract business.

Clothes are put on sale for many reasons. *General sales* are often held throughout stores during holiday times to lure people in. Retailers have sales for almost every holiday and special event. Other sales are held during slow seasons. Examples are January *white sales* and *promotional sales* during August.

Stores want to sell leftover inventory at the end of the season. If merchandise is no longer selling well at full price, a store will not want to keep it for the next season. *Clearance, inventory,* and *end-of-season sales* clear out old stock to make room for new merchandise. See **16-15**. Items can be picked up at great savings.

Sometimes leftover garments are in unusual sizes or colors. These are often of good quality and are bargains if needed anyway. By waiting until after fashions have reached their peak popularity, shoppers can find good-quality

16-15 Sales that are held at the end of a fashion season encourage consumers to buy items at lower clearance prices. Retail shelf and hanging space then becomes available for new merchandise.

items at fractions of their original prices. This is especially a good deal if the style will be popular for a long time.

New items are sometimes put on sale to encourage customers to become acquainted with them. Such sales might offer good bargains. Other times, stores buy quality garments at lower-than-regular prices for *special-purchase sales*. Stores can offer lower prices because they bought large amounts, but certain sizes and colors may be limited. On the other hand, sometimes great quantities of cheap or inferior merchandise are brought into stores just to be sold at low prices.

Sometimes garments are marked up artificially and then marked down to a regular level and said to be on sale. They are *preticketed* with high prices that consumers are led to believe are the retail selling prices. Those prices are then crossed off, and lower prices are marked to make consumers feel they are getting bargains. Some of these methods seem unethical. However, they are widely used in the retailing world. This is why it is always important to compare quality and prices.

A retailer might hold a *fire sale* when part of a store or warehouse has burned. The sale goods might have water damage or smell like smoke. They could, however, be very good items.

A store might also hold a *going-out-of-business sale*. The retailer might have lost its lease. It might have gone bankrupt. In any case, the owners must sell all their merchandise. Bargains may be available, but consumers should look closely before buying. Sometimes cheap, low-quality merchandise is brought in to be sold with the items already on hand.

Some stores offer coupons to customers. For example, a coupon may give the holder 20 percent off any one merchandise purchase. This could result in savings for the customer if he or she would have bought the item anyway. However, coupons often have exclusions. For example, a coupon may only be good on certain days or expire after a specified date. Consumers should read the fine print on a coupon before heading for the store.

Impulse Buying

As mentioned in the previous chapter, consumers may be tempted to buy impulsively, as in **16-16**. Impulse buying occurs when people

16-16 Unusual designs, favorite colors, or special prices might tempt consumers to buy impulsively.

buy things as soon as they see them, without thinking carefully. These types of purchases are not part of anyone's plans, budget, or needs. They are emotional purchases rather than logical ones. People buying on impulse do not consider their needs or other wardrobe items. They just buy on a whim.

Fad items are often bought impulsively. Sometimes buyers are influenced by advertising displays, salespeople, or friends with whom they are shopping. One impulsive splurge could ruin a whole shopping plan. People may spend more than they had budgeted and end up with garments they do not need and will never wear.

To guard against impulsive buying when shopping, consumers should ask themselves, "Do I like this enough that I would come back on another day to buy it?" If it is on sale, they should ask, "Do I like it enough that I might have paid full price for it?" If the answers are *yes*, it is probably a good purchase.

Questions to Ask When Buying Apparel

Is it the correct style for my shape and personality?

Is it functional and appropriate for my lifestyle?

Does it fit into my color schemes?

Does it fill a need listed in my wardrobe plan?

Does it provide comfort and easy care?

Have I gathered information and comparison shopped?

Does the quality meet my requirements?

Is it my size?

Have I tried it on to evaluate its fit and look?

Is it a brand name that I like?

Is it a bargain with a reasonable price for the quality and for the amount of use I expect to get from it?

Am I buying impulsively (emotionally) or logically?

16-17 Consumers can avoid purchasing mistakes by asking themselves these questions.

The questions in **16-17** can help consumers make wise, planned purchases. Items purchased will be wanted and needed. They will fit into a total plan. Consumers should be able to purchase things they like if they can do so with confidence and without overspending.

How to Pay

Buying is the exchange of money or credit for goods or services. Consumers who buy carefully avoid overspending. Making unplanned purchases can leave no money for emergencies and necessities.

Cash Purchases

In a *cash purchase*, money is used to pay the full cost of merchandise bought. The transaction is then complete. The buyer is not in debt for that purchase. He or she is not sent a bill and is not responsible for added credit charges. Paying with cash forces people to develop discipline. They must save money until they have what they need to make a purchase. People who use cash avoid spending more money than they have. They have an easier time controlling their expenditures. (Gift cards may also be used toward cash purchases at the retailers that issue them.)

Paying with cash also has its drawbacks. For example, expensive items are often difficult to pay for with cash. Consumers who spend unwisely can run out of cash and be unable to pay for things they really need. Also, cash can be stolen or lost. The only record of a cash purchase is a sales slip. Additionally, purchases made with cash may not be used to establish and build a person's credit rating.

Writing a Check

Cash purchases are also made by check. Using a check gives the consumer more evidence of his or her spending than using money. Cancelled checks and records of checks are good receipts. Paying by check eliminates the need to carry large amounts of money or to send money through the mail.

People record the amounts of the checks they write so their accounts do not become overdrawn. When an account is overdrawn, the total of the withdrawals and checks written against it is greater than the funds available in the account. Checks written on an overdrawn account will usually *bounce*. The bank will not cover the payment, and the check writer will still owe the money to the merchant. Plus, he or she will probably owe both the merchant and the bank an extra penalty charge.

When a store clerk receives a check, he or she may run it through a special machine. The voided check is handed back to the customer with a receipt. This is *electronic check conversion*. The machine reads the bank identification, account number, and check number. That information is used to instantly transfer an electronic payment from the customer's bank account to that of the merchant. In the customer's bank statement, the transaction will be shown as an electronic debit to the merchant rather than a check payment.

Using Debit and Smart Cards

Cash purchases can also be made electronically with a debit card. The card looks similar to a credit card. When a purchase is made, the customer swipes his or her card and enters a personal identification number (PIN). The money is deducted from the customer's bank account and goes into the retailer's account without the need to withdraw cash or write a check. This enables people to buy items without carrying cash and without paying bills and interest payments later. These transactions and others are included in a statement the bank creates for each account. Customers should always check to make sure the transactions listed in their statements are accurate. To do this, they should keep their own records of purchases and deductions from their accounts.

A *smart card* has an electronically stored cash value built-in. This reloadable prepaid cash card looks like a credit card but has a computer chip embedded in the plastic. The chip might be programmed to hold a certain amount of money after the consumer gives that sum to the card issuer. Retail checkout terminals read the information stored on the card's chip. After the cashier rings up the purchase, the terminal requests verification of the purchase total. The consumer pushes an *okay* or *yes* button, and the cash amount is electronically deducted from the value of the card. The purchase amount is stored in the retailer's terminal for settlement with the card issuer.

Consumers find smart cards to be fast and easy for purchases. There is no personal identification number to enter, no paper, no signatures, and no online authorization. It is faster than making a cash purchase with money. Plus, most smart cards can be reloaded after their value has been depleted. Those that also contain a credit-card magnetic strip can be reloaded at automated teller machines (ATMs).

Retailers like these cards because bad payments are less likely. As retailers replace their checkout terminals with new equipment, they will install versions that can accept credit, debit, and smart cards.

Layaway Purchases

When a customer makes a layaway purchase, he or she puts down a deposit on an item and the store puts the item away for a certain length of time. During that time, the customer makes payments to the retailer. When the retailer has been paid in full, the customer receives the exact merchandise he or she originally picked. By putting the item aside, the store prevents other customers from buying it. However, there are consequences if layaway customers change their minds or cannot finish making the payments. Customers either forfeit the money already paid or get only part of it back. This is because the retailer kept the merchandise off the selling floor for a period of time.

Layaway may be a good method of buying items consumers do not need immediately. It encourages budgeting. Successfully using layaway can help people establish a credit record. Consumers do not pay interest and do not go into debt. However, the retailer has the consumers' money ahead of time. When buying this way, consumers should always be sure to have a written agreement with the retailer.

Credit Purchases

A *credit purchase* is a promise by the buyer to pay the seller for goods or services in a specified way at a later date. It is a buy now, pay later arrangement. A credit agreement is used rather than cash. The agreement states how the amount owed will be paid. For example, consumers may be required to pay the amount in full when they receive the bill. Other agreements state that consumers may pay portions of the total in monthly installments with interest added.

Credit Cards

Credit cards are plastic cards that establish the holder's ability to charge goods and services at participating businesses. They are available from financial institutions and credit card agencies. Some retailers issue their own credit cards. Some credit cards have annual fees while others do not. They are used for merchandise and services bought around the world. See **16-18**.

Newer credit cards and those used internationally contain an embedded microchip as well as the traditional magnetic stripe. For purchases, they are used at chip-enabled terminals. The embedded chip encrypts information. This increases data security about purchases and makes it very hard to copy or counterfeit a card. The chip communicates with the terminal to determine whether or not the card is authentic.

Applying for a credit card involves filling out an application or contract. Applicants should always give truthful information on their applications. They will be asked about their income, bank accounts, and other credit cards. They should carefully read the credit application. If they have any questions, they should ask a representative of the financial institution, agency, or retailer for clarification, as in **16-19**. Consumers should be certain they can meet their obligations before they sign.

StockLite/Shutterstock.com

16-18 Name three actions that someone should take if he or she is a victim of identity theft.

In order to be approved to use credit, consumers must have a good financial standing or credit rating. That means they have a good record of paying their bills—credit card bills, rent, car loan payments, utility and medical bills, and others—according to agreed-upon terms. A poor credit rating can result from missing payments and bouncing checks. It is also caused by sending payments in late or in amounts that are less than what the contracts specify.

The *credit limit* is the maximum amount a person may have outstanding on a charge or other credit account. It is set when a credit card account is opened and is determined by a person's ability to pay. Any number of purchases can be made as long as the total does not exceed the credit limit.

When a purchase is made with a credit card, the cardholder usually signs a *charge slip*. It tells what was bought, where and when it was bought, and the amount of the purchase. The merchant keeps a signed copy and gives the cardholder a copy. All credit card purchases are itemized on a bill at the end of the pay period.

There is usually no interest added if the bill is paid in full and on time. However, if a cardholder does not pay the entire balance after the bill arrives, a finance charge is added. A finance charge is the fee and interest for credit—in other words, the cost of borrowing. Some finance charges are lower than others, so it is wise to shop around for the lowest finance charge and the best credit arrangements. When finance charges are paid, purchasing something with a credit card costs more than purchasing the same thing with cash.

Finance charges are expressed as percentages. These fees can be high and may add significantly to the cost of using a credit card. For example, a 1½ percent per month rate of interest is sometimes charged on the unpaid balance of a credit card account. That is the same as a whopping 18 percent annual charge. This finance charge adds that much more to the purchase price of apparel and other items bought this way. Sometimes accounts charge 1 percent per month, which is a 12 percent annual interest rate. Consumers should check credit card costs before using them.

Installment Plans

Retail credit is also offered through installment plans. These are used most often for specific large items. The consumer makes a down payment when he or she takes the item. A contract or agreement is written for the amount of the purchase. The total cost of the finance charges and the number of periodic (usually monthly) payments are specified. The least expensive way to use installment credit is to make the largest down payment possible and to have short payment periods.

Consumers should never sign a contract or agreement they do not fully understand. All verbal promises by the merchant or party extending the credit should be put into writing by him or her. Consumers should cross out all blank spaces and mark them with the date and their initials. Also, consumers should receive and keep a copy of the signed contract.

Financial Loan

A loan from a bank, credit union, or other financial institution can also provide the money for large purchases. Interest rates for these credit agreements vary, so it is wise to look for the best loan arrangements.

BELK CREDIT APPLICATION

EMPLOYEE NO.	DATE

Type of Account Requested:
☐ INDIVIDUAL   ☐ JOINT

PLEASE TELL US ABOUT YOURSELF

FIRST NAME (TITLES OPTIONAL)	MIDDLE INITIAL	LAST NAME		AGE

STREET ADDRESS (IF P.O. BOX — PLEASE GIVE STREET ADDRESS)	CITY	STATE	ZIP

☐ OWN ☐ LIVE WITH RELATIVE	MONTHLY PAYMENT	YEARS AT PRESENT ADDRESS	HOME PHONE NO.	NO. OF
☐ RENT ☐ OTHER	$		( )	DEPENDENTS

PREVIOUS ADDRESS	CITY	STATE	ZIP	HOW LONG

NAME OF NEAREST RELATIVE NOT LIVING WITH YOU	RELATIONSHIP	PHONE NO.
		( )

ADDRESS	CITY	STATE

NOW TELL US ABOUT YOUR JOB

EMPLOYER OR INCOME SOURCE	POSITION/TITLE	HOW LONG EMPLOYED	MONTHLY INCOME
		YRS. MOS.	$

EMPLOYER'S ADDRESS	CITY	STATE	TYPE OF BUSINESS	BUSINESS PHONE
				( )

MILITARY RANK (IF NOW IN SERVICE)	SEPARATION DATE	UNIT AND DUTY STATION	SOCIAL SECURITY NO.

SOURCE OF OTHER INCOME (Alimony, child support, or separate maintenance need not be revealed if you do not wish to have it considered as a basis for repaying this obligation)	SOURCE	INCOME	☐ MONTHLY
		$	☐ ANNUALLY

AND YOUR CREDIT REFERENCES ARE

NAME AND ADDRESS OF BANK/SAVINGS AND LOAN	☐ CHECKING ☐ SAVINGS ☐ LOAN	PREVIOUS BELK OR LEGGETT ACCOUNT? ☐ YES ☐ NO ACCOUNT NO. HOW IS ACCOUNT LISTED?

List Bank cards, Dept. Stores, Finance Co.'s, and other accounts:	NAME	ACCOUNT NO.	BALANCE	PAYMENT
			$	$
			$	$
			$	$
			$	$

INFORMATION REGARDING JOINT APPLICANT

COMPLETE THIS AREA IF   ☐ JOINT ACCOUNT IS REQUESTED   ☐ YOU ARE RELYING ON SPOUSE'S INCOME OR CREDIT HISTORY TO OBTAIN CREDIT

FIRST NAME	MIDDLE INITIAL	LAST NAME	AGE	RELATIONSHIP	SOCIAL SECURITY NO.

JOINT APPLICANT'S ADDRESS IF DIFFERENT FROM APPLICANT ADDRESS	CITY	STATE	ZIP

JOINT APPLICANT'S PRESENT EMPLOYER	ADDRESS	HOW LONG EMPLOYED
		YRS. MOS.

BUSINESS PHONE ( )	POSITION/TITLE	MONTHLY INCOME $

YOUR SIGNATURE PLEASE

Store Stamp Below

I have read and agree to the Terms and Conditions of the Belk Retail Charge Agreement as set forth on attached. Belk is authorized to investigate my credit record and exchange credit experience with other creditors and Credit Reporting Agencies. This information is given to obtain credit, and is true and complete.

FOR OFFICE USE ONLY

Letter _____
CB. RPT. _____
EMP. VER _____

Applicant's Signature   Date

DATE	EMP.	#CARDS	T/C	CR/LN.	APPROVED

Joint Applicant's signature
(required if joint applicant section completed)   Date

16-19   Credit applications should be read carefully and filled out honestly.

Electronic Payments

When buying services and merchandise via computer or mobile devices, several methods of payment can be used. If paying with a debit or credit card, the customer types in his or her name, account number, the card's expiration date, and other information asked for. Some people prefer not to give this information to lots of vendors or have it transmitted in cyberspace, for fear it might get stolen.

Online payment services can be used to provide more secure electronic debit or credit payments to merchants. The customer's bank account or credit card must be linked to an online payment service. Examples of such companies are PayPal, Bill Me Later, and Google Checkout. The customer may later pay online (or send a check) to the services used.

When people finish selecting online purchases, they go to a retailer's check out page, then the payment page. They should make sure the website is secure. After entering a user name and password (set up separately), they are prompted to approve the payment details. The transaction information is then encrypted into bits of code and sent over the Internet. An electronic funds transfer results, removing money from a customer's bank account and putting it into the merchant's account. The customer receives verification of the transaction (a receipt) via e-mail.

Evaluating the Use of Credit

There are many advantages to using credit to make purchases. People who purchase with credit have use of the merchandise before they pay for it. Payment with credit is convenient; money does not have to be carried. Wise uses of credit include making planned purchases and taking advantage of sales. Also, it may be easier to return goods when they are bought with credit. Monthly statements provide a permanent record of expenses.

A disadvantage of credit is that people using it tend to overbuy. They buy impulsively and charge their purchases. They buy what they really cannot afford or do not need. They decide to figure out how to pay for the items later. Note the pros and cons of using credit listed in **16-20**.

Consumers should never charge more than they can afford. They can end up in trouble if they cannot pay their bills. Possible consequences

16-20 The use of credit has both pros and cons. Before using credit, consumers should understand all of the agreement terms and how to follow them properly.

Pros and Cons of Using Credit

Pros (Advantages)
- Can pay later and have merchandise now
- Don't have to carry cash
- Can write just one check to pay a bill that covers several purchases
- May be easier to return unwanted purchases
- Can give you a good credit rating if bills are paid on time
- Provides a permanent record of purchases with monthly statements

Cons (Disadvantages)
- Need a special card or loan agreement
- Is easy to buy too much or impulsively
- Involves risk, since card or number can be used fraudulently by others
- May be more expensive to use than cash because of fees and finance charges
- Can give you a poor credit rating if bills are not paid on time
- Might limit where you make your purchases

include high penalty charges. Consumers can be denied credit in the future. Also, the finance charges can add up quickly. To reduce interest payments, people should pay as much as possible toward the bill each month. Every dollar spent on finance charges is one less dollar to spend on more merchandise. Sometimes it is worth it; sometimes it is not.

The *Truth in Lending Act* says that consumers must be informed of the finance charges for credit accounts, installment contracts, and cash loans in uniform, easy-to-understand terms. The method of calculating finance charges must be disclosed. Consumers can then compare the terms and choose the type of credit they want. Also, the *Credit Card Accountability, Responsibility, and Disclosure Act* makes it harder for banks to promote credit cards to younger consumers. Credit cards cannot be issued to consumers under age 21 unless they have an income or their parents cosign on the account.

If a credit card is lost or stolen, the cardholder should immediately contact the retailer, bank, or other institution that issued it. Otherwise, if it is used dishonestly, the cardholder may be responsible for paying the first $50 of charges placed on it.

Identity Theft

Many consumers are concerned about the crime of identity theft. That is when a consumer's personal, identifying information is stolen—to be used fraudulently. Stolen information can include Social Security numbers, driver's license numbers, credit or debit card and bank account numbers, PINs, user names, passwords, birth dates, and addresses. Using this information, criminals can fraudulently open new credit accounts and get loans in a victim's name. They may also steal money from bank accounts. Identity thieves can ruin a person's credit rating, deplete financial accounts, and destroy his or her good name. Restoring an identity can take a victim of this crime much time and money.

Identity theft is often committed by organized crime rings or by people with access to sensitive information. Computer hackers sometimes steal large amounts of data from financial institutions and retail companies. Businesses need to protect their electronic files containing peoples' information. Documents listing customer information should be shredded before disposal. If a data breach occurs, those involved should be immediately notified. Meanwhile, consumers can protect themselves by only purchasing goods from reputable firms. Also, they should monitor their incoming bills and financial accounts. They should watch out for unusual or unauthorized transactions.

Some consumers do not want to reveal financial information to unknown third parties or share their private data on the Internet due to possible identity theft. They avoid online shopping and banking for this reason. Identity theft can also happen at stores, restaurants, bank ATM machines, and other locations. To prevent theft, consumers should keep credit card and debit receipts, as well as printouts of all online transactions. They should limit the information they give out. Also, they should keep up-to-date virus protection software on their digital devices.

If someone is a victim of identity theft, he or she should immediately contact the local police and file a crime report. Banks, credit card companies, and any other lenders should be notified as soon as possible. The three major credit reporting agencies—Equifax, Experian, and TransUnion—should be notified to put a security freeze on the person's credit history. This is free, as long as the consumer has a police report. The security freeze prevents any changes of name, address, date of birth, or Social Security number in a credit report without the approval of the person whose name is on the report. This makes it much harder for identity thieves to commit crimes such as taking out credit in other people's names. The consumer will still have access to his or her credit history for specified uses. Each year, consumers are entitled to one free copy of a credit report from each of the three major credit reporting agencies.

For questions about identity theft, or to seek protection if personal data is lost, contact the Federal Trade Commission (FTC). The FTC provides answers and publications that help consumers deter, detect, and defend against identity theft.

Summary

Level-headed judgments at the time of purchase enable consumers to make the right decisions. Consumers can compare the qualities and prices of the same or similar items from different retailers. They can use this information to determine the availability and prices of items before buying.

In clothing, the best value is the item that has the highest quality for the lowest price. Whether quality is high, medium, or low depends on the item's construction, materials, and design. Consumers should pay only for the quality wanted and needed for various items. Specific points of quality should be checked carefully on garments. Also, consumers may consider political/social viewpoints about imports, environmental issues, and ethics when making purchases.

To evaluate whether or not clothes fit properly, consumers should know their general size category. With body measurements, a specific size can be determined. When shopping, fit can be checked by trying on clothes while wearing the underclothes and shoes to be worn with the garment.

Knowledge of trademarks helps consumers evaluate quality and fit, too. Designer labels almost always have higher prices than similar nondesigner items.

A bargain can result in money savings and increased consumer satisfaction. Consumers should evaluate sale merchandise in terms of whether it fills a genuine need. Various types of sales are held. Impulse buying of sale items should be avoided, especially if the item is not part of a plan or budget or is not needed.

Buying is the exchange of money or credit for goods or services. A cash purchase is made when the full cost of the purchase is paid for with money, a check, a debit card, or a smart card. A layaway purchase involves a down payment by the consumer and an agreement that the item is put away until periodic payments by the consumer are completed. Credit purchases include credit cards, installment plans, and financial loans. The pros and cons of using credit should be carefully considered. Electronic payments are used for purchases made via computer or mobile devices. Also, consumers need to take precautions to protect themselves from the crime of identity theft.

Fashion Recall

Write your answers on a separate sheet of paper.

Short Answer: Write the correct response to each of the following items.

1. How can looking at quality clothes in expensive stores help people do their comparison shopping?

2. Explain what best value means in terms of clothing.

3. List five characteristics of high-quality garments.

4. *True* or *False*. Quality is always related to price.

5. When judging the quality of a garment, list five points to consider about its seams.

6. List five points to consider when judging the quality of a garment with a lining.

7. When trying on a garment, name five ways to check the fit.

8. *True* or *False*. A low price is always the sign of a real bargain.

9. Why do stores have clearance or inventory sales?

10. What is the cause of an overdrawn checking account?

11. When you make a deposit toward buying an item, and the store puts the item away for you for a certain length of time, what kind of purchase are you making?
    A. Debit card.
    B. Layaway.
    C. Credit.
    D. Mail-order.

12. A credit rating is _____.
    A. the percentage rate of finance charge on credit purchases
    B. a person's financial standing or record of paying bills
    C. an evaluation system that ranks credit companies and banks
    D. the ratio of a consumer's credit purchases to his or her cash purchases

13. What is the difference between a credit rating and a finance charge?

14. List three advantages and three disadvantages of using credit.

15. Name three actions that someone should take if he or she is a victim of identity theft.

Fashion Vocabulary

16. Work with a partner to write the definitions for the *Fashion Terms* on the chapter opening based on your current understanding. Then, pair up with another pair to discuss your definitions and any discrepancies. Finally, discuss the definitions with the class and ask your instructor for necessary corrections or clarification.

Critical Thinking

17. **Judge value and quality** Describe how successfully you would be able to judge value and quality in a knock-off. Give an example, citing text evidence to support your judgments.

18. **Analyze economic factors** Analyze how imported garments affect the economy of the United States. In your opinion, should U.S. consumers buy fewer imported garments? Explain your opinion. Cite text and other evidence from reliable resources to support your opinion.

19. **Evaluate credit use** Evaluate the advantages and disadvantages of teens using credit. How do the disadvantages outweigh the advantages? Write a brief summary of your evaluation.

Core Skills

20. **Math practice** Comparison shop for two different apparel items in three types of stores. Compare quality as well as prices (including the cost-per-wearing). Decide which items would be the best buys based

on your calculations. Write a report that includes descriptions and calculations.

21. **Speaking and listening**   In class, discuss how people shop for clothes at regular and sale prices. Are shoppers more cautious when they cannot return items? Do they settle for lower quality when they buy items at low sale prices?

22. **Research and writing**   Investigate sources of credit, including installment plans, credit cards, and financial loans. Compare eligibility requirements, interest rates, extra finance charges, and payment schedules. Present your findings in a written report.

23. **Technology**   Choose an apparel or accessory item. Enter its identifying information, including the brand name, into a comparison-shopping website. The site should return a list of retailers that sell the item, along with prices charged. Report the results to the class. Discuss how using technology for comparison shopping saves resources, including time and money.

24. **Math practice**   Find an online credit card minimum-payment calculator. Enter a balance amount, an interest rate, and a minimum balance. How long will it take to pay the balance? How much interest will be paid? Repeat using different numbers. Share your findings with the class.

25. **CTE career readiness practice**   Suppose you volunteer at a community workforce development program. The director of the program overheard you talking with another volunteer who is looking for several garments that can be worn for job interviewing. You were explaining to the other volunteer how to evaluate proper garment fit and evaluate bargains. The program director asks you to put together a demonstration for the program clients on how to purchase business-appropriate garments that fit well and are budget-friendly. Think about the following as you prepare for your demonstration, including

- types of workplace-appropriate garments to show clients
- visuals to use to demonstrate proper fit
- accessories to use to change the look of an outfit
- ways to save when buying quality garments

After putting together your presentation, do a trial run for a group of friends or coworkers (your classmates).

Fashion in Action

26. **Portfolio builder**   Select three garments you will need to buy. Plan how you can get the best value. Determine what quality each garment should be. Decide where you should shop and when you should buy. Figure out the best method to pay for each garment. Prepare your purchase plan and keep a copy in your portfolio.

27. **Design activity**   Use a school-approved application to design a digital, interactive bulletin board display that prompts other students to post ideas on how to prevent identity theft.

Self-Assessment Quiz ↗

Complete the self-assessment quiz online to help practice and expand your knowledge and skills.

Apparel for People with Special Needs

While studying, look for the activity icon **to:**

- **practice** key fashion terms with e-flash cards, vocabulary games, and matching activities
- **assess** what you learn by completing self-assessment quizzes

www.g-wlearning.com/clothingandfashion/

Fashion Terms 📩

grippers   toddlers   growth features
layette   preschoolers   trunk
infant kimono   self-help features   maternity fashions
infant gown   safety features   travel wardrobe

Objectives

After studying this chapter, you will be able to
➤ evaluate the apparel needs and sizes for infants.
➤ judge the clothing needs and sizes for children.
➤ describe wardrobe selection guidelines for older adults.
➤ discuss the special apparel needs of people with disabilities.
➤ explain attributes of maternity fashions.
➤ put together and pack a wardrobe for travel.

Some people need special features in their apparel because of their age or physical limitations. Enabling these people to dress with ease and to look their best helps them gain self-confidence and pride. Appropriate clothing can enhance their physical, social, and emotional well-being.

Apparel Needs of Infants

Infant growth is rapid, and wardrobe needs change quickly. Shopping for slightly larger sizes will best accommodate a fast-growing baby. The garments can then be worn longer. However, garments that are far too big are dangerous, since they can become tangled.

Many factors influence the selection of baby clothes. Comfort, practicality, and safety are important. Other considerations include the climate, finances, and availability of laundry facilities.

FamVeld/Shutterstock.com

Comfort

Comfort is a must for infant clothing. Tight garments, or too many garments, will make the baby uncomfortable. Soft, durable garments are best for the baby's delicate, sensitive skin because harsh fabrics can cause skin rashes. Fabrics that are extremely fuzzy can irritate the nose and throat. Babies are most comfortable when dressed in supple, nonirritating garments.

Infant garments should be constructed of fabrics that are absorbent and let moisture evaporate. Cotton flannelette, as shown in **17-1**, challis, batiste, plissé, terry cloth, and jersey are good. Modacrylics have good hand and natural flame resistance. Nylon gives good strength and wearability. Blends of these fibers and others add the needed characteristics to garments. The fabric should be preshrunk or shrink-resistant.

Knit garments are very popular because of the built-in fabric stretch that expands with infant growth. Knits also provide warmth and ventilation.

Practicality

Infant clothing should be designed for ease of changing. It is important to keep the baby clean and dry. Most infants dislike clothing that has to be pulled over the head. Dressing and undressing will be easier if the baby's clothing has front openings. Shirts often have open shoulders that overlap, or fronts that overlap and snap near the side. Blanket sleepers and coveralls usually have a front zipper that extends down into one leg, as in **17-2**, to allow for easy dressing. Some have grippers, which are heavy-duty types of snaps.

The time of year the baby is born and the climate are important considerations when purchasing clothes. It is best to buy only what is needed for each season as the baby grows.

Warmth is necessary, since new babies lie still and sleep most of the time. Their garments provide their protection.

Fewer garments are needed if they can be laundered frequently. When buying clothes, washability is important. Easy care is necessary for all infant items.

Safety

The flammability of baby clothes has been a concern in recent years. The federal government has taken action to require flame-resistant sleepwear. Flammability standards have been set for infant sleepwear in sizes larger than nine months. These garments must be either snug-fitting or flame resistant. Garment packages, tags, and permanent labels indicate whether a garment is flame resistant or must fit the infant snugly. Another safety concern is the type of fasteners on infant clothing. Lightweight zippers or gripper snaps are best. Buttons and trims

17-1 These pajamas of 100 percent cotton are absorbent and comfortable.

Stephen Mcsweeny/Shutterstock.com

17-2 The long zipper from the neckline to one ankle gives a large opening for dressing the baby or for changing diapers.

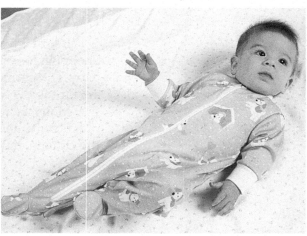

The Right Start Catalog, Los Angeles

that can be pulled off are not practical and may be dangerous. They can be swallowed or poked into a nose or ear by the baby if they become loose. Trimmings should be soft and safe. They should be washable in the same way as the fabric.

The Layette

A layette is the assembled minimal needs of clothing and textile goods for a newborn. It consists mostly of *onesies*, as in **17-3**, *diapers*, and standard sleeping clothes. Diapers are made of folded cloth, or other absorbent material, that is drawn up between the legs and fastened near the waist. Only a few dressy clothes are needed for outings. Use **17-4** as a guide in selecting what should be included in a basic layette.

Diapers

Two common types of diapers are disposable diapers and cloth diapers. Disposable diapers are popular, since moisture is drawn away from the skin to minimize rashes. These diapers come in different sizes to fit newborns through toddlers. Thicker ones are available for nighttime wear. Disposable diapers are convenient for travel or to use for spares in emergencies. However, disposable diapers are expensive to use and waste natural resources. They also create millions of tons of garbage that go into landfills each year and take hundreds of years to biodegrade.

Cloth diapers come in a variety of fabrics and styles. Rectangular diapers that fold in several different ways as the baby grows are usually preferred. It is essential that diapers

A Sample Layette	
6 Onesies	2 Blanket sleepers
36 Cloth diapers	3 Bibs
4 Waterproof pants	4 Diaper pins
Disposable diapers	4 Crib sheets
4 Gowns or kimonos	1 Crib blanket
4 Coveralls or stretch suits	3 Receiving blankets
Shawl, bunting, or	2 Waterproof pads
topper set	3 Washcloths
Bonnet or cap	6 Towels
Socks	Sweater and bootie sets

17-4   After getting the items in a basic layette such as this one, fun and cute extras can be added as desired.

be soft, absorbent, washable at hot temperatures, and quick drying.

Most parents do not consider cloth diapers to be convenient. However, cloth diapers are less expensive to use, even with all the washings. New disposable inserts for cloth diapers have been developed that biodegrade in only 50–150 days. They contain no plastic, chlorine, latex, or perfumes. These inserts can be flushed, composted, or thrown in the garbage to be reabsorbed into the ecosystem. Disposable inserts are now widely available online and at many stores.

Waterproof Pants

Waterproof pants are used over cloth diapers. They are usually made of soft, sturdy vinyl. They should have sealed seams and soft finished edges on all openings. Waterproof pants either pull on or snap on both sides. Most are machine washable.

Kimonos and Gowns

A full-length infant garment that looks like a long dress is called an infant kimono. It is closed in the front or back with snaps or ties. It has sleeves and is often made of lightweight flannel. An infant gown is similar but has a drawstring at the bottom to keep it closed. This provides warmth yet allows the baby to have kicking room inside the garment. The drawstring is untied to open the entire garment bottom for the changing of clothes or diapers.

17-3   *Onesies* are basic undergarments for infants. They serve as an undershirt and they snap over diapers at the crotch.

sjgh/Shutterstock.com

Cuffs on the sleeves can fold over the hands to serve as mittens for extra warmth or to stop fingernails from scratching the face. Drawstrings should never be used at the neck since they are dangerous.

Bibs

Bibs for infants are small (drool or teething bibs) or large (mealtime bibs). Bibs usually have absorbent terry cloth on one side and wipe-clean vinyl on the other. The smaller bib is worn most of the day during the baby's teething months. The vinyl side of larger bibs often has a catch-all pocket. The adjustable neck opening of bibs either snaps or ties in the back.

Stretch Suits or Coveralls

These are made of two-way stretch terry fabric in assorted designs. Some have zippers. Some have snaps or grippers along the entire crotch inseam. They have enclosed feet. They are long- or short-sleeved for various climate conditions.

Towels and Washcloths

Towels and washcloths for infants are 100 percent cotton. They are not as thick or heavy as regular towels. Most have extra fabric across one corner, like a hood, to put over the baby's head for warmth after the bath, as in **17-5**. The towels often come in white or have a small printed design.

17-5 The corner hood on a baby towel can be quickly placed over the infant's head for warmth as the rest of the towel is used to dry and wrap the baby.

BlueOrange Studio/Shutterstock.com

Infant Apparel Sizes

Manufacturers base their infant apparel sizes on the average heights and weights of infants. The clothing sizes are actually listed by age in months. However, clothing should be selected by height and weight rather than by age. Figure **17-6** gives the most widely used categories of sizes for infant clothing.

The smallest sizes are not very practical and may be outgrown before being worn. Also, as with other types of apparel, there are differences among the sizing systems of various manufacturers. The garment label and package information can guide in evaluating a manufacturer's specific size. Sizing charts are also included in mail-order catalogs.

Clothing for Young Children

The selection of clothes for toddlers and preschoolers must emphasize comfort. Young children should be dressed in simple and functional clothes, as in **17-7**, rather than in fussy or complicated attire. Their clothing needs are based on growth, constant movement, and the development of their coordination to dress themselves.

Toddlers are children who are actively moving or walking. They are usually between the ages of 1 and 3 years. They have short bodies, short legs, and a protruding abdomen.

17-6 Infant sizes are based on average heights and weights of infants of different ages. However, individual babies vary in their growth rates. Whenever possible, buy infant clothes according to a baby's actual height and weight, not age.

Infant Sizes		
Size	Height (in inches)	Weight (in pounds)
Extra Small	18½–20½	up to 6
0–3 Months	20½–23½	6–12
3–6 Months	24–26½	12½–16
9 Months	27–28½	16½–18
12 Months	29–30½	18½–20
18 Months	31–32½	20½–24
24 Months	33–34	24½–29

17-7 This colorful outfit is comfortable, durable, and machine washable.

shupian/Shutterstock.com

Preschoolers are taller than toddlers and not as round. They are starting to have a defined waistline. They are between the ages of 3 and 5 years.

Appropriateness

Toddlers and preschoolers need clothes built for comfortable, constant action. Their garments should be easy to launder, and they should not be scratchy or itchy. Garments should have adequate fullness where needed for freedom of movement. Tight clothing binds and restricts movement. Extra room should be provided at the seat, armholes, pant legs, and crotch. Elastic inserts should be included to hold garments in place. Soft, unstructured styles are good, such as one-piece playsuits that hang from the shoulders. Shoulder straps should be wide and crisscross in the back. Some shirts have shoulder tabs to keep up straps of pants or skirts.

Pants and straps that keep falling off cause frustration and can create resentment toward dressing.

Clothing for preschoolers must be easy for them to manage. Sometime during the third year, children become aware of clothing and show an interest in dressing and undressing themselves. Children develop greater independence and responsibility when they can get into and out of their clothes by themselves. For this reason, children's clothes should have **self-help features**. Armholes should be large. The backs and fronts of pants, shirts, and undershirts should be different or well marked. Closings should be easy to fasten and located in front, so they can be seen and manipulated. Grippers and hook-and-loop fasteners, such as Velcro®, are the easiest fasteners for children to handle. Zippers and medium-sized flat buttons can be used. Elastic waistlines enable children to pull pants on and off by themselves.

Children's garments should be attractive in color and style. Children generally like clear, bright colors, as in **17-8**. Prints should be in proportion to the size of the child.

Corduroy, textured fabrics, and prints help hide wrinkles and soil. Pockets are important features because children need places for the treasures they collect. A sense of identity and self-worth is gained by children from compliments received on their clothing or on the special details of their garments.

17-8 Most children prefer bold, bright colors. These colors are also more visible for safety.

Tracy Whiteside/Shutterstock.com

Safety

Children's clothes should provide safety features. If possible, they should be of flame-resistant fabrics. This is especially required of sleepwear that is not snug-fitting. The designs of children's apparel should not cause the child to trip or catch on corners. Avoid styles with long, flowing skirts, tie belts, drawstrings, or very full sleeves. Trims should be firmly attached and placed where they will not hamper the child.

Children's outerwear must provide protection from severe weather. This means water repellency as well as warmth, without heavy weight. Heavy strain should not be placed on the shoulders. Bulky clothes are tiring and can restrict proper posture. Brightly colored outer garments are readily noticed by motorists.

Practicality

Economy of the wardrobe is also important. Children's garments receive very hard wear. Reinforcements should be included at the points of strain (pocket corners, placket ends, knees, and elbows). For longer wear, the clothes should be of durable, sturdy materials. The best fabrics have soil and stain resistance. They should be made of permanent-press fabric, which provides wrinkle resistance and easy care.

Ease of care is important for children's clothes, just as it is for infants' apparel. Children are apt to get extremely dirty, and the clothing must be laundered frequently. Children's garments must be durable enough to withstand both the actions of the children and repeated washings. They should be washable without shrinking or losing their color. Even snowsuits and coats for children are available in washable fabrics. Try to avoid purchasing clothing that must be dry-cleaned.

Growth Features

Children's clothes are expensive and are outgrown fast if they do not have built-in growth features. These features allow garments to be expanded as children grow. This does not mean parents should buy or make clothes that are far too big. Children's clothes should fit well when worn and have features for growth.

Garments with growth features should be of simple designs. They should have large necklines. Raglan or kimono sleeves or sleeveless armholes allow for expansion since there is no defined end to the shoulder in those designs. Elastic waistbands and stretch fabrics adapt to growth. Wrap styles are good.

Since children grow taller much faster than they grow wider, length adjustments are the most important. Garments should have wide hems and cuffs that can be let down. They should not have defined waistlines. If clothes have shoulder straps, they should be adjustable so they can be lengthened.

Try to keep a young child's wardrobe down to a minimum amount of apparel. Children often outgrow clothes before they are worn out.

Children's Self-Esteem

In child care, preschool, or school, conformity is important. Children become conscious of what their peers are wearing, and they want to look like others. Approval by their friends gives a sense of belonging and security, as in 17-9. Clothing contributes to a feeling of self-confidence and self-esteem. It encourages good emotional development. Clothes that make the child look different from others may cause him or her to feel strange, be ridiculed, and become withdrawn or rebellious.

Reinforce interest in appearance by giving children some choice in what they wear. Giving helpful, tactful guidance will help them develop

17-9 These children are happy being well dressed. Feeling good about themselves will help them do productive schoolwork.

good taste. Clothing selection can be a shared experience between parent and child. Allowing preschoolers to help choose the clothes at the time of purchase ensures that they will wear the garments. The teaching of clothing care can also be started at this age. Provide hooks on which to hang outer garments and a hamper in which to deposit dirty clothes.

Children's Apparel Sizes

Sizes of clothes for toddlers are 1T, 2T, 3T, and 4T. They are based on age, but children do not necessarily fit into the size that corresponds with their age. Order or purchase by correct measurement, not by age. Garments for toddlers are made to go over diapers or training pants. They fit children who have not lost their baby roundness. They usually have a snap crotch with grippers.

Clothing for preschoolers is sized from 2 to 6X. These sizes are also related to age. However, always buy or make children's apparel in sizes according to height rather than age indicators.

Height is the most important measurement for determining size. Children grow faster in height than in width. The length of the arms, legs, and trunk (measurement from shoulder to crotch) change much more quickly than the width of the shoulders, chest, and hips.

Figures **17-10** and **17-11** show the most widely used approximate measurements (in inches) of clothing sizes for toddlers and young children. Toddlers' and children's sizes 2, 3, and 4 basically only differ in the diaper allowance, length, and width through the shoulder and back. Sometimes preschooler clothing sizes are labeled *Small (S), Medium (M), Large (L),* and *Extra Large (XL).* Typically, (S) relates to sizes 2 and 3 in the chart. (M) means sizes 4 and 5, (L) means sizes 6 and 6X, while XL addresses the needs of those preschoolers who are more generously proportioned. However, all sizing can vary slightly by manufacturer.

Elastic waist garments will fit waistlines approximately one inch smaller to one inch larger than shown in the size chart.

17-10 The measurements shown here are similar to those used by apparel manufacturers and commercial pattern companies to determine clothing sizes for toddlers.

Clothing Sizes for Toddlers				
Toddler Size	Height (in inches)	Chest (in inches)	Waist (in inches)	Approximate Weight
1T	29½–32	20–20½	19½	25
2T	32½–35	21–21½	20	29
3T	35½–38	22–22½	20½	33
4T	38½–41	23–23½	21	38

17-11 Garments in sizes 2 to 6X are for young children who are taller and more slender than toddlers.

Clothing Sizes for Young Children					
Children's Size	Height (in inches)	Chest (in inches)	Slim Waist (in inches)	Regular Waist (in inches)	Husky/Plus (in inches)
2	33–35½	21	18	20	22
3	36–38½	22	18½	20½	22½
4	39–41½	23	19¼	21¼	23¼
5	42–44½	24	20	22	24
6	45–47½	25	20½	22½	24½
6X	48–50½	25½	21	23	25

More two-piece outfits are needed at this stage. Interchangeable separates will give the greatest wardrobe mileage for the least cost.

Children's shoes are in sizes 6 to 13 and then start over at size 1 of a new scale as they get bigger. They then continue into adult sizes. Be sure to have the child's foot measured by a well-trained salesperson for an accurate fit. Nothing should ever be put on a child's foot that restricts the normal growth of the bones, muscles, or nerves. Children's shoes need to be checked, and often bought, every few months to avoid later deformity or discomfort. Socks must also fit properly. See **17-12**.

Sewing Children's Apparel

Children's clothes are fun and easy to sew, and a great deal of money can be saved by making them. The investment for fabric is small. Cute patterns are available that are quite simple to make. Creative touches can be added that will make the child love each garment. If a sewing mistake is made, simply cover it up with an appliqué or some trim. If a tear appears during wearing, there will be fabric scraps to use to put on a matching patch. In addition, leftover fabric can always be used for mending, lengthening, and adding decorations.

By adding growth features and using durable sewing techniques, garments can be created that will last a long time. For instance, include several decorative rows of tucks parallel to the hemline of a skirt or dress to be let out later for more length. Choose designs and fasteners that make the garments easy to change. Include flat seams for comfort. Put extra layers or padded appliqués at the knees.

Good fabrics for children's garments are those that are absorbent and either firmly woven or closely knitted. Corduroy, denim, poplin, gingham, seersucker, and broadcloth are good choices. Knit and stretch fabrics are especially good for comfort, action, and growth. Also, children enjoy soft fabrics, such as brushed flannel and terry cloth. Cotton blends are wise choices. Clothing made from fabrics that contain nylon, acrylics, and polyester fibers wear well and have easy care. Strive for comfort without bulkiness and warmth without weight.

Hand-me-downs can help stretch clothing dollars. These can be adjusted to fit. New trim, appliqués, or other personal touches can make them special for the child. Permanent marks, such as lines where the hem has been let down, can be covered with preshrunk ribbon, rick-rack, or topstitching that coordinates with the design of the garment.

17-12 New shoes and socks that fit properly and are easy to put on also help children feel self-reliant.

matka_Wariatka/Shutterstock.com

Clothing for Older Adults

It is important for older adults to maintain their self-esteem by looking attractive. Some may lose interest in their appearance, possibly due to poor health, weight changes, or even loneliness. Being well dressed helps older adults retain a greater interest in life.

Americans are living longer now than ever before. Improved medical practices are extending life expectancies and increasing the number of people well past retirement age. This ever-growing population group tends to stay active in recreational and community activities and requires up-to-date stylish clothes, as in **17-13**.

Many older adults live in retirement communities where there are frequent social activities. Fashionable apparel is still important to

Monkey Business Images/Shutterstock.com

17-13 Many older adults lead active lives and need versatile wardrobes.

these adults. Compliments on their attire can increase wearers' self-esteem and provide feelings of well-being.

Physical Changes

As adults pass middle age, they can become less agile, and their body proportions may change gradually. For some, the abdomens and hips get larger, the face and legs get thinner, and waistlines thicken. See **17-14**. Older women can develop stooped shoulders, which then lowers the bust line. Older men can develop protruding stomachs. These changes become more accentuated with time until the older person can sometimes no longer wear standard-sized, ready-to-wear clothing.

If physical changes in body proportions with advancing age become extreme, alterations to standard-sized garments are often necessary. Sewing garments at this stage in life can be a good way to occupy extra time and achieve a better fit. However, sometimes eyesight and finger dexterity has diminished.

For people with arthritis or partial paralysis, getting dressed and undressed is often difficult. These people may also lack energy or feel weak due to infrequent physical activity. They need large, accessible openings with easy-to-close fasteners. Many older people have trouble with

Jack.Q/Shutterstock.com

17-14 Older adults sometimes have to adjust their wardrobes to different body types.

closures in the back of garments. They may not be able to extend their arms over their heads or reach to the back. Outfits that have jackets provide for easier dressing and protection against temperature changes. Cardigan sweaters are also good.

Older people often feel cold temperatures more intensely than the young. However, heavy clothing may not be comfortable for them. Therefore, lightweight fabrics that provide warmth are needed. Acrylic and modacrylic sweaters and polyester fleece garments can provide needed warmth without weight.

Older people with physical disabilities may require clothes that have self-help and accessibility features. These people need safety features and fabrics that feel soft to the skin. As glandular secretions decrease, their skin often becomes thin, dry, and inelastic. Heavy fabrics and rough textures may irritate delicate skin.

Personal coloring in later years may be different from coloring earlier in life. Gray and white hair enables different colors to be worn attractively. See **17-15**. Yellow and brown seldom look good if skin is pale. Colors and styles that focus attention on the face are helpful in drawing attention away from any physical disabilities.

Selecting Apparel for Older Adults

Certain style features are generally recommended for older adults who are sedentary or have any physical issues with caring for themselves. These include shift-style dresses without fitted waistlines, A-line skirts, and looser necklines. Men's trousers should be less fitted for more wearing ease. Garments with elasticized waistbands, long center front closures, and large patch pockets are good. Also, raglan sleeves and straight long sleeves without cuffs reduce fitting and buttoning problems. Knit fabrics and blends with polyester are more durable and have ease of care.

17-15 Silver hair goes with many color schemes.

Shopping must be done carefully for older adults, to satisfy their special clothing needs. This may not be easy for an older person who might be uncomfortable with today's complex consumer decisions, or who may not have available transportation. Also, many retirees living on reduced incomes have extra concerns about the price and durability of their garments.

Apparel for older adults should be attractive as well as functional; conservative, and yet fashionable. Clothes should have simple care requirements and be easy to put on and take off. The physical and psychological needs of older adults for proper clothing must always be considered.

Apparel for People with Disabilities

Millions of adults and children have disabilities that may limit their activities. They need clothes that are comfortable, functional, and attractive. See **17-16**. Appropriate apparel can enhance people's independence and productivity.

Easy care is an important factor in clothing selection for many people with disabilities. Those who are weak and inactive need clothes that provide warmth without weight. Garment fabrics should be soft and absorbent. Unsuitable or tight clothing can hinder movement, produce discomfort, make the wearer feel unattractive, and negatively affect the wearer's self-image and morale.

17-16 People with disabilities also need fashionable and professional business clothing.

goodluz/Shutterstock.com

People with physical limitations need apparel that simplifies the task of dressing. Some disabilities cause reduced manual dexterity and strength. Those with such disabilities feel better psychologically when they can dress themselves.

Specific Garment Features

For people with disabilities, choose styles without fussy details and with a minimum of fastenings. Self-help features may include easy-to-handle front or side closures. Grippers and zippers are good fasteners. Small loops stitched to the garment near the bottom and top of zippers can be used as leverage when zipping and unzipping. A decorative zipper pull, such as a ring, yarn tassel, or braided ribbon can be added to the existing zipper pull as an aid in grasping it. Velcro® fastening pieces are convenient. However, a long tape of Velcro® might be hard to pull apart.

Buttons may be difficult for some to fasten. If buttons seem necessary, they should be large and can be sewn with elastic thread for easy maneuvering. *Mock buttons* are also a good alternative. They are created by removing the existing buttons and sewing the buttonholes closed. Velcro® squares or dots are then affixed under the sewn-closed buttonholes and where the buttons were removed. The removed buttons are sewn on top of the closed buttonhole. This simple alteration allows the Velcro® to easily perform the closure, yet the buttons are still visible. Whichever method is used, there should be as few fasteners as possible above mid-chest level.

Raglan and dolman sleeves are easy to slip on and off, and they allow for ease of movement. Large armholes may be needed. Shoulder openings, longer neck openings, and drawstring necklines and waist closures often add convenience. Elastic bands can be used at the waistlines of pants and skirts. Garments will then slip on and off easily, as well as have roomy fullness. Also, a longer back rise can make pants fit better for someone who must remain in a sitting position.

Wrap-around styles are easy for many people with disabilities to handle. Pockets are more usable if they are slightly larger than normal. An air opening in the back of a waterproof rain suit gives ventilation needed for those in wheelchairs. It can be covered with a flap to keep out the rain. A built-in sling can support a weak or paralyzed arm.

Trousers with few or no seams on the back or sides are more comfortable for those who must spend hours every day in a wheelchair. A pocket just below the pants knee is useful to hold loose tickets, bills, and other items. For foot or leg casts, the pants leg seam may have to open its entire length. Pants and underwear may need added seam openings.

Knitted fabrics allow for both ease of wear and ease of dressing. Woven fabrics may be needed if braces or crutches snag knits. Double-knit jersey, velour, and stretch terry are good washable fabric choices. Avoid sheer, flowing fabrics that can catch fire or become caught in wheelchairs or doorways. See **17-17**.

Shape and Fashion

Clothing for people with disabilities may have to go over mechanical devices or body casts. Some bodies may not be symmetrical, so clothing camouflage techniques may be effective. In many cases, separates are a good choice so one size on top can be paired with a different size on the bottom.

17-17 Comfortable and breathable cotton woven fabrics are best for those who need assistance with movement.

Clothing for people with disabilities should help the wearer project a fashionable image. Most people who have special clothing needs prefer to wear the latest fashions. Looking good gives their spirits a lift.

Apparel chosen for people with disabilities should not call attention to any type of difference. For instance, wearing daytime clothing, instead of pajamas or loungewear, can help to create a feeling of health. Protective cover-ups for students with disabilities have been designed to resemble a turtleneck shirt, a football jersey, overalls, a jumper, or an apron, for example. They are functional, durable, attractive, and appropriate in design for the ages of the students. The garments should be current in style, functional, and include appropriate modifications that adapt to various everyday needs, as in **17-18**.

17-18 This rain poncho, available online, is waterproof, flannelette-lined, accommodates headrests, and has tie downs and a built-in carrying pouch.

www.epiphanydesign.ca

Obtaining Apparel for People with Disabilities

It can be difficult to find appropriate and attractive self-help clothing for people with disabilities. There is a definite need for specially-designed clothing to be manufactured and promoted for people with disabilities. Although there is a sizable demand, it is not large enough for manufacturers to produce special items on a mass scale. Manufacturers understand that few people need exactly the same adaptations. Some ready-to-wear apparel items, such as wrap-around skirts and certain types of action wear, are already suitable. Specialized garments are available on several websites.

For example, a group of Japanese firms has designed and manufactured a line of clothing specifically for people with disabilities. Each company produces one category of garment, such as pajamas, raincoats, shirts, or underwear. The products meet foreign regulations and are being exported to other parts of the world. Retail prices are about 30 percent higher due to the complicated sewing processes, as well as reduced production runs. High-fashion designers in Rome have also created collections for people with disabilities. These fashions are shown on the runways by real people/models with disabilities in their own wheelchairs.

Special clothing needs can often be met by modifying ready-to-wear clothing. For instance, set-in sleeves can be adapted to include an action pleat that allows more room for arm movement from a seated position. This is shown in **17-19**. Instructions for such modifications, as well as publications, videos, specialized mail-order catalogs, and other resources for selecting or changing clothing to meet specific physical needs, are available through *extension agents*. (Extension agents are state university employees who provide help in communities. They can be located by calling your county administrative office or searching online for "extension agent" and your county and state.)

It is feasible to successfully adapt home sewing patterns to the individual needs of people with disabilities. Several booklets have been written on how to do this. Helpful information is also available on the Internet.

West Virginia University/Nora MacDonald

17-19 This action pleat allows greater freedom of arm movement from a seated position. When the arm is at rest, the action pleat folds inside and does not show.

Knowledge of clothing modifications can also provide a community service opportunity. By combining interests in clothing design and social service, garments can be developed that are suitable for people with disabilities.

Maternity Fashions

Maternity fashions are for pregnant women. They usually have soft pleats, gathers, and added fullness in front, as shown in **17-20**. Maternity skirts and pants have an elasticized panel across the front with an expandable elastic waistband. Maternity apparel designers are continually updating designs for the business professionals' needs, both in the office and for social events.

Entire shops, websites, and mail-order catalogs cater to only maternity fashions. Department stores usually have a maternity apparel section that carries fancy attire as well as casual wear. Fashionable home patterns are also offered for pregnant women.

Since maternity clothes are worn for about five months during a pregnancy, they are often only needed for one or two seasons of the year; for instance, summer into fall, or winter into spring. Some maternity dresses can continue to be worn after the baby is born by adding a sash or belt to the waistline. See **17-21**.

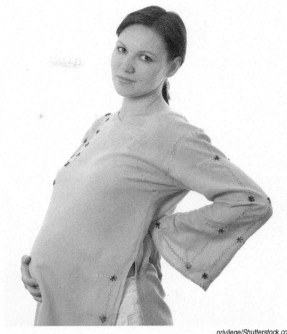

privilege/Shutterstock.com

17-20 This casual maternity outfit has plenty of fullness for comfort and a stylish appearance throughout a pregnancy.

Travel Wardrobes

A travel wardrobe is all the apparel a person takes on a trip. Good travel wardrobes should be lightweight, well coordinated, and wrinkle resistant. Many people attempt to pack entirely too much clothing for trips, resulting in excess luggage and potential airline fees. Careful planning is the key. Paring down a travel wardrobe to a few coordinated pieces will eliminate unnecessary items and reduce the amount of luggage.

Mix and Match

Clothes for trips must be appropriate, as well as good travelers. There is no need to purchase a lot of new clothes. Present apparel will look new to people elsewhere. Simply mixing and matching familiar favorites tends to make people feel more comfortable when traveling.

When packing, select coordinated separates and simple garments that can be accessorized for many options. Three tops and three bottoms can make up to nine different combinations. Travel light with a small number of items that complement each other, so outfits are interchangeable.

McCall Pattern Company, Vogue American Designer® / Donna Karan New York

17-21 This comfortable dress can be worn before, during, or after pregnancy. It has fullness that expands in the front or can be belted for a fashionable, slim look.

bikeriderlondon/Shutterstock.com

17-22 By mixing and matching several favorite garments, different outfits that will be comfortable for the various activities of a trip can be created.

Travel wardrobes should be planned around the traveler's most becoming colors and silhouettes. Use only one or two basic colors, if possible, for easier coordination, as in **17-22**. Bright colors can accent neutral garments. Wardrobe options will also be stretched by creatively using belts, scarves, jewelry, neckties, and other smaller accessories that are easy to pack.

Be Practical

Fabrics with dull finishes and moderate textures show less soil and fewer wrinkles. They are also appropriate for many different places and occasions. Stretchy fabrics and knits are good. Small prints, checks, and tweeds also hide soil and wrinkles. Bright (or light-colored) accessories, such as scarves or jewelry, positioned near one's face also serve to de-emphasize any travel weariness.

Comfortable shoes are a must, because travel often includes much walking in unfamiliar areas. Never attempt to break in new shoes on

a trip. Since shoes and boots are heavy, only pack those that are absolutely necessary. A pair of dress shoes and a different pair of walking shoes are required for regular travel. Hiking or sports activities will have different footwear requirements, as in **17-23**.

Determine Travel Needs

Travel wardrobe needs are determined by the destination(s), weather, trip length and types of transportation. Learn about the trip's

17-23 Your planned travel activities may require special footwear or other gear.

Golden Pixels LLC/Shutterstock.com

activities and dress code ahead of time, and then make a list of what to wear for each occasion. See **17-24**.

For traveling long distances, wear an outfit that does not bind while sitting for a long time and looks fresh on arrival. Consider the proper attire for sight-seeing stops and restaurants along the way. Plan to arrive at destinations dressed presentably and appropriately. Metropolitan areas may require more sophisticated clothes than rural resorts.

On an extended trip, a larger wardrobe is generally unnecessary. By taking several well-chosen outfits, the same clothes can be worn over again at different locations. Provisions will have to be made for laundering, but then exhaustion from carrying excess luggage is avoided.

Some small garments may be washed in a bathroom sink and hung to dry overnight. Plan to take travel-sized packets of detergent, a small stretch clothesline with a few clothespins, or plastic hangers.

Lightweight travel irons have assorted plugs for different electric currents in foreign countries. Other clothing care items to consider taking include a clothes brush, a small shoe cleaning kit, and a small bottle of cleaning solvent. Large, plastic zipper bags may serve as see-through organizers when starting the trip. They also come in handy if some items are damp or dirty when they have to be packed for the return trip.

Before packing, check that buttons are secure, hems are intact, and seams are not coming unstitched, to avoid clothing repairs while travelling. However, bring a small sewing kit and some safety pins just in case. Also, be sure all clothes are clean and without stains.

Packing Tips

If a trip includes many stops, organize the suitcase to eliminate unpacking items from the bottom as much as possible. In other words, pack last what will be used first.

Before putting items in the suitcase, stuff shoes with socks, hose, belts, or soft items. Turn the tops of the shoes toward each other with heels at opposite ends. Place the shoes in plastic or fabric bags to prevent them from soiling packed clothes. Match the leg seams on pants to preserve the center front and back creases.

A good deal of wrinkling can be avoided with proper packing techniques. Pack by layering or rolling the garments, or a combination of the two.

In a hard-sided suitcase, pack the odd-shaped and heavy items on the bottom, preferably near the edge opposite the handle. Then pack the large apparel. Pants and other long items should be laid in alternating directions across the suitcase, as in **17-25**. One end of each garment should be at a *wall* or side of the case. The remainder can hang out the other side, to be folded around all the other items later. Add tissue paper or dry cleaning bags on top and along the edges of the suitcase to prevent creasing when the ends are eventually folded.

Roll up sweaters, lingerie, and other non-wrinkling items. Make a layer of rolled items on top of the pants layer. Stuff pajamas and underwear around the rolls to fill in the spaces. This keeps items from shifting.

Now place dress shirts, jackets, skirts, and dresses flat on top of the rolled items layer. Alternate the edges of each piece so collars, shoulders, waistbands, or other bulky parts do not pile up in one area. The sleeves, ends, and sides should be left hanging over the edge of the suitcase. Lay any delicate items on top. Then complete the packing job by alternately folding in the shirts, dresses, skirts, and pant legs, one over the other. This system provides a neat arrangement that travels well and protects garments from wrinkles.

17-24 Could anything be added to this travel wardrobe, possibly for more casual activities?

Karkas/Shutterstock.com

StockLite/Shutterstock.com

17-25 Careful packing will keep travel wardrobes pressed and ready to wear whenever needed.

An alternative packing method for large roomy suitcases is to hang pants, skirts, shirts, and dresses on individual hangers. Cover each garment with a dry-cleaning bag. Lay the entire pile centered lengthwise across the suitcase, hanging out on both sides. Then fold the pile in thirds, hanger side first. Upon arrival, shake out and hang up the garments. The plastic bags are amazing crease fighters since they trap air that provides a buffer cushion for the clothes.

To pack a smaller duffel or sports bag, make one big roll of soft items. Slacks, skirts, and blouses that wrinkle should be on the outside (bottom) of the roll. Lay them on a bed or other flat surface first. Then place knits and underwear so they are on the inside (top) before everything is rolled together. Start rolling from the thicker end toward the flatter end. Then place the roll into the bag as one smooth, round bundle. Shoes and a toiletry pack can fit into an edge or end of the bag.

Other Considerations

In addition to a large suitcase, a tote or shoulder bag for last-minute items—such as a magazine or book, hairbrush, and cosmetics—is a good idea. Jewelry, electronic devices, and other valuables should not be in a checked bag. Keep them with you. Airline companies usually do not compensate you for the loss of or damage to such items. When traveling by plane, pack some necessities, such as toiletries, any medications, and a change of underwear, in a carry-on bag. Also include the suit you need for the next day (business suit or swimsuit) plus power cords and chargers for your electronic devices. Having these items with you will be lifesavers if luggage is lost or delayed.

Additional considerations include taking an empty water bottle to fill after going through airport security, so you do not need to buy an expensive bottle of water on the way to the gate. A compact umbrella will serve you well for rain in all locations. You may also want a pair of rubber flip-flops for the hotel room and bathroom. Finally, for packing, place a business card or note with contact information on top of your clothes inside your suitcase. If your suitcase name tag and baggage claim tag are torn off by airline baggage machinery, your suitcase will be opened to try to identify the owner. Airline employees will know immediately how to reach you.

Always plan to hang up packed clothing as soon as possible after arrival. If some clothes have wrinkled, let the steam of a hot shower relax the wrinkles. Some people travel with a portable steamer. Many hotels/inns provide an iron and an ironing board in the rooms, or may loan them when requested.

When traveling by plane and checking luggage, it is helpful to mark bags with a bright piece of tape on the sides or ribbon on handles. See **17-26**. This provides easy identification when claiming baggage at the other end. If there is room, consider adding an empty lightweight duffel bag in the suitcase. It can be used to take home those cherished treasures, mementos, or additional clothing acquired on the trip.

Trips are more enjoyable when people are dressed comfortably and appropriately, and are carrying minimal luggage. See **17-27**.

17-26 The yellow ribbons on these suitcases will make them easy to spot at the airport baggage claim.

MJTH/Shutterstock.com

17-26 Traveling can be a memorable and fun experience if people plan in advance for their apparel needs.

Summary

Appropriate apparel for people with physical limitations of any kind can enhance physical, social, and emotional well-being. Infants need the comfort of soft, durable, absorbent fabrics. Practicality of infant clothing gives ease of changing and laundering. Safety considerations are flammability and safe fasteners and trimmings. The layette includes onesies, diapers, waterproof pants, kimonos and gowns, bibs, stretch suits or coveralls, towels and washcloths, and other items of choice. Infant apparel sizes should be selected by height and weight.

Simple, functional clothes for toddlers and preschoolers must also emphasize comfort. They should be appropriate for constant action and laundering. They should have self-help features, safety features, and growth features. Economical, durable wardrobes for young children should also have styles similar to those worn by friends. Children's apparel in toddler and preschooler sizes should be purchased by height rather than age. Children's clothes can also be fun and easy to sew.

Clothing for older people should enable them to look attractive to maintain high self-esteem. Physical differences in older adults can include changed body proportions and coloring, as well as motor skill restrictions. Certain style features can help to make it easier for older adults to dress themselves, look attractive, and function better in their everyday lives.

People with disabilities need clothes that are comfortable, functional, and attractive. Specific garment features include self-help fasteners, a longer back rise, wraparound styles, added seam openings, and other considerations. Sometimes clothing must hide figure irregularities or mechanical devices, so camouflage techniques and separates are good choices. Since it may be difficult to find appropriate and attractive clothing for people with disabilities, ready-to-wear clothing or sewing patterns can be modified appropriately.

Maternity fashions, with added fullness in front, are available from department stores, specialty shops, mail-order catalogs, websites, and home sewing patterns. Travel wardrobes should be lightweight, well coordinated, and wrinkle resistant. Plan to mix and match separates and simple garments in flattering colors that can be accessorized for many options. Be practical and comfortable. Determine travel needs ahead of time, considering the destination(s), weather, type(s) of transportation, trip's activities, and available laundering facilities. Suitcases should be organized to eliminate unpacking from the bottom at interim stops. If taking a large suitcase, have an additional tote bag with necessary items. After arrival, unpack as soon as possible to minimize wrinkling.

Fashion Recall

Write your answers on a separate sheet of paper.

Short Answer: Write the correct response to each of the following items.

1. Why are knit garments popular choices for infants?

2. Name two safety concerns related to infants' clothes.

3. Describe two kinds of bibs worn by infants.

4. On what do manufacturers base infant sizes?

5. What factor is of least importance when choosing infant apparel?
   A. Fabric type.
   B. Comfort.
   C. Fashion interest.
   D. Flame resistance.

6. What quality is least desirable in young children's clothing?
   A. Comfort.
   B. Fussiness.
   C. Growth features.
   D. Self-help features.

7. Name three self-help features in children's clothes.

8. Describe three safety features in children's clothes.

9. List three growth features in children's clothes.

10. How can clothes contribute to a child's self-esteem?

11. Name two physical changes that occur as people age, and explain how those changes influence clothing needs.

12. List three style features that are generally recommended for older people.

13. Name two kinds of fasteners that are often used on clothes for people with physical disabilities.

14. Explain how trousers can be constructed to be more comfortable and practical for people who are confined to wheelchairs.

15. What special features are common in maternity clothes?

16. List three tips for selecting items for a travel wardrobe.

17. Why should a person avoid wearing new shoes on a trip?

18. If traveling by plane, what items should be packed in a carry-on bag?

Fashion Vocabulary

19. With a partner, use the online resources to locate photos or graphics that depict the *Fashion Terms* on the chapter opening. Print the graphics or use presentation software to show your graphics or photos to the class, describing how they depict the meaning of the terms.

Critical Thinking

20. **Evaluate options**   Evaluate the primary considerations when selecting clothing for infants. Summarize your evaluation and suggestions for the class. Cite evidence to support your summary from the text and other reliable resources.

21. **Assess garment needs**   Describe a disability and assess types of garments or garment modifications that would be appropriate for that disability. Use online resources to locate visual examples of your assessment of garments or garment modifications. Use presentation software and your digital visuals to share your assessment with the class.

22. **Create a plan**   If you were packing for a weekend trip that involved flying to a friend's wedding, what factors would you take into consideration as you packed? Create a plan for packing, listing items you would require for the wedding. Identify how you would pack your suitcase to maximize the space to accommodate your apparel needs for the weekend.

Core Skills

23. **Speaking and listening**   Debate the issue of cloth diapers versus disposable diapers. Discuss convenience, cost, environmental issues, and babies' comfort. To prepare for your debate, use reliable online resources to research key issues on both sides of the debate. Note key evidence (and sources) to cite during the debate.

24. **Speaking and writing**   Interview an older neighbor or relative about his or her clothing likes and dislikes. If you were going to give that person a gift of clothing, what would it be? Describe its features, cost, colors, and other details. Explain why you think it would be a good choice for that person. Write your findings in a short report.

25. **Technology**   Plan a vacation (real or imaginary) and identify the location. Determine a suitable travel wardrobe for your destination. Coordinate specific apparel items and accessories. Use a school-approved infographic application to create a poster that includes pictures or drawings as well as explanations, to show how the garments and accessories would go together for all the types of planned vacation activities.

26. **Research and writing**   The U.S. Consumer Product Safety Commission (CPSC) lists and reports on dangerous products, including clothing, on its website. Read the lists of adults' and children's apparel. Using a desktop publishing program, create a brochure summarizing dangerous clothing features for consumers. With approval, consider posting your brochure to the class or school website for peer and community review.

27. **Technology**   Working with a group, choose a specific population—young children, older people, or people with a particular disability. Research their clothing needs. Obtain permission from a retailer to shoot a video of apparel in a local store that shows viewers what type of clothing is appropriate for this population. Then, edit and post your video to the class website for peer and instructor review.

28. **CTE career readiness practice**   Your job in marketing for a local clothing retailer involves writing a monthly blog showcasing various clothing and accessory products your store features to meet customer needs. Your assignment this month is to write about clothing items your store features for people who have disabilities. Write and illustrate your blog post and share it with your readers (the class).

Fashion in Action

29. **Portfolio builder**   Develop a fashionable collection of clothing for a person with a physical disability. Draw or collect pictures of garments that accommodate the person's disabilities. Describe any special features of the garments. Keep this in your portfolio to demonstrate your knowledge of apparel needs for people with special needs. For a digital portfolio, scan or use digital images to create a photo essay with descriptions of special garment features.

30. **Design activity**   Interview parents of preschool children about apparel needs. Then, design what you consider to be a good outfit for a preschool boy or girl. Include a sketch, a written description, and (if possible) swatches of fabrics and trims for your design. Mount your sketch, description, and swatches to a display board to present to the class.

Self-Assessment Quiz ☞

Complete the self-assessment quiz online to help practice and expand your knowledge and skills.

Caring for Clothes

G-WLEARNING.com

While studying, look for the activity icon to:

- **practice** key fashion terms with e-flash cards, vocabulary games, and matching activities
- **assess** what you learn by completing self-assessment quizzes

www.g-wlearning.com/clothingandfashion/

laundering   soaps   fabric softeners
wash load   biodegradable   ironing
detergents   enzymes   pressing
surfactants   bleaches   dry cleaning
builders   water softeners

Objectives

After studying this chapter, you will be able to
➤ describe how to provide daily and weekly care for clothes.
➤ discuss the proper storage of clothing.
➤ evaluate the best ways to treat and remove stains.
➤ explain how to keep apparel clean and pressed.

Considerable time and effort go into selecting clothes and building wardrobes. Caring for clothes properly is just as important. Getting into the habit of treating clothes right with regular cleaning and upkeep is essential. Taking good care of clothes helps them last longer, thus saving time, money, and energy in finding replacements. Most garments today have easy care requirements. Giving them regular attention stretches apparel dollars and ensures a well-groomed, neat appearance.

Daily Care of Clothes

A daily pattern of clothing care should be established. Preventive care keeps soiling and damage to a minimum. Simple and immediate procedures are important for prolonging garment life and reducing maintenance costs. Routine care of clothes will keep garments and accessories in good condition and ready to wear, as in **18-1**.

While Dressing and Undressing

When dressing and undressing, be careful not to ruin clothes by snagging, ripping, or stretching them. Put a towel around the

StockLite/Shutterstock.com

PathDoc/Shutterstock.com

18-1 Regular care of clothes keeps them in good condition.

After Wearing

After clothes are worn, put them with the dirty clothes, on a hanger, or in a drawer. Wrinkles added from tossing a garment onto a chair or the floor may not hang out later.

After taking clothes off, check to see if they need to be brushed, laundered, spot-cleaned, dry-cleaned, pressed, or mended. If they need special attention, put them where the necessary care will not be forgotten. Only put away clothing that is ready to be worn again.

Brush good suits, jackets, and pants after each wearing. If dust and lint are left in the fibers, the life of a garment will be shortened, and the garment's appearance will be affected. With a soft-bristled clothes brush, brush with the nap (or grain) of the fabric. The upholstery attachment of a vacuum cleaner is also good for removing loose dirt. A lint roller with a sticky-tape surface can be used to remove lint. Turn the pockets inside out to shake or brush out accumulated dirt and lint. Then put the pockets back to their usual positions. If the garment has cuffs, do the same with them.

Hang clothes carefully and squarely onto sturdy hangers. Clothes that are hung correctly on firm hangers will keep their shape and press. Padded hangers, as in **18-2,** or broad hangers

shoulders, over clothing, to catch any hairs, dandruff, or powder when fixing hair or putting on makeup after dressing. If clothes must be pulled on over makeup or creams, put a large scarf around the hair and face when slipping clothes on. Let a freshly applied deodorant or antiperspirant dry before putting on clothes to avoid staining them.

Also, when dressing or undressing, open fasteners fully so garments will slip on or off easily. Extra strain from unopened fasteners can cause rips, broken zippers, and missing buttons. When putting on hose, gather up the leg portion in both hands and slip the foot into the toe. Then gently draw the stockings over the legs. Make sure hands and fingernails are smooth to prevent runs.

18-2 Hangers such as these give excellent support to apparel for good care of clothes, plus they look pretty in the closet.

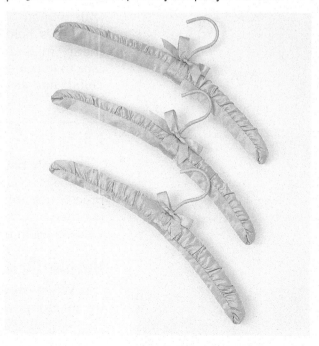

of shaped wood or plastic are best for most garments. Thin wire hangers may leave ridges across the shoulders or droop under heavy coats and jackets. They may cause garments to lose their shape. Some may even leave rust marks.

When hanging garments, make sure lapels are flat and pocket flaps are pulled out (not tucked in) and lying smooth. Empty pockets so the garments will not be stretched out of shape.

Fasten zippers and buttons of garments when they are on the hanger. This keeps them from twisting, wrinkling, or slipping off. Skirts can be hung on special hangers with clips, or they can be secured on regular hangers with clothespins, safety pins, or straight pins. Do not fold them over a hanger, because that causes wrinkles and takes up more space in the closet. If closet space is limited, try using multiple skirt, shirt, or slacks hangers.

Trousers can be hung upside down with the hem area held between the two sides of a pants hanger. See **18-3**. They can also be hung over hangers that have a thick or round bottom bar.

Until the Next Wearing

Allow recently worn clothes to air in an open room, outside, or in front of a fan before putting them away in a closet or drawer. Airing helps remove odors and wrinkles. By being exposed to air for a time, garments will stay fresher longer. Also, let wool garments and woven stretch fabrics rest for a day between wearings to regain their original shape.

18-3 These hangers are especially designed for hanging skirts or trousers. The bottoms of the hangers are double, to separate for inserting the garment. Then they lock tightly together to hold the garment for hanging in the closet.

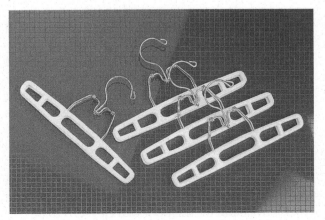

If garments are badly wrinkled, give them a quick and easy bathroom steam press. Hang them in the bathroom while taking a shower. Be sure the garments are fully dry before putting them away.

Fold sweaters and knit garments and place them neatly in drawers or on shelves. Store them flat and loosely to retain proper shapes and minimize wrinkles. If placed on a hanger, they may sag and stretch out of shape.

Avoid overcrowding closets and drawers. Clothes will wrinkle when stuffed into jammed spaces. If possible, keep seldom-worn or out-of-season garments in a different location. This allows more space for clothes worn more often.

When coming in from wet weather, neatly hang damp clothes to dry immediately on removal. Hang them in a well-ventilated area away from direct heat. With heat, they could start to steam or shrink. Stuff wet pockets lightly with tissue paper to help them dry faster. Prevent woolen gloves from shrinking by inserting wooden clothespins in the fingers. All rainwear should be kept where there is plenty of ventilation to avoid mildew.

Stuff wet shoes and leather boots with wads of paper to help them retain their original shape. A shoetree might cause damp footwear to change shape or stretch unnaturally. If the leather starts to harden, rub on some oil. Polish as usual when the footwear is dry. The inside of shoes can be dried faster by using the *cool air* setting on a hair dryer.

Weekly Care of Clothes

Upkeep of clothing should be done during a set time each week. If a weekly schedule is established, clothing care will become routine and easier to accomplish.

Sew on loose buttons, hooks and eyes, and snaps. Replace lost ones. Mend small rips and tears before they become large holes. These repairs should be made before garments are laundered or cleaned. Otherwise the broken stitches will pull loose, rips will fray and get bigger, and fasteners will get lost.

Remove spots and stains. Launder the washable clothes that are dirty. Hand wash sweaters and other delicate items. Take soiled garments that cannot be washed to a dry cleaner. Also take good clothes with stains that have not come out when using home spot removal methods. Tell the dry cleaner which types of stains are present and where they are, so the correct stain removal treatments can be used.

If outerwear has lost its water repellency, apply a new coating by using a water-repellent spray. Such a spray can also be used to protect parts of garments from perspiration damage. Follow the directions on the container carefully.

If some garments have become pilled, brush them carefully with a stiff-bristled brush to remove the pills. Press clothes that are wrinkled. If shoes are dirty and scuffed, clean them with a dry cloth and a brush. Then polish them. If the heels or soles need replacing, take them to a shoe repair shop as in **18-4**. Replace old, worn shoelaces with new ones.

Home Storage Areas

Home storage areas, such as closets, shelves, and drawers, should be neat and well organized. The saying, *a place for everything and everything in its place*, applies here. Good use of storage helps a home look neat and keeps apparel in its best condition. Look at the well-organized closet in **18-5**.

California Closet Company

18-5　All of the apparel items in this closet are clean and organized. They are easily seen and ready to be worn.

18-4　Shoe repair shops are available in most areas, either in malls or in their own independent locations.

Storage areas should provide adequate space for both hanging and folded clothes. Store items as close as possible to the place where they will be used or put on. For instance, coats should be near the door. Jewelry should be near the mirror.

Store similar items together, or at least near each other, if they are worn together. All underwear items should be in the same or adjoining drawers. Shirts should be together, as well as sweaters, slacks, jackets, and so on.

Closet space should be big enough to hold a season's wardrobe without crowding. Traditionally, a sturdy horizontal pole is attached from end to end of the closet to hold hanging clothes. The pole should be high enough for long garments. Sometimes a second pole extends only partway across the closet. This allows double space for shorter items, such as shirts and skirts.

Using all available closet space to good advantage can sometimes be a challenge. A shoe rack can be put on the floor of a closet. A shoe bag can be hung on a wall or on the inside of a closet door. A storage box can be placed under hanging shirts, since these garments are not full length. A tie and belt rack can go on the back of a door. Make sure to utilize all shelves in the top area of a closet. Can you get any ideas from **18-6**?

Several hooks in a closet provide handy places to hang pajamas, belts, and scarves. Hooks usually screw into a wooden frame area of a closet for strength. Adhesive-backed hooks can be placed at other spots, but cannot hold as much weight.

Store items so they are easy to find at a glance. Frequently used items should be the easiest to reach. Cover closet shelves with washable paper so they look nice, have no splinters, and are easy to clean. Shelves are good places to store boxes containing seldom-worn shoes, hats, or purses. Be sure to label the boxes so their contents are readily known. A light in the closet helps to locate these items when they are needed.

Closets should be kept clean and dry to prevent mold or mildew from damaging clothes and shoes. People living in a damp climate may benefit from additional items that should keep closets dry and mildew free. These can include a heating rod, a low-watt lightbulb always left on, or special kinds of absorbent materials. Large walk-in closets can be kept fresh with a dehumidifier or simply with good ventilation to circulate air freely.

Drawers should be free of dust, lint, and dirt. Line them with shelf paper or special liner. Do not use newspaper, since the printer's ink can rub off onto clothes. Treated shelf paper absorbs grease and repels moisture.

If a living space does not have enough closet or drawer space, create new additional storage. For example, to form an attractive storage unit in an open space, tack or glue fabric to a bookcase. Add a coordinating shade across the front. When the shade is pulled down over the shelving, a unique room divider is created. To carry out the scheme, use matching fabric for the window treatments or to make throw pillows for the bed. A small chest of drawers used for storing out-of-season items can easily become a bedside table. Simply put a circle of plywood or particleboard on top of it with fabric or a floor-length tablecloth.

18-6 See-through bins and a covered rolling cart can store items wherever space is available. A mirror in the dressing area is a great convenience.

IKEA

Seasonal Clothing Storage

Seasonal clothing storage usually happens in the spring and the fall to prepare for temperature and weather changes. Apparel that will not be worn for several months should be put away. Closets and drawers should be cleaned and prepared for the current season.

Never store clothing that is dirty. Dirt sets over time and with heat. It may even become permanently embedded in the fabrics. Food stains attract insects. Even the substances found in deodorants, perfumes, body lotions, and perspiration break down fibers over time. Therefore, always wash or dry-clean garments before storage. Also, make any needed repairs before storing out-of-season garments. Some dry cleaners provide a clothing repair service for a fee. See **18-7**.

To prepare clothes for storage, empty all pockets and remove belts. Close all fasteners so garments will maintain their shape.

18-7 If you cannot make the necessary repairs to clothing, dry cleaners sometimes offer this service.

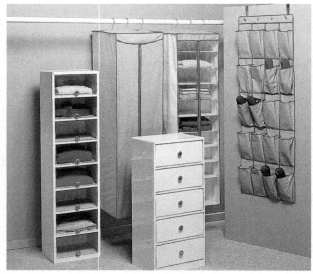

18-8 Garment storage bags and other closet accessories can be purchased in various sizes and styles, and at different prices.

Knitted garments should be folded, not hung. Insert layers of flat tissue paper into the folds of garments to prevent fold marks. Folded items can be kept in trunks and suitcases, or stored in boxes.

Store hanging clothes in zippered garment bags of the right length. These may be purchased, as shown in **18-8**, or made. Make sure there is sufficient room between garments to allow the items to breathe. Plastic dry cleaning bags may suffocate the fibers in clothing. To store purses and shoes, fill them with wads of tissue paper and protect them from dust.

Thoroughly mothproof all apparel to be stored. Put mothballs into the closet or storage containers. Moth protection also comes commercially in pouches, boxes, fragrant sachets, and vacuum-sealable plastic bags. Additionally, dry cleaners can mothproof garments after cleaning them.

Put items to be stored in a clean, dry, cool, and dark place. The storage location should be dust free to keep garments clean. It should be dry and cool to prevent mildew, and out of direct sunlight to keep colors from fading. Spray storage spaces with bug repellent to prevent the hatching of insects.

Cedar closets or cedar chests provide good seasonal storage, especially for those who find mothball odor to be offensive. Insects avoid garments surrounded by cedar. However, cedar will not kill the eggs of moths or silverfish if they are already in the clothing.

Some dry cleaners provide sealed storage vaults with controlled humidity and temperature for a fee. Furs and leathers can be specially cleaned, reconditioned, and stored. Cold storage keeps fur strong and supple, and it prevents cracking and mildewing of the skins. Furs should not be sprayed with moth or insect repellent. Some repellents contain oil that may harm fur. Garments are returned from the dry cleaner at the end of the season clean, pressed, and ready to wear. Professional clothing storage might be a good storage option if space at home is limited and if the cost can be afforded.

Removing Spots and Stains

If a garment gets a spot, treat it as quickly as possible. Stains are harder to get out the longer they stay in fabrics. If treated correctly, most stains can be removed from washable fabrics at home. The wrong treatment, or delayed treatment, can often make the stain permanent.

Treat all stains before laundering or dry-cleaning a garment. Pretest the stain removal method on the item's seam allowance, facing, or other hidden area before using it on a visible part. This test ensures the color or appearance of the fabric will not change.

When a spill occurs, immediately absorb excess liquid with a napkin, towel, tissue, or other absorbent material. Gently blot, and do not rub. Do not apply pressure. That could force the stain further into the fabric. Also, never iron over a stain or expose a stained garment to heat or sunlight. Heat can permanently set stains.

Identify the Fiber and the Stain

Spots and stains on clothing have many causes and cures. Correct removal depends on the fiber content of the garment and the source of the stain. Stain removal often takes some time to accomplish successfully.

First, identify the fiber content. Determine if the fabric is washable or bleachable by checking the care label and any saved hangtags. Stains on dry-cleanable fabrics should be treated with cleaning fluid or cleaned by reputable dry cleaners. Dry cleaners have special equipment, products, and knowledge to remove most stains. Do not attempt to remove stains on antique or extremely delicate articles.

Stains on fabrics with manufactured fibers or permanent-press finishes are often hard to remove. Most manufactured fibers do not absorb water, so the outside of the fibers are cleaned by water, but not the inside. If the fibers absorb an oily stain, special treatment with a prewash soil and stain remover is needed.

Next, identify the nature of the stain, to remove it. If the stain is on a washable fabric, refer to **18-9** for the specific removal procedure.

Treat an unidentified stain on a washable garment with a prewash soil and stain remover. Rinse out the soil and stain remover and let the garment air dry. If the spot remains, treat it with a dry-cleaning solvent. After treating the stain, air or rinse out all spot-removing products. Launder all washable items to make sure the spot remover and stain are gone. Another stain removal method and a rewash may be necessary for complete removal. Do not put items in a dryer until the stains are gone.

Stain Removal Supplies

Before using a cleaning product, be sure to read the manufacturer's directions and warnings. Many products are poisonous and flammable. Some treatments could damage certain fibers or cause fading or bleeding of dyes. Some cause shrinkage, stretching, or a loss of luster. Some come as a gel and dry to a powder. Use a medicine dropper or glass rod to apply liquid cleaning preparations to very small areas.

Some safety precautions are necessary when working with cleaning products. Always work in a well-ventilated area. Do not breathe more solvent vapors than necessary. Wear rubber gloves to protect hands. Do not let cleaning agents come in contact with the skin, eyes, or mouth. Keep them away from electrical outlets and open flames. Never use dry-cleaning solvents in a washing machine. Also, do not put articles in the dryer that are damp with solvent.

When using stain removal products, work in a clean, well-lit area. Have a hard work surface that will not be affected by the chemicals. Never leave any spot or stain removers or other cleaning products within reach of children or pets. Store them closed and in their original containers in a cool, dry place away from food products. If any products are spilled, wash the skin and/or work surface immediately.

Stain removal supplies should be kept together near the laundry area. Absorbent materials should include clean white cloths and white paper towels. Necessary supplies include a heavy-duty liquid detergent, a bar of white soap, chlorine bleach, and oxygen (all-fabric) bleach. Also stock a prewash soil and stain remover, laundry detergent, spot lifter, cleaning fluid, and rust stain remover. These and other stain removal supplies can be purchased at most food, drug, and variety stores.

Also keep a small flat brush with nylon bristles, a medicine dropper, rubber gloves, and a tub or pail for soaking stained articles. Glass or unchipped porcelain containers are best for stain removal treatments. Do not use plastic with solvents. Never use a rusty container.

Stain Removal Methods

There are many stain removal methods. The most common are sponging, chilling to harden, scraping, and soaking.

For *sponging*, place the stained side down over a clean, dry, absorbent material. Dampen another piece of absorbent material with water or the appropriate stain remover. Then sponge lightly from the center of the stain toward the edge to minimize the formation of rings. Apply

18-9 If one of these stains appears on a washable fabric, carefully follow the suggested treatment as soon as possible.

Stain Removal Guide for Washable Fabrics

Adhesive Tape
Rub with ice; scrape with dull knife; sponge with cleaning fluid; wash.

Ballpoint Ink
Soak with hair spray; rinse; hand scrub with liquid detergent; rinse well; can also try rubbing alcohol, glycerin, or prewash spray.

Blood
Soak in cool water with enzyme presoak; rub with detergent; rinse; can also try hydrogen peroxide, ammonia solution or heavily-salted water, wash.

Candle Wax, Paraffin
Freeze and scrape; place between paper towels or tissues and press with warm iron; place facedown on paper towels and sponge with cleaning fluid or rubbing alcohol; wash.

Chewing Gum
Put item in freezer overnight with gum side out or harden with ice; scrape with dull knife; can soften with egg white; sponge facedown on paper towels with cleaning fluid; wash.

Chocolate, Cocoa
Soak in club soda or cool water with enzyme presoak; sponge with cleaning fluid, later with detergent; launder in hot water.

Coffee, Tea
Soak with enzyme presoak, oxygen bleach, or dab with mixture of ¼ c. white vinegar, ¼ c. cold water, and 1 tsp. laundry detergent; rinse with cold water and launder.

Cosmetics
Dampen and rub with detergent; rinse; sponge with cleaning fluid; rinse; wash in water as hot as fabric care permits.

Crayon
Scrape (can loosen with cooking oil); spray with prewash or rub with detergent; rinse; sponge with cleaning fluid facedown on paper towels; rinse; launder hot with bleach.

Deodorants
Scrub with vinegar or alcohol; rinse; rub with liquid detergent; launder in hot water.

Egg
If dried, scrape with dull knife; soak in cool water with enzyme presoak; rub with detergent; launder in hot water.

Felt-Tip Ink
Rub with strong household wall and counter cleaner; rinse; repeat if needed; launder; this stain may not come out.

Fingernail Polish
Sponge white cotton with polish remover and all other fabrics with amyl acetate (banana oil); scrape with dull knife; wash.

Fruits and Juices
Soak with enzyme presoak; wash; if stain remains, cover with paste of oxygen bleach and a few drops of ammonia for 15–30 minutes; can also try white vinegar; wash as hot as possible.

Grass
Soak in enzyme presoak; rinse; rub with detergent; hot wash with bleach; if stain remains, sponge with alcohol.

Gravy
Scrape with dull knife; soak in enzyme presoak; rub with detergent, later cleaning fluid; hot wash with bleach if safe.

Grease
Scrape off excess or apply absorbent powder (talcum or cornstarch) and brush off; pretreat with strong detergent; rinse; sponge with cleaning fluid; hot wash with extra detergent; bleach if safe.

Ice Cream
Soak in enzyme presoak; rinse; rub with detergent; rinse and let dry; sponge with cleaning fluid if needed; hot wash with bleach if safe.

Ink
Spray with hair spray or squeeze lemon on stain; place out in sunshine; repeat if needed.

Lipstick
Moisten with glycerin, petroleum jelly, or mineral spirits; blot with paper towel; wash; bleach if safe.

Margarine
Same as for grease.

Mayonnaise, Salad Dressing
Rub with detergent; rinse and let dry; sponge with cleaning fluid; rinse; hot wash with bleach if safe for fabric.

Mildew
Rub with lemon juice; dry in the sun; rub with detergent; hot wash with bleach; if stain remains, sponge with hydrogen peroxide.

Milk
Soak in enzyme presoak; rinse; rub with detergent; launder.

Mud
Let dry and scrape off. Soak in water with dishwashing detergent and 1 Tbsp. white vinegar; rinse; sponge with rubbing alcohol; rinse; soak in enzyme presoak; wash with bleach if safe.

Mustard
Spray with prewash or rub with bar soap or liquid detergent; rinse; soak in hot water and detergent; launder with bleach if safe.

Oil
Same as for grease.

Paint
Do not let paint dry; sponge oil-based types with turpentine or paint thinner; rub with bar soap; launder.

(continued)

18-9 (continued)

Peanut Butter
Saturate with mineral oil to dislodge oil particles from fibers; blot; apply cleaning fluid and blot between absorbent mats; rinse and launder.

Perspiration
Soak in water with salt, enzyme presoak, or rub with baking soda paste; rinse; rub with detergent; can apply ammonia to fresh stain and white vinegar to old stain; rinse and launder.

Scorch
Soak with enzyme presoak or wet with hydrogen peroxide and a drop of ammonia; let stand 30–60 minutes; rinse well; wash in hot water; rub with suds; bleach; dry in sunshine; may not come out.

Shoe Polish
Scrape off excess; rub with detergent; wash.

Soft Drinks
Dampen with cool water and rubbing alcohol or enzyme presoak; launder with bleach if safe; stain may appear later as a yellow area.

Tomato Products
Sponge with cold water; rub with detergent; launder with bleach if appropriate.

Water Ring
Rub with rounded back of silver (not stainless steel) spoon.

Wine
Same as for fruits; sprinkle a red wine spill immediately with salt.

---

stain remover to the underside of the fabric, so the stain will be sponged off the garment surface rather than through the fabric. If the stain has hardened, soften it by soaking the spot first. Sponge irregularly around the edges of the stain so there will be no definite line when the fabric dries. Change the under pad and sponge pad frequently, so the stain will not be redeposited on the fabric. When the spot is gone, blot up as much excess moisture as possible.

Hardening a substance is a method to remove substances and stains, such as candle wax and gum, from textile products. To do this, gently rub an ice cube across the area. When the material hardens, lift or scrape it off the fabric. If the garment is small enough, it may be wrapped in a plastic bag and placed in the freezer until the stain hardens.

Scraping is a method of removing a substance off a fabric by using a dull knife or a spoon. Place the fabric (stain side up) directly on the work surface. After applying stain remover, gently scrape back and forth over the stain. Do not press hard. This procedure should not be used on delicate fabrics because damage could result.

If a garment is washable, *soaking* it in cool water for about 30 minutes is another stain removal method. An enzyme presoak may be helpful. Prewash sprays work well on the insides of collars and cuffs. If necessary, repeat any treatment until all the stain is removed.

When using an enzyme presoak product or a prewash soil and stain remover, follow the instructions on the package. When using bleach, dissolve it in water first. Do not apply bleach directly to a garment's spot. It will cause uneven color removal or make thin spots in the fabric. Then put the garment in the water/bleach solution. The color of the entire garment may get lighter, but at least the change will be uniform. White fabrics that picked up dye from colored fabrics might be restored by using a fabric color remover.

Do not combine chlorine bleach and any detergent full strength. These two products combine safely only when properly diluted. Do not put chlorine bleach on any fabric's rust stains. Instead, apply a rust stain remover.

A *spot lifter* is sprayed or rubbed into a dry stain. Dampened talcum powder, cornstarch, or a commercial product may be used. After the spot lifter dries, it is brushed away. If successful, the spot is lifted out and brushed away with the dried spot lifter. If a stain cannot be removed from a nonwashable garment, take it to the dry cleaner as soon as possible.

Laundering Clothes

Laundering is washing apparel and other textile items with water and cleaning products. Good laundering procedures and equipment, as in **18-10**, extend garments' wearability and keep them looking newer longer. Front-loading, tumble-type automatic washers use less water than top-loading agitator machines. Both types launder clothes well when used properly.

Clothes that are allowed to get too dirty may be hard to clean. Also, when soil becomes ground into them, fibers can weaken. With proper laundering, the original size, shape, color, and overall appearance of apparel items should be maintained.

Check the fiber content and washing and drying instructions of garments before laundering them. The chart in **18-11** explains the meanings of terms used on labels. The symbols shown in **18-12** are from an international code for care labels. Read and follow the directions on care labels, laundry products, and appliances.

Keep the laundry area well organized, as in **18-13**. Store cleaning and laundry supplies where they are handy, but out of the reach of children and pets. A place to hang up garments as they are removed from the dryer will minimize ironing time later.

Prepare clothes for washing by closing fasteners and emptying pockets. A marking pen or facial tissue can affect every item in the wash load with stains or lint. Shake dirt from cuffs and pockets. Loosely tie long belts and sashes to prevent tangling. Turn knits inside out to prevent snagging.

18-10 Automatic washers and dryers make the task of doing laundry fairly easy.

VGstockstudio/Shutterstock.com

Sort Clothes

Sort clothes carefully to separate items that could damage other items. For instance, if colored dyes run onto white garments, the resulting marks could be permanent.

Separate clothes into piles that are suitably sized wash loads. A wash load is the clothing and other washable items put into a machine to launder together. Wash loads should be large enough to make good use of water, but not overly large, which prevents thorough cleaning. Washable items should move freely in the wash water. To save energy and money, coordinate the water level adjustment on the washer with the size of each wash load.

Sort by Color

Wash white clothes and other items in a separate load. Colorfast prints and pastel solids should be in another load. Dark colors are still another category. The dyes in bright or dark-colored fabrics can bleed into the wash water to discolor whites or pastels. Manufactured fibers have an especially strong tendency to pick up traces of dyes in the wash water.

Colored clothes are most likely to bleed when they are new. To help items hold their dye, soak them in heavily salted, cool water for 10 to 15 minutes. To test for colorfastness, wash them separately to see whether color appears in the wash or rinse water. If color appears, wash them separately or only with garments of the same color and intensity.

Sort by Type of Fabric and Garment Construction

Delicate items that might snag or tear should not be washed with sturdy items that require stronger washing action.

Lint-producing fabrics, such as new towels, terry cloth robes, or chenille spreads, should be washed alone. They will transfer lint onto items washed with them, especially onto *lint-attracting fabrics*, such as linen, corduroy, dark cotton, fabric with manufactured fibers, and fabric with permanent-press finishes. It may also help to turn lint-attracting items inside out when washing them.

Sorted groups should contain a mixture of large and small items to provide good washing

18-11 This chart explains the meanings of the terms printed on the care labels of apparel.

	When Label Reads:	It Means:
Machine Washable	Machine wash	Wash, bleach, dry, and press by any customary method including commercial laundering and dry cleaning.
	No chlorine bleach	Do not use chlorine bleach. Oxygen bleach may be used.
	No bleach	Do not use any type of bleach.
	Cold wash Cold rinse	Use cold water from tap or cold washing machine setting.
	Warm wash Warm rinse	Use warm water or warm washing machine setting.
	Hot wash	Use hot water or hot washing machine setting.
	No spin	Remove from washer before final machine spin cycle.
	Delicate cycle / Gentle cycle	Use appropriate machine setting; otherwise wash by hand.
	Durable press cycle / Permanent-press cycle	Use appropriate machine setting; otherwise use warm wash, cold rinse, and short spin cycle.
	Wash separately	Wash alone or with like colors.
Non Machine Washable	Hand wash	Launder only by hand in lukewarm (hand comfortable) water. May be bleached. May be dry-cleaned.
	Hand wash only	Same as above, but do not dry-clean.
	Hand wash separately	Hand wash alone or with like colors.
	No bleach	Do not use bleach.
	Damp wipe	Clean surface with damp cloth or sponge.
Home Drying	Tumble dry	Dry in tumble dryer at specified setting—high, medium, low, or no heat.
	Tumble dry / Remove promptly	Same as above, but in absence of cool-down cycle, remove at once when tumbling stops.
	Drip dry	Hang wet and allow to dry with hand shaping only.
	Line dry	Hang damp and allow to dry.
	No wring / No twist	Hang dry, drip dry, or dry flat only. Handle carefully to prevent wrinkles and distortion.
	Dry flat	Lay garment on flat surface.
	Block to dry	Maintain original size and shape while drying.
Ironing or Pressing	Cool iron	Set iron at lowest setting.
	Warm iron	Set iron at medium setting.
	Hot iron	Set iron at hot setting.
	Do not iron	Do not iron or press with heat.
	Steam iron	Iron or press with steam.
	Iron damp	Dampen garment before ironing.
Misc.	Dry-clean only	Garment should be dry-cleaned only, including self-service.
	Professionally dry-clean only	Do not use self-service or home dry cleaning.
	No dry-clean	Use recommended care instructions. No dry-cleaning materials to be used.

The American Apparel Manufacturers Association, Inc.

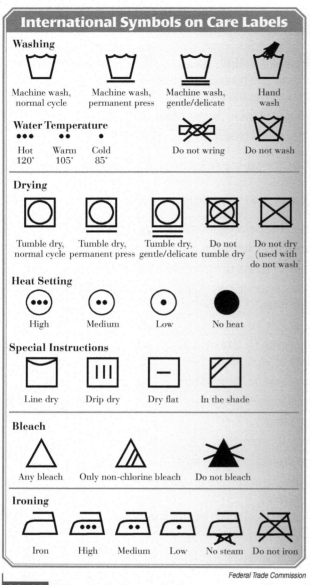

International Symbols on Care Labels

Washing

Machine wash, normal cycle | Machine wash, permanent press | Machine wash, gentle/delicate | Hand wash

Water Temperature

●●● Hot 120° | ●● Warm 105° | ● Cold 85° | Do not wring | Do not wash

Drying

Tumble dry, normal cycle | Tumble dry, permanent press | Tumble dry, gentle/delicate | Do not tumble dry | Do not dry (used with do not wash)

Heat Setting

High | Medium | Low | No heat

Special Instructions

Line dry | Drip dry | Dry flat | In the shade

Bleach

Any bleach | Only non-chlorine bleach | Do not bleach

Ironing

Iron | High | Medium | Low | No steam | Do not iron

Federal Trade Commission

18-12 These symbols give universal messages without having to write explanations in any language.

Elena Elisseeva/Shutterstock.com

18-13 A well-organized laundry area can be safe and minimize the effort of clothing care.

action. Also, different textures should be combined, if feasible, so more cleaning will result as they rub against each other.

Sort by Type and Amount of Soil

Extremely dirty items can make lightly soiled garments look dingy after washing. Wash heavily soiled garments separately. Do not wash polyester or nylon fibers with oily or greasy items, since they have a tendency to pick up oily substances.

Choose Correct Products

Choose the correct laundry products for the job. There are several kinds of laundry products with different purposes. Each category has several brands from which to choose, meeting the various needs, preferences, and budgets of consumers. The products are compatible with different types of laundry equipment, the hardness of the water, and the types of clothing washed. Use only the appropriate products, depending on the job at hand. Always read and follow package directions.

Detergents are made synthetically from chemicals that break up oils, help water penetrate solids, and suspend and hold dirt away from clothes. They are granular or liquid. They dissolve readily in water of all temperatures and degrees of hardness. Technology has made them more effective in cooler water (to save energy) and safer for the environment. They can be high or low sudsing.

High-sudsing detergents are all-purpose and popular. However, they are only for top-loading washers.

Low-sudsing detergents contain suds-control agents and are recommended for washers that are suds sensitive. They are especially recommended for front-loading, tumbler-type washing machines. However, they can be used in all washers. For new "high efficiency" washing machines, low-sudsing detergents contain an oval with a lowercase *h e* on the label.

The most important ingredients in detergents are surfactants (surface active agents). They reduce the surface tension of water, allowing the water to penetrate soiled fabrics more easily. Surfactants loosen and remove soil with the aid of the wash action. They also dissolve or suspend the removed soil in the water until the wash is over, when it goes down the drain.

Detergents may also contain builders that inactivate hard water minerals. Builders prevent the formation of insoluble residues that could be redeposited onto clothes during the wash cycle. Sometimes an extra amount of detergent must be used in very hard water to ensure proper cleansing.

Some detergents contain perfumes, and some have fabric softeners that reduce static cling and help control wrinkles. Bluing aids are additives that provide extra whitening and brightening.

Cold-water detergents are sometimes used for fabrics that are made of manufactured fibers or dark colors that could fade in hot water. Cold water detergents can also be used for other wash loads, but they may not be as effective. They save energy costs since cold water is used.

Light-duty dish detergents can be used for hand washing lightly soiled, delicate laundry items. They should never be used in an automatic washing machine because of their high-sudsing characteristics.

Soaps are made mostly from natural products (fats and oil). They come in bar and granule forms. They are mild on hands and clothing. They do not work well in hard water, since they react with the minerals to form cloudy white curds. Bar soaps are good for pretreating some types of stains before laundering. Soaps are biodegradable. That is, they break down into natural waste products that do not harm the environment.

Enzymes are proteins that speed up chemical reactions. In laundry products, they help break down certain soils and stains into simpler forms. The soils can then be removed easily in the wash.

Enzymes are found in some all-purpose laundry detergents as well as in presoak products. Look for the words *protease* or *amylase* on the product's label. Enzymes are inactivated by chlorine bleach, so their purpose is defeated when used with chlorine bleach.

Bleaches are either of a chlorine type or an oxygen type, as in **18-14**. The least expensive is liquid chlorine bleach, used mainly for white cotton fabrics. Oxygen bleach, available in liquid form or boxes of dry powder, is safe for most fabrics. Bleach substances are now often premixed with detergents when purchased. If using such a detergent, do not add more bleach.

Chlorine bleach whitens clothes and helps remove soils and stains. It also disinfects and deodorizes laundry. Do not use bleach if the water supply contains iron. Use it for items that have care labels that say they can be laundered with chlorine bleach. Never use chlorine bleach on silk, wool, mohair, or spandex. Bleach interacts chemically with those fibers and can destroy them. It can also destroy flame-retardant finishes. Bleach may also cause polyester fibers to turn yellow, and reduces the effectiveness of permanent-press finishes. It shortens the life of a garment by weakening the fibers when used too often. However, bleach is a very good laundry aid when used correctly, especially for white cotton products.

18-14 Chlorine bleach is used on white cotton fabrics. Oxygen bleach is safe for most fabrics.

Many automatic washing machines have dispensers for adding liquid chlorine bleach to wash loads. These dispensers dilute the bleach before it enters the wash water. Some machines delay adding the bleach until the last few minutes of the wash cycle. This enables any other products that may be used in the wash, such as enzymes, to do their work. If chlorine bleach needs to be added manually at the beginning of a wash cycle, either dilute it or mix it into the water before adding clothes. When poured directly onto fabrics, chlorine bleach can cause holes and ultra-white spots.

Oxygen (all fabric) *bleaches* can be used on all fabrics and, when used properly, for most colors. They are considered to be less effective, or weaker, than chlorine bleaches. Adding oxygen bleach to regular laundry loads keeps clothes looking their best. Just as for chlorine bleach, do not pour oxygen bleaches directly onto clothes.

Packaged water softeners may be necessary for households with hard water. They neutralize the mineral ions found in hard water or hold them in solution, enabling soaps and detergents to work better. Without them, the clothes could get rust marks or become gray, dingy, and stiff. Powdered water softeners can be added directly to the wash water.

A mechanical water softening device can be installed in homes. The water supply runs through it and is softened by a chemical reaction before it comes out of the faucet. This is probably the most effective long-term solution for people with very hard water.

Water hardness varies from region to region. To determine an area's water hardness, consult the local water company, cooperative extension office, or agricultural university.

Fabric softeners give softness and fluffiness to washable fabrics by preventing fibers from getting stiff and harsh. They have nothing to do with water softening. They control static electricity and manage static cling. However, with repeated use, they can build up on fibers and reduce the fabric's absorbency.

Some fabric softeners are added directly to the wash water. Sometimes they are included in the detergents. Some liquid fabric softeners are added during the rinse cycle of the washing machine. Other fabric softeners are put into the dryer with the laundry. They are in the form of sheets that tumble with the clothes and transfer softness and fragrance to them.

Starches and *fabric finishes* are *sizings*. They restore body and crispness to fabrics that have become limp from laundering and wear. They cause the fabrics to have a fresh, smooth appearance after being pressed. Spray starches and fabric finishes are generally applied when clothes are ironed.

Disinfectants are not essential for regular laundering. They are recommended if there is illness in the family or some other reason that clothes must be sanitized. Disinfectants reduce or kill microorganisms to control or eliminate infections. Chlorine bleach does some disinfecting. Household liquid disinfectants can also be used. Be sure to follow package directions.

Use Laundry Products Correctly

The containers in which detergent, bleach, and other laundry products are sold have instructions for their use. Read them and follow directions. For best results, measure amounts of laundry products accurately, as in **18-15**. If the cap of the product is not intended for measuring, use a measuring cup that is used only for laundry products. Use separate cups for different

18-15 To use laundry products properly, read the instructions on the labels and measure accurately.

types of products so chemicals do not mix with each other. If only one cup is used, rinse it thoroughly between measuring different products.

Package recommendations are based on average washing conditions. However, water hardness, laundry equipment, amount of soil on the clothes, and size of the wash load varies. Use more than the recommended amount for very hard water, a large wash load, extremely dirty clothes, or the extra water volume of a large washing machine. Use less than the recommended amount for soft water, a small wash load, very light soil, or the reduced water volume of a small washer or a partial fill. Too little detergent can cause graying, yellowing, or dingy laundry. Too much detergent can cause clothes to become stiff and harsh.

Use the Right Water Temperatures

The water temperatures of wash and rinse cycles directly affect the cleaning, wrinkling, and durability of clothes. Although most detergents work in all water temperatures, they clean best in warm or hot water. However, the heating of water uses energy and increases cost.

Most automatic washers offer a choice of three wash temperatures (cold, warm, or hot) and a choice of two rinse temperatures (cold or warm). However, some machines have water temperatures programmed into the cycles. In such a case, review the instruction book about the options of the machine. Water temperature is controlled manually when hand washing.

The *cold* wash setting is best for dark colors that bleed, lightly soiled loads, and delicate items. See **18-16**. It helps prevent fading and shrinkage. It draws water only from the cold water line as it enters the house. This temperature varies depending on climate areas and seasons of the year. The colder the water, the harder it is to accomplish cleaning.

The *warm* setting gives a mixture of cold and hot water. Warm water is about halfway between the temperatures of the cold and hot water. It varies depending on the temperatures of the incoming hot and cold water. Warm water provides effective cleaning for most wash loads. Most people wash their laundry in warm water. It is good for washing garments made of manufactured fibers and those with

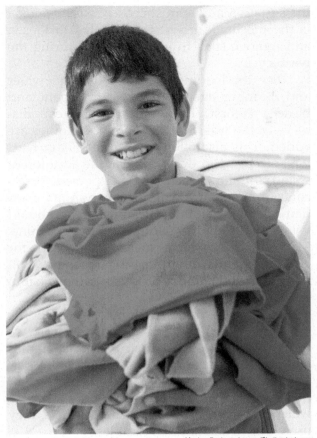

Monkey Business Images/Shutterstock.com

18-16 This load of dark and brightly colored clothes should be washed and rinsed using the cold water cycle.

permanent-press finishes. It cleans moderately soiled items well.

The *hot* setting draws water only from the hot water line coming from the water heater. Hot water provides the best soil removal and sanitizing. However, it may set stains, cause shrinkage, fade colors, and encourage wrinkling of some fabrics. It should be used only for white or colorfast fabrics and heavily soiled loads.

For energy reasons, it is most practical to rinse clothes in cold water after washing. It is also better for the clothes and lessens wrinkling of permanent-press items.

Follow the Correct Laundering Procedures

Know about and utilize the features of available laundry equipment. Controls on many washers allow selection of the best water temperature, water level, length of wash time, and the agitation and spin speeds. *Washer agitation* is the mechanical action that helps to loosen and remove soils from the clothes during the wash cycle.

For top-loading washers, put the water and cleaning agents (such as detergent and bleach) in first. Then the products can dissolve in the wash water before the clothes are added. This also allows any minerals in hard water to be neutralized prior to the addition of soiled clothing. Bleach can be dispersed, too, so concentrations of it will not cause spotty color damage on the clothes. Cleaning agents should *not* be poured over clothes in the machine. Many machines have special dispensers for cleaning agents. Front-loading machines will mix water and laundry products as they go into the revolving tub.

For top-loading machines, be sure the selected water level and size of the load are right for the washer. Distribute the clothes evenly around the machine's agitator to balance the load. Never wrap large items around the agitator. Front-loading machines use less water than top-loading machines since they use water in a drum that tumbles.

For all types, overloading reduces cleaning and causes extra wrinkling. It is better to underload than to overload the washer. Garments need room to circulate in the water for optimal cleaning. Soil and lint can then be washed away. There should always be enough wash and rinse water to cover the clothes.

Select the proper washing action cycle on the machine. A regular or normal setting is good for most items. Choose a longer washing time for heavily soiled, sturdy items. A shorter, slower washing time (or gentle speed) is best for delicate garments, such as lingerie. There may also be cycles for knits and permanent-press items. These cycles automatically provide a cool-down period and a cold rinse to minimize wrinkles.

Rinse the clothes thoroughly with clean water. This carries away dissolved laundry products, suds, and loosened soil and lint.

In automatic machines, water is extracted from the clothes after each of the wash and rinse cycles by spinning. These machines have a regular spin speed for most fabrics and a slow speed for permanent-press or delicate clothing. On washers with only one speed, the spin time is longer for the regular cycle than for the gentle cycle. After using the washing machine, clean the lint filter if it has one.

Hand Washing

Any clothing that can be washed in a washing machine can also be hand washed in a large container or sink. Delicate items and wool garments are typically washed by hand, unless indicated otherwise on the garment's care label. Woolens can shrink from agitation as well as hot water. Before washing shrinkable garments, trace around them with pencil on a large sheet of heavy paper or a paper sack cut open, as in **18-17**. Do not use newspaper.

Hand wash in cool water. Use a light-duty detergent or soap. Several special cold water solutions are available with the correct pH for animal fibers, such as wool and silk. Swish the water to dissolve the laundry product, then add the garment and squeeze the suds through it gently. Rub softly only if necessary to remove soil. Soak up to 20 minutes. If the fabrics are of dark colors that bleed, only soak for 5 minutes. Never wring or twist delicate articles.

Rinse hand-washed articles in cool water at least twice, or until the water is clear. Then roll them in an absorbent towel to remove as much water as possible. Block (shape) shrinkable garments to their original size according to the previous paper tracings when laid flat to dry. Occasionally during drying, reshape the garments by stretching to match their outlines.

If wool garments have shrunk, they may not be permanently damaged. Try soaking them for 10 minutes in 1 gallon of lukewarm

18-17 By tracing around a shrinkable garment before it is washed, its size and shape are recorded for use later.

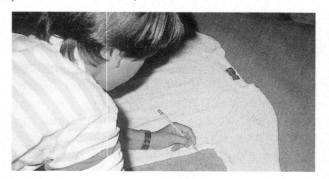

water containing 2 tablespoons of baby shampoo. Without rinsing, blot out all excess water with a dry towel and lay them on fresh towels. Reshape them slowly, carefully stretching back to their original size.

Drying Clothes

Clothes can be dried with heat and a tumbling action in an *automatic dryer*. They can also be drip-dried on a hanger, line dried (outside or inside), or laid flat to dry. Usually, items washed together are dried together. Dark items should be turned inside out to prevent lint from adhering and showing on the right side.

Automatic dryers usually have regular, permanent-press, and air-fluff cycles, **18-18**. The regular cycle is for items that are not heat sensitive. The permanent-press cycle provides a cool-down tumble time with no heat at the end to reduce wrinkles. Remove and hang up permanent-press items as soon as the dryer stops. See **18-19**. Smooth the seams, collars, and cuffs. Permanent-press garments should not need to be ironed when removed immediately. If clothes are accidentally left in the dryer after drying, they can be retumbled for a few minutes with a damp towel to restore their permanent-press smoothness.

The air-fluff cycle on automatic dryers provides tumbling in unheated air. Some delicate garments may need a cool temperature, gentle tumbling, and a short drying time. Elastic materials should be dried on the air setting only. This setting can also be used between washings to fluff items.

Drying clothes in an automatic dryer costs money but saves time and effort. It makes clothes

www.ImprovementsCatalog.com

18-19 If permanent-press items are put on hangers as soon as the dryer stops, they should not need ironing. They can be hung in the closet and look good when worn.

soft and comfortable, helps remove wrinkles, and is not dependent on the weather.

Do not overload the dryer, because the clothes would not be able to tumble freely. They would take a long time to dry and could become wrinkled and twisted. Do not set the heat too high. A hot temperature can ruin buttons and trims and can cause shrinkage and wrinkles. Also, do not allow clothes to overdry. This makes fabrics harder to handle. Remove clothes immediately, smooth the wrinkles, and either hang or fold them. Be sure clothes are completely dry before putting them away in closets and drawers. Also, be sure to clean the dryer's lint filter after each use.

Line drying, or hanging laundered items on an outdoor clothesline, is economical and is especially good for large, flat items. It can give clothes a fresh smell, but is not recommended in heavy air pollution. Also, some items become stiff. Others fade if they are in direct sunshine.

Before hanging clothes on the line, wipe the line with a damp cloth. Be sure the clothespins are clean. Shake the clothes, smooth out wrinkles, and straighten the seams. Hang items carefully

18-18 When using an automatic dryer, choose the setting that is appropriate for the garments that are being dried.

by their firmest parts to avoid creases, stretching, or imprints from the clothespins. Distribute the weight of heavy items over several lines. Dry colored garments in the shade, if possible, and take them down as soon as they are dry to avoid fading. Take items to be ironed off the line while they are a little damp to make ironing easier.

Line drying inside is good for only a few small items. Clothes take longer to dry inside and may become stiff because of the limited air movement.

Few garments require *drip-drying*. However, if this is recommended on the care label, hang the item on a wooden or plastic hanger or over a rack. Metal hangers can cause rust marks and leave indentations. Usually garments that require drip-drying are hung up dripping wet without squeezing or wringing.

Flat drying is good for wool, knit, and leather items, such as gloves. Sweaters are often dried flat. This helps prevent shrinkage but takes up household space. Lay garments away from direct heat on a clean, absorbent surface such as a large towel. Shape the items to their original dimensions.

Ironing and Pressing

Ironing is the process of using an iron to remove wrinkles from damp, washable clothing. Heat and pressure are used to flatten the fabric. Ironing is done with a gliding motion. It is done to entire garments after laundering.

Pressing involves no sliding of the iron. The iron is placed on the fabric and then lifted. Moisture is added from a pressing cloth or steam in the iron. This procedure is good for wool clothing and loose or bulky textures. It is often done to apparel between wearings. It is also done while constructing garments.

A well-ironed or well-pressed garment should be free of all wrinkles. The original garment shape and fabric texture should be preserved. There should be no outline of the edges of seams, facings, hems, or other structural details on the right side.

Ironing and Pressing Equipment

Proper ironing and pressing equipment is needed to do a good job. Basic equipment is needed to iron most laundry items. See **18-20**.

Lisa S./Shutterstock.com

18-20 For proper ironing of laundry, a steady ironing board is needed. The iron should have both dry and steam settings, a water-level gauge, and a temperature guide for various fabrics.

More specific equipment may be necessary for tricky garments and sewing projects.

Many *irons* have both dry and steam settings. The dry setting is used at low temperatures for fabrics made of acetate, acrylic, nylon, polyester, rayon, silk, and some blends. It is also used if the fabric being ironed is damp, or if a damp pressing cloth is used between the iron and garment.

For ironing and pressing with steam, the soleplate of a steam iron has holes that allow steam to escape. Some steam irons have a button that, when pushed, gives either a shot of steam spray or a sprinkling of water when needed for stubborn wrinkles. Distilled water is recommended for most steam irons, since mineral deposits can build up in the iron. However, some manufacturers recommend tap water, for which their irons are designed. Some have an automatic jet steam clean-out feature to help remove lint or solids that can collect and clog the steam holes. Read and follow your iron's use and care directions carefully.

Most irons have a dial with a wide variety of fabric settings. Use this dial to prevent scorching or melting fabrics. When not in use, store the iron on its heel rest to protect the ironing surface. Clean the soleplate by using a damp cloth with liquid detergent, powdered cleaner, or silver polish, but do not scratch the soleplate. If needed, a special metal soleplate cover (converter) that prevents sticking, scorching, and shine can be attached.

Lightweight travel irons are small, so they fit nicely into suitcases. They press small areas well but are not recommended for complete laundry ironing.

A good, sturdy, flat *ironing board* should not rock when ironing. If it is on legs, it should be adjustable to various heights. A smooth, thick, well-fitting pad with a silicone-treated cover gives good results.

A *pressing cloth*, as in **18-21**, protects the right side of garments and prevents shine from forming on fabrics. It is placed between the item being pressed and the hot surface of the iron. Pressing cloths can be bought in several weights and sizes. A handkerchief, a cotton/linen dish towel, or a piece of cheesecloth can also serve as a pressing cloth. It is usually used dry with a steam iron, and damp with a dry iron. If the cloth is damp, its moisture provides added steam when combined with the heat of the iron. Be sure to evenly dampen and wring out the cloth, rather than saturating it with water. A cloth that is too wet can cause spotting. A moistened cloth is recommended for cottons and linens. For silks and woolens, it is best to use two cloths, a damp cloth over a dry cloth.

A *sleeve board*, shown in **18-22**, looks like a miniature, double ironing board. It fits nicely on top of a standard ironing board. It is designed for pressing sleeve seams, hard-to-reach areas, such as necklines, cuffs, and small flat areas of a garment. It should be well padded and have a clean cover.

Specialized pressing equipment is needed for some jobs. For instance, a *tailor's ham*, **18-23**, is used to press curved areas. A *pressing mitt*

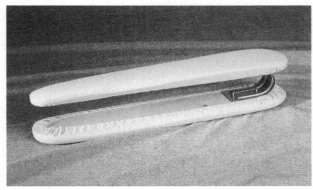

June Tailor, Inc.

18-22 A sleeve board is convenient when pressing sleeves, the legs of pants, or other hard-to-iron areas.

can be slipped over the hand or onto the end of a sleeve board and used instead of a tailor's ham. A *velvet board* has a surface of needles to maintain the plushness of velvet, corduroy and other napped fabrics.

Ironing Techniques

It is important to use correct ironing techniques. Insert the plug of the iron firmly into the electrical outlet. Unplug it by grasping the plug, not by pulling on the cord. Always iron with the right equipment to maintain the shape of all garment parts.

Iron with the grain of fabrics to prevent stretching garments out of shape. If ridges or impressions result on the right side of the fabric from the edges of seam allowances or facings, place brown paper between the inside garment fabric and structural edges.

18-21 A pressing cloth is placed between the iron and the fabric to protect the fabric as it is being pressed.

18-23 A tailor's ham has a rounded shape for pressing curved areas. Usually one side of the tailor's ham is covered with a wool fabric, while the other side has a heavy canvas surface.

When ironing a garment, start with the multiple-layer areas, such as collars and cuffs. Then do small garment parts, such as yokes and sleeves. Finish by doing the large, flat areas. If the large areas were done first, they would get wrinkled again during the ironing of the small areas.

Iron dark, dull fabrics on the wrong side or use a pressing cloth on the right side to prevent shiny areas. Press wool with moisture. Use steam, but no pressure, on napped fabrics. Iron linens, cottons, and silks damp.

The best use of energy is to complete one batch of ironing at a time. Start with garments that require a low heat setting on the iron, such as those made of manufactured fibers. Work up to those that require higher heat, such as cottons and linens. An iron heats faster than it cools, so it is quicker to go from low to high heat. This also prevents scorching items with an iron that has not cooled down from the last piece.

Spray starches and fabric finishes are convenient. They are applied while ironing. They add stiffness and restore body lost in laundering. If desired, they can be used only on certain areas, such as collars and cuffs.

Spray starches provide firm crispness for natural fibers. Fabric finishes give body, but less stiffness, to manufactured fibers, cottons, and blends. Both can be used on either damp or dry clothes. They help the iron glide easier. However, sticking and scorching can result from excess moisture or improper iron temperature.

When using aerosol sprays, shake the contents before using. Line up the markers on the spray button (nozzle) and the can. Hold the container upright about 6 to 12 inches from the fabric. Spray lightly and evenly using a back-and-forth motion. Too much will lead to flaking and stickiness.

Clean the spray opening of an aerosol can when finished ironing. To do this, hold the can upside down and spray out the last residue in the hose. If this is not done, the spray feature could be clogged for the next use.

Dry Cleaning

Dry cleaning is the process of cleaning textile items with nonwater liquid solvents or absorbent compounds. Dry-cleaning solvents kill living bacteria. Properly dry-cleaned garments do not smell of the solvents when they are finished. Dry cleaning minimizes shrinkage, preserves tailoring details, and maintains the fine characteristics and finishes of fabrics.

All garments can be dry-cleaned unless the care label states otherwise. When the label says *dry-clean only*, the garment should not be washed in water. Clothes can be professionally dry-cleaned; cleaned manually in a self-service, coin-operated machine; or done at home.

With *professional dry cleaning*, payment for service is per garment. Cleaners should have trained employees and proper equipment, so expect skillful spot and stain removal as well as professional pressing. They should know how to care for various fabrics, dyes, finishes, and tricky garment construction, such as in **18-24**.

Tell the dry cleaner if clothing has stains, what the stains are, and how long they have been there. If requested, fabric pills can often be removed by the dry cleaner's industrial fabric brush. Sizing (for more body) or a water-repellent finish can usually be requested for an additional fee.

18-24 A professional dry cleaner has the skills and equipment to care for special garments of fine fabrics.

Coin-operated dry cleaning is faster and less expensive than professional dry cleaning. However, the advantage of professional spot removal, special care for delicate items, or thorough pressing is missing. These machines are similar to coin-operated washing machines.

Prepare clothes carefully by emptying pockets, repairing loose stitches and buttons, and brushing off dirt and lint. Remove belts or fancy buttons that should not be cleaned. Pretreat spots and stains. Sort the clothes into similar types and colors. Follow the directions for the machine. Loads may need to be weighed, so the proper amount of clothing is put into the machine.

Coin-operated dry cleaning can be dangerous, so take extra precautions. The machines use a chemical that can be poisonous in strong doses. In the past, the machines were sometimes poorly maintained. Large amounts of the cleaning solvent remained in the clothes, especially if the machines were overloaded or bulky items were cleaned. Almost all coin-operated machines now limit solvent exposure, and there is stricter regulation of inspection and maintenance of the machines. Industrial and retail dry cleaners use machines with recovery systems that greatly reduce solvent consumption and emissions. They also have trained operators and regularly monitor workplace exposure levels.

When the clothes are finished, hang them up immediately. Shake them and pat out wrinkles. To minimize chemical fumes, open a car window on the drive home. Shape and press the clothes, and air them, before storing them in a closed space.

Home dry-cleaning kits are available at many discount and other stores. These are designed specifically for use in home dryers on the *no heat* or *air dry* setting. After preparing the clothes, as for coin-operated dry cleaning, follow the kit directions carefully. Great care must be taken not to ruin good garments when drycleaning in the home.

Home dry-cleaning kits include a special bag for the clothes and several cleaning sheets. The consumer unfolds and opens a dry-cleaning sheet, and places it in the bag with one or more garments. The bag is tumbled in the dryer for about 10 minutes. The clothes are then removed from the bag, shaken, and hung up to prevent wrinkles.

Home dry-cleaning kits are simple to use and offer time and money savings over traditional dry cleaning. They remove odors and many spots, but not serious stains. This procedure can be done conveniently in the home. The chemicals in the kit are not as harmful for people and the environment as those used by most drycleaning establishments. However, home pressing must be done. Professional dry cleaning is still needed on most garments occasionally.

Summary

Taking good care of a wardrobe means clothing dollars can be stretched and a well-groomed, neat appearance is easier to maintain. Daily care of clothes keeps soiling and damage to a minimum. When dressing and undressing, be careful not to snag, rip, stretch, or stain garments. After wearing, hang up garments or put them where they will be washed or otherwise treated properly. Let clothes get air circulation and avoid wrinkling. Clothing repairs and laundering are easiest done during a set time each week.

Home storage areas, such as closets, shelves, and drawers, should be neat, handy, and well organized. Seasonal wardrobe storage usually takes place in the spring and fall to prepare for temperature and weather changes. Spots and stains should be removed from garments as quickly as possible. First, identify both the fiber content of the fabric and the source of the stain. Have stain removal supplies on hand and know how to use them properly.

Good laundering procedures and the proper equipment extend the life and appearance of garments. Before washing, sort clothes by color, by type of fabric and garment construction, and by type/amount of soil. Choose the right laundry products for the job, such as proper detergents, enzymes, bleaches, water softeners, fabric softeners, disinfectants, and starches or fabric finishes. Use laundry products correctly and select the right wash and rinse water temperatures. Also, know how to hand wash delicate items and wool garments.

Clothes can be dried by tumble action in an automatic dryer, drip-dried on a hanger, line dried, or laid flat to dry. Ironing and pressing should remove all wrinkles from garments. Correct ironing and pressing techniques are important for different fabrics and types of garments.

Dry-cleaning jobs can be given to professionals, done in coin-operated machines, or at home with dry-cleaning kits.

Fashion Recall

Write your answers on a separate sheet of paper.

Short Answer: Write the correct response to each of the following items.

1. List five guidelines for the daily care of clothes.
2. List five guidelines for the weekly care of clothes.
3. List five guidelines for clothing storage.
4. Name three of the most commonly used stain removal methods.
5. Name three guidelines for sorting garments into wash loads.
6. Explain the difference between water softeners and fabric softeners.
7. Name three ways of drying clothes.
8. Name and describe two pieces of specialized pressing equipment.

True/False: Write *true* or *false* for each of the following statements.

9. It is best to hand wash knit garments so they don't wrinkle.
10. It is wise to line drawers with newspapers so no splinters will harm your clothes.
11. Stains often fade or disappear if left alone.
12. To save energy and money, coordinate the water level selector on the washer with the size of the wash load.
13. It is best to use soap rather than a detergent for laundering in hard water.
14. Chlorine bleach is safe for use on all fabrics.
15. Starches and fabric finishes are sizings that restore body and crispness to fabrics that have become limp from laundering and wear.
16. Cold water should be used to wash white and colorfast fabrics and heavily soiled loads.
17. Hot water should be used to wash most wash loads.
18. Pour the detergent over the clothes in the washing machine when starting a load of laundry.
19. The lint filter of an automatic dryer should be cleaned after each use.
20. When ironing a garment, start with the large flat areas.

Fashion Vocabulary

21. Work with a partner to locate small images online that visually describe or explain each of the *Fashion Terms* on the chapter opening. To create flash cards, write each term on a note card and paste the image that describes or explains the term on the opposite side of the card.

Critical Thinking

22. **Plan storage**   Describe a garment you plan to store. What is the proper method of storing the garment? Explain.
23. **Analyze stain removal**   Analyze how you would identify a stain of unknown origin and remove it from a washable fabric. If possible, demonstrate how to remove the stain using a stained swatch of fabric.
24. **Predict outcomes**   Predict what might happen if you failed to sort clothes properly before washing them. Cite the text and other reliable resources as evidence to support the outcomes of your predictions.

Core Skills

25. **Math practice**   Compare costs of clothing care options. Call, visit an appliance store, or use a store's website to find out the approximate purchase price of a basic washer and dryer, and the life expectancy of these appliances. Check the energy-use label to determine their annual energy costs of operation. Also, the cost of using

washers and dryers at a Laundromat®, including round-trip transportation. For your wash loads done each week, is it more economical to do laundry at home or in a Laundromat? Share your findings with the class.

26. **Science**   Test various stain removal products and techniques. Cut some light-colored washable fabrics of natural and manufactured fibers into 10-inch squares. Make a stain on each with some of the sources of stains listed in Figure 18-9. Try the appropriate stain removal treatments for each. Document the procedures and results and discuss your findings with the class.

27. **Writing**   Create a four-column chart with the following headings: *Terms*, *Definitions*, *Product Names*, and *Ingredients*. Write each of the following terms in the appropriate column in the chart: all-purpose (high-sudsing) detergent, low-sudsing detergent, cold water detergent, soap, chlorine bleach, oxygen bleach, water softener, fabric softener, and fabric sizing. Write the definitions for the terms in the second column. Then, write the brand names of products that fit in each category and the lists of typical ingredients in the correct column.

28. **Writing and speaking**   Locate a closet, perhaps your own, to clean out and organize using tips you read in the text. Use a digital camera to take before and after pictures to use in creating a presentation to share with the class. As you prepare your presentation, explain why the new organization is an improvement.

29. **Technology**   Research washers and dryers online. List and compare the features of various models. Report any new features. Predict what features may be available in 10 years. Share your findings and predictions with the class.

30. **CTE career readiness practice**   Presume you write a monthly feature for a fashion magazine. This month your editor indicated many readers have been requesting information on using environmentally friendly methods for removing stains and laundering clothes, especially items made from delicate fabrics. Your assignment is to research environmentally friendly methods for stain removal and laundry and write an article for your readers identifying the best methods you find. Be sure to express these concepts clearly and effectively for your readers.

Fashion in Action

31. **Portfolio builder**   Make a list of at least five apparel items that need special care or storage. Write a summary describing how to maintain and store them. Add your summary to your portfolio to demonstrate your understanding of caring for clothes.

32. **Design activity**   Design the ideal storage for your wardrobe items, including drawings or photos and written descriptions. Include shelf space, drawer space, and hanging space. Use a school-approved digital application to express your ideas through drawings and written descriptions. Cite the text and other reliable resources to support your storage design decisions. Then, share your digital plan with your peers and instructor for review.

Self-Assessment Quiz ↪

Complete the self-assessment quiz online to help practice and expand your knowledge and skills.

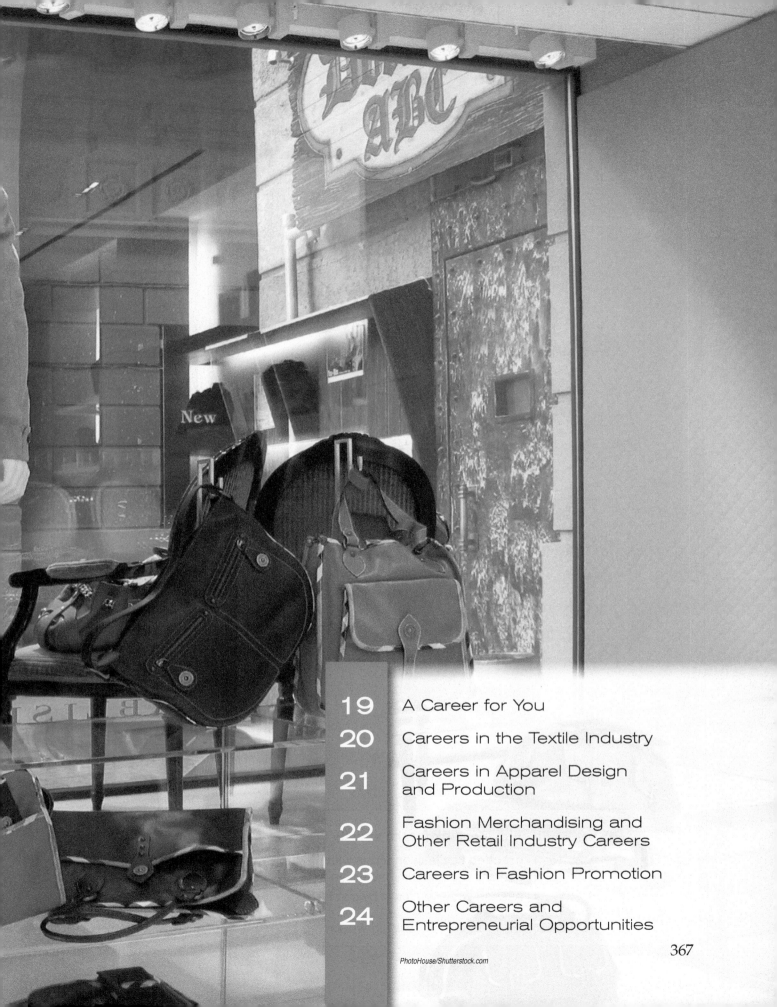

19 A Career for You

20 Careers in the Textile Industry

21 Careers in Apparel Design and Production

22 Fashion Merchandising and Other Retail Industry Careers

23 Careers in Fashion Promotion

24 Other Careers and Entrepreneurial Opportunities

While studying, look for the activity icon **to:**

- **practice** key fashion terms with e-flash cards, vocabulary games, and matching activities
- **assess** what you learn by completing self-assessment quizzes

www.g-wlearning.com/clothingandfashion/

FASHION TERMS ↪

occupation
career
interests
aptitudes
abilities
career clusters
job shadowing

mentor
work-based learning
  programs
technical schools
trade schools
salary
hourly wage

fringe benefits
networking
résumé
references
portfolio
cover message
ethical behavior

Objectives

After studying this chapter, you will be able to
➤ explain how to find out about yourself, specific careers, and educational resources.
➤ evaluate careers that might interest you.
➤ create a résumé and a cover message.
➤ prepare a job application form correctly.
➤ create a portfolio.
➤ summarize the process of interviewing for a job.
➤ identify the personal traits needed to become a success.

Many people seek employment in the fashion industry because there is such variety of opportunities. There is something for everyone. Many people like the excitement of being part of a dynamic and fast-moving field. Those who show interest in the business and have talent, ambition, and ability can succeed in a wide variety of jobs. A *job* is the work a person does to earn a living. With careful planning and preparation, you should be able to find an occupation (type of work) that suits you. You should be able to enjoy the work and achieve success in it.

Fashion offers some of the world's most fascinating, challenging, high-paying, and exciting careers, as in **19-1**. A career is a progression of related jobs in a person's field of work. Maybe you have dreamed of becoming the president of a large retail firm, a famous designer, or a top fashion model. These highly competitive positions are difficult to achieve. They may be obtained, however, with lots of hard work, strong ambition, personal sacrifices, and skill. What steps can you take now to improve your chances of success in the field of fashion?

crystalfoto/Shutterstock.com

19-1 The fashion world offers glamorous jobs such as modeling.

Choosing a Career

Preparation for your career should include careful planning and study. Your career decision is very important. It will determine where you will live, what free time you will have, and how much money you will make. It will also influence the friendships you will develop. Your career choice will affect all aspects of your adult life.

The most satisfying career for you will include work activities that you enjoy. It can be a source of continued learning and pleasure from the day you begin.

To choose a career that is right for you, first get to know yourself. Then learn as much as possible about various fields of work. With an understanding of your own interests and abilities, and information about various career paths, you can make the best possible career choices. You can get the education and develop the skills needed for a career in the area that seems most satisfying to you.

Find Out About Yourself

A sincere self-assessment is needed to determine the type of work you can do and would like to do. One way to do this is to determine your interests, aptitudes, and abilities. Take the time to think seriously about times, events, or jobs that may have provided you with good learning experiences. List your accomplishments in school, at work, and during leisure activities. What skills did you use to achieve your accomplishments? What did you like or dislike in each situation? You will make interesting discoveries as you take stock of yourself.

Your Interests

Your interests are the activities, ideas, and experiences you like the most. Do you like to work alone or with others? Do you like to travel, or work at the same place every day? Would you want to live in a large city, in a small town, or near a university? Do you like to do scientific experiments? Do you like to sew, draw, sell, or write?

Think about your job-related interests. Do your interests seem to revolve around people, data, objects, or all three? Do you like organized activities, such as office work? Do you prefer repeated activities, such as factory work? Do you enjoy a variety of changing activities, such as sales or administrative work? Do you like calm times, or do you handle pressure well? Reviewing your likes and dislikes should help to identify careers you might find interesting.

Your Aptitudes and Abilities

Aptitudes are your natural talents and potential for learning. If you have an aptitude for a skill, you will be able to learn the skill quickly and easily. You can determine your aptitudes by taking aptitude tests. These tests can help you predict your suitability to different jobs. Aptitude tests are often given in schools by a guidance counselor. The results indicate the types of work in which you would probably excel.

For instance, suppose you have an aptitude for writing. You would probably be successful in the fields of fashion or retail advertising, fashion journalism, public relations, and audiovisuals. With an aptitude for science, you might develop new textile fibers and finishes or research new products. With a natural talent for working with people, you might want a career in sales, education, or human resources. Creative or artistically talented people may do well in design, display, advertising, photography, and illustration jobs, as in **19-2**. Some people have aptitudes for logical thinking and working with numbers. They may be successful in managing retail units, planning factory production, or doing market research.

Your *abilities* are skills you develop through training or practice. An ability is developed more easily if you have a related aptitude for a skill. For instance, if you have an aptitude for art, you will probably excel quickly in a painting class. If you have a low aptitude for art, you may need much more training and practice to develop the ability to paint.

Consider your interests, aptitudes, and abilities when planning your career. Ideally, you will choose a career that interests you, and uses your aptitudes and abilities.

Research Careers

To make wise and realistic career choices, you must investigate specific careers. Analyze job possibilities that exist within different career fields. Understand the personal qualifications and educational requirements needed for the jobs that interest you. Evaluate earning levels and employment outlook. You must plan ahead to find the most meaningful career for *you*.

The Career Clusters

When examining careers, you will encounter the career clusters. The *career clusters* are 16 groups of occupational and career specialties, **19-3**. Each cluster includes occupations that have common knowledge and skill requirements (called *essential knowledge and skills*). These occupations are further grouped into subsets, called *career pathways*. Occupations in these pathways often have more specialized knowledge and skill requirements.

Knowledge of the career clusters will help as you plan and prepare for your career. The skills you need for one job may also be needed for another job within the same pathway. This will help in your job search. If you are unable to obtain the job you want, your skills will be useful in another position. Learning about related occupations now will help you more easily adjust to job changes later.

The career clusters most closely related to the fashion industry include
- Arts, Audio-Video Technology & Communications
- Business, Management & Administration
- Manufacturing
- Marketing
- Science, Technology, Engineering & Mathematics

Careers in the fashion industry can also be found in other career clusters. You can learn more about your career options by exploring all the career clusters online.

Other Career Research Sources

In addition to using the career clusters, read books that describe various careers. Review sections of this book that describe individual jobs that especially interest you. Use your guidance counselor as a resource. Check what information is available in the library or on file at nearby career centers. Search the Internet to learn more about careers. Several online career sources are shown in **19-4**.

19-2 This teen's creativity and aptitude for sewing can help her be a successful fashion designer.

AVAVA/Shutterstock.com

Sixteen Career Clusters

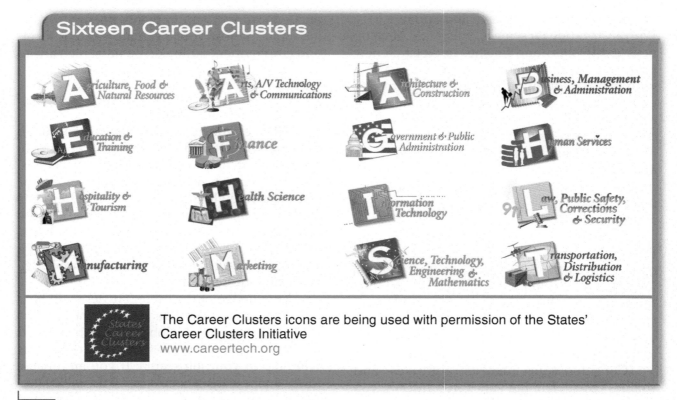

The Career Clusters icons are being used with permission of the States' Career Clusters Initiative
www.careertech.org

19-3 Explore the career clusters to find careers that might interest you.

Talk with people in the careers that interest you. Ask about jobs, the needed education and training, and possible advancement opportunities. Check with your state employment office. Request information from trade associations and organizations in the fields you are considering.

Finally, try some jobs to test your career interests. You can learn about different jobs through job shadowing. In a job shadowing experience, you will follow a worker on the job to observe the duties and responsibilities. This type of experience may last for a few hours, a day, or several days. An employer must always approve this arrangement. You may also want to find a mentor. A mentor is a faithful counselor who values your abilities and potential. He or she guides you along your career path.

19-4 To be able to make wise career choices, use websites such as these to find out information about a career.

Online Career Resources	
Source	**Internet Address**
USAJOBS, the official job site of the U.S. Federal Government	www.usajobs.gov
Career Outlook, U.S. Department of Labor	www.bls.gov/careeroutlook
Occupational Outlook Handbook, U.S. Department of Labor	www.bls.gov/ooh
Career Builder	www.careerbuilder.com
U.S. Department of Labor Employment and Training Administration	www.doleta.gov
The Occupational Information Network (O*NET™)	www.onetcenter.org
CareerOneStop	www.careeronestop.org
Mapping Your Future	www.mappingyourfuture.org
Career Resource Center	www.careers.org

Determine Needed Education and Training

Some apparel industry jobs need no advanced education beyond high school. Some require occupational training. Other jobs may require college degrees. When planning your career, you must determine the amount of education and training you need.

Work-Based Learning Programs

Many schools offer work-based learning programs that place students in a job while they are still taking classes. A program coordinator works with the student and the job site to make the work experience successful. Work-based learning programs make the transition from the classroom to a full-time career position easier.

Work-based learning programs at the secondary level of education are often called *co-op programs*. In co-op programs, coordinators arrange to place students in paid part-time jobs. Students in these programs will often attend classes for approximately a half-day and then work the remainder of the day. Through co-op programs, students are better able to recognize the realities and responsibilities of a job.

Work-based learning programs at the *postsecondary level* of education (after high school) are often called *internships*. An internship is a supervised work experience that can be either paid or unpaid. Students must often enroll for an internship as they would a class. Students might work several days a week while taking a reduced course load, or spend a summer on a particular job. Through internships, students are able to earn credits toward graduation. They also gain valuable work experience, learn about different jobs, and make important contacts in the industry. See **19-5**.

Occupational Training

Students who receive *occupational training* are preparing for a job in a specific field. Occupational training can be received through programs such as technical schools, trade schools, and apprenticeships. Some businesses may offer on-the-job training.

Technical schools provide training for jobs at the secondary and postsecondary levels

Iowa State University/AESHM Department

19-5 An internship in New York City with a publisher of fashion journals is a great way to get on-the-job experience and make contacts in the industry. It also looks good on your résumé when you search for full-time career employment.

of education. Students who attend a secondary technical school will often receive a high school diploma and a certificate for a particular job. Those who attend a technical school at the postsecondary level may receive an *associate's degree* (a two-year degree) or a certificate.

Trade schools provide job-specific training at the postsecondary level. *Certificate courses* in trade schools usually take one, two, or three years to complete. Associate degrees are available in such fields as merchandising, fashion design, apparel production management, and apparel production engineering.

Through an *apprenticeship program*, students may spend many months or years learning all aspects of a trade by practical experience under skilled workers. Requirements for entry into an apprenticeship program vary from state to state and from one trade to another.

Clothing-related businesses often have *on-the-job training programs*. An employee receives specific training to learn how to do a particular job. He or she might spend a day, a week, or longer working with a more experienced employee before being asked to work independently.

Colleges and Universities

For many creative and challenging career positions, higher education is desirable. These jobs, especially those with potential for career advancement, can be highly competitive. Needed education for these jobs may include a college degree from a community college, four-year college, or university.

Students who attend a community or two-year college can earn an associate's degree. They can earn a *bachelor's degree* from a four-year college or university. Students may then choose to take additional courses to receive a *master's degree*, also called a *graduate degree*. A master's degree usually takes another one or two years of study. Certain professional occupations may require a *doctorate*, or *Ph.D.* This degree usually requires an additional three to six years of study beyond a master's degree, especially if done part-time while also working.

Four-year college bachelor's degrees offer majors in textile science, fashion design, merchandising, and other textiles and clothing specializations. These programs are offered by colleges of art or family and consumer sciences within universities.

Some universities that are not near fashion centers have *reciprocal agreements* with schools in such cities as New York City, Paris, Rome, and London. Students go to these schools for a semester, year, or some other recommended length of time. They see and learn about the actual workings of most aspects of the apparel industries. They receive credits that transfer to their original institutions.

To find out about schools that offer training and education in fashion, consult your guidance counselor or a librarian and do research online. Several handbooks and websites are available that index schools in many ways. They describe each school's curriculum, size, costs, student body, housing, and financial aid programs. They also provide contact information for each school's admissions office.

You might want to talk about schools with people who work in apparel careers that interest you. They can tell you which schools have the best reputations and the best results in placing their graduates into good jobs. See **19-6**.

Jacob Lund/Shutterstock.com

19-6 After finding out what preparation is needed for the career you choose, take your studies seriously. Then you will be able to seek the right job to begin your successful career path.

Consider Earning Levels

The earning levels for fashion careers are as varied as the jobs themselves. Some apparel employees are salaried. Some are paid commissions, and others are paid by the hour. Taxes and other deductions are taken out of employees' paychecks. Also, some jobs have better fringe benefits than others.

A **salary** is a fixed amount of pay, usually received once or twice a month, for services performed on the job. A salary is determined by the company's need for a person's services, education, and work experience. Most jobs requiring college degrees are salaried. They are considered professional positions.

A salaried employee usually does not receive overtime pay for extra hours worked. On the other hand, pay is not deducted if the employee takes a long lunch break or leaves work early for a personal reason. Thus, a salary is the amount of money paid for a particular person to do a particular job.

Some employees receive an **hourly wage**. Their wage is the amount of pay for each hour they spend doing the job. *Wage earners* usually punch in and out on a time clock. If they work overtime, they are paid an extra amount. In fact, overtime is usually paid at one-and-a-half times the regular hourly wage. Work on Sundays and holidays is sometimes paid at two times the regular rate. On the other hand, wage earners who work fewer hours than normal during a pay period are paid only for the time they worked.

A *commission* is a percentage paid to an employee of the dollar amount of goods sold by that employee. Commissions serve as incentives for sales employees to sell as much as possible. The more a person sells, the more he or she earns. Often a small base salary or hourly wage is paid, with a commission added to it.

Fringe benefits are additional inclusions, such as disability insurance, life insurance, medical insurance, and pension plans. Benefits may also include paid vacation time, sick leave, bonus payments, and discount privileges for merchandise purchased. Perquisites (perks) are extras, such as free parking spaces.

Learn About the Employment Outlook

In general, apparel industry occupations offer less job security than many other businesses. Employees tend to change jobs frequently because of the changeability and seasonal nature of much of the industry. Few jobs offer a typical nine-to-five workday. Production schedules or other deadlines must be met at peak times. Also, retail sites must be staffed when other businesses are closed. Freelancers, consultants, and other self-employed people must provide their own benefits, such as health insurance and retirement accounts.

Look at the expected job prospects and working conditions for different occupations that interest you. Will the need for a certain career still exist in 10 years? You will often have less job options if the employment outlook for a career is declining. Through careful research and planning, however, you can focus on careers that offer better employment options. The U.S. Department of Labor's *Occupational Outlook Handbook* provides detailed information about employment prospects and working conditions for a variety of jobs.

Landing That Job

Finding the type of job you desire is not always easy. First, you must know how to find job leads. You should also know how to showcase your qualifications and accomplishments to potential employers. Finally, you need to be well prepared for interviews. You will benefit from the experience of each try for a job, even if you are not hired. You will gain confidence and maturity needed for just the right opportunity.

Job Hunting

An important aspect of job hunting is networking. Networking is the exchange of information or services among an interconnected group of people. Lines of communication flow throughout such a network of friends, relatives, and former school acquaintances who are already employed in the industry. When looking for a job within a certain field of work, contact acquaintances you have in that field.

In addition to networking, there are many ways to locate job openings. Check with the offices of trade associations as well as professional and technical societies. Find out if your school has a *placement office* that arranges contacts for jobs. Look for a job through *employment agencies*. Read the *classified ads* in newspapers and trade publications. Place a *situation-wanted ad* about yourself in some publications. Describe the type of job you are seeking and list your qualifications.

Stores and factories sometimes post job openings in a window, on a bulletin board, or near the entrance, as in **19-7**. The general news section of the paper might even help you. If there is an article about a new or expanding business in your chosen field, apply for a related job.

Contact the *human resources offices* of large industrial firms and department stores. Pleasantly ask about any possible job openings. Tell them about your interests and abilities. Try to make a strong, personal impression so they will remember you. If no jobs are available, ask if you could fill out an application for them to keep on hand in case something opens up. Follow this with a letter thanking them for allowing you to fill out the application.

The Internet is a great source for employment information and listings. Specialized job-search sites describe openings by category and job title.

19-7 Retail stores sometimes put a sign in their window to entice shoppers to apply for a sales job while they are going past the store.

They describe the jobs available, list educational requirements, allow job seekers to post their qualifications, and provide links to the companies. Government websites also offer information and listings about jobs. Businesses post employment opportunities directly on their websites. Social networking sites may also provide information on businesses and employment opportunities.

Preparing a Résumé

A résumé is a brief account of your education, work experience, and other qualifications for a job. Be sure you are very honest about all the information in your résumé. Never misrepresent your experience or work history. Focus on your strong points that are related to the job.

The résumé should include your name, address, telephone number, and e-mail address at the top. (Avoid using an e-mail address that sounds unprofessional.) A well-written résumé should include a job objective. Be sure to list an occupational goal that is in keeping with the job for which you are applying. Describe your education, listing the most recent first. Include general dates, degrees, and honors. List special achievements both in and outside of school.

Indicate in your résumé any work experience that you have. List the most recent first. Volunteer work is equally important. Also, list any special skills. Special skills might include your computer proficiency, skills with machines or instruments, or ability to speak a foreign language. A sample résumé is shown in **19-8**.

A neat, organized résumé is very important. It can bring attention to you and persuade an employer to grant you an interview. Try to keep the information limited to one page. The résumé should not have any spelling or grammatical errors. Ensure accuracy by having someone proofread it for you after you do an electronic spell check.

You should also create an electronic résumé that can be posted to business websites or online job-search sites. Some businesses may want you to send your résumé via e-mail. In this case, save your electronic résumé as *text only* without formatting. Save this file separate from your formatted résumé. Be sure to check your electronic résumé for accuracy. Businesses will often review electronic résumés by searching for key terms that identify applicants who may be more qualified for the position.

In addition to your résumé, you should have a list of at least three references. These are people who know you well enough to recommend you for a job. They can vouch for your work attitude and character. They must be adults, but not relatives. The best choices are former bosses, teachers, your counselor, or another adult who knows you well. Ask these people for permission before you list their names as references. Only share this information with interviewers who ask for your references.

The references who know you the best can write *letters of recommendation* for you. These letters should provide more detailed information about your abilities. Make sure the letters are well written. If you receive numerous letters, you can choose the best ones to give to prospective employers.

Creating a Portfolio

A professional-looking portfolio should contain a collection of your best and most creative work. Your portfolio should show a balanced representation of your current styles of art and abilities.

John W. Gordon

2119 Cedar Drive

Hillsboro, Oregon 97799

(503) 555-1234

jwgordon@hills.net

Job Objective	Seeking a job that will lead to a position as a retail department manager
Education	Portland Technical College, Portland, Oregon, 20XX to Present
	Completing retail management course, graduating June 20XX in upper quarter of class. Computer skills include keyboarding and Microsoft Word, Excel, and PowerPoint.
	North County High School, Hillsboro, Oregon, 20XX to 20XX
	Focus on business management courses. Graduated May 20XX.
Work Experience	Apparel Stock Clerk, Tallmore Discount Store, Reedville, Oregon, 20XX to 20XX
	Responsible for recording inventory, stocking shelves, and transporting incoming apparel to proper areas.
	Sports Activities Counselor, Camp Tockovista, Batterson, Oregon, summers of 20XX and 20XX
	Responsible for organizing and leading sports activities for resident campers, ages 8–14.
Honors and Activities	Member, Future Business Leaders of America (FBLA), North County High Chapter, 20XX to 20XX
	North County High School Honor Roll, 20XX and 20XX
	Team Captain, North County High School Football Team, 20XX to 20XX
	Athletic Leadership Award, 20XX

19-8 A résumé should be brief, truthful, positive, and neatly prepared.

Your portfolio should also showcase the best samples of your work related to the job you seek. For instance, you may want to include drawings, photographs, or reports about involvement in community projects. Your portfolio should include your résumé and any letters of recommendation. Make sure to include any certificates of completion and awards you have received.

Your work should be neat and organized. You can keep your portfolio in a folder or binder for protection. You can also store and present your portfolio electronically. Each portfolio piece should have your name on it. Keep your portfolio up-to-date by adding new items and replacing others.

Writing a Cover Message

A cover message is a short business letter sent with your résumé. The purposes of the message are to express your interest in a job and to persuade a potential employer to read your résumé and grant you an interview.

The cover message should be positive and polite. It should introduce you in a way that makes you stand out above the others who want the job. It should tell why you are interested in and qualified for the job.

To make a good impression, the cover message must be neatly prepared. It must not have any spelling, grammar, or typographical errors. It must not be a photocopy. Each message sent must be an original. A sample cover message is shown in **19-9**.

Send a cover message and résumé only to places where you are really interested in working. Try to learn the name of the person who is doing the hiring. Address your message to that person, rather than just sending it to the company in general. When answering a job ad, follow the specific instructions that are given. In all cases, enclose your résumé and ask for an interview.

Filling Out a Job Application

You may be asked to fill out a job application before having an interview. An *application form* requests the applicant's personal, academic, and employment information. Some of the questions may duplicate information already given in your résumé. The company may, however, still require you to complete an application form.

Fill out the form completely and neatly. Follow the directions exactly. If you do not understand a question, ask for an explanation. Do not give an incomplete response. Refer to an extra copy of your résumé for dates of previous jobs and other information you need for the application. Additional tips for filling out a job application are found in **19-10**.

Some companies choose to use electronic job applications. This allows companies to screen employment applications more easily by searching for key words. Applicants for some retail jobs may be expected to use kiosks in stores that are equipped with computer terminals and online connections. This systemizes the hiring of hourly employees for retailers and provides easy access to the process for anyone looking for a job.

The Interview

A *job interview* is a face-to-face meeting between you and the person who hires employees for a company. It is the time when you try to present yourself as the best candidate for a particular job. It is also the time to find out what the company has to offer you.

Getting Ready

Preparing yourself for the interview is extremely important for a successful outcome. Try to be ready for all interview questions by practicing the answers. As shown in **19-11**, you may be asked about your goals, career plans, previous jobs, school background, and special skills. You should also be familiar with questions you legally do not have to answer. These may include questions about age, marital status, religion, or family background.

Think about your answers to interview questions in advance. Practice talking about your educational background, work experience, professional interests, and future plans. Try this with a friend or family member, or alone in front of a mirror. Take note of your body language since that also tells a lot about you.

Learn all you can about the firm ahead of time. Find out what the company makes or sells, what the customers are like, and if there are branch operations. You can do this by talking to friends who work there or by doing some research online. Large firms may have annual reports or other descriptive materials available on their websites. If you are interviewing at a store, browse at its various branches ahead of time. If the firm makes products, familiarize yourself with them at stores that stock them.

Decide why you are suitable for the job. Review your qualifications and experiences. Be mindful of your special skills and talents. Be

2119 Cedar Drive
Hillsboro, Oregon 97799
April 20, 20XX

Mr. Fredrick Ashton, Human Resources Manager
Kroley's Department Store
2006 East Augusta Road
Portland, Oregon 97790

Dear Mr. Ashton:

Through an online job listing, I learned your company plans to hire a retail department manager. I know your company is a community retail leader and I would like to apply for this position.

To prepare for a retail management position, I will be receiving an associate's degree in Retail Management from Portland Technical College next month. As an apparel stock clerk at Tallmore Discount Store, I gained on-the-job experience in the retail field. I feel confident my education and work experience qualify me for the opening with your company.

Enclosed is my résumé. I would appreciate the opportunity to meet with you for an interview. I can be reached at (503) 555-1234 or at jwgordon@hills.net. I look forward to hearing from you and talking with you in the near future. Thank you for your kind consideration in this matter.

Sincerely,

John W. Gordon

John W. Gordon

19-9 Your cover message might be similar to this one. Each one must be prepared individually since the content must be geared to a specific job.

rested when you go to the interview so your thinking is sharp. You will then be ready mentally and physically.

Take time to dress properly for the interview. In most cases, you should dress as you would dress for the job. A basic tailored suit is often good, even if more casual garments might be worn after you are employed. Avoid casual, dressy, or gaudy extremes. Cleanliness and good grooming show that you take pride in yourself. This is very important, especially in apparel businesses. The interviewer will often judge you on your appearance and behavior as well as your professional qualifications.

Tips for Filling Out a Job Application

- Read the entire application before you begin to fill out the form.
- Ask for clarification of any questions you do not understand.
- Follow instructions provided on the form.
- Fill out the form as neatly as possible. Do not write in any spaces marked for *employer use only*.
- Provide a response for all questions. If a question is not applicable to you, write *N/A* or *does not apply*.
- Omit your social security number to protect your identity. Instead, write *will provide if hired*.
- Unless specifically requested, do not provide a specific wage or salary expectation. Write *open* or *negotiable* so you do not commit to an amount that is too high or too low.
- Remember to include any part-time jobs.
- Check your application for accuracy before you submit it. If you need to make any changes, neatly draw a line through the incorrect information.

19-10 Follow these tips as you fill out an application form for employment.

Before you go to the interview, write down the company's address. Also, write the time of your interview and the name of the person you are to see. Have these details with you so you do not have to rely on your memory. If you need a portfolio, have it in perfect order. Take an extra copy of your résumé. Also, take a small pad of paper and a pencil or pen so you can take notes.

Allow extra time to get to the interview in case you have traffic problems or difficulty finding the address. You will then arrive relaxed and in plenty of time. Showing up late for an interview is not acceptable. Immediately notify the interviewer's office, however, if you must be delayed.

During the Interview

Let the interviewer lead the conversation. Be courteous and alert. Maintain eye contact. Clearly answer all questions in a pleasant tone of voice with complete, informative sentences. Answer honestly; do not just say what you think the interviewer wants to hear. After all, you want a job that suits you, not the interviewer. Sell yourself by being quietly confident about your qualifications. Emphasize all information that relates to the job. Indicate your flexibility and willingness to learn. Try to be businesslike and positive in your speaking.

Some interviewers will discuss your portfolio with you to learn about your abilities and

ideas. Others might look at it without any discussion or comments. It is not recommended that you leave your portfolio with an employer. Instead, arrange to bring it back another time so others in the firm can see it and evaluate your work.

Ask any necessary questions at appropriate times during the interview. These may be about the duties and responsibilities of the job. You may also want to know more about the background and operations of the company. These questions give you information about the firm while you are giving information about yourself.

Do not ask about salary, raises, vacations, lunch breaks, or fringe benefits. Someone will fill you in on those details if you are offered a job. At that time, you should ask any questions that are still unanswered in your mind.

An interviewer may ask you to take one or more tests. Some are *performance tests*. They test technology or other skills that are needed for the job. *Written tests* check aptitudes for the job and general knowledge.

At the end of the interview, stand up and shake hands with the interviewer. Smile. You should have a clear understanding of what happens next. Most likely, the interviewer will want to take some time to consider the qualifications of all applicants. The interviewer may promise to contact you with a hiring decision by a certain date. Sometimes you may be asked to contact him or her.

Questions Often Asked at Job Interviews

About work experience:
What was your most recent job?
What were your job duties and responsibilities?
What did you like the most about your previous jobs? the least?
How would you describe the ideal job for you?
Why did you leave your last job?
Why should you be considered over other applicants for this position?

About education and training:
Do you intend to further your education?
What subjects did you enjoy the most? the least?
Did you participate in co-curricular activities? If so, which ones?

About your interests:
Why have you chosen this career field?
Why do you want to work for this firm?
What would you like to be doing one, five, and ten years from now?
Do you want to manage others? create? do detail work? be outdoors? be at a desk? have regular or irregular hours?
Do you usually prefer to work alone or with a lot of people?
What are your feelings about being transferred to other locations?
What do you feel your strengths and weaknesses are as a person?
What are your favorite leisure-time activities?

19-11 These and other questions might be asked during job interviews. They should be answered with well thought-out answers.

After the Interview

After the interview, do not just wait to hear if you get the job. Send a thank-you letter within 24 hours, like the sample one in **19-12**.

Keep a record of which employers expect you to call them and which ones will call you about their hiring decisions. If you do not hear from a company within a week or so, call the interviewer's office to thank him or her again for seeing you. At this time, you may also ask if anyone has been hired for the job. Show your interest, but do not be pushy. Sometimes the person who shows the most interest is the one who ends up with the job.

If you are offered a job, and you are sure you want it, give a definite acceptance with thanks. If you are not sure about accepting a job offer, thank the employer and ask if you can take some time to think about it. Clarify any questions about the job and specify when you will respond with your answer. If you decline, express your appreciation graciously. You may be interested in considering employment with that firm some time in the future.

A number of job rejections can be discouraging. However, you learn a great deal from your early interviews and do better as you gain experience. You may get an exciting job offer when you least expect it. Actively pursue all leads that interest you. Follow up in a persistent, but businesslike, manner. Go after what you want.

Becoming a Success

Success is obtained with hard work, strong ambition, and diverse skills. Whatever career you choose, you must give it your best effort. Apparel-related jobs require a neat appearance, good grooming, and good health. You need energy, pride, a cooperative manner, and sincere enthusiasm, **19-13**. The responsibility of confidentiality must also be taken seriously, so new fashion designs, company policies, or research discoveries are not given to the wrong people. To get ahead, you must follow instructions accurately, take suggestions and criticism well, and finish all tasks promptly. You must be willing to do more than you are asked and

2119 Cedar Drive
Hillsboro, Oregon 97799
May 30, 20XX

Mr. Fredrick Ashton, Human Resources Manager
Kroley's Department Store
2006 East Augusta Road
Portland, Oregon 97790

Dear Mr. Ashton:

Thank you for giving me the opportunity of interviewing with you yesterday. It was a pleasure to meet you and to hear about the operations of Kroley's Department Store.

My interest in working for your firm is high, and I would appreciate being able to prove my worth in a top-notch retail firm such as yours.

I look forward to hearing from you soon.

Sincerely,

John W. Gordon

John W. Gordon

19-12 Sending a thank-you letter to follow up on a job interview will show that you are polite and interested in the job.

respect the work of others. Enthusiasm, perseverance, and ambition are important traits for success. It is no small order, but you can do it!

Develop Positive Personal Traits

To become a success, work on developing the following positive personal traits. If perfected, they will become highly valued habits, and you will be on your way to the top.

Drive is the energy and persistence to accomplish goals. It causes you to have the best attitude and to put forth the most effort toward your job.

Self-esteem is a deep conviction of your own worth. With honesty, high ethics, and hard work, you will always be proud of your actions. Keep a positive attitude about yourself and your abilities.

Reliability is dependability. It means you can be trusted to do as you say you will do. People are confident that you will not let them down.

A *sense of responsibility* is the ability to complete assigned tasks and account for your own behavior and decisions. You accept blame for your mistakes and learn from them. (No one is perfect.) On the other hand, you are entitled to praise for your accomplishments.

Dedication is a devotion of your time and enthusiasm to the job and to the firm. Be willing to learn new skills. Accept new ideas. Try your best.

Monkey Business Images/Shutterstock.com

19-13 Pleasure and satisfaction result when you enthusiastically give your best effort toward your job.

Awareness is the knowledge of what is happening. Observe the job, the people, and other operations so you always know what is going on. You may learn many valuable details about your work and the entire operation.

Cheerfulness is the tendency to look for the good side of every situation. Be optimistic. Have a positive attitude and good expectations for yourself and others. Being pleasant and courteous makes everyone feel better, as in **19-14**.

Cooperation allows you to get along with others. Be considerate, pleasant, and concerned about those around you. This creates cooperation and makes the work easier for everyone. Pitch in and help coworkers when you can without interrupting your own work schedule. You can then ask them for help when you need it. Experienced employees have wonderful amounts of information and advice. Use them as resources and appreciate their experience.

Other Important Factors

Besides the personal traits just mentioned, a few steps can be taken to further your fashion career. These steps may take time and effort on your part. They include using effective communication, customer relations, and decision-making skills. They also include demonstrating leadership skills, ethical behavior, and presenting a professional image. Knowing your rights in the workplace is important, too.

Use Effective Communication Skills

Jobs rely heavily on the accurate exchange of information. You need reading skills to understand directions and other written information. You need good writing skills so you can give directions and messages to others. Learning to listen well and speak clearly is also very important. Skills in technology are a must to communicate effectively.

Develop Customer Relations Skills

Working with customers requires you to remain courteous and patient. You need to be pleasant as you answer their questions. If a customer is upset, you must remain polite and be able to handle the situation efficiently. In order for customers to return, they must receive satisfactory service from you. Customers need to know you appreciate their business.

19-14 A cheerful attitude about work helps you become a success and helps those around you feel good.

Pressmaster/Shutterstock.com

Display a Positive Response to Pressure

This is easier by nature for some people than for others. It is essential for many jobs in the apparel industries. Producing good, creative results under pressure is a valuable ability. Meeting deadlines and filling sales quotas are types of pressure. See **19-15**. Some people enjoy this challenge and are able to perform their best. On the other hand, pressure makes some people nervous and unable to perform well. Learn to control your emotions.

Use Decision-Making Skills

Decision making is the determining of a course of action from all the options. It is the process of choosing what seems to be the best of several alternatives. It requires an understanding of the situation and may involve some risk. It also involves accepting the responsibility for the decision after it is made.

Demonstrate Leadership Skills

Leading others involves motivating and managing them. This means getting members of a group to work together to further the group's interests. A skillful leader gives employees the opportunity to attain individual goals and rewards while they are performing well for the company.

19-15 Many workers in apparel careers face the pressure of interacting with customers and making good sales. It is important for these workers to display positive attitudes and encourage customers to return for repeat business.

Pressmaster/Shutterstock.com

Present a Professional Image

By presenting a businesslike image of yourself through your appearance and actions, you can further your career. When you look and feel professional, you will perform and be viewed as a successful member of your profession.

Demonstrate Ethical Behavior

Ethical behavior refers to accepted standards of fairness and good conduct on the job. Employers seek workers who have a strong work ethic. These workers strive to do their best. They are honest and dependable. They understand the importance of confidentiality in the workplace. They care about the quality of their work.

Unfortunately, some workers do not have a strong work ethic. They may steal from the company. Theft may include office supplies, money, or even time. These employees may arrive late, take extended breaks, or leave early. They may use office computers for personal reasons instead of completing their duties. Be aware of company policies that address these issues. If you do not demonstrate ethical behavior, you will be much more likely to lose your job. You may also have difficulty finding new employment.

Know Your Rights

Employee protection is provided by government legislation, labor unions, and private agencies. The Equal Employment Opportunity Act, Fair Labor Standards Act, Equal Pay Act, and Americans with Disabilities Act are a few of the laws that protect employees. These laws are explained in **19-16**.

Making Job Changes

At different times in your career, you may decide to leave a job. You might not be happy in your current position, or you may feel you are stuck in a dead-end job and want to move higher in your career. Whatever the reason, you need to think carefully about your future career plans before making any decisions. Try to leave your job on good terms. Avoid quitting without any notice. It is not fair to your employer, and it could hurt your future job chances.

Laws That Provide Employee Protection

Equal Employment Opportunity Act—Prohibits employers from discriminating against any employee or job applicant because of race, color, religion, national origin, sex, physical or mental disability, or age.

Fair Labor Standards Act—Sets the national minimum wage and overtime pay practices.

Equal Pay Act—Requires that men and women be paid the same amount for doing the same jobs under the same conditions.

Americans with Disabilities Act—Prohibits employers from discriminating against people with disabilities, and mandates that the work environment be made physically accessible for workers with disabilities.

19-16 The intent of these laws is to provide fairness to those being employed.

racorn/Shutterstock.com

19-17 Make sure your letter of resignation is respectful, clear, and honest. Your letter of resignation is one way of ensuring you and your former employer have positive future relations.

If you do decide to leave your job, try to give your employer at least a two-week notice. If you are leaving during a busy season, you might even try to give more notice. You should prepare a *letter of resignation* that states your reason for leaving the job. See **19-17**. This letter should also include the date you intend to leave. Your employer can then look for your replacement. If a new employee is hired quickly, you may have time to train him or her before you leave. When you leave a job on good terms, you often find that your former employer becomes a great help when you need a good reference for another job.

Summary

The fashion industry offers a variety of job opportunities. Do careful planning and study to choose your career. First, get to know yourself with a self-assessment of your interests, aptitudes, and abilities. Then investigate fields of employment that match you. There are many resources available to help you learn about careers. As you research careers, you should determine the level of education and training you will need. You should also consider the earning levels and employment outlook for these careers.

You can use networking and placement offices to find jobs in your chosen field. You might use the help of employment agencies. Classified or situation-wanted ads may help you find a job. The Internet is also a good source to use.

Carefully prepare a résumé to give to prospective employers. Create a portfolio that includes samples of your best work. Send a cover message to the correct person at each firm that interests you. Fill out job applications completely and neatly. For job interviews, be ready to answer questions, and take performance and written tests. Try to be relaxed and honest during interviews.

Hard work, strong ambition, and diverse skills are needed to become a success. Develop positive personal traits, such as drive, self-esteem, reliability, a sense of responsibility, dedication, awareness, cheerfulness, and cooperation. Also, present a professional image and develop effective communication and customer relations skills. A positive response to pressure, decision-making skills, and leadership skills are also needed. Develop ethical behavior and know your rights in the workplace. When you are ready to leave a job, try to give at least a two-week notice. Continue to learn and grow through your career to gain the success you deserve.

Fashion Recall

Write your answers on a separate sheet of paper.

True/False: Write *true* or *false* for each of the following statements.

1. Abilities are your natural talents and potential for learning.
2. Each career cluster includes occupations that have common knowledge and skill requirements.
3. A mentor is a faithful counselor who guides you along your career path.
4. Two-year colleges and trade schools offer bachelor's degrees.
5. If salaried employees work overtime, they are paid an extra amount.
6. Apparel industry occupations offer less job security than many other businesses.
7. Networking is the exchange of information or services among an interconnected group of people.
8. Volunteer work should not be mentioned in a résumé.
9. It is wise to ask for an interview in a cover message.
10. During an interview, only give answers you think the interviewer wants to hear.

Short Answer: Write the correct response to each of the following statements.

11. List four ways your career decision will affect your life.
12. List five sources to use as you research careers.
13. List four ways to receive occupational training.
14. List five personal traits that people need to achieve success.
15. Name four laws that protect employees.

Fashion Vocabulary

16. With a partner, create a T-chart. In the left column, write each of the *Fashion Terms* found on the chapter opening. In the right column, write a *synonym* (a word that has the same or similar meaning) for each of the terms. Then, discuss your synonyms with the class.

Critical Thinking

17. **Draw conclusions**   For yourself, describe what you think would be the opportunities and rewards of a career in fashion. Write a summary citing the text and other reliable resources as evidence for your conclusions.
18. **Assess skills and interests**   Use such online self-assessments as the *Skills Profiler, Interest Profiler,* or *Work Importance Locator* on the CareerOneStop and O*NET websites. Take the assessments. Then, evaluate how these assessments can help you locate a career that matches your skills and interests. Write a summary of your findings.
19. **Differentiate careers**   Differentiate among a variety of fashion-related career choices that you find appealing. Explain why choosing a career is such an important decision. How can such decisions impact your career life?
20. **Analyze factors**   Analyze factors that can lead to career success or failure. Discuss your analyses with the class.

Core Skills

21. **Reading and writing**   Select two careers related to fashion to research on O*NET. Read the summary reports for these careers, especially the knowledge, skills, abilities, and interests required to do the work. Analyze whether your personal interests, skills, and abilities are a logical fit with one or both fashion careers. Write a summary explaining why you think you are well suited for either career.
22. **Writing**   Work independently and search online for examples of different types of résumés that can be used when applying for jobs. Print an example of each. Analyze the similarities and differences among

the documents. Then, write a summary indicating when you might use each type of résumé in applying for employment related to fashion.

23. **Speaking and writing**   Contact professional references to acquire recommendations. Practice your professional communication skills by contacting these persons to seek permission to list them as references. If they agree, verify their contact information. Then, prepare an electronic list of references to give to potential employers. Also, ask each reference if he or she would write a letter of recommendation for you. Store these letters in your portfolio.

24. **Speaking and listening**   With a classmate, conduct a mock interview in front of the class for a specific fashion-related position. Practice job-related questions and answers beforehand. Ask the class and your instructor for feedback regarding ways to improve your interview skills.

25. **Speaking**   Search online for opportunities to take free interview quizzes. Practice your responses aloud. Take the quizzes and analyze your answers with the recommended responses. Practice until your score reaches 90 percent.

26. **Research and speaking**   Examine the Americans with Disabilities Act (ADA). Give an oral report to the class telling when the law was enacted, what protections it provides for employees with disabilities, and how companies must comply.

27. **Writing**   In the counselor's office or reference section of the library, or on an Internet website, look through lists of trade schools and colleges. Find five schools that offer courses to prepare students for apparel and fashion careers. Write an article, comparing their curriculums, sizes, costs, settings, and other specifics. Submit the article to your school newspaper or website for publication consideration.

28. **Research and writing**   Enter the name of a fashion career and different geographic areas into a job search engine. For each area, note salary information as well as cost of living. Using presentation software, create a bar graph illustrating the variation in salaries and cost of living by area.

29. **Research and writing**   Search for an educational and training program in a fashion career area that is delivered via the Internet. Track down all the information you can about the program, including student feedback. Describe the pros and cons of such a program.

30. **CTE career readiness practice**   Setting reasonable, attainable goals is an important skill. Note that goals should be specific and positive, be measurable, and have a target deadline. In writing, set a career goal for five years from now. Determine how you will measure achievement of this goal, and identify a deadline for meeting it. Create a personal plan of study to outline how you can help meet your career goal.

Fashion in Action

31. **Portfolio builder**   Prepare your own résumé, listing your education, honors and activities, work experience, skills, and interests. Then write a cover message to an imaginary company asking for an interview for a specific job that might really suit you. Keep copies of these documents in your portfolio.

32. **Design activity**   Design an apparel-related job-openings bulletin board. Look through the classified ads in a local newspaper or use online sources for job descriptions. Obtain photos of people in apparel-related jobs to place next to the job descriptions. Present your bulletin board to the class and discuss the variety of career opportunities available in your area from entry-level jobs to management positions.

Self-Assessment Quiz ↗

Complete the self-assessment quiz online to help practice and expand your knowledge and skills.

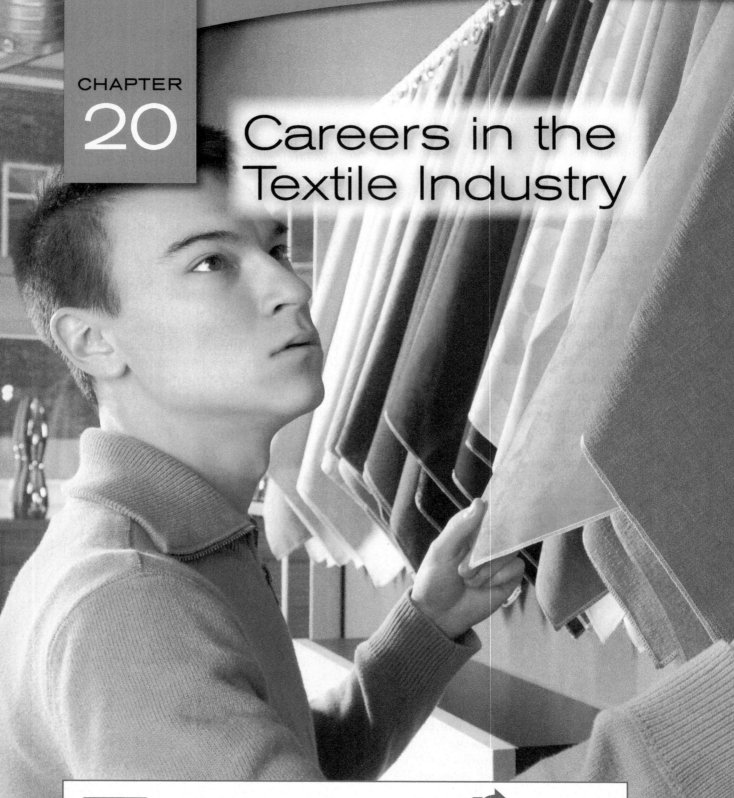

CHAPTER 20

Careers in the Textile Industry

G-WLEARNING.com

While studying, look for the activity icon to:

- **practice** key fashion terms with e-flash cards, vocabulary games, and matching activities
- **assess** what you learn by completing self-assessment quizzes

www.g-wlearning.com/clothingandfashion/

Fashion Terms

research scientists
freelance jobs
textile designer
textile colorists
textile stylists
production
 supervisors

machine operators
machine technicians
plant engineers
industrial engineers
market research
 analysts

sales representatives
administration
human resources
 manager
data processors

Objectives

After studying this chapter, you will be able to
➤ discuss the wide range of careers in the textile industry.
➤ explain the requirements needed for various textile-related careers.
➤ discuss professions in textile research and development.
➤ describe opportunities in textile design and textile production.
➤ explain careers in textile marketing, sales, and administration.

Many millions of people share in the world's apparel industries. Researchers develop fibers and fabrics. Engineers design machines, and computer experts program systems to mass-produce huge quantities of garments. Workers cut, sew, press, and ship merchandise. Promoters write, photograph, illustrate, display, and model items. These people, and many others, make the apparel industries what they are today.

The textile industry includes every aspect of making, finishing, and selling fibers, yarns, and fabrics. The industry employs artists, chemists, engineers, managers, merchandisers, and many more. It offers jobs at all levels of skill and education. Its constant changes in products and methods keep creating new opportunities.

Salaries in the textile industry vary, but are usually higher for people with more education and experience. Fringe benefits usually include medical benefits, retirement plans, paid vacation time, sick leave, and some life insurance. Sometimes tuition reimbursement plans are available for further education.

Colleges and technical schools offer textile majors in manufacturing, chemistry, engineering, design, and other subjects. Some textile careers require only a high school diploma and on-the-job training. Most companies run their own training programs. However, advancement is more difficult for those without college degrees. As in most industries, production workers outnumber management.

The textile industry also offers employment opportunities worldwide. The main U.S. textile sales offices are located in New York City. Branch offices are in many other major U.S. cities and in foreign capitals. The salespeople spend much of their time traveling. Most textile manufacturing plants, or mills, are located in industrial towns throughout the world. The *textile belt* of the U.S. stretches from New England, down through the Carolinas and Georgia, and across to Texas.

Figure **20-1** lists many, but not all, of the career opportunities in the textile industry. Many of the jobs are described in this chapter.

Textile Research and Development

The purpose of *research and development (R and D)* is to provide new knowledge, develop new products, and improve old products. Employees in R and D usually work in modern, well-equipped labs, such as the one shown in **20-2**. They search for facts and then analyze them. They use their findings to make better products. Through research, they try to develop goods that will satisfy the changing wants and needs of consumers, while providing a profit for the company.

The personal traits for a career in R and D include creativity, curiosity, and attention to details. Researchers should like to work independently. They should also be able to clearly communicate their findings to others in a precise, realistic, and practical way. Patience and persistence in working toward a solution are also needed. Sometimes it takes many years to invent a product or to solve a technical problem.

20-1 Most of the jobs in the textile industry are listed here. Other specific ones may be created as new technology causes changes in textile industry procedures.

Careers in the Textile Industry

Accountants	Human resources managers	Public relations specialists
Administrators	Industrial engineers	Purchasing agents
Advertising and promotion agents	Information specialists	Quality control inspectors
Business operations specialists	Knitting machine technicians	Research scientists
Card technicians	Laboratory technicians	Safety experts
Chemists	Loom technicians	Sales managers
Cloth inspectors	Machine operators	Sales representatives
Colorists	Machine technicians	Screen printers
Computer programmers	Managers	Spinners
Converters	Market research analysts	Stylists
Data processors	Office managers	Systems analysts
Designers	Office support workers	Textile testers
Doffers (bobbin changers)	Plant engineers	Transportation (shipping) specialists
Dyeing supervisors	Product developers	Warehouse workers
Electricians	Production supervisors	Weavers
Engravers		

20-2 People who work in research and development try to develop new products or improve existing ones.

People who work in the field of textile R and D are employed by fiber manufacturers, textile mills, and private testing laboratories. Government agencies hire chemists and lab technicians to see that textile products on the market meet government standards. At times, researchers must develop the specifications for the standards. A great deal of research is also done at universities. Research positions give graduate students the opportunity to work and gain experience while earning advanced degrees.

Textile Research Scientist

Research and development is done in several different textile areas to satisfy needs for specific end uses. Textile research scientists develop new synthetic fibers that have certain characteristics. They blend fibers in new and better ways to create desired qualities. They work on different fabric constructions and find new finishes for better fabric performance.

R and D is technical work, as indicated in **20-3**. Researchers must enjoy science and like to conduct lab experiments. They study consumer complaints to improve upon existing products and to create new products. Their work must be done several years before the products will be offered to the retail market. They must be patient and flexible enough to see a project through from the initial idea to actual installation in a manufacturing plant. Researchers keep up with the latest work of their peers through related trade journals and scientific writings on credible websites. They write reports about their own findings and recommend changes.

To become a textile research scientist, a bachelor's degree in the sciences, such as chemistry, chemical engineering, or physics, is required. Many research jobs also require a master's degree or Ph.D. Manufacturing experience in a textile plant during the summers, or as part of a work-based learning program, is a great asset.

Salaries and fringe benefits vary for textile research scientists, depending on the scientist's level of education and place of employment. There are sometimes opportunities to broaden a person's career into other areas of company activity, such as manufacturing supervision or marketing. Also, personal satisfaction can be very high when complex problems are solved or something new is created. Work hours are usually regular, with some overtime demands.

20-3 Textile researchers can compare the drape of fabric weights with computer simulation. Pseudo-coloring shows how far from the body each fabric drapes for the same skirt design. Here, heavy denim stands away from the body as it goes downward from the waist turning to yellow and red.

Fiber Science & Apparel Design/Cornell University

Textile research scientists usually belong to professional organizations, such as the American Association of Textile Chemists and Colorists (AATCC). They often attend seminars and conferences about their subject areas. Expenses for these are usually paid by the companies that employ the scientists.

Textile Laboratory Technician

Textile *laboratory technicians* help conduct research, often working under the supervision of research scientists. See **20-4**. An associate's degree or a technical or trade school certificate in the sciences is often required. Many of the specific procedures laboratory technicians do are repetitive and are learned on the job.

In the lab, technicians set up equipment, write computations, and help categorize and analyze experiment results. They may duplicate each step of a future manufacturing operation to evaluate its quality and efficiency. They may also test the durability and serviceability of finished fibers, yarns, and fabrics.

Technicians who are *textile testers* work for textile mills or independent testing laboratories. They test new products against the specifications that must be met. They are responsible for checking different fibers, fabrics, or finishes after they have been developed, but before they are introduced to the public. They also perform tests during the textile manufacturing process to assure good and uniform quality.

20-4 The important jobs done by technicians depend on reliable work.

Burlington Industries, Inc.

Textile technicians and testers should be organized and able to work independently. They should enjoy working with equipment and chemicals. They must be able to follow precise instructions, do detailed work accurately, and write thorough reports of their test results.

Textile Design

Textile design employees should have a fine sense of color, a creative imagination, and artistic ability. They also need knowledge of and interest in the fashion field. They should have a fascination for beautiful patterns that are woven, knitted, or printed onto fabrics.

Most jobs in textile design are located in New York City and other fashion centers, where the designing and styling departments of the major textile firms are located. Although most of these jobs are offered on a full-time basis, it may be possible for experienced people to find freelance jobs. These are short-term jobs done for various firms that end when each assignment is completed. Freelancers must build a network of client companies for whom they provide services so they can work steadily. They must be able to complete highly professional work, while meeting tight deadlines. Therefore, most companies prefer to only hire workers with much on-the-job experience.

Textile Designer

A textile designer creates new patterns and designs, or redesigns existing ones for fabrics. The designer creates new looks in fabrics for wearing apparel as well as for home and commercial furnishings. The fabric designs are usually directed toward a specific end use or market. The designer tries to anticipate coming fashion trends in fabrics. Designers develop a seasonal line of new fabrics for textile manufacturers.

Surface designs are applied on top of a fabric, usually by printing. First, the designer sketches one motif, or repeat, of the design on paper or with a computer design program, as in **20-5**. A sample can be silk-screened or roller printed to show how the final design will look for mass printing. Then it goes into printing production on a large scale.

Textile designers also create *structural designs* through knitted patterns or special weaves. Yarns

20-5 Training is needed to effectively use the exciting capabilities of electronic design systems.

20-6 This textile student is learning about structural design by weaving a sample of the idea directly on a loom.

of different textures or colors are combined in interesting ways. Less need for fine drawing ability is required for this. However, more knowledge of yarns, technical processes, machine capabilities, and programming software is needed.

The use of technology is widespread for structural design. With older methods, patterns were designed on hand looms, as in **20-6**, or knitting machines. Small quantities were produced to show the finished effect in sample swatches. The designer or a technician then transferred the design into a computer. The computer controlled the loom or knitting machine to produce large quantities of fabric with the design. However, now the entire process can be done on computers or other digital devices. The textile designer creates a design on an electronic system, which then weaves or knits the fabric. This is very fast and accurate.

A textile designer must know about new fibers, dyes, and finishes. He or she must understand the latest machinery, as well as new styles and fashion trends. The designer must know how to select, mix, and combine colors. He or she must know how to plan repeats. All processes of textile manufacturing must be understood so the designs can go into factory production within a specific price category.

Textile designers often get their creative ideas by observing the world around them. They must be sensitive to trends, fads, and current events. They may also look through older fabrics and works of art for inspiration. Many firms have their own fabric libraries for this purpose.

To become a textile designer, educational requirements usually include an associate's or bachelor's degree in textile design. The curriculum covers basic art and design courses. Color theory, computer design, apparel, fibers, and fabric construction courses are also needed. Advancement opportunities may be available after gaining experience in the field.

To obtain a job in the textile design field, a person must demonstrate technical skills and textile knowledge to complement their artistic creativity. Competition is keen in the textile design field. There are a limited number of new openings each year. However, the jobs that are available are very rewarding.

Textile Colorist

You may have seen a particular textile design that was offered in several different color combinations. See **20-7**. Textile colorists decide which combinations of colors will appeal to consumers. They skillfully add those colors into the original textile design electronically or with paints on paper. There might be many changes before final approval is given for production. Then specific instructions are sent to the mill for the manufacturing process.

The position of textile colorist is often an entry-level job for graduates with an associate's degree or technical or trade school certificate in textile design. These programs usually include the study of woven and printed fabrics, color fundamentals, as in **20-8**, and creative design principles. A portfolio of textile colorings and designs must be submitted when applying for this position.

A textile colorist learns to match and paint various color combinations or arrangements on a design created by a textile designer. This gives employees who are new to the field a chance to increase work speed and better develop a sense of color. The colorist is an important member of

Fashion Institute of Technology

20-8 A textile colorist might make up several sample swatches for fabric designs in the same colors. These might be coordinated or combined in apparel outfits or manufacturer's garment lines.

the designer's team. He or she becomes aware of how colored dyes look on almost any type of fabric. Records of color samples and fabric swatches must be kept. Often, textile colorists research older textiles to get color information about designs used in the past.

Textile colorists must be neat and careful workers. They must be able to follow precise instructions. They must often work at a fast pace to meet deadlines that keep the expensive fabric production on schedule.

Textile colorists who gain experience in the field and prove their skill may advance to a textile design job. Eventually, they might even fill a managerial position with a textile mill or design studio.

Textile Stylist

Textile stylists have responsibility over the fabric line from its start to finish. Textile stylists guide textile designers, as in **20-9**, to fulfill consumer desires. They are responsible for most long-range fashion planning of fabric colors, weights, and textures. They sometimes act as a colorist, technician, merchandiser, salesperson, and even designer. They must have an extensive knowledge of the textile industry and a wide range of industry contacts and resources.

Stylists must understand the textile marketplace. They must know what consumers want. They can sometimes even stimulate consumer desires. Successful company sales depend on

20-7 These three fabrics have the same print, but each is done with different color combinations.

Tania Anisimova/Shutterstock.com

Monkey Business Images/Shutterstock.com

20-9 Textile stylists coordinate the designs, colors, and end-use projections with those who are creating the fabrics.

wavebreakmedia/Shutterstock.com

20-10 Before planning their fabric lines, textile stylists check fashion forecasting information for expected future colors and trends.

the stylists' abilities to gauge consumer demand and to stimulate interest in new fabrics.

The stylist determines the proper look, or overall concept, of the fabric line. He or she might tell designers and colorists exactly what types of patterns to develop and what fashionable colors to use. The stylist then coordinates the design and color work with the efforts of the production staff at the mill or print plant, often many miles away.

The stylist may supervise one or many designers and colorists in the design studio. In addition, frequent contact with plant employees where the fabric is being produced or printed is needed. Accuracy of the designs and colors must be checked at the mill site to eliminate costly production errors and to assure high sales.

The textile stylist works closely with the company's merchandising department in planning the future fabric lines. Frequent contact must be made with garment manufacturers to learn what kinds of fabrics they will want in order to produce their items. The stylist might also suggest to the manufacturers ways in which particular fabrics can be used.

Stylists learn about new directions that fashion and color will take from forecasting services, as in **20-10**. They also get information from fabric editors of trade publications, fashion magazines, or industry associations. The stylist's own good taste and fashion sense are combined with doing research of the marketplace and trade resources. To be a success, this person needs

many years of textile industry experience predicting what the public will want to buy more than a year in the future.

Training in the fine arts and textile science is required to be a textile stylist. The varied work requires courses in art, advertising, apparel, textiles, and CAD. Creative talent is a must. Retail sales experience with fabrics of ready-to-wear is helpful. Also, experience in a textile mill, to understand production methods and machinery, is valuable.

Textile styling jobs are highly desirable and very competitive. They pay extremely well. The sales and profits of textile firms depend to a great extent on the talents of the stylist. The position is often reached only after many successful years in the textile field. Large textile manufacturing firms may hire several stylists. Each one is responsible for a specific group of fabrics, such as those for children's wear, menswear, or women's wear.

Assistant Stylist

An *assistant stylist* is a person who is being trained to be a stylist. Assistants set up appointments with customers. They have regular contact with the mills to check on production schedules or problems. They may handle clerical details and correspondence.

Assistant stylist positions are often filled by people who have completed college programs in textile design or textile technology. They also usually have experience as a successful textile colorist or designer.

Textile Production

As already mentioned, first the researchers must develop the fibers, yarns, and fabrics. Next, the designers must create the weaves, knits, and prints in the desired weights and colors. Then the yard goods can be produced. Textile production involves the largest single portion of textile industry employees. Much textile production is done overseas in low-wage countries.

Textile plant operations include opening the bales of fibers, cleaning and straightening the fibers, and spinning the fibers into yarns. Then the yarns are woven, knitted, or matted into fabrics. See **20-11**. The textile goods must also be chemically or mechanically finished. Each manufacturing step needs special machinery and trained employees.

Many textile mills run six or seven days a week with three 8-hour work shifts. Shift work schedules often rotate, so employees share the day, evening, and night shifts. Employees may work six days in a row and have three days off in the middle of the week. That enables them to take care of personal business or enjoy recreation without usual weekend crowds. Also, extra pay is given to those who work the evening and night shifts.

A textile mill often handles just one part of production—spinning, weaving, knitting, or finishing. The majority of U.S. textile production jobs are located in the Southeast, such as in the Carolinas and Georgia. A few are in New England. Many companies have plants in more than one town or country, so employees are subject to transfer if their expertise is needed elsewhere.

Most firms encourage and pay for their management personnel (higher engineers and supervisors) to attend seminars, workshops, and classes to help keep them abreast of current developments in the textile industry, as in **20-12**. Otherwise, not much traveling is done by manufacturing employees.

Salaries and fringe benefits are good in textile production jobs. Recognition is given for responsibilities handled well. Working conditions are generally pleasant in modern plants. Many plants even sponsor recreational, social, and athletic activities for employees and their families.

More technical jobs are being created as new technology is introduced into the textile industry. New machines and processes are being developed. Computers are involved in almost all manufacturing operations. Electronic equipment is used to forecast amounts of raw materials needed, compute how much of each type of fiber or fabric to produce, and give statistics on quality control. Computers also control much of the textile manufacturing machinery.

Textile Converter

A key person in textile production is the converter. *Converters* are finishing experts. At finishing plants, they decide how various amounts of fabrics should be dyed, printed, or otherwise finished. Converters must be aware of all the needs of customers, so the right finished textiles are made.

Converters calculate the amounts of fabric that will be bought by the firm's customers. They plan the fabric construction and decide on suitable finishes and dyes based on the end uses.

20-11 This textile production employee is setting up a circular knitting machine that will produce many yards of knitted fabric.

Burlington Industries

ITMA International Textile Machinery Association

20-12 Many seminars and professional meetings are offered for managers employed by textile firms.

Quality standards are calculated for various fabrics, depending on how each fabric will be used. Converters also help set prices based on the costs of supplies and production.

Large textile firms employ more than one converter. Each converter is a specialist in a certain fabric area for a particular market. Each knows what is current in that marketplace and keeps in touch with the customers of those goods. Each must be able to quickly sum up new economic trends relating to his or her particular textile market.

Textile converters must be good at details, figures, and record keeping. They should be well organized and have excellent communication skills. They must be calm and levelheaded when working under pressure.

Assistant Converter

Assistant converters must also be familiar with all the textile production procedures, especially finishing processes. If they perform the duties of assistant well, they can move up to a textile converter's position. They should have completed a two- or four-year textile technology program. College courses are needed in the areas of textile science, fabric construction, mathematics, and textile chemistry. Assistant converters also should have studied dyeing, color analysis, textile testing, marketing principles, and other related areas.

Assistant converters are responsible for keeping accurate production and inventory records. They handle many clerical duties for the textile converter. They also help establish prices based on all the costs involved, plus a margin of profit. This is known as *costing the fabric*. Assistant converters also need to maintain contact with fiber mills from whom they buy, as well as with customers wanting to know the status of their orders.

Production Supervisor

Many college graduates entering the textile industry begin their careers as production supervisors. They usually have degrees in engineering, textile technology, business, or chemistry. In addition, they can take production management training programs given by the companies that hire them. They coordinate and direct the various mill departments to maintain the highest production and the best quality.

A production supervisor must have qualities of leadership. This ability is needed to motivate others to be loyal to the team or firm and give their best efforts toward the finest possible results. Production supervisors must be able to organize work and to solve problems. Supervisors who prove their capabilities can move up to plant management positions or move into sales or development jobs.

Machine Operator

Under the supervisors, there are many workers called machine operators. They operate the machines that do the manufacturing procedures, as shown in **20-13**. They do not need college degrees, but they do important, specialized

20-13 Machine operators in textile manufacturing plants run the production machinery. This woman works in a weaving mill.

Sulzer Ruti, Inc.

jobs. They generally have a high school education and are trained on the job. However, as the need for skilled workers increases with computerized, high-tech procedures, more employers are emphasizing formal training in trade or technical schools. Complicated machines must be handled with a high degree of skill and responsibility.

Machine operators must use their minds and their hands. They should have good mechanical aptitude, physical coordination, manual dexterity, and normal vision. There are also numerous opportunities for people with disabilities. There is ample job advancement from hourly, paid operator jobs to salaried, managerial jobs for those who work hard and have a good attitude. Most textile production operators are people who enjoy routine tasks and like to work independently.

Quality Control Inspector

Quality control inspectors work in all phases of textile production to analyze the quality of the products. They try to find solutions to quality problems when necessary, as shown in **20-14**. They carefully examine the fibers, yarns, or fabrics as they come from the extruders, looms, knitting machines, or finishing operations. They check to see that precise standards and specifications are met. Imperfect goods cannot be sold. Thus, inspectors identify production-

related problems at different stages of the manufacturing process and write reports based on their findings.

People who choose quality control work for a career should have good analytical skills. They should enjoy detail and follow-up work. They should also complete a textile technology or apparel production program.

Machine Technician

Machine technicians keep the complex textile production equipment in good working order. They are often former operators with especially good mechanical skills. They are either trained at the plant or in technical schools. They do regular maintenance on the machinery. They are also called on to diagnose problems in every type of production machine in the plant. This applies to large gear chains as well as delicate weaving or knitting machine controls. The pay is usually higher than for operators.

Plant Engineer

Plant engineers make sure all environmental systems are operating properly. They are responsible for the heating, air conditioning, electrical, materials handling, and other systems. If these operations are not functioning properly, they must be modified or repaired. Sometimes plant engineers are also consulted by the machine technicians if complex problems occur in production machinery.

Plant engineers must be expert problem solvers. A college degree in engineering is usually required. The job involves a great deal of responsibility. Pay is quite good.

Industrial Engineer

Industrial engineers are cost and efficiency experts. They save companies time and money. They study each operation, as in **20-15**, and determine the most efficient and least expensive method of getting tasks done. Industrial engineers decide what machines are needed for the operations of the mill. They are constantly looking for better ways of doing production jobs without reducing the quality of the final product. They also try to improve the safety of operations.

Industrial engineers must have a complete understanding of the operation of the plant. They must be experts in work methods and

20-14 When problems in production arise, they are analyzed. Then recommendations are made for solutions. This enables the best possible products to be produced.

Burlington Industries, Inc.

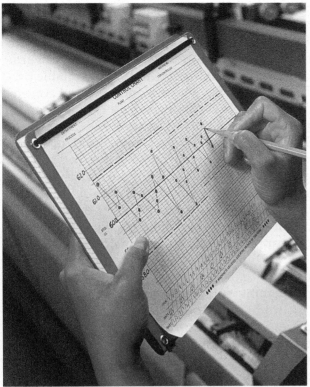

20-15 Industrial engineers study textile production operations to determine the most efficient methods of doing the tasks.

job design. They work with plant management and plant engineers to develop the best ways to put new procedures into effect.

For this job, companies prefer college graduates with industrial engineering or textile manufacturing degrees. In addition, companies usually provide their own training programs. Industrial engineers are usually people who like scientific or technical work. They enjoy planning and controlling activities.

Textile Marketing and Sales

As defined in Chapter 5, *marketing* is the business of finding or creating a market for the textiles produced. It includes identifying customers, determining the wants and needs of customers, and providing satisfying products at acceptable prices. Marketing also incorporates promotion and distribution at a profit.

It helps develop the sales strategy of the firm. *Sales* refer to the actual exchange of goods from the supplier to the customer for money.

Marketing and salespeople must be fully familiar with their firm's lines, as well as policies and procedures. They must try to satisfy the ever-changing needs and tastes of those who purchase their company's textile products. They must stay on the leading edge of rapid changes in fashion and style.

Market Research Analyst

Market research analysts conduct market research by studying consumer tastes and changing trends. They try to discover future textile needs for all markets. Market research analysts are alert to any shift in supply and demand. They keep the research scientists informed of what must be developed. Market research analysts work closely with their firm's textile stylists. They assist the textile converters in keeping production of the proper finished goods at peak levels. Market research information must be supplied far in advance so the textiles will be ready at the time of demand.

Market research analysts help predict the trends of special colors, looks, weights, and textures of fabrics. They coordinate the activities of their textile companies with the rest of the fashion world. They often travel to foreign fashion showings. Market research analysts also keep on top of what their competitors are doing in long-range pricing and supply. With a knowledge of general consumer preferences and a great deal of experience, they can make accurate predictions. Their work can be especially exciting if they have been a prime influence behind a successful marketing idea.

Market research analysts should have education and training in textiles, business, marketing, economics, psychology, and statistics. They also need to know every aspect of the textile industry.

Textile Sales Representative

Textile sales representatives are the actual salespeople at various levels of the textile chain. Fiber producers sell to yarn producers or fabric manufacturers. Greige goods manufacturers sell their unfinished fabrics to finishers. Finally, the finished yard goods are sold. To do this, sales representatives show cloth samples, and sometimes finished garments, to apparel manufacturers, as shown in **20-16**. They also sell to retail fabric stores and to industrial and household goods producers.

Textile salespeople are the link between their firm and its customers. A continuing relationship is sought with each customer, so the salesperson can be the company's eyes and ears. Salespeople try to advise their managers and market research analysts on fashion directions in the marketplace. They stay alert to the activities of competitors and supply-demand situations. They must give attention to both the needs of the customers and the interests of the company.

Sales personnel are important representatives of their companies. They must be knowledgeable about their products and able to talk intelligently to give reputable advice and direction to each particular customer.

20-16 This textile salesperson is taking notes about her client's preferences in fashionable fabrics.

bikeriderlondon/Shutterstock.com

Sales is the most competitive area of the textile industry. It is not the career for everyone. However, for those who have an aptitude for sales, the opportunities and financial rewards can be great. It is a respected and profitable profession for those who are outgoing, yet sincere.

Sales representatives must have personalities that can stimulate desires for their products. They must have poise, self-confidence, and maturity. They must be able to meet and get along with people. Sales representatives need good, convincing communication skills, intelligence, adaptability, and an alertness to current cultural trends. They must be able to make their own appointments and set their own hours.

Textile salespeople must have integrity in order to gain and keep the trust and respect of customers. Honesty in dealing with factors of current sales (quality, dates of delivery, and price) will set the groundwork for future sales to be made. Creativity to make the best of each situation is needed. Sensitivity to respond to the views of others is necessary. Also, proper personal appearance is very important. This means being well groomed and fashionable rather than sloppy, flashy, or out of style.

Many textile salespeople work in New York City or in corporate offices near their companies' production plants. Also, regional or district sales offices are located in other major cities throughout the world. Travel is usually part of a salesperson's life since he or she must be in constant contact with customers and the market.

A sales career requires a certain amount of stamina and ability to withstand stress. Salespeople must have a strong desire to sell in this highly competitive business. Sometimes they have to work under pressure, while always keeping high enthusiasm and interest in the lines they are selling.

Sales representatives are given earnings and responsibilities in proportion to their performance on the job. For the right hardworking person, this exciting field is both personally and financially rewarding. Pay is either a flat salary or a salary plus a commission on the amount sold. There are opportunities to advance into a sales manager's job.

Sales Trainee

The entry-level job in textile sales is that of a *sales trainee*, or person learning sales work. Most are hired with a college degree, often in business administration, marketing, the sciences, or liberal arts. They have usually had courses in business, economics, and psychology. Some are textile graduates.

All textile sales personnel are given a period of training by their companies. Some training programs follow a strict schedule, while others are more casual. All of them teach sales trainees about the firms' products and production processes. They cover merchandising techniques and customer needs.

Sometimes sales trainees begin their careers as customer service representatives. Sometimes they are technical service troubleshooters who try to solve problems. This gives them maturity and time to learn about the products before they actually go out to sell them.

Sales trainees perform any duties related to the sales operation. They hang up fabric samples and keep the showroom in shape. They greet customers in the showroom and help present the line. They go out on sales calls to manufacturers with an experienced salesperson. During these calls, they carry the samples, do clerical work related to sales, and assist with the billing, shipping, and handling of orders.

Textile Sales Manager

Sales managers supervise several sales representatives. They might be in charge of the sales of a geographic district or of all the sales of a particular division of the company. They set sales quotas and guide their salespeople to achieve or surpass those quotas.

Sales managers help plan and direct the smooth flow of products from the textile plant to the customer. They must understand every step from research, through design and production, to the final customer. Most successful sales managers have a good sense of fashion and sound judgment about what customers want, as shown in **20-17**.

Sales managers must relate easily to people. They must have strong administrative abilities to achieve top sales. The job is demanding and stressful. Success in the job can lead to top management.

Sulzer Ruti, Inc.

20-17 A good sales manager takes time to meet with customers to help satisfy their important needs.

Textile sales managers should have a college degree. They may also have an advanced degree, often an MBA (master of business administration). They should have experience in sales and also understand production. They typically earn high salaries.

Textile Advertising and Promotion Specialists

Textile *advertising and promotion specialists* help boost sales by telling the firm's customers that there is something wonderful to buy. They try to create demand for their textile products. They place ads in apparel trade publications and have displays or exhibits at trade shows. They plan fashion shows or other publicity events to show garments made from the company's fabrics. They prepare instructional materials to show special sewing or handling techniques for their fabrics.

Advertising and promotion specialists must have creativity and excellent communication skills. These are needed to plan, develop, and execute campaigns that announce and encourage sales of their textile products. They must meet people easily and have a sincere interest in the company's products. They usually have a college degree in liberal arts, advertising, communications, or journalism.

Textile Administration

Administration is the overall managing of the textile company. Administrators oversee the entire operation. They organize and coordinate the development, manufacturing, and marketing of the fabrics so the company's functions run smoothly. They manage the employees in their departments. This enables the company to stay in business with a profit.

Men and women reach management positions in administration after they have acquired maturity and a thorough knowledge of all aspects of the textile business. They are the junior and senior executives all the way up to the president of the firm. See **20-18**.

Administrators must have an interest in business and commerce. They must have the ability to make sound decisions, to see how all aspects of the company fit together, and to understand how specific procedures will affect the firm.

Human Resources Manager

The human resources manager oversees the people employed by the company. He or she sees that the employees are hired, or fired, if necessary. This person also makes sure employees are paid, insured, given benefits, and given retirement compensation.

20-18 Company administrators manage the operations of companies. Each one shown here might be in a different department, such as human resources, accounting and finance, information systems, public relations, purchasing, and others.

Pressmaster/Shutterstock.com

Human resources managers must get along well with people. They should have the ability to understand employee problems and to communicate with employees in a friendly and honest manner. They may be in charge of training, work incentives, and award programs. They may work with union grievances, management development programs, insurance claims, continuing education programs, and health and safety programs.

Accounting and Finance Employees

Accounting and finance employees keep track of the funds of the company. They keep records of all the money earned and paid out. They manage the company's investments, monitor the cash flow, and deal with financial institutions, such as banks. They also supervise the company's operating statements and financial reports.

Accounting and finance jobs are great for people who enjoy routine and organized work. People in these professions often use calculators, computers, and other electronic devices. The work is very exacting. Education beyond high school is required. For more advanced jobs, a college degree in accounting, finance, or mathematics is desired.

Data Processors

In the textile industry, data processors keep track of sales, shipping, billing, inventories, employee records, and payroll through electronic systems. Data processors may also use electronic programs to monitor textile production processes and design fabrics.

Data processors have basic computer skills since they routinely type information into computers, as in **20-19**. They are sometimes high school graduates with technical school training. *Computer programmers* (also called *developers*) write program software and set up the firm's computer systems. These professionals usually have college degrees in computer science. *Computer systems administrators* keep all technology within a company in good running order. A specialized trade school education is needed for these careers, with possible repair training from the company's technology provider.

Pressmaster/Shutterstock.com

20-19 Data processors put company-specific information into computer systems for their firms.

Kiselev Andrey Valerevich/Shutterstock.com

20-20 Business operations specialists make important decisions about production and sales forecasting that affect their companies' bottom lines.

Other Administrative Employees

Many other positions in the administration of textile firms are similar in titles and duties to those in other industries. For instance, *office managers* supervise the sales offices or plant sites around the country. They manage equipment and supplies, negotiate with vendors, oversee the company cars, and so on.

Business operations specialists gather data on the company's operations, as in **20-20**. After analyzing the information, they make recommendations of action to the company's management to meet business goals.

Public relations specialists tell the company's story. They promote the positive attributes of the company and, if necessary, explain negatives to employees, customers, the community, and the government. They write press releases, schedule speaking engagements, plan publicity events, manage business contacts, respond to consumer concerns, and try to diffuse potential conflicts.

Purchasing agents are buyers of goods and services. They may specialize in buying fibers to be made into fabrics. They may be in charge of buying chemicals, dyes, and equipment. They may also buy office equipment, vehicles, machinery, parts, and other materials used by the textile manufacturer. They try to get the

best value for each dollar spent. They must be organized, tough, and good with numbers.

Transportation managers plan, direct, and coordinate the incoming and outgoing shipments of goods for their companies. They dispatch trucks, route goods on trains and planes, and track all shipments. See **20-21**. If necessary, they resolve delivery problems or arrival disputes.

Upper-level executives oversee various aspects of businesses. In different companies, their titles are *director* or *vice president*. For instance, the *Vice President of Sales* oversees all sales procedures, representatives, and managers. The *Director* or *Vice President* of Finance supervises the budget, income, and spending of the firm, including managing credit and collections, paying bills and wages, and getting loans if needed. The *VP/Director of Operations* oversees the physical buildings and grounds, security, and movement of goods. The *Information Technology (IT) Director* oversees all computer operations, including data processing, evaluation and purchases of electronic systems, and company website design and maintenance. Upper-level executives are also the bosses of marketing, human resources, and other areas of businesses.

Textile Careers

Career Cluster	Sample Occupations	
Agriculture, Food & Natural Resources	• Quality Control Inspector	
Arts, A/V Technology & Communications	• Computer Programmer • Computer Technician • Information Technology (IT) Director	• Public Relations Specialist • Textile Designer • Textile Stylist
Business, Management & Administration	• Accounting and Finance Employees • Business Operations Specialist • Data Processor • Human Resources Director • Office Manager • Public Relations Specialist	• Purchasing Agent • Textile Administration • Textile Advertising and Promotion Agent • Textile Sales Manager
Finance	• Accountant • Director or Vice President of Finance • Financial Analyst	
Information Technology	• Computer Programmer • Computer Technician • Information Technology (IT) Director	
Manufacturing	• Business Operations Specialist • Director of Operations • Industrial Engineer • Machine Operator • Machine Technician	• Plant Engineer • Production Supervisor • Quality Control Inspector • Textile Stylist
Marketing	• Market Research Analyst • Marketing Director • Public Relations Specialist • Purchasing Agent • Quality Control Inspector • Sales Trainee	• Textile Advertising and Promotion Agent • Textile Sales Manager • Textile Sales Representative • Vice President of Sales
Science, Technology, Engineering & Mathematics	• Industrial Engineer • Machine Technician • Plant Engineer • Quality Control Inspector • Textile Colorist	• Textile Converter • Textile Laboratory Technician • Textile Research Scientist • Textile Tester
Transportation, Distribution & Logistics	• Business Operations Specialist • Transportation Manager	

NOTE: *Occupations may link to additional career clusters.*

The Career Clusters icons are being used with permission of the States' Career Clusters Initiative.
www.careertech.org

Christian Lagerek/Shutterstock.com

20-21 Transportation managers determine the tactics and strategies for timely product delivery, such as the goods in these shipping containers. They must be very detail oriented.

surface and structural patterns or redesign existing ones for the making of fabrics. Textile colorists develop fashion color design combinations electronically or with paints on paper. Textile stylists have responsibility for entire fabric lines from the beginning stages to completion. Assistant stylists handle details for textile stylists.

Production at textile mills involves the largest single portion of textile industry employees. Textile converters decide how various amounts of fabrics should be dyed, printed, or otherwise finished for end-use demand. Assistant converters keep accurate production and inventory records and handle many clerical duties for textile converters. Production supervisors coordinate and direct the various mill departments to maintain the highest production and the best quality. Machine operators do the manufacturing procedures. Quality control inspectors analyze the quality of the products as they go through manufacturing. Machine technicians keep the complex equipment in good working order. Plant engineers make sure all environmental systems are operating properly, and industrial engineers are cost and efficiency experts.

Textile marketing finds or creates markets for the textile products. Market research analysts study consumer tastes and changing trends. Sales representatives sell the firm's products to customers. Sales trainees are learning sales work. Textile sales managers supervise several sales representatives in a geographic district or a division of the company. Textile advertising and promotion specialists try to create demand for their firm's textile products through advertising, trade show exhibits, special events, and instructional materials.

Textile administration is the overall managing of the company. Accounting and finance employees keep track of the funds of the company. Data processors record sales, shipping, billing, inventories, employee records, and payroll on computers. Other administrators include office managers, business operations specialists, public relations specialists, and purchasing agents. Upper-level executives are directors or vice presidents who oversee specific segments of their company.

Summary

Millions of people work in the textile industry, in many locations and with good pay and fringe benefits. Textile research and development provides knowledge, develops new products, and improves old products. Research scientists develop new synthetic fibers, blend fibers in new and better ways, work on different fabric constructions, and create finishes for better fabric performance. Textile laboratory technicians help research scientists by setting up equipment, writing computations, and helping to categorize and analyze experiment results.

Textile design employees should have a fine sense of color, a creative imagination, and artistic ability. Textile designers create new

Fashion Recall

Write your answers on a separate sheet of paper.

True/False: Write *true* or *false* for each of the following statements.

1. Textile-related jobs are available at all skill levels.
2. Most textile firms run their own training programs.
3. In most industries, management personnel outnumber production workers.
4. The textile belt stretches from Texas across to California.
5. A good way for beginners to enter the field of textile design is to seek freelance jobs.
6. Fabric designs are usually directed toward a specific end use or market.
7. The position of textile colorist is often an entry-level job for graduates of college or trade school textile design programs.
8. A textile stylist is responsible for determining the proper look, or overall concept, of the company's fabric line.
9. Textile design involves the largest single portion of textile industry employees.
10. Market research analysts study consumer tastes and changing trends.

Multiple Choice: Write the letter of the best response to each of the following statements.

11. R and D stands for _____.
    A. review and decide
    B. recycle and deliver
    C. recolor and design
    D. research and development

12. Textile converters mainly _____.
    A. update or convert production machines so they can produce the latest textile products
    B. decide how various amounts of fabrics should be dyed, printed, or finished
    C. change old production machinery to computerized systems
    D. convert the colors of last year's textile designs to the colors of the upcoming season

13. The person who determines the most efficient method for each operation of textile production is a(n) _____.
    A. production supervisor
    B. quality control inspector
    C. plant engineer
    D. industrial engineer

Fashion Vocabulary

14. Write each of the *Fashion Terms* from the chapter opening on a separate sheet of paper. For each term, quickly write a word you think relates to the term. In small groups, exchange papers. Have each person in the group explain a term on the list. Take turns until all terms have been explained.

Critical Thinking

15. **Analyze a career**   What career in the textile industry do you find most interesting? Use the text and online resources to analyze details about this career. Write a summary explaining why this career is of interest to you, citing the text and other resources as evidence to support your analysis.

16. **Generate requirements**   Name a career within the textile industry. What are the educational requirements for that career? Use the text and online resources to research your response. Discuss your findings with the class.

17. **Evaluate jobs**   Using the content in this chapter, evaluate opportunities for acquiring an entry-level job in the textile industry. Write a summary of your evaluation to post to the class website for peer and instructor review.

Core Skills

18. **Research and writing**   Make a list of the colleges and technical or trade schools near you that offer training for the careers described in this chapter. Obtain a catalog from one or more of the schools, or review an online catalog. Write a short report explaining the specific courses that are required to graduate in a particular textile-related curriculum.

19. **Research**   Use online resources to examine textile job opportunities advertised in your area. Use one or more references from the U.S. Department of Labor to investigate the education, training, or skills required. What are the responsibilities of the positions? What is the job outlook for these positions? Do the ads mention salaries? How do these compare to salary potentials listed on the government sites? Use presentation software to report your findings to the class.

20. **Speaking**   Choose a specific textile product, such as a certain fiber or a fabric with a particular look or end use. Give a sales presentation to the class that includes textile samples and garments, or pictures to support your message. Organize your thoughts to speak knowledgeably about the positive aspects of and uses for your textile line.

21. **Technology**   Create a textile design using a CAD fabric design program, or download a free program or application that enables you to create designs using your computer or other digital device. Write a report describing the program you used and critique its ease of use.

22. **Design a poster**   Go to the website of the American Association of Textile Chemists and Colorists (AATCC) and click on the *Students* tab and review the "Awards & Competitions" requirements page. Create your own textile design using past C2C competition winner's projects as a guide. Use a school-approved application to create your poster and upload it to the class website for peer and instructor review.

23. **CTE career readiness practice**   Suppose you are a manager who works for a textile design and manufacturing firm. Your firm is looking to hire a textile colorist. Write a job description for this position you can use for an online job board. Use the text and U.S. Department of Labor resources to help guide your description. Then, post your description to the job board (the class website).

Fashion in Action

24. **Portfolio builder**   Pick a specific job in the textile industry that interests you. Study it further and prepare a written report about the job. Include the qualifications needed to get the job, the type of company that might hire you, and the tasks you would perform. Estimate the salary range and fringe benefits you could expect. Determine the possible opportunities for advancement. Add this information to your portfolio.

25. **Design activity**   Imagine you are a textile designer. Sketch one design motif for a certain type of garment. First, list several ideas to help shape your design. Then, make rough sketches of your ideas. Finally, develop your best idea into a finished design. Find a fabric swatch with the texture you want. Use paints or felt-tip pens to show the desired colors. Assemble your papers from each step of the designing process in a booklet.

Self-Assessment Quiz ↗

Complete the self-assessment quiz online to help practice and expand your knowledge and skills.

CHAPTER 21

Careers in Apparel Design and Production

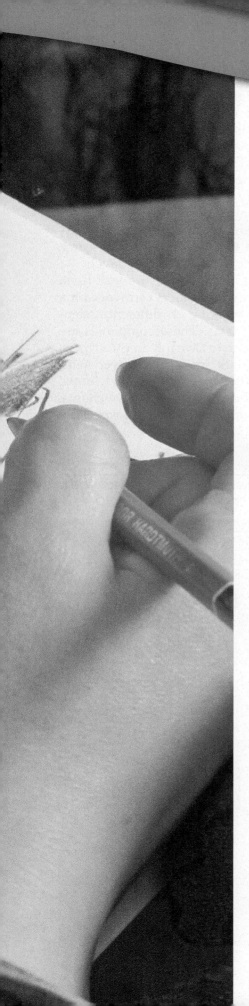

fashion designers
sample maker
value added
pattern maker
pattern graders
assorters
alteration hands

product manager
plant manager
piece goods buyers
costing engineers
distribution
showroom
　salesperson

outside sales
　representatives
　(reps)
jobbers
CEO (chief
　executive officer)
division director

Objectives

After studying this chapter, you will be able to
➤ describe the work of a fashion designer and the qualifications needed for that career.
➤ discuss the many types of jobs in apparel manufacturing.
➤ explain production management careers.
➤ identify positions in sales and distribution of manufactured apparel merchandise.
➤ name top management and administration jobs and their responsibilities.

Apparel production is the making of fabric into clothing. It is a major industry worldwide. Manufacturing jobs enable new apparel designs to be produced in large quantities and sold to retailers. Many workers are needed with different skills to perform all of these tasks.

Apparel Design

Apparel design is the field of creating new fashionable garments and accessories with customer appeal. New ideas are needed to make the items original and different from others. The success of a manufacturer's business depends on its designs selling well in the marketplace. See **21-1**.

© Lilly Pulitzer

21-1 Jane Schoenborn is now the design talent for the Lilly Pulitzer label. She has continued the same look of Florida colors and cheerful designs as the firm's founder, who retired and sold the business.

Fashion Designer

Fashion designers (also called *apparel designers*) create new ideas for garments and accessories. They try to design functional and beautiful items that will be at the leading edge of fashion when produced. Designers might specialize in men's, women's, or children's wear. They might concentrate on even more specific areas, such as swimwear, bridal attire, shoes, lingerie, or evening dresses, as in **21-2**.

Couture designers usually create two major collections each year. Large U.S. manufacturing firms may have four or five seasonal lines a year. Most lines contain 40 to 75 items.

The greatest number of design employees work for manufacturers that mass-produce lower-priced items. These *design stylists, sketchers/stylists,* or *copyists* seldom originate ideas. Instead, they adapt current higher-priced designs to meet their customers' price ranges. They may select the fabrics, coordinate the lines, and oversee other details. They receive lower salaries and less prestige than designers of high-end lines. However, these entry-level jobs are often available to gain experience in the industry.

Moderately priced apparel is usually produced by medium-sized manufacturers with one or more designers. Each designer has an assistant or a design room staff. Most of these designers are not well known, because their names are not publicized or sewn into their creations. They are still important employees in their firms, however.

Very high-priced and exclusive apparel firms employ only the most talented designers. These opportunities are limited, and competition is great. A designer must be recognized as gifted in the field to land one of these scarce positions. Salaries can be high at this level.

Most fashion design jobs are full-time. However, experienced designers can work on a freelance basis by working on different assignments for several firms. These companies are usually not big enough to have full-time designers. Also, a few designers are self-employed with their own labels. They may hire sewers to make the items they sell directly to exclusive clients. Others sell their creations through specialty boutiques.

21-2 Most fashion designers concentrate on a specific type of clothing, such as evening dresses.

Fashion Institute of Technology

Apparel designers work in cities that are fashion centers. Over one-half of U.S. designers work in the fast-moving fashion scene of New York City. Most of the rest are in Los Angeles, San Francisco, Chicago, Atlanta, Dallas, Miami, St. Louis, Kansas City, Minneapolis, and Cleveland.

The Work of a Fashion Designer

The idea is the first step in creating an apparel design. Many designers are inspired by swatches of fabrics and information from forecasting services and textile firms. Others find new fashion ideas by doing research about vintage fashions in museums, art galleries, and libraries. Some ideas even come from world events, from nature, or by observing people on the streets of fashion-forward cities. Ideas also come from movies, stage plays, TV shows, rock stars, and sports figures. Fashion designers are always searching for new ideas. They keep up with art and fashion news through various trade media and websites.

Some designers sketch their ideas by hand. There are those who prefer this method, since their creativity flows onto the paper better through their pencils or pens, as in **21-3**.

More and more designers, however, are visualizing their ideas through computer-aided design (CAD) programs. Using CAD, they can easily add more or less fullness where desired, play with colors, and add various trims for different looks. When the design is just right, it can be saved and printed digitally. The image can be enlarged and the colors altered, if needed.

Several rough sketches (called *croquis*), and later completed drawings, are done to show the details of a new design. The croquis and drawings indicate the types of fabrics, trims, construction details, and color combinations the designer has in mind.

The sketched or computer-generated designs are shown to top management for approval. When approved, each design can be made into a paper pattern or draped onto a dressmaker's form, usually in muslin fabric. The muslin outline and markings can also turn into the pattern. The pattern is then cut and sewn. Further details are worked out, and the *prototype* is altered as needed. At this point, the item is made with the chosen fashionable fabric. It is shown to top management again and becomes a *sample* for merchandisers and salespeople to view and discuss. If the sample is approved and included in the line, it will be shown to buyers. Some of the equipment used by fashion designers is shown in **21-4**.

Designers must plan and supervise the work of their staff members. In a large firm, they might have one or more assistant designers and sketchers, as well as several sample hands. They work with buyers and fabric salespeople in addition to management, production, and publicity teams.

21-3 Some fashion designers express their creative talent best by drawing directly on paper, rather than by using technology.

21-4 Basic equipment used by fashion designers helps them work accurately and efficiently.

Designers select fabrics and trims, and they help with the costing of their garment designs. They work with production and marketing people. They present their ideas and samples to salespeople and clients at meetings. Designers often work long hours and have hectic days, especially when a line is being finished for a showing. The work might be intense and tiring, but it can be very rewarding.

One personal reward of design work is the opportunity to express creativity. Another is the pride felt when the products of that creativity are accepted, purchased, and worn by other people.

The financial rewards of a design career vary greatly. Experience, talent, the company size, and its market and location are all factors. Salaries are very high for successful top designers.

Qualifications to Be a Fashion Designer

Fashion designers must be imaginative and have a flair for clothing. They should love fashion, fabrics, and style. They must be creative artists who can draw the human form. A strong sense of color, line, texture, balance, and proportion is necessary. Designers must be able to generate a constant flow of ideas. Successful designers are aware of changing social and economic trends, so their designs meet the public's demands. Some of this fashion awareness, or flair, is natural aptitude. The rest is gained through experience and education, as in **21-5**.

Fashion designers must understand the technical aspects of fabrics, trimmings, and fit. Also important are technical skills in pattern making, draping, and sewing. Designers must understand manufacturing processes and garment costing. Understanding their firm's production capabilities, budget, and marketing plans is essential. They must be able to visualize the finished garment before it is made. The job requires patience, since design specifications (specs) often have to be revised.

Designers should be enthusiastic, determined, and ambitious to succeed in this demanding career. They need to be able to work easily and comfortably with others. Flexibility and cooperation are extremely important, especially in a busy and crowded design room. However, designers must also be decisive and believe firmly in their own creativity. They

Dept. of Consumer Studies, University of Delaware

21-5 Fashion design students learn about how well-known designers have achieved their success and fame.

must be able to think on their feet and sell their design ideas to others.

To be an apparel designer, a degree in fashion design is needed from a college or technical trade school. These programs include courses in the history of costume, drawing, pattern making, draping, CAD, and sewing. Programs also cover fabrics and trimmings, the elements and principles of design, and the production and costing of garments. Some schools have study tours or student exchange programs in the United States or abroad. The industry is international in scope and highly computerized. Higher education and developed creativity enable higher success.

Assistant Designer

Designers usually serve apprenticeships as *assistant designers* first. This provides entry-level, on-the-job training in the business. A great deal can be learned while working for experienced designers.

An assistant designer might start by following through on a designer's sketched idea. This can involve CAD work, draping, pattern making, sample cutting, or sample making, as in **21-6**. Clerical duties might involve keeping records of fabric, notions, and trim purchases. Assistants may also make appointments, answer the phone, and run errands for designers.

Fashionware Technologies Corp.

21-6 Assistant designers help fashion designers with whatever needs to be done, such as CAD work, draping designs onto mannequins, making patterns, and cutting and making samples.

Later, assistant designers may help the designer select fabrics and trimmings. They might visit retail stores and fashion shows to keep up on new trends. They must follow precise directions and work well with many people, sometimes under pressure, and often in cramped design rooms. Eventually, they are asked to contribute their own original ideas.

It is important for an assistant to establish a reputation as a good designer. Then he or she can either move up in the firm, or get a job as a higher-level designer with a different firm. Designers tend to change companies often. There is little job security for those who have not become highly recognized.

Opportunities for assistant designers exist in ready-to-wear manufacturing firms or pattern companies in large cities. Sometimes assistant designer positions are available as internships during college, or as part of work-based learning programs. When applying, present a neat portfolio with your own best designs.

Sketching Employees

Exclusive fashion houses sometimes employ *sketchers*. Sketchers create illustration-quality renderings of a designer's ideas, often from fabric draped on dressmaker's forms. They might use CAD programs or draw freehand. The work of sketchers can also include meeting customers, doing promotion work, and assisting with presentations of new collections.

Sketching assistants are hired by large manufacturing firms and pattern companies, mainly to record designs. They illustrate the fashion designers' rough sketches in precise, technical detail, as in **21-7**. Their drawings point out all construction and design features and add fashion touches. They draw a season's line of samples to be kept with the company records. The assistants *swatch* the renderings by attaching samples of the actual fabrics and trimmings. They also fill out a spec sheet of construction details for each item.

Sketching jobs may include a fair amount of clerical work. Technical ability is more important than creativity. These jobs are good for people who can draw precise and accurate accounts of other people's ideas at a fast pace.

Sketchers and sketching assistants need professional training and education in fashion design after high school. The programs of study should be strong in the areas of art, design, textiles, and sewing construction. Sketchers should also study draping and pattern making to move up into fashion design jobs.

Sketchers compete for a limited number of jobs. Hours are often long and irregular. Salaries are generally low. However, good experience is gained, along with learning about how important design houses or manufacturing firms operate. Also, good contacts can be made for other positions in the industry.

These jobs require outstanding sketching skills and a very high level of fashion sense. When applying, a portfolio of fashion sketches must be presented to the employer. Candidates must look fashionable and be extremely well groomed. They should be articulate, poised, and interact well with high-level executives.

21-7 A sketching assistant must be able to include all the details of an outfit in a fashion drawing.

makar/Shutterstock.com

Sample Maker

A sample maker (also called a *sample hand*) sews sample garments together to make the designer's vision a reality. The sample maker proceeds according to the designer's pattern, sketch, and specs. He or she does all the required machine stitching and hand sewing. This tests the designer's pattern in the chosen fabric. The garment is then put onto a dress form, as in **21-8**, and changes or refinements may be made. Later the sample garment may be worn by a fitting model and shown to management.

Sample hands must be skilled in all construction techniques and be able to turn someone else's ideas into garments. In many cases, a factory sewing machine operator has moved up to this position due to skill, hard work, and good attitude. Sometimes he or she has taken technical trade school courses in apparel construction.

21-8 A sample garment is sewn, taken apart if needed, and refitted until it is just right.

Sample making is exacting work. The pay is modest to good. It is higher than those of most other sewing machine operators in the factory. Someone who does outstanding work and pursues more education could move up to assistant designer.

Apparel Manufacturing

Apparel manufacturing is the production of large quantities of garments. Ready-to-wear apparel is mass-produced along factory assembly lines. Most producers specialize in one type of apparel.

Apparel manufacturing is *labor intensive*, requiring many workers. However, worldwide competition encourages fast, flexible, and accurate high-tech production. Older methods are being replaced, and trained workers with specialized computer knowledge are hired. The trend is toward fewer workers with higher skill levels to operate more advanced technologies.

Apparel production plants are located in small towns and large cities in the United States and in almost every country. Some American apparel manufacturers cut garments in the United States and then ship them to lower-wage countries for sewing. Other U.S. companies develop the design and construction specs of garments and have all cutting and production done overseas. The finished garments are shipped to the United States, and the apparel firms sell the garments to their retail accounts.

When garments re-enter the U.S. after being manufactured in another country, *duties* (taxes on incoming goods) are paid to the U.S. government only for the *value added*. Value added is the increase in the worth of products as a direct result of a particular work activity. In this case, it is the value of only the work (such as sewing) that was done outside the country, not the full value of the garments. For example, if the cut, fabric parts of a dress are worth $20 when they are shipped out of the country, and the wholesale worth of each sewn dress is $30 when it comes back into the U.S., the value added while it was out of the country is the difference, or $10 per dress. The original $20 of value is already credited to the U.S. apparel firm.

Pattern Maker

A pattern maker translates an apparel design into the pattern pieces used for mass production. The pattern maker cuts a set of heavy manila paper or fiberboard pattern pieces for each part of the garment, as in **21-9**. Every detail of the final design is included in this master pattern. It is made in the basic size the manufacturer uses for sample garments.

Pattern makers must make patterns that keep fabric yardage to a minimum. They must be as efficient and precise as possible. They produce the shape, size, and number of pattern pieces needed to make the garment.

Most apparel manufacturers now make their patterns using technology. The pattern maker selects the right garment parts needed from the multitude of choices offered in a software program. The software program combines those choices and shows a picture of the finished garment. The design can still be changed at this point. If no more changes are desired, the software program makes the garment's master pattern. However, some feel the flair and judgment of a skilled pattern maker cannot be duplicated by a machine.

Pattern makers need a good background in fitting, flat pattern making, draping, design, and fabrics. They must understand body proportions and work well with others. They should have at least two years in a technical trade school studying pattern-making technology. These programs offer courses in industrial draping, pattern making, and pattern grading. They also cover the pricing of garments, apparel production processes (construction), and textile science. After learning pattern-making skills, students receive training on pattern-making technology.

Pattern makers are hired by apparel manufacturers. The pay for experienced pattern makers is quite good. Assistant pattern makers learn the trade by working closely with experienced pattern makers after finishing their education. Those who are trained to use pattern-making technology equipment may earn even higher pay.

Pattern Grader

Working from the master pattern, pattern graders cut patterns in all of the different sizes produced by the manufacturer. By enlarging or reducing the pattern within a figure-type category, all the pattern pieces of the design are made for each size to be manufactured. For instance, the same dress may be produced in misses' sizes 6 to 20. The exact additions or deletions must be graded in the right places to give the same effect as the original design in all sizes.

Pattern grading is highly technical and precise work. It must be done neatly and often at a fast pace, under the pressure of production schedules. Pattern makers, or their assistants, often do the grading of the patterns they make. Almost all large manufacturers use technology to do the grading work quickly. However, some believe that to keep a design's intended look and feel, the artistry of the pattern grader is needed.

Pattern graders need skills in drafting, pattern making, and clothing construction. These skills are obtained from at least two years of training at a fashion or technical school. Full-time positions for pattern graders are mainly found with sizeable manufacturers in large cities.

Marker Makers

Marker makers are the employees who figure out how the pattern pieces can be placed most efficiently on fabric for cutting. They trace the pattern pieces onto a long sheet of paper in the

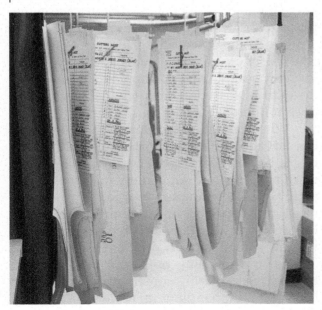

21-9 A set of heavy manila paper patterns is made for each garment design. Here, several are hanging with work-order sheets attached.

tightest possible layout, called a *marker*. In the ready-to-wear manufacturing industry, almost no fabric is wasted. Computerized plants have systems that do this electronically.

Spreader

Spreaders lay out the chosen fabric for cutting. They guide bolts of fabric back and forth on a machine that spreads the fabric smooth and straight, layer upon layer. The marker is laid across the top of the layered fabric. In the past, this job required no higher education, since the skills were learned at the plant. However, with electronic equipment, technical training is needed to operate the systems. This job is done by cutters in small plants with fewer employees.

Cutter

Cutters use power saws or electric cutting machines to carefully cut around the pattern pieces. They cut through all layers in the stack of fabric, which is often many inches thick. Sometimes they use knives. Shears may be used for just a few layers.

Some firms may use jets of water or laser beams for cutting out garment parts quickly and accurately. Plants with the latest technology do computer cutting, without needing a paper marker on the top of the fabric stack. In such a case, the layout arrangement and pattern piece outlines are in the memory of the computer, as shown in **21-10**.

Cutters who use power saws or electric cutting machines need physical strength, good manual dexterity, and excellent eyesight. They must take pride in accuracy. They often have some technical training, but actually learn the skills on the job from experienced cutters. However, as plants increase computerized functions, more employees trained in those technologies are needed. These employees need education in computer operations and programming, combined with apparel production technology.

Assorter

Assorters (also called *assemblers*) prepare the many fabric cutout parts for sewing, if the progressive bundle system is being used. Assorters sort the garment parts and mark any construction details. They tie the pieces into bundles of 12, according to color and size,

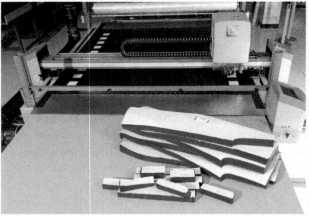

Gerber Technology, Inc.

21-10 After an operator puts the proper information into the computer system, this equipment does garment cutting automatically.

before the bundles go to the sewing machine operators. Later in the production process, assorters bring parts together, such as shirts with their corresponding collars and pockets. Some assorters may also fold and package items after they are finished.

Factories that are mechanized with computer-aided manufacturing (CAM) do not need as many assorters. They have overhead carriers that automatically take garment parts through the operation.

Sewing Machine Operator

Sewing machine operators construct apparel on heavy, fast, industrial-power sewing machines. Large numbers of operators work in rows in the factory. For low- and medium-priced ready-to-wear lines, the operators perform just one specific task over and over again. Certain operators sew only seams. Others just put in zippers. Then the work is passed on to another operator who does a different task.

When operators develop more skills, they can advance to more complicated jobs. They might be moved to specialized double-needle machines or power embroidery machines. They might also be promoted to a job as a sample hand, an inspector, or a training supervisor. Modular work groups also require operators who are skilled in many different sewing tasks.

Sewing machine operators need a basic knowledge of sewing construction. They must be skilled in handling materials and using equipment, as in **21-11**. They must have good finger dexterity, coordination, and eyesight. They must be able to do neat, steady, and accurate work at a fast pace in a compact work area. Operators should enjoy doing routine tasks and not be affected by the loud noise of many machines.

Sewing machine operators usually work regular weekday hours. Their work can be tiring due to the rapid pace. Some are paid on a piecework basis. This encourages faster work, because the more pieces they finish, the higher their paychecks. The most complicated procedures, which require more skill, receive a higher rate of piecework pay. Operators' earnings compare to those of office support workers, but may not be as high as factory jobs in other industries. However, pay scales are increasing with the higher skills needed to match the latest industry technologies. Also, sewing machine operators often belong to employee unions.

A high school diploma is needed to be a sewing machine operator. Technical schools offer training on power-driven industrial machines. Manufacturing companies give on-the-job training in the specific construction techniques for their garments, as in **21-12**. Robotics operations are being perfected to automate more sewing functions. This may replace some operators, but will never replace them all, because fashions always change.

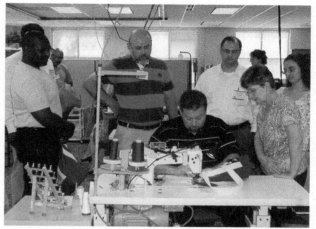

21-12 Training is being given at an apparel industry educational facility, so industry employees can learn effective sewing procedures.

Finisher

Finishers are employed mainly by better-quality, higher-priced lines. They hand sew whatever is required to finish garments. They may specialize in one technique, such as attaching fasteners, adding trimmings, putting in hems, or securing linings. There are few opportunities, but the hourly pay may be higher than that of a machine operator.

Hand finishers must have the ability to do rapid, accurate hand sewing. They need to have good eyesight and manual dexterity. No higher education beyond high school is required.

Trimmer and Inspector

Trimmers and *inspectors* are sometimes called *cleaners* and *examiners*. Trimmers cut off loose threads and pull out any basting stitches. They also remove lint and spots from finished apparel items. Inspectors examine unfinished garment parts during production, as well as finished garments. They check for construction flaws and imperfections. They remove any garments that do not meet the company's quality standards. They try to prevent items from being labeled as seconds or imperfects, which would have to be sold cheaply or thrown out.

The jobs of trimmer and inspector are combined in small factories. These employees arrange for minor repairs, or send the garments to alteration hands in the factory who correct the defects or mistakes.

21-11 Dexterity and skill are needed to operate the many varieties of industrial sewing machines.

Alteration Hand

Alteration hands repair garment defects that happen during factory production. They must be able to skillfully perform all basic construction techniques. Experience in clothing construction is needed to perform this job well and prevent waste. If a garment cannot be restored to first quality, it is marked as a second. Only items that cannot be repaired are thrown out.

Presser

Pressers flatten seams, iron garment surfaces, and shape garments with steam pressing machines, as shown in 21-13. Pressing is done during construction only in better garments. A final pressing is given to garments in all price ranges at the end of the construction process.

Pressers need a high school diploma. Technical or trade school training is an asset. Pressers learn the specifics of the tasks on the job from a supervisor. They need a tolerance for steam and heat.

Production Management

Management jobs involve planning, organizing, coordinating, and overseeing the work of others. Managers supervise the various areas of production. They study and prepare reports, attend business meetings, and use production planning software. See 21-14. They guide people

Gerber Technology, Inc.

21-14 Computerized apparel production planning systems are used in design rooms and factories throughout the world.

and operations so the company can reach its goals. It is demanding work with good compensation.

Most managers have a college background in apparel management, apparel production, or engineering technology. Good math, communication, and problem-solving skills are needed. A combination of production, technical, administrative, and marketing knowledge is required.

A production manager may start as a management trainee. Maturity, the ability to work with varied personalities, and good organizational skills enable educated employees to advance fairly quickly.

Managers hired by large manufacturers may be transferred to several different factory locations over time. They may move several times during their careers to plants across the U.S. or in other countries. Opportunities for high-paying apparel production management careers are much greater for those willing to move wherever they are needed. A bachelor's degree in business management is necessary.

Product Manager

A product manager may be in charge of every aspect of one of the company's lines, or a specific category of garments within a line. The manager oversees the design, manufacturing, sales, and delivery of that line or category.

Product managers must keep up with the latest market trends related to their products. Before production begins, a product manager must

21-13 Steam pressing machines are made specifically for the types of garments being constructed and needing pressing.

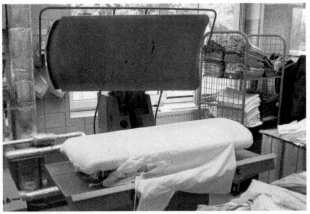

xtrekx/Shutterstock.com

decide how items coordinate with apparel produced by other firms. He or she must also make sure items fit into the company's total line. Do the colors mix and match with other clothes being sold by the company and other firms this year? Are the products related to the total line of the manufacturer, so the same production machinery can be used to manufacture them? Can similar sales methods and retail outlets be used?

Product managers study the competition. The products must be competitive to sell well and be profitable. The manager may reject a designer's idea because it is not practical or would cost too much to produce. Also, the production schedules must allow delivery dates to be met. The goods must be ready and delivered to the retailers on time. All stages of design, manufacturing, and distribution must be planned and carried out.

A product manager must be practical, organized, and good at making business decisions. He or she needs a college degree in business management. Fashion training is also helpful. Often the manager has been a successful production supervisor before being promoted to this level. This position has a good salary.

Plant Manager

The plant manager (also called *production manager*) is responsible for all operations at the plant. This person is in charge of the employees, equipment, and procedures for production. Tasks include estimating production costs, scheduling the flow of work, and hiring and training new workers. The plant manager must also oversee quality control of the products and supervise all other aspects of production.

It is a complex task to oversee the purchasing, cutting, sewing, pressing, and shipping functions. This position is achieved after many dedicated years of working as a production assistant and supervisor. The plant manager's salary is very high.

Production Assistant

Production assistants do detail work and record keeping for plant managers. They keep track of fabric, trim, and notion samples for the design room. They also assist with the production schedules and keep tabs on the flow of work in the factory. Production assistants are in charge of inventory control. They check incoming materials deliveries to the factory and outgoing merchandise shipments to customers. They must keep clients informed on the progress of orders and expedite certain deliveries.

Production assistants have an excellent overview of the entire manufacturing process. They need good math and technology skills. They must be able to communicate well with many people, especially by phone and e-mail. It is helpful to be organized, accurate, assertive, thorough, and able to tolerate stress. A college degree in apparel production management, engineering, or fashion merchandising is usually required.

Supervisors

Production supervisors oversee and direct the sewing machine operators and other workers on the factory floor or workroom. They work in the factory, solving operators' problems. They try to make sure there is a smooth flow of work for the operators at the machines. They need the ability to motivate others in order to achieve the highest quality and speed of production.

Training supervisors train new operators on specific tasks or to use specialized machines. They help all workers with procedures when needed. They must know how to do all of the sewing operations in the plant. This usually comes from experience and a technical or trade school education in apparel production.

Production supervisors and training supervisors report to the plant manager.

Piece Goods Buyer

Piece goods buyers are purchasing agents for the materials needed to produce garments. They research and buy the fabrics, trims, and notions chosen by the design staff and approved by management. They find the latest information available about textiles and trims. The buyers try to get the highest quality textile products for the lowest prices to produce the firm's lines. They also keep tabs on any production problems that might occur with the fabrics or trims.

Assistant piece goods buyers keep clear and accurate ordering and inventory records and swatch files. They assist buyers with the ordering of fabrics, trims, and notions. They follow up on materials deliveries. Sometimes they must place reorders or consider substitutions. Employees in this entry-level job often learn from buyers on visits to fabric and trim markets.

Piece goods buyers and their assistants should have an interest in, and knowledge of, fabrics. They should have good math, communication, and organizational skills. Specialized training in textiles, fashion merchandising, or apparel production management is recommended.

Industrial Engineer

Industrial engineers in the apparel manufacturing industry select the most efficient machinery and operational methods. They perform similar duties to industrial engineers in the textile industry. They find ways to cut costs and improve plant safety. They analyze techniques to use the least amount of raw materials. They work out time and motion studies to establish the piece rate pay for each sewing and production task. Industrial engineers are involved in the physical layout of the plant by designing production lines, storage areas, and workstation progression. They also do production forecasting and planning.

A college degree in industrial engineering or apparel production management is needed for this position. Manufacturers usually supplement that education with their own training programs.

Costing Engineer

Costing engineers determine the overall price of producing each apparel item. This includes the cost of fabrics and notions, the pay for each construction operation, and all other production fees. They price each separate design in an upcoming line. They may have to travel to various plants to view production operations and consult with plant managers. They sometimes have *costing clerks* who assist them by noting and analyzing the figures on spec sheets.

Quality Control Engineer

Quality control engineers develop specs for items to be manufactured. They make sure that those standards of quality are met during all of the production phases. They identify quality problems and work with the production staff to correct them. They are also charged with ensuring that the materials purchased from other companies for garment construction meet their firm's quality standards. To do this, they may need to travel to many different plant locations. Quality control engineers must understand textile technology and garment construction. They must be thorough, well organized, and good with both details and follow-up.

Plant Engineer

Just as in the textile industry, apparel production factories have *plant engineers*. These people oversee the physical plants. They maintain the heating, lighting, noise reduction, and other environmental operations.

Sales and Distribution

Manufacturing firms sell their finished goods to retail stores so consumers can buy them. This is sometimes done through wholesale distributors. However, most sales are done directly from apparel manufacturers to the retailers, as in **21-15**. Sales positions offer a great variety of interesting tasks at a fast pace.

Manufacturers' sales offices and showrooms are located in fashion centers, with many in New York City. They might also be in such cities as Los Angeles, Dallas, Chicago, San Francisco,

21-15 Sales employees who work for apparel manufacturers show their company's garments to retail buyers on live models, display mannequins, hangers, and display tables.

zhu difeng/Shutterstock.com

Miami, Minneapolis, Philadelphia, and St. Louis. Some salespeople represent one large corporation with many lines. Others sell the goods of several firms.

Distribution is the process of getting the merchandise to the proper locations. For apparel, orders are fulfilled from the manufacturer to each retail store in the correct quantities of colors, sizes, and other specs.

Showroom Salesperson

A showroom salesperson has an in-house sales position at the firm's sales offices. This employee presents the line of goods to buyers who visit the manufacturer's showroom. Buyers are shown the newest styling features, fabrics, and colors that are part of the line.

Showroom salespeople get to know the buyers of their important, active accounts. They take orders and provide customer service. They sometimes suggest ways for retailers to present and display their merchandise in the stores. They may also act as a communication link between the design staff and the retail buyers.

Showroom salespeople must be friendly, outgoing, and service oriented. They must be able to communicate well and follow through on details. To do this, they must understand both the manufacturing and retailing of apparel. They must be well groomed, dress fashionably, and have poise and confidence. They must be able to react quickly to buyers' needs, and present an apparel line with flair and enthusiasm.

Hours for showroom salespeople are regular most of the time. However, during market weeks, when much of the buying for each season occurs, the hours can be long. See 21-16. It is desirable for these employees to have completed a program in fashion merchandising or business development. These programs teach techniques for showing a line, making a presentation, handling objections, and closing a sale. Previous sales experience is also beneficial.

Other Showroom Sales Employees

Being a *showroom sales trainee* is a good way to break into apparel production sales. By working with experienced salespeople, trainees learn to present the merchandise to buyers in appealing ways. They sometimes model the apparel.

Chicago Apparel Center

21-16 During market weeks, salespeople work long hours showing their lines to many prospective customers.

They must write orders accurately, as in **21-17**, and later follow up on shipments. They also work with buyers by phone and e-mail, act as receptionists, schedule appointments, and perform other clerical duties.

With experience, a trainee may advance to the position of showroom salesperson and then to *showroom manager*. The manager supervises all staff and activity in the showroom. He or she must make sure the showroom displays are attractive and changed regularly. The manager also makes sure that samples are in stock for the buyers. He or she handles any buyer issues and trains new showroom staff members. An alert showroom manager also keeps the design staff informed of market trends and buyers' feedback.

Outside Sales Representative

Outside sales representatives (reps) are the salespeople who work outside of the firm's sales office and showroom. They travel to buyers at department stores and other retailers who cannot go to the showroom.

The sales reps are given sample garments and color swatches at company sales meetings. The meetings are held at the home office several times a year before each new line is launched. The product manager shows and describes the new line's garments to the reps. The reps learn about the garments' construction, any special features, the type of care needed, and how the garments should be worn. Each item is given an order number. Any questions about the line are answered. Also, ideas are given to the reps to help them sell the line(s).

Pressmaster/Shutterstock.com

21-17 Showroom sales trainees learn how to write orders. All style numbers, colors, sizes, and other details must be checked before the items being ordered are entered into a purchase-order form via computer.

Outside sales reps sell mainly to retail buyers. A great deal of selling is done during market weeks, when retail buyers visit market centers. The reps may be responsible for planning exhibits, displays, or demonstrations to promote their lines during market weeks. At such shows, salespeople get buyers' feedback about the wants and needs of their retail companies. This information is brought back to the product managers, so production can be adjusted accordingly.

Between trade shows, sales reps keep in contact with their accounts (retail companies) and make sales appointments. They inform the buyers about recent developments, such as price changes, new styles, trends, and fabrics added to the line. They get to know the buyers well and try to expand their markets by getting new accounts. Sales reps sometimes provide displays for special product promotions. They can also give presentations about their apparel lines, or present fashion shows at stores. They take orders and follow up to make sure the delivery commitments are kept. They must also deal politely with customer complaints.

Independent sales reps often handle several different lines for many small manufacturers. These manufacturers are not large enough to have their own salespeople. Independent reps are called jobbers, if they actually buy quantities of goods directly from the manufacturers and resell them to retailers. For example, a jobber in men's apparel might sell a line with the shirts, slacks, neckties, and sweaters made by different manufacturers. Thus, the lines of the companies they represent are not in competition with each

other, but blended for more sales to the same type of retail customers.

Independent sales reps are self-employed, but have the same contacts and knowledge as the manufacturers' salespeople. They work on a commission basis. By *repping* many lines, if one is not selling well, they still get income from the others. Also, they can drop less successful lines and find replacements as needed.

An outside sales rep usually works in a certain geographical *territory*, or selling area, for the company. He or she travels within that territory, mostly by car. Most reps are away from home much of the time. They often work long and unusual hours, especially during peak times. The job is exhausting, but exciting. It is very satisfying for those who enjoy working with people as well as fashion. Financial rewards for successful reps can be great, depending on their sales numbers.

Qualifications to Be an Outside Sales Representative

Sales reps must be outgoing and likable. They should be excited about their lines and eager to sell. They must have a thorough knowledge of fashion and garments and have good sales skills. They must also be hardworking and organized, since they usually work independently.

Sales reps must be willing to work long and irregular hours. They should like to travel, rather than being in a showroom or office. They must also be willing to move to a different territory, if asked to transfer.

Sales reps must be honest to develop longstanding accounts and generate repeat orders. They must know and believe in their product lines, and be able to speak about them with confidence. They must represent their company in a professional manner, while providing their clients with good service.

Most sales reps are college graduates. They have studied such courses as textiles, economics, marketing, psychology, mathematics, merchandising, and computer science.

Sales Manager

A *sales manager* supervises several sales reps in a large firm. He or she has usually been promoted after being a successful, hardworking sales rep. The pay and prestige are high.

Market Research Employees

Market researchers (also called *market analysts*) study and analyze consumer buying habits, as well as consumer needs and wants. They spend time in the marketplace and consult with fashion resources, such as forecasters and textile manufacturers. They access market trend reports to find out what is selling now, the expected future sales, and why. They research consumer choices. In direct focus groups, they learn how long certain items are worn, where they are worn, and the preferred colors. They also study their firm's competitors. Sometimes telemarketers are hired to gain specific information.

Market researchers discuss the results of their work with product managers. They try to predict the success or failure of various fashions or apparel items. Their goal is to produce only those items that will sell well in the market.

Sometimes the person in charge of market research is called a *merchandiser*. Merchandisers determine the direction a manufacturer's seasonal line should take, based on market research. In small firms, market research is done by designers or stylists.

Market researchers and merchandisers should have a keen fashion sense and an understanding of styles, colors, and fabrics. They need self-confidence and good communication skills. They also need to understand the production process and have excellent industry contacts. Market researchers or merchandisers tend to have degrees in fashion merchandising, fashion design, or apparel production. They are analytical and organized.

Merchandise control specialists monitor sales flows of specific items in different geographic areas to predict trends and production needs. They generally chart sales electronically and analyze the figures to determine results. They might suggest that salespeople stress certain items or colors in one part of the country and different ones in other areas.

Jobs in Distribution

Many jobs in warehouse distribution earn hourly wages. Racks of garments must be moved from place to place. Finished merchandise is taken either to storage areas or to the shipping department. Then it is packed and shipped, based on orders from the sales departments.

It is important to fill orders correctly and meet delivery dates in order to satisfy retailers and their electronically. Records of the shipments are kept electronically. Garments are loaded onto trucks for delivery to stores, **21-18**.

Most of these jobs do not require education beyond high school. These workers must be accurate, detail oriented, and want to do a good job. Some of the job titles for these workers include clerk, order picker, checker, packer, and transportation specialist.

Top Management

Like other businesses, apparel manufacturing firms have several executive positions. They include members of the board of directors and the president, or CEO (chief executive officer), who runs the firm. Most firms also have several vice presidents. Each vice president is in charge of a department, such as sportswear, or a business segment, such as overseas operations. There can be several levels of top management, depending on firm size. All executives should have good problem-solving skills and the ability to communicate clearly and accurately.

Division Director

A division director supervises the product managers, plant managers, and sales managers. This person manages the design, production,

21-18 Distribution employees are needed to load finished apparel onto trucks for delivery to retailers.

and sales functions of an entire line or company division. Sometimes he or she is a vice president. In large firms, several division directors may work under one vice president.

Division directors must analyze the total scope of their assigned business and make important decisions with confidence. They must be hardworking and able to direct people with pleasant authority.

Division directors should have a college degree, possibly in business or engineering. They most likely have experience in both production and sales. A master of business administration (MBA) degree is also an asset. The salaries for division directors are high.

Administrative Employees

Positions for administrative employees in apparel manufacturing companies are similar to those described for the textile industry. Such positions are found in human resources, accounting and finance, and data processing. Those specializing in public relations are in this category as well.

Summary

Apparel design employees create the ideas for new fashionable garments and accessories. They design men's, women's, and children's wear, or specialize in such areas as swimwear, bridal attire, shoes, or evening dresses. Fashion designers get ideas from fabrics, forecasting information, art events, and world news. They must have fashion flair and knowledge of fabrics and fit. Assistant designers help fashion designers with all details, including office support work. Sketching employees record designers' ideas, or draw and sketch each season's line of samples for the company records. A sample maker sews designers' ideas into sample garments.

Apparel manufacturing is the mass production of garments. A pattern maker translates an apparel design into pattern pieces for factory production. A pattern grader cuts pattern pieces in all of the different sizes to be produced. Marker makers are employees who figure out how the pattern pieces can be placed most efficiently for cutting. Spreaders lay out bolts of fabric for cutters, who use power saws or other machines to cut around the pattern pieces. Assorters put the cutout parts into bundles or onto carriers for sewing. Sewing machine operators construct the garments on industrial sewing machines. Finishers do any needed hand sewing, and trimmers remove loose threads and basting stitches. Inspectors check for construction flaws and imperfections, and alteration hands repair defects. Finally, pressers flatten seams, iron surfaces, and shape the garments.

Production management jobs involve planning, organizing, and coordinating the work of others. Product managers oversee the design, manufacturing, selling, and delivery of a line or category of garments. Plant managers are responsible for all employees and functions at a plant site. Production assistants do detail work and record keeping for plant managers. Production supervisors oversee and direct all machine operators, while training supervisors teach specific tasks and the use of specialized machines to workers. Piece goods buyers and their assistants research and buy the fabrics, trims, and notions for apparel production. Engineering positions in the plant include industrial engineers to calculate the most efficient machinery and operational methods. Costing engineers determine the price of procuring items. Quality control engineers develop production standards, and plant engineers oversee the physical plants.

Manufactured apparel is moved to retail locations by distribution employees according to sales orders. Showroom salespeople present goods to buyers who visit manufacturers' showrooms. Other showroom sales employees are showroom sales trainees and showroom managers. Outside sales reps and jobbers go to retail locations to sell manufacturers' lines, often working long and unusual hours. A sales manager supervises the sales reps. Market research employees might be market analysts, merchandisers, or merchandise control specialists. Distribution jobs deal with getting the merchandise to the proper locations.

Top management of apparel manufacturing firms include members of the board of directors, the president or CEO, vice presidents, division directors, and others. Administrative jobs are similar to those in textile firms.

Apparel Design and Production Careers

Career Cluster	Sample Occupations	
Agriculture, Food & Natural Resources	• Assistant Piece Goods Buyer • Piece Goods Buyer	
Arts, A/V Technology & Communications	• Assistant Designer • Assorter • Couture Designer, Fashion Designer • Inspector	• Pattern Maker • Public Relations Specialist • Sketcher • Sketching Assistant
Business, Management & Administration	• Accountant • Assistant Piece Goods Buyer • Chief Executive Officer • Data Processor • Division Director • Human Resources Manager • Independent Sales Representative	• Jobber • Outside Sales Representative • Piece Goods Buyer • Product Manager • Sales Manager • Showroom Manager • Showroom Salesperson
Education & Training	• Showroom Sales Trainee • Training Supervisor	
Finance	• Accountant	
Manufacturing	• Alteration Hand • Assembly Line Worker • Assistant Designer • Assorter • Cutter • Finisher • Hand Finisher • Industrial Engineer • Inspector	• Marker Maker • Pattern Grader • Pattern Maker • Plant Engineer • Plant Manager • Presser • Production Assistant • Production Manager • Production Supervisor • Quality Control Engineer • Sample Maker • Sewer • Sewing Machine Operator • Spreader • Training Supervisor • Trimmer
Marketing	• Market Researcher • Merchandise Control Specialist • Outside Sales Representative • Piece Goods Buyer • Product Manager • Public Relations Specialist • Sales Manager • Showroom Manager • Showroom Sales Trainee • Showroom Salesperson	
Science, Technology, Engineering & Mathematics	• Accountant • Costing Engineer • Industrial Engineer	• Plant Engineer • Quality Control Engineer
Transportation, Distribution & Logistics	• Checker • Clerk • Industrial Engineer • Order Picker	• Packer • Transportation Specialist • Wholesale Distributor

NOTE: *Occupations may link to additional career clusters.*

The Career Clusters icons are being used with permission of the States' Career Clusters Initiative.
www.careertech.org

Fashion Recall

Write your answers on a separate sheet of paper.

Matching: Write the letter of the general category that matches each specific job.

1. Outside sales representative.
2. Pattern maker.
3. Sample maker.
4. Piece goods buyer.
5. Sketcher.
6. Cutter.
7. Order picker.
8. Fashion designer.
9. Plant manager.
10. Assorter.

A. apparel design
B. apparel manufacturing
C. production management
D. sales and distribution

True/False: Write *true* or *false* for each of the following statements.

11. A design stylist creates original fashions within a certain style category.
12. Assistant designers are employed by manufacturing firms and pattern companies to record designs with precise, technical illustrations.
13. Working from the master pattern, pattern graders cut patterns in all of the different sizes produced by the manufacturer.
14. Spreaders are employees who figure out how the hard paper pattern pieces can be placed most efficiently for cutting.
15. Production supervisors oversee and direct the sewing machine operators and other factory workers.
16. Costing engineers determine the overall price of producing each apparel item.
17. Salespeople who work for apparel manufacturers sell mainly to retail buyers.
18. Showroom sales trainees are also known as jobbers.
19. Most jobs in distribution do not require education beyond high school.
20. A division director tries to divide the work tasks properly among the plant workers.

Fashion Vocabulary

21. With a partner, use online resources to locate photos that depict the *Fashion Terms* on the chapter opening. Print the photos or use presentation software to show your photos to the class, describing how they depict the meaning of the terms.

Critical Thinking

22. **Analyze a career**   What career in apparel design and production do you find most interesting? Use the text and online resources to analyze details about this career. Write a summary explaining why this career is of interest to you, citing the text and other resources as evidence to support your analysis.

23. **Outline requirements**   Name a career within the apparel design and production industry. What are the educational requirements for that career? Use the text and online resources to research your response. Discuss your findings with the class.

24. **Evaluate jobs**   Compare opportunities for acquiring an entry-level job in the apparel design and production industry. Write a summary of your evaluation to post to the class website for peer and instructor review.

Core Skills

25. **Writing** Use a school-approved infographic application to design a digital poster display to show the wide range of career possibilities in apparel design and production. Upload your completed poster to the class website for peer and instructor review.

26. **Research and speaking** Research apparel design and production jobs that people held during the Industrial Revolution. How do they compare to apparel design and production jobs of today? Give an illustrated oral report to share your findings with the class.

27. **Writing** Study the job listings in your local newspaper or online to find out about apparel production jobs. Prepare an informational brochure describing careers available in apparel design and production.

28. **Research and speaking** Cut out a picture of a garment from a magazine, catalog, or advertisement, or print it from a website. Using presentation software, identify the production workers who probably contributed to its creation and completion. Briefly describe the ways in which each person contributed. Share your presentation with the class.

29. **Technology** Design an apparel item using a school-approved CAD program or other drawing application. Present your design to the class. Explain how you used the elements and principles of design in creating the garment.

30. **CTE career readiness practice** Obtain a copy of a career search book (such as the latest edition of *What Color Is Your Parachute?*). Read the book. Then, write a book report identifying the important guidelines for finding meaningful employment. Select two topics you found most valuable that apply to apparel design and textile production, and share these topics with the class.

Fashion in Action

31. **Portfolio builder** Pick a specific job in the apparel manufacturing industry of interest to you. Study it further in the library, with materials from your guidance counselor, by talking to people who are in that field, and on the Internet. Prepare a written report about the job. Include the qualifications you would need to get the job, the type of company that might hire you, and the tasks you would perform. Estimate the salary range and fringe benefits you could expect. Determine the possible opportunities for advancement. Add this information to your portfolio.

32. **Design activity** Clip or print fashion drawings (not photos) of three different garments from newspapers, catalogs, or websites. Imagine you are a design stylist. Trace each of the drawings and show any changes you would make to lower their production costs. What seams or trims would you change to eliminate some sewing procedures? Mount the fashion drawings and your new designs on paper. In an oral report, describe the changes you made. Cite the text and other resources as evidence to support your change.

Self-Assessment Quiz ↗

Complete the self-assessment quiz online to help practice and expand your knowledge and skills.

Fashion Merchandising and Other Retail Industry Careers

While studying, look for the activity icon **to:**

- **practice** key fashion terms with e-flash cards, vocabulary games, and matching activities
- **assess** what you learn by completing self-assessment quizzes

www.g-wlearning.com/clothingandfashion/

G-WLEARNING.com

Fashion Terms ⮕

Chapter 11
  bankruptcy
retail buyers
vendors
executive trainees
retail salesperson
commission

customer service
  representative
comparison shoppers
personal shopper
stock clerk
head of stock

checkout cashier
merchandise
  manager
fashion coordinator
store manager
branch coordinator

Objectives

After studying this chapter, you will be able to
➤ list the career opportunities in fashion merchandising and retailing.
➤ describe the work of a retail buyer and the qualifications needed for that career.
➤ explain the duties of persons involved with direct selling and other store operations.
➤ distinguish between the management positions of merchandise manager, fashion coordinator, store manager, and branch coordinator.

As described earlier, the giant field of *fashion merchandising* involves all of the functions of planning, buying, and selling apparel items. Figure **22-1** gives an overview of merchandising. Large numbers of merchandising jobs exist in the retail industry, which sells goods to individual consumers in exchange for money or credit. Stores do this through direct selling. The indirect selling part of merchandising is promotion, which includes advertising and publicity. Those careers will be discussed in the next chapter.

Many career opportunities exist in the retail industry. People who are interested in textiles and fashion, and who understand the

22-1 All segments of the textile and apparel industries involve merchandising. However, merchandising functions are the primary focus of the retail industry. Work in apparel retailing is often referred to as *fashion merchandising*.

needs and wants of consumers, are the most likely to succeed. Employees plan the merchandise that will sell the best. Then they buy it from manufacturers or other wholesale sources and promote and sell it to consumers. They must keep a steady flow of merchandise going through their stores as efficiently and profitably as possible.

Retail Job Generalities

Jobs in retailing are found in all geographic locations. Opportunities exist in large and small department stores, chain stores, discount stores, variety stores, and specialty shops. They are also in mail-order houses, online retail firms, manufacturers' outlet stores, and some home-based businesses.

Retailing went through a period of fast growth in the late 1900s. Many types of stores, mail-order businesses, and shopping malls prospered and expanded. However, in the early 2000s, the U.S. economy slowed. At the same time, the industry became oversaturated with too many retailers. Some retailers had to file for Chapter 11 bankruptcy protection. In other words, their debts and management were restructured so they could try to regain their strength. Other retailers went out of business.

Now the industry is experiencing a reduction to fewer, but larger, retail companies. Some retail companies have bought other retailers, causing this consolidation in the industry. Also, new technology has automated many

retail tasks. For these reasons, the growth of traditional retail jobs has slowed, and different types of retail jobs have been created. People without any experience must be willing to start at the bottom. Those with education and training can move up quickly and to higher level jobs. The opportunities for advancement are good for talented, hardworking people.

Retailing jobs are varied and have different degrees of responsibility. The division of job duties varies among different retailers. Employees buy merchandise and work with stock. Others promote goods, sell merchandise, and oversee safety and security systems. Still others design catalogs, websites, and stores, as in **22-2**.

In small shops, many retail duties are combined. A single owner or employee may do all of the planning, buying, receiving, pricing, advertising, displaying, and selling. He or she may also keep accounts and inventory records.

In large stores or chains, specialized tasks are assigned to many different employees. There are also executive and supervisory opportunities, since people are needed to direct the work. Most large retailing firms offer executive training programs for those with college degrees in retail management or merchandising. Some of the best career opportunities are with discount chains and mass merchandisers, although many college graduates prefer jobs with upscale fashion stores.

As a general rule, people with jobs in retail merchandising and retailing work long hours. However, these jobs also come with job benefits and other rewards. Pay is competitive and employees usually receive discounts on personal

22-2 Retailing offers career opportunities for people with many different talents and interests, including storefront and layout design.

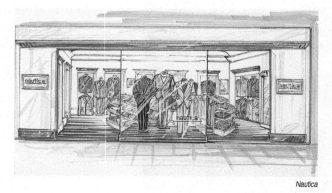

Nautica

purchases. Some employees experience adventure and recognition, and many see the direct results of their efforts. Often those in retailing get caught up in the excitement of the work and would be unhappy doing anything else.

Qualifications for Retail Work

To succeed in retailing, workers need to be well organized. They should handle figures and details well and be able to move and think quickly. Energy and stamina are essential. They must work well with customers, value cultural diversity, and work well under stress. Workers with good leadership abilities and self-confidence can advance to higher positions. Also, having excellent grooming and a sense of fashion are important.

Someone preparing for a professional career should consider a two- or four-year program in fashion merchandising or retailing. Courses include fashion marketing, sales promotion, fashion buying, merchandise math, and consumer motivation. Other subjects studied are merchandise planning, retail operations, business law, computer science, and small store management. Knowledge of textiles, garment construction, advertising, economics, accounting (as in **22-3**), and psychology are valuable for anyone in retailing. Many colleges offer work-based learning programs. Students alternate on-the-job, retail work experience with their academic studies.

Experience in any retail store is valuable and transferable. Summer or part-time work in sales, even as a teen, gives a person a taste of this industry and puts experience on a résumé.

Once people have training in retailing procedures, they can switch from one retail company to another in any part of the country. They may work in mail-order, online, or in their own retail business.

Those who want to pursue retail careers should heed one warning. Anyone with a record of shoplifting or employee theft will have a hard time finding work. See **22-4**. Such information is noted by the security departments of retail organizations. It is kept for many years and checked when employment applications are reviewed. Anyone whose name is on file is considered to be a security risk.

Merchandise Planning and Buying

Planning and buying are key activities of fashion merchandisers. These tasks are performed by retail buyers, resident buying office buyers, buying assistants, and executive trainees in all retail business formats.

22-4 Shoplifting and employee theft are crimes punishable by the law. People involved in such activities will be caught.

22-3 Having a sound understanding of business subjects can help a person move up in the retail industry. Important knowledge includes accounting principles and the ability to read and analyze financial spreadsheets.

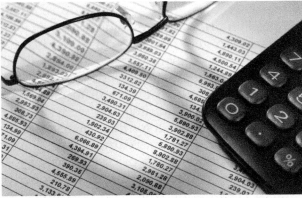
Olivier Le Queinec/Shutterstock.com

Sensormatic

Retail Buyer

Retail buyers are merchandising employees who select and purchase goods for their companies to sell. See **22-5**. Their goal is to make a profit for the company when the goods are sold, so good decision making is important. Retail buyers must estimate future demand for the merchandise they buy. The two main types of retail buyers are departmental and classification buyers.

Departmental buyers work in traditional department stores. They plan and purchase all the goods for their own departments. They manage their inventory, pricing, and promotions. They are accountable for sales and profits. They serve as *department managers*, overseeing the salespeople in their departments. This position only exists in small companies these days.

Classification buyers are more common today. They are central buyers who specialize in only one category of goods, such as infant sleepwear or men's casual trousers. They do all the buying of that category for a retail company. Larger retail organizations have centralized buying procedures, plus sophisticated systems to distribute items to their many stores. This type of buying is also done by mail-order and online retailers.

Classification buyers work at a central office, often at the corporation's headquarters. They visit major markets, locate new and exciting sources of merchandise, make selections, and place orders. They reorder the goods that sell well. They are not responsible for publicizing or selling the merchandise.

Planning the merchandise involves determining quantities for various styles, colors, sizes, prices, and fashion emphasis. This must be done within a certain budget. Timing is also important. For quick and profitable sales, merchandise must be in stores when consumer demand is high. The store image, as well as activities of competitors, must be watched.

To purchase goods, buyers must locate reliable sources, called vendors. They visit these suppliers' or manufacturers' showrooms to view and select items, and to negotiate prices and delivery dates. Buyers *go to market* several times a year in New York, Los Angeles, Chicago, or other cities. They might also travel to such places as Europe, Asia, or South America to find interesting new items at good prices. Sometimes a resident buyer from the market city may accompany a retail buyer to see goods of manufacturers and wholesalers at the market center. Other times sales representatives call on buyers at their stores or offices.

Before merchandise is ordered, buyers estimate how much of it can be sold from their stores, catalogs, or websites. To make accurate estimates, buyers look at different factors. These include current fashion trends and past sales records. They also examine the characteristics of their customers—age and socioeconomic level, for example. Buyers are aided by electronic data processing equipment that collects ongoing sales data. Knowing how fast particular products are selling helps buyers decide when and how much of it to reorder. Competition drives buyers to do their best job. They strive to generate more sales than competing retailers. They also try to surpass their own records from previous years.

Buyers ensure that orders from manufacturers are delivered on time and ready to sell. They authorize payment for the merchandise or issue instructions for its return if it is defective. Buyers decide what prices to charge for different items and see that prices are properly marked. They decide when and how much to

22-5 Retail buyers purchase merchandise for their departments and work with store employees. They also spend many hours in their offices taking care of important details.

In Cooperation with The Fashion Shop

reduce the price of goods that are not selling well. They also help promote, display, and advertise the merchandise.

Buyers instruct the retail salespeople about new merchandise at meetings. They train employees in the most effective sales techniques. They supervise the handling of complaints about the merchandise. Sometimes they can be found on selling floors doing direct selling, as in **22-6**. This helps them keep in touch with the views of customers.

The role of retail buyers has changed. Merchandise is now often reordered from manufacturers automatically using electronic data interchange linkages. Also, more private-label merchandise is sold by retailers. Therefore, buyers spend less time doing direct selling. Instead, they do more long-range market planning and help develop the specifications of items to be produced. They also consult with the primary sources of merchandise, which sometimes requires international travel.

Buyers' Schedules and Benefits

Buyers put in long, irregular hours. Besides their long work days, they may work some weekends and holidays. However, there are many job perks. For example, a buyer may have opportunities to travel to the fashion centers of the world. Also, a buyer can feel enormous

satisfaction when a retailer sells hundreds of items he or she helped to develop or bought on a hunch. There are also fringe benefits, such as discounts on personal merchandise purchases, paid vacation time, and group insurance.

Buyers are paid monthly salaries rather than hourly wages. As they prove their abilities and assume more responsibilities, their salaries increase. The pay also depends on the size and type of retailer for which the buyer works. However, most buyers will say that someone should not enter this field for the paycheck alone. He or she must love this competitive, stimulating, exacting work making fashion decisions. Top-level buyers develop an enormous range of contacts with fashion writers, manufacturers, fabric houses, designers, and buying offices. A retail company usually picks its top executives from the best buyers.

Qualifications to Be a Buyer

Buyers need fashion sense and good taste to anticipate what styles and prices will be accepted by their customers. They must keep abreast of fashion trends to know when something has reached its peak and is starting to lose popularity. They should be able to generate original ideas about promoting and selling merchandise. In their personal appearance, they also need to show good grooming and flair. They must always be attractively and appropriately dressed.

Buyers need technical knowledge about the merchandise, as well as a keen business sense. They must be creative and able to organize their work and that of others. It helps to be outgoing and self-confident. They must make sure staff members work together as a cooperative team. They must also have patience and tact to deal with customers and manufacturers' representatives.

It is often said that buyers need strong feet and a sense of humor. They do need good emotional and physical health and lots of energy. Buyers must be enthusiastic and dedicated to their work. They must remain unruffled when working closely with many people under pressure. They must be fascinated with the business of planning, buying, and selling. People who like this work would be bored in many other types of jobs.

22-6 Retail buyers sometimes work directly with customers in a store, to hear their thoughts and see their reactions to available merchandise. Buyers also like to get ideas for future items that should be ordered to satisfy customer desires.

Monkey Business Images/Shutterstock.com

Buyers must be good with figures and details to compute ongoing sales, margins, markdowns, and inventories. They must have computer skills, as in **22-7**, and the ability to interpret trends indicated in computer-generated reports. They need mature judgment and the ability to respect other people's opinions and points of view. They must be able to take and give directions clearly, respect authority, and demand respect.

To become a buyer, it is best to have a college degree in merchandising, fashion, or business. Experience, talent, and hard work are also prerequisites. Most buyers are former assistant buyers. Some were fashion editors for magazines before going into retail work. Some had responsible jobs with fabric or apparel manufacturers.

Assistant Retail Buyer

Assistant retail buyers help buyers with many different tasks. They help present the merchandise and promotions to the selling staff at sales meetings. They help supervise the sales and stock staffs. They record the sales for the week. They keep track of garments in each style in the department or at all branch stores. With that information, they coordinate transfers of merchandise when needed. They help trace items during shipment, return unsatisfactory items to vendors, and place reorders. They keep the books for the buyer and keep track of items ordered, prices, style numbers, and items sold. They help the buyer stay within budget.

As assistant buyers gain experience, they can identify merchandise that sells well—either in their department or in a particular classification. They learn about profitable price ranges. They accept responsibility in the buyer's absence. At other times, they go to market with the buyer to help select merchandise. In this way, they learn the buying techniques and manufacturing sources of their type of apparel.

Assistant buyers also help with the displays and advertising for merchandise. They get samples from the manufacturers ahead of time so they can help prepare copy for ads. They continually check ads to see that their products are presented accurately and with the proper mood and image.

Assistant buyers must be organized and carry out jobs accurately and quickly. They must communicate well, get along with all kinds of people, and remain calm under pressure.

An assistant buyer is usually a college graduate who has completed an executive training program. Someone with less education must have successful sales and stock experience, plus enthusiasm and initiative. An assistant buyer's salary is fair to good.

Resident Buying Office (RBO) Buyer

Resident buying office (RBO) buyers help the buyers from their member retail companies do a better job of buying. They research wholesale markets and report on trends through written fashion news bulletins, as in **22-8**. They arrange appointments and recommend suppliers. They get samples for retail buyers to help them make buying decisions. Sometimes they go with out-of-town buyers into the market. If requested, they make their own buying decisions for their customer retailers. They follow up on deliveries, adjustments, and complaints about merchandise. They also place reorders. They sometimes present *merchandise clinics*, or previews of items from leading vendors. See **22-9**.

RBO buyers should have excellent communication skills. They must multitask under pressure. They must possess a highly developed sense of fashion, both personally and professionally. These buyers usually work regular

22-7 Almost all jobs in retailing and other fashion careers require good computer skills. Merchandise buying careers require computer use.

yuri4u80/Shutterstock.com

22-8 Resident buying offices send bulletins to their retail clients about fashion looks in the marketplace. RBO buyers must know the availability and sources of these and similar garments and accessories in the wholesale market.

weekday office hours, with longer days during market weeks. Their offices are located in New York City, Los Angeles, and other fashion centers. Assistant buyers may be hired to help the buyer and to do follow-up tasks.

22-9 RBO buyers need knowledge of the apparel and retail industries. These jobs go to talented graduates of related college programs.

Iowa State University / AESHM Department

Executive Trainee

Executive trainees, also called *management trainees*, receive on-the-job training for potential buyer and management positions. They are interviewed and selected carefully by retail managers. They are almost always college graduates. Some may have completed two-year retailing or fashion programs in technical trade schools.

To be considered for executive training, candidates need intelligence, leadership abilities, maturity, initiative, and alertness. Applicants must be serious about their choice of retailing as a career. The final selections of executive trainees are usually made by a committee of the retailer's top managers.

The executive trainee program acquaints participants with all aspects of merchandising and develops their management skills. They learn about the company's branches, selling departments, and nonselling jobs. Executive trainees spend months in training, learning the business from the ground up. They usually start out selling in a retail department or store. They rotate through every type of department at a fast pace. This acquaints them with the operations and customers of every department. They also do a stint in the stockroom, as in **22-10**, and study the retailer's promotional techniques. Usually they take a trip to the market with buyers and present their own merchandising promotions to encourage retail sales.

22-10 Executive trainees learn about all aspects of retail operations, including warehouse operations.

Monkey Business Images/Shutterstock.com

Executive trainees must be able to take constructive criticism and withstand stress. They should be goal oriented, decisive, and self-confident. They must be enthusiastic, flexible, energetic, and not easily discouraged. They must look like professional fashion experts. They should be able to work with all of the retailer's employees. They should be available for evening, weekend, and holiday work.

An executive training position is salaried. However, the salary is low during the training period. An executive trainee who meets the retailer's high standards of performance may emerge from the program as head of stock or assistant buyer. In several more years, he or she could become a buyer or move into the ranks of management.

Direct Selling

The greatest number of employees in most retail companies are involved with direct selling. They either work under departmental merchandise buyers or branch or chain store managers.

Retail Salesperson

A retail salesperson, or *sales associate*, deals directly with customers. This is often a job for someone just starting out in retailing. It can be a stepping-stone to a higher-level merchandising job. However, a person may spend his or her entire career as a sales associate.

Retail salespeople are valuable employees. They meet the public and represent the retailer. They project the company's image to the outside world. They help customers find what they want.

To help shoppers make selections, sales associates must know every aspect of the merchandise in their department or store. They should be able to show, explain, and recommend merchandise in enticing ways. Top salespeople can answer every question about the goods, as in **22-11**.

Salespeople must make sure all merchandise stays in good condition. Displays must be replenished as merchandise is sold. Salespeople may assist in stock counts and suggest reorders of fast-selling items. Most retailers use electronic checkout systems. Salespeople scan or type in a product code from a merchandise tag. The code is converted into electronic signals that

In Cooperation with J⁰S. A. Bank

22-11 In some stores, the store manager also sells to customers and knows all the specifics about each piece of merchandise.

can be read by a computer. The computer looks up the item's price and computes the sales tax and total. At the same time, the item is subtracted from the retailer's inventory records. Salespeople who work for small retailers may still write out sales slips and compute sales tax.

Salespeople handle payments, such as cash, checks, debit cards, credit cards, and gift cards, according to store policy. They must be able to make change accurately and package purchases neatly. They may also have to accept returns and refund money.

Retail sales work can be physically tiring, with much time spent standing or walking. Part-time, holiday, and summer sales work can provide good experience. For a permanent job, a high school diploma may be needed.

Retailers give in-store training to new salespeople. New employees are taught how to handle sales, exchanges, and refunds. They learn about merchandise, stock arrangements, and about dealing with customers. They learn what should and should not be said to customers. The instructional program might be short, followed by on-the-job training.

The pay for apparel sales work is generally low to medium. It may be based on an hourly wage, a commission, or on a combination of the two. If pay is based on a commission, an employee's pay is a percentage of the dollar amount of the goods he or she sells. Most salespeople work some weekends, evenings, and holidays. Longer hours may be necessary during busy times, such as the holiday season, special sales, and inventory time. A job perk for almost all salespeople is the employee discount they receive on merchandise they buy from the retailer for which they work. Other benefits for full-time employees are paid vacation time, sick days, and health insurance.

There are quite a few job opportunities in retail sales because of the rapid turnover of employees. Jobs are available in every city in the world. The working environment for most retail sales jobs is pleasant. Stores and offices are usually well lit, air-conditioned, and clean.

Qualifications to Be a Retail Salesperson

Salespeople should be neat and well-groomed, since they represent the retailer. They should get along with many types of people. Salespeople should be quick to understand what the customer does and does not want. They must always be courteous and pleasant.

Retail salespeople must be enthusiastic about the products they sell. They need good communication skills to describe merchandise. Basic arithmetic skills are necessary to handle payments by customers. Reliability, honesty, good health, and physical endurance are also required.

Sales work provides an excellent background for almost any higher-level job in the apparel industries. The training value of selling experience should not be underestimated. With good performance, a salesperson may advance to assistant buyer or head of stock. To move up fast, or to get into top positions, a college education is usually needed.

Other Store Operations

There are many other important jobs in retailing. For instance, people are needed to train new employees, handle customer problems, and keep tabs on the competition. Employees are needed to do stock control, customer checkout, and office work. Maintenance and security jobs are also available.

Training Supervisor

Training supervisors give orientation classes to newly hired salespeople. They also give programs that inform current salespeople about new equipment, procedures, or other matters. For example, a program may be held to educate employees about a season's new colors, styles, terms, and promotional plans. The training supervisor may work with the fashion director to present this information. Training supervisors also help plan and run classes for executive trainees.

The training supervisor position is usually only available in large retail companies. With smaller retailers, these duties are folded into the job description of another supervisor. The training supervisor job is a combination of office work, teaching, and promotional activities.

This is a salaried position with good pay. A college degree is usually required. Retail experience is a must. A training supervisor must be self-confident, organized, and businesslike. He or she must be at ease when meeting people and communicate ideas clearly.

Customer Service Representative

A customer service representative serves as an intermediary between the retailer and its customers. He or she handles customer complaints and deals with special needs, such as credit purchases, gift wrapping, special orders, or home delivery.

Customer service representatives investigate problems consumers have with the retail site or its merchandise. They try to solve problems for customers, so customers continue to like, trust, and patronize the company. Customer service representatives oversee the return of items by customers and answer general questions. They make sure that each salesperson treats shoppers of all backgrounds fairly and courteously. They take action, if needed, to protect customers from illegal business practices. They also keep records of all such dealings.

This position is usually gained after much retail experience. People with problem-solving abilities and a talent for dealing effectively with people can move into this job. Its salary is medium to high.

Alterations Expert

An *alterations expert*, or tailor, is employed by large stores that do their alteration work in-house. This person takes in, lets out, and reshapes garments that do not fit the purchasing customer properly.

An alterations expert must be proficient at all sewing procedures. Such skills are learned from high school or technical trade school courses, and from lots of sewing experience. A complete understanding of garment fit and adjustment techniques is necessary. This work can be more complicated than sewing new garments from scratch. The pay is low to medium.

Comparison Shopper

Comparison shoppers peruse the stores or retail sites that employ them, as well as competitive retailers. A *competitive retailer* carries similar merchandise and serves the same clientele.

Comparison shoppers compare the merchandise offered by competitive retailers with that of their own company or store. They note the amounts of merchandise offered. They evaluate whether or not a retailer's merchandise is up-to-date and contains a season's new items. They also look at the colors, size ranges, and prices offered.

Comparison shoppers note displays and advertisements. They buy merchandise from their company and others to evaluate sales techniques and service provided. If possible, they also study the reactions of other consumers.

Comparison shoppers collect facts that are necessary to answer customers' questions and complaints about products, prices, and services among competitive companies. They keep management informed, so problems can

be anticipated and eliminated, and good programs can be expanded.

A comparison shopper might work for one or several departments of a large store or chain. In a smaller retail outlet, he or she would work for the entire store, probably under the head of stock or assistant buyer. Sometimes this is part-time employment or a temporary job. The pay is fairly low.

There are limited positions available for comparison shoppers. They do not need higher education, but must be able to communicate clearly. They should be organized enough to evaluate their findings and reach meaningful conclusions. Some retailing experience, such as a sales background and a knowledge of merchandise value, is desired.

Personal Shopper

A *personal shopper* selects merchandise for customers. One type of personal shopper works on the staff of a retailer and receives a commission on sales. The other type has an independent business, shops many places, and charges by the hour.

Consumers who employ personal shoppers are often busy professionals or entertainers who do not have time to shop, but want to appear stylish. Sometimes personal shoppers accompany their customers throughout stores or malls. They offer fashion advice and help customers select the best items for their needs. A personal shopper may be hired to create gift packages for a customer's family or business acquaintances.

Personal shoppers must know current fashion trends and the standards of dress for various professions and lifestyles. They must be pleasant, tactful, and understanding about customers' lifestyle and budget needs. Education beyond high school may not be required. However, extensive retail experience and a flair for fashion are necessary.

Stock Clerk

Stock clerk is an entry-level position for someone without college training. They receive merchandise from delivery trucks that bring apparel to retailers. They open containers, unpack items, and compare delivery records with goods actually received.

The stock clerk checks apparel for damage or soiling. If goods are damaged or lost, a report is filed. New stock items must be entered into the records. These stock control lists are kept digitally. The increased use of computers and stockroom automation has led to fewer opportunities in this work. Stock clerk jobs are not increasing in numbers the way they once were.

Stock clerks prepare merchandise for selling. They affix price tags and place some items on hangers. The merchandise is then taken to the proper departments as needed. They update stockroom records again when goods are delivered to the sales floor. Stock clerks also place items on shelves or racks in the sales area so all displays are neatly filled, as in **22-12.**

Most retailers conduct occasional physical inventories when each item on the sales floor and in stockrooms must be counted. Stock clerks usually help count items during this time. They handle returned merchandise by sending it back to the manufacturer or repairing

it. Some of these items are returned to the sales floor at full price, and others are marked down. Records must be adjusted accordingly.

A stock clerk must always know what is on hand and where to find it. The inventory in the stockroom must be kept in the proper order. Sometimes special orders must be filled. Transfers of merchandise might be made between branches of a chain store. All movements of goods must be recorded immediately.

The job of stock clerk must be performed methodically and accurately. Merchandise must be handled carefully and quickly. There may be a lot of lifting, bending, and pushing involved. It may be physically tiring, heavy work. Those who do it must have good health, stamina, and fine eyesight.

Stock clerks usually work regular hours and receive hourly wages. The pay is not very high. However, as retail employees, stock clerks usually receive employee discounts on merchandise purchases. Other benefits for full-time workers can include paid vacation time and group insurance.

A high school diploma is usually required for this job. A stock clerk should be familiar with mathematics, typing, filing, and computer use. Companies give training in their stockroom procedures, records, and forms. Dependability, a helpful attitude, and legible handwriting all help a person do the job well.

Head of Stock

Head of stock is a job with more duties, responsibilities, and pay than that of a stock clerk. This person may be in charge of the stock for one department of a large store, an entire small store, or a catalog or online retailer. He or she may have been a stock clerk or salesperson with a proven ability to get a job done well and quickly. The head of stock works closely with buyers and assistant buyers to make sure stock is always available for customers to buy.

Heads of stock supervise and coordinate all the activities of stock clerks. They decide how inventory is stored, such as by size, color, or number. They establish procedures so that damaged or soiled goods are repaired or cleaned. They also make sure that goods returned by customers are sent back to manufacturers or put back into the system for sale.

22-12 A stock clerk must make sure all new merchandise is tagged and ready to sell. Job satisfaction is achieved when the inventory has been sent to the correct departments, ready to be sold to consumers.

Monkey Business Images/Shutterstock.com

Heads of stock help with inventory, supervise stock labeling, and process reorders. They make sure merchandise is presented to customers in an orderly, attractive way. They also update stock records, so the whereabouts of every item is known.

This is an entry-level job for a college graduate. A degree in retailing or merchandising is helpful. With experience and proven abilities, a high school graduate could move into this job.

The head of stock must be well organized and have good record-keeping skills. He or she should be tactful and able to motivate others. The head of stock must pay close attention to details. This supervisory job involves both written work and footwork.

The head of stock is salaried. The pay is fair. A store discount is an added benefit. The work might be tiring. If this person does a good job, he or she might move up to a merchandise buying job.

Checkout Cashier

A checkout cashier, as shown in 22-13, rings up customers' purchases. He or she collects and records customers' payments, and bags or wraps purchases.

A cashier is usually a high school graduate who was trained to use the checkout equipment. This might include merchandise bar code and debit/credit card scanners, an electronic cash register, a tool to remove security tags from merchandise, and other such equipment.

22-13 Checkout cashiers are important because they have direct contact with the stores' customers. They handle the merchandise and accept payment in sales transactions.

Monkey Business Images/Shutterstock.com

Since they handle money, checkout cashiers must be honest and trustworthy. They must perform their checkout duties thoroughly. They should be personable and have a pleasant appearance.

Checkout cashier jobs are available in retail stores across the country. These jobs require a great deal of standing, and the pay is quite low. However, experience as a cashier can be an asset for those who plan to move into other retail jobs.

Office Support Workers

Administrative assistants are needed for top executives of retail firms. A person in this job can develop a broad picture of a company's operations. He or she often has opportunities to meet important retailing people. The job can be a stepping-stone to a direct selling or other retail job.

Other office support positions include *billing agent*, *accountant*, and *office manager*. Resident and corporate buying offices have *buyer's office support staff* who answer telephones, reply to e-mails, schedule appointments, follow up on shipments, and do filing. They may also handle problems with late deliveries or damaged goods. Retail chains hire *distributors/planners* to keep track of thousands of units of merchandise through precise, computerized records. They allocate stock to the branches that need them.

Office support workers should be well organized and good with details. They need a good memory and the ability to communicate well in person, by phone, and electronically. For most of the jobs, an aptitude for working with figures and strong computer skills are needed. Salaries vary according to the educational level, job duties, experience, and expertise of the employee.

Maintenance Workers

Maintenance workers clean facilities on a regular basis. They may also paint and repair facilities as needed. Knowledge of carpentry and plumbing is recommended. Some workers are electricians. However, for large or specialized jobs, outside tradespeople may be hired. This work is often done at night when businesses are closed.

Security Guard

Security guards protect against shoplifters while stores are open and against break-ins when stores are closed. They also work to prevent employee theft. Security guards watch for pickpockets, vandals, and other people engaging in undesirable activities. They also handle customer safety in emergencies, such as an evacuation of a store in case of fire.

Shopping malls hire security guards to patrol the common areas. Some retail stores post security guards near doors. Others use electronic devices that activate an alarm if tags attached to store goods pass through doors. Closed-circuit television cameras and mirrors also help security workers do their jobs.

Security guards must be calm, alert, and efficient. Some wear uniforms, and others work in street clothes. They are usually trained in first-aid techniques, as well as security work.

Retail Management

Management employees, as pictured in **22-14**, are executives who oversee and coordinate the various parts of a firm. They have college educations and often advanced degrees. They are usually promoted to their jobs after being successful, hardworking employees of the company for a long time. The pay and prestige are high.

22-14 Retail management positions are filled by experienced, knowledgeable people who can plan, organize, and control a firm's operations.

Monkey Business Images/Shutterstock.com

Merchandise Manager

A merchandise manager is responsible for coordinating several departments or classifications of goods. This person supervises a group of buyers. For independent department store organizations, as in **22-15**, he or she may also oversee the fashion coordinator, sales staff, and stock workers.

Merchandise managers compete with each other for larger sales and profits. They also try to outdo their own previous sales records. To do this, they search out new and different sources of merchandise. They try to develop new areas or special selling departments. For example, merchandise managers may devise new glamorous looks or use other approaches to draw customers to their departments. They hope to make their parts of the business grow and prosper.

Merchandise managers have a great deal of responsibility. They act as consultants and teachers by sharing their knowledge and ideas with those under them. They have to organize their duties effectively and work overtime when necessary. They must gain and keep the respect of employees at all levels in the company. They need patience, diplomacy, and enthusiasm.

Being a merchandise manager is exciting, yet it demands a great deal of time and energy. Educational requirements are high. The prestige and salary are also high.

Fashion Coordinator

A fashion coordinator is sometimes called a *fashion director*. Working in a large retail business, this person makes sure that all fashion departments are updated on the latest trends. Besides advising buyers and merchandise managers about new fashions, he or she assists the promotion departments.

Fashion coordinators tie the merchandise of retail departments together to create a fashion whole. For example, when a store features a color or style of clothing, the fashion coordinator makes sure the right accessories are also available in the store. He or she sees to it that merchandise throughout the store can be coordinated into pleasing wardrobes.

Most fashion coordinators assemble and harmonize the merchandise on display. An overall look and feeling is created for each

Independent Large Store Organization

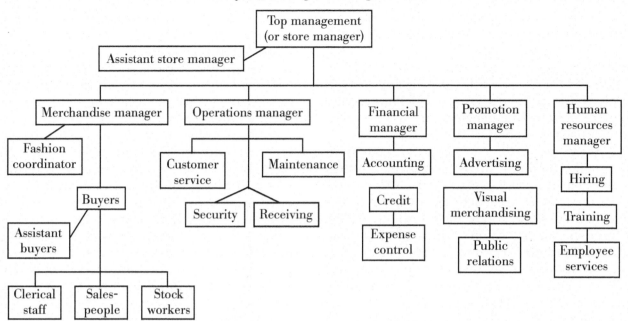

22-15 Although the organizational charts of retail companies vary, the job of merchandise manager is an executive position. He or she oversees the planning, buying, and selling of goods.

season. These themes are suggested to display managers. Fashion coordinators choose garments and accessories for window and interior displays, as in **22-16**. They work with publicity departments by informing them about new

22-16 A fashion coordinator makes sure that items and accessories available in the store are shown to shoppers by selecting compatible items for store displays.

fashion trends and products. They give direction to copywriters and illustrators and advice for radio and television commercials. Fashion coordinators use information from fashion forecasters to decide which clothes to offer consumers. They also use their own tastes, ideas, and fashion instincts. To get what they want, they sometimes make suggestions to designers or manufacturers.

When fashion shows are held, as in **22-17**, the fashion coordinator selects the models, clothing, and accessories. He or she supervises the publicity and preparations for the shows, and often fills the role of commentator. The commentator tells the audience about fashion news and gives ideas about how different fashion items can be combined.

Even before the buyers go to market, fashion coordinators monitor worldwide fashion centers to get the best advanced information. They attend trade shows to see the new fabrics and products being introduced. By studying product research and development information, fashion coordinators know about goods before they become available. They then develop buying

22-17 Fashion coordinators supervise all aspects of store-sponsored fashion shows. They give audiences tips about the latest styles, and hope they are inspired to buy items from their stores.

the24studio/Shutterstock.com

and selling strategies for each part of the total look. The fashion story must then be transmitted to the employees who buy, promote, and sell the merchandise.

A fashion coordinator teaches buyers and salespeople about new silhouettes, colors, fabrics, styles, and accessories. Sometimes talks about trends and changes in fashion are given to community groups. The job also may incorporate the duties of a training supervisor.

The job of fashion coordinator is time-consuming and demanding. It requires long hours of work, often under considerable pressure. Yet, there is stiff competition for the few positions. It is glamorous and challenging. It has an interesting variety of duties. The excitement of this job is sought after by most aspiring retail people.

Fashion coordinators have a great deal of prestige. Their salaries are high, although they vary among different types and sizes of retailers. Fashion coordinators also receive the usual company discounts and other fringe benefits.

Qualifications to Be a Fashion Coordinator

Fashion coordinators must have a highly developed fashion sense. They must be familiar with fashion cycles and with style lines that leading designers will be using. They must understand what affects consumers' acceptance or rejection of fashions and merchandise. They must know the contents of all national and international fashion magazines.

Fashion coordinators must be resourceful and flexible. For instance, they might spot an unusual scarf and visualize an entire retail display or promotion around that item. They must be aware of general social and economic trends that can impact apparel trends and consumer demand. If more consumers are dining in restaurants as opposed to eating at home, for example, they may want different types of apparel.

Fashion coordinators are expected to be at important social events attended by fashion leaders. They participate in a wide range of activities so they can better relate to how their customers live. Understanding their customers' wants and needs helps them determine what merchandise to carry.

Fashion coordinators must be tactful and schedule their time well. They must be comfortable and confident about speaking to large audiences. They must have poise and good grooming. They must adapt to many situations and make sound decisions. Good health and energy are needed. A sense of humor is a must.

Fashion coordinators should be enthusiastic, curious, and sensitive. They need imagination, creativity, and initiative. They need a background of successful retail experience. They are always selling, even at the executive level.

A sound educational background is needed to be a fashion coordinator. It is best to have a college degree. People usually work their way up to this position after having broad merchandising experience. Someone may move into this job after being an assistant fashion coordinator or a buyer.

Assistant Fashion Coordinator

An *assistant fashion coordinator* helps a fashion coordinator, mainly by taking care of details. He or she sets appointments, makes telephone and e-mail contacts, books models, and runs errands. The assistant helps put on fashion shows and helps write fashion bulletins. He or she spends time observing market trends and new looks.

Assistant fashion coordinator jobs are scarce and the competition to get them is fierce. The positions are only available in large retail firms. Excellent grooming and a keen sense of fashion are required, since the assistant must sometimes stand in for the fashion director. Poise, self-confidence, and a good speaking voice are important.

Store or Site Manager

The jobs described so far are related to merchandise. Store or site management is a different type of retail career. It falls under operations management—one of the two tracks taken by executive trainees moving into retail management positions. See each career path in **22-18**.

The store manager is often named to this position after being a successful assistant store manager or department manager. He or she is in charge of every aspect of the store's operation. The store manager oversees buying and selling activities, as well as the hiring, training, and scheduling of workers. He or she is in charge of promotional activities, financial accounts, and security. Internet-based companies would have a site manager overseeing the operations of electronic retailing.

A store or site manager must sometimes work evenings, weekends, and holidays. However, with dependable and well-trained employees, operations should run smoothly without the manager present. Large problems will still be brought to the manager to solve. Also, credit for a smoothly running operation is given to this person.

Store or site managers must have initiative, leadership abilities, and lots of energy. They should possess a good memory, clear writing, and good communication skills. They need an outgoing personality and a fashionable appearance. They must deal with many people, and should do so in a firm, yet friendly, manner. See **22-19**. They should have good fashion-business sense. They may have to relocate if transferred to business units in different geographic locations.

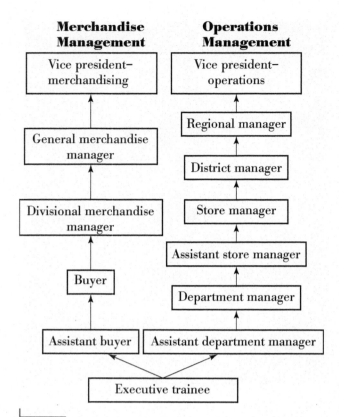

Merchandise Management / **Operations Management**

22-18 Retail managers either move up the merchandise career path or the operations track. The path they take depends on their interests, aptitudes, and skills.

Other Retail Management

The job of branch coordinator, or *district manager*, is becoming more important and more common in stores as they expand. One store might have several branches. At least one full-time employee is required to keep tabs on them all. He or she sees that there is consistency across branches in stock, selling techniques, and general operations. There must also be coordination between the branches and the main store or central office. This executive position is gained after much retail and management experience.

In centralized retail corporations, a branch coordinator might be responsible for up to a dozen stores in a geographic area. Above him or her might be a *regional manager* who oversees several districts containing a total of maybe 75 or 80 stores. Regional managers report to the highest store management executive, the *vice president of operations*.

Dragon Images/Shutterstock.com

22-19 Store or site managers must have excellent communication skills to collaborate with vendors, know the merchandise, lead employees, and assist customers.

Goodluz/Shutterstock.com

22-20 Finding, recruiting, and interviewing potential employees are just a few of the functions of the human resources manager position.

In the merchandise management track, buyers move up the track into management. These employees might be promoted to *divisional merchandise manager (DMM)*. This person supervises a group of buyers or a segment of the merchandise the company offers. The next move up would be to *general merchandise manager (GMM)*, who is responsible for the total retail merchandising of the company. The GMM reports to, or has the title of, the *vice president of merchandising*.

As in other industries, a retail *human resources manager* oversees the hiring of new employees. See **22-20**. Sometimes this person must dismiss an employee who has done an unsatisfactory job, is unreliable, or has been dishonest. The human resources manager also oversees the fringe benefit programs for employees.

The human resources manager position requires a college education in human resources, human resources administration, industrial and labor relations, or a related area. The human resources manager may not have advanced through either the merchandise or operations management chain of jobs. However, he or she knows what tasks each job entails and what qualifications a person must have to do those tasks.

All good-sized retail firms have *chief financial officers (CFOs)*. They oversee their companies' financial planning, cash flow, and accounting functions. Other retail management jobs exist in specific types of businesses. For example, a mail-order company has a *catalog manager*. He or she is in charge of photographs, copy, layout, and printing. The *distribution manager* is in charge of catalog distribution, as well as the workers who fill and ship orders and receive returns. An important executive in an Internet retailing company is the *chief information officer (CIO)*. He or she is in charge of computer operations.

Retail firms need dynamic, fashion-oriented executives. The vice presidents and president, like the salespeople, should be thrilled about selling. They must be creative and appreciate creativity in others. They must be selective and make decisions based on thorough knowledge of the latest business and fashion trends. They must know what resources are available and how to use them. They must know and understand the firm's customers, products, employees, promotional programs, and all other details.

Summary

Fashion merchandising involves the planning, buying, and selling of apparel items. Jobs are available in different types of retail businesses in all geographic locations. Being well organized and detail oriented are qualifications for retail work.

Retail buyers may do planning and buying exclusively. Departmental buyers oversee the goods for their own department, while classification buyers specialize in one category of goods for all of a company's sites. Buyers put in long, irregular hours and receive good salaries and benefits. Buyers must have fashion and business sense, as well as technical knowledge about merchandise. Assistant retail buyers help buyers with all the details of the job. Resident buying office buyers are based in market centers to help the buyers of their member retailers. Executive trainees are college graduates learning to do merchandising jobs.

The greatest number of retail employees do direct selling. Retail salespeople help customers find what they want. Retail salespeople should be neat and well-groomed and get along well with people. They should be quick to understand customer wants, and always be courteous and pleasant.

There are many other store-operations jobs. Training supervisors give orientation classes to new salespeople. Customer service representatives serve as intermediaries between the store and its customers. Alterations experts remake garments to fit customers. Comparison shoppers analyze merchandise and services of their own and competitive stores. Personal shoppers select requested merchandise for customers. Stock clerks receive, unpack, check, record, prepare, and move goods for selling. The head of stock is in charge of the stock for one department of a large store, or for an entire small store or a catalog or online retailer. Checkout cashiers ring up customer purchases, record payments, and bag items. Office support workers include administrative assistants, billing agents, accountants, office managers, buyer's office support staff, distributors/planners, and others. Additionally, maintenance workers keep company locations clean and in good repair, while security guards protect against theft and safety hazards.

Just as for other industries, managers oversee and coordinate the various parts of retail firms. Merchandise managers coordinate the business of several departments or classifications of goods. Fashion coordinators keep all fashion departments of large retail businesses updated on the latest trends. This prestigious job requires a deep understanding of fashions and consumer acceptance of products. Assistant fashion coordinators follow up on details for fashion coordinators. Store managers are in charge of every aspect of their store's operation. Other retail managers include branch coordinator, district manager, divisional and general merchandise managers, human resources managers, and specific mail-order and Internet-based company managers.

Fashion Merchandising and Other Retail Industry Careers

Career Cluster	Sample Occupations		
Architecture & Construction	• Maintenance Worker		
Arts, A/V Technology & Communications	• Assistant Fashion Coordinator • Catalog Manager	• Fashion Coordinator • Fashion Merchandiser	
Business, Management & Administration	• Accountant • Administrative Assistant • Assistant Fashion Coordinator • Assistant Retail Buyer • Billing Agent • Branch Coordinator • Classification Buyer • Customer Service Representative	• Departmental Buyer • Distributor • District Manager • Divisional Merchandise Manager • Executive Trainee • General Merchandise Manager • Management Trainee • Merchandise Manager	• Office Manager • Planner • Regional Manager • Resident Buying Office Buyer • Retail Buyer • Store Manager • Training Supervisor • Vice President of Operations
Education & Training	• Human Resources Manager • Training Supervisor		
Finance	• Chief Financial Officer		
Human Services	• Alterations Expert • Customer Service Representative • Personal Shopper		
Information Technology	• Chief Information Officer • Internet Retailers Operations Manager		
Law, Public Safety, Corrections & Security	• Security Guard		
Marketing	• Assistant Fashion Coordinator • Assistant Retail Buyer • Classification Buyer • Customer Service Representative • Departmental Buyer	• Divisional Merchandise Manager • Fashion Coordinator • Fashion Merchandiser • General Merchandise Manager • Merchandise Manager	• Personal Shopper • Planner • Resident Buying Office Buyer • Retail Buyer • Retail Salesperson • Sales Associate
Transportation, Distribution & Logistics	• Distribution Manager • Distributor		

NOTE: *Occupations may link to additional career clusters.*

The Career Clusters icons are being used with permission of the States' Career Clusters Initiative.
www.careertech.org

Fashion Recall

Write your answers on a separate sheet of paper.

True/False: Write *true* or *false* for each of the following statements.

1. Fashion merchandising is a giant field that involves all of the functions of planning, buying, and selling apparel items.

2. In direct selling, goods are sold to consumers in exchange for money or credit.

3. Retailing is currently experiencing a period of fast growth with many new companies that are prospering and expanding.

4. Retail buyers spend most of their time on the selling floor of the store to find out what consumers want.

5. The position of retail buyer is an entry-level job requiring only a high school degree.

6. A classification buyer does the buying of a specific merchandise category for all the chain stores of one particular company.

7. A customer service representative deals with special customer needs, complaints, and problems.

8. Comparison shoppers peruse the store or site that employs them, as well as those of competitive retailers.

9. A personal shopper selects merchandise for customers.

10. Maintenance workers guard against shoplifting, employee theft, and vandalism.

11. A merchandise manager is responsible for coordinating the business and functions of several departments of a store.

12. A branch coordinator updates fashion departments on the latest trends and ties the merchandise of retail departments together to create a fashion whole.

Short Answer: Write the correct response to each of the following items.

13. List five duties of retail salespeople.
14. List five duties of stock clerks.
15. List five duties of fashion coordinators.

Fashion Vocabulary

16. For each of the *Fashion Terms* on the chapter opening, identify a word or group of words describing a quality of the term—an *attribute*. Pair up with a classmate and discuss your list of attributes. Then, discuss your list of attributes with the whole class to increase understanding.

Critical Thinking

17. **Analyze a career**   What career in the fashion merchandising or other retail industry do you find most interesting? Use the text and online resources to analyze details about this career. Write a summary explaining why this career is of interest to you, citing the text and other resources as evidence to support your analysis.

18. **Outline requirements**   Name a career within fashion merchandising or other retail industry. What are the educational requirements for that career? Use the text and online resources to research your response. Discuss your findings with the class.

19. **Evaluate jobs**   Compare opportunities for acquiring an entry-level job in fashion merchandising or other areas of retailing. Write a summary of your evaluation to post to the class website for peer and instructor review.

Core Skills

20. **Speaking and listening** Interview the manager of a local retail store about how current economic factors are affecting his or her business. Share what you learn with the rest of the class in an oral report.

21. **Speaking and listening** Interview three experienced apparel sales associates from different stores. Ask what help they offer customers. How do they stay informed about the merchandise they sell? What training have they had for their jobs? Compare your findings in a class discussion.

22. **Writing** Look for local job openings in retailing by checking postings online or the classified ads in your local newspaper. Print out or clip the ads and divide them into specific job categories, such as salesperson, checkout cashier, and stock clerk. Follow up on three of the ads to find out about pay and qualifications needed to get the jobs. Compare local findings with national information from the U.S. Department of Labor or the U.S. Bureau of Labor Statistics. What are the similarities and differences? Prepare a written report about your findings to share with the class.

23. **Technology** Have class members form teams to prepare a report about upcoming fashion trends. Assign one person in each team to be the fashion coordinator for a retailer with stores around the world. Use school-approved software to hold a virtual meeting in which the coordinator describes the trends to his or her staff (other team members). Discuss the benefits of using technology to hold virtual meetings.

24. **Research and writing** Find reliable statistics on retailer losses due to shoplifting spanning the past 20 years. Using online tools, create a graph showing the year on the x-axis and the dollar amount of losses (in millions) on the y-axis. Are shoplifting losses going up or down over time?

25. **CTE career readiness practice** Imagine you are a retail buyer for a specific department of a local department store. In a written report, describe items you would buy for your department to sell. Explain why you selected those particular items. Keep a copy of this document in your portfolio to demonstrate your understanding of the duties of a retail buyer.

Fashion in Action

26. **Portfolio builder** Begin assembling your portfolio to use for work-based learning opportunities and postsecondary education applications. Choose an attractive binder or case in which to display your work. Be sure to include the following in your portfolio: letter of introduction, résumé, references, letters of recommendation, and work samples that showcase your abilities in understanding and using industry tools and communication. In addition, compile any special recognition, work experiences, awards, or honors you have received for your work or academics.

27. **Design activity** Visit the human resources office of a large department store. Ask for a list of all the different kinds of jobs in the store. Use this information and a school-approved digital application as the basis for creating a poster display. Locate digital images of people working in various positions along with text descriptions to use with your poster. Then, upload your poster to the class website for peer and instructor review.

Self-Assessment Quiz ⤴

Complete the self-assessment quiz online to help practice and expand your knowledge and skills.

Careers in Fashion Promotion

While studying, look for the activity icon to:

- **practice** key fashion terms with e-flash cards, vocabulary games, and matching activities
- **assess** what you learn by completing self-assessment quizzes

G-WLEARNING.com

www.g-wlearning.com/clothingandfashion/

Fashion Terms 👆

account executive (AE)
art director
graphic designers
advertising directors
display designer
fashion illustrators

fashion models
fashion photographers
photo stylists
fashion writers
press kits

copywriters
editors
audiovisual
publicity
public relations
   specialist

Objectives

After studying this chapter, you will be able to
➤ **discuss** careers in fashion advertising and display.
➤ **explain** the work of fashion illustrators, models, and photographers.
➤ **describe** employment in the fashion journalism and audiovisual fields.
➤ **discuss** the field of fashion publicity.

Fashion promotion is the indirect selling part of merchandising, informing all potential and current customers about new fashions and convincing them to buy. This area of employment has unlimited, diverse career possibilities. Some are glamorous and exciting. Most are creative and competitive. All are challenging.

A firm can have the best products in the world, but if they do not sell, there is no profit. Thus, a demand must be created. Indirect selling helps create demand through promotion, such as advertising and publicity. With e-mail, ads can be sent to targeted audiences.

Indirect selling is aimed at the general buying public. It does not happen one-on-one with consumers, as in retail sales. People in indirect selling jobs show, draw, model, photograph, write about, and discuss fashions to create interest in the products. Sometimes promotional activities attract people to a certain store or mall by using a band, car show, or personal appearance by a designer. Resturants and movie theaters also bring consumers to shopping areas, as in **23-1**.

23-1 Movie theaters and special attractions are often placed near or in shopping malls. This creates an upbeat feeling that encourages people to shop and enjoy themselves.

Indirect selling is done by a network of supporting businesses to the apparel industries. The network includes advertising agencies and various print and broadcast media that spread the news of fashion trends.

Fashion Advertising

People who work in advertising attract and inform audiences in the hope of selling products. To succeed, they must know the merchandise and its outlets. They need to be familiar with the best approaches to reach the target markets for different products. They formulate and follow complete advertising programs for fashion products.

Account Executive

An advertising agency employee in charge of handling specific advertising accounts is called an account executive (AE). AEs work closely with merchandising and marketing people from the businesses they represent (the agency's clients). Some ad agencies have a fashion expert or advisor on staff, while other agencies are devoted entirely to apparel industry clients. Their accounts tend to be medium to large textile or apparel manufacturers and small to medium retailers. Most large retailers have their own advertising departments.

Account executives manage entire corporate advertising campaigns. These consist of a series of ads or promotions designed to create a special impact. Usually a campaign has a theme with all advertising channels (TV, radio, print, billboard, and Internet) supporting that theme. The advertising is aimed at reaching and enticing as many customers of the manufacturing or retail business as possible.

Successful AEs continue to work with the same businesses year after year. They must be innovative and up-to-date on all the fashion news and trends for those businesses. It is important for AEs to identify the target markets and know their buying habits. AEs work with the ad agency's media buyers to place the ads for the greatest impact and potential sales.

AEs also relate their client's campaign goals to the agency's creative staff. AEs help to decide the best ways to reach those goals and stay within budget. They specify the feeling the client's advertising should evoke, and the message(s) most likely to increase sales. Then the creative staff takes over. It is the AE, however, who brings the agency's work back to the client for approval.

Art Director

Art directors decide how to present a concept visually, so that it is organized, appealing, and attention grabbing. They create the overall look and feel of campaigns. Ads might be for newspapers, magazines, direct-mail flyers, or billboards and signage, as in **23-2**. Art directors also design the look of electronic media, including radio, television, apps, or website ads. Art directors try to design the best advertising for the budget. They also design collateral materials. These include brochures, annual reports, package designs, hangtags, logos, and other corporate image projects. The collateral materials often accompany products for sale. They usually contain important information, sometimes required by law, while they catch the consumer's eye to help sell the product.

Career opportunities for fashion art directors are with ad agencies, trade magazines, and in retailers' advertising departments. Only a few art directors are employed by textile producers, apparel manufacturers, trade groups, and buying offices.

23-2 The concept for this advertisement was suggested by an art director who wanted to convey a certain message and feeling.

23-3 Audiovisual labs give students hands-on experience with equipment they might use in promotional jobs after graduation.

Graphic Designer

Graphic designers prepare sketches or layouts—by hand or digitally—to illustrate their vision for the direction given by the art director. They select colors, sound, art, photography, animation, typestyle, and other visual elements for ads and collateral materials. See **23-4**. They often come up with several different options. The best ideas are then chosen by the art director and approved by the client before a campaign is launched. Finally, the finished artwork is prepared by the graphic designer or junior members of the staff.

A graphic designer must have a degree in art or advertising design. At some colleges, a BFA degree is offered with a major in packaging

23-4 Graphic designers work with other advertising employees to create the most effective advertisements possible.

There is stiff competition in advertising design. Job titles and duties differ, depending on the size of the agency/firm, and the types of projects. Salaries, fees, or commissions vary widely. Creative work is often done under the pressure of deadlines. There may be long hours and limited vacations.

Art directors need a Bachelor of Fine Arts (BFA) degree with an advertising design major from a college or technical trade school. Courses include basic design, drawing, painting, lettering, photography, typography, advertising, and promotion. Audiovisual skills are also learned. Many schools have electronic commercial printing systems and equipment. Many also have well-equipped radio and television studio labs, as shown in **23-3**.

Studies in computer design and graphics are essential for advertising graduates, too. Digital design technology is used throughout the advertising field. All college-level art and advertising programs require students to create portfolios of their work, based on their specific majors.

design. This degree has art, design, and advertising courses. In addition, other classes are offered in packaging materials, such as glass, plastic, paper, and industrial materials.

Other Advertising Design Employees

Entry-level jobs that can lead to graphic design positions include those of layout artists and paste-up/mechanical artists. These people create the finished artwork and prepare it for reproduction. In some ad agencies, this work can be done by the same person.

Layout artists design the physical layouts for ads, usually under the supervision of a graphic designer or art director. They specify the typefaces and do comp renderings (computer depictions) and storyboards to show how the finished ads will look.

Paste-up/mechanical artists put together the elements of the layout, such as the words, line drawings, and photographs. They arrange the art and words based on direction from the graphic designer or art director. People seeking these positions should have a degree in advertising design or illustration. Their portfolios should show a high degree of precision and accuracy in layout work. They need to have the ability to work quickly under pressure to meet deadlines. They should be good at details and following instructions. They must do neat, accurate, precise, and thorough work.

Advertising Director

Advertising directors work for retail companies and publications. They oversee all the advertising activities. People with similar duties in manufacturing firms are often called *marketing specialists*.

Some advertising directors work with account executives at advertising agencies. Others supervise their companies' own ad departments. They direct the planning of advertising and promotional campaigns. This includes the preparation of print and broadcast ads, as well as the creation of sales pieces, labels, signs, and packaging.

The advertising director of a retail firm coordinates the design and distribution of all the newspaper ads, catalogs, and other direct-mail pieces. He or she also helps plan promotions,

keeps track of each buyer's advertising budget, and manages the art department. This position requires both advanced education and experience. Experience may be gained either at an ad agency or by working up through the retailer's advertising or fashion promotion departments.

The advertising director of a publication is in charge of selling and arranging ad space in that publication. He or she interacts a great deal with the media buyers and AEs at ad agencies. This person also works with the advertising directors of industry businesses (the advertisers) to coordinate their advertising in the publication.

Advertising directors must be organized in order to meet constant deadlines. They need self-confidence, persuasiveness, and the ability to communicate ideas. Other helpful traits are having a good imagination, and the ability to work well with creative people. Advertising directors originate and develop ideas that are sound and practical, yet new and unusual. They might also do market research, media analysis, and mass communications planning.

Advertising directors are usually college graduates with degrees in marketing or advertising. They have taken courses in advertising, psychology, fashion, business, marketing, writing, printing, photography, and art.

Fashion Display

A *display* is a visual presentation of merchandise. It might be in the window of a store or in an interior location, as shown in **23-5**.

Displays show customers the available merchandise and how items can be combined and accessorized. Each display should be eye-catching to encourage consumers to select and buy merchandise.

Display Director

Display directors are sometimes called *visual presentation directors*. They consult with the store buyers, public relations specialists, creative artists, and photographers to supervise displays of accessorized outfits. They prepare rough sketches, outline ideas, and make blueprints or models for the display staff to follow. They sometimes arrange for monitors to be placed in particular locations and select the videos for customers to view.

23-5 Interior and window displays for fashion items are planned and put together by display designers and directors.

The display director needs a thorough knowledge of retail markets. He or she decides which trends and items to promote in displays, and how to make them appealing.

A college degree in the visual arts is preferred for this position. Small stores and businesses with no display staff sometimes hire display agencies to do this work, when needed.

Display Designer

Display designers, sometimes called *visual display artists*, create eye-catching displays for store interiors and windows. They usually gear their work toward special events or promotional activities, as shown in **23-6**. They often emphasize seasonal and holiday themes, such as summer vacation, back-to-school, and New Year's Eve. Sometimes displays stress a new color, fashion trend, or cultural event.

Display designers must study and understand lighting techniques, accessorizing, and the use of props. They need training in design elements and principles, as well as window trimming. They must have a good imagination and be able to show their ideas with sketches

or computer renderings. Knowledge of carpentry and sewing is helpful. They should also be familiar with the related areas of photography, lettering, painting, fashion, and merchandising.

Some technical trade schools offer specific programs in display design. Education is usually followed by an apprenticeship in the actual use of lighting, mannequins, and props under a display designer or display director.

Other Fashion Promotion Careers

Other forms of promotion go hand-in-hand with advertising and display to announce and help sell the latest fashions. They include fashion illustration, modeling, photography, journalism, publicity, and audiovisual activities.

Fashion Illustrator

Fashion illustrators draw garments that have been designed and produced by others.

23-6 Designers created this special display to spotlight linen garments at a Paris festival.

Complete outfits are usually shown with fashionable accessories. Illustrators show the good points of apparel to promote and sell the fashions.

Fashion illustrators are employed mainly by retailers, pattern companies, and advertising agencies. Some are hired by fashion magazines and other publications. Design or display studios, buying offices, and textile and apparel manufacturers also use fashion illustrators.

When illustrating for a pattern company, emphasis is given to seams and to trimming details of the apparel. The intent is to give the sewer an idea of the construction required. For fashion magazines or trade publications, the illustrator might focus on the fabric textures, accessory trends, or garment features described by the fashion writers. For retail uses and in advertising, exotic background touches might be added, often by computer. Good illustrators catch the attention of viewers and invite them to buy the fashions shown.

Illustrators who work for buying offices show the latest fashions for their member retailers. Those who are employed by textile firms illustrate fashionable uses for the line of textiles. In manufacturing firms, the illustrators' drawings often record a season's line.

Competition for illustration jobs is keen. Most opportunities are located in big cities. Illustration jobs are usually paid by salary, depending on talent and the size or type of firm. The hours are usually regular.

Good illustrators who become well-known often decide to be independent freelance artists. They make this choice after having much on-the-job experience and making many good contacts. Freelance work can be more profitable than staff work. It can be more challenging and satisfying, but less steady. A freelancer may have many or few assignments and must complete them within set deadlines.

Qualifications to Be an Illustrator

Fashion illustrators must be artistic and understand fabrics and fashion. It also helps to have flair, initiative, and the ability to work rapidly under the pressure of deadlines. Illustrators remain current on art and fashion news through trade publications, magazines, websites, art and costume exhibits, fashion shows, and displays.

To succeed in this field, natural artistic talent should be refined at a college or technical trade school. In these programs, art courses concentrate on drawing the human figure, as shown in **23-7**. There is also training in advertising design, all art media, computer graphics, and the use of art studio equipment. Many students develop their own unique styles of illustration.

Fashion illustration jobs are obtained by submitting a neat portfolio with the best examples of illustrations that will interest the employer. Technical ability is often judged on the basis of portfolio presentations.

Fashion Model

Fashion models wear garments and accessories to show them to potential buyers. Modeling is a combination of the fashion, advertising, and performing worlds. Models stand, turn, and walk to demonstrate the best features of garments. Fashion shows can be at restaurants, department stores, seminars, trade shows, and conventions.

Some models show companies' lines in the showrooms of designers or manufacturing firms. This is called *mannequin work*. These models usually work full-time, regular daily hours for the firm. They receive salaries and company benefits. Extra part-time models are employed for several weeks during the retail buying seasons.

Runway work takes place in front of live audiences, as in **23-8**. These models appear in fashion shows, usually walking and turning on a runway. Some of this work is done at fashion trade shows, conventions, and luncheon events.

23-7 Students in fashion illustration courses often develop their skills by drawing live models.

1000 Words/Shutterstock.com

Gina Smith/Shutterstock.com

23-8 These models are doing runway work in a fashion show for a live audience.

Modeling clothing in front of cameras is called *photography work*. Photographic models pose for pictures used in press releases from manufacturers and other firms, as in **23-9**. These photographs might appear in fashion magazines, trade publications, newspapers, print ads, and pattern catalogs. They are also used in mail-order catalogs and direct-mail flyers, as well as on companies' websites, garment packaging, and billboards.

23-9 Photographic models have their pictures taken to show consumers the types of merchandise that an apparel firm or retailer offers.

Photographee.eu/Shutterstock.com

Modeling is competitive and demanding work. It can be glamorous. However, employment is often erratic with uncertain earnings. Runway and photographic models are paid on an hourly or daily basis. Models' incomes increase with experience and name recognition.

Many models are in their late teens and twenties, but there is a growing demand for models of all ages and body builds. Some very young models are needed to model children's clothes.

A modeling career may only last a few years, but it can be a great stepping-stone to other apparel careers. Also, part-time modeling can add to the regular income from another job.

Qualifications to Be a Model

Successful models need good health, posture, and grooming. They must have physical stamina as well as plenty of determination and patience. Employers look for models with self-confidence, poise, style, and a flair for proper movement in their clothing. A pleasant, outgoing personality is also a plus. Photographic models generally have photogenic features. Models need the ability to convey feelings, as directed, for long hours under bright lights and often in hard-to-hold poses. They must be responsive to direction and able to move with spirit and grace.

Most models have body builds that are tall, well proportioned, and long-waisted, as in **23-10**. Photos can make the figure look larger than it really is.

Models are hired by manufacturers to fit the company's clothing. The smaller sizes of a fashion line are usually modeled. Female models are usually 5'9" or taller for runway or photographic work.

Some people strive too hard to become a model because this career seems so glamorous. In reality, there is a great deal of pressure to conform to a certain physical image. To maintain optimal fitness, models need plenty of sleep, balanced meals, and regular physical activity. They must be ready for a job at any time and able to adapt to changing schedules. The career demands self-discipline and sometimes the sacrifice of personal pleasures.

Professional models often attend accredited modeling schools after high school. They learn the technical aspects of modeling, such as how

JCPenney

23-10 A long-waisted body with long legs is desirable for models to show most fashions the best.

to stand, pose, and move properly. Correct posture, speech, hairstyling, and makeup techniques are also studied. Additional training or experience in dance, drama, art, fashion design, and retail sales is helpful.

Modeling school courses, however, do not guarantee a modeling career. Many modeling schools have job placement services. Those schools are the best choices. Learn to thoroughly read and understand any job contracts before signing. Also, be prepared for some rejection, since this is a very competitive field.

Another way to get started in this career is by registering with a modeling employment agency. This requires a personal portfolio with several enlarged, unretouched photos in various poses. One should be full-length, one close-up, and one smiling. The photos should be taken by a professional, and is at the model's own expense. Agencies use an application form listing name, address, age, height without shoes, weight, and body measurements. Often modeling agencies also train models.

Most professional models are employed in major cities. Although New York City has the greatest number, models are also needed in most other cities. Large businesses almost always hire models through agencies. However, models may apply directly to advertising agencies, newspapers, retail stores, or apparel manufacturers. In each case, include portfolio photographs and a résumé with training, experience, and personal specifications.

Fashion Photographer

Fashion photographers take pictures that show fashionable clothes and accessories looking their best. They also try to express mood through the settings and compositions of their photos. They use creative props and interesting backgrounds. Photographers may take pictures of fashion apparel on live models or still shots of fashion merchandise.

When using models, a fashion photographer often tries to create more visual interest by having them appear to be in motion. The models move and pose in front of the camera while many pictures are taken. After review, the best ones are chosen for use.

Some fashion photographers shoot motion footage digitally or on film. These are used for television ads, educational purposes, and other promotions. They may be played on monitors in retail stores to update consumers and to help sell merchandise.

Photography is considered to be one of the most flexible forms of artistic expression in fashion communication. Photographers work with photo studios, advertising agencies, publications, and large retail firms. Their jobs might require travel. They may work as salaried employees or as freelancers. Only top talent receives top pay.

A fashion photographer should have an interest in all art forms, fashion trends, and people. Besides artistic talent and imagination, photographers need sound technical training. They must understand lighting techniques and how to use professional cameras and other film-related equipment, as in **23-11**. They must be able to use both black-and-white and color images effectively. Knowledge of digital photography technology and darkroom procedures is also necessary.

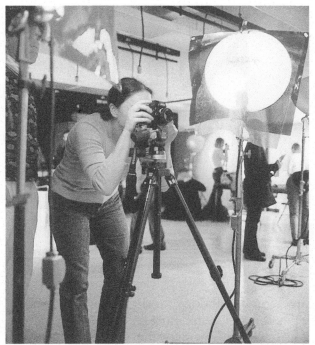

Fashion Institute of Technology

23-11 Professional photographers must know how to use many types of cameras, lighting techniques, props, and other equipment to get expert results.

Fashion photographers need technical trade or art school training after high school. They must learn the technical aspects of photography. They should also study fashion display and advertising design. A fashion photography degree is helpful, but not always required for success in the field. A portfolio must be prepared to show prospective employers the types and quality of their work.

Other Fashion Photography Employees

Assistant photographers are apprentices getting on-the-job experience under professional photographers. They test the lighting, take sample photos, and help prepare sets and props for backgrounds. They may clean the studio and make minor repairs to equipment. When they have proven their technical abilities, they also work with the digital equipment.

Photo stylists work in photography studios, in advertising agencies, or as freelancers. They book models, accessorize apparel, obtain props, pin up hems, iron garments, and pick up and return merchandise. They may work long hours during heavy work periods. They must understand both fashion and photography. They need enthusiasm, stamina, flexibility, ingenuity, a high tolerance for stress, and a strong sense of style and color.

Fashion Writer

Fashion journalists pass along textile and apparel information through the mass media. Fashion writers work mainly for newspapers and fashion magazines. Some publish books on related topics, such as wardrobe planning, personal color, or general fashion information, like this textbook.

A fashion reporter/writer for a newspaper may write a daily or weekly column, or periodic feature stories. He or she may write about fashions seen at important social and cultural events. Some fashion writers work on freelance assignments and travel where needed. For monthly magazines, full-time writers usually submit more than one article. These often include several fashion photos or illustrations.

Fashion writers plan, research, and write their assigned articles. They gather material by conducting personal interviews, making phone calls, and attending fashion events. Some fashion news items come international agencies, as well as from fashion websites. Press kits (also called *media kits*) contain promotional materials sent to the media by manufacturers and advertisers. Fashion writers often use them as sources of information. A typical press kit includes photos along with descriptions and/or short articles about a company's latest apparel.

A writer often covers a specific subject area, such as textiles, accessories, coats, knitwear, or certain designers. Sometimes the fashion writer gives technical advice to other writers, staff members, photographers, and advertising people. The writer might travel to get a firsthand look at the latest fashions during the semiannual Fashion Press Weeks. He or she must keep in touch with key people in fashion, textile production, and apparel manufacturing.

Qualifications to Be a Fashion Writer

Fashion writers must be creative. They need to write precisely while under the pressure of meeting strict deadlines. They research the latest interesting and useful information and relay it to the proper audience. The information must always be presented clearly and thoroughly.

Members of the *fashion press* have a flair for writing and a keen sense of fashion. They keep up with changes in the industry and can spot newsworthy trends or feature material. Enthusiasm is needed. Writers must be organized and work independently. They arrange and conduct interviews. Writers must be able to think and act quickly to obtain as much information as possible from each interview.

To become a fashion writer, obtain a college degree in journalism, combined with retail merchandising and apparel courses. Advertising courses are also helpful. Good computer skills are required.

When researching a career in fashion writing, read fashion publications and well-known blogs to note various writing styles. Writing samples are requested by every publication that hires fashion writers. Become familiar with the publication or website before applying for a job or submitting writing samples. Research helps to determine the required qualifications and a person's fit with the job.

Beginning salaries in fashion journalism are moderate, with higher pay for more education, experience, and writing ability. Fringe benefits vary by employer. Working hours may be irregular, depending on the deadlines and events covered. The work is exciting and offers challenges and variety. However, the competition is steep for a limited number of jobs. Most opportunities are located in large cities. Sometimes telecommuting is available.

Copywriter

Copywriters compose the messages that describe items being promoted in ads and catalogs. They write the information as text, or as blurbs that accompany photographs or illustrations. See **23-12**. *Copy* includes the words, lettering, and numbers that appear in print or electronic media.

Copywriters work for the same types of companies and ad agencies as art directors and graphic designers. In fact, copywriters work very closely with those in the art department when creating ads and other promotional materials. Industry manufacturers and retailers need compelling copy for websites, brochures,

23-12 Copywriters are needed to write the descriptions that describe merchandise in mail-order catalogs.

direct mail, catalogs, and other publications. Often, apparel items must be described precisely in as few words as possible. Copywriters work from essential information, such as garment and fabric descriptions, prices, sizes, or locations where available.

Copywriters should be creative, with the ability to quickly turn ideas into words and meet deadlines. They must be thorough, flexible, and able to spot trends and identify resources. They also need good computer skills.

A copywriter should have a college degree in advertising or journalism, with a fashion emphasis. Technical trade schools also offer training in advertising and communications. When applying for a job, a copywriter should have a portfolio with his or her best writing samples.

Editor

Editors usually supervise fashion writers and copywriters. They might be in charge of one or more departments of a publication, such as fabrics or accessories. They are administrators as well as journalists with fashion expertise. Editors set policies, make assignments, and can supervise photography sessions. They ensure that all information is correct and appealing to their readership. Eventually, they might become editor-in-chief of a fashion magazine.

The activities of fashion editors vary by publication and the importance of fashion to the readers. For large general publications, the fashion editor is assisted by a fashion staff that might include photographers, illustrators, and writers. The editor is the publication's authority on all aspects of fashion and apparel. He or she interprets fashion news, influences trends, and advises manufacturers about which fashions their readers want. Editors must have imagination, integrity, vision, and good management skills. Besides flair and proven ability, editors benefit from well-rounded social and cultural experiences. Editors need to understand business, know the apparel industries, and be willing to work hard, often on weekends. However, they enjoy high prestige and pay.

Audiovisual Jobs

Apparel-related audiovisual (AV) jobs include those in radio, television, and multimedia presentations. These jobs involve planning programs, writing scripts, getting props, and producing and/or being in the presentations. These promotions may be commercials, promotional fashion films, online videos, TV shopping programs, or entertainment talk shows with fashion themes. They could feature interviews with fashion experts or coverage of designer collection runway shows. The productions might be educational, such as consumer fashion programs or sewing shows. They could be aimed at staff training, such as instructing or updating retail store employees.

Those working in fashion AV jobs must know about fashion and its related industries. Writing, speaking, and dramatic skills are also required. They need to write descriptive, informational dialogue quickly and accurately, as well as present ideas clearly and simply. They must be confident and outgoing on screen, while appearing natural and sincere with a pleasing voice.

Being organized and staying current on fashions trends is important. There are frequent deadlines, long rehearsals, and tight and irregular schedules. Instinctive timing is necessary, as well as the ability to think and act professionally in any situation. Other important traits include poise, self-confidence, and the ability to get along with others, even under pressure.

Those who work in audiovisual jobs must also be able to constantly adapt to new technologies. AV professionals must understand digital settings and calibrations for audio and visual equipment. They often solve problems relating to production aspects and troubleshoot equipment to bring about audiovisual technology solutions.

A degree in audiovisual or communications is recommended. Courses in writing, speech, drama, and visual communications are needed. Some people enter this field after gaining fashion, advertising, or journalism expertise. Employment might be with a broadcast station, ad agency, marketing firm, video production company, or fashion website.

These competitive jobs are challenging and may include some travel. There is contact with interesting people. Every day is different. The limited positions go to those with ambition and the ability to convince others.

Fashion Publicity

Publicity is time, space, or editorial coverage given by various media because the message is newsworthy. Publicity differs from advertising, which is paid promotion. This free exposure also enhances sales appeal, just like other forms of promotion. Sometimes it is even preferable, and free publicity saves advertising budget dollars.

Public Relations Specialist

Public relations (PR) specialists, or *publicists*, tell the story of a firm, or its products or services, to various media outlets. They strive to get editorial mention and photographs in publications, plugs on broadcasts, and favorable remarks in public speeches. They speak about products at meetings, conferences, and conventions. PR specialists may plan product demonstrations and special events for their companies, such as fashion shows. They know how to get exposure by providing free products for use by schools, colleges, sports teams, and professionals. Sometimes they give training courses for retail salespeople and buyers.

PR employees prepare and send out press releases to the media, as in **23-13**. They produce and send out videos, posters, booklets, and press kits. They publish and distribute newsletters, reports, and bulletins for teachers, researchers, store buyers, students, and consumers. PR specialists also give technical advice to writers, photographers, and artists. They study the market to seek new product

dotshock/Shutterstock.com

23-13 A public relations specialist might send this photo along with supportive copy to local newspapers and websites. The press release would serve as publicity for a charity fashion event in which these community members will model.

uses. They try to present their products better than the competition and counteract any bad publicity.

Creative people are hired by public relations firms or the public relations departments of manufacturers, retail stores, and trade groups. PR specialists for fabric houses, pattern companies, sewing machine manufacturers, and other apparel-related firms travel around the country. They are always alert for opportunities to mention and promote their companies' products and receive free publicity. They also relate consumer needs and desires back to their firms.

PR specialists must have imagination and good writing skills. They must have a thorough understanding of their products and be able to anticipate and predict trends. PR specialists know how to find or create news value to promote products. They must be familiar with all types of advertising media and selling techniques.

PR specialists must be convincing, yet tactful. They should have confidence and drive and schedule their time wisely. Good public speaking skills with the ability to use visual aids is helpful. They should also enjoy some traveling.

Most public relations employees have college degrees in communications. The courses are similar to those offered in other advertising and promotion programs. A portfolio of successful publicity campaigns is needed when applying for a public relations job. Pay is high, once experience and success are achieved.

Summary

Fashion promotion helps create market demand in the buying public. Advertising tries to sell specific products by attracting and informing audiences. Account executives with advertising agencies handle specific accounts. An art director conceptualizes ads to put into various media. Graphic designers create the ads based on the ideas of the art director. Other advertising design employees include layout artists and paste-up/mechanical artists.

Fashion display is a visual presentation of merchandise. Display designers create displays based on special events, promotional activities, holidays, or seasons. Display managers often work for retail stores, planning and arranging displays showing the latest merchandise.

Other promotional careers include fashion illustrations and models. Fashion illustrators draw garments that have been designed and produced by others. Illustrators must be artistic and know about fabrics and fashions. Modeling combines fashion, advertising, and performing to show off garments. Models might do mannequin, runway, or photography work. For modeling, you need good health, grooming, posture, and appearance.

Fashion photographers take pictures that show clothes and accessories at their best. Assistant photographers do photo preparation and testing work, while photo stylists book models and gather merchandise and props for photo shoots.

Fashion writers work mainly for newspapers and fashion magazines, sometimes using press kits for information. Members of the fashion press must prepare concise, creative copy under the pressure of deadlines. Copywriters compose descriptive messages used in ads, catalogs, and other promotional materials. Editors supervise fashion writers and copywriters. Those in audiovisual communications plan programs, write scripts, get props, and produce or appear in commercials, promotional fashion videos, TV programs, or other presentations.

Fashion publicity is free promotion by the media when the information is deemed newsworthy. Public relations specialists, or publicists, strive to get comments and photos in publications, on broadcasts, and in public speeches.

Fashion Promotion Careers	
Career Cluster	**Sample Occupations**
Architecture & Construction	• Display Director • Visual Display Director
Arts, A/V Technology & Communications	• Advertising Account Executive • Advertising Director • Art Director • Assistant Photographer • Broadcast Producer • Copywriter • Display Designer • Display Director • Editor • Fashion Illustrator • Fashion Model • Fashion Photographer • Fashion Writer • Freelance Artist • Graphic Designer • Layout Artist • Mannequin Model • Multimedia Specialist • Paste-up/Mechanical Artist • Public Relations Specialist • Visual Display Artist • Visual Display Director
Business, Management & Administration	• Advertising Account Executive • Advertising Director
Marketing	• Advertising Account Executive • Advertising Director • Art Director • Copywriter • Display Director • Editor • Fashion Illustrator • Fashion Writer • Multimedia Specialist • Public Relations Specialist

NOTE: *Occupations may link to additional career clusters.*

The Career Clusters icons are being used with permission of the States' Career Clusters Initiative.
www.careertech.org

Fashion Recall

Write your answers on a separate sheet of paper.

Matching: Match the general categories to the specific job titles.

1. Account executive.
2. Graphic designer.
3. Display designer.
4. Art director.
5. Public relations specialist.

   A. fashion advertising
   B. fashion display
   C. fashion publicity

True/False: Write *true* or *false* for each of the following statements.

6. Indirect selling is aimed at the general public rather than dealing individually or personally with consumers.
7. Account executives with advertising agencies keep the financial books.
8. Advertising directors oversee all the advertising activities for their companies.
9. A display manager decides which trends and items to promote in displays and what feeling the displays should have.
10. Fashion illustrators draw garments that have been designed and produced by others.
11. Runway work is the term for modeling a manufacturer's line of clothes in a showroom.
12. Most female models are 5'9" or taller.
13. Editors compose the message that describes items promoted in ads and catalogs.
14. Audiovisual employment is involved with radio, television, and multimedia presentations.
15. Public relations specialists are constantly alert for opportunities to mention and promote their companies' products.

Fashion Vocabulary

16. Read the text passages that contain each of the *Fashion Terms* from the chapter opening. Then, write the definitions of each term in your own words. Double-check your definitions by rereading the text and using the text glossary.

Critical Thinking

17. **Analyze a career**   What career in fashion promotion do you find most interesting? Use the text and online resources to analyze details about this career. Write a summary explaining why this career is of interest to you, citing the text and other resources as evidence to support your analysis.
18. **Outline requirements**   Name a career in the fashion promotion field. What are the educational requirements for that career? Use the text and online resources to research your response. Discuss your findings with the class.
19. **Evaluate jobs**   Compare opportunities for acquiring an entry-level job in fashion promotion. Write a summary of your evaluation to post to the class website for peer and instructor review.
20. **Analyze magazines**   Study several fashion magazines. Using spreadsheet software, create a chart describing the differences between the magazines—the articles, advertising, photos, graphic design, and other elements. Determine the target audience of each.

Core Skills

21. **Reading** Read three current articles on fashion promotion from reliable sources. Write a brief summary about the content of each. As you read, remember to identify the following:

    - *Author/writer credibility.* Is the author/writer well-known? Is the author, writer, or publisher known for reliable fact-checking?
    - *Verify details.* Can you verify facts from other reliable sources?
    - *Identify bias.* Is the information presented from only one point of view? Avoid articles that lack objectivity.

    Then select the article you found most beneficial and explain why.

22. **Research and writing** Ask local modeling schools or agencies about their programs and policies. What modeling courses do they offer? Are job placement services available? As an alternative, review the websites of modeling schools or agencies about their programs. Prepare a written report about your findings to share with the class.

23. **Writing** Suppose your latest assignment as a fashion writer is to write a fashion article for a fashion blog of a newspaper or fashion magazine. Choose a new fashion or accessory item that interests you. If possible, talk with manufacturers and retailers about it or review information on the manufacturer's website. Locate available information from the library or on the Internet about its popularity. Inform your audience about it in your article, enthusiastically telling about its fashion appeal.

24. **Technology and writing** Create a sales campaign for an apparel item you created. Use a school-approved video application to develop a commercial, using words and video. Upload your video to the class website for peer and instructor review.

25. **CTE career readiness practice** The elements and principles of design can have a psychological impact on fashion and how fashions are presented through photography. Draw conclusions about how a photographer uses the elements and principles of design when photographing the latest fashions. Cite examples and locate photos that support your conclusions to share with the class.

Fashion in Action

26. **Portfolio builder** Pick a specific job in fashion promotion that interests you. Use online or print resources to learn more about the job. Prepare a written report about the job. Include the qualifications you need to get the job, the type of company that might hire you, and the tasks you would perform. Determine the possible opportunities for advancement. Add this information to your portfolio.

27. **Design activity** Design a newspaper advertisement for an apparel product that you like. Begin by gathering information about it. Clip a photograph or illustration from a magazine, newspaper, or catalog, or print one from a website. Paste it onto a piece of heavy paper or cardboard. Add lettering for headlines as well as some advertising copy. Target the ad toward a certain audience you are trying to reach.

Self-Assessment Quiz ⤴

Complete the self-assessment quiz online to help practice and expand your knowledge and skills.

Other Careers and Entrepreneurial Opportunities

While studying, look for the activity icon **to:**

- **practice** key fashion terms with e-flash cards, vocabulary games, and matching activities
- **assess** what you learn by completing self-assessment quizzes

www.g-wlearning.com/clothingandfashion/

extension agents

consumer education

home sewing industry

notions

costume curators

theatrical costuming

entrepreneurs

sole proprietorship

partnership

corporation

business plan

cottage industry

trading company

freelancing

consulting

Objectives

After studying this chapter, you will be able to

➤ **discuss** careers in the areas of education and extension.

➤ **list** and **describe** careers in the home sewing industry.

➤ **describe** the job duties of textile and clothing historians and theatrical costumers.

➤ **discuss** careers in the clothing care field.

➤ **explain** how to become an entrepreneur of an apparel-related business.

Many apparel-related careers fall outside the areas of the textile industry, apparel design and production, retailing, and fashion promotion. People with these careers have various duties and must possess a number of different personal qualifications. One of these careers may be especially suited to you.

Apparel Educators

Apparel educators are instructors of clothing and merchandising classes, extension work, and adult and consumer education courses. These educators need a thorough knowledge of apparel. Different types of teaching positions require various amounts of education and work experience.

Classroom Teacher

Classroom teachers in the apparel area of Family and Consumer Sciences (FACS) are in charge of clothing classes at the middle school and high school levels. They teach textiles, fashion, grooming, clothing selection, consumer education, apparel care, clothing careers, and sewing construction.

Teachers in technical and trade schools teach courses in commercial clothing construction, clothing alteration and repair, pattern making, modeling, art, and retailing skills. Trade school teachers also might instruct students in fashion design, illustration, apparel production, photography, and other fashion subjects.

Colleges and universities need apparel instructors and professors. These experts teach courses in textiles, apparel design, market research, merchandising, family and consumer sciences education, fashion journalism, advertising, and other areas.

Teachers are professionals who have many roles. Besides instructing classes, apparel teachers demonstrate products and procedures. They must make purchasing decisions about textbooks, sewing machines, mannequins, and other equipment and supplies. When fashion concepts are taught, they might assume the role of designer, stylist, or fashion coordinator. Teachers have the opportunity to spread knowledge and enthusiasm to others, as in **24-1**.

Teaching provides a routine with variety. The formal teaching day may end in mid-afternoon, but teachers often have to correct papers or prepare lessons during other hours. Instructional plans follow a certain master curriculum. However, as fashions change and different students enroll in the classes, the specific content of the courses vary. Teachers learn continually as they read and study to stay up-to-date. They have a fair amount of flexibility and freedom in their work. Teachers are needed in every state. They can work in small towns or large cities.

Fringe benefits for teaching jobs often include group insurance rates and retirement programs. Generous vacation times are scattered throughout the year. Teachers who are parents of school-age children have more time to spend with them.

Monkey Business Images/Shutterstock.com

24-1 Teachers share their knowledge with others in interesting, informative ways.

College instructors have shorter teaching hours, but they have other duties in professional areas. They are assigned to be advisors to certain students. Sometimes they conduct research or write for professional publications.

The salary for teachers varies depending on a person's level of education, field of study, and geographic location. However, the great amount of vacation time is a bonus. Teachers can use that time to conduct personal business, enjoy hobbies, travel, or pursue further studies.

Qualifications to Be a Classroom Teacher

Teachers must like working with people and helping them. They need good communication skills to explain facts, give directions, demonstrate procedures, answer questions, and discuss ideas. Teachers should be flexible, fair, and patient. They should be able to gracefully accept and give criticism.

Clothing teachers at middle schools and high schools need at least a bachelor's degree and a teaching license or previous work experience. Many have master's degrees. Therefore, they receive higher salaries. Teachers in technical and trade schools should have education beyond high school. However, their work experience and job expertise are very important, too. To teach at the college level, a master's degree is required. A doctorate (Ph.D.) is preferred and is rewarded with a higher salary and better opportunities for advancement.

If you think you might be interested in teaching, get involved now in school organizations such as Family, Career and Community Leaders of America (FCCLA). This group highlights career opportunities and stresses leadership. Another helpful organization might be Educators Rising. Test your teaching ability by doing volunteer work with young people. Evaluate how you feel and react in teaching-related activities.

Extension Agent

Extension agents are hired and paid by state land-grant universities under the U.S. Department of Agriculture. They serve both urban and rural areas. Among their many important duties, they teach apparel, family, and consumer subjects to groups such as 4-H clubs, community organizations, and individual families. See **24-2**. They also focus on agriculture, health, the environment, and many other issues. Extension agents work informally in communities, sometimes holding classes or workshops. They develop programs and provide research-based information to help people be better informed.

Most extension agents work at the county level. A few, including clothing specialists, work at the state or federal level. They might be on a university staff, teach college courses, and do extension work throughout their territory. Extension agents speak to groups, attend meetings, and plan and put on demonstrations. They write columns for newspapers and websites and prepare booklets and educational materials. They prepare information for radio and television programs, and they often appear on the programs. They analyze research data and report the findings. Extension agents also coordinate their work with other public agencies and spend lots of time traveling within their jurisdictions.

Extension agents' salaries vary by level, but are similar to those of teachers. Extension agents usually have longer work hours and shorter vacations than classroom teachers do. They have a great deal of freedom to plan and work on their own. They usually get deep satisfaction from working closely with the people in their communities.

Crystal Terhune, University of Maryland Extension/Jennifer Guy, photographer

24-2 One job of extension agents is to empower people to become smart consumers who make wise choices. Clothing specialists sometimes collect gowns from the community for students going to prom.

Qualifications to Be an Extension Agent

Teaching experience is excellent preparation for this work. Extension agents should be organized and efficient. They should be able to get along well with others and want to help them. However, they should also like to work independently. They must be resourceful, imaginative, and good at solving problems.

Extension agents need good communication skills to be able to present material in a clear and interesting way through all media. They should have a pleasant personality and poise in making public appearances. Extension agents must have a genuine interest in family and consumer sciences and a willingness to learn and teach.

Extension agents must have at least a bachelor's degree in family and consumer sciences, with some courses in education. Advanced degrees are needed for state and national extension careers. All extension agents need experience in the practical use of the skills they teach. They should be knowledgeable in communications, advertising, psychology, and art.

Adult Education

Adult education courses are usually held at a school or community center in the evenings or on weekends. This is because most of the people who take the courses have work or family responsibilities. Teaching these courses is often a part-time or extra job.

An apparel-related adult education teacher might instruct adults about pattern alteration, basic construction, tailoring, or sewing with new fabrics. He or she might teach clothing care, clothing repair and alteration, consumer skills, or other subjects.

Adult education teachers usually have developed the skills they teach through work experience. Some are high school or technical teachers during the regular workday.

Consumer Education

Consumer education combines teaching with business. It is a full-time professional position with manufacturing firms. It can sometimes be done part-time with retail stores. Employees who do this work are often called *educational representatives*.

Educational representatives promote their firms' products by teaching about them. They instruct dealers and consumers about sewing machines, patterns, notions, textiles, laundry equipment, or other products. They teach about their products at in-store classes and demonstrations. They give presentations at trade shows, special seminars, and other events. They are important links between their companies and consumers.

Educational representatives for manufacturers assist dealers by helping with store events. They prepare the retail staff for special sales, sewing programs, and fashion shows. They answer consumers' questions.

When they are not out in the field, educational representatives work in the consumer education offices of their firms. There they plan the informative programs that are presented around the country. They also prepare educational and promotional materials about the use and care of their products.

A consumer educator employed by a retail store might teach sewing classes to the store's clientele, as in **24-3**. For instance, specialty classes might be taught in a fabric store during the month before a major holiday. In a yarn store, one might teach knitting, crocheting, or macramé to promote the store's products. The educators often have to prepare instructional materials, make samples to show, or demonstrate the use of tools, as in **24-4**. Pay is either a flat fee per session or a percentage of the total fees collected. Sometimes the educator is given all the fees since the class brings customers into the store to buy supplies for the course.

Consumer educators should be well-groomed and well mannered. They should have poise and a pleasing voice and personality. They should be creative, have good personal taste, and cooperate well with others. They need good communication skills, self-confidence in front of large groups, and loyalty to their firms.

Earnings vary greatly for consumer educators according to job responsibilities and personal

24-3 Consumer educators at retail fabric stores hold classes to teach customers how to sew.

Monkey Business Images/Shutterstock.com

24-4 Educators are more effective if they show samples that illustrate the points they are teaching.

qualifications. A bachelor's degree in textiles and clothing, fashion, or a related field is usually needed to work for a manufacturer. A high level of skill may be the only requirement to teach at a store.

The Home Sewing Industry

Businesses in the home sewing industry sell nonindustrial sewing machines, notions, fabrics, and patterns to home sewers. Notions are useful small items sewn into or used on garments. Examples of notions are thread, zippers, buttons, snaps, ribbon, elastic, and trim. Also available for home sewers are related books, magazines, radio and television shows, and videos. Some mail-order firms cater to home sewers and professional dressmakers. They sell specialized items through magazine and Internet ads, direct-mail campaigns, and catalogs. All the businesses in the home sewing industry need fashion-oriented personnel.

Employees of commercial pattern companies design, produce, package, and sell the patterns that are purchased by home sewers. These people combine their artistic talent and technical expertise as a team to create the patterns. Many

of the job duties are similar to the related positions in apparel manufacturing and fashion promotion. The educational and staff requirements are also similar. The office staff and top management jobs for these firms have similar duties and personal qualifications, too.

Commercial Pattern Development

The marketing departments of major pattern companies collect consumer statistics. *Fashion information directors* gather and interpret the latest fashion information about silhouettes, colors, fabrics, and accessories. *Merchandising directors* determine what companies' customers will want in patterns.

With this information in hand, *designers* create fashionable garments within the many pattern categories offered, as in **24-5**. They might specialize in such design areas as dresses, sportswear, or children's patterns. *Pattern makers* create heavy paper patterns for the parts of the new designs, as shown in **24-6**. They also use technology for this work. Then *garment makers* construct the muslin prototype and fashion

24-5 Development of commercial patterns involves precise designs and drawings of each detail, such as this coat with princess seamlines.

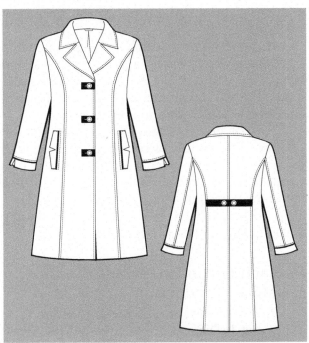

The McCall Pattern Company

24-6 Pattern makers work out every detail of each design via technology and in heavy paper pattern pieces.

fabric samples of each design. Finally, *fitting models* try on the samples to check fit, drape, and movability. They model for the design staff and members of management.

Design directors supervise the designers, pattern makers, and garment makers in producing the new pattern designs. Design directors are in charge of the initial designs. They also check the fit and approve the final garments.

Simultaneously, *fabric editors* obtain samples of the latest fabrics. They catalog, display, and supervise the samples in the company's fabric library. They also order fabrics and help *swatch* patterns for dressmaking. This means they recommend fabrics to be used for the sample of the design.

Accessory editors research and obtain the latest available styles in shoes, scarves, buttons, and belts. They organize the items in the accessories room. The accessories are used to create finished ensembles for illustration and photography.

Pattern graders make larger and smaller versions of the pattern pieces for each design, with the help of a computer. *Checkers* look over patterns to see if notches line up and if facings match necklines or other garment edges. They also check to see that other cutting and sewing markings have been properly included.

Pattern Guide Sheet and Envelope Production

Technical writers create clear sewing directions that must be easy to read and follow. These writers must have journalism skills as well as

knowledge of sewing construction, fabrics, notions, and patterns. They also need technology skills, since some standardized *how to* copy is preprogrammed. *Diagram artists* sketch the technical drawings to accompany the written directions of the guide sheet.

Illustrators make a finished fashion drawing of each design. Garments are shown in the fabric selected by the designer. The artwork appears in the company's counter catalog and on the pattern envelope. *Marker makers* calculate pattern layouts and fabric requirements for the designs. These are done with design software, and the best versions are printed on the guide sheets.

Finally, *layout designers* mount the guide sheet copy and diagrams on layout sheets for printing. See **24-7**. They also prepare the layouts for pattern envelopes. *Printing plant employees* produce the finished pattern pieces, guide sheets, and envelopes. Special machines fold the pattern pieces and insert them into the envelopes. The counter catalogs are also printed and bound at the printing plant.

Pattern Sales and Promotion

Sales and promotion employees include home office and field staff members who call on accounts in geographic territories. *Retail coordinators* are fashion and promotional liaisons between pattern companies and retail fabric

24-7 The finished pattern envelope is shown here in the upper left. The guide sheet is in the lower left, with technical sketches and written instructions. A pattern piece is along the right side.

stores. They provide the retail stores with promotional help. *Educational representatives* prepare educational materials and teaching aids such as booklets, posters, and videos. They respond to e-mails and phone questions from people using the company's patterns. They must have top construction skills to be able to answer customers' questions about sewing problems.

Fabric Sales

Salespeople in fabric stores, as shown in **24-8**, have similar duties to other retail salespeople. However, they must have a thorough understanding of fibers, fabric construction, finishes, care of textiles, and sewing procedures. They must be able to interpret information from pattern envelopes in order to advise customers. Today, some fabric stores are placing more emphasis on home decorating fabrics than apparel fabrics.

Online fabric sales personnel work at central website offices and warehouses of their companies. They do not deal face-to-face with customers since all sales are made digitally. Some employees may give advice via chat rooms. Others buy and stock quantities of fabrics. These fabrics must be added to the website for sale. Sometimes online fabric sales personnel cut swatches and prepare periodic mailings to send to certain customers. They may also send out e-mails about special deals. Employees do website setup and updating, and create design advertisements to put onto other websites and into sewing publications.

Fabric website personnel measure and cut the fabrics that are ordered. They also fill orders for patterns, notions, and sewing tools, and then ship the items to the customers. They receive merchandise returns from customers who are not satisfied. Fabric website personnel must be organized and good with details.

Video Demonstration Work

Home sewing videos are available with information on wardrobe planning, pattern alterations, and sewing techniques. Some give step-by-step directions in various sewing procedures for particular fabrics, garments, or notions. They go into more detail than most pattern guide sheet instructions. Some videos demonstrate beginning sewing skills. Others give instruction in advanced techniques and tailoring.

Sewing videos offer flexibility of use. Viewers can watch them whenever they have time. They also have the option of stopping and reviewing portions when needed.

Videos may be offered for rent or purchase through fabric stores, mail-order firms, schools, 4-H groups, or extension agents. Some can be viewed in retail stores or online.

To create videos, preproduction planning is very important. The right equipment and supplies must be on hand. Knowledge and experience in electronics and communications are needed. The demonstrators must be experts in the subjects being discussed. They should seem pleasant and fashionable. They also need self-confidence and good communication skills.

Textile and Clothing Historians

Fabrics and apparel of the past represent the living patterns of people long ago. Such antique textiles and clothing give a special richness to the fine art collections of museums and libraries.

Costume curators as well as historians, scientists, and conservators work with fabrics and apparel of the past. They locate, identify, and determine the ages of textiles, apparel, and accessories from past cultures. Scanning electron microscopes are often used to determine the age and condition of fibers and stitching threads.

24-8 Retail salespeople who work in fabric stores assist home sewing customers.

mangostock/Shutterstock.com

Costume curators and conservators carefully restore old textiles and garments. They repair broken and frayed areas. They also remove soil that could prematurely age and damage the fabrics, as in **24-9**. Dust, dirt, and insects are harmful to old textiles.

Costume curators and conservators record their findings. Then they store the clothing and textiles in places with proper temperature and humidity. They use archival, acid-free paper products for storage. Curators also make sure the items are kept in darkness or under low light levels. Ultraviolet rays are screened out to minimize fading.

Costume curators and conservators work in museums to develop and care for historic costume collections. They prepare exhibits that display the historical garments as accurately as possible. They must know every detail of the apparel of past eras and other cultures. They often deal with inaugural gowns, wedding gowns, and other ceremonial garments because these special ones have been saved. Everyday clothes from long ago are quite rare, but they often tell a great deal more about what life was like in former times than special garments do.

Costume scholars also work for large city and university libraries. They collect and catalog old and new fashion drawings, clippings, slides, photos, films, and books. They often give lectures with slides depicting historic costumes and their influences on modern fashions and fabrics. They have access to detailed information that can date, describe, authenticate, and classify old apparel, as in **24-10**. They help people find

Dept. of Consumer Studies, University of Delaware

24-10 The ages and origins of historic garments can be determined by costume scholars.

specific information by researching what has been written about various aspects of clothing. Sometimes they assist the wardrobe designer of a historic film.

Costume curators and conservators generally have college degrees in science, textiles and clothing, history, or art history. Many have master's or doctoral degrees. Apprenticeship training or graduation from an art conservation training program is recommended for this work. Also, one must have patience to do a job carefully. For employment in a library, a background in library science is recommended. Interests in textiles, science, history, and fashion are needed.

Work with historic textiles and costumes can be stimulating and personally rewarding. The hours are sometimes long and are often spent working independently. The pay is average. Professional esteem, however, may be very high.

24-9 Wet cleaning of antique silk damask fabric is done by trained conservators using special equipment.

The Henry Francis DuPont Winterthur Museum

Those with experience and expertise might also be instructors for others, such as apprentices going into this career.

Theatrical Costumers

Theatrical costuming is done for opera, ballet, stage plays, circuses, movies, advertisements, television productions, and parades, as in **24-11**. A costumer might work for a theater company, a movie studio, a costume shop, or a television network. Sometimes outside costume designers are hired to work with the wardrobe staff of certain shows.

Theatrical costumers work from scripts to learn about the types of activities for which outfits are needed. They should know the culture and time period being represented, the income level of the characters, and the mood or desired effect. Designers must create complete costumes that give the right look under various lighting conditions. They have to work within certain limitations, such as the size of the stage or screen. They have to coordinate the costumes with the props. All of this must be done within a specified budget.

There are several levels of responsibility and pay in theatrical costuming. A beginner may start as a *wardrobe helper*, sometimes called a *costume technician*. Wardrobe helpers organize the costumes and accessories by character and scene. They shop and do other footwork to collect everything that is needed. They help with research to make sure the designs are authentic. They help the actors and actresses dress for the production and care for the wardrobes afterward. They also repair costumes before, during, and after performances. All members of the wardrobe crew must work together as a team.

With experience, a wardrobe helper might eventually advance to the position of *wardrobe designer*. The person in this position, as head of the costume department, earns much higher pay and has greater professional esteem. Recognition is given in the credit lines of a movie or the program of a stage production. However, as in other types of fashion designing, a very small percentage of people advance to a career of this high level. There are important contributions and enjoyable careers for those at all levels of theatrical costuming.

Theatrical costumers should have great flair and creative imagination. They must be able to work with emotional and artistic personalities. They need a thorough knowledge of lighting, staging, and special techniques. They also need a solid background in art, design, and history.

To work in theatrical costuming, fashion school training and an apprenticeship are necessary. A wide range of skills, including sketching, pattern making, draping, and sewing, is needed. It may even be necessary to glue or staple once in a while, as in **24-12**.

24-12 A proficiency at many different sewing and craft skills is needed to assemble professional-looking costumes.

24-11 Although theatrical costumers do not always create flamboyant or historical costumes, such as these classic French shoes and the garments that go with them, their work often involves interesting designs.

Clothing Care

Textile care and maintenance is a leading service industry. Most of these businesses are small and privately owned. There are many jobs in commercial laundries and dry-cleaning establishments. Sometimes several jobs are combined for one person to do.

A high school diploma is needed for careers in clothing care. Many require training or experience from skilled workers in the field. Some technical schools and the Drycleaning & Laundry Institute International train people in basic fabric knowledge, spot removal, and the use of clothing care equipment.

In most clothing care jobs, good eyesight and hand coordination are needed. The work must be accurate, and a person must be able to concentrate well as tasks are repeated. It is important to have a thorough knowledge of textiles and a good attitude to maintain high standards.

Dry-Cleaning and Laundry Businesses

With dry cleaners, a *checker* receives and returns the garments. This is a front-counter job with lots of customer contact. Checkers represent their companies to the public. They also handle payment, minor complaints, and telephone calls. They should have a neat appearance, a pleasing voice, and patience. They should be courteous, like people, and have knowledge of clothing and cash register procedures.

A *marker* puts identity tags on the clothes and sorts them. The garments are inspected for stains, damage, and items left in pockets. Trims or buttons are removed, if necessary, for the cleaning process. Garments are classified according to fiber content, color, and type. This determines how each will be cleaned. Some items are marked for special handling.

A *spotter* treats stains with proper spot removal methods. The fabric of the garment must not be damaged. He or she must understand fibers, finishes, dyes, and stain removal. The spotter should have an interest in fashion and some knowledge of clothing construction.

A *dry cleaner* is responsible for cleaning the garments. The garments are weighed to determine the poundage of each load. Then they are cleaned in special solvents that must be kept pure and clear. Specialized cleaning equipment is used. Some clothes are tumble dried, and some are dried in the air.

A dry cleaner must have physical strength and mechanical ability. An understanding of chemistry and mathematics is helpful. A person may start as a helper and advance to this job.

A *washing operator* does laundry with wet washing and drying equipment. The proper water level, temperature, and amounts of detergents and chemical agents must be selected for each load. Each load must be balanced to prevent equipment damage. A washing operator must have physical strength and mechanical ability.

A *finisher* restores the cleaned garments to their original appearance and shape using various kinds of finishing equipment. Finishers soften fabrics and remove wrinkles by using steam and various types of presses in combination with hand irons. Skill is needed to handle the equipment on the many different garment designs and fabrics. The garments are then hung on hangers or folded neatly.

A *sewer* makes any needed repairs or alterations. He or she might restitch seams and attach linings that have become loose. A sewer may also replace buttons, secure shoulder pads and trims, and put in hems. A person in this position must have complete knowledge of sewing construction.

An *inspector* examines the apparel after the cleaning and finishing processes. Garments are returned to the proper departments for correction if they do not meet the plant standards. Memos to the customers are sometimes attached regarding special garments. An inspector needs to understand the expected standards as well as the dry-cleaning and laundry operations. He or she needs to have good judgment as well as tact.

An *assembler* gathers all the pieces of a customer's order. He or she matches invoice descriptions and numbers with garment tags. An assembler's job must be done carefully and accurately so no items are lost or misplaced.

A *wrapper* (sometimes called a *bagger*) packages the finished apparel to maintain the quality of cleaning or finishing. This person places garment bags over dry-cleaned items and wraps laundered clothes. He or she then attaches invoices to the packages that are ready to be returned to customers.

Commercial Laundries

A few jobs are available in self-service laundries. *Attendants* make change, sell laundry products, and assist customers with laundry problems and the use of machines. They should have a general knowledge of fibers, fabrics, and clothing. Attendants must be courteous and well-groomed. They may have to work some evenings, holidays, and weekends.

Institutions, such as hospitals and hotels, employ *laundry specialists* to work in their on-site laundries. Laundry specialists maintain the linens, such as uniforms, aprons, sheets, towels, tablecloths, and napkins. Also, some outside laundry businesses specialize in commercial work and clean only items from institutions and large businesses. Laundry specialists need formal training or experience in an apparel care establishment.

Linen Supply Service

Linen supply services own linens and rent them to institutions and businesses. These types of firms have pickup, laundering, and delivery services. Panel truck drivers are needed, as well as laundry equipment operators and maintenance workers. Office employees schedule pickups and deliveries, purchase new and replacement linens, and handle the financial accounts.

Entrepreneurs

Entrepreneurs are people who start their own businesses. More and more people want to work for themselves. As owners, they assume the risk and management of their enterprises. A business might be run from home, an office, or a store. It may focus on retail sales, provide a service, or manufacture a product. The business might be set up as a sole proprietorship, with only one owner. It could be a partnership, with two or more owners, as in **24-13**. The business could also be a corporation, which is a separate legal entity that gives the owner certain protections. A lawyer may be needed to set up the company.

Entrepreneurs need to look at all the factors involved in starting and running a business. They should take business courses and specialized education classes to get all the preparation

Stephen Coburn/Shutterstock.com

24-13 A company with two owners is set up legally as a partnership. It could have a few more owners and still be a partnership.

possible. They should have work experience in another firm that deals with the same type of product or service. They should analyze such questions as those in **24-14** before starting an entrepreneurial endeavor.

An entrepreneur should develop a business plan that defines the idea (purpose), operations, and financial forecast of the proposed company. The business plan will help the entrepreneur crystallize his or her thinking about the venture. Also, it is needed in order to get business loans from lending institutions.

Entrepreneurs need to have good communication skills to deal with employees and customers. They need to have effective management and problem-solving skills. They must have good math skills to keep track of the business's finances. Entrepreneurs need to have an understanding of insurance, taxes, and government regulations. See **24-15**. Information and guidance might be available from the local chamber of commerce or small business association.

Self-employment is a big responsibility. Discipline is needed to schedule work and meet deadlines. Long hours must often be worked,

Some Questions to Ask Before Starting a Business

Does the business fill a gap or real need in the market?

Is the timing right, so the demand is growing?

Do I have enough education and experience in this type of work?

What are my strengths and weaknesses in this type of work?

Where can I get the extra expertise I need (such as courses, workshops, and consultants)?

Do I have helpful industry contacts?

What is my target market and the image I want to project?

What are my promotional and pricing strategies?

Who are my competitors, and what are their strong and weak points?

Where will the business be located, and why should it be there?

How and where will I get the capital I need to finance the venture?

Are there organizations that I should join (such as chamber of commerce or trade associations)?

Am I willing to put in lots of hard work?

24-14 These questions are important to answer as a person considers starting a business.

Regulations to Check Before Starting a Business

Licenses or Permits—State or local licenses are often needed to make or sell certain items or to provide certain services. Your local Economic Development Office or Department of Public Health should be able to help you with this.

Zoning Ordinances—In almost all communities, certain areas are designated for residential use (for homes), and other areas are designated for commercial use (for businesses). Most businesses cannot be located in a residential zone. Also, commercial zones are often further restricted to certain types of businesses, such as offices, light industry, or heavy manufacturing. For zoning information, check with your local planning commission.

Sales Tax—Many states have a sales tax on certain categories of items that are sold directly to consumers. If your goods or services are within one of the categories, you must collect the tax from your customers and pay it to the state. Check with your County Clerk's Office about sales tax procedures.

Labeling—If you plan to manufacture apparel items, even on a small scale, certain information must be included on permanent garment labels. The Federal Trade Commission can provide you with specific details about this.

Registering a Business Name—The name of your business can be registered if no one has already registered it for their use. This protects the name for your use only. Your County Clerk's Office can get you started on this procedure.

24-15 Local, state, and federal laws affect businesses. Owners must find out about official regulations and obey them or face penalties. A lawyer may be needed.

and concerns about work usually linger after hours. Employees sometimes have to be hired and trained, and work must be delegated. Expenses must be kept down, while efforts are made to increase profits. Great satisfaction is received from a business venture that becomes a success. However, many small businesses fail each year because of poor planning, poor business skills, and lack of money for a solid start.

A Home-Based Business

More and more people are earning some or all their income from working at home. Some people use knitting machines to produce sweaters, or monogramming machines to personalize jackets. Some write fashion articles for publications. Some specialize in making quilts or seasonal craft items. Some buy items wholesale to combine into new products or provide a service, such as consulting.

One type of home-based business is a *home handiwork business*, also called a cottage industry. The labor force of a cottage industry consists of family units working in their homes with their

own equipment. It can be just one person working at home or many people who are hired to work individually in their own homes. This reduces overhead and provides flexibility for the hiring company. It might serve as a way to do small-scale contract manufacturing.

For a home-based business in which goods are produced independently at home, selling might be done directly to consumers or by consignment. For *consignment*, you would place your goods for sale in a store. You would be paid a percentage of the retail price if and when the goods are sold. You might also consider renting a booth at fairs or shows to sell your products directly to consumers. Many home-based businesses now sell their products online or by mail order.

You may be able to sell products made at home to regular retail outlets. To do this, you must make appointments with buyers to meet at their convenience. You must make sales presentations, pack and unpack samples, and fill out order forms. This is time consuming, often frustrating, and sometimes rewarding. You might even pay commissions to sales representatives to sell your products in various parts of the country. As a business grows, sales outlets and methods change. In all cases, you must supply items of consistent quality in the amounts needed after the orders have been taken.

Most of the time, home-earned income is lower than that earned from employment with an outside firm. However, there are many advantages. Home-based businesses allow you to dress comfortably, eliminate commuting costs, and combine some family responsibilities with work activities. Income is earned without losing the flexibility and personal rewards that being at home offers.

There are some tax advantages related to home-based businesses. Check with an accountant or tax expert about home expenses that may be allocated to the business. Publications by the Internal Revenue Service or Small Business Administration are also helpful. Keep careful records of business-related travel, legal and professional fees, supplies, business publications, educational expenses, and so on.

Some trade schools and colleges offer courses to prepare people to own home-based businesses. Some have continuing education classes in the evenings for adults already in the workforce. Students prepare financial, marketing, and feasibility studies to see if their business ideas are sound. They look at the realities of taxes, insurance, patents, liabilities, and investment capital. They also consider their personal values and lifestyles, to evaluate the effects of a home-based business on family members.

A Retail Store

Great amounts of textile and apparel products are distributed by specialty stores. Some are privately owned and successful for many years. However, apparel shop entrepreneurship is risky and has a high failure rate. Lack of working capital and poor management are often the reasons for failure. There is sometimes too much optimism combined with too little experience and knowledge. To open a retail shop, you first need a sound background in the business.

As a general rule, if a store can get through the first two years, the chances for survival are good. The rewards with a successful shop are many. It can be wonderful to be your own boss. You can decide where the shop is located, what image and merchandise it has, and how it is run. See **24-16**.

There are various ways to establish ownership of a retail shop. People can buy a business that is already in operation or buy into a partnership in it. This takes some negotiating after the assets and profitability of the store have been evaluated. Another way is to start a retail business from scratch. A store facility must be rented or bought, merchandise must be ordered, advertising must announce the store, and employees may have to be hired and trained.

Another way to own a retail establishment is to buy a franchise. A *franchise* is a business in which a person enters into a contractual agreement with an existing company (the *franchisor*) to buy into the business and to sell its products. The buyer (the *franchisee*) can then operate the business using the trade name of the franchisor. This type of business has a lower rate of failure, since the franchisee receives some guidance and protection from the franchisor. A capital loan will probably have to be acquired from a lending institution for start-up costs.

24-16 Owning your own retail store can be exciting, yet a challenge. Expertise is needed in merchandising and all business principles. Much time and energy is needed to make it a success.

Hurst Photo/Shutterstock.com

Small shop owners often employ only one or two others to help operate the store. They perform all the retail functions of buying, stock control, promotion, and direct selling. The owner must locate sources, price the goods, and offer credit and personal services to customers. He or she probably does all the paperwork, arranges displays, and possibly even sweeps the floor. There may be low or inconsistent income for the owner until the store becomes well established with satisfied customers.

Owners of retail shops must know their target market and their competition. They must carry goods that meet a need or are in demand. They must cater to their market segment of customers with the proper merchandise and image. For long-term success, they must adapt to changing market conditions.They should have good relations with people in the community.

Independent store owners need expertise in many areas, as outlined in **24-17**. They have to be able to maintain and analyze business records. They must be able to interpret financial data in order to improve business performance. They have to update their inventory control systems when needed. They must know how to develop seasonal merchandise plans. They must know how to control costs and build sales, so the bottom line shows a profit.

24-17 These areas of expertise, and others, are needed for owners of apparel retail stores. They can be gained through reading, attending courses and seminars, and having work experience in similar businesses.

Areas of Expertise Needed to Own a Small Retail Shop

How to maximize your buying dollars to get appropriate quantities, assortments, and styles for your target customers

How to merchandise your store according to the *fashion calendar*

How to maintain proper inventory levels and overcome slow- or nondeliveries of merchandise

How to calculate open-to-buy and stock-to-sales ratios

How to build and keep good credit and financial health

How to establish and maintain good relationships with suppliers

How to maximize an image of high customer service

A Dressmaking or Tailoring Shop

Professional *dressmakers* and *tailors* do custom sewing, alterations, and repairs for others. Some people do the work in their homes. Others have storefront operations.

Custom sewers make garments for individual clients. Sometimes they specialize by creating only wedding gowns or tailored suits. They help the customer choose a flattering style and fabric. They take the person's measurements. They construct the garment, check fit, and include all finishing touches.

Dressmaking is much more than following a printed pattern. Many are designers and tailors who build a clientele on their ability to create a garment according to customer specifications. Sometimes they make apparel with just a sketch or photograph to follow. To do this, they must understand form, proportion, fit, and color. They must also be good at pattern making and draping.

Dressmakers and tailors must have a keen interest in clothes and enjoy sewing, as in **24-18**. They must be experts at all the skills of construction. They should know professional techniques and shortcuts. With experience, they develop speed and accuracy. Good eye-hand coordination is needed, as well as finger dexterity and a fashion sense.

Dressmakers and tailors must have knowledge of the types of fabrics that are suited to various garment designs. They must be neat, accurate, and patient. They must be tactful with people and work well under pressure.

24-18 To have a successful dressmaking or tailoring shop, you must take your work seriously to do an expert job on each project.

Lucian Coman/Shutterstock.com

Dressmakers and tailors sometimes master this trade through apprenticeships. However, technical or trade school courses in fashion design, pattern making, construction, and textiles are helpful. The best preparation is to study textiles and clothing in college with business courses taken as electives. Sometimes extension clothing specialists or adult education courses offer *sewing for profit* workshops.

Special books and magazines are also available. They provide information about how to start a business and make it profitable. They give helpful advice and keep people up-to-date. These materials can often be found online or at local fabric stores. If you are interested in a career as a dressmaker or tailor, you might want to join an association such as the Custom Tailors and Designers Association (CTDA).

A dressmaking or tailoring shop can be started with a relatively small investment. It has good potential for growth. With so many people employed outside the home, apparel services that offer quality work and proper fit are in demand. Dressmakers and alterations experts may also work with department stores, specialty clothing shops, and dry-cleaning establishments.

An Apparel Production Business

Despite the existence of many giant garment firms, the apparel manufacturing industry has an abundance of small, privately-owned businesses. It is possible for enterprising and creative people to set up businesses and prosper. Some capital is needed for office space and to purchase fabric. The cutting and sewing can be sent out to contractors.

To succeed, small apparel manufacturers must produce styles that will find acceptance. They have as good a chance to create popular designs as large firms. In fact, they often have the advantage of being able to react quickly to sudden fashion shifts. They buy smaller amounts of fabrics and produce only a few designs in small lots. They often set the fashion pace for the industry because they create more fashion-forward or future-inspired designs. Profits can be high with the right ingenuity. However, a single season with a bad line can wipe out a small, under-capitalized firm.

Apparel production entrepreneurs should become personally acquainted with store buyers, fashion editors, suppliers, and contractors. Personal appearances in stores that carry the products can help promote the line. Such visits also give the entrepreneurs customer feedback for improvements or changes. Plugs in fashion articles can be a big boost.

Small business centers and trade schools offer courses in how to start apparel production businesses. Students are often people with design talent and experience with large firms who want to go out on their own. In the courses, students learn how to develop a sales force, manage personnel, and work with contractors. They also learn various finance methods relating to sales and production. Workshops are taught by industry leaders and consultants, with guest speakers in specific fields of expertise.

At the contracting end of the business, capital is required for machinery, rent, utilities, and employees' wages. Sometimes there is demand for a specialized type of production, such as sewing appliqués or monograms onto garments. In such a case, a niche can be filled very successfully by a manufacturing entrepreneur.

A Trading Company

A **trading company** is an import/export business. Trading companies contract for, or buy, merchandise from other countries. They arrange for shipments of goods to the United States, as in **24-19**. They sell the merchandise to domestic retailers who, in turn, sell it to consumers. Most trading companies specialize in a particular product category, such as silk apparel from Hong Kong or hand-knit items from Scotland.

24-19 Goods that trading companies have bought or sold in other parts of the world are shipped into and out of the United States on container ships.

National Cotton Council

A trading company may be run by one or two people who have some warehouse space and a small office. To start this type of a business, product line expertise is needed. Contacts are needed with overseas suppliers and domestic retail accounts. A great deal of traveling has to be done. The costs of the travel are business expenses.

A Mail-Order or Online Business

Many people find a market through mail-order or website sales for the apparel-related products they produce. Such products include specialized patterns, supplies, manufactured garments, kits to be made into apparel, and how-to books for home sewers. Mail-order businesses advertise in publications that are read by consumers who can use what they have to offer. Sometimes they send out advertising materials to a targeted mailing or e-mail list of names. Postage costs for this can add up quickly. Other times, businesses supply their products to an existing mail-order house or website that reaches their target audience. In that case, they get about 40 percent of the retail selling price.

Inventory planning for a mail-order or online sales business can be tricky. There is no sure way of knowing how many orders will be received. A business could be swamped with orders that cannot be filled fast enough. However, if the business builds a large inventory to fill orders that do not materialize, it could be stuck with unsold goods.

A small mail-order business can be run from home. Basement or garage space can be used as a warehouse. Additional space and equipment are needed to produce whatever is being sold. Packing materials and office supplies are also required, as in **24-20**. A post office box is usually rented and used as the address for the business.

Mail order is a relatively simple way to start a business. It requires organizational abilities and a willingness to work hard. It also requires a talent for selecting products that people will want badly enough to call to place an order or fill out a paper or website order form. Customers pay by check, online payment service, or credit card. A toll-free phone number may be needed. The business can be started on a part-time basis

Yeko Photo Studio/Shutterstock.com

24-20 Prompt and professional delivery is important for a small mail-order business.

until it grows into a full-time job. The owner can dress as desired and work whatever hours are convenient.

Products sold through mail-order and online marketing should be fairly lightweight and easy to package. They should be easy to show with photos and to describe technically and creatively in words. The market for the products must be identifiable and easy to reach. The prices must attract customers while making a realistic profit for a person's time and effort.

Owners of mail-order and online businesses must obey Federal Trade Commission and post office regulations. Products and prices cannot be misrepresented in advertisements. Items must have proper labeling. All products must be safe for consumers to use. Also, all orders must be filled within 30 days of receipt. If this cannot be done, customers must be contacted. Each customer must be given the opportunity to cancel the order with a refund or to accept later shipment.

Freelancing and Consulting

Freelancing is the selling of expert skills. Consulting is the selling of expert ideas and advice. Both are service businesses that offer help to companies or consumers. Freelancers and consultants sell expertise rather than merchandise. A great deal of successful experience is needed to establish credentials as an expert.

Freelancing and consulting can be done to serve any of the apparel industry segments. (Previous chapters have mentioned freelance work in fashion design, illustration, and photography.) These positions can also serve consumers. For instance, *color analysis consultants* find the best colors for specific clients. They guide clients in the color coordination of their apparel and cosmetics, as in **24-21**. *Wardrobe consultants* show consumers how to combine fashion items, and help them plan and manage their wardrobes and purchases. See **24-22**. They are especially helpful in establishing personal image programs for busy career people.

wavebreakmedia/Shutterstock.com

24-22 Wardrobe consultants may work with clients face-to-face, through video conferencing, or over the phone, depending on how often they want to travel.

Freelancing and consulting jobs generally have few inventory requirements, since they are service businesses. Advertising materials are usually distributed to announce and promote the service. The work can be full or part time. Sometimes it is started during free time from other employment until enough contacts have been made to make it a steady career.

Evening courses offer instruction in establishing freelancing or consulting businesses. See **24-23**. They teach people how to promote themselves and their talents, develop client lists, and minimize financial risks. Methods of building personally and financially rewarding businesses are discussed.

24-21 Color analysis consultants are trained to determine what colors are the most flattering for individuals' apparel and cosmetics.

BeautiControl

24-23 Courses in freelancing and consulting can teach prospective business owners important skills for establishing, maintaining, and marketing their services. They can also provide prospective business owners with helpful contacts and networking opportunities.

bikeriderlondon/Shutterstock.com

Summary

There are fashion careers outside of textiles, apparel, retailing, and promotion. Classroom teachers instruct students about fashion, grooming, clothing selection, sewing, and other apparel subjects. Teachers should have good communication skills, flexibility, patience, and the desire to help people. Extension agents with state land-grant universities develop educational programs for people in their counties. Extension agents should be organized, resourceful, and work well independently. State and federal clothing specialists coordinate apparel extension work.

Adult education teachers teach courses in the evenings, usually at schools or community centers, to local residents who sign up. Consumer educational representatives teach about and promote products of manufacturing firms for whom they work.

The home sewing industry sells nonindustrial sewing machines, patterns, fabrics, and notions to home sewers. Employees in commercial pattern development include fashion information directors, merchandising directors, designers, pattern makers, garment makers, fitting models, design directors, fabric editors, accessory editors, pattern graders, and checkers. Pattern guide sheet and envelope production workers include technical writers, diagram artists, illustrators, markers, layout designers, and printing plant employees. Coordinators with retail stores and educational representatives who prepare teaching aids are sales and promotion employees. The home sewing industry also has retail fabric salespeople and video demonstration employees.

Costume curators, as well as historians, scientists, and conservators, locate and identify old apparel, record their findings, and do repairs and restoration work. Theatrical costumers work for theater companies, movie studios, costume shops, and television networks as wardrobe helpers.

Clothing care is a service industry with jobs in commercial laundries and dry-cleaning firms. Workers for dry cleaners include checkers, markers, spotters, dry cleaners, washing operators, finishers, sewers, inspectors, assemblers, and wrappers/baggers. Commercial laundries have attendants and laundry specialists. Linen supply services own linens they pick up, launder, and deliver to institutions and businesses.

Entrepreneurs are self-employed, and they assume the risk and management of their enterprises. A home-based business can be a cottage industry, sell items on consignment, or earn money from home another way. Owning an apparel retail store has a high risk of failure, but many specialty stores are independently owned. A dressmaking or tailoring shop does custom sewing, alterations, and repairs for others. An apparel production business can be started with good designs, with the cutting and sewing sent out to contractors.

A trading company buys merchandise from other countries and sells it to domestic retailers. A mail-order or online business takes orders via mail, telephone, or a website and ships items to the customers. Freelancing and consulting are service businesses that sell expert skills or expert ideas and advice to those who pay for the service.

Other Careers and Entreprenearial Opportunities

Career Cluster	Sample Occupations		
Arts, A/V Technology & Communications	• Accessory Editor • Color Analysis Consultant • Commercial Pattern Designer • Costume Curator • Costume Technician • Design Artist • Design Director	• Entrepreneur • Fabric Editor • Fitting Model • Freelance Illustrator • Home Sewing Magazine Editor • Home Sewing Media or Video Producer	• Illustrator • Layout Designer • Marker Maker • Pattern Maker • Theatrical Costumer • Wardrobe Consultant • Wardrobe Designer • Wardrobe Helper
Business, Management & Administration	• Franchisee • Home Sewing Products Director • Import/Export Business Operator • Mail-Order Business Operator	• Merchandising Director • Retail Coordinator • Website Sales Manager	
Education & Training	• Adult Education Teacher • Apparel Educator • Classroom Teacher • College/University Professor • Educational Representative	• Entrepreneur • Extension Agent • Home Sewing Video Demonstrator • Trade School Teacher	
Human Services	• Alterations Expert • Color Analysis Consultant • Customer Sewer • Dry Cleaner • Entrepreneur	• Finisher • Inspector • Laundry Specialist • Linen Supply Service Manager • Marker	• Professional Dressmaker, Spotter • Tailor • Wardrobe Consultant • Washing Operator • Wrapper
Information Technology	• Internet Marketing Specialist • Online Fabric Sales Personnel	• Website Technician • Technical Writer	
Manufacturing	• Apparel Production Entrepreneur • Garment Maker • Pattern Grader	• Pattern Maker • Printing Plant Technician • Sewer	
Marketing	• Accessory Editor • Fabric Editor • Fabric Salesperson • Fashion Information Director • Franchisee	• Entrepreneur • Home Sewing Products Marketing Specialist • Internet Marketing Specialist	• Merchandising Director • Subscription Fabric Club Marketing Director • Website Sales Manager
Science, Technology, Engineering & Mathematics	• Costume Conservator • Costume Curator • Entrepreneur		
Transportation, Distribution & Logistics	• Entrepreneur • Home Sewing Mail-Order Distributor	• Mail-Order Fulfillment Clerk • Subscription Fabric Club Warehouse Manager	

NOTE: *Occupations may link to additional career clusters.*

The Career Clusters icons are being used with permission of the States' Career Clusters Initiative.
www.careertech.org

Fashion Recall

Write your answers on a separate sheet of paper.

True/False: Write *true* or *false* for each of the following statements.

1. Work experience and job expertise are more important than advanced degrees for teachers in technical schools.

2. Extension agents work only in rural areas.

3. Technical writers create clear sewing directions for commercial patterns.

4. Online fabric sales personnel work at central website offices and warehouses of their companies.

5. Video demonstration work is sometimes done for a home sewing audience.

6. Costume curators locate, identify, and determine the age of textiles, apparel, and accessories from past cultures.

7. Wardrobe helpers are consultants who do color analysis and personal image wardrobe planning.

8. Linen supply services own linens and rent them to institutions and businesses.

9. Entrepreneurs are people who start their own businesses and assume the risk and management of their enterprises.

10. Sole proprietorships are small manufacturing firms that make and sell shoe parts in the footwear industry.

11. Selling something by consignment is when you are paid to sign over the ownership of your product idea to a manufacturing firm.

12. Small apparel manufacturers often have the advantage over large firms to create popular designs because they can act quickly to respond to sudden fashion shifts.

Fashion Vocabulary

13. In teams, play picture charades to identify each of the *Fashion Terms* listed on the chapter opening. Write the terms on separate slips of paper and put the slips into a basket. Choose a team member to be the *sketcher*. The sketcher pulls a term from the basket and creates quick drawings or graphics to represent the term until the team guesses the term. Rotate turns as the sketcher until the team identifies all terms.

Critical Thinking

14. **Analyze a career**   What career described in this chapter do you find most interesting? Use the text and online resources to analyze details about this career. Write a summary explaining why this career is of interest to you, citing the text and other resources as evidence to support your analysis.

15. **Outline requirements**   Name an apparel-related career in one of the areas described in this chapter that might appeal to you. What are the educational requirements for that career? Use the text and online resources to research your response. Discuss your findings with the class.

16. **Evaluate self-employment**   Create an illustrated report (digital or print) to describe an apparel-related business you would like to start. Who would be your target market? What product or products would you sell? Who would be your competitors? In your report, evaluate and summarize the advantages and disadvantages of self-employment (being an entrepreneur).

Core Skills

17. **Speaking**   Imagine you are an educational representative. Plan an informative program demonstration for an apparel-related product. Demonstrate the product in class. Be prepared to answer audience questions about the product.

18. **Research and writing**   Visit the website of a museum with apparel collections, such as the Smithsonian. Take a virtual

tour of their apparel collection. Choose an apparel item from history and prepare an illustrated report about it using a school-approved digital application. Describe the details of the garment, including fabrics and trims. Use other online sources to report on who wore the garment and the events to which it was worn. Share your report with the class.

19. **Writing**   Develop a plan to start an apparel-related online business. Write a report and complete the following:

   - Describe the products and explain how you would produce them. What supplies would you need?

   - Create a sample advertisement.

   - Identify your target market and the publications or websites where you would place your ads.

   - Determine the cost for a post office box. Also, check postage rates for the size and weight of the packages you would ship.

20. **Business simulation**   Use a school-approved free online simulation or game in which users pretend to be owners of small businesses. Without revealing personal information, research the site and create a presentation for your class on what it teaches users about entrepreneurship and running a small business.

21. **Research and writing**   Go to the website of the U.S. Small Business Administration. Choose a course from the list of free online courses. Register and spend 30 minutes on the course. Write a report summarizing what you learned.

22. **CTE career readiness practice**   Choose a specific job in fashion promotion of interest to you. Use print or online resources to learn more about the job. Prepare a written report about the job. Include the qualifications you need to get the job, the type of company that might hire you, and the tasks you would perform. Determine the possible opportunities for advancement. Save this information to your portfolio.

Fashion in Action

23. **Portfolio builder**   As you assemble your final portfolio for this course, keep the following in mind. Include a table of contents with your portfolio. This will allow the person reviewing your portfolio to find items easily. Continue to add and remove documents and projects as you complete assignments or gain new skills. Update the table of contents when you make changes to your portfolio. Keep items that are for your own use separate, such as your contacts database and sample interview answers. Complete the following:

   A. Review the items you have collected for your portfolio. Select the items you want to include and remove the others. Make copies of certificates, diplomas, and other important documents. Keep the originals in a safe place.

   B. Create the table of contents and a title page for each section of your portfolio.

   C. Place the items in a binder, notebook, or other presentation container.

24. **Design activity**   Using an old commercial pattern, mount the pattern pieces, guide sheet pages, and envelope on poster board. In an oral report, describe the jobs of at least six employees who contributed to the design, production, packaging, and selling of the pattern. Ask classmates to describe the jobs of any other employees who contributed to the finished pattern.

Self-Assessment Quiz

Complete the self-assessment quiz online to help practice and expand your knowledge and skills.

Following is a comprehensive glossary of fashion and apparel terms used in the context of this textbook. For descriptions of specific fabrics, consult the *Glossary of Popular Apparel Fabrics* in this textbook.

A

abilities. Skills developed through training or practice. (19)

abrasion. Surface wear and rubbing. (8)

absorbent. Having the ability to take up moisture. (8)

accented neutral color scheme. Color plan that combines white, black, or gray with a bright color accent. (10)

accessories. Items worn with garments, such as belts, hats, jewelry, shoes, gloves, and scarves, to complete or enhance an outfit. (2, 14)

accessory editors. Commercial pattern company employees who research and obtain the latest styles; accessories are used to create finished ensembles for illustration and photography. (24)

account executive (AE). Advertising agency employee responsible for handling specific clients' accounts. (23)

accountant. Administrative support employee who records and summarizes business transactions and reports the results. (22)

accounting and finance employees. Employees who keep track of the funds of the company. (20)

acetate. Manufactured cellulosic fibers. (8)

acrylic. Manufactured fiber with wool-like qualities. (8)

added visual texture. Surface design printed onto fabrics. (11)

administration. Overall management functions of a company. (20)

administrative assistant. Administrative support employee who handles correspondence and manages other work for an executive. (22)

adornment. Decoration or ornamentation. (1)

adult education. Educational courses for adults. (24)

advertising. Paid promotional message by an identified sponsor. (7, 23)

advertising and promotion specialists. Employees who create a demand for products through advertising and promotion. (20)

advertising directors. Retail and publications employees who oversee all the advertising activities. (23)

agile manufacturing. The future of apparel production; seamless data capture system of information, production, and delivery for individuals. (6)

A-line dresses. Dresses that are narrow (fitted) at the shoulders, have no waistline seam, and become wider at the hemline. (3)

A-line skirts. Skirts with extra width at the hem on each side; the silhouette resembles the letter *A*. (3)

alteration hands. Apparel manufacturing employees who repair garment defects that happen during factory production. (21)

alterations. Modifications, such as by sewing, to change the fit of garments. (16)

alterations expert. Retail store employee who takes in, lets out, and reshapes standard-sized garments so they fit the customers who buy them. (22)

American Fashion Critics' Awards. See *Coty Awards* and *Cutty Sark Awards*. (4)

American Fiber Manufacturers Association, Inc. (AFMA). Trade organization for producers of manufactured fibers in the United States. (8)

Americans with Disabilities Act. A law that prohibits employers from discriminating against people with disabilities; mandates that the work environment must be made physically accessible for workers with disabilities. (19)

analogous color scheme. Color plan using adjacent or related colors on the color wheel. Also called *related color scheme.* (10)

anchor stores. Large, well-known stores that provide the attraction needed to draw customers to shopping malls. (7)

angora. Fiber made from Angora rabbit fur. (8)

antistatic. Chemical finish applied to fabrics to prevent the buildup of static electricity so garments will not cling to the body of the wearer. (9)

Note: The numbers in parentheses following the definitions represent the chapter in which the terms appear.

Glossary

apparel. General term that includes men's, women's, and children's clothing. (2)

apparel designers. See *fashion designers*. (21)

apparel educators. Instructors of clothing and merchandising classes, extension work, and adult and consumer education courses. (24)

apparel industries. Businesses that center around textiles, garment manufacturing, and retailing. (4)

apparel manufacturing industry. The firms that design and construct garments. (4, 21)

apparel marts. Buildings or complexes that house permanent showrooms and sales offices of apparel manufacturers. (6)

application form. Employer form requesting personal, academic, and employment information to be filled out by a job applicant. (19)

applied lines. See *decorative lines*. (11)

appliqués. Cutout decorations applied to garments by stitching or fusing with an iron. (14, 17)

apprenticeship program. Months or years spent learning all aspects of a trade by practical experience under skilled workers. (19)

aptitudes. A person's natural talents and potential for learning. (19)

aramid. Manufactured fiber that is lightweight, tough, and resistant to flames and chemicals. (8)

armchair shopping. Gathering product and availability information at home through catalogs and public media, often as a planning step before doing the actual shopping. (15)

art directors. Advertising agency employees who create the overall look and feel of advertising campaigns. (23)

artificial suedes. Nonwoven fabrics composed of polyurethane with fine fibers of polyester; can be finished to look like leather or woven fabrics. (9)

as ready. A promise to fill (ship) orders as they are completed, rather than by an exact date. (7)

assembler. See *assorters*. (21); dry-cleaning firm employee who gathers all the pieces of a customer's order. He or she matches invoice descriptions and numbers with garment tags. (24)

assistant fashion coordinator. Employee who helps a fashion coordinator, mainly by taking care of details. (22)

assistant retail buyers. Employees who assist the retail buyers with all the functions of buying merchandise, sales planning, and promotion. (22)

assistant stylist. A person who is in training to become a stylist. (20)

associate's degree. Two-year college or technical/trade school degree. (19, 20)

assorters. Apparel manufacturing employees who sort and prepare the cut garment parts for the sewing assembly line. Also called *assemblers*. (21)

asymmetrical. A design in which the right side is not the same as the left side. (3); see *informal balance*. (12)

attitudes. A person's feelings about or reactions to people, things, or ideas as formed by that person's values. (1)

audiovisual (AV) jobs. Employment involving aspects of radio, television, and multimedia presentations. (23)

automatic dryer. Laundry appliance that dries fabric items with heat and a tumbling action. (18)

autumn season. Most diverse personal color category; for people with warm undertones and lighter, sometimes reddish, hair with dark or light eyes. (10)

avant-garde clothes. Daring and wild designs that are unconventional and startling. (2)

B

bachelor's degree. Postsecondary school degree from a four-year college or university. (19, 20)

back fullness silhouette. Fashion dress style with a skirt that puffs out in back, but not in front. (2)

bagger. See *wrapper*. (24)

balance. Principle of design that implies equilibrium or steadiness among the parts of a design. (12)

balanced plaid. Plaid design running the same in both the lengthwise and crosswise directions; design will match if a corner is folded back across the center of any repeat. Also called *even* plaid. (9)

bales. Large bundles of closely pressed and bound raw natural fibers, such as cotton. (8)

bamboo. Inexpensive bast fiber. (8)

bar codes. See *universal product code (UPC)*. (7)

bargain. Favorable purchase; a high value of merchandise in exchange for a relatively small amount of money. (16)

basic apparel. Garments that are worn most often; the core of a person's wardrobe. (14)

basic stock. Retail merchandise that is constantly in demand. It is stocked continuously on an ongoing basis. (7)

basket weave. Common variation of the plain weave; formed by using two or more yarns as one. (9)

bast fibers. Strong, woody fibers that lie in bundles just under the bark in the stems of various plants. (8)

bateau neckline. See *boat neckline*. (3)

batik. Form of resist dyeing in which wax covers the area where dye is not wanted. (9)

batting. Nonwoven fabrics produced by machines that mechanically tangle fibers into a mat for use as filler for quilts. (9)

batwing sleeves. Type of kimono sleeve style that are very low and loose at the underarm, with only a gradual curve between the side waistline and the sleeve bottom. (3)

beauty. Quality that gives pleasure to the senses and creates a positive emotional reaction in the viewer. (1)

beetling. Mechanical finishing process where linen or cotton fabric is pounded to give a flat effect; gives a harder surface with increased sheen. (9)

bell silhouette. Fashion dress style with a fitted waist and full skirt. It is wide at the bottom. (2)

belt pack. A small bag that has loops to attach to a belt, often for a camera or other small devices. (14)

benchmarking. The continuous process of measuring a company's products, services, and practices against those of other companies that are extremely good. (6)

bias grain. Diagonal grain of fabric. See *true bias*. (9)

bicomponent fibers. Fibers of two different polymers extruded in the same filaments through a spinneret. (8)

billing agent. Office support employee in charge of keeping track of amounts due and sending out bills for those amounts. (22)

biodegradable. Ability to be broken down into natural waste products that do not harm the environment. (18)

blazers. See *sport coats*. (3)

bleaches. Chlorine- or oxygen-based laundry products used to clean, whiten, and brighten fabrics. (18)

bleaching. Chemical process that removes color, impurities, or spots during fabric finishing or garment laundering. (9, 18)

blend. A combination of two or more different fibers (usually staple fibers) before spinning into yarn. (8)

block printing. Handcraft type of fabric printing. A carved design on a block is inked and then placed onto the fabric to create a design. (9)

blouson dresses. Dresses with a blousy fullness above the waist, usually with a fitted skirt and a belt. (3)

boat neckline. Neckline shape that goes straight across from shoulder to shoulder. It is high at the front (and usually back) and is wide on the sides. Also called *bateau neckline*. (3)

bodice. Apparel area above a waistline seam, usually closely fitted. (2)

body build. The relationship among the different areas of the total human form. (12)

body scanning. A procedure to collect individual sizing information electronically; virtual fit technology using 3-D modeling computer software. (7, 15)

bolls. Seed pods of cotton plants where the cotton fibers grow. (8)

bonding. Method of permanently fastening (laminating) together two layers of fabric. (9)

border print. Design that forms a distinct border, usually along one or both sides of the fabric. (9)

boutique. Small shops that sell few-of-a-kind apparel and accessories. (7)

box loom. Loom with shuttles carrying different colors of yarn that are housed in boxes at the sides of the loom. Specific shuttles are used at certain times to produce the desired pattern in the fabric. (9)

braiding. Interlacing three or more yarns to form a regular diagonal pattern down the length of the resulting cord. Also called *plaiting*. (9)

branch coordinator. Retail executive who coordinates several branch stores of a company. Also called *district manager*. (22)

branch stores. Additional stores receiving merchandise and operations direction from the original flagship department store. (7)

bridge jewelry. Jewelry made to look like fine jewelry using good metals and semiprecious stones, but less expensive. (14)

bridge lines. Designer ready-to-wear apparel priced between the better and couture categories. (4)

brushing. Fabric is swept mechanically with stiff metal-bristled brushes, removing loose fibers, threads, and lint from the surface; produces a soft, fuzzy, napped finish. Also called *napping*. (9)

buckles. Parts of belts used to fasten the belt ends together; can be plain or elaborate. (14)

builders. Ingredients in laundry products that inactivate hard water minerals. (18)

business operations specialists. Employee who gathers data on the company's operations, analyzes information, and makes recommendations to company management. (20)

business plan. Written plan that defines the idea (purpose), operations, and financial forecast of a proposed company. (24)

business-to-business (B2B) e-commerce. The transacting of business between companies through the Internet. (6)

button-down collar. Collar style with points that button to the shirt. (3)

buyer. See *retail buyer*. (22)

buyer's office support staff. Retail employees who answer telephones, reply to e-mails, schedule appointments, follow up on shipments, and do filing for the buyers. (22)

C

CAD. See *computer-aided design*. (6, 21)

caftans. Long, flowing, robe-like garments. (3)

calender printing. See *roller printing*. (9)

calendering. Mechanical finishing process where fabric is passed between heated cylinders or rollers; gives the fabric a lustrous, smooth, polished surface; also used to *emboss*. (9)

CAM. See *computer-aided manufacturing*. (6)

camel's hair. Specialty wool made from the two-humped Bactrian camel. (8)

cap sleeves. Very short sleeves, like a sleeveless armhole at the underarm and a short kimono sleeve going out from the shoulder. Also called *French sleeves*. (3)

capes. Cloaks that hang from the neck and shoulders and have no sleeves. (3)

capital. Financial worth or accumulated investment cash needed to start, expand, or run a business. (5, 24)

cardigans. Sweaters that open down the front. (3)

carding. Machine process that cleans and straightens raw cotton and wool. (8)

career. A progression of related jobs in a person's field of work. (19)

career clusters. Sixteen groups of occupational and career specialties. Each cluster includes occupations that have common knowledge and skill requirements. (19)

career pathways. Subsets of career clusters. Occupations in career pathways often have more specialized knowledge and skill requirements. (19)

cargo pants. Loose pants with pockets on the outer sides of the legs. (3)

cash purchase. Transaction in which goods or services are bought by paying the full amount with cash, check, or automatic fund transfer. (16)

cashmere. Luxurious specialty wool from the cashmere goat. (8)

catalogs. Booklets that list, show, and describe products for sale. (22)

cellulosic natural fibers. Fibers derived from the cellulose of plants, such as cotton and flax (linen). (8)

CEO. Chief executive officer of a company. (21)

certificate courses. Trade school training programs that take one to three years to complete. (19)

chain stores. Groups of stores that are owned, managed, and controlled by a central office and that handle the same goods at similar prices. (7)

Chambre Syndicale. (shom'br sin-dee-kall') Trade association for top designers of the Paris couture. (4)

channel of distribution. Route that goods and services take from the original source, through all middle people, to the ultimate user. Also called *supply chain*. (7)

chapter 11 bankruptcy. Situation in which debts and management of a failing company are restructured to try to regain the company's strength. (22)

charge slip. A record retailers give to customers that describes details of a credit transaction. (16)

checker. A dry-cleaning firm employee who receives and returns garments. (24)

checkout cashier. Retail store employee who rings up customers' purchases. He or she collects and records customers' payments, and bags or wraps purchases. (22)

chemical finishes. Finishing agents that become part of the fabrics through chemical reactions with the fibers. (9)

chemical spinning. Three methods (wet, dry, and melt) that cause extruded chemical solutions to become fibers by hardening and solidifying filaments coming from the spinneret into continuous strands. (8)

chemise dresses. See *shift dresses*. (3)

chevron. Angles of seams having the shape of the letter *V*. (11)

chief financial officer (CFO). Executive who oversees the company's financial planning, cash flow, and accounting functions. (22)

chief information officer (CIO). Executive in charge of computer operations for a firm. (22)

circular skirt. Very full skirt that forms a circle when laid flat. (3)

class market. The few consumers who buy very expensive high-fashion clothing. (2)

classic. Clothing that continues to be popular even though fashions change. (2)

classification buyer. Central office retail buyer for one category of goods across all company stores. (22)

classified ads. Ads in newspapers and trade publications that are divided into classes or categories; source of lists of job openings. (19)

classroom teacher. Instructor who teaches in a school classroom. (24)

cleaners. See *trimmers*. (21)

clearance sale. A lowering of retail prices to clear out old stock and make room for new merchandise. (6)

closures. Zippers, buttons, snaps, hooks and eyes, Velcro®, or any other fasteners that enable the wearer to get into and out of garments. (3)

coatdresses. Heavy dresses that look like coats, but are worn as dresses. (3)

coats. Warm, weatherproof garments that are worn over regular clothing. (3)

cold-water detergents. Laundry products designed to clean fabrics in cold water, usually those made of manufactured fibers or dark colors. (18)

collaboration. All companies in an industry sharing information and working together to ensure the whole supply chain works better. (6)

collateral materials. A company's printed promotional materials, such as brochures, annual reports, packaging, hangtags, logos and trademarks, and corporate image projects. (23)

collections. A manufacturer's or designer's group of lines that include all of their designs for a specific season. (4, 5)

color. Element of design; hue. (10)

color analysis. Studying a person's skin tone and hair and eye colors to determine which colors are most flattering for that person to wear. (10)

color analysis consultants. People who find the best colors for specific clients and guide in the color coordination of their clothing. (24)

color schemes. The different ways that colors are used together. (10)

color tricks. Using different colors to appear to change the size and shape of the person wearing them. (10)

color wheel. A circle segmented to show hues and how they can be mixed or used with each other. (10)

colorfast. Term designating that the color in a fabric will not fade. (9)

combination yarns. Ply yarns composed of two or more different yarns. (8)

combing. Process that filters out short fibers before forming the long fibers into a sliver; done for high-quality fibers of exceptional smoothness, fineness, and strength. (8)

commission. A percentage of the dollar amount of goods sold by that employee and paid to him or her. (19, 22)

commissionaires. Agents in foreign countries functioning like an overseas buying office, often working for many manufacturing firms. (7)

communication. The giving and receiving of verbal and nonverbal messages. (13)

comparison shoppers. Employees who peruse the stores or retail sites that employ them, as well as competitive retailers, to compare the merchandise, prices, and customer services. (22)

comparison shopping. Comparing the qualities and prices of the same or similar items from different retailers before buying. (16)

complementary color scheme. Color scheme that uses hues located opposite each other on the color wheel. (10)

completion date. Date designated on a purchase order by a retailer to a manufacturer, after which the order is subject to cancellation. (7)

composite garments. Garments made by a combination of the tailored and draped methods. (2)

compressive shrinkage. Finishing process of permanent shrinkage control for fabrics made of cellulosic fibers. Trademarked as Sanforized®. (9)

computer-aided design (CAD). Computer software used to create new designs for textiles, apparel, or other products. (6, 21)

computer-aided manufacturing (CAM). Manufacturing system that utilizes electronics (computers at each workstation) for the production of textiles, apparel, and other goods. (6)

computer imaging. CAD function that enables a design to be seen on a monitor in three dimensions. The graphics allow the drawing to turn to any angle, so all sides of the fashion design can be seen. (6)

computer-integrated manufacturing (CIM). Manufacturing that combines CAD, CAM, robotics, and company information systems to approach *hands-off* production. (6)

computer programmer. Employee who writes computer programs and sets up computer systems for organizations. (20)

confined. When certain manufactured goods are sold to only one retailer in a certain trading area on an exclusive basis. (6)

conformity. Act of obeying, or agreeing with, some given standard or authority. (1)

conjugate fibers. See *bicomponent fibers*. (8)

conservators. See *costume curators*. (24)

consignment. Placing merchandise for sale in a store and being paid a percentage of the retail price, if and when it is sold. (14, 24)

consulting. The selling of a person's expert ideas and advice as a service business. (24)

consumer aids. Educational information provided by manufacturers, retail firms, or trade associations to inform consumers about their products. (15)

consumer education. The combining of teaching with business, often done for a manufacturing firm or a retail store. (24)

consumer protection agencies. Government agencies that work to improve merchandise standards and create new and better products; they also run quality and durability tests and determine wearability of garments. (15)

consumers. People who buy and use goods and services. (1, 2, 15)

contractors. Independently owned sewing factories that do some, or all, of the cutting, sewing, and finishing work for garments according to the manufacturing firm's designs and specifications. (6)

converters. Textile employees who plan the fabric construction and decide on suitable finishes and dyes based on the end uses. (20)

convertible collar. Collar style that can be worn buttoned at the neck or open to form a *V* shape with a lapel. (3)

cool colors. Hues, such as green, blue, and violet; reminders of water or the sky. (10)

co-op programs. Secondary and postsecondary school programs to place students in paid part-time jobs relating to their areas of study. (19)

cooperative advertising. Advertising done jointly by a manufacturer and retailer with the costs shared. (6, 7)

copies. Fashions that look similar to original haute couture garments, but are mass-produced in factories and much less expensive. (2)

copy. The words, lettering, and numbers in print or electronic advertising and media. (23)

copyists. See *sketchers*. (21)

copywriters. Employees who compose messages describing items for ads, collateral materials, and catalogs. (23)

cords. Jeans made of corduroy fabric. (3)

cord yarn. The result of twisting together a number of ply yarns. (8)

corporation. Business set up as a separate legal entity, giving the owners certain protection. (24)

co-spun fibers. Different polymers extruded through different holes in the same spinneret. (8)

costing. Determining the actual expenses of producing a design. (6)

costing engineers. Apparel manufacturing employees who determine the overall price of producing each apparel item. (21)

cost-per-wearing. The purchase price, plus upkeep, divided by the number of times an item is worn. (16)

costume curators. Employees who carefully restore and exhibit old textiles and garments, usually employed by a museum. (24)

costume jewelry. Inexpensive, trendy, obviously fake jewelry; often of unusual materials or plated with metals. (14)

costume technician. See *wardrobe helper*. (24)

cottage industry. A type of home-based business where families work in their homes using their own equipment. (24)

cotton. A natural cellulosic fiber obtained from mature seed pods of the cotton plant; the most widely used natural fiber. (8)

cotton belt. Band of southern states in the U.S. where cotton is grown. (8)

Cotton Incorporated. The marketing and research organization for cotton growers. (8)

Coty Awards. Another name for the American Fashion Critics Awards presented annually from 1943 to 1978 for the most creative and outstanding designers of women's wear, accessories, and menswear. (4)

Coty Hall of Fame. Honor bestowed on designers who won a Coty Award three different years. (4)

courses. Lines of loops that run crosswise on knit fabric. (9)

couturiers. Designers of exclusive, high-fashion garments. (2, 4)

cover message. Short business letter sent with a résumé to apply for a job. (19)

cowl neckline. Neckline style that is draped with flowing folds. (3)

crabbing. Woolen fabrics are given the correct width and length by drying and stretching. (9)

craze. Passing love for a new fashion that is accompanied by a display of emotion or crowd excitement. (2)

crease resistance. The baking of some fabrics with a resin to help them resist and recover from wrinkles. (9)

credit cards. Plastic cards that establish the holder's ability to charge goods and services at participating businesses; a buy now, pay later arrangement. (16)

credit limit. Maximum amount a person may have outstanding on a charge or other credit account; determined by the person's ability to pay. (16)

credit purchase. A promise by the buyer to pay the seller for goods or services in a specified way at a later date. Interest is charged to the consumer on unpaid balances. (16)

credit rating. Evaluation of the financial standing of a person or business based on past records of debt repayment, financial status, and other factors. (16)

crimp. The natural curl in wool fibers that looks like wavy lines or coil springs under a microscope; gives fibers elasticity and resiliency. Also the mechanical process of curling or waving manufactured *tow* filaments. (8)

croquis (crow-key). First rough sketches of a garment design showing any special details. (5, 21)

cross-channel shopping. Shopping for items across more than one retail channel, such as stores, mail-order catalogs, TV shopping channels, websites, and apps. (15)

cross dyeing. Method of piece dyeing where two or more fibers with different dyeing properties are combined in a fabric. (9)

crosswise grain. Direction of the filling yarns that run parallel to the fabric selvages. (9)

cuff. Band at the bottom of the sleeve, pant leg, or other area. (3)

cuff links. Worn in place of shirt buttons at the wrist through buttonholes on French cuffs. (14)

culottes. Pants made to look like a skirt. (3)

cultures. Customs and beliefs of certain groups of people. (1)

curved lines. Lines that are rounded and circular, or somewhat flattened out. (11)

custom-designed. Garments made with a special fit, design, and fabric for the one person who ordered them. (2)

custom-made. A product made for a particular person who has ordered it, usually after seeing a sample sketch or picture. See *made-to-order*. (2)

custom patterns. Patterns made to fit individual measurements. (5)

customer service representative. Retail employee in charge of handling customer complaints and returns, as well as special requests, including gift wrapping, home delivery, and special orders. (22)

cutters. Apparel manufacturing employees who cut out fabric garment parts for production. Also, the machines that do the cutting. (21)

cutting. In fabric finishing, a process that creates a cut pile; the ribs of floating filling yarns are cut down the center with razor-sharp cutting discs. (9); in apparel production, the cutting out of garment fabric parts before sewing. (21)

Cutty Sark Awards. Another name for the American Fashion Critics Awards presented from 1979 to 1988 to designers voted to be the most creative and outstanding by fashion editors of newspapers and magazines. They replaced the Coty Awards. (4)

cylinder printing. See *roller printing*. (9)

D

dart loom. Weaving loom using many darts that shoot across at the right time with individual lengths of yarn from a package beside the loom. (9)

darts. Short, tapered, stitched areas that provide shape for a garment to fit a figure. (2)

data processors. Employees who use computers to keep track of sales, shipping, billing, inventories, employee records, and payroll. In textile firms, they use computers to monitor textile production processes and create fabric designs. (20)

debit card. Card used for electronic transfer of money from a customer's bank account to that of a retailer to pay for purchases. (16)

décolleté. The French term for a low neckline, often with bare shoulders. (3)

decorative lines. Lines added simply to decorate garments and create interest. (11)

denier. Term used to describe a fiber's thickness or diameter. (8)

department managers. Retail employees who oversee the salespeople in their store departments. (22)

department store. Retail establishment that offers a large variety of many types of merchandise placed in appropriate departments. (7)

departmental buyers. Traditional retail buyers who plan and purchase all the goods for certain departments. They manage the inventory, pricing, and promotions and are accountable for sales and profits. (22)

design. The plan, or artistic arrangement, used to put an idea together. (12); selecting and combining the design elements of color, shape, line, and texture to create a fashion style concept. (21)

design directors. Home sewing pattern company employees who supervise the designers, pattern makers, and garment makers in producing the new pattern designs. (24)

design stylists. People who rework existing garment designs, rather than creating new fashion designs. (21).

designer labels. Designers' logos appear on the apparel to denote quality and status. (16)

designer patterns. Patterns for couturiers' fashions offered to home sewers by commercial pattern companies. (4, 5)

designers. People who create new versions of concepts, patterns, or styles in fabrics, apparel, and accessories. See *fashion designers*. (4, 21, 24)

detergents. Laundering products made synthetically from chemicals that break up oils, help water penetrate solids, and suspend and hold dirt away from clothes (18)

diagonal lines. Elongated marks that slant rather than being vertical or horizontal. (11)

diagram artists. Commercial pattern company employees who sketch the technical drawings to accompany the written directions of the guide sheet (24)

diapers. Basic garments for infants of folded cloth or other absorbent material drawn up between the legs and fastened near the waist. (17)

directional print. Fabric design in an up-and-down direction. (9)

direct printing. See *roller printing*. (9)

direct selling. The exchange of merchandise to individual consumers in return for money or credit. (7)

direct-mail marketing. See *mail-order retailing*. (7)

dirndl skirts. Skirt style that is gathered only slightly for minimum fullness. (3)

discharge printing. Variation of roller printing; a bleaching paste is applied to the rollers, which removes dye from certain areas of dyed fabric to result in a white design on a colored background. Also called *extract printing*. (9)

discount store. Retail outlet that sells merchandise at consistently low prices, usually in a simple building with low overhead, and utilizes mass retailing methods with few customer services. (7)

disinfectants. Sanitizers, sometimes used in laundering, that reduce or kill microorganisms to control or eliminate infections. (18)

display. Visual presentation of merchandise. (23)

display designers. Retail employees who create eye-catching displays for store interiors and windows. Also called *visual display artists*. (23)

display director. Employee in charge of the creation of all visual displays at a retail store; prepares rough sketches, outlines ideas, and makes blueprints or models for the display staff to follow. Also called *visual display directors*. (23)

distribution. Process of getting merchandise to the proper locations. (21)

distributors/planners. Retail chain employees who keep track of merchandise through precise, computerized records and allocate the stock items to the branches that need them. (22)

division director. Management employee who supervises the product managers, plant managers, and sales managers for a company's division. (21)

dobby attachment. Electronic loom attachment that weaves geometric forms into fabric. (9)

doctorate. The highest earned degree, usually requiring an additional three to six years of study beyond a master's degree. (19)

dollar stores. Bargain retailers with more locations and smaller discount layouts. (7)

dolman sleeve. Kimono type of sleeve with a lowered underarm. (3)

domestic production. The manufacturing of goods in one's own country. (6)

double-breasted. A front closure that laps over and has two vertical rows of buttons. (3)

double knit. Fabric produced on a weft knitting machine with two sets of needles and yarns; loops are drawn through from both directions to knit two fabrics as one. (9)

double ticketing. Garment sizing that combines two or more specific numbered sizes into general categories, such as small, medium, and large. (16)

doupion silk. Silk fibers made from two silkworms that have spun their cocoons together. It has irregular, thick-thin filaments producing a slubbed effect. Also see *shantung*. (8)

down. The light, fluffy feather undercoating of geese and ducks that is an extremely effective insulator. (8)

draped garments. Garments that are wrapped or hung on the human body and have characteristic folds of soft fabric. (2)

drawing. Process in textile manufacturing that combines several slivers into a strand that is drawn out, without twisting, and reduced to about the same diameter as the original sliver; it blends the fibers, arranges them in parallel order, and increases uniformity. (8)

dress codes. Written or unwritten rules of what should or should not be worn by certain groups of people. (1)

dressmakers. Expert sewers who do custom sewing, alterations, and clothing repairs for others. Also called *tailors*. (24)

drip-drying. Method of drying laundered items by hanging them up dripping wet, without squeezing or wringing, on nonrusting hangers or racks. (18)

dropped shoulder sleeves. Sleeve style with a horizontal seam going around the upper part of the arm. (3)

dry cleaner. Employee in a dry-cleaning firm who does the actual cleaning of garments with specialized equipment and solvents. (24)

dry cleaning. Process of cleaning textile items

with nonwater liquid solvents or absorbent compounds. (18)

dry spinning. Chemical spinning process that solidifies extruded filaments by drying them in warm air. (8)

dry-clean only. Means the item should not be washed, even by hand. (15)

durable finish. Fabric finish that lasts through several launderings or dry cleanings, but loses its effectiveness over a period of time. (9)

durable press. See *permanent press*. (9)

duties. See *tariffs* and *import taxes*. (6, 21)

dyeing. Method of giving color to a fiber, yarn, fabric, or garment by using either natural or chemical color agents. (9)

E

easy-to-sew patterns. Simple designs offered by commercial pattern companies; developed for beginners or busy sewers. (5)

e-commerce. See *business-to-business (B2B) e-commerce*. (6)

editors. Administrative journalists who supervise fashion writers and copywriters. (23)

educational representative. Consumer educator who promotes the products of a firm by teaching about them and their uses. (24)

Egyptian cotton. High-quality fabric with a smooth, silklike texture made from cotton grown in Egypt. (8)

elasticity. Ability to stretch, compress, and recover an original shape without damage. (8)

electronic data interchange (EDI). Secure computer linkages between companies to automatically communicate inventory levels, purchase needs, and other information throughout the supply chain. (6)

electronic merchandising. Promotion via electronic devices. (7)

electronic retailing (e-tailing). Online selling to consumers via computer and mobile devices. (7)

elements of design. Building blocks of design that include color, shape, line, and texture. (11)

emboss. To give a permanent raised and indented design to fabric using a calendering process; heated rollers have engraved sections that form the design. (9)

emphasis. Principle of design that uses a concentration of accent for a center of interest in a particular area of a design. (12)

empire. (om-peer) Dress with a high waistline. (3)

employee protection. Safeguards provided to workers by labor unions, private agencies, and government legislation. (19)

employment agency. Company that matches available jobs with qualified job applicants. (19)

empowers. When a manufacturing system gives workers the authority and autonomy to make the decisions needed to ensure the highest group productivity. (6)

entrepreneurs. People who start their own businesses and assume the risk and management of their enterprises. (24)

environmental sustainability. Preserving the well-being of our planet through responsible processes and uses of resources. (16)

enzymes. Proteins that speed up chemical reactions. In laundry products, they help break down certain soils and stains into simpler forms that can be removed more easily. (18)

epaulet sleeve. See *saddle sleeve*. (3)

ergonomics. Design of manufacturing systems that matches human performance to the tasks being done, the equipment used, and the environment for efficiency and safety. Also called *human engineering*. (6)

e-tailing. Selling to consumers electronically. (7)

ethical behavior. Accepted standards of fairness and good conduct on the job. (19)

ethics. Moral principles, or rules of conduct, that distinguish right from wrong. (16)

even plaid. See *balanced plaid*. (9)

examiners. See *inspectors*. (21)

executive trainees. Retail employees who receive on-the-job training for potential buyer and management positions. Also called *management trainees*. (22)

export incentives. Tax exemptions, rebates, and preferential financing plans offered by governments to producers who export goods. (6)

exports. Commercial products sent out of a country to other countries. (5)

extenders. Less expensive garments and accessories used to expand a wardrobe. Also called *multipliers*. (14)

Glossary

extension agents. Educators who teach apparel, family, and consumer subjects to groups such as 4-H clubs, community organizations, and individual families. They are hired and paid by state land-grant universities under the U.S. Department of Agriculture. (17, 24)

extract printing. See *discharge printing*. (9)

extruded. Forced out in the desired thickness; liquid chemical substances are extruded through spinnerets to make manufactured fibers. (8)

F

fabric. Cloth made from textile fibers or yarns by weaving, knitting, or other methods. (5, 9, 16)

fabric editors. Commercial pattern company employees who obtain samples of the latest fabrics for the firm's fabric library and recommend fabrics to be used for design samples. (24)

fabric softeners. Laundry products that give softness and fluffiness to washable fabrics and control static cling. (18)

factory outlet. See *outlet stores*. (7)

fad. Temporary, passing fashion or item with great appeal to many people for a short period of time; dies out quickly. (2)

fanny pack. A small bag that is worn around the waist with a buckle strap, usually for casual or athletic use. (14)

fashion. The prevailing type of clothing that is favored by a large segment of the public at any given time. (2)

fashion conscious. State of being aware of and wanting new fashionable items, usually for self-expression and peer approval. (15)

fashion coordinator. Retail executive who ensures all fashion departments are updated on the latest trends. Besides advising buyers and merchandise managers about new fashions, he or she assists the promotion departments. Also called a *fashion director*. (22)

fashion cycle. Periodic popularity, disappearance, and later reappearance of specific styles or general apparel shapes. (2)

fashion designers. Design entrepreneurs and employees who create new ideas for garments and accessories. Also called *apparel designers*. (4, 21)

fashion forward. Phrase implying the leading edge of fashion trends. (6)

Fashion Group International, Inc. (The). Organization of women who are influential in American women's fashions. (4)

fashion houses. Couture firms, each with a designer who creates original, individually designed fashions. See *haute couture*. (4)

fashion illustrators. Artists who draw garments that have been designed and produced by others. (23)

fashion information directors. Commercial pattern company employees who gather and interpret the latest fashion information about silhouettes, colors, fabrics, and accessories. (24)

fashion leaders. Men, women, and trendy young people with enough status and credibility to start new styles. (2)

fashion merchandising. The planning, buying, promoting, and selling of apparel and other goods to meet customer demands on price, quantity, quality, style, and timing. (7, 22)

fashion models. People who wear garments and accessories to show them to potential buyers. See *runway work* and *mannequin work*. (23)

fashion obsolescence. A fashion that has fad qualities that will soon date it. (15)

fashion photographers. Creative people who take pictures that show fashionable apparel and accessories looking their best. (23)

fashion piracy. The stealing of original design ideas, or the use of a design without the consent of the originator. (2, 4)

fashion shows. Planned presentations of a group of styles, often as part of the promotion of a season's new merchandise, usually with live models. (6, 23)

fashion trend. Direction in which fashion is moving. (2)

fashion writers. People who write about fashion for newspapers and magazines, or publish books on the topic. (23)

fast fashion. Small lots of new designs that are brought to market quickly through automated information transfer and collaborating partners. (6)

fasteners. Items to close garment openings, such as buttons, snaps, and hooks and eyes. (16)

Federal Trade Commission (FTC). Governing body over textile and apparel legislation and labeling; files complaints against violators of the trade practice rules. (15)

Glossary

felt. Process using a combination of heat, moisture, chemicals, and pressure, so the scales of the wool (or other) fibers interlock and mat together; felt fabrics are thick, somewhat stiff, and can be molded. (9)

fiber dyeing. Imparting color to fibers before they are spun into yarns. (9)

fiberfill. Manufactured crimped staple fibers used as filling without being made into yarns. (8)

fibers. The long, thin, hair-like strands that are the basic units in textiles. Different raw materials (natural or chemical) are processed into various fibers. (5, 8)

figure. Shape of a female's body. (12)

filament. A very long, fine, continuous thread; either found naturally as in silk or extruded from chemical solutions for manufactured fibers. (8)

filling knits. See *weft knits*. (9)

filling yarns. See *weft yarns*. (9)

films. Thin sheets, usually of vinyl or urethane, finished to look like leather or woven fabrics; sometimes used as coatings on fabrics. (9)

finance charge. The fee and interest charged to consumers for using credit to purchase goods or services; the cost of borrowing. (16)

fine jewelry. Expensive jewelry made of gold, silver, or platinum; may contain precious stones. (14)

finisher. Apparel manufacturing employee with better quality, higher-priced lines who does any hand sewing needed to finish garments. (21); also a dry-cleaning firm employee who restores the cleaned garments to their original appearance and shape using finishing equipment. (24)

finishes. The processes through which fibers, yarns, and fabrics are passed to improve their appearance, feel, and/or performance in preparation for their end uses. (9)

first impression. What others think when they first see or meet a person; a feeling or reaction. (13)

fit. How tight or loose a garment is on the person who is wearing it. (2)

fitted. Garment or garment part that is shaped to follow the lines of the body. (2)

fitting models. People employed by an apparel manufacturing firm or pattern company who try on garment samples to check fit, drape, and movability. See *mannequin work*. (24)

flagship store. Original department store that provides the operations direction and merchandise to its branch stores. (7)

flame resistant. A chemical fabric finish that prevents fabric from supporting or spreading a flame; causes the fabric to be self-extinguishing when removed from the flame source. (9, 15)

Flammable Fabrics Act. Law that specifies burning standards for household textiles and apparel. (15)

flaps. Decorative fabric pieces that fall down over the openings of pockets. (3)

flared. Garment, that widens near the bottom and has some fullness at the hem. (3)

flat drying. Method of drying laundered garments, usually used for wool, knit, and leather items such as gloves and sweaters. Items are laid on a flat, absorbent surface away from direct heat and shaped to their original dimensions. (18)

flax. Plant from which linen is obtained from the fibrous materials of the stalk. (8)

fleece. One year of sheep's wool growth. (8)

flocking. Printing a glue substance onto fabric in a pattern, so small pieces of fluffy material can adhere. (9)

forecasting services. Information consultants who predict coming fashion trends in colors, textures, silhouettes, and accessories. (5)

formal balance. Both sides are the same to create a centered balance. Also see *symmetrical*. (12)

franchisee. The owner-operator of a franchise business. (7, 24)

franchises. Business arrangement in which a firm grants retailers the right to use a famous or established name and trademarked merchandise in return for a certain amount of money. (4, 7, 24)

franchisor. The brand company that provides the name goods for a franchise business. (7, 24)

freelance jobs. Short-term jobs done for various firms that end when each assignment is completed. (20)

freelancing. The selling of expert skills as a service business. (24)

French sleeves. See *cap sleeves.* (3)

fringe benefits. Extra compensation other than pay, such as vacation time, insurance, sick leave, and pension plans. (6, 19, 20)

full-fashioned. Description of knits that are shaped during knitting; reduces garment seam construction to make a finer garment. (9)

full skirts. Skirts that are pleated or gathered for fullness. (3)

fulling. Mechanical finishing that shrinks some wool fabrics lengthwise and widthwise under carefully controlled conditions; makes the fabrics stronger and gives them body by tightening the weave. (9)

Fur Products Labeling Act. Law that requires descriptive labels on fur garments or garments containing fur trim; lists the names of the animals, if the fur was bleached, dyed, or otherwise artificially colored, and if scrap or waste fur was used. (15)

fusible web. A sheet of binder fibers that fuses two layers of fabric together when it is placed between them and pressed with a heated iron. (9)

G

garment. Any article of apparel, such as a dress, suit, coat, evening gown, or sweater. (2)

garment districts. Areas within a fashion city where apparel businesses are located. (4)

garment dyeing. The dyeing of apparel manufactured in various styles, but made from raw, undyed yarns. (9)

garment industry. Another name for the apparel manufacturing industry. Also called the *rag trade* or *needle trades.* (4)

garment makers. Sewers for commercial pattern companies or designers who construct muslin prototypes for approved designs, and then the samples in fashion fabrics. (24)

garment parts. The sleeves, cuffs, collar, waistband, and other components that make up a complete garment. (2, 3)

gathered skirts. Skirts that have the fullness of the fabric pulled together at the waist without structured folds. (3)

gaucho pants. Pants that end just below the knee with legs like wide tubes. (3)

gauge. Number of stitches or loops per inch in a knitted fabric. (9)

generic name. The identification for each group of manufactured fibers with similar chemical compositions. (8)

gored skirts. Skirt style with panels formed by vertical seam lines. (3)

gradation. A gradual increase or decrease of similar design elements used to create rhythm in a design; progression. (12)

grading. Scientific process of making garment patterns into larger or smaller sizes. (5)

graduate degree. See *master's degree.* (19)

grain. The direction that yarns run in a fabric. (9)

graphic designers. Advertising artists who prepare sketches or layouts, by hand or electronically, to illustrate their visions for the directions given by the art directors. (23)

greige goods. Unfinished fabrics. (5)

grippers. Heavy-duty types of snaps. (17)

grooming. Clean nails, hair, teeth, and body. (13)

growth features. Attributes of garments that allow them to be expanded as children grow. (17)

guide sheets. Illustrated printed directions for all cutting and sewing steps that are included in commercial patterns for home sewers. (5)

gusset. Wedge-shaped piece of fabric added to give more ease of movement at a kimono sleeve underarm or other area of a garment. (3)

H

hackled. The combing of flax fibers to straighten and clean them. (8)

haircloth. Fabric made from *horsehair.* (8)

halters. Brief garments worn on the upper body, usually in hot weather. (3)

hand. The way fabric feels to the touch. (9)

handling trucks. Canvas bins with wheels. (6)

hangtags. Detachable signs, usually affixed to the outside of garments, that provide manufacturers' promotional information. (15)

hardening a substance. Method to remove substances, such as candle wax and gum, from textile products by chilling the material so it can be easily scraped off. (18)

harem pants. Flared pants that are gathered in at the ankles. (3)

harmony. Pleasing visual unity of a design; the tasteful relationship among all parts within the whole. (12)

haute couture. (oat koo-tur´) French term that literally means *finest dressmaking*; has come to mean the high-fashion industry. See *fashion houses*. (2, 4)

head of stock. Retail store employee responsible for the stock (inventory) for one department of a large store, or an entire small store, and for coordinating the activities of stock clerks. (22)

heat setting. Process of drying and stretching manufactured fibers to give them the correct width and length. (9)

heat transfer printing. Transfer of colors and designs from special preprinted paper to fabric through the use of heat and pressure. (9)

Hemline Index. Theory that links the rise and fall of fashion hemlines to the rise and fall of stock market indexes. (2)

hemp. Inexpensive bast fiber. (8)

herringbone. Weave pattern where the wale changes direction at regular intervals to produce a zigzag effect. (9)

high-fashion. The very latest or newest fashions; fine quality and made with beautiful fabric, therefore expensive. Also called *high-style*. (2)

high quality. Items that have the best construction, materials, and design. (16)

high-sudsing detergents. All-purpose laundry detergents used primarily in top-loading washers. (18)

hip-huggers. Pants with waistlines that sit on the hips. (3)

hipster. A small bag on a long strap that crosses the body diagonally from the opposite shoulder. (14)

home sewing industry. Businesses that sell nonindustrial sewing machines, notions, fabrics, and patterns to home sewers. (24)

hood. Head covering that is attached at the garment neckline. (3)

horizontal lines. Elongated marks that go from side to side like the horizon. (11)

horsehair. Fibers made from the manes or tails of horses. (8)

horseshoe neckline. Neckline that is high at the back neck, but shaped like a *U* in front. (3)

hosiery. Panty hose, tights, anklets, knee-highs, leg warmers, and all other stockings or socks. Also called *leg wear*. (14)

hourly wage. The amount of pay for each hour an employee spends doing a job. (19)

house boutiques. Small retail shops owned by couturiers that sell items with the couturiers' labels. (4)

hue. The name given to a color. (10)

human engineering. See *ergonomics*. (6)

human resources manager. Oversees the hiring of the people employed by the company and manages the department handling all employee-related issues. (20, 22)

human resources offices. Firm department that deals with employment and all employee concerns. (19, 20)

hypermarkets. Large stores that sell almost every type of merchandise, including apparel and groceries. (7)

I

identification. The process of establishing or describing who someone is or what someone does. (1)

identity theft. The stealing of a person's identifying information to use it fraudulently. (16)

image. What others see when they look at the person and remember them later. (13)

import taxes. Taxes paid to government when the merchandise enters the U.S. to be sold. Also called *duties* and *tariffs*. (6)

imports. Goods that come into the country from foreign sources. (5, 7, 16)

impulse buying. Making unplanned purchases that are sudden and not carefully thought out. (15)

independent sales reps. See *jobbers*. (19)

indirect selling. Promotion to the general public. (7)

individuality. The quality that distinguishes one person from another; self-expression. (1)

industrial engineers. Cost and efficiency experts who coordinate people, materials, equipment, operations, space, and energy to save time and money. (20, 21)

Industrial Revolution. The time, roughly between the late 1700s and mid-1800s, when the hand-crafting economy changed to a machine-manufacturing economy for mass production. (4)

infant gown. Full-length garment for infants with sleeves and a drawstring closing at the bottom. (17)

infant kimono. A full-length infant garment that looks like a long dress; has sleeves; closes in the front or back with snaps or ties. (17)

informal balance. Created when design details are divided unequally from the center. Also see *asymmetrical*. (12)

ink-jet printing. Computer-driven ink-jet textile printers using thousands of micronozzles to spit droplets of the basic colors into designson fabrics moving through them. (9)

innovation. The creative, forward-thinking introduction of new ideas. (5)

inseam. Seam on the inside of pant legs from crotch to bottom of hem. (3, 16)

inspectors. Apparel manufacturing employees who check garment parts during production, as well as finished garments, for flaws and imperfections. Also called *examiners*. (21); dry-cleaning firm employees who examine apparel after the cleaning and finishing processes. (24)

installment plans. Credit arrangement by which a down payment is made toward a specific large purchase, and a contract specifies the periodic payments and finance charges. (16)

intensity. The brightness or dullness of a color; color purity. (10)

interests. The activities, ideas, and experiences people like the most. (19)

interfacings. Fabric pieces between the outer cloth and lining or facing of a garment, usually to give support and extra strength. (9, 16)

interlock knit. Lightweight and stretchy double-knit fabric with a smooth surface on both sides and a very fine lengthwise rib. (9)

intermediate hues. Colors made by combining equal amounts of adjoining primary and secondary hues. Examples are blue-violet, yellow-green, and red-orange. Also called *tertiary hues*. (10)

internships. A supervised work experience that can be either paid or unpaid. (19)

inventory. Supply of goods to be sold. (7, 21); an itemized list of a person's possessions. See *wardrobe inventory*. (14)

inventory control. See *stock control*. (7)

inverted triangle. A body build with an upper body that is larger in proportion to the lower body. (12)

investment dressing. Owning several basic high-quality garments that will last a long time and not go out of style. (14)

invoicing. Billing for goods or materials that were ordered and sent. (6)

ironing. Process of using a heated iron to remove wrinkles from damp, washable clothing using movement and pressure. (18)

ironing board. Flat, padded, cloth-covered surface, usually on legs, that is used for ironing. (18)

irregulars. Articles of merchandise with slight imperfections or defects that are sold to consumers at reduced prices. (2)

J

jabot. (ja-bow) Ruffled or lace trimming effect on the front of men's or women's shirts on the collar or going down from the neckline. (3)

jackets. Short coats. (3)

Jacquard loom. Type of shuttle loom that weaves large and intricate designs; the fabric pattern is programmed on a computer that controls when each individual warp yarn is raised for every passage of the shuttle. (9)

jagged lines. Lines that change direction abruptly and with sharp points like zigzags. (11)

jeans. Sturdy pants, usually made of denim. (3)

jewel neckline. Plain, rounded neckline that encircles the base of the neck. Also called *round neckline*. (3)

jewelry. Decorative accessories for personal adornment; necklaces, rings, pins, bracelets, and earrings. (14)

job. The work a person does to earn a living. (19)

job interview. Face-to-face meeting between a job applicant and the person who hires employees for a company. (19)

job lots. See *odd lots*. (7)

job shadowing. Following a worker on the job to observe the duties and responsibilities. (19)

jobbers. Independent sales reps who buy quantities of goods from different manufacturers to resell them to retailers. Also called *independent sales reps*. (21)

joint venture. Partnership of two firms for combined advantages, such as a domestic firm and a foreign producer for production and sales overseas. (6)

jumpers. Low-necked, one-piece garments with shoulder straps; worn over a blouse or knit top. (3)

jumpsuit. Garment with a bodice attached to pants. (3)

jute. Inexpensive bast fiber used in burlap. (8)

K

kapok. Natural cellulosic fiber extracted from seed pods. (8)

kimono sleeves. Sleeves that are continuous extensions out from the armhole areas with no seam line connecting them to the garment bodice. (3)

knickers. Pants that end just below the knee where they are gathered to a band or strap. (3)

knitting. Method of fabric construction done by looping yarns together. (9)

knockoffs. Lower-priced copies of garments that are produced in great volume using lower-quality materials and construction. (2)

L

label. Small piece of ribbon or cloth permanently attached to a garment that provides necessary information, most of which is required by law. (15)

labor intensive. When a big portion of finished products' total cost is due to large amounts of human effort, as compared to other expenses. (6)

laboratory technician. Employee who helps conduct research, often working under the supervision of research scientists. (20)

lamb's wool. Wool from a lamb up to seven months old. (15)

laminated. Fabric layers joined with an adhesive. (8)

lap. A continuous wide sheet of loose, natural fibers to prepare for carding. (8)

lapel. Pointed part of the front neckline of a garment below the collar that is folded back with the collar and looks like a continuation of it; forms a "V" notch along the outer collar edge. (3, 16)

lapel pin. Pin worn in the buttonhole on the lapel of a suit. (14)

laser cutter. A device that cuts out garment parts with an intense, powerful beam of light that quickly vaporizes the fabric. (6)

laundering. Washing apparel or other textile items with water and laundry products. (18)

laundry specialists. People employed on-site by institutions such as hospitals or hotels to maintain the linens, including uniforms, aprons, sheets, towels, tablecloths, and napkins. (24)

layaway purchase. Deferred purchase arrangement; the consumer makes a deposit and the store puts merchandise away for a certain length of time. During that time, the consumer makes payments to the retailer and receives the merchandise when paid in full. (16)

layette. Assembled minimal needs of clothing and textile goods for a newborn infant. (17)

layout artists. Advertising department employees who design the physical layouts for ads; they specify the typefaces and do comp renderings. (23)

layout designers. Commercial pattern company employees who mount the guide sheet copy and diagrams on layout sheets for printing. (24)

lead time. Amount of time customers must order ahead to receive the merchandise by the time they need to sell it. (6)

leased department. Department within a retail store operated by an outside firm for a percentage of the sales. (7)

leg wear. See *hosiery*. (14)

lengthwise grain. The warp yarns in a fabric running parallel to the selvages. (9)

leno weave. Weave variation where the warp yarns do not lie parallel to each other; they are used in pairs, with one crossing over the other before the filling yarn is inserted. (9)

letter of resignation. Letter to an employer that states the reason for leaving a job. (19)

letters of recommendation. Letters from references that provide more detailed information about a job applicant's abilities. (19)

licensing. Arrangement whereby manufacturers are given exclusive rights to produce and market goods bearing a famous name as a stamp of approval. In return, the person or firm whose name is used receives a percentage of wholesale sales. (4, 6)

lifestyle. A person's activities, including school, work, social, and leisure. (13)

line. Element of design that is a distinct, elongated mark as if drawn by a pencil or pen. (11); a collection of styles and designs that will be produced and sold as a firm's new selections for a given season. (6, 18)

line drying. Method of drying laundered items by hanging them on a clothesline, usually outside. (18)

linen. Natural fiber obtained from the fibrous materials of the stalk of the *flax* plant. (8)

linen supply services. Companies that own linens and rent them to institutions and businesses. (24)

lingerie. Feminine undergarments and nightwear. (3)

lining. Layer of lightweight fabric sewn inside a garment. (16)

lint. Cotton fiber after it has been ginned (separated from the seeds and cleaned). Also, any fuzz from the fiber ends of a natural fabric's surface. (8)

logo. Symbol that represents a person, firm, or organization. (4)

loom. Machine for weaving fabric. (9)

loss leaders. Items priced so low that the retailers make little or no profit on them, used to attract shoppers to their retail site. (7)

low quality. Items of only fair standards of construction, materials, and design. (16)

lowered waistline style dress. Dress with a long torso and a waistline seam close to the hips. (3)

low-sudsing detergents. Laundry detergents containing suds-control agents, especially recommended for front-loading, tumbler-type washers that are suds sensitive. (18)

lyocell. A biodegradable, cellulosic manufactured fiber made from wood pulp from trees grown in managed, constantly replanted forests. The chemical agents used to manufacture it are recycled. (8)

M

machine operators. Production workers who operate machines for manufacturing procedures. (20, 21)

machine technicians. Plant technicians who keep the complex manufacturing equipment in good working order. (20)

Made in the USA. Labels placed in domestically produced apparel. (6, 15)

made-to-order. See *custom-made.* (2)

mail-order retailing. Sales business done by selling to consumers through a catalog; direct-mail marketing. (7, 24)

maintenance workers. Employees who clean, paint, make repairs, and otherwise keep the physical structures of a business in good condition. (22)

management. Supervisory employees who plan, organize, coordinate, and oversee the work of others. (21)

management trainee. See *executive trainee.* (22)

mannequins. A lifelike figure used to display clothing. (7); the French term for human fashion models. (23)

mannequin work. Live fashion modeling to show companies' lines in the showrooms of designers or manufacturing firms. See *fashion models.* (23)

manufactured fibers. Fibers made by industrial processes from substances such as wood cellulose (the fibrous substance in plants), oil products (petroleum), and chemicals. (8)

margin. Profit; the amount of money made. (7)

markdown money. Funds given to retailers from manufacturers as compensation for losses when the selling prices of goods must be reduced. (7)

markdowns. Retail price reductions that are made in the hope of selling certain merchandise; most often made at the end of a season. (7)

marker. Long piece of paper that lays out all the various pieces and sizes of a garment pattern for economical cutting. (6, 21)

marker makers. The apparel manufacturing employees who figure out how the pattern pieces can be placed most efficiently on fabric for cutting. (21); also pattern company employees who calculate pattern layouts and fabric requirements for the designs. (24)

market. Group of potential customers. Also, the city or merchandise mart in which buyers and sellers congregate. (7, 20)

market researchers. Employees who conduct research by studying consumer tastes and changing trends. Also called *market analysts.* (20, 21)

market weeks. Periods of time when retail store buyers travel to look at collections shown by manufacturers in their showrooms. (6, 7)

marketing. The business of finding or creating a profitable market for specific goods or services. (5); identifying customers, determining the wants and needs of customers, and providing satisfying products at acceptable prices. (20)

marketing specialists. Advertising directors for manufacturing firms. (23)

markup. The difference between a company's cost of goods bought (purchase price) and the retail price of goods sold. (7)

mass market. The bulk of consumers; those who buy lower-priced, mass-produced garments. (2)

mass production. Factory manufacturing of large numbers of the same items at the same time, which lowers the production costs. (6)

mass retailing. Impersonal selling used by retailers to save money, since fewer salaries need to be paid; vast amounts of merchandise are put on racks and shelves, or are available in catalogs and on websites. (7)

master's degree. Post-college degree received after completing one or two more years in a specific program. Also called *graduate degree.* (19)

maternity fashions. Apparel for pregnant women. (17)

mechanical finishes. Fabric finishes that are applied using mechanical methods, rather than with chemicals. (9)

mechanical spinning. Process that pulls (draws) and twists fibers together to obtain a continuous length sufficient for weaving or knitting. (8)

medium quality. Items of reliably good construction, materials, and design. (16)

melamine. Manufactured chemical fiber that is flame resistant, has low thermal conductivity, and is stable at high heat; used for protective clothing. (8)

melt spinning. Chemical spinning process that solidifies the melted, extruded filaments by cooling them. (8)

mentor. Faithful counselor who values a person's abilities and potential and who guides that person's career. (19)

mercerization. A caustic soda treatment used on cellulosic textiles, such as cotton, linen, and rayon; increases the luster, strength, absorbency, and dyeability of the fibers. (9)

merchandise control specialists. Employees who monitor the sales flows of specific items in different geographic areas to predict trends and production needs. (21)

merchandise manager. Retail executive responsible for coordinating several departments or classifications of goods, plus supervises a group of buyers. (22)

merchandise plan. Each season's business plan for a manufacturer's line of designs; aimed at meeting the final consumers' demand for the goods. (6)

merchandisers. Employees who determine the direction a manufacturer's line will take each season, based on current market research. (21)

merchandising directors. Executives who lead a company's merchandising activities and determine which products/styles the firm's customers will buy. (24)

microdenier fibers. Very thin fibers; used to make wrinkle-resistant and water-repellent yet breathable fabrics that are soft, luxurious, and drapable. (8)

microelectronics. Miniature electronic components that result in smaller, faster, and cheaper computerized devices. (5)

mildew resistance. Metallic chemicals applied to fabrics that prevent mildew from forming. (9)

mills. Textile production plants that spin fibers into yarns and/or manufacture fabrics from yarns. (5)

mix-and-match items. Garments and accessories that can be combined in different ways with several other wardrobe items to provide flexibility and extend a person's wardrobe. (13, 17)

modacrylic. Modified acrylic fibers that resist flames and most chemicals. (8)

modesty. The covering of a person's body according to the code of decency of that person's society. (1)

Glossary

modular manufacturing. Apparel manufacturing system that divides the production employees into independent teams, or module work groups, for increased efficiency. (6)

mohair. Specialty wool from the long silky fleece of Angora goats. (8)

money conscious. Wise consumers' awareness of how much items cost and their monetary resources. (15)

monochromatic color scheme. Color plan that uses different tints, shades, and intensities of one color. (10)

monofilament yarns. Single filament strands, usually of a high denier. (8)

moth resistant. Chemical finish that discourages moths and carpet beetles from attacking wool fibers. (9)

motif. One unit of a design that is usually repeated. (11)

multifilament yarns. Yarns formed by twisting the many continuous strands of fiber being extruded through the spinneret at the same time. (8)

multipliers. See *extenders*. (14)

multisize patterns. Home sewing patterns with several sizes printed together on the same pieces. (5)

N

nanotechnology. The science of altering materials atom by atom, such as at the molecular level of chemicals. (5, 9)

nap. A layer of fiber ends raised from a fabric surface, appearing differently when viewed from different directions. (9)

napping. See *brushing*. (9)

natural fibers. Fibers made from natural (animal or plant) sources, the most common of which are cotton, linen, wool, and silk. (8)

need. Something necessary for a person's continued existence or survival. (14)

needle punched. Process that creates a mechanical interlocking of fibers with a needle loom; used for some nonwovens to hold their fibers tangled together. (9)

needle trades. See *garment industry*. (4)

networking. The exchange of information or services among an interconnected group of people. (19)

neutrals. Variations of black, white, and gray, rather than true hues. (10)

niche retailing. Dividing the total consumer market into narrow target markets by specific tastes or lifestyles. (7)

nightgown. Loose garment worn in bed. (3)

nightshirt. Nightgown that resembles a shirt. (3)

nonverbal communication. Type of personal messaging through facial expressions, hand gestures, body movements, and clothes. (13)

nonwoven fabrics. Fabrics made directly from fibers, rather than from yarns; sometimes formed when a chemical binder is added as a glue-like substance. Manufactured fibers can be melted together. (9)

notions. Small useful items sewn into or used on garments, such as thread, zippers, buttons, snaps, ribbon, elastic, and trim. (5, 24)

National Retail Federation (NRF). The trade association for leading American retailers. (7)

nylon. The first manufactured, noncellulose, test-tube fiber. (8)

O

occupation. The type of work that suits a person. (19)

Occupational Outlook Handbook. U.S. Department of Labor handbook that provides detailed information about employment prospects and working conditions for a variety of jobs. (19)

occupational training. Training received through programs such as technical schools, trade schools, and apprenticeships. (19)

odd lots. Incomplete assortments of manufacturers' goods, such as overruns or discontinued items, bought by retailers for reduced prices and sold as sale items. Also called *job lots*. (7)

odd-figure pricing. The practice of pricing retail merchandise a few cents lower than the next higher dollar, such as $2.99 or $19.98, to make the merchandise seem less expensive in shoppers' minds. (7)

office managers. Administrative employees who supervise the sales offices or plant site offices around the country. (20, 22)

off-price discounters. Retailers that sell moderate- to higher-priced brand-name apparel at lower-than-normal prices by purchasing odd lots and paying cash. (7)

offshore production. Manufacturing that is done overseas. (6)

offshore sourcing. The purchasing of goods from overseas producers. (7)

olefin. Nonabsorbent, shrink-resistant manufactured fiber that resists dyeing; lightweight with good *wicking* power. (8)

omni-channel retailing. The selling of identical products to consumers seamlessly across all channels of a retail company (such as stores, mail-order catalogs, and websites). (7)

online fabric sales personnel. Workers who sell goods from central offices and warehouses of online fabrics and notions companies. (24)

open-to-buy. The amount of merchandise (in dollars or units) that retail buyers are permitted to order for their store, department, or apparel category during a specified time period. (7)

opposition. The design rhythm created when lines meet to form right angles, such as in checks or plaids. (12)

optical illusion. A visual impression or perceived image that is misleading. (11)

organic cotton. Fibers from cotton plants where no chemical fertilizers or pesticides were used and which were not genetically modified. (8)

organic wool. Fibers from sheep that were not genetically engineered, with which no chemical pesticides were used, and from farms where only a certain number of sheep are grazed. No chemical processes can be used, from farm production to finished garments. (8)

outlet stores. Retail stores owned by the manufacturers that sell overruns, seconds, and some discount lines produced just for those stores. Also called *factory stores.* (7)

outside sales representatives (reps). The salespeople who work outside of the firm's sales office and showroom. (21)

overall print. A printed design that is the same across the entire fabric. (9)

overdrawn. An account in which the total amount of withdrawals and checks written against it is greater than the amount of money it contains. (16)

overruns. The extra items that were produced by manufacturers, but were not ordered for regular season selling. (2)

P

package priced. Each garment, or package of items, has an individual price marked on it for customers to read. (7)

packaging. The covering, wrapper, or container in which some merchandise for sale is placed. (15)

padding. Bulky, stuffed material placed inside a garment to give added shape. (16)

pajamas. Loose, usually two-piece, lightweight garment worn for lounging or sleeping. (3)

palazzo pants. Pants that are flared from the waist and very full at the bottom. (3)

pants. Garment that covers each leg separately. Also called *slacks* and *trousers.* (3)

parka. Heavy winter jacket with a hood and a warm fuzzy lining. (3)

partnership. Business structure with two or more owners. (24)

paste-up/mechanical artists. Advertising employees who put together the elements of a layout, such as the type, line drawings, and photographs. (23)

pattern graders. Apparel manufacturing or commercial pattern company employees who make patterns in all the different sizes to be produced, with the help of a computer. (21, 24)

pattern makers. Apparel manufacturing employees who create heavy paper patterns for the parts of new designs to be mass-produced. (21, 24)

peer pressure. Social influence from others in a person's age group. (1)

performance standards. The ratings of suitability of various textiles for specific end uses. (5)

performance test. Test given to some job applicants; determines the level of computer proficiency or other skills that are needed for the job. (19)

Permanent Care Labeling Rule. Law that requires manufacturers to attach clear and complete permanent care labels to all textile and apparel items. (15)

permanent finish. A fabric finish that lasts for the lifetime of the garment. (9)

permanent press. A chemical finish that helps fabric retain its original shape and resist wrinkling. Also called *durable press.* (9)

personal selling. Moves cosmetics, jewelry, clothing lines, and other merchandise directly to customers through parties or showings in homes. (7)

personal shopper. Retail employee who selects merchandise for customers. (22)

personal style. A person's appearance when design is used to the best advantage for that individual. (12)

personality. The total unique characteristics that distinguish an individual, especially his or her behavioral and emotional tendencies. (1, 13)

P.F.D. When garments are manufactured preshrunk and *prepared for dye*. (9)

photo stylists. Employees who book models, accessorize apparel, obtain props, pin up hems, iron garments, and pick up and return merchandise for photo shoots. (23)

photography work. Fashion modeling done in front of cameras. See *fashion photographers*. (23)

physique. Shape of a male's body. (12)

piece dyeing. Greige goods are placed in a dye bath before being cut and made into garments. (9)

piece goods buyers. Purchasing agents for the materials needed to produce garments. (21)

piecework system. Manufacturing method in which each specific task is done by a different person along an assembly line. (6)

pile. Fabric with loops or yarn ends projecting from the surface, such as terry cloth; velvet is made when the loops are cut. (9)

pill. To form an accumulation of little balls on the surface of a natural fabric through wearing or from rubbing. (8)

pima cotton. Cotton fibers of very high quality that are naturally long. (8)

pinsonic thermal joining. Quilting of some fabrics by a machine that uses ultrasonic energy to join (fuse) layers of thermoplastic materials. (9)

placement office. Office within a school in which people specialize in arranging contacts for placing students in appropriate jobs. (19)

placket. Decorative strip of fabric over a sleeve vent, closure, or fastener. (3)

plain weave. Simplest and most common fabric weave in which each filling yarn passes successively over and under each warp yarn. (9)

plaiting. See *braiding*. (9)

plant engineers. Employees responsible for manufacturing plants' heating, air conditioning, electrical, materials handling, and other systems. (20, 21)

plant manager. Manufacturing management employee who is responsible for all operations at a plant site. Also called a *production manager*. (21)

pleated skirts. Skirts that have structured folds of cloth. The pleats either hang open from the waist or are stitched down for a snug fit from the waist to the hips. (3)

ply. One strand of yarn. (8)

ply yarns. Yarns formed by twisting together two or more plies; multiple-ply yarns provide extra strength, added bulk, or unusual effects. (8)

pockets. Built-in envelopes in a garment to hold items. (3, 16)

policies. Action plans that guide decisions and outcomes. (15)

polybenzimidazole (PBI). A manufactured fiber that does not burn, melt, or drip; used for protective apparel. (8)

polyester. Versatile manufactured fiber known for its outstanding wrinkle resistance and easy care qualities; most widely used manufactured fiber. (8)

polylactide (PLA). Renewable manufactured fiber that uses natural lactic acid from plants as its polymer material; lightweight fiber with good wicking and low flammability properties. (8)

polymers. Chemical compounds made from linked molecules of various combinations of carbon, hydrogen, nitrogen, and oxygen. (8)

poncho. Unshaped, blanket-like outer garment with a slit or hole in the middle so it can be slipped over the head. (3)

portfolio. Contains a collection of a person's best and most creative work. (19, 20, 23)

postsecondary level of education. Education after high school. (19)

preschoolers. Young children between the ages of 3 and 5 years. (17)

preshrinking. Procedure done with heat and moisture to prevent fabric shrinkage of no more than three percent in either direction. (9)

press kits. Print or electronic informational packages containing promotional materials and sent to the media by manufacturers and retail advertisers. Also called *media kits*. (7, 23)

pressers. Apparel manufacturing employees who flatten seams, iron garment surfaces, and shape garments with steam pressing machines. (21)

pressing. Placing a heated iron on fabric and then lifting, rather than using a gliding motion as in ironing. (18)

pressing cloth. Piece of fabric placed between the hot surface of an iron and the item being pressed to prevent shine or other damage to garment fabrics. (18)

prêt à porter. (pret-ah-por-tay') The French ready-to-wear apparel (or *pret*) industry. (4)

price markets. Categories into which merchandise is placed according to the retail selling prices. (2)

primary hues. The three basic, pure colors of red, yellow, and blue; colors that cannot be made from any other color. (10)

princess dresses. Dresses with seam lines going up and down the entire length from the shoulder or the armhole and no horizontal waistline seam. (3)

principles of design. Balance, proportion, emphasis, and rhythm; the guidelines for the use of the elements of design: color, shape, line, and texture. (12)

printing. Process for placing color, pattern, or design onto the surface of fabrics. (9)

priority. Something that is most important and should be considered first. (14)

private label. Merchandise produced specifically for a retailer with the special trademark or brand name owned by the store or chain. (7)

product development directors. Retail management employees who work with the buyers to establish the basic items and fashion copies for their company's private label merchandise. (7)

product manager. Management employee who is in charge of every aspect of a product line or a specific category of items within a line. (21)

production assistants. Manufacturing employees who do detail work and record keeping for the plant managers. (21)

production manager. See *plant manager*. (21)

production supervisors. Plant employees who coordinate and direct the various departments and operators to maintain the highest production and the best quality. (20, 21)

production throughput time. The time required to turn raw materials into completed products. (6)

productivity. The measure of how efficiently and effectively resources, such as labor supply, machines, and materials, are used. (6)

profit. The incoming money that is left over in a business after all the outgoing expenses have been deducted. (6)

progressive bundle system. Piecework apparel manufacturing method in which cut garment parts are packaged into bundles of dozens to go through the sewing operations. (6)

promotion. Indirect selling to encourage public acceptance and purchasing through the use of advertising, displays, exhibits, and/or publicity. (7)

promotions. National or local advertising and merchandising efforts to increase sales. (2)

proportion. The spatial, or size, relationship of all the parts in a design to each other, as well as to the whole. Also called *scale*. (12)

protective clothing. Apparel that gives physical protection to the body. (1)

protein natural fibers. Natural fibers of animal origin, such as wool, silk, and specialty hair fibers. (8)

prototype. The original correct version from which others are made; the first full-scale trial garment of a new design. (5, 6, 21)

public relations specialists. Publicists who tell the story of a firm or its products or services through various media or in person. Also called *publicists*. (20, 23)

publicity. The free time, space, or editorial coverage given by various media because the message is newsworthy. (7, 23)

pullovers. Garments, such as sweaters, that slip over the head when put on or taken off. (3)

purchase order. Document written by a buyer that authorizes a seller to deliver certain goods at specified prices. (7)

purchasing agents. Employees who buy supplies and equipment for a company. (20)

pure silk. Silk fabric with no metallic weightings and no more than 10 percent by weight of dyes or finishing materials. (Black silk may have up to 15 percent.) (8)

pure wool. Fabrics that are made from all-wool fibers or yarns that have never been used before. Also called *virgin wool* and *100% wool.* (8)

purl knit. Knitted fabric with pronounced horizontal (crosswise) ridges with superior stretch and recovery in both directions. (9)

Q

quality. The degree to which a product meets desired standards of excellence and performance. (16)

quality control. Maintaining high standards of product design and manufacturing through product analysis and problem solving. (15)

quality control engineers. Production management employees who develop specifications for items that will be manufactured. (21)

quality control inspectors. Employees who ensure that precise standards and specifications are met for the manufactured products. (20)

quality standards. The ratings of textiles according to levels of defects. (5)

quilted fabrics. Two layers of fabric with batting in between, usually held together by machine stitching. (9)

quotas. Limitations set by the government on certain goods (by categories of products) that can enter the country during a particular time span. (6)

R

radial arrangement. Design rhythm created by lines emerging from a central point like rays. (12)

rag trade. See *garment industry.* (4)

raglan sleeves. Sleeve style with shaped seams in the garments originating from the underarms. (3)

ramie. Bast fiber sometimes used as a linen or cotton substitute. (8)

raschel knit. A type of coarse or open knit; often lace or net. (9)

ravel. When fabric comes unwoven at the edges. (8)

rayon. The first commercially manufactured fiber; made from cellulose. (8)

ready-to-wear (RTW). Apparel that is mass-produced in factories according to standard sizes. (2, 4)

reciprocal agreement. A cooperative pairing of services, such as a school in a fashion center offering parts of its program for credit to students from a university away from the fashion scene. (19)

recycle. To use again, often in a new and different way or after reprocessing. (14)

recycled wool. Wool fibers from previously made wool fabrics. (8, 15)

redress. Correction of, or a remedy for, wrongdoing. (15)

reeling. Process of unwinding the unbroken silk threads from water-softened cocoons and putting them on large reels. (8)

references. Adults (but not family members) who know a person well enough to recommend him or her for a job. (19)

registered number (RN). Identifying number of the producer of goods. (15)

reinforcements. Strengthening materials or supports at a garment's points of strain. (16)

related color scheme. See *analogous color scheme.* (10)

renewable. The ability to regrow fairly fast. (8)

renewable finish. Fabric finish that is temporary, but can be replaced or reapplied. (9)

repetition. The repeat of lines, shapes, colors, or textures in a garment; method of creating rhythm. (12)

resale shops. See *thrift shops.* (7)

research and development (R and D). The business department that develops new goods and improves old ones to satisfy consumer demand, while providing a profit for the company. (5, 20)

research scientists. Employees with advanced degrees in the sciences. In textile firms, they develop new synthetic fibers for certain characteristics and improve existing ones. (20)

resident buying offices (RBOs). Business organizations located in a market center that serves client retailers with market information and buying help. (7, 22)

resilience. Retaining shape or bouncing back when crushed. (8)

resin. Chemical substance applied to fabrics to increase both crease and wrinkle resistance. (9)

resist dyeing. Fabric coloring procedure in which areas that are not to be colored are restricted from the dye, while areas to be colored are left exposed to the dye. (9)

resources. The money, time, and skills a person has available to make wardrobe improvements or carry out other plans. (14)

response time. The amount of time it takes a manufacturer to produce and deliver merchandise after it has been ordered. (6)

responsibilities. Personal duties for proper courses of action. (15, 19)

résumé. Brief account of a person's education, work experience, and other qualifications for a job. (19)

retail buyers. Merchandising employees responsible for selecting and purchasing goods for a retail company, with the goal of making a profit for the company when the goods are sold. (22)

retail coordinators. Commercial pattern company employees who function as the fashion and promotional liaisons between pattern companies and retail fabric stores. (24)

retail salesperson. Employee who deals directly with customers by selling merchandise and handling payments—cash, checks, debit cards, credit cards, gift cards, etc.—according to store policy. Also known as a *sales associate.* (22)

retailers. Businesses that sell merchandise directly to the final consumers through a store or other sales methods. (2, 7)

retting. Bundles of flax stalks are soaked in water tanks—to allow bacterial action to loosen the outside flax fibers for removal from the rotting woody center stem. (8)

rhythm. The pleasing arrangement of design elements, so the eye moves easily over the apparel; one of the principles of design. (12)

rib knit. Double-knit fabric with pronounced vertical (lengthwise) ridges and great crosswise stretch. (9)

rib weave. Weave that uses filling yarns that are quite different in size from the warp yarns, giving a ribbed look. (9)

rights. Legal or moral privileges. (15)

robe. Long, loose garment worn over nightwear. (3)

robotics. Mechanical equipment that automates tasks so human workers are not required. (5)

roller printing. The application of designs to fabric using a machine with a series of engraved metal rollers around a large padded cylinder from which one color of dye paste is applied at a time. Also called *direct, calender,* or *cylinder printing.* (9)

rotary screen printing. A mechanized combination of roller and screen printing; dye is transferred to the fabric through porous, cylinder-shaped, nylon screens using separate screens for each color. (9)

round neckline. See *jewel neckline.* (3)

royalty fees. The percentage of wholesale sales received by designers in *licensing* agreements. (4)

roving. Process where cotton slivers are twisted slightly and drawn into smaller strands before being fed into spinning frames. (8)

rubber. Fibers that are made from the sap (latex) of certain plants; used in boots, raincoats, and elastic. (8)

rubbing. Passing fabric between calender rolls that are revolving at different speeds; produces soft, polished surfaces. (9)

runway work. Live modeling of new designer fashions, usually on a long platform, in front of an audience. See *fashion models.* (23)

S

saddle sleeve. A specific type of raglan sleeve. Also called *epaulet sleeve* or *strap-shoulder sleeve.* (3)

safety features. Attributes of garments that reduce the chances of injury or other hazardous occurrences. (17)

salary. Fixed amount of pay for an employee to perform the duties of a particular job. (19)

sale. Reduction in retail price made to clear out goods and/or bring in more customers. Also, a retail promotional event with merchandise offered at reduced prices. (7, 16)

sales. The exchange of goods from the supplier to the customer for money. (7, 20)

sales associate. See *retail salesperson.* (22)

sales managers. Management employees who supervise the sales representatives. (20)

Glossary

sales representatives. Employees who sell the products of a company to the next level of user in an industry's supply chain. (20)

sales resistance. Self-control to avoid making unplanned purchases while shopping. (15)

sales trainee. Person learning to do sales work; often an entry-level position. (20)

sample makers. Skilled sewers who make sample garments from a designer's vision. Also called *sample hands*. (6, 21)

samples. The initial trial garments made up by sample makers exactly as they will look when sold. (6, 21)

samplings. Small quantities of garments that are made and placed in retail stores to gauge consumer reaction. (6)

Sanforized®. See *compressive shrinkage*. (9)

sateen. Silk-weave fabrics using spun yarns; the floats run in the filling direction producing a lower-luster surface. (9)

satin. Silk-weave fabrics using filament fibers with low twist; the floats run in the warp direction producing a high-luster surface. (9)

satin weave. Weave with long yarn floating on the surface; fabric is composed almost entirely of yarns running in only one direction. (9)

scale. See *proportion*. (12)

scoop neckline. Neckline style that is lowered and round in front. (3)

scoured. Raw wool is washed to remove sand, dirt, and the natural oil, called lanolin. (8)

scraping. Method of removing a substance off a fabric by using a dull knife or a spoon. (18)

screen printing. Printing method similar to stenciling in which the dye paste is forced through untreated areas of a fabric screen; each color has a separate screen. (9)

scutched. After retting, rollers crush flax stalks to complete the separation of the soft linen fibers from the harsh, woody parts. (8)

seam. A stitched line that joins two garment parts together. (2, 16)

seasonless clothes. Clothing that can be worn during most of the year: fall, winter, and spring. (14, 15)

secondary hues. The colors of orange, green, and violet made by mixing equal amounts of two primary hues together. (10)

seconds. Apparel items that are soiled or have flaws, therefore priced lower than perfect goods. (2)

security guard. Employee who protects against shoplifters while stores are open and against break-ins when stores are closed. (22)

self-concept. The mental image people have of themselves. (13)

self-help features. Attributes of garments that enable children, as well as older adults or people with disabilities, to dress themselves. (17)

selvage. Side edges of woven fabrics, formed when the filling yarns turn to go back the other direction; strong and will not ravel. (9)

sericin. The gum released by silkworms when spinning cocoons to hold them together. (8)

sericulture. Science of the cultivation of silkworms; carefully controlling the cycle from moth to silk fiber. (8)

set-in sleeves. Sleeves that are stitched to the garment around the regular armholes. (3)

Seventh Avenue. The center of New York City's fashion industry; nearby streets and avenues are home to textile firms, menswear showrooms, fashion accessories companies, and the fur district. (4)

sewer. Dry-cleaning firm employee who repairs garments. (24)

sewing machine operator. See *machine operator*. (21)

shade. Darkened value of a hue from adding black. (10)

shape. Element of design; form or silhouette; the overall outline. (11)

shantung. Fabric made from *doupion silk* filaments. (8)

sheared. Removal of wool fleece from sheep. (8); mechanical finishing procedure where projecting fibers are cut or trimmed from the face of fabric. (9)

sheath dresses. Dresses that hang from the shoulders and have inward shaping at the waist, but no waistline seam. (3)

shift dresses. Straight, loose-fitting dresses that have no inward shaping at the waist and no waistline seam. Also called *chemise dresses*. (3)

shirt-sleeve measurement. The length from the back center base of the neck, across the shoulder, and down the arm around the bent elbow to the wrist bone. (16)

shirtwaist dresses. Dresses that look like long, semifitted, tailored shirts and usually have a belt or sash at the waist. (3)

shoplifting. The stealing of merchandise from a store. (15)

shoppertainment. Term for drawing people to a store or mall for the entertainment value of shopping; providing socialization, recreation, and an enjoyable escape. (7)

shopping cart. Electronic means for buyers to place their selected items when shopping on websites. (7)

shoulder bag. A bag that has a long enough strap to go over a person's shoulder. (14)

showroom manager. Employee who supervises the sales staff and all activity in a manufacturing firm's showroom. (21)

showroom salesperson. Employee who makes in-house sales presentations of a line of goods to buyers visiting the manufacturer's showroom. (21)

shrinkage control. Chemical finishes used to give a fabric dimensional stability. (9)

shuttle. The part of a loom that weaves crosswise yarns back and forth from edge to edge; it pulls the threads through the warp yarns. (9)

shuttleless loom. Weaving device that carries the filling yarns by steel bands attached to wheels or other methods without using shuttles. (9)

signature line. A collection of apparel or commercial patterns that has the endorsement of a celebrity. (5)

silhouette. The shape of a clothing style shown by its outer lines. (2)

silk. Luxurious natural fiber obtained by unwinding the cocoons of silkworms; fabric made by weaving the natural silk filament fibers. (8)

silk screening. See *screen printing*. (9)

singeing. Passing fabric over a series of gas jets, a flame, or heated copper plates to singe off any protruding fibers; gives a smooth, uniform surface. (9)

single knit. Stretchy knit fabric constructed on a single-needle, weft-knitting machine. (9)

single-breasted. A front closure that laps over and is held shut with one row of buttons. (3)

sisal. Cellulosic natural fibers extracted from plant leaves. (8)

sizing. Solution of starch or resin used to fill up spaces between yarns; applied to fabrics to increase weight, body, and luster. (9)

sketchers. Fashion house employees who make freehand, illustration-quality renderings of a designer's ideas, often from fabric draped on dressmaker's forms. Also called *copyists*. (21)

sketching assistants. Employees of an apparel manufacturing firm or pattern company who draw a season's line of samples and swatch them to be kept with the company records. (21)

skorts. Shorts combined with a skirt panel across the front. (3)

slacks. See *pants*. (3)

sleeve board. Miniature ironing board used for pressing sleeve seams and other hard-to-reach areas. (18)

sleeveless. Garment design that has no sleeves. The armhole hits the top of the shoulder where a set-in sleeve would ordinarily join the bodice. (3)

sliver. Molded, round, rope-like strand of natural fibers formed after carding or combing; about the diameter of a person's finger. (8)

sloper. A company's basic pattern size, programmed into computer software, from which all designs in a category start. (5)

smart card. A plastic payment card with an electronically stored cash value; looks like a credit card, but is reloadable with a computer chip embedded in the plastic. (16)

soaking. Method to remove stains from washable fabrics. (18)

soaps. Biodegradable cleaning products made mostly from natural fats and lye. (18)

social media. Websites and other electronic tools that allow people to communicate and share information. (16)

social responsibility. Idea that individuals and businesses should contribute to the welfare of the larger society. (16)

social saturation. A period when a fashion is worn by almost everyone, after which it starts to decline in popularity and eventually becomes obsolete. (2)

soft sell. Subtle (or background) sales efforts. (7)

soil release finish. Chemical finish for fabrics that eases the removal of soil and stains. (9)

sole proprietorship. Business with only one owner. (24)

solution dyeing. Process of adding color to a chemical fiber solution before it is extruded; provides clear, rich color with high colorfastness since the pigment is an integral part of the fiber. (8, 9)

sonic joining. Fusing seams together by using radio-wave, supersonic sound. (6)

spandex. Strong and lightweight manufactured fiber with great elasticity. (8)

specialty retailer. Retailer that carries a specific kind of merchandise or one category of goods, such as shoes, bridal attire, or children's apparel. (7)

specialty wools. Fibers from the hair of goats, camels, llamas, or other animals. (8)

spinneret. Device made from corrosion-resistant metals that extrudes liquid into fibers; has hundreds of tiny holes, each forming one fiber. (8)

spinning. Process by which twisted slivers are fed into a frame, where they are drawn out to the final size and twisted into yarn. (8)

split-complementary color scheme. The use of one color with the two colors on each side of its complement on the color wheel. (10)

sponging. The dampening and drying of wool fabrics to prevent them from shrinking during dry cleaning. (9); also, a method of removing stains from fabrics. (18)

sport coats. Classic, suit-type jackets. Also called *blazers*. (3)

spotter. Dry-cleaning firm employee who treats stains with proper spot removal methods. (24)

spreaders. Machines that move bolts of yard goods back and forth on long tables, in high stacks, for garment piece cutting. (6); apparel manufacturing employees who lay out fabric for cutting. (21)

spring season. Personal color category for people with warm undertones and lighter skin/eyes. (10)

spun silk. Silk made from pierced cocoons (cut filaments) or waste silk. (8)

spun yarns. Yarns made with *staple fibers*, which are usually bound together by *mechanical spinning*; more irregular than filament yarns. (8)

stain resistance. Ability to resist spills and other soiling because of chemical finishing that makes the fibers less absorbent. (9)

standards. The criteria set by authorities who judge products to verify certain levels of quality. (15)

staple fibers. Short fiber pieces, usually between one and four inches; cotton, linen, wool and other natural fibers occur normally as staple, while manufactured fibers are cut into staple. (8)

starches. Sizings that restore body and crispness to fabrics that have become limp from laundering and wear. (18)

status. One's position or rank compared with that of others. (1)

stock clerk. Entry-level retail employee who receives and marks merchandise, moves it to the selling floor, maintains inventory records, and otherwise handles merchandise inventory. (22)

stock collar. Collar style that is an imitation of an ascot; accessory added at the neck like a necktie. (3)

stock control. The receiving, storing, and distributing of merchandise in a retail store. Also called *inventory control*. (7)

stock dyed. When color is added to the loose natural fibers before spinning. (9)

stock keeping unit (SKU). Numbers that give the style, color, size, vendor, and other chosen information for each item; basic unit of inventory. (7)

store manager. Retail executive responsible for the profitable operation of an entire store and all its functions. (22)

STORES Magazine. Trade publication of the NRF. (7)

straight lines. Elongated marks that are not curved or jagged. (11)

straight skirts. Skirts that go down straight from the hipline with no added fullness and a slim silhouette. (3)

strap-shoulder sleeve. See *saddle sleeve*. (3)

structural designs. Knitted patterns or special weaves used by textile designers to create structural interest in woven fabrics. (20)

structural lines. Lines formed when parts of the garment are constructed (seams, darts, pleats, tucks, and garment edges). (11)

structural texture. The texture created when fabrics or garments are manufactured. (11)

style. A particular design, shape, or type of clothing item; distinct features that create a garment's overall appearance. (2)

stylish. In vogue; wearing the styles that are currently popular and fashionable. (2)

stylists. See *design stylists*. (6)

summer season. Personal color category for people with cool undertones and lighter skin/eyes. (10)

sundresses. Dresses for hot weather with a brief bodice, often with shoulder straps and a low neckline. (3)

supply chain. See *channel of distribution*. (7)

surface designs. Designs applied on the right side of fabrics, usually by printing. (20)

surfactants. Surface active agents in detergents that reduce the surface tension of water, help loosen and remove soil, and suspend the soil in the water until it is drained. (18)

surplice. A diagonally overlapping neckline or closing. (11)

sweater. A knitted (or crocheted) covering for the upper body, usually worn for warmth. (3)

sweater knits. A loosely knitted, stretchy fabric made with large denier yarns to resemble hand knitting. (9)

sweatshops. Manufacturing plants that pay less than fair wages, use child labor, do not recognize overtime worked, have unclean conditions, or violate workers' rights in other ways. (6)

symmetrical. Containing formal balance, or design details that are identical on both sides and an equal distance from the center. (12)

synthetic. Noncellulosic. (8)

T

tabs. Decorative fabric pieces that go out from the edge of pockets or other areas of a garment. (3)

tailor. See *alterations expert* and *dressmaker*. (22)

tailor system. Apparel manufacturing system in which all sewing tasks for a garment are done by one person; for custom-made or high-priced garments. (6)

tailored garment. Garment that is made by cutting garment's fabric pieces and then sewing them together to fit the shape of the body. (2)

tapered pants. Pants that narrow near the bottom or hem. (3)

target market. The group of consumers who are most likely to buy specific goods. (7)

tariffs. Government import taxes paid when goods enter a country to be sold. See *duties*. (6)

technical schools. Provide training for jobs at the secondary and postsecondary educational levels. (19)

technical writers. Employees with commercial pattern companies who create clear, easy-to-read and -follow sewing directions. (24)

technology. Creation, modification, or application of products, methods, and systems, usually advanced through research and development. (5)

television retailing. Retailing that combines entertainment and sales to show and describe merchandise on certain home shopping television channels. (7)

temporary finish. Fabric finish that lasts until washing or dry cleaning. (9)

tent dresses. Large, billowy dresses that hang loosely from the shoulders. (3)

tentering. Process that gives some fabrics their final shapes by passing them through heat, and sometimes moisture, while in a stretched condition. (9)

tertiary hues. See *intermediate hues*. (10)

textile/apparel pipeline. The specific apparel channel of distribution. (7)

Textile/Clothing Technology Corporation [(TC)2]. An industry-wide, not-for-profit, textile/apparel coalition that researches high-tech innovations in apparel production processes and helps the industry to implement them. (6)

textile colorists. Textile industry employees who decide which color combinations in textile designs are most likely to appeal to customers. (20)

textile converters. Firms or individuals that buy or handle greige goods for finishing. Also see *converter*. (5)

textile designer. Textile industry employee who creates the patterns and designs, or redesigns existing ones, for new fabrics. (20)

Textile Fiber Products Identification Act. Legislation requiring all fibers, including their generic group names, to appear on textile product labels; must be listed in order of content by weight. (15)

textile industry. Businesses that work with any or all processes needed to produce fibers, yarns, and finished fabrics. (4, 20)

textile stylists. Textile industry employees responsible for the long-range fashion planning of fabric colors, weights, and textures. (20)

textile tester. Technician with a textile mill or an independent testing laboratory who tests new products against specifications. (20)

texture. Element of design; the surface quality of goods, or how they feel and look; the quality of roughness or smoothness, dullness or glossiness, or stiffness or softness. (11)

texturing. Process of turning straight, rod-like fibers into crimped, coiled, or looped forms. (8)

theatrical costuming. Job of finding or creating appropriate apparel for opera, ballet, stage plays, circuses, movies, advertisements, television productions, and parades. (24)

thermoplastic materials. Materials that soften when heated and harden again when cooled. (9)

threads. See *yarns*. (9)

thrift shops. Shops that sell items that have been owned and used by others. Also called *resale shops*. (7)

throwing. The process of tightly twisting silk filaments together for a heavier weight before it is woven into fabric. (8)

tie dyeing. A form of resist dyeing using tight folds to form barriers to the dye where desired. (9)

tint. A lightened color made by adding white to a hue. (10)

toddlers. Young children, usually between 1 and 3 years of age, who are actively moving or walking. (17)

Tokyo Collection. Association organized to introduce Japanese designers to international buyers, the public, and the press. (4)

top management. A firm's highest executives. (21, 22)

tow. Manufactured fibers that are extruded from the spinneret in large continuous filament bundles before being cut into staple. (8)

trade associations. Groups that promote or further the interests of a certain industry or trade. (4)

trade deficit. A negative economic condition; the amount of a country's imports is greater than the amount of exports. (5)

trademark. A distinctive symbol or name that identifies the goods of a particular producer or manufacturer; registered with the U.S. Patent Office. (8, 16)

trade publications. Magazines, newspapers, and books that deal specifically with a certain industry or trade. (4)

trade schools. Provide job-specific training at the postsecondary level. (19)

trading company. Import/export business that contracts for, trades, or buys merchandise from other countries to sell in the U.S. (24)

training supervisors. Manufacturing plant employees who train new operators for specific tasks or how to use specialized machines. (21); also, large retail store employees who give orientation classes to new salespeople, train executive trainees, and update current employees. (22)

transition. Fluid design rhythm created when a curved line leads the eye over an angle. (12)

transportation managers. Employees who plan, direct, and coordinate the incoming and outgoing shipments of goods for their companies. (20)

travel wardrobe. All of the apparel a person takes on a trip. (17)

trendsetters. People who lead by example within their social groups. (2)

triacetate. See *acetate*. (8)

triad color scheme. Color plan that uses three colors equidistant on the color wheel. (10)

triangular. A body build where people have broad hips that are large in proportion to their upper bodies. (12)

tricot. Drapable, warp-knit fabric with fine, vertical wales on the front and crosswise ribs on the back. (9)

trimmers. Apparel manufacturing employees who cut off loose threads, pull out basting stitches, and remove lint and spots from finished apparel items. Also called *cleaners*. (21)

trimmings. Various types of ornamentation added to garments. (16)

trousers. See *pants*. (3)

true bias. Grain line that runs at a 45 degree angle, or halfway between the lengthwise and crosswise grains of a fabric. See *bias grain*. (9)

trunk. Measurement from shoulder to crotch. (17)

trunk show. A complete collection of designer samples brought into a store for a limited amount of time. Orders are taken directly from customers by a key company salesperson. (6)

Truth in Lending Act. Federal statute requiring grantors of consumer credit to reveal the true cost of credit in uniform, easy-to-understand terms. (16)

tubular silhouette. Fashion dress style that hangs straight from the shoulders to the hem without being belted. (2)

tunic. A hip-length or longer blouse or shirt that extends down over pants or a skirt and is often belted. (3)

tussah. Fabric woven from *wild silk* fibers. (8)

twill weave. Weave type where the yarns in one direction pass over two or more yarns in the other direction at regular intervals; creates a diagonal rib or cord pattern. (9)

U

ultrasonic energy. Sound energy that is higher in frequency than can be heard by the human ear; used to join layers of thermoplastic materials. (9)

umbrella skirts. Skirt style with many narrow gores that open and close as the wearer moves. (3)

understated design. Garments with subtle colors, simple lines, and little decoration. (12)

undertone. Subdued trace of a color seen through another color or modifying the other color. Every skin color has an undertone of either yellow (warm) or blue (cool). (10)

uneven plaid. A plaid design that is different in one or both directions. (9)

uniforms. Outfits or articles of clothing that are specific to everyone in a certain group of people. (1)

unit production system (UPS). Computerized piecework apparel manufacturing system; cut pieces of each garment are hung (loaded) together onto an overhead product carrier, which is moved through the manufacturing steps by a conveyor system. (6)

universal product code (UPC). Standardized bars on merchandise to be scanned for instant computerized inventory updates and sales tracking. Also called *bar codes*. (7)

upper-level executives. Presidents, vice presidents, and directors of companies; oversee various departments or aspects of the business. (20)

V

value. The lightness or darkness of a color, ranging from almost white to almost black. (10); the degree of worth or measure of benefit of something, such as highest quality of garment materials, construction, and fashion for the lowest price. (16)

value added. The increase in the worth of products as a result of a particular work activity. (21)

values. The ideals and beliefs important to individuals. (1)

variants. Manufactured fibers that are modified versions of the generic group composition. (8)

variety store. Store with wide assortments of inexpensive merchandise, such as clothing, stationery, plants, and toys. (7)

vat dyeing. Piece dying for cellulosic fiber textiles; the color develops (oxidizes) after the vat dyes are inside (or combined with) the fiber; vat-dyed fabrics are very colorfast. (9)

vendors. Suppliers that sell goods to manufacturers or wholesalers. Also, the manufacturers from whom retail store buyers purchase goods. (22)

vent. An opening that goes up into a sleeve from the opening of the cuff. (3)

vertical lines. Elongated marks that go up and down. (11)

vests. Sleeveless, close-fitting, jacket-like garments that cover the chest and back. (3)

vice president. A high-level management executive in charge of certain large functions within a business. (22)

video demonstration work. Employment in the production of videos such as those that give information on wardrobe planning, pattern alterations, and sewing techniques. (24)

video merchandising. The use of videos in retail stores to show new fashion trends, promote merchandise, and build customer traffic. (7)

Glossary

virgin wool. Wool fibers that have never been used before. Also called *pure wool* or *100% wool*. (8)

virtual product development (VPD). The practice of developing products in a fully digital environment. (6)

virtual reality. Technology that allows users to create, access, and interact with computer simulated objects and environments. (16)

visual merchandising. Presenting goods in an attractive and attention-getting manner through displays, exhibits, and special promotional activities. (7)

visual presentation director. See *display manager*. (23)

W

waistband. Band of fabric that fastens together at the waistline of a garment. (3, 16)

wale. In woven fabrics, a diagonal rib or cord pattern. (9)

want. Desire for something that gives personal satisfaction, but is not necessary. (14)

wardrobe. The apparel a person owns, including all garments and accessories. (2)

wardrobe consultants. People who show consumers how to combine fashion items to enhance personal or professional images and help them plan and manage their wardrobes and purchases. (24)

wardrobe designer. The head of theatrical costuming for an entertainment production organization. (24)

wardrobe helper. Theatrical worker who helps to obtain, make, and organize costumes and accessories by character and scene and to help the actors dress for the production. Also called a *costume technician*. (24)

wardrobe inventory. Itemized list of apparel and accessories that a person owns. (14)

wardrobe plan. A blueprint of actions needed to update or complete a person's wardrobe in the best way. (14)

warehouse clubs. Discount retailers that specialize in bulk sales of nationally branded merchandise; membership fees apply. (7)

warm colors. Hues, such as red, orange, and yellow that appear to be hot like the sun or fire. (10)

warp knits. Fabrics made on flat-knitting machines using many yarns and needles, with loops interlocking in the lengthwise direction. (9)

warp yarns. Yarns that run lengthwise (parallel to the selvage) in woven fabrics. (9)

wash load. The clothing and other washable items put into a laundry machine to be washed together. (18)

washer agitation. The mechanical action that helps to loosen and remove soils during laundering. (18)

washing operator. Employee who does laundry with wet washing and drying equipment. (24)

waste fur. Fur taken from the ears, throats, paws, tails, or bellies of animals. (15)

water repellent. Fabric finish that provides partial protection; not completely waterproof. (9)

water softeners. Chemical agents or mechanical devices that neutralize or remove the mineral ions found in hard water. (18)

waterproof. Finish that provides complete water protection on a fabric. (9)

wearing ease. The extra room built into a garment, beyond that needed to accommodate actual body measurements, that allows the wearer to move comfortably. (16)

weaving. Procedure of interlacing two sets of yarns placed at right angles to each other on a loom. (9)

weft knits. Fabrics knit with one continuous strand of yarn going crosswise. Also called *filling knits*. (9)

weft yarns. Crosswise yarns running from selvage to selvage at right angles to the warp yarns in a woven fabric. Also called *filling yarns*. (9)

weighted silks. Silk fibers with salts from tin, lead, or iron added to make them heavier. (8)

weskits. See *vests*. (3)

wet spinning. Chemical spinning process that hardens extruded filaments in a chemical bath. (8)

wholesalers. Businesses that sell goods in large lots to retailers. (2)

wicking. The ability to pull moisture away from the body and onto the surface of a fabric where it can evaporate quickly. (8)

wild silk. Fibers from uncultivated silkworms; strong with a distinctive rugged appearance when woven; stiff, coarse texture and difficult to bleach or dye. (8)

window shopping. Browsing stores and evaluating merchandise and displays, without purchasing. (15)

winter season. Personal color category for people with cool undertones and dark skin/eyes. (10)

Women's Wear Daily **(WWD).** The premier trade newspaper covering all aspects of the women's fashion industries. (4)

woof yarns. See *filling yarns.* (9)

wool. Natural protein fiber obtained from the fleece of sheep or lambs; the most commonly used animal fiber. (8)

wool pools. Collection points organized throughout the country for fleece from many producers. (8)

Wool Products Labeling Act. Law requiring labels to specify the percentage of each type of wool, virgin wool, and recycled wool; imported wool must be labeled as such, and include the country of origin. (15)

woolen yarn. Less expensive yarn made from short wool fibers (less than 2 inches). Fabrics made from woolen yarns are relatively dense and have soft, fuzzy surfaces. (8)

work-based learning programs. Programs offered by schools that place students in a job while they are still taking classes. (19)

worsted yarns. Higher-priced wool yarns made from long staple fibers. Fabrics made from these are smooth and compact. (8)

wrap skirts. Skirts that wrap around the body, overlap at the side-back or side-front, and are fastened with a tie or button. (3)

wrapper. Dry-cleaning firm employee who packages the finished apparel to maintain the quality of cleaning and finishing. Also called a *bagger.* (24)

written test. Test of general knowledge and aptitudes. (19)

Y

yang. Chinese term that represents the active, rugged, extroverted elements of personality. (13)

yard goods. Manufactured lengths of fabrics. (9, 20)

yarn dyeing. Placing spools of yarns into a dye bath. (9)

yarns. Continuous strands, usually of multiple fibers, ready for knitting, weaving, or other processing into cloth. (5, 8)

yin. Chinese term that represents the passive, timid, sensitive, and delicate elements of personality. (13)

yoke. A band or shaped piece, usually at the shoulders or hips, to give shape and support to the garment below it. (3)

Index

A

Abilities, 371
Absorbent, 146
Accented neutral color scheme, 204
Accessories, 38, 266–271
    belts, 268
    definition, 266
    eyewear, 270
    footwear, 267
    gloves, 270–271
    handbags, 267–268
    handkerchiefs, 269
    headwear, 268
    hosiery, 271
    jewelry, 270
    neckties, 268–269
    scarves, 268
    using to advantage, 266–267
Accessories magazine, 72
Accessory editors, 472
Account and finance employees, 402
Accountant, 440
Account executive (AE), 452
Acetate, 157, 158, 161, 165
Acrylic, 158, 162, 164
Action wear, 334
Added visual texture, 225
Administration, textile, 402
Administrative assistants, 440
Administrative employees, 424
Adornment, 23–24
Adult education, 470
Advertising, 28, 126, 182
Advertising and promotion specialists, 401
Advertising directors, 454
Agile manufacturing, 121
Alpaca, 146, 153
Alteration hand, 418
Alterations, 310
Alterations expert, 438
American Association of Textile Chemists and Colorists (AATCC), 392
American Fashion Critics' Awards, 76
American fashion designers and firms, 80
American Fiber Manufacturer's Association, Inc., 157
Americans with Disabilities Act (ADA), 384
Amylase, 355
Analogous color scheme, 203
Anchor stores, 133
Angora, 146, 153
Anidex, 158, 163
Antistatic, 187
Apparel
    appropriate, 253–255
    changeability of colors, 205
    choices, enjoy, 257
    climate, 254–255
    community standards, 255
    definition, 36
    evaluate current, 261–263
    industries, scope, 71–73
    infants, 323–326
    international care labels, 353

    lifestyle, 253
    maternity fashions, 335
    older adults, 330–332
    people with disabilities, 332–335
    people with special needs, 323–341
    sizes, 308
    travel wardrobes, 335–338
    using colors, 204–207
    wardrobe inventory, 262
    yin and yang traits, 251
    young children, 326–330
Apparel design and production
    administrative employees, 424
    careers, 409–427
    design, 409–414
    management, 418–420
    manufacturing, 414–418
    sales and distribution, 420–423
    top management, 423–424
Apparel designers, 410
Apparel educators, 467–471
    classroom teacher, 468–469
    extension agents, 469–470
Apparel fabrics glossary, 189
Apparel magazine, 72
Apparel marts, 114
Apparel production
    business, 104, 481
    designing process, 106–107
    establishing merchandise plans, 104–106
    factory production, 109–112
    innovation, 118–121
    manufacturing, 71, 414–418
    overseas manufacturing, 115–118
    planning systems, 418
    plants, 414
    preparation, 107–109
    selling the apparel, 112–115
Apparel retail outlets, 132–137
    branch, 133
    chain, 133–134
    department stores, 132
    discount, 134
    electronic retailing, 136–137
    franchises, 135
    less common types, 136–137
    mail-order houses, 136
    specialty, 135
    television retailing, 136
Application form, 378
Applied lines, 222
Appliqués, 264
Apprenticeship program, 373
Aptitudes, 370
Aramid, 158, 163, 165
Argyle, 37
Armchair shopping, 281
Art director, 452–453
Artificial suede, 179
As ready, 129
Assembler
    dry cleaning, 476
    manufacturing, 416
Assistant converter, 397

Assistant designers, 412
Assistant fashion coordinator, 443
Assistant photographers, 459
Assistant piece goods buyers, 419
Assistant retail buyers, 434
Assistant stylist, 395
Associate's degree, 373
Assorters, 416
Asymmetrical, 232
Asymmetrical dress, 52
Attendants, 477
Attention, avoiding and attracting, 237
Attitudes, 28
Audiovisual (AV) jobs, 461
Audiovisual labs, 453
Automatic dryer, 359
Avant-garde clothes, 36

B

B2B e-commerce, 120
Bachelor's degree, 374
Bagger, 476
Balance, 231–232
    definition, 231
    types, 232
Bales, 146
Bamboo fibers, 158
Bankruptcy, Chapter 11, 430
Bar codes, 129
Bargains
    definition, 311
    evaluate, 311–314
    shopping at sales, 311–312
    types of sales, 312–313
Basic apparel, 271
Basic stock, 129
Bast fibers, 150
Batik, 183
Beetling, 187
Belts, 268
Benchmarking, 112
Bicomponent fibers, 163
Billing agent, 440
Biodegradable, 355
Bleaches, 355
Bleaching, 181
Blend, 166
Block printing, 185
Bodice, 38–39
Body builds, 236
    general guidelines, 242–243
    large lower body, 241
    large upper body, 240–241
    short and heavy, 239
    short and thin, 239
    tall and heavy, 238
    tall and thin, 237–238
    thick middle, 241
    types, 237–243
Body measurements, know and use, 307–309
Body scanning, 139, 284
Body shape illusions, 237
Bolls, cotton, 146
Bonded fabrics, 179–180

Index

Border prints, 183
Box loom, 175
Braided fabrics, 181
Branch coordinator, 444
Branch stores, 133
Bridge jewelry, 270
Bridge lines, 79
Brushing process, 187
Builders, 355
Business
    apparel production, 104
    home sewing patterns, 95–96
Business operations specialists, 403
Business plan, 477
Business-to-business (B2B)
    e-commerce, 120
Buttonholes, 303
Buyer qualifications, 433–434
Buyer's office support staff, 440
Buyers' schedules and benefits, 433

C

Calculations and decisions, 105–106
Calendering, 186–187
Calender printing, 184
California Apparel News, 72
Camel's hair, 146
Capital, 95, 104
Cardigans, 63
Carding, 147, 151
Career
    apparel design and production,
        409–427
    becoming a success, 381–384
    changing jobs, 384–385
    choosing, 370–375
    definition, 369
    entrepreneurial opportunities,
        484–485
    fashion merchandising and other
        retail careers, 408–425
    fashion promotion, 451–465
    interview, 378–381
    landing that job, 375–381
    letter of application, 378
    portfolio, 376–378
    researching, 371–375
    résumé, 376
    textile industry, 389–407
Career clusters
    apparel design and production
        careers, 425
    entrepreneurial and other
        careers, 485
    fashion merchandising and other
        retail careers, 447
    fashion promotion careers, 463
    textile careers, 404
Career pathways, 371
Career research sources, 371–372
Care labels for apparel, 353
Cargo pants, 60
Cashmere, 146
Cash purchases, 314
Catalog manager, 445

Catalogs, 95
Cellulosic fibers, 146
CEO (chief executive officer), 423
Ceremonial garments, 26
Certificate courses, 373
Chain stores, 133–134
Chambre Syndicale, 76
Channel of distribution, 128
Chapter 11 bankruptcy, 430
Character of the fabric, 224
Charge slip, 316
Checker, 472, 476
Checkout cashier, 440
Checks, bounce, 314
Check writing, 314
Chemical finishes, 187
Chemical spinning, 159
Chevron, 221
Chief financial officers (CFOs), 445
Chief information officer (CIO), 445
Children's clothing, 326–330
    appropriateness, 327
    growth features, 328
    practicality, 328
    safety, 328
    self-esteem, 328–329
    sizes, 329–330
Children's self-esteem, 328
Children's sizes, sewing children's
    apparel, 330
China grass, 150
Chlorine bleach, 355
Classic, 38
Classification buyers, 432
Classified ads, 375
Class market, 42
Classroom teacher, 468–469
Cleaners, 417
Clearance sale, 312
Closures, 64
Clothes
    adornment, 23–25
    drying, 359–360
    evaluate proper fit, 307–311
    identification, 25–26
    modesty, 26–27
    needs, 28–30
    protection, 22–23
    reasons for, 22–28
Clothing as communication, 250
Clothing business terms, 40–43
    haute couture, 40
    prêt à porter, 79
    ready-to-wear, 41
    retailers, 42
    wholesalers, 42
Clothing care, 343–365, 476–477
    commercial laundries, 477
    daily care, 343–345
    dry cleaning and laundry
        businesses, 476
    drying clothes, 359–360
    hand washing, 358
    home storage areas, 346–347
    ironing and pressing, 360–363

laundering, 351–358
    linen supply service, 477
    removing spots and stains, 348–351
    seasonal storage, 347–348
    weekly care, 345–346
Clothing construction terms, 38–40
    composite garments, 40
    draped garments, 39
    fit, 38
    tailored garments, 40
Clothing, for older adults, 330–332
    physical changes, 331–332
    selecting apparel, 332
Coat and jacket styles, 61
Cocoon of silkworm, 156
Cold-water detergents, 355
Collaboration, 119–120
Collars, 303
Collar styles, 53–55
Collections, 74
Color, 199–215
    changeability, 205
    color schemes, 202–204
    color wheel, 201–202
    creating illusions, 205–207
    design element, 199–200
    enhancing personal coloring, 207–213
    psychological associations, 200
    symbolism, 200–201
    terms, 201
    using in apparel, 204–206
Color analysis, 207
Color analysis consultants, 482
Coloring, enhancing, 207–213
Color schemes, 202–204
    accented neutral, 204
    analogous, 203
    complementary, 203
    definition, 202
    monochromatic, 202–203
    split complementary, 203–204
    triad, 204
Color tone, 207
Color value, 201
Color wheel, 201
Combination yarns, 166
Combing, 147
Commercial pattern development,
    471–472
Commission, 375, 437
Commissionaires, 138
Communication, 250, 358
    clothing, 250
    skills, 383
Community standards, 255
Comparison shoppers, 299, 438
    shopping, 299
Competitive retailer, 438
Complementary color scheme, 203
Completion date, 129
Composite garments, 40
Compressive shrinking, 186
Computer
    automation, 118
    imaging, 118

programmers, 402
systems administrators, 402
Computer-aided design (CAD), 107
Computer-aided design programs, 92, 411–413, 416
Computer-aided manufacturing (CAM), 111
Computer-integrated manufacturing (CIM), 118
Confined, 114
Conformity, 29–30
Conjugate fibers, 163
Consignment, 137, 265, 478
Consulting, 483
Consumer, 21, 41, 279–297
    aids, 281
    education, 470
    government legislation, 289–291
    hangtags, labels, and packaging, 287–289
    prepare ahead, 280–282
    protection agencies, 293
    shopping considerations, 286–287
    when and where to shop, 282–286
Consumer rights and responsibilities, 291–295
    to be informed, 292
    safety, 292
    to be heard, 293–295
    to choose, 292–293
Contractors, 104, 107
Converters, 396
Cool colors, 201
Cooperative advertising, 114, 126
Co-op programs, 373
Copies, 41
Copy, 460
Copyists, 410
Copywriters, 460
Cord, 166
Corporation, 477
Correct care label, 291
Co-spun fibers, 163
Costing, 107
Costing engineers, 420
Cost-per-wearing, 302
Costume
    curators, 473
    jewelry, 270
    technician, 475
Cottage industry, 478
Cotton, 146–148, 156
    belt, 146
    characteristics and uses, 148
    production and processing, 146–148
Coty Hall of Fame, 76
Couture, 73–79
    American high-fashion designers, 74
    business of high fashion, 74–76
    development of high fashion, 73–74
    fashion associations and awards, 76
    French couturiers of the past, 74
    recent changes for growth and income, 77–79
Couturiers, 40

Coveralls, 326
Cover message, 378
Crabbing, 186
Craze, 38
Crease resistance, 187–188
Credit
    evaluating, 318
    limit, 316
    pros and cons, 318
    purchase, 315
    rating, 316
Credit Card Accountability, Responsibility, and Disclosure Act, 318
Crimp, 152
Croquis, 97, 411
Cross-channel shopping, 284
Cross dyeing, 182
Crosswise grain, 173
Cuff, 57
Cuff links, 270
Cultures, 22
Curators, costume, 473
Customer relations skills, 383
Customer service representative, 437
Custom-designed, 41
Custom-made, 41
Custom patterns, 99
Cut of garment, 302
Cut pile fabrics, 175
Cutters, 416
Cutting, 187
Cutty Sark Awards, 76
Cylinder printing, 184

D

Dart loom, 172
Darts, 38, 310
Data processors, 402
Debit card, 314
Decision-making skills, 384
Decorations, 304
Decorative lines, 222
Denier, 159
Departmental buyers, 432
Department managers, 432
Department stores, 132
Design
    definition, 231
    directors, 472
    elements of, 199–227
    options, 63
    principles of, 231–243
    stylists, 410
Designer
    labels, 311
    patterns, 77, 96
    ready-to-wear, 79–82
Designing process, 106–107
    adapting designs, 107
    sources of inspiration, 106
Detergents, 354–355
Diagonal lines, 221
Diagram artists, 472
Diapers, 325
Direct-mail marketing, 136

Direct Marketing News, 132
Direct selling, 125, 436–437
Disabilities, apparel for people with, 332–334
Discharge printing, 184
Discount stores, 134
Disinfectants, 356
Display, 44
Display designer, 455
Distribution, 421
Distribution manager, 445
Distributors/planners, 440
District manager, 444
Divisional merchandise manager (DMM), 445
Division director, 423
Dobby attachment, 175
Domestic production, 117
Double-breasted, 61
Double ticketing, 309
Doupion silk, 155
Down feather, 157
Draped garments, 39
Drawing, 147
Dress codes, 26
Dress styles, basic, 51–52
Dressmakers, 480
Dressmaking or tailoring shop, 480–481
Drip-drying, 360
Dry cleaning
    and laundry businesses, 476
    clothes, 360, 362–363
Dry-clean only, 290
Drying and stretching, 186
Drying clothes, 359–360
Dry spinning, 159
Dyeing, 181–183
Duties, import taxes, 414

E

Earning levels, careers, 374–375
Easy-to-sew, 96
E-commerce, 120
Economic views on imports, 94, 117
Editors, 460
Educational representatives, 470, 473
Education and training, 373
Egyptian cotton, 147
Elasticity, 152
Electronic check conversion, 314
Electronic data interchange (EDI), 119
Electronic merchandising, 128
Electronic payments, 317
Electronic retailing, 136–137
Elements of design, 199–206, 217–229, 232
    color, 199–206
    line, 219–224
    shape, 217–219
    texture, 224–227
Emphasis, 234–235
Employability skills, 381–384
Employee protection laws, 385
Employee theft, 431
Employment agencies, 375
Employment outlook, 375

End-of-season sales, 312
Entrepreneurial opportunities, 467–487
Entrepreneurs, 477–483
Environmental sustainability, 305–306
Enzymes, 355
E-research, 284
Ergonomics, 112
E-tailing, 135–136
Evaluate proper fit, 307–310
Ethical behavior, 384
Ethics
    behavior, 384
    definition, 306
    piracy, 41, 75, 107
    shoplifting, 287, 431
    social responsibility, 306–307
    sweatshops, 109
Examiners, 417
Executive trainee, 435–436
Export incentives, 116
Exports, 94
Extenders, 272
Extension agents, 334, 469–470
Extruding, 159
Eyewear, 270

F

Fabric
    coloring and printing, 181–185
    definition, 89
    glossary, 189–193
    grain, 172
    production and distribution, 88–89
    quality, 302
    sales, 473
    sizings, 356
    softeners, 356
Fabric construction, 171–181
    finishes, 171–195
    coloring and printing, 181–185
Fabric editors, 472
Facial shapes, 219
Factory outlets, 134
Factory production, 109–112
    cutting, 109
    finishing, 112
    latest production methods, 111–112
    piecework system, 110–111
    tailor system, 110
Fad, 37
Fashion
    apparel industries, 71–73
    clothing business terms, 40–43
    clothing construction terms, 38–40
    considerations, 90–92
    couture, 73–79
    cycles, 43–45
    definition, 36
    designer ready-to-wear, 79–82
    development, 71–85
    leaders, 43
    obsolescence, 280
    popularity, 44
    social and economic influences, 45–47
    timing, 285

understanding, 35–49
Fashion advertising careers, 452–454
    account executive, 452
    advertising director, 454
    art director, 452
    graphic designer, 453
    other employees, 454
Fashion conscious, 285
Fashion coordinator, 441–443
    assistant fashion coordinator, 443
    qualifications, 443
Fashion cycles, 43–45
    definition, 43
    how cycles occur, 43–45
Fashion designers, 410–412
    definition, 410
    qualifications, 412
    the work, 411
Fashion director, 441
Fashion display, 454–455
    display designer, 455
    display director, 454–455
Fashion fabric sales, 92
Fashion Group International (FGI), 76
Fashion houses, 40, 73
Fashion illustrators, 455–456
Fashion information directors, 471
Fashion leader, 43
Fashion merchandising, 128, 429
    and other retail industry careers,
        429–449
Fashion model, 456–458
Fashion photographer, 458
    other photography employees, 459
Fashion piracy, 41, 75, 107
Fashion promotion, 451–465
    advertising, 452–454
    careers, 451–465
    display, 454–455
    other forms, 455–461
    publicity and press, 461–462
Fashion retailing, 125–141
    apparel retail outlets, 132–137
    how retail works, 128–132
    retail imports, 137–138
    retailers' future, 138–139
    store promotions, 125–128
Fashion silhouettes, 44–45
    back fullness silhouette, 45
    bell silhouette, 44
    tubular silhouette, 45
Fashion terms, 35–38
    apparel, 36
    avant-garde, 36
    classic, 38
    fad, 37
    garment, 36
    high-fashion, 36
    silhouette, 36
    style, 35
    trend, 36
    wardrobe, 38
Fashion writer, 459–460
Fasteners, 303
Fast fashion, 120

Federal Trade Commission (FTC), 289, 319
Fiber dyeing, 182
Fiberfill, 160
Fiberglass, 163
Fiber production, 88
Fibers, 88, 145
Filament, 153
Filling yarns, 172
Finance charge, 316
Finance, vice president, 403
Fine jewelry, 270
Finisher, 417, 476
Finishes, 185–188
Fire sale, 313
First impression, 252
Fit, 38
Fitted garment, 38
Fitting models, 472
Flagship store, 133
Flame resistance, 188
Flammable Fabrics Act, 291
Flat drying, 360
Flax, 148
Fleece, 151
Flocking, 185
Fluid designing, 118
Footwear, 267
Footwear News (FN), 72
Forecasting information, 395
Forecasting services, 91
Formal balance, 232
Franchise, 78, 135, 479
Franchisee, 135, 479
Franchisor, 135
Freelance jobs, 392
Freelancing, 410, 456, 458, 483
French fashion houses, 79
Fringe benefits, 116, 375
Fulling, 186
Fur Products Labeling Act, 291
Furs, 157, 291
Fusible web, 180
Future Educators Association (FEA), 469

G

Garment
    districts, 72
    dyeing, 183
    industry, 72
    makers, 471
    parts, 36
Garments
    basic, 271–272
    recycle, 263–264
    try on, 309–310
    with growth features, 328
Garment styles and parts, 51–67
    basic dress styles, 51–52
    coat and jacket styles, 61
    collar styles, 53–55
    design options, 64
    miscellaneous, 61–64
    neckline styles, 52–53
    pants styles, 58–61
    skirt styles, 57–58

Index

sleeve styles, 55–57
Gauge, 176
General merchandise manager (GMM), 445
Generic name, 158
Gift card, 314
Glass fibers, 158, 163
Gloves, 270
Going out of business sale, 313
Gores, 57
Gore-Tex®, 158
Go to market, 432
Government legislation, fabrics, 289–291
    Flammable Fabrics Act, 291
    Fur Products Labeling Act, 291
    Permanent Care Labeling Rule,
      290–291
    Textile Fiber Products Identification
      Act, 289–290
    Wool Products Labeling Act, 291
Gradation, 235
Graded, 108
Grading, 98, 108
Graduate degree, 374
Graphic designers, 453
Green facilities, 306
Greige goods, 89
Grippers, 324
Grooming, 249
Grouping of clothes, 263–265
    not worn in past year, 265
    repairs or cleaning, 264–265
    worn occasionally, 263–264
    worn often, 263
Growth features, 328
Guide sheets, 95
Gusset, 55

H

Hackled, 149
Haircloth, 156
Hand, 186
Handbags, 267–268
Handling trucks, 110
Hands-off production, 119
Hand washing, clothes, 358–359
Hangtags, labels, and packaging, 287–289
Harmony, 235
Haute couture, 40, 73
Head of stock, 439
Headwear, 268
Heat transfer printing, 185
Hem, 303
Hemline Index, 47
Hemp, 146, 150
Herringbone pattern, 174
High-fashion items, 36
High-style items, 36
High-sudsing detergents, 355
Historic clothing, 28, 46
Home dry cleaning, 363
Home handiwork business, 478
Home sewing industry, 471–473
Home sewing patterns, 95–99
    breadth of pattern companies, 96
    business, 95–96

designing, 97
finishing, 98
innovation for future, 98–99
perfecting, 97–98
Home storage areas, 346–347
Horizontal lines, 221
Horsehair fiber, 146, 156
Hosiery, 271
Hourly wage, 374
House boutiques, 77
Hue, 201
Human engineering, 112
Human resources manager, 402, 445
Hypermarkets, 134

I

Identity theft, 318–319
Illustrators, 472
Image, positive, 249
Imports
    and overseas manufacturing,
      115–118
    definition, 93
    political and social viewpoints,
      304–305
    retail, 137–138
Import taxes (duties), 116
Impulse buying, 286, 313
Independent sales reps, 422
Indirect selling, 125, 451
Individuality, 29–30
Industrial engineers, 398–399, 420
Industrial Revolution, 71
Infant apparel, 323–326
    bibs, 326
    comfort, 324
    kimonos and gowns, 325–326
    layette, 325
    practicality, 324
    safety, 324–325
    sizes, 326
    stretch suits or coveralls, 326
    waterproof pants, 325
Informal balance, 232
Information Technology (IT), 403
Ink-jet printing, 185
Innovation, 93
Inseam, 58
Inspector, 417, 476
Installment plans, 316
Intensity, 201
Interests, 370
Interfacings, 304
Intermediate hues, 201
International fashion names, 81
International trade, competition, 116
Internships, 373
Intimate Apparel News, 72
Inventory control, 29
Inventory sale, 312
Inverted triangle figure, 240
Investment dressing, 271
Ironing and pressing, 360–363
Ironing board, 361
Ironing techniques, 361–362

Irregulars, 42
Italian fashion names, 80

J

Jacquard loom, 175
Job. *See also* Career
    application, 378
    changes, 384–385
    definition, 369
    interview, 378
    shadowing, 372
Jobbers, 422
Job lots, 129
Joint venture, 117
Jute, 146, 150

K

Kapok, 146, 150
Kimono sleeves, 55
Knitting, 176
Knitting machines, 95
Knockoffs, 41, 107

L

Labels, 288–289
Laboratory technicians, 392
Labor intensive, 414
Laces and nets, 181
Lap, 147
Lapel, 54, 304
Lapel pin, 270
Laser cutter, 110
Laundering clothes, 351–358
    choose correct products, 354–356
    clothing care, 351–358
    definition, 351
    follow correct procedures, 357
    sort, 352
    type and amount of soil, 354
    use products correctly, 356–357
    water temperatures, 357
Laundry specialists, 477
Layaway purchase, 315
Layette, 325
Layout artists, 454
Layout designers, 472
Leadership skills, 384
Lead times, 119, 137
Leased department, 137
Legwear, 271
Leno weave, 176
Letter of resignation, 385
Letters of recommendation, 376
Licensing, 78, 117
Lifestyle, 253
Line, as element of design, 219–224
    applications, 222
    creating illusions, 222–223
    definition, 219
    further use of lines, 223–224
    line directions, 220–221
    types, 219–224
Line drying, 359
Line, fashion collection, 105
Linen, 146, 148–150, 156

characteristics and uses, 150
definition, 148
production and processing, 148–149
Linen supply service, 477
Lining, 304
Lint, 146, 352
Llama, fibers, 146
Logo, 75
Loom, 172
Loss leaders, 129
Low-quality garments, 301
Low-sudsing detergents, 355
Lyocell, 158, 162, 165

M

Machine operators, 397–398
Machine technicians, 398
Made-to-order, 41
Mail-order
businesses, 482
houses, 135–136
Maintenance workers, 440
Management trainee, 435
Mannequins, 126
Manufactured fibers, 157–164
categories, 158–159
development, 157–158
generic characteristics, 160
present and future, 158
processing, 161
producing, 159–160
Markdown, 128
Marker, 109, 416, 478
Marker makers, 415, 472
Marketing and sales, 90, 399–401
Marketing specialists, 454
Market research analysts, 399, 423
Market weeks, 113, 129
Markup, 128
Mass market, 43
Mass production, 109
Mass retailing, 132
Master's degree, 374, 401
Maternity fashions, 335
Mechanical finishes, 186
Mechanical spinning, 166
Media kits, 459
Medium-quality garments, 301
Melamine fibers, 158, 163
Melt spinning, 159
Mentor, 372
Mercerization, 188
Merchandise
clinics, 434
control specialists, 423
manager, 441
plan, 104
Merchandise planning and buying jobs,
431–436
assistant retail buyer, 434
buyer qualifications, 433–434
buyers' schedules and benefits, 433
executive trainee, 435–436
resident buying office buyer, 434–435
retail buyer, 432–433

Merchandiser, 423
Merchandising
directors, 471
functions, 430
Metal rivets, 303
Microdenier fibers, 159
Microelectronics, 93
Mildew resistance, 188
Mix-and-match items, 256
Mock buttons, 333
Modacrylic, 158, 162
Model
fashion, 456–458
fitting, 472
Modesty, 26–27
Modular manufacturing, 111
Mohair fiber, 146, 153
Money conscious, 285
Monochromatic color scheme, 202
Monofilament yarns, 161, 166
Moth resistance, 188
Mothproofing apparel, 348
Motif, 92, 227
Multifilament yarns, 161, 166
Multipliers, 272
Multisize patterns, 98
Muslin proof, 97

N

Nanotechnology, 93, 186, 188
Nap, 175
National Retail Federation (NRF), 132
Natural fibers, 146–157
cotton, 146–148
linen, 148–150
other natural materials, 156–157
other plant fibers, 150
silk, 153–156
wool, 150–154
Neckline styles, 52–53
Neckties, 268–269
Need, 265
Needle punched, 179
Needles trades, 72
Networking, 375
Neutrals, 201
Niche retailing, 138
Nonwoven fabrics, 179
Notions, 95, 471
Nylon, 157, 158, 161, 164

O

Occupation, 369
Occupational Outlook Handbook, 375
Occupational training, 373
Odd-figure pricing, 128
Odd lots, 129
Office manager, 403, 440
Office support workers, 440
Off-price discounters, 134
Offshore production, 117
Offshore sourcing, 137
Olefin, 158, 162, 165
Omni-channel retailing, 138
Onesies, 325

On-grain, 302
Online business, 482
Online fabric sales personnel, 473
Open-to-buy, 129
Opposition, 235
Optical illusion, 222
Organic cotton, 146
Organic wool, 151
Outlet stores, 134
Outside sales representatives, 421
Overall prints, 183
Overdrawn, 314
Overlock sewing machines, 99
Overruns, 42
Overseas manufacturing, 115–118
competition, 116
differences, 115–116
labeling, 117
no clear-cut answers, 117–118
using, 116–117
Oxygen bleaches, 356

P

Package priced, 132
Packaging, 289
Paddings, 304
Pants styles, 58–61
Partnership, 477
Paste-up/mechanical artists, 454
Pattern companies
breadth of, 96
business of, 95
graders, 415, 472
guide sheet and envelope
production, 472
maker, 415, 471
Pattern-making resources, 99
Patterns
brands, 95
designing home sewing, 97
finishing, 98
innovations for future, 98
perfecting, 97
sales and promotion, 472–473
Payment
cash purchases, 314
credit cards, 315–316
debit card, 314–315
gift card, 314
electronic payments, 317
financial loan, 316
how to, 314–318
installment plans, 316
layaway purchases, 315
writing a check, 314
PBI, 163, 165
Peer pressure, 29
Performance
standards, 93
tests, 380
Permanent Care Labeling Rule, 290–291
Permanent press, 188
Personal color categories, 208
Personality, 30, 250–251
Personal selling, 137

Index

Personal shopper, 438
Personal style, 236
Personal traits, develop positive, 382–383
Petrochemicals, 161
Photographer, fashion, 457–458
Photo stylists, 459
Physique, 236
Piece dyeing, 182
Piece goods buyers, 419
Piecework system, 110–111
Pill, cotton fabric, 148
Pima cotton, fibers, 147
Pinsonic thermal joining, 180
Piracy, 41, 75, 107
Placement office, 375
Plaid, 303
Plaid pattern, 175
Plain weave, 173
Plaiting, 181
Plant engineers, 398, 420
Plant fibers, 150
Plant manager, 419
Ply yarns, 166
Pockets, 304
Policies, 287
Political/social viewpoints, 304–307
   dilemmas of imports, 118, 304–305
   environmental sustainability, 305–306
   ethics and social responsibility, 306–307
Polyactide (PLA), 158, 163
Polybenzimidazole (PBI) fibers, 158, 161, 163, 165
Polyester, 158, 161, 164
Polymers, 158
Portfolio, 376
Postsecondary level, 373
Prepared for dye (P.F.D.), 183
Preschoolers, 327
Pressers, 418
Pressing, 187, 360
   cloth, 361
   mitt, 361
Press kits, 126, 459
Prêt à porter, 79
Prêt collections, 79
Price markets, 42–43
Primary hues, 201
Principles of design, 231–245
   balance, 231–232
   create best look, 236–237
   definition, 231
   emphasis, 234–235
   harmony, 235–236
   proportion, 232–234
   rhythm, 235
   total design for individuals, 237–243
Printing, fabric, 183–185
Priority, 266
Private label, 131
Private label brand merchandise, 131–132, 433
Product development directors, 131
Product manager, 418
Production

finishing, 112
   preliminary procedures, 108–109
   preparation, 107–109
   samples, 108
Production management jobs, 418–420
   assistant, 419
   manager, 419
   supervisors, 397, 419
Production throughput time, 112
Productivity, 111
Professional dry cleaning, 362
Professional image, 384
Profit, 104
Progressive bundle system, 110
Promotion, 125–128
   advertising, 126
   definition, 125
   publicity, 126
   visual merchandising and special events, 126–127
Promotional sales, 312
Promotions, 42
Proportion, 232–234
   definition, 232
   in apparel, 233–234
Protease, 355
Protective clothing, 22–23
   definition, 22
   environmental dangers, 22
   from enemies, 23
   occupational hazards, 22–23
   weather, 22
Protein fibers, 146
Protein natural fibers, 146
Prototype, 97, 105, 108, 411
Psychological uniform, 26
Publicity, 126, 461
Public relations (PR) specialists, 403, 461
Pullovers, 63
Purchase orders, 129
Purchasing agents, 403
Purchasing, political/social viewpoints, 304–307
Pure silk, 156
Pure wool, 153

Q

Quality, 300
Quality control, 293
   engineers, 420
   inspectors, 398
Quality, specific points, 301–304
Quality standards, 93
Quilted fabrics, 180
Quotas, 116

R

Radial arrangement, 235
Raglan sleeves, 56
Rag trade, 72
Ramie, 146, 150
Raschel knits, 179
Ravel, 150
Rayon, 157, 158, 162, 165
Ready-to-wear (RTW), 41, 79

Reciprocal agreements, 374
Recycle, 263
Recycled wool, 153
Redress, 293
Reeling, 154
References, 376
Regional manager, 444
Registered numbers (RN), 290
Regulations, starting a business, 478
Reinforcements, 303
Reorders, 115, 138
Resale shops, 137
Research and development (R and D), 93, 390–392
   textiles, 390–392
Research scientists, 391
Resident buying offices (RBOs), 130, 435
   buyers, 434
Resilience, 157
Resist dyeing, 183
Resources
   available, 273–275
   definition, 273
   planning available, 273–275
   sewing as an option, 274–275
Response times, 119
Responsibilities, consumer, 291
Résumé, 376
Retail, 128–132
   business considerations, 132
   buyers, 129–131, 432–433
   careers, 430–445
   coordinators, 472
   future of, 138–139
   imports, 137–138
   private label brands, 131–132
   terms, 128
   timing and pricing for demand, 129–131
Retailers, 42, 128
Retail management, 441–446
   fashion coordinator, 441–443
   merchandise manager, 441
   other jobs, 444–446
   store or site manager, 444
Retail salesperson, 436–437
   qualifications, 431, 437
Retail store, owning, 479–480
Retting tanks, 149
Rhythm, 235
Rights, consumer, 291
Robotics, 93, 118
Roller printing, 184
Rotary screen printing, 185
Roving, 147
Royalty fees, 78
Rubber, 158, 163
Runway work, 456

S

Safety features, 328
Safety, right and responsibility, 292
Salary, 374
Sales, 287, 312–313
   resistance, 287

types of retail, 312–313
Sales positions, 399–401, 422, 436
associate, 436
manager, 401, 422
representatives, 399–400, 422
trainee, 401
Sample, 411
Sample hand, 108, 414
Sample maker, 108, 414
Samples, fashion design, 105
Samplings, 106
Satin weave, 174
Scal, 232
Scarves, 268–269
Scored, wool, 151
Scraing, stain removal method, 351
Screen printing, 185
Scuthed, 149
Sea Island Cotton, 147
Seam, 38, 302
Seasonal clothing storage, 347–348
Seamless clothes, 273, 280
Secondary hues, 201
Seconds, 42, 112
Security guard, 441
Self-concept, 251
Self-esteem, children's, 328
Self-help features, 327
Selling apparel, 112–115
promoting lines, 114–115
showing the lines, 113
Selvage, 172
Serge, 109
Sericin, 154
Sericulture, 154
Set-in sleeves, 55
Sewer, 476
Sewing, 274–275, 416, 481
an option, 274–275
profit, 481
machine operators, 416
Sewn-in labels, information, 289
Shade, 201
Shape, 217–219
condition, 217
flat shapes, 219
form, 218
use in clothing, 218
Shears, 361
Shearing, 187
Shoplifting, 287, 431
Shopping environment, 138
Shopping
by mobile apps, 284
comparison shopping, 299–300
considerations, 286–287
consumer decisions, 285
cross-channel, 284
gauge quality, 301–302
judge value and quality, 300–304
list,
location and store hours, 283
malls, 287
price versus quality and service, 282
specific points of quality, 302–304

types of merchandise, 283
when, 285–286
where to, 282–285
Showroom sales positions, 421
manager, 421
trainee, 421
salesperson, 421
Shrinkage control, 188
Shuttle, 172
Shuttleless loom, 172
Signature lines, 96
Silhouettes, fashion, 36
Silk, 146, 153–156
characteristics and uses, 155–156
definition, 153
natural insulator, 155
production and processing, 154–155
Singeing, 187
Single-breasted, 61
Sisal, 146, 150
Size range categories, 307–308
Sizings, fabric finish, 188, 356
Sketchers, 410, 413
Sketching assistants, 413
Skirt styles, 57–58
Sleeve board, 361
Sleeves, styles of, 54–57
Sliver, 147
Sloper, 97
Smart card, 315
Smart consumer, 279–297
Soaking, 351
Soaps, 355
Social and economic influences on
fashion, 45–47
Social media, 300
Social responsibility, 306
Social saturation, 43
Soft sell, 127
Soil release, 193
Sole proprietorship, 477
Solution dyeing, 159, 182
Sonic joining, 118
Spandex, 158, 162, 165
Special-purchase sales, 313
Specialty hair fibers, 146
Specialty retailers, 135
Specialty wools, 153
Spinneret, 159
Spinning, 147
Split complementary color scheme, 203
Sponging, 349
Sportswear International, 72
Spot lifter, 351
Spots and stains, 348–351
identify fiber and stain, 349
stain removal methods, 349–351
stain removal supplies, 349
Spotter, 476
Spreaders, 109, 416
Spun silk, 155
Spun yarns, 166
Stain resistance, 193
Stains and spots, 348–351
Standards, 292

Staple fibers, 160
Starches, 356
Status, 27
Steam pressing machines, 418
Stitching, 302
Stock clerk, 438
Stock control, 129
Stock dyed, 182
Stock keeping units (SKUs), 130
Store displays, 281
Store manager, 444
STORES magazine, 132
Straw, 146
Stretching, 159
Structural designs, 392
Structural lines, 222
Structural texture, 225
Style, 35
Stylish, 36
Stylists, 107
Supervisors, 419
Supply chain, 128
Surface designs, 392
Surfactants, 355
Surplice, 52, 221
Sweatshops, 109
Symbolism, color, 200
Symmetrical, 232
Synthetic fibers, 158

T

Tailored garments, 40
Tailors, 480
Tailor's ham, 361
Tailor system, 110
Target customer, 310
Target market, 132
Tariffs, 116
Technical schools, 373
Technical writers, 472
Television retailing, 136
Territory, sales, 422
Tertiary hues, 201
Textile and clothing historians, 473–475
Textile belt, 390
Textile corporations, 89–90, 92–93
development, 89–90
technology, 92–93
Textile Fiber Products Identification Act,
289–290
Textile fibers and yarns, 145–169
manufactured fibers, 157–164
natural fibers, 146–157
yarns, 164–167
Textile industry
administration, 402–405
careers, 389–407
design, 392–395
development of textile corporations,
89–90
fabric manufacturing, 89
fabric production and distribution,
88–89
fashion considerations, 90–92
fiber production and distribution, 88

fibers and yarns, 145–169
future of, 93–95, 158
marketing and sales, 90, 399–401
research and development, 390–392
Textile laboratory technician, 392
Textile production jobs, 396–399
assistant converter, 397
colorists, 394
converters, 89, 396
industrial engineer, 398–399
machine operators, 397–398
machine technicians, 398
plant engineer, 398
production supervisor, 397
quality control inspector, 398
Textile Research Journal, 93
Textile research scientist, 391–392
Textile stylists, 394
Textile testers, 392
Textile World magazine, 72, 93, 94
Texture, 224–227
added visual texture, 226–227
definition, 224
structural texture in clothing, 225–226
Textured yarns, 167
Texturing, 167
Theatrical costumers, 475
Thrift shops, 136–137
Throughput time, 112
Throwing, silk production, 154
Tie dyeing, 183
Tint, 201
Toddlers, 326
Tokyo Collection, 76
Trade
associations, 71
deficit, 94, 117, 305
journals, 94
publications, 72
schools, 373
Trademarks, 159, 310–311
definition, 310
designer labels, 311
Trading company, 481
Training supervisor, 419, 437
Transition, 235
Transportation managers, 403
Travel wardrobes, 335–338
be practical, 336
definition, 335
mix and match, 335–336
other considerations, 338
packing tips, 337–338
travel needs, 336–337
Trendsetters, 43
Triacetate, 158, 162
Triad color scheme, 204
Triangular figure, 241
Tricot warp knit, 179
Trimmers, 417
Trimmings, 304
True bias, 302

Trunk, 329
Trunk show, 115
Truth in Lending Act, 318
Tussah fiber, 155
Twill weave, 174

U

Ultrasonic energy, 180
Understated design, 238
Undertone, 207
Uniforms, 25
Unit production system (UPS), 111
Universal Product Code (UPC), 138
Upper level executives, 403

V

Value, 201, 300
Value added, 414
Value and quality, judging, 300–304
Values and attitudes, 28–29
Variants, 159
Variety stores, 137
Vat dyeing, 183
Velvet board, 361
Vendors, 432
Vertical lines, 220
Vice president of merchandising, 445
Vice president of sales, 403
Vicuña fiber, 146, 153
Video demonstration work, 473
Virgin wool, 153
Virtual product development (VPD), 120
Virtual reality technology, 300
Visual display artists, 455
Visual merchandising, 126
Visual presentation directors, 454

W

Wage earners, 374
Waistband, 57, 304
Want, 265
Wants, versus needs, 265–266
Wardrobe
appropriate apparel, 253–255
benefits, 255–257
definition, 38
enjoy apparel choices, 257
gain flexibility, 256–257
planning, 261–277
positive image, 249–253
project best self-image, 255–256
save money, 256
wardrobe inventory, 261
wardrobe plan, 271–273
Wardrobe consultants, 482
Wardrobe designer, 475
Wardrobe helper, 475
Wardrobe planning, 261–277
accessories, 266–271
available resources, 273–275
evaluate advertising, 282
evaluate current apparel, 261–263

future plan, 271–273
gather information, 281
group clothes, 263–265
make a list, 280–281
prepare ahead, 280–282
wants, versus needs, 265–266
Warehouse clubs, 134
Warehouse distribution, jobs, 423
Warm colors, 201
Warp knits, 179
Warp yarns, 172
Washer agitation, 358
Washing operator, 476
Wash load, 352
Waterproof, 193
Waterproof pants, 325
Water repellent, 193
Water softeners, 356
Wearing ease, 310
Wearing the best color, 213
Weaves, types, 173
Weaving, 172
Weft knits, 177
Weighted silks, 155
Wet spinning, 159
White sales, 312
Wholesalers, 42
Wicking, 162
Wild silk, 154
Window shopping, 281
Women's Wear Daily (WWD), 72
Woof yarns, 172
Wool, 146, 150–154, 156
categories, 153
characteristics and uses, 153
definition, 150
production and processing, 151–152
Woolen yarn, 152
Wool pools, 151
Wool processing, 152
Wool Products Labeling Act, 29
Work-based learning programs, 3
Worsted yarns, 152
Wrapper, 476
Written tests, for job evaluation, 80

Y

Yang, 251
Yard goods, 171
Yarn dyeing, 182
Yarn production, 88
Yarns, 88, 145, 164–167, 182
combination yarns and blends, 166
definition, 163
dyeing, 182
types, 166
yarn textures, 167
Yin, 251
Yoke, 64

Z

Zipper, 303